EUROPEAN POLITICAL, ECONOMIC, AND SECURITY ISSUES

THE EUROPEAN UNION AND THE GLOBAL FINANCIAL CRISIS

A VIEW FROM 2016

EUROPEAN POLITICAL, ECONOMIC, AND SECURITY ISSUES

Additional books in this series can be found on Nova's website
under the Series tab.

Additional e-books in this series can be found on Nova's website
under the eBooks tab.

EUROPEAN POLITICAL, ECONOMIC, AND SECURITY ISSUES

THE EUROPEAN UNION AND THE GLOBAL FINANCIAL CRISIS

A VIEW FROM 2016

GRAEME SCOTT BABER, PHD

publishers

New York

Library of Congress Cataloging-in-Publication Data

Names: Baber, Graeme, author.
Title: The European Union and the global financial crisis : a view from 2016
   / editor, Graeme Scott Baber (Researcher in Financial Law).
Description: Hauppauge, New York : Nova Science Publishers, Inc., [2016] |
   Series: European political, economic, and security issues | Includes
   bibliographical references and index.
Identifiers: LCCN 2016017089 (print) | LCCN 2016022545 (ebook) | ISBN
   9781634850261 (hardcover) | ISBN 9781634852388 ()
Subjects: LCSH: Financial institutions--Law and legislation--European Union
   countries. | Global Financial Crisis, 2008-2009
Classification: LCC KJE2188 .B33 2016 (print) | LCC KJE2188 (ebook) | DDC
   346.24/082--dc23
LC record available at https://lccn.loc.gov/2016017089

Published by Nova Science Publishers, Inc. † New York

The Cotswold town of Northleach, Gloucestershire, United Kingdom, became prosperous in medieval times, with earnings from the supply of the wool from its local sheep to merchants of continental Europe.

To my family, especially my mother, for loyalty and support in the preparation for and writing of this work

CONTENTS

PREFACE

When the president of Nova Science Publishers kindly invited me to contribute a chapter to the then forthcoming book 'Global Financial Crisis: Causes, Consequences and Impact on Economic Growth', I was pleased to do so, but anticipated before completion that it would be difficult to report and discuss all that was required within the space of 35,000 words. Thus, the seed of the current monograph was sown.

The original chapter uncovered interesting findings, which include issues with the Treaty basis of aspects of the post-GFC legislation and a good fit between the primary and the secondary rules under the new architecture of the European financial sector – using one detailed example. Bearing this in mind, the monograph attempts a fuller treatment of this legislation. The emergence of the new rules is put into context by looking at the EU before the GFC and by considering the international response to the crisis. Aspects of the recent provisions are then reported and discussed, and, on the basis of these considerations, concluding thoughts are made.

The book aims to state and review the position as at March 2016. In practice, there may be updates which I have not been able to reach within the months between starting this work and completing it. I ask that you bear with me in this respect, as it is difficult to assimilate information as fast as the European Commission publishes it.

Do let me know if you have feedback, questions or comments on the issues discussed within the book, or any helpful suggestions for improvement. I wish you well in your reading of the material, and hope that you find it both interesting and informative.

Graeme Baber
June 2015

ACKNOWLEDGMENTS

The author and publishers wish to thank the following, who have kindly given permission for the use of copyright material:

Mr. James K. Jackson for the quotation from CRS Report for Congress R40415.

The [global financial]. crisis has underscored growing interdependence between financial markets and between the U.S. and European economies. ... The United States and the EU share a mutual interest in developing a sound financial architecture to improve supervision and regulation of individual institutions and of international markets.
- Jackson, J.K., 2010. The Financial Crisis: Impact on and Response by The European Union, Congressional Research Service (CRS) Report for Congress R40415, March 17, 2010, Washington D.C., United States: Congressional Research Service, 1-35, 3.

LIST OF ABBREVIATIONS

AIF	Alternative Investment Fund
AIFM	Alternative Investment Fund Manager
AIFM Directive	Directive 2011/61/EU of the European Parliament and of the Council of 8 June 2011 on Alternative Investment Fund Managers and amending Directives 2003/41/EC and 2009/65/EC and Regulations (EC) No 1060/2009 and (EU) No 1095/2010
BCBS	Basel Committee on Banking Supervision
BCD	Directive 2006/48/EC of the European Parliament and of the Council of 14 June 2006 relating to the taking up and pursuit of the business of credit institutions (recast) (Banking Consolidation Directive)
BIS	Bank for International Settlements
BRRD	Directive 2014/59/EU of the European Parliament and of the Council of 15 May 2014 establishing a framework for the recovery and resolution of credit institutions and investment firms and amending Council Directive 82/891/EEC, and Directives 2001/24/EC, 2002/47/EC, 2004/25/EC, 2005/56/EC, 2007/36/EC, 2011/35/EU, 2012/30/EU and 2013/36/EU, and Regulations (EU) No 1093/2010 and (EU) No 648/2012, of the European Parliament and of the Council (Bank Recovery and Resolution Directive)
CARD	Directive 2001/34/EC of the European Parliament and of the Council of 28 May 2001 on the admission of securities to official stock exchange listing and on information to be published on those securities (Consolidated Admissions and Reporting Directive)
CCP	Central counterparty
CDR	Commission Delegated Regulation
CIR	Commission Implementing Regulation
CMU	Capital Markets Union
Commission	European Commission

Council	Council of the European Union
CRD	Directive 2006/49/EC of the European Parliament and of the Council of 14 June 2006 on the capital adequacy of investment firms and credit institutions (recast) (Capital Requirements Directive)
CRD IV	Directive 2013/36/EU of the European Parliament and of the Council of 26 June 2013 on access to the activity of credit institutions and the prudential supervision of credit institutions and investment firms, amending Directive 2002/87/EC and repealing Directives 2006/48/EC and 2006/49/EC (Fourth Capital Requirements Directive)
CRR	Regulation (EU) No 575/2013 of the European Parliament and of the Council of 26 June 2013 on prudential requirements for credit institutions and investment firms and amending Regulation (EU) No 648/2012 (Capital Requirements Regulation)
CSDR	Regulation (EU) No 909/2014 of the European Parliament and of the Council of 23 July 2014 on improving securities settlement in the European Union and on central securities depositories and amending Directives 98/26/EC and 2014/65/EU and Regulation (EU) No 236/2012 (Central Securities Depositaries Regulation)
EBA	European Banking Authority
EEA	European Economic Area, comprising the European Union, Iceland, Liechtenstein and Norway
EEA State	Contracting Party to the European Economic Area Agreement
EEC Treaty	Treaty Establishing the European Economic Community
EIOPA	European Insurance and Occupational Pensions Authority
ELTIF	European Long-term Investment Fund
ELTIF Regulation	Regulation (EU) 2015/760 of the European Parliament and of the Council of 29 April 2015 on European long-term investment funds
EMIR	Regulation (EU) No 648/2012 of the European Parliament and of the Council of 4 July 2012 on OTC derivatives, central counterparties and trade repositories (European Market Infrastructure Regulation)
ESA	European Supervisory Authority – i.e., the European Banking Authority, the European Insurance and Occupational Pensions Authority, or the European Securities and Markets Authority
ESMA	European Securities and Markets Authority
EU	European Union
FSB	Financial Stability Board
FSF	Financial Stability Forum
GBP	Great British Pounds

G7	Group of Seven
G20	Group of Twenty
GFC	Global financial crisis
IMF	International Monetary Fund
IOSCO	International Organization of Securities Commissions
ITS	Implementing Technical Standard
JPY	Japanese Yen
MAD	Directive 2003/6/EC of the European Parliament and of the Council of 28 January 2003 on insider dealing and market manipulation (market abuse)
MAD II	Directive 2014/57/EU of the European Parliament and of the Council of 16 April 2014 on criminal sanctions for market abuse (market abuse directive)
MAR	Regulation (EU) No 596/2014 of the European Parliament and of the Council of 16 April 2014 on market abuse (market abuse regulation) and repealing Directive 2003/6/EC of the European Parliament and of the Council and Commission Directives 2003/124/EC, 2003/125/EC and 2004/72/EC
Member State	Member State of the European Union
MEP	Member of the European Parliament
MiFID	Directive 2004/39/EC of the European Parliament and of the Council of 21 April 2004 on markets in financial instruments amending Council Directives 85/611/EEC and 93/6/EEC and Directive 2000/12/EC of the European Parliament and of the Council and repealing Council Directive 93/22/EEC (Markets in Financial Instruments Directive)
MiFID II	Directive 2014/65/EU of the European Parliament and of the Council of 15 May 2014 on markets in financial instruments and amending Directive 2002/92/EC and Directive 2011/61/EU (recast) (Second Markets in Financial Instruments Directive)
MiFIR	Regulation (EU) No 600/2014 of the European Parliament and of the Council of 15 May 2014 on markets in financial instruments and amending Regulation (EU) No 648/2012 (Markets in Financial Instruments Regulation)
MP	Member of Parliament
MTF	Multilateral trading facility
OECD	Organisation for Economic Co-operation and Development
OTC	over-the-counter
Parliament	European Parliament
PD	Directive 2003/71/EC of the European Parliament and of the Council of 4 November 2003 on the prospectus to be published when securities are offered to the public or

	admitted to trading and amending Directive 2001/34/EC (Prospectus Directive)
PDR	Commission Regulation (EC) No 809/2004 of 29 April 2004 implementing Directive 2003/71/EC of the European Parliament and of the Council as regards information contained in prospectuses as well as the format, incorporation by reference and publication of such prospectuses and dissemination of advertisements (Prospectus Directive Regulation)
PRIIPs	Packaged retail and insurance-based investment products
PRIIPs Regulation	Regulation (EU) No 1286/2014 of the European Parliament and of the Council of 26 November 2014 on key information documents for packaged retail and insurance-based investment products (PRIIPs)
PSD	Directive 2007/64/EC of the European Parliament and of the Council of 13 November 2007 on payment services in the internal market amending Directives 97/7/EC, 2002/65/EC, 2005/60/EC and 2006/48/EC and repealing Directive 97/5/EC (Payment Services Directive)
PSD II	Directive (EU) 2015/2366 of the European Parliament and of the Council of 25 November 2015 on payment services in the internal market, amending Directives 2002/65/EC, 2009/110/EC and 2013/36/EU and Regulation (EU) No 1093/2010, and repealing Directive 2007/64/EC (Second Payment Services Directive)
RTS	Regulatory Technical Standard
SME	Small and medium-sized enterprise
TD	Directive 2004/109/EC of the European Parliament and of the Council of 15 December 2004 on the harmonisation of transparency requirements in relation to information about issuers whose securities are admitted to trading on a regulated market and amending Directive 2001/34/EC (Transparency Directive)
TDID	Commission Directive 2007/14/EC of 8 March 2007 laying down detailed rules for the implementation of certain provisions of Directive 2004/109/EC on the harmonisation of transparency requirements in relation to information about issuers whose securities are admitted to trading on a regulated market (Transparency Directive Implementing Directive)
TEU	Treaty on European Union
TFEU	Treaty on the Functioning of the European Union
Third countries	Countries outside the European Economic Area
UCITS	Undertakings for Collective Investments in Transferable Securities

UCITS Directive	Council Directive 85/611/EEC of 20 December 1985 on the coordination of laws, regulations and administrative provisions relating to undertakings for collective investment in transferable securities (UCITS)
UCITS V Directive	Directive 2009/65/EC of the European Parliament and of the Council of 13 July 2009 on the coordination of laws, regulations and administrative provisions relating to undertakings for collective investment in transferable securities (UCITS) (recast)
USD	United States Dollar

Chapter One

THE EUROPEAN UNION BEFORE THE GLOBAL FINANCIAL CRISIS

ABSTRACT

The European Union has pursued the completion of the internal market in financial services through following its Financial Services Action Plan. Although the Commission was already empowered to enact subordinate legislation – the original authority being in Article 155 of the EEC Treaty, a special procedure called the Lamfalussy process was introduced for the Commission to be able to adopt detailed secondary legislation in the securities sector. The subsequent founding of the Committee of Banking Supervisors and the Committee of European Insurance and Occupational Pensions Supervisors, together with the extension of the advisory power of the Committee of European Securities Regulators to include the preparation of draft implementing legislation relating to UCITS, ensured that committees were in place to advise the Commission on the content of subordinate legislation in the fields of securities, banking and insurance. This structure formed the foundation upon which the post-GFC European Union architecture for the financial sector is based.

The majority of the chapter is devoted to describing the legislation for the securities and banking sectors immediately prior to the GFC. This provides a basis upon which to examine the laws that are currently in place, which is the subject of Chapter 4 of the monograph. Whilst the pre-GFC legislation is extensive and detailed, these instruments do not form a unified system for European financial regulation – even though they display common features. Thus, in 2006 or 2007, there is a developing framework, but a fair way to go before the sector is comprehensively and integrally supervised.

Keywords: European Community, directive, securities, investment, bank, credit institution

INTRODUCTION

In June 1985, the Commission published a White Paper, which outlined completion of an internal market for the free movement of goods, services, persons and capital by 1992 [1]. Article 13 of the Single European Act 1986 introduced this goal into EU law [2]. By the 1990s, it was clear that, with periodic enlargement of the European Communities (as they then were), the internal market was an on-going project which required refinement and progression. Development of the regulation of the financial sector was a significant part of this process, in respect of the free movement of services.

In May 1999, the Commission published the Financial Services Action Plan [3]. In addition to a programme for updating existing rules and for the development of new initiatives in the interests of the internal market, the plan proposed the creation of a securities committee, [4] which heralded the development of the specific regulatory environment for the sector – building upon the founding in December 1997 of the Forum of European Securities Commissions [5].

THE LAMFALUSSY PROCESS

The *Final Report of The Committee of Wise Men on the Regulation of European Securities Markets* recommended, amongst other things, the introduction of a process for the implementation of detailed secondary legislation over the area of securities' regulation [6]. This is known as 'the Lamfalussy process' – named after the Chairman of the Committee, Baron Alexandre Lamfalussy.

The Lamfalussy process has 4 levels, as follows. At level 1, framework principles are to be enacted by the co-decision procedure – the predecessor to the Ordinary Legislative Procedure in Article 294 of the TFEU in which the Commission proposes draft legislation to the Parliament and the Council, which are responsible for agreeing a final version of the instrument [7].

At level 2, an EU Securities Committee and an EU Securities Regulators Committee are to be founded. In the light of the output from level 1, and after consulting the EU Securities Committee, the Commission is to request the EU Securities Regulators Committee to start work on the technical details and to agree the time in which its advice is to be formulated. The Commission is to consider this advice, and to send a proposal to the EU Securities Committee, whilst informing the Parliament of the details of each event and document. If the EU Securities Committee agrees by qualified majority voting with the Commission's proposal, then the Commission may decide to enact the latter. The Parliament has one month from the vote of the EU Securities Committee in order to consider whether the final draft measures would exceed the Commission's implementing powers as defined by the output from level 1. The Parliament may pass a resolution which states that the measures surpass these powers – in which case the Commission is to re-examine its proposal, taking careful account of the Parliament's position [8].

At level 3, the EU Securities Regulators Committee is to ensure the consistent implementation of Community rules, by publishing consistent guidelines for administrative regulations that Member States will adopt, issuing interpretative recommendations, comparing and reviewing regulatory practices, and periodically carrying out peer reviews of these regulations and practices [9]. At level 4, the Commission is to check that Member States comply with EU legislation, and may bring a case before the European Court of Justice (as it then was)[1] for alleged breach of this law [10].

---

[1] The European Court of Justice has been renamed the Court of Justice of the European Union.

The MiFID [11] and Directive 2006/73/EC implementing Directive 2004/39/EC as regards organisational requirements and operating conditions for investment firms[2], [12] provide examples of level 1 and level 2 outputs from the Lamfalussy process, respectively. For instance, Article 13(10) of the MiFID states the following.

In order to take account of technical developments on financial markets and to ensure the uniform application of paragraphs 2 to 9 [of Article 13]., the Commission shall adopt implementing measures which specify the concrete organisational requirements to be imposed on investment firms performing different investment services or combinations thereof. ...

The level 2 Directive contains this statement.

The Commission of the European Communities, ... Having regard to Directive 2004/39/EC of the European Parliament and of the Council of 21 April 2004 on markets in financial instruments ... , and in particular Article 4(2), Article 13(10), Article 18(3), Article 19(10), Article 21(6), Article 22(3) and Article 24(5) thereof, ... has adopted this Directive ... [13].

Thus, a connection is made between Article 13(10) of the MiFID and its implementing instrument, Directive 2006/73/EC. The first of the 2 above quotes indicates that secondary measures may be enacted pursuant to paragraphs 2 to 9 of Article 13 of the MiFID. Article 13(2) of the MiFID is as follows.

An investment firm shall establish adequate policies and procedures sufficient to ensure compliance of the firm including its managers, employees and tied agents with its obligations under the provisions of this Directive as well as appropriate rules governing personal transactions by such persons.

Each implementing Article of the level 2 Directive contains the name of the Article of the level 1 Directive that gives rise to the former. Thus, Article 10 of Directive 2006/73/EC is an implementing provision of Article 13(2) of the MiFID, and appears thus.

Article 10

(Article 13(2) of Directive 2004/39/EC)

Complaints handling

Member States shall require investment firms to establish, implement and maintain effective and transparent procedures for the reasonable and prompt handling of complaints received from retail clients or potential retail clients, and to keep a record of each complaint and the measures taken for its resolution.

The level 1 and level 2 Directives fit together well. In the example, it is clear that Article 10 of Directive 2006/73/EC is enacted pursuant to Article 13(2) of the MiFID, on authority that Article 13(10) of the MiFID provides.

---

[2] Directive 2006/73/EC is known as the 'MiFID Implementing Directive'.

By 2008, 4 Lamfalussy level 1 Directives were in place, and 5 Lamfalussy level 2 Directives [14]. The 4 level 1 Directives are the MiFID, the MAD, [15] the PD [16] and the TD, [17] which are important components of the Financial Services Action Plan. Note, however, that the MiFID and the MAD are soon to be replaced, mainly by Regulations[3], and that the Commission is seeking to reform the PD, too[4] [18].

The content of level 2 Lamfalussy instruments may be considerable. For example, the Annexes to the PDR contain lists of the items that the issuers of different types of securities must place in the prospectus for the sale to the public or admission to trading of those securities [19].

EUROPEAN SUPERVISORS FOR BANKING AND INSURANCE ACTIVITIES

The European Communities founded the proposed Lamfalussy level 2 'EU Securities Committee' as the European Securities Committee, [20] and the planned levels 2 and 3 'EU Securities Regulators Committee' in the form of the Committee of European Securities Regulators [21] This process must have been deemed to be successful. For the European Communities founded 2 new institutions to provide advice to the Commission "in particular as regards the preparation of draft implementing measures in the field of banking activities" [22] and "in particular as regards the preparation of draft implementing measures in the fields of insurance, reinsurance and occupational pensions" [23] – namely the Committee of European Banking Supervisors [24] and the Committee of European Insurance and Occupational Pensions Supervisors, [25] respectively. In addition, the advisory power of the Committee of European Securities Regulators was amended to include the preparation of draft implementing legislation relating to UCITS, [26] thus extending the scope of the securities' advisory committee to investment funds[5].

These developments are the seeds of the European sectoral architecture that Chapter 3 is to discuss. From 1st January 2004, committees were in place to advise the Commission on the content of subordinate legislation in the fields of securities, banking and insurance[6].

---

[3] MiFID is to be superseded by MiFID II and the MIFIR. The MAD is to be repealed in favour of the MAR. Chapter 4 provides comments on the new legislation.

[4] In February 2015, the Commission issued a consultation document, which sought views from EU citizens and organisations on possible changes to the PD, in the light of its wish to pursue a Capital Markets Union. The consultation closed in May 2015. The results are available at https://ec.europa.eu/eusurvey/publication/ prospectus-directive-2015?language=en#.

[5] "[I]n November 2003 ... the Commission launched a package of measures designed to extend the Lamfalussy process to the areas of investment funds, banking and insurance ... . The fact of this extension is a positive reflection of the effect that the Lamfalussy process is perceived to have had in the area of securities, where it was first used." (European Commission (2007), FSAP Evaluation Part I: Process and implementation, p.11, <http://ec.europa.eu/internal_market/finances/docs/actionplan/index/070124_part1_en.pdf>.).

[6] The Committee of European Securities Regulators took up its duties on 7th June 2001 (Commission Decision 2001/527/EC, Article 8). The Committee of European Insurance and Occupational Pensions Supervisors commenced its role on 24th November 2003 (Commission Decision 2004/6/EC, Article 8). The Committee of European Banking Supervisors started to carry out its obligations on 1st January 2004 (Commission Decision 2004/5/EC, Article 8).

A Pause to Consider: The Role of the Commission in the Enactment of Secondary Legislation

The Lamfalussy process and subsequent developments in the sectoral architecture depend upon the power of the Commission to pass secondary legislation. The Council granted the Commission this power in 1987, [27] and formalized it in 1999[7] [28]. From the latter time, these implementing powers could be exercised by an advisory procedure, [29] a management procedure, [30] a regulatory procedure [31] or a safeguard procedure [32]. From July 2006, the Commission could alternatively exercise its implementing powers by a regulatory procedure with scrutiny [33]. Since 1st March 2011, a simpler, clearer process for the enactment of secondary legislation has applied with 2 alternative procedures – an advisory procedure and an examination procedure – together with the introduction of an appeal committee [34].

In all of these committee procedures, there is an element of representation from outside the EU institutions; for each committee contains representatives of the Member States – although chaired by a member of the Commission [35-38]. It may be informative to examine the original basis for the exercise of these powers – i.e., under the EEC Treaty[8]. Article 155 of the EEC Treaty states the following.

En vue d'assurer le fonctionnement et le développement du marché commun, la Commission: ... – exerce les compétences que le Counseil lui confère pour l'exécution des règles qu'il établit[9].

In 1958, the Assembly – now the Parliament – had mainly advisory capacity. This explains why it is the Council that confers competence on the Commission. Article 155 of the EEC Treaty makes it clear that Commission was, in principle, able to implement rules made under the Treaty.

The legislative basis for Council Decision 87/373/EEC was Article 145 of the EEC Treaty, [39] which is as follows.

En vue d'assurer la realization des objets fixés par le présent Traité et dans les conditions prévues par celui-ci, le Conseil: ... – dispose d'un pouvoir de décision[10].

Thus, provided that Treaty objectives and conditions are respected, the implementing powers contained in the Decision are legitimate. It is submitted that the principle to carry forward is that delegated legislative procedures, and, indeed the secondary legislation itself, must respect the objectives and the terms of the relevant Treaty – which was the Treaty

---

[7] The Council's Decision of 28 June 1999 provided criteria for the choice of committee procedures, clarified these procedures, and increased the involvement of the European Parliament in the secondary decision-making process (Council Decision 1999/468/EC, Recitals 5, 9 and 10).

[8] The EEC Treaty was superseded by the Treaty Establishing the European Community, and subsequently by the TFEU.

[9] With a view to ensuring the functioning and development of the common market, the Commission is to exercise the powers that the Council has conferred upon it for the implementation of the rules that the Council has established.

[10] With a view to ensuring the objectives of this Treaty and under the conditions that prevail under it, the Council may delegate a power of decision.

Establishing the European Community in the years immediately before the GFC, and is the combined TEU and TFEU today.[11]

By the time of arrival of the GFC, the Commission was able to pass secondary legislation either through the Lamfalussy process or through its general power to do so under Council Decision 1999/468/EC. The forerunner of today's European supervisory structure for the financial sector was present in the form of the Committee of European Securities Regulators, the Committee of European Insurance and Occupational Pensions Supervisors and the Committee of European Banking Supervisors. Chapter 3 will continue this theme.

SECURITIES LEGISLATION

Market Abuse

The European Community enacted the MAD, in order to further the development of an integrated services market, and to introduce provisions concerning market manipulation, which had not been addressed previously [40, 41]. It considered a single market for financial services to be essential for the creation of jobs and for economic growth within its territories, and market abuse to damage integrity and public confidence in financial instruments [42].

Member States are to prohibit any person who possesses inside information from using it in the purchase or sale of financial instruments[12] [43]. 'Inside information' includes specific information which has not been made public that would be likely to have a "significant effect" on the price of financial instruments or related derivatives[13] [44]. For persons who carry out orders which concern financial instruments, 'inside information' also includes precise information that a client conveys and which relates to his/her orders [45]. This prohibition does not apply to the discharge of a duty to purchase or sell financial instruments that originates from an agreement made before the relevant person possessed inside information [46].

Member States are also to prohibit any person from conducting market manipulation [47]. 'Market manipulation' includes orders to trade or transactions that provide false or misleading indications as to the price of, supply of, or demand for, financial instruments, or which secure the price of one or more financial instruments at an exceptional or artificial level, unless the person concerned demonstrates that his/her reasons for acting thus are valid and that the orders to trade or transactions are accepted market practice on the relevant regulated market [48]. It also includes transactions or orders to trade which make use of "deception or contrivance," [49] and the spread of information through the media that provides, or is likely to give, false or misleading signals in respect of financial instruments – as long as the person who disseminated the information knew, or ought to have known, the information to be false or misleading [50].

---

[11] The TEU and the TFEU are the Treaties upon which the EU is founded, and have the same legal value (TEU, Article 1; TFEU, Article 1(2)). Article 3 of the TEU contains the EU's objectives.

[12] This prohibition relates to the offence of insider dealing, which includes possession of the inside information by virtue of criminal activities, even when the person with the information is not connected (for instance, by employment or membership) to the person to whom the information relates (MAD, Article 2(1)(d)).

[13] A 'derivative' is a financial instrument whose price depends upon (i.e., 'derives from') the price of an underlying asset.

These prohibitions do not apply to share buy-back programmes or to the stabilisation of a financial instrument[14], as long as this trading is conducted in accordance with implementing measures adopted under the regulatory procedure[15] of Council Decision 1999/468/EEC[16] [51, 52]. Each Member State is to ensure that "appropriate administrative measures can be taken or administrative sanctions be imposed" if its provisions that transpose the MAD are breached; these measures are to be "effective, proportionate and dissuasive" [53]. As the harmonisation of sanctions is "outside the scope of Community competence," the MAD introduces a general duty for Member States to determine and impose suitable administrative and criminal penalties in order to ensure compliance with its provisions [54].

The Prospectus

The PD introduced a single European passport regime for prospectuses in relation to the offer of securities to the public or the admission of securities to trading on a regulated market, which was an increase in the level of harmonisation from the mutual recognition scheme that previously operated within the European Community for prospectuses [55, 56]. Member States are to require the publication of a prospectus before the securities that it promotes are offered to the public [57]. The duty to publish a prospectus does not apply to an offer of securities that is addressed only to qualified investors[17], to less than 100 non-qualified investors per Member State and/or to investors who purchase securities for a total sum of at least 50,000 Euros per investor per offer, and/or whose denomination per unit amounts to 50,000 Euros or more, and/or whose total consideration is for less than 100,000 Euros – calculated over one year [58]. Member States are also to ensure that all admissions of

---

[14] The MAD does not explain what is meant by 'stabilisation of a financial instrument'. The Directive states the following: "Stabilisation of financial instruments or trading in own shares in buy-back programmes can be legitimate, in certain circumstances, for economic reasons and should not, therefore, in themselves be regarded as market abuse. Common standards should be developed to provide practical guidance." (MAD (original version), Recital 33).

[15] In March 2008, this was changed from the regulatory procedure to the regulatory procedure with scrutiny (Directive 2008/26/EC of the European Parliament and of the Council of 11 March 2008 amending Directive 2003/6/EC on insider dealing and market manipulation (market abuse), as regards the implementing powers conferred on the Commission, Articles 1(3), 1(5)(a) and 2).

[16] The resulting measures are contained in Commission Regulation (EC) No 2273/2003 of 22 December 2003 implementing Directive 2003/6/EC of the European Parliament and of the Council as regards exemptions for buy-back programmes and stabilisation of financial instruments, Recital 11 of which explains that 'stabilisation' means "providing support for the price of an offering of relevant securities during a limited time period if they come under selling pressure, thus alleviating sales pressure generated by short term investors and maintaining an orderly market in the relevant securities. ...." Whilst this Regulation was enacted under the Commission's general power to pass legislation under Council Decision 1999/468/EC, the MAD is also accompanied by 3 Commission Directives which were enacted through the Lamfalussy process. Thus, the MAD is supported by secondary legislation that results from the use of both methods.

[17] Before the GFC, i.e., in the original version of the PD, 'qualified investors' was defined therein (rather than by reference to Annex II to the MiFID), as legal entities that are authorised or regulated to function in the financial markets, governments, central banks, international organisations, companies that are not SMEs, individuals with a securities portfolio of more than 500,000 Euros who have conducted large transactions on securities markets at 10 or more per quarter on average over the past year and who work or have worked as a professional with required knowledge of securities investment in the financial sector for at least one year – subject to mutual recognition and the permission of the requesting person's home Member State, and SMEs similarly subject (PD (original version), Articles 2(1)(e), 2(1)(f) and 2(2)).

securities to trading on regulated markets within their territories are subject to the publishing of a prospectus [59]. There are no exceptions to this latter rule.

The prospectus is to contain all information that is necessary to enable investors to conduct an informed assessment of the issuer's assets and liabilities, financial position, profit and losses, and prospects, and of the rights attached to the securities, and is to present this information clearly and comprehensibly [60]. Whilst the Annexes to the PDR specify data that the securities' issuer must include in the prospectus, the home Member State's competent authority "may authorise the omission from the prospectus of certain information," if, in its view, disclosure of this information would be "seriously detrimental" to the issuer (as long as the omission would be unlikely to mislead the public) or against the public interest, or the information is only of minor importance and will not influence the financial position of the issuer, offeror or guarantor [61].

Other than for non-equity securities with a denomination of at least 50,000 Euros, the prospectus is to include a summary that concisely and clearly conveys the essential features and risks with which the issuer is associated [62]. Whilst Member States are to ensure that their rules on civil liability apply to the persons who are responsible for the information in a prospectus, they are also to make sure that no civil liability attaches to anyone exclusively on the basis of the summary – unless this is inaccurate, inconsistent or misleading when read in conjunction with the rest of the prospectus [63]. In instances in which the final offer price and amount of securities to be offered to the public are unable to be included in the prospectus, Member States are to ensure that the conditions and/or the criteria in accordance with which this price and amount will be determined, and the maximum price, are placed therein [64]. In that situation, the acceptances of the acquisition of securities may be revoked for up to 2 working days after the final offer price and amount of securities which are to be offered to the public have been filed with the home Member State's competent authority [65].

A prospectus is valid for one year after its publication, as long as it is completed by any required supplements [66]. Each "significant new factor, material mistake or inaccuracy" that relates to the information included in the prospectus, is capable of affecting the appraisal of the securities, and arises before the final closing of the public offer or the time at which trading on a regulated market commences, is to be included in a supplement to the prospectus [67]. Issuers whose securities are admitted to trading on a regulated market are to supply at least annually a document that contains or refers to information that they have published or made available to the public over the preceding year – unless these securities are non-equity items with a denomination per unit of at least 50,000 Euros [68].

The competent authority of the issuer's home Member State must approve the prospectus, before the latter can be published [69]. Member States are to ensure that "appropriate administrative measures can be taken or administrative sanctions be imposed" against the persons who are responsible, if the national provisions that transpose the PD have been contravened; these measures are to be "effective, proportionate and dissuasive" [70].

Financial Instruments

The Commission proposed the MiFID, in order to further the single passport regime for investment services[18] and to provide a comprehensive supervisory system to govern the conduct of transactions in financial instruments[19] [71, 72]. By introducing the MTF[20] as an authorised forum for trading financial instruments, the MiFID enables investment firms[21] in all Member States to carry out the orders of clients other than on a regulated market[22] [73].

Each Member State is to require that the provision of investment services "as a regular occupation or on a professional basis," and the running of an MTF by a market operator[23], to be subject to prior authorisation in accordance with Articles 5 to 15 of the MiFID[24] [74]. Authorisation is to cover the investment services and ancillary services that the firm is to provide, although permission is not to be granted for supplying only ancillary services[25] [75]. The authorisation is valid throughout the whole of the European Community, and is to permit an investment firm to supply the services for which it has been authorised throughout this area [76].

Conditions for authorisation are as follows. Each Member State is to require an investment firm that is a legal person to locate its head office in the same country as its registered office, and that any other investment firm has its head office in the Member State in which it conducts its business [77]. The investment firm is to supply all information that is necessary for the competent authority to be satisfied that the applicant has established all of the necessary arrangements to fulfil its obligations under Articles 5 to 15 of the MiFID [78]. The competent authority is to refuse authorisation, if it is not satisfied that the persons who are to direct the investment firm's business "are of sufficiently good repute or sufficiently experienced," or if there exist "objective and demonstrable grounds" to believe that proposed

---

[18] 'Investment services' are the reception and transmission of orders in respect of financial instruments, the carrying out of orders on behalf of clients, dealing on own account, portfolio management, investment advice, the underwriting of and the placement of financial instruments, and the operation of MTFs (MiFID (as amended to 21/09/07), Article 4(1)(2) and Annex I, Section A).

[19] 'Financial instruments' comprise transferable securities, money market instruments, UCITS, derivative contracts (with specified exceptions) and financial contracts for differences (MiFID (as amended to 21/09/07), Annex I, Section C).

[20] An 'MTF' is a multilateral system which assembles third-party interests in the purchase and sale of financial instruments in a manner that results in a contract in accordance with Title II of the MiFID (MiFID (as amended to 21/09/07), Article 4(1)(15)).

[21] 'Investment firm' means any person (excluding natural persons in specified exceptional circumstances) whose regular business or occupation is the supply of investment services to third parties on a professional basis (MiFID (as amended to 21/09/07), Article 4(1)(1)).

[22] A 'regulated market' is a multilateral system which collects third-party interests in the purchase and sale of financial instruments in a manner that results in a contract, and which is authorised and operates regularly and in accordance with Title III of the MiFID (MiFID (as amended to 21/09/07), Article 4(1)(14)).

[23] 'Market operator' means a person or persons who operate(s) and/or manage(s) the business of a regulated market (MiFID (as amended to 21/09/07), Article 4(1)(13)).

[24] The market operator of an MTF need not comply with Articles 11 and 15 of the MiFID (MiFID (as amended to 21/09/07), Article 5(2)).

[25] 'Ancillary services' are the safekeeping and administration of financial instruments on behalf of clients, the grant of loans or credits to an investor to conduct a transaction in financial instruments in cases in which the firm that provides the credit or loan is a party to the transaction, advice to firms on capital structure and industrial strategy, advice and services to entities that concerns mergers and acquisitions, foreign exchange services which are connected to the supply of investment services, investment research, financial analysis, services that are related to underwriting, and investment and ancillary services that are connected to the underlying assets of derivatives – if these are associated with the provision of investment or ancillary services (MiFID (as amended to 21/09/07), Annex I, Section B).

changes to the applicant's managers are a danger "to its sound and prudent management" [79]. The competent authority is also to refuse permission, if it is not satisfied as to the appropriateness of the shareholders or members that have qualifying holdings[26] in the investment firm, given the need to ensure the applicant's "sound and prudent management"; if there are close links[27] between the investment firm and other persons, then the authority is only to grant authorisation if these connections do not stop the effective exercise of the latter's supervisory duties [80]. Furthermore, the competent authority is to refuse permission if the rules of a third country that governs at least one person with whom the firm has close links, or problems with the enforcement of these provisions, hinder the effective use of the authority's supervisory functions [81]. The competent authority must verify that any applicant for authorisation as an investment firm satisfies its obligations under the Directive on Investor Compensation Schemes[28] [82]. Member States are to ensure that the competent authority does not grant permission, unless the investment firm has sufficient initial capital in accordance with the applicable Capital Requirements Directive[29] [83]. The home Member State[30] is to require investment firms to comply with specified organisational requirements, which include, for instance, the need for each firm to have sound accounting and administrative procedures, internal control mechanisms, effective processes for risk assessment, and effective safeguard and control arrangements for systems that process information [84]. There are additional requirements for the authorisation of investment firms or market operators that run MTFs; for instance, Member States are to require these applicants to establish transparent rules concerning the criteria for determining the financial instruments which can be traded on the relevant MTF [85].

The MiFID's operating rules for investment firms comprise general provisions[31], measures to ensure investor protection[32], and duties regarding market transparency and integrity[33]. The general provisions include a direction to Member States to require each investment firm to continuously observe the conditions for authorisation [86]. Member States are to require competent authorities to establish suitable methods to monitor that firms are adhering to this duty [87]. Member States are to ensure that their competent authorities

---

[26] 'Qualifying holding' means any holding in an investment firm that represents at least 10% of its voting rights or capital, or which makes it possible to exert a "significant influence" over the firm's management (MiFID (as amended to 21/09/07), Article 4(1)(27)).

[27] 'Close links' means a situation in which 2 persons are connected by ownership of 20% or more of the voting rights or capital of a company, control –which is the relationship between a parent undertaking and a subsidiary, and a situation in which at least 2 persons are permanently connected to a third person by a control relationship (MiFID (as amended to 21/09/07), Article 4(1)(31)).

[28] This is Directive 97/9/EC of the European Parliament and of the Council of 3 March 1997 on investor-compensation schemes; see the subsection 'Deposit guarantee and investor compensation schemes', in the section 'Banking Legislation', below in this chapter.

[29] This is Council Directive 93/9/EEC of 15 March 1993 on the capital adequacy of investment firms and credit institutions – although the MiFID-amending Directives should have changed this to Directive 2006/49/EC of the European Parliament and of the Council of 14 June 2006 on the capital adequacy of investment firms and credit institutions – which applied from 20th July 2006, and subsequently to the CRR – which has applied since 1st January 2014.

[30] 'Home Member State' means the country in which the registered office (or, in its absence, the head office) of an investment firm is situated (MiFID (as amended to 21/09/07), Article 4(1)(20)(a)). This phrase also means the Member State in which a regulated market is registered (or, if the regulated market has no registered office, the country in which its head office is located) (MiFID (as amended to 21/09/07), Article 4(1)(20)(b)).

[31] These are Articles 16-18 of the MiFID.

[32] These are Articles 19-24 of the MiFID.

[33] These are Articles 25-30 of the MiFID.

monitor investment firms' activities in order to appraise the compliance of those firms with the MiFID's operating rules, and that suitable measures are in place to enable these authorities to acquire the information needed to assess this compliance [88]. Member States are to require investment firms to take all reasonable actions to identify internal conflicts of interest [89]. If a firm's arrangements for the management of these conflicts are insufficient to reasonably ensure that the risks of harm to the interests of clients will be averted, then it is to clearly disclose the sources and/or the general nature of conflicts of interest to each customer before undertaking business on the latter's behalf [90].

Measures to ensure investor protection include the following. Member States are to require investment firms to "act honestly, fairly and professionally in accordance with the best interests of their clients" when supplying services to customers [91]. Further to this duty, each firm is to comply with specified principles, which include, for instance, the duty to provide its clients with "adequate reports" on the work that it performs for them [92]. Member States are to require investment firms to "take all reasonable steps" to achieve the optimal result for their customers, taking into consideration any factor that is relevant to the execution of the order – although each firm must follow a specific instruction that the client gives [93]. Member States are to require firms to set up and implement an order execution policy, in order to enable the latter to obtain this optimum outcome [94]. Member States shall require investment firms to implement arrangements and procedures that enable "the prompt, fair and expeditious execution of client orders" [95]. Member States are to ensure that firms may enter into transactions with eligible counterparties without being obliged to observe the duties described above in this paragraph, in respect of these transactions and any ancillary service that is "directly related" to them [96]. The MiFID defines 'eligible counterparties' widely, to include, for instance, financial institutions that are authorised or regulated under Community law or the provisions of a Member State [97].

Obligations of investment firms concerning market transparency and integrity include the following. Member States are to make sure there are "appropriate measures" in place to allow the competent authority to monitor investment firms' activities, in order to ensure that these organisations "act honestly, fairly and professionally and in a manner which promotes the integrity of the market" [98]. Member States are to require investment firms to keep available to the competent authority, for 5 years or more, the relevant data concerning all transactions in financial instruments that they have conducted [99]. Member States shall require firms that carry out transactions in any financial instruments that have been admitted to trading on a regulated market – whether or not the transactions were conducted on a regulated market – to report details of these deals to the competent authority by the close of the next working day [100]. The reports are to include the names and numbers of the financial instruments purchased or sold, the dates and times of the deal's execution, the transaction prices, and ways of identifying the relevant investment firm(s) [101]. Member States are to require entities that operate an MTF to set up and maintain effective arrangements and procedures for monitoring its users' observance of its rules [102]. These organisations are to monitor the transactions carried out on the MTF, in order to identify contraventions of these rules, disorderly conditions for trading, or possible market abuse – which they are to report to the competent authority [103]. They are to promptly supply all relevant information to the authority which is responsible for the investigation and prosecution of market abuse, and to give full assistance to the latter in respect of possible market abuse taking place on or through the MTF [104]. Member States are to require systematic internalisers[34] that deal in transactions of up to "standard market size"[35] to publish a firm quote for shares in which they trade and which are admitted to trading on a regulated market for which "a liquid market" exists[36] [105]. Systematic internalisers are to be permitted to decide, in an objective non-discriminatory manner and in accordance with their commercial policy, the investors to whom they allow access to their quotes [106]. Member States are to require investment firms that carry out transactions in shares admitted to trading on a regulated market, but outside an MTF or a regulated market, to promptly and accessibly publish the price and volume of these deals and the time at which they were made [107]. Member States are to require entities which operate an MTF to make public current bid and offer prices, and the extent of trading interests on the MTF at these prices, in respect of shares that are admitted to trading on a regulated market [108]. Member States are also to require organisations which operate an MTF to publish the time, price and volume of the transactions concluded under this MTF's systems in respect of shares that are admitted to trading on a regulated market[37] [109].

A firm may use the 'investment services passport' in order to provide investment (and associated ancillary) services for which it has been authorised by the competent authority of its home Member State, to other Member States without requiring further permission. These services may be supplied with or without the founding of a branch, whose establishment of in the host Member State[38] requires additional formalities.

Thus, Member States are to ensure that any investment firm which is authorised and supervised by the competent authority of another Member State in accordance with the MiFID, and any credit institution that is licensed to provide financial services in agreement with the applicable Banking Directive[39], may supply investment and associated ancillary services within their territories, as long as these services are within the scope of its authorisation; they are not to place any additional requirements on such an investment firm or credit institution in respect of matters that the MiFID covers [110]. An investment firm that wishes to begin to provide services within the territory of another Member State, or which would like to alter the range of services that it supplies there, is to communicate the name of

---

[34] 'Systematic internaliser' means an investment firm which, on a systematic, frequent and organised basis, deals on own account by conducting client orders outside a regulated market or an MTF (MiFID (as amended to 21/09/07), Article 4(1)(8)).

[35] Article 27(1) of the MiFID provides guidelines on how to group shares into classes and compute 'standard market size' for each of these.

[36] If there is no liquid market for the relevant shares, then systematic internalisers are to disclose quotes to their customers on request (MiFID (as amended to 21/09/07), Article 27(1)). A 'liquid market' is one in which there are buyers and sellers who are ready to relinquish, and pay for, the securities, respectively, at the stated price.

[37] This requirement does not apply to details of trade conducted on an MTF that are published under the systems of a regulated market (MiFID (as amended to 21/09/07), Article 30(1)).

[38] 'Host Member State' means the Member State (other than the home Member State) in which an investment firm runs a branch or provides services, or the Member State in which a regulated market makes suitable arrangements so as to facilitate access to trading on its system by remote members that are established there (MiFID (as amended to 21/09/07), Article 4(1)(21)).

[39] This is Directive 2000/12/EC of the European Parliament and of the Council of 20 March 2000 relating to the taking up and pursuit of the business of credit institutions – although the MiFID-amending Directives should have changed this to the BCD – which applied from 20th July 2006, and subsequently to CRD IV – which has applied since 1st January 2014. A 'credit institution' is an entity whose business is to receive repayable funds from the public and to provide credits for its own account, or an electronic money institution within the meaning of Directive 2000/46/EC of the European Parliament and of the Council of 18 September 2000 on the taking up, pursuit and prudential supervision of the business of electronic money institutions (MiFID (as amended to 21/09/07), Article 4(1)(23); Directive 2000/12/EC (as amended to 09/03/06), Article 1(1)).

the host Member State, a programme of operations which states the investment and ancillary services that it intends to deliver there, and whether it intends to use tied agents[40] in the host Member State, to its home Member State's competent authority [111]. Within one month of receiving the information, the latter is to forward it to the host Member State's competent authority – after which the investment firm may provide the relevant investment services in that country [112].

Without further legal or administrative requirements, Member States are to permit entities that operate MTFs from other Member States to provide suitable arrangements on their territory so as to enable access to, and use of, their systems by remote users established there [113]. The investment firm or the market operator that runs an MTF is to communicate to the competent authority of the MTF's home Member State the country in which it intends establish these arrangements; within one month, this authority is to forward that information to the host Member State[41] [114].

Member States are to ensure that investment and associated ancillary services may be supplied within their territories in accordance with the MiFID and the applicable Banking Directive[42] through the founding of a branch, as long as these services are covered by the authorisation that the home Member State's competent authority has granted to the investment firm or the credit institution; they are not to place any additional requirements on the organisation and functioning of the branch in respect of issues that the MiFID covers, other than those that Article 32(7) of the MiFID permits [115]. Under Article 32(7), the competent authority of the Member State in which the branch is situated is responsible for ensuring that the services which the branch provides within its territory comply with the obligations contained in Articles 19, 21. 22, 25, 27 and 28 of the MiFID[43] and in provisions enacted pursuant thereto[44] [116].

Member States are to require an investment firm that wishes to establish a branch in the territory of another Member State to notify the competent authority of the entity's home Member State and to furnish it with the following information: the name of the host Member State, a programme of operations that sets out the investment and ancillary services to be offered, the branch's organisational structure and whether the branch will be using tied agents, the address in the host Member State from which documents may be acquired, and the names of the branch's managers [117]. Unless the home Member State's competent authority "has reason to doubt the adequacy of" the firm's financial circumstances or administrative structure – taking the planned activities into consideration, within 3 months of receiving all of the information it shall forward these data to the host Member State's competent authority and inform the firm accordingly [118]. The home Member State's competent authority shall

---

[40] 'Tied agent' means a person who, under the full, unconditional responsibility of a single investment firm on whose behalf it acts, promotes investment and/or ancillary services to clients or prospective customers, receives and transmits orders and instructions from the client in respect of financial instruments or investment services, places financial instruments and/or furnishes advice to clients or prospective customers in respect of those financial instruments or services (MiFID (as amended to 21/09/07), Article 4(1)(26)).

[41] At the request of the host Member State's competent authority, the competent authority of the MTF's home Member State is to notify the former of the identity of the MTF's members who are established in the host Member State (MiFID (as amended to 21/09/07), Article 31(6)).

[42] See fn 39.

[43] These provisions are some of the operating conditions for investment firms – see above in this subsection.

[44] In carrying out its responsibilities under the MiFID, each host Member State may require the branches of investment firms to supply the information that is necessary for the monitoring of their compliance with the standards which it sets pursuant to Article 32(7) of the MiFID (MiFID (as amended to 21/09/07), Article 61(2)).

also send details of the investment firm's accredited compensation scheme to the host Member State's competent authority [119]. If the former refuses to forward the information to the latter, then it is to give reasons for this decision to the investment firm within 3 months of receiving all of the data [120]. On receipt of a communication from the host Member State's competent authority, or after 2 months have passed from the date of transmission of the information to this entity, the branch may be founded and may start business [121].

The 'investment services passport' extends to the right to trade on regulated markets that are situated in other countries of the EU. Member States are to require that investment firms from other Member States which are authorised to carry out client orders or to deal on own account, have the right of access to regulated markets established in their territory by way of either of the following arrangements: by establishing branches in the host Member States, and by becoming remote members of the regulated market [122]. Member States are not to lay down any additional requirements on firms that exercise this right, in respect of the issues covered by the MiFID [123].

Each Member State is to require that investment firms from other countries of the EU have the right of access to central counterparty, clearing and settlement systems in its territory in order to conclude transactions in financial instruments, and that access to these facilities is subject to the same transparent, objective, fair criteria as apply to local participants [124]. Member States are to allow entities that operate an MTF to enter into suitable arrangements with a central counterparty, clearing house or settlement system of another country of the EU, in order to prepare for the clearing and/or settlement of some or all of the trades that market participants conduct on the MTF [125].

In addition to the authorisation of investment firms, and of entities that run MTFs (whether these are investment firms or market operators), the MiFID also provides for the authorisation of regulated markets. Authorisation as a regulated market is only to be granted if its home Member State's competent authority is satisfied that both the market operator (whether this is the regulated market itself or another person) and the regulated market's systems comply with the requirements of Articles 36 to 47 of the MiFID; the market operator is to present all information which enables this competent authority to be satisfied that the regulated market has established all of the necessary arrangements to fulfil these duties[45] [126]. Member States are to ensure that their competent authorities regularly review the continuing observance of regulated markets with those obligations [127]. The competent authority is to refuse to authorise the regulated market if it considers that the latter's decision-takers are of inadequately good repute and insufficient experience so as to ensure its "sound and prudent management," and to reject proposed changes in these personnel if "there are objective and demonstrable grounds for believing that they pose a material threat to" this management and to the regulated market's operation [128]. Member States are to require the persons who are positioned to exert "significant influence" on the regulated market's management to be "suitable"[46] [129]. The competent authority is to reject planned alterations to the regulated market's and/or the market operator's controlling interests in instances in which "there are objective and demonstrable grounds for believing that they would pose a threat to the sound and prudent management of" that market [130]. Member States are to

---

[45] This information is to include a programme of operations, which sets out the types of business planned and the organisational structure (MiFID (as amended to 21/09/07), Article 36(1)).
[46] The MiFID defines neither 'significant influence' nor 'suitable'.

require the regulated market to have the following organisational features in place: (a) arrangements for the identification and management of possible detrimental consequences of any conflict between the interests of the regulated market, its owners, its operator and its "sound functioning," (b) an effective system for the identification, management and mitigation of risks, (c) arrangements for the "sound management of" the system's technical operations, (d) transparent, obligatory rules and procedures for fair, orderly and objectively efficient trading, (e) effective systems to assist the competent, timely finalization of transactions, and (f) adequate financial resources to enable the "orderly functioning" of the regulated market [131]. Member States are to require regulated markets to have clear, open rules concerning the admission of financial instruments to trading, which ensure that the latter are able to be "traded in a fair, orderly and efficient manner" − in particular that transferable securities[47] are freely negotiable, and that derivative contracts permit the tidy pricing of these instruments and the presence of the conditions for "effective settlement" [132]. Member States are to require the regulated market to draw up and maintain transparent, fair, objective rules to govern access to the latter [133]. Member States are to require each regulated market to establish and preserve effective arrangements and procedures for monitoring its members' observance of its rules [134]. This market is to monitor the transactions conducted by its members on its systems, in order to identify contraventions of these rules, disorderly conditions for trading, or possible market abuse − which its operator is to report to the competent authority [135]. The market operator is to swiftly supply all relevant information to the authority that is responsible for the investigation and prosecution of market abuse, and to give full assistance to the latter with regard to possible market abuse taking place on or through the regulated market's systems [136]. Member States are to require regulated markets to publish current bid and offer prices, and the volume of trading interests at these prices that are advertised through their systems, in respect of shares which are admitted to trading [137]. Member States are also to require regulated markets to make public the price, time and volume of the transactions which are concluded in respect of shares that are admitted to trading on a regulated market [138].

MiFID includes a 'regulated markets passport', which is similar to that provided for MTFs under paragraphs 5 and 6 of Article 31 of that Directive[48]. Without further requirements, each Member State is to permit regulated markets from other Member States to put suitable arrangements in place on its territory, in order to enable remote members established in the former to trade on these markets; the regulated market is to inform the competent authority of its home Member State of the name of the host Member State, which forwards this information to the latter's competent authority within one month [139]. Member States are to require the market operator to regularly send the list of the regulated market's members to the competent authority of that market's home Member State [140]. In addition, Member States are to permit regulated markets to agree suitable arrangements with a central counterparty, clearing house or settlement system of another country within the EU, in order to provide for the clearing and/or settlement of some or all of the trades that participants conclude on the systems of those markets [141].

---

[47] 'Transferable securities' means categories of securities that are negotiable on the capital market − other than payment instrument; examples include shares in companies and bonds (MiFID (as amended to 21/09/07), Article 4(1)(18)).

[48] See above in this subsection, for Article 31 of the MiFID.

Each competent authority is to be given all powers of investigation and supervision that it requires in order to perform its functions [142]. These powers are to be exercised in accordance with national law; they shall include, for instance, the rights to access and receive any document, question any person, request the immobilization and/or the sequestration of assets, and require a financial instrument to be suspended or withdrawn from trading [143].

Member States are to ensure that, in accord with their domestic law, suitable administrative measures may be taken or administrative sanctions be laid on the persons responsible, if provisions enacted in the transposition of the MiFID have been breached; these measures are to be "effective, proportionate and dissuasive" [144]. They are also to ensure that, any decision taken under rules enacted in conformance with the MiFID is thoroughly reasoned and "subject to the right to apply to the courts"[49] [145].

Member States are to ensure that competent authorities, their present and former employees, and auditors and experts whom these authorities instruct, are bound by the duty of professional secrecy – no confidential information received in connection with their work may be disclosed to any person or authority, other than in summary or aggregate form such that individual persons are unable to be identified[50] [146]. The competent authorities, and other persons who receive confidential information pursuant to the MiFID, may only use it "in the performance of their duties and for the exercise of their functions"[51] [147].

Competent authorities of different Member States are to co-operate with each other as necessary for the purposes of performing their duties under the MiFID, and of exercising their powers set out there or in their domestic law [148]. A competent authority may request another Member State's competent authority to co-operate with the former in a supervisory activity, an investigation or an on-the-spot verification; in the latter 2 schemes, the recipient may carry out the procedure itself, permit the requesting authority to conduct it, or allow auditors or experts to undertake it [149].

The competent authority is to consult the competent authority of the other Member State before the former grants authorisation to an investment firm that is a subsidiary of, a subsidiary of the parent company of, or controlled by the same persons as control, another investment firm, a credit institution[52], or an insurance firm, which is supervised by that latter authority [150]. These competent authorities are to exchange all information that concerns "suitability of shareholders or members and the reputation and experience of persons who effectively direct the business," for both the granting of an authorisation and the continuing assessment of conformity to operating conditions [151].

Article 62 of the MiFID, which is entitled "Precautionary measures to be taken by host Member States," is separated into 3 paragraphs, the first of which considers this procedure in respect of the free movement of investment services – and the freedom of establishment in instances in which power is not conferred upon the host Member State's competent authority, the second of which details the process in relation to the operation of a branch in another Member State in instances in which there is such a transfer of power, and the third of which lays down the procedure in relation to the provision of services by a regulated market or an MTF to members in other countries of the EU. Any measure adopted pursuant to one of these

---

[49] This probably means the courts of the Member State in which the decision is taken.

[50] This is without prejudice to the application of the criminal law and to the other provisions of the MiFID (MiFID (as amended to 21/09/07), Article 54(1)).

[51] This is without prejudice to the application of the criminal law (MiFID (as amended to 21/09/07), Article 54(2)).

[52] See fn 39, for the applicable definition of a 'credit institution'.

paragraphs which involves sanctions or restrictions on an investment firm's, or a regulated market's, activities must be "properly justified" and notified to that entity [152].

If the host Member State's competent authority has "clear and demonstrable grounds for believing that" the investment firm is in contravention of the duties arising from the national provisions that transpose the MiFID, or that the investment firm's branch within its territory is in transgression of the obligations originating from such rules which do not confer powers on this authority, then it is to refer these findings to the home Member State's competent authority. If, despite the measures that the latter authority takes or because those measures prove to be insufficient, the firm persists in acting in a way that is clearly prejudicial to the interests of investors in the host Member State or "the orderly functioning of markets," then the host Member State's competent authority, after notifying the home Member State's competent authority, is to take all of the suitable measures that are needed in order to shield investors and "the proper functioning of the markets," and is to promptly inform the Commission of these measures [153].

If the host Member State's competent authority ascertains that an investment firm which has a branch within its territory that is in contravention of the national provisions that transpose the MiFID which confer powers on that country's competent authority, then these authorities are to require the firm to "put an end to its irregular situation." If the firm does not "take the necessary steps," then this competent authority is to take all suitable measures to ensure that the firm "puts an end to its irregular situation," and to inform the home Member State's competent authority of "the nature of those measures." If, despite these measures, the firm persists in its transgression of these national provisions, then the host Member State's competent authority may, after informing the home Member State's competent authority, take suitable measures "to prevent or penalize further irregularities," and is to swiftly notify the Commission of these measures [154].

If the competent authority of the host Member State of a regulated market or of an MTF has "clear and demonstrable grounds for believing that" this market or MTF is in contravention of the duties arising from the domestic provisions that transpose the MiFID, then it is to refer these findings the competent authority of the home Member State of the regulated market or the MTF. If, despite the measures that the latter takes or because these are insufficient, the regulated market or the MTF continues to act in a way that is biased against the interests of investors in the host Member State or "the orderly functioning of markets," then the host Member State's competent authority, after notifying the home Member State's competent authority, is to take all the suitable measures that are required in order to safeguard investors and "the proper functioning of markets," and is to quickly inform the Commission of these measures [155].

Member States may make co-operation agreements that provide for the exchange of information with the competent authorities of third countries, and with other specified entities from those states, only if the information divulged is "subject to guarantees of professional secrecy at least equivalent to those required under Article 54" of the MiFID[53]; this exchange of information must be intended for the performance of the duties of these entities [156]. These data may only be disclosed with the express agreement of the competent authorities that have communicated them, and only for the purposes for which these authorities have agreed [157].

---

[53] See above in this subsection, for paragraphs 1 and 3 of Article 54 of the MiFID.

Member States are to transpose the MiFID into national law by 31st January 2007, and to apply these provisions from 1st November 2007 [158]. Thus, the rules considered in this subsection reflect approximately the state of the law for financial instruments within the EU at the start of the GFC.

The Official Listing of Securities

The CARD was enacted in order to codify 4 earlier Directives[54], which had been substantially amended [159]. These latter Directives have been repealed [160].

Member States are to ensure that securities may not be admitted to official listing on a stock exchange that is located or functioning within their territory, unless the conditions that the CARD states are met and the issuers[55] of these securities are subject to the obligations for which this Directive provides [161]. The admission of shares to official listing are subject to the conditions in Articles 42 to 51 of the CARD; the admission of debt securities to official listing is governed by Articles 52 to 63 of the Directive [162].

Member States may subject the admission of securities to official listing to stricter conditions than those which Articles 42 to 63 of the CARD set out, or to additional conditions, as long as these apply to all issuers or to specified classes of issuer and have been published before the application for admission to official listing is made [163]. Member States may make liable to additional duties the issuers of securities admitted to official listing, as long as these further obligations apply to all issuers or to stated classes of issuer [164]. Member States may authorise derogations from the additional or stricter conditions and duties, provided that any detractions from the conditions for the admission of securities to official listing apply to all issuers in instances in which the circumstances justifying them are similar [165].

A Member State may, "solely in the interests of protecting the investors," grant its competent authority the power to subject the admission of a security to official listing to "any special condition" which this authority considers to appropriate and of which it has notified the applicant [166]. A competent authority may reject an application for the admission of a security to official listing if, in its opinion, the issuer's circumstances are such that acceptance would harm the interests of investors [167]. The authority may refuse to admit a security to official listing, if its issuer does not fulfil the obligations that result from its earlier admission to official listing in another Member State [168].

An issuer whose securities are admitted to official listing is to give the competent authority all of the information that the latter considers to be "appropriate in order to protect investors or ensure the smooth operation of the market" [169]. The competent authority may

---

[54] These Directives are Council Directive 79/279/EEC of 5 March 1979 coordinating the conditions for the admission of securities to official stock exchange listing, Council Directive 80/390/EEC of 17 March 1980 coordinating the requirements for drawing up, scrutiny and distribution of the listing particulars to be published for the admission of securities to official stock exchange listing, Council Directive 82/121/EEC of 15 February 1982 on information to be published on a regular basis by companies the shares of which have been admitted to official stock-exchange listing, and Council Directive 88/627/EEC of 12 December 1988 on the information to be published when a major holding in a listed company is acquired or disposed of (CARD (as amended to 24/03/05), Recital 1).

[55] 'Issuers' means any entity whose securities are the subject of an application for admission to official listing on a stock exchange (CARD (as amended to 24/03/05), Article 1(a)).

suspend the listing of a security in instances in which "the smooth operation of the market is, or may be, temporarily jeopardized," or "where protection of investors so requires" [170]. It may discontinue the listing of a security, if it is satisfied that "owing to special circumstances" usual transactions in this instrument are henceforth impossible [171]. Each Member State must ensure that decisions of its competent authority to refuse admission of a security to official listing or to discontinue this listing, are to be "subject to the right to apply to the courts"[56] [172].

This paragraph concerns conditions for admission of shares of a company to official listing. The firm's legal position must conform to the laws and regulations that govern that entity, in respect of both its formation and its working [173]. The estimated market capitalisation[57] of the shares for which admission to official listing is sought, is to be one million Euros or more[58] [174]. Member States may allow admission to official listing in the absence of fulfilment of this condition, as long as the competent authority is content that the shares will have "an adequate market" [175]. The condition is not to apply to the admission to official listing of a further issue of shares of a class which has already been admitted [176]. The company is to have filed or published its annual accounts in agreement with national law for the previous 3 financial years [177]. The shares' legal position must conform to the laws and regulations to which they are liable [178]. The shares are to be freely negotiable [179]. If the public issue of shares precedes their admission to official listing, then the listing may only take place subsequent to the period during which applications for subscription for a holding of the shares may be submitted [180]. "A sufficient number of shares" are to have been dispensed to the public in at least one Member State by the time of their admission[59] [181]. If the shares are admitted to official listing in at least one country that is not a Member State, then the competent authority may permit their admission to official listing in the relevant Member State if "a sufficient number of shares" are distributed to the public in the former lands [182]. 'A sufficient number of shares' are distributed either if the shares in respect of which application for admission to official listing has been made are issued to the public to the extent that 25% or more of the subscribed capital of shares of this class are owned by the public, or if the market will function properly with a smaller percentage [183]. The application shall cover all of the shares of the same class that have already been issued [184]. For a new public issue of shares of the same class as those already officially listed, the firm must (if necessary) apply for their admission to the same listing either within one year of their issue or at the point at which they become freely negotiable [185].

This paragraph considers conditions for the admission of debt securities that are issued by a company to official listing. The legal position of these securities must conform to the laws and regulations to which these instruments are subject [186]. The debt securities are to be freely negotiable [187]. If their public issue precedes their admission to official listing, then this listing may only be made beyond the period during which applications for subscription

---

[56] These are the courts of the Member State in which the relevant decision is taken.

[57] If an assessment of anticipated market capitalisation is impossible, then the company's capital and reserves from the previous financial year are used instead (CARD (as amended to 24/03/05), Article 43(1)).

[58] A Member State may only require a higher anticipated market capitalisation (or capital and reserves), if that country contains another functioning, regulated market with requirements that are no greater than those to which paragraph 1 of Article 43 refers (CARD (as amended to 24/03/05), Article 43(3)).

[59] If admission to official listing is sought for further shares of the same class, then the competent authority may examine whether a "sufficient number of shares" has been dispensed to the public in relation to all of the issued shares of this class (CARD (as amended to 24/03/05), Article 48(3)).

for a holding of the instruments may be submitted[60] [188]. The application for admission to official listing is to cover all of the debt securities that rank *pari passu*[61]. The principal of the loan must be at least 200,000 Euros[62] [189]. Member States may permit admission to official listing in the absence of this condition, provided that the competent authority is satisfied that "a sufficient market" for the instruments will exist [190]. Convertible debentures, exchangeable debentures, and debentures with warrants may be admitted to official listing, only if the related shares are already listed on a "regulated, regularly operating, recognised open market" or are admitted for listing on such a market at the same time as the hybrid instrument is listed [191]. Nevertheless, Member States may allow these hybrids to be admitted to official listing, if the competent authority is satisfied that the holders possess all of the information that is required to come to a view about the value of the shares to which the hybrids relate [192].

This paragraph concerns conditions for the admission to official listing of debt securities that are issued by a government body or a public international organisation. The debt securities are to be freely negotiable [193]. If public issue of these instruments precedes their admission to official listing, then listing may only be made following the period during which applications for subscription for a holding may be submitted [194]. The application for admission to official listing is to include all of the debt securities which rank *pari passu*[63] [195].

Competent authorities of different Member States are to co-operate whenever this is required for the purpose of carrying out their obligations, and shall exchange any information that is useful for this purpose [196]. Member States are to require all persons employed or previously employed by the competent authority to be subject to the obligation of professional secrecy – no confidential information that they receive during the course of their duties may be disclosed to any person or authority, other than in accordance with "provisions laid down by law" [197]. This obligation does not prevent competent authorities from exchanging information in accordance with the CARD [198].

Market Transparency Requirements for Listed Securities

The TD increases the amount and the frequency of financial information that companies whose securities are officially listed will be required to publish [199]. The Commission considers that the TD improves the quality of information which is available to investors on the performance and financial situation of companies and on changes in large shareholdings, thereby contributing to improved protection for investors, higher investor confidence and better operation of European capital markets [200].

---

[60] This rule shall not apply to tap issues of debt securities, when there is no fixed closing date for subscription (CARD (as amended to 24/03/05), Article 55).

[61] Thus, the debt instruments to be included in the application are those with a similar priority in terms of payment of interest and repayment of principal.

[62] This rule shall not apply to tap issues of debt securities, because the amount of these loans is variable (CARD (as amended to 24/03/05), Article 58(1)).

[63] See fn 61.

The TD establishes requirements for the disclosure of periodic and continuing information that concerns issuers whose securities[64] have been admitted to trading on a regulated market[65] which is located or functioning within a Member State [201]. This Directive is inapplicable to units issued by, or acquired or disposed of in, UCITS[66] [202].

Whilst a home Member State may subject an issuer or a shareholder to stricter requirements than those which the TD lays down, a host Member State may not do so [203]. The TD introduces this 'home Member State principle' in order to protect investors, whilst enabling obstacles to the admission of securities to regulated markets within Member States to be removed[67] [204].

The issuer is to publish its annual report within 4 months of the end of each financial year, and is to ensure that this document remains available to the public for at least 5 years [205]. The annual report is to comprise the audited financial statements, the management report, and statements made by the responsible persons that to the best of their knowledge the financial statements provide "a true and fair view of the assets, liabilities, financial position and profit or loss of the issuer and [its group]." and that "the management report includes a fair review of the development and performance of the business and position of the issuer and [its group, and]. a description of the principal tasks and uncertainties that they face" [206]. The financial statements, and consolidated accounts (if required) are to be audited in accordance with the applicable EU legislation[68] [207].

The issuer is to publish a half-yearly financial report which covers the first 6 months of the financial year – no later than 2 months thereafter, and is to ensure that this item is available to the public for 5 years or more [208]. This report is to comprise "the condensed set of financial statements," an interim management report, and statements made by the responsible persons that to the best of their knowledge these statements "give a true and fair view of the assets, liabilities, financial position and profit or loss of the issuer or [of its group].," and that "the interim management report includes a fair review of" the significant

---

[64] 'Securities' means transferable securities as defined in Article 4(1)(18) of the MiFID (TD (original version), Article 2(1)(a)). See fn 47, for Article 4(1)(18) of the MiFID. As money market instruments tend to have maturities of no more than one year, it is unclear why Article 2(1)(a) of the TD explicitly excludes money market instruments with a maturity of less than one year from the definition of 'securities'.

[65] 'Regulated market' means a market as defined in Article 4(1)(14) of the MiFID (TD (original version), Article 2(1)(c)). See fn 22, for Article 4(1)(14) of the MiFID.

[66] Article 1(2) of the TD refers to 'collective investment undertaking other than the closed-end type', whose definition in Article 2(1)(g) of the TD is the same as that of 'UCITS' in Article 1(2) of the original version of Council Directive 85/611/EEC on the co-ordination of laws, regulations and administrative provisions relating to undertakings for collective investment in transferable securities (UCITS). By the time of the GFC, the definition of 'UCITS' had been slightly modified – see the subsection entitled 'UCITS', next in this section. 'Units of a collective investment undertaking' means securities that a collective investment undertaking issues, which represent rights of its participants over its assets (TD (original version), Article 2(1)(h)).

[67] The 'home Member State principle', together with the passporting requirements for regulated markets under the MiFID, builds the internal market for the services of regulated markets. These passporting requirements include the extension of the 'investment services passport' to regulated markets under Article 33 of the MiFID, and the 'regulated markets passport' in Article 42(6)-(7) of the MiFID; see the subsection entitled 'Financial instruments', above in this section.

[68] At the onset of the GFC, the applicable legislation for financial statements was the Fourth Council Directive 78/660/EEC of 25 July 1978 based on Article 54(3)(g) of the Treaty on the annual accounts of certain types of companies, and for consolidated accounts was Seventh Council Directive 83/349/EEC of 13 June 1983 based on Article 54(3)(g) of the Treaty on consolidated accounts. Both of these Directives were subsequently repealed by Directive 2006/34/EU of the European Parliament and of the Council of 26 June 2013 on the annual financial statements, consolidated financial statements and related reports of certain types of undertakings, amending Directive 2006/43/EC of the European Parliament and of the Council and repealing Council Directives 78/660/EEC and 83/349/EEC (TD (original version), Article 4(4)).

activities which have taken place during the first 6 months of the financial year and their effect on the condensed statements, a description of the main risks and uncertainties for the second 6 months of the financial year and (for issuers of shares) substantial transactions with related parties [209]. If the issuer is required to draw up consolidated accounts, then the condensed statements are to be prepared in accordance with the applicable EU legislation[69]; if the issuer is not required to construct consolidated accounts, then the half-yearly statements must include a condensed profit and loss account, a condensed balance sheet, and explanatory notes [210]. In the latter case, the condensed profit and loss account and the condensed balance sheet must show all of the headings and subtotals that are included in the issuer's most recent annual financial statements[70], and comparative information for the profit and loss account and the balance sheet from the preceding financial year [211]. The explanatory notes must contain enough data to ensure the comparability of the condensed half-yearly statements with the annual financial statements and "sufficient information and explanations to ensure a user's proper understanding of any material changes in amounts and of any [reflected]. developments" [212]. The audit report or auditors' review is to be included; if the half-yearly financial report has not been audited or reviewed by auditors, then the issuer is to state this in the report [213].

An issuer whose shares are admitted to trading on a regulated market is to publish an interim management report during the first 6 months of its financial year, and another during the second 6 months of that year, which provides an explanation of material transactions and events and their impact on, and a description of the performance and financial position of, the issuer and its subsidiaries, from the start of the 6-month period to the statement's date of publication [214]. If an issuer publishes quarterly financial reports in accordance with national law or the regulated market's rules, then it will not be required to publish interim management reports as well [215].

Member States are to ensure that "the issuer or its administrative, management or supervisory bodies" assume responsibility for the information to be collected and published in accordance with the rules in the previous 3 paragraphs, and that the national rules on liability apply to the issuer, those bodies and[71] "the persons responsible within the issuers" [216]. These rules do not apply to countries, their regional and local authorities, public international organisations of which one or more Member States are members, the European Central Bank,

---

[69] The applicable legislation is Regulation (EC) No 1606/2002 of the European Parliament and of the Council of 19 July 2002 on the application of international accounting standards, Article 6(2) of which empowers the Commission to use the regulatory procedure in Council Decision 1999/468/EC. Whilst this was current law at the start of the GFC, Article 6(2) Regulation (EC) No 1606/2002 was subsequently amended by Article 1(2)(b) of Regulation (EC) No 297/2008 to substitute the regulatory procedure with scrutiny – which was inserted by Council Decision 2006/512/EC into Council Decision 1999/468/EC – for the regulatory procedure. Regulation (EU) No 182/2011 of the European Parliament and of the Council of 16 February 2011 laying down the rules and general principles concerning mechanisms for control by Member States of the Commission's exercise of implementing powers has repealed Council Decision 1999/468/EC, simplifying to 2 procedures the processes for enactment of secondary legislation as from 1st March 2011; see the section 'A Pause to Consider: the Role of the Commission in the Enactment of Secondary Legislation', above in this chapter.

[70] Additional line items are to be included if, in consequence of their omission, the semi-annual financial statements would provide a misleading view of the issuer's assets, liabilities, financial position and profit or loss (TDID (original version), Article 3(2)). The drafters of this instrument probably meant 'a misleading view of the issuer's assets, liabilities, financial position *or* profit or loss'.

[71] The text of Article 7 of the TD uses 'or' in this place rather than 'and'. It is submitted that it is the intention of the drafters of this legislation to make both the issuing company and the responsible persons within it liable for the publication of misinformation.

the central banks of Member States, and issuers "exclusively of debt securities admitted to trading on a regulated market" with a denomination of at least 50,000 Euros per unit[72] [217].

The home Member State is to ensure that, if a shareholder purchases or sells shares of an issuer that "are admitted to trading on a regulated market and to which voting rights are attached," then the shareholder must notify the issuer of the proportion of the latter's voting rights that are held by the former consequent to the acquisition or disposal – if this proportion attains or crosses at least one of the thresholds of 5%, 10%, 15%, 20%, 25%, 30%, 50% and 75%[73] [218]. This rule is not to apply to the purchase or sale by a market maker (who acts in this capacity) of a substantial shareholding that reaches or crosses the 5% threshold, as long as this market maker is authorised by its home Member State under the MiFID, does not interfere in the management of the issuer, and does not exercise any influence on the latter to buy these shares or "back the share price"[74] [219]. This notification is to include a statement of the voting rights after the event, "the chain of controlled undertakings" by way of which voting rights are held, the date on which the threshold was attained or crossed, and the shareholder's identity [220]. It is to be made within 4 trading days, the first of which is to be the day after the date on which the shareholder learns, or should have learned, of the acquisition or disposal[75] [221]. The shareholder shall be deemed to have learned of this event no later than 2 trading days after the transaction takes place [222]. The notification requirements are also to apply to a person who holds financial instruments which entitle their holder to acquire shares that have already been issued and to which voting rights attach, of an issuer whose shares have been admitted to trading on a regulated market [223]. 'Financial instruments' comprise derivative contracts as referred to in Section C of Annex I to the MiFID[76] and transferable securities, as long as they entitle the holder to acquire, solely on his/her initiative, under a formal agreement, such shares [224].

The issuer of shares admitted to trading on a regulated market is to promptly publish any change in the rights attached to these shares, including those connected to derivative contracts that it issues which provide access to its shares [225]. The issuer of debt securities is to swiftly publish any modifications to the rights of their holders, which result in particular from an alteration in interest rates or in the terms of the loan [226]. The issuer of securities that are admitted to trading on a regulated market is to quickly publish new loan issues and, in particular, any security or guarantee in respect thereof [227].

The issuer of shares admitted to trading on a regulated market is to ensure that all shareholders "who are in the same position" are given equal treatment [228]. It is to make sure that all information and facilities which are necessary to enable shareholders to exercise their rights are available in the home Member State, and that the integrity of data is maintained [229].

---

[72] It is submitted that the quoted phrase means that the issuer only lists its debt securities – i.e., the equity that it has issued is not listed.

[73] A similar requirement applies, if an alteration in a shareholder's voting rights results from "events changing the breakdown of voting rights (TD (original version), Article 9(2)). If the home Member State applies a threshold of one-third, then it does not need to apply the 30% threshold; if it applies a threshold of two-thirds, then it need not apply the 75% threshold (TD (original version), Article 9(3)).

[74] It is submitted that 'back the share price' means publish a statement which proclaims that the issuer agrees with the price that the market-maker is asking for purchase of the shares that the latter holds.

[75] For the circumstances in Article 9(2) of the TD (see fn 73), the first trading day is to be the day after the date on which the shareholder is informed of these events (TD (original version), Article 12(2)(b)).

[76] Fn 19 summarises the list of 'financial instruments' in Section C of Annex I to the MiFID.

The issuer of debt securities admitted to trading on a regulated market is to ensure that all holders of equal-ranking instruments are accorded equal treatment in respect of the rights which attach to these securities [230]. It is to make sure that all information and facilities which are indispensable to debtholders for the exercise of their rights are available to the public in the home Member State, and that data integrity is preserved [231].

If an issuer's registered office is in a third country, then the home Member State's competent authority may exempt that issuer from requirements under Articles 4 to 7, 12(6) and 14 to 18 of the TD, as long as the law of the third country lays down equivalent requirements or the issuer observes legal provisions of a third country which the home Member State's competent authority considers to be equivalent [232]. Articles 13 to 22 of the TDID contain guidance as to these equivalence requirements for third countries. For example, a third country is to be deemed to set requirements that are equivalent to those which Article 6 of the TD contains if, under that state's law, an issuer is required to publish quarterly financial reports[77] [233]. Nevertheless, an issuer whose registered office in a third country is to be exempted from preparing its financial statements in compliance with Article 4 or Article 5 of the TD, if it draws up its financial statements "in accordance with internationally accepted standards" to which Article 9 of Regulation (EC) No 1606/2002 on the application of international accounting standards refers[78] [234].

Each competent authority is to be granted all of the necessary powers for the performance of its functions. These include the power to require specified persons to supply information and documents, require the issuer to divulge information to the public by the means and within the time limits that the competent authority considers to be necessary, require specified persons to notify information requested under the TD or its transposed domestic law, suspend trading in securities for periods of up to 10 days "if it has reasonable grounds for suspecting that" the issuer has contravened provisions of the TD or of its transposing legislation, forbid trading on a regulated market "if it finds that" provisions of the TD or its transposing legislation have been breached or "if has reasonable grounds for suspecting that" provisions of the TD have been transgressed, examine that the information to which the TD refers is constructed in harmony with the applicable reporting framework, and conduct on-site inspections within its jurisdiction in accordance with domestic law in order to verify observance of provisions of the TD and its implementing measures [235].

The duty of professional secrecy is to apply to all persons who work or have worked for the competent authority and for entities to which it has delegated functions; information to which this duty applies may not be divulged to any other person or authority – other than in accordance with the rules of a Member State [236]. Nevertheless, competent authorities may exchange confidential information; these data are subject to the duty of professional secrecy [237]. Competent authorities of different Member States are to co-operate with each other,

---

[77] See above in this subsection, for Article 6(1)-(2) of the TD.

[78] Article 9(b) of Regulation (EC) No 1606/2002 states: "By way of derogation from Article 4 [which provides that companies within the EU are to construct their consolidated accounts in accordance with international accounting standards], Member States may provide that the requirements of Article 4 shall only apply for each financial year starting on or after January 2007 to those companies … (b) whose securities are admitted to public trading in a non-member State and which, for that purpose, have been using international accepted standards since a financial year that started prior to the publication of this Regulation in the *Official Journal of the European Communities*." As Article 9 of Regulation (EC) No 1606/2002 is a transitional provision, the extent to which the definition of 'internationally accepted standards' applies needs to be clarified; the content of Article 23(2) of the TD remains unchanged at the time of writing from prior to the GFC, which indicates that the definition of this term in Article 23(2) remains valid.

whenever this is necessary, for the purpose of undertaking their obligations and using their powers; each competent authority is to assist competent authorities of other Member States [238]. Member States may make co-operation agreements for the exchange of information with an entity of a third country whose legislation enables it to conduct any of the tasks that the TD assigns to competent authorities; the information exchange is to be intended for the performance of the supervisory task of this entity, and is to be "subject to guarantees of professional secrecy" that are "at least equivalent to those" to which this paragraph refers [239].

UCITS

The objectives of the UCITS Directive, which stood until the introduction of the UCITS V Directive after the GFC, were to co-ordinate national laws that govern UCITS "with a view to approximating the conditions of competition between those undertakings at Community level," whilst ensuring that unitholders are more uniformly and more effectively protected [240]. This co-ordination "will help to bring about a European capital market" [241]. This theme of a European capital market continues to prevail in the form of the recent Commission initiative for a capital markets union. Its prominence may explain why harmonising measures in the form of the UCITS Directive were enacted over a specialised financial area as early as 1985.

'UCITS' are entities that function "on the principle of risk-spreading" whose only purpose is the collective investment in transferable securities and/or "other liquid financial assets" to which Article 19(1) of the UCITS Directive refers[79], of capital raised from the public, and the units of which are redeemed or re-purchased out of the assets of those entities at the request of the unitholders [242]. The Member States are to forbid UCITS that are subject to the UCITS Directive from converting themselves into entities that are outside this Directive's scope [243]. UCITS which are not subject to the UCITS Directive comprise closed-ended funds, UCITS that raise capital without advertising the sale of their units to the public within the EU, UCITS which may be sold only to the public in third countries, and classes of UCITS that the rules of Member States in which these funds are located[80] lay down – for which the rules in Section V[81] and Article 36[82] of the UCITS Directive are unsuitable in the light of their policies on investment and borrowing [244]. The UCITS Directive is not a 'maximum harmonisation' Directive – i.e., Member States may apply requirements that are stricter than, or additional to, those which the Directive contains, to UCITS located within

---

[79] Whilst Article 19(1) of the UCITS Directive does not contain this phrase, it specifies 3 subcategories of 'money market instruments' immediately after mentioning 'transferable securities' in each case. These items are likely to be at least some of the 'other liquid financial assets' to which Article 1(2) of the UCITS Directive refers. For the purposes of that Directive, 'money market instruments' are "instruments normally dealt in on the money market which are liquid, and have a value that can be accurately determined at any time" (UCITS Directive (as amended to 19/03/08), Article 1(9)).

[80] For the purposes of the UCITS Directive, an UCITS is deemed to be located "in the Member State in which the investment company or management company of the unit trust has its registered office" (UCITS Directive (as amended to 19/03/08), Article 3).

[81] Section V of the UCITS Directive is entitled 'Obligations concerning the investment policies of UCITS', and comprises Articles 19-26. See below in this subsection, for the essence of this material.

[82] See below in this subsection, for section 36 of the UCITS Directive.

their territories, as long as these "are of general application" and are compatible with the Directive's provisions[83] [245].

An UCITS must be authorised by the competent authority of the Member State in which it is located, in order for it to conduct its activities; this authorisation is valid for all Member States [246]. For a unit trust to be authorised, the competent authority must have approved the management company, the fund rules and the depositary[84]; for an investment trust to be licensed, the competent authority must have approved its instruments of incorporation and the depositary [247].

The management company is to comply with the preconditions in Section III[85] of the UCITS Directive. The investment company is to observe the preconditions in Section IV[86] of this Directive [248].

The competent authority is not to authorise an UCITS, if the depositary's directors "are not of sufficiently good repute or are not sufficiently experienced" in respect of the class of UCITS to be managed[87] [249]. It is not to license an UCITS, if a legal provision precludes the latter from marketing its shares or units in its home Member State[88] [250].

"Access to the business of management companies" requires prior authorisation from the home Member State's competent authority[89], which is to be valid for all Member States [251]. The activity of management of unit trusts/common funds and of investment companies includes investment management, administration[90] and marketing [252]. Member States may authorise management companies to provide the following additional services: management of portfolios of investments, investment advice, and safekeeping and administration in respect

---

[83] The idea of 'maximum harmonisation' brings to mind an academic point in respect of EU competences. Shared competence between the EU and its Member States applies to the internal market (TFEU, Article 4(2)(a)). Over areas of shared competence, "[t]he Member States shall exercise their competence to the extent that the [European] Union has not exercised its competence" (TFEU, Article 2(2)). If there is 'maximum harmonisation' then the Member States are implementing identical rules. It might be argued that, in practice, this is exclusive competence, rather than shared competence: over areas of exclusive competence, "only the [European] Union may legislate and adopt legally binding acts, the Member States being able to do so themselves only if so empowered by the Union or for the implementation of Union acts" (TFEU, Article 2(1)). Of course, if the 'internal market' is taken as a whole, there will be a part of it over which the EU has not legislated (or legislated with 'minimum harmonisation' as in the case of the UCITS Directive) – so 'maximum harmonisation' over other sectors of the internal market can be brought within the ambit of shared competence.

[84] A 'depositary' is any institution that is entrusted with the obligations that Articles 7 and 14 of the UCITS Directive contain, and which is subject to the other provisions that Sections IIIa and IVa of this Directive (UCITS Directive (as amended to 19/03/08), Article 1a(1)). Sections IIIa and IVa are both entitled 'Obligations regarding the depositary', and comprise Articles 7-11 and 14-18, respectively. See below in this subsection, for these duties.

[85] Section III of the UCITS Directive is entitled 'Obligations regarding management companies', and contains Articles 5-6c. See below in this subsection, for the kernel of this material.

[86] Section IV of the UCITS Directive is entitled 'Obligations regarding investment companies', and contains Articles 12-13c. See below in this subsection, for the core of this material.

[87] 'Directors' are those persons who represent the depositary, or who "effectively determine" the depositary's policy (UCITS Directive (as amended to 19/03/08), Article 4(3)).

[88] A 'UCITS home Member State' means in respect of an UCITS established as (a) a unit trust/common fund – the Member State in which the registered office of the management company is situated, (b) an investment company – the Member State in which that company's registered office is located (UCITS Directive (as amended to 19/03/08), Article 1a(5)).

[89] A 'management company's home Member State' means the Member State in which that entity's registered office is located (UCITS Directive (as amended to 19/03/08), Article 1a(3)).

[90] 'Administration' comprises legal and fund management accounting services, customer enquiries, valuation and pricing, the monitoring of regulatory compliance, the maintenance of a register of unitholders, the distribution of income, the issue and redemption of units, the settlement of contracts, and the keeping of records (UCITS Directive (as amended to 19/03/08), Annex II).

of units of collective investment undertakings – although each of these 3 may only be provided with the management of unit trusts/common funds and/or investment companies, and the latter 2 may only be supplied together with the management of portfolios of investments [253]. The competent authority is not to grant authorisation to a management company unless the latter has an initial capital[91] of 125,000 Euros or more – rising to a maximum of 10 million Euros as the value of the portfolios of the management company increases[92], the management company's directors "are of sufficiently good repute and are sufficiently experienced" in relation to the category of UCITS to be managed, the company has at least 2 directors, the application for authorisation is accompanied by a programme of operations that includes the management company's organisational structure, and the management company's registered office and its head office are situated in the same Member State [254]. If there are close links[93] between the management company and other persons, then the competent authority is only to grant authorisation if these permit the effective exercise of its functions of supervision; the authority is to refuse authorisation if the rules of a third country that govern one or more persons with which the management company has close links, or problems involved in their enforcement, preclude the exercise of its duties of supervision [255]. The competent authority is not to grant authorisation to a management company to take up its business, until the former has been notified of the identities of the shareholders or members who have qualifying holdings[94] and the size of these holdings; it is to refuse authorisation if, taking into consideration "the need to ensure the sound and prudent management of a management company," it does not consider these shareholders or members to be suitable [256]. The competent authority of the other Member State is to be consulted beforehand on an issue which concerns the authorisation of any management company that is a subsidiary of, or of the parent company of, or controlled by the same persons who control, another management company, an investment firm, a credit institution or an insurance company – which is authorised in another Member State [257].

Operating conditions for management companies include the following. The competent authority of a management company's home Member State is to require the management

---

[91] 'Initial capital' comprises paid-up equity share capital, share premium accounts, reserves, and profits and losses brought forward consequential to the application of the final profit or loss, but excludes cumulative preference shares (UCITS Directive (as amended to 19/03/08), Article 1a(14); Directive 2000/12/EC (as amended to 09/03/06), Article 34(2)(1)-(2)(2); Directive 86/635/EC (as amended to 16/08/06), Articles 22-23).

[92] 'Portfolios of the management company' for the purposes of Article 5a(1)(a) of the UCITS Directive comprise unit trusts/common funds that the management company oversees, investment companies for which the management company is the specified management company, and other collective investment undertakings that the management company organises (UCITS Directive (as amended to 19/03/08), Article 5a(1)(a)).

[93] 'Close links' means circumstances under which at least 2 persons are connected by (a) participation – which is the ownership, directly or "by way of control," of 20% or more of the capital or voting rights of a company, (b) 'control' – which is the relationship between a parent company and a subsidiary, a similar relationship to this, and a relationship between a parent company and its subsidiary's subsidiary, or (c) circumstances under which at least 2 persons are "permanently linked" to a third person by a control relationship (UCITS Directive (as amended to 19/03/08), Article 1a(9); European Parliament and Council Directive 95/26/EC of 29 June 1995 amending Directives 77/780/EEC and 89/646/EEC in the field of credit institutions, Directives 73/239/EEC and 92/49/EEC in the field of non-life insurance, Directives 79/267/EEC and 92/96/EEC in the field of life assurance, Directive 93/22/EEC in the field of investment firms and Directive 85/611/EEC in the field of undertakings for collective investment in transferable securities (Ucits) with a view to reinforcing prudential supervision, Article 2(1)).

[94] 'Qualifying holdings' means any holding in a management company that represents at least 10% of the voting rights or of the capital, or which enables the exercise of "a significant influence over the management of" this entity (UCITS Directive (as amended to 19/03/08), Article 1a(10)).

company that it has authorised to comply continuously with the conditions for the grant of the permission [258]. The management company's prudential supervision is to be the responsibility of the competent authority of its home Member State – without prejudice to provisions of the UCITS Directive that accord responsibility to its host Member State's competent authority[95] [259]. Each home Member State is to construct prudential rules that management companies – in respect of their management of UCITS – are to continuously observe; in particular, the home Member State's competent authority is to require every management company to have in place "sound administrative and accounting procedures, controls and safeguard arrangements for electronic data processing and adequate internal control mechanisms," and to be "structured and organised in such a way as to minimise the risk of UCITS' or clients' interests being prejudiced by conflicts of interest between the company and its clients." [260]. Each Member State is to draw up rules of conduct which management companies that are authorised in that Member State are to respect at all times; these precepts are to ensure that every management company "acts honestly and fairly in conducting its business activities" and "with due skill, care and diligence" in the furtherance of market integrity and of the UCITS' best interests, attempts to refrain from conflicts of interests and if this is impossible, ensures that the UCITS which it manages are treated justly, and observes all regulatory requirements that apply to the conduct of its business activities – in order to advance market integrity and its investors' best interests [261].

This and the next 4 paragraphs concern passporting rights and responsibilities for management companies. Member States are to ensure that a management company which has been authorised in accordance with the UCITS Directive by another Member State's competent authority, may conduct within their territories the activity that it has been licensed to undertake – either through the founding of a branch or by the free movement of services [262]. Member States may not subject the establishment of a branch or the supplying of the services to a requirement for authorisation or for the provision of "endowment capital," or to any equivalent measure [263].

To found a branch in the territory of another Member State, the management company must fulfil the conditions that Articles 5 and 5a of the UCITS impose[96], and must notify its home Member State's competent authority of its intention to establish this branch [264]. When effecting the notification, the management company must furnish the following documents and information: the name of the host Member State, a programme of operations that sets out the planned services and activities and the branch's organisational structure, the address in the host Member State from which documents may be acquired, and the names of the branch's managers [265]. Unless the home Member State's competent authority has "reason to doubt the adequacy of" the management company's organisational structure or financial circumstances, taking into consideration the proposed activities, it is to communicate the information (together with details of any investor compensation scheme) to the host Member State's competent authority within 3 months of receiving it, and to inform the management company that it has done this; if the home Member State's competent authority refuses to forward the information, it is to give reasons for that refusal to the

---

[95] A 'management company's host Member State' means the Member State (other than its home Member State) within the territory of which this firm has a branch or supplies services (UCITS Directive (as amended to 19/03/08), Article 1a(4)).

[96] See above in this subsection, for Articles 5 and 5a of the UCITS Directive.

management company within 2 months of receipt[97] [266]. Before the management company's foreign branch commences business, the host Member State's competent authority shall, within 2 months of receiving the information, prepare for its supervision of the management company and, "if necessary," state the conditions under which, "in the interest of the general good," this business must be conducted in the host Member State[98] [267]. On receipt of a communication from the host Member State's competent authority or on expiry of the 2 months in the absence of the former, the branch may be founded and may start business [268].

A management company that wishes to commence business in territory of another Member State under the free movement of services must pass to its home Member State's competent authority the following information: the name of the host Member State, and a programme of operations which sets out the planned services and activities [269]. Within one month of receiving this information, that authority is to communicate it to the host Member State's competent authority, together with details of any investor compensation scheme [270]. Then, the management company may begin business in the host Member State[99]; "When appropriate," the host Member State's competent authority is to make known to the management company the conditions which, "in the interest of the general good," the latter must observe in the host Member State[100] [271].

In carrying out their responsibilities under the UCITS Directive, host Member States may require branches of foreign management companies to furnish the same particulars as national management companies for this purpose. Host Member States may require management companies that conduct business within their territories under the free movement of services, to supply the information which is necessary for the monitoring of their observance of the standards that the host Member States set for them. These requirements are to be no stricter than those that the same Member State applies to "established management companies" in order to monitor their compliance with those standards [272].

If a host Member State's competent authority finds that a management company, which owns a branch or supplies services within that country's territory, has contravened its rules enacted pursuant to those provisions of the UCITS Directive which confer powers on this authority, then the latter is to require the management company "to put an end to its irregular situation." [273]. If the management company "fails to take the necessary steps," then the host Member State's competent authority is to inform the home Member State's competent authority, which is to promptly "take all appropriate measures" in order to make sure that the management company "puts an end to its irregular situation" and to communicate these to the former authority [274]. If, despite these measures or because they are insufficient or unavailable in the home Member State, the management company continues to breach the

---

[97] The management company may apply to the home Member State's courts against a refusal or a non-reply (UCITS Directive (as amended to 19/03/08), Article 6a(3)).

[98] The host Member State's competent authority is to supervise the branch that is established there, rather than the management company as a whole.

[99] This is "notwithstanding the provisions of Article 46" (UCITS Directive (as amended to 19/03/08), Article 6b(3)). See below in this subsection, for Article 46 of the UCITS Directive.

[100] It is understandable that the host Member State's competent authority may wish to impose local business conditions on newly-established branches of management companies – as these branches are to operate within that Member State. It is less clear that any host Member State will need to introduce local business conditions for the provision of cross-border services there – as the management and operational aspects of these services are within the domain of the management company's home Member State. These conditions must not be so onerous as to be, in effect, requirements for a further authorisation – i.e., a license from the competent authority of the host Member State to open a branch or to provide cross-border services in that jurisdiction.

relevant provisions, then the host Member State's competent authority may, after notifying the home Member State's competent authority, "take appropriate measures" to preclude or to punish further transgressions, and insofar as is necessary, to prevent the management company from continuing to do business within its territory [275]. Before following this procedure, the host Member State's competent authority "may, in emergencies, take any precautionary measures necessary to protect the interests of" persons for whom the services are supplied[101] [276]. In addition, a host Member State may "take appropriate measures" to preclude or to punish contraventions committed within its jurisdiction that breach "legal or regulatory provisions adopted in the interest of the general good." [277]. Reasons are to be given for any non-emergency measure, which is to be "subject to the right to apply to the courts in the Member States which adopted it" [278].

This paragraph considers the authorisation and operating conditions of investment companies. Access to investment companies' business requires prior authorisation from the home Member State's competent authority [279]. Investment companies may only purchase transferable securities and/or "other liquid financial assets" to which Article 19(1) of the UCITS Directive refers[102] [280]. If the investment company has not specified a management company that is authorised under the UCITS Directive, then the following authorisation conditions apply: the former must hold initial capital[103] of 300,000 Euros or more, a programme of operations which states the investment company's organisational structure must accompany the application for its authorisation, the investment company's directors[104] are to "be of sufficiently good repute and be sufficiently experienced" with respect to the firm's business, there must be at least 2 directors, close links[105] between the investment company and other persons are not to prevent the competent authority from effectively exercising its supervisory duties, and rules of a third country that govern one or more persons with whom the investment company has close links – or problems involved in their enforcement – preclude the competent authority from effectively exercising its supervisory obligations [281]. Each Member State is to put in place rules of conduct that investment companies authorised there are to observe at all times[106] [282]. Investment companies may not receive a mandate to manage assets on a third party's behalf [283]. Every Member State is to construct prudential rules that investment companies which have not specified a management company are to respect continuously; in particular, the home Member State's competent authority is to require the investment company to have "sound" accounting and administrative procedures, safeguard and control arrangements for processing data electronically, and "adequate" mechanisms for internal control [284].

This paragraph concerns obligations of, and in respect of, the depositary. The assets of a unit trust, and those of an investment company, are to be entrusted to a depositary for their safekeeping [285]. A depositary is to carry out a management company's legally-compliant

---

[101] The host Member State's competent authority must swiftly inform the Commission and the competent authorities of the other Member States involved; the Commission may, after consulting the latter, require the former to correct or abolish the emergency measures (UCITS Directive (as amended to 19/03/08), Article 6a(8)).

[102] See fn 79, for a possible meaning of 'other liquid financial assets'.

[103] See fn 91, for a description of 'initial capital' under the UCITS Directive.

[104] 'Directors' are those person who represent the investment company, or who determine the firm's policy (UCITS Directive (as amended to 19/03/08), Article 13a(1)).

[105] See fn 93, for the definition of 'close links' under the UCITS Directive.

[106] Article 5h of the UCITS Directive applies to investment companies (UCITS Directive (as amended to 19/03/08), Article 13b). This Article specifies the content of the rules of conduct for management companies, and is considered above in this subsection.

instructions, and to ensure that the sale, issue, redemption, repurchase and cancellation of units which are undertaken by or on behalf of an investment company, on behalf of a unit trust or by a management company, are conducted in accordance with the law, the investment company's incorporation documents and the fund rules, that in transactions concerning an investment company's or a unit trust's assets any payment is remitted to it within the normal time constraints, that an investment company's or a unit trust's income is used in accordance with the law, the investment company's incorporation documents and the fund rules, and that (in the absence of an investment company) the value of units is computed in accordance with the fund rules [286]. Any Member State may decide that investment companies located within its territory which advertise their units solely through one or more stock exchanges on which their units are admitted to the official list, are not to be required to use depositaries[107] [287]. A depositary is either to have its registered office in the same Member State as that of the investment or management company, or to be founded in that Member State – if its registered office is in another Member State [288]. A depositary is to be an institution that is "subject to public control"; it must "furnish sufficient financial and professional guarantees" to act in practice as depositary [289]. A depositary shall be liable to the investment/management company and the unitholders for any loss incurred by them in consequence of unwarranted non-performance of its duties [290]. No company is to act as both investment/management company and depositary [291]. A depositary is to act independently, and exclusively in the unitholders' interests [292].

Section V of the UCITS Directive considers the legal framework for the investment policies of UCITS. The investments of an investment company or a unit trust are to comprise transferable securities and money market instruments[108] that are traded on a regulated market, recently issued transferable securities (subject to 2 conditions), units of UCITS authorised in accordance with the UCITS Directive, units of other collective investment undertakings that satisfy the description in Article 1(2) of the UCITS Directive[109] (subject to 4 conditions), deposits with credit institutions[110] that are repayable on demand and which mature in less than one year (subject to 2 conditions), financial derivative instruments[111] (subject to 3 conditions), and/or money market instruments other than those that are traded on a regulated market (subject to 5 conditions) [293]. An UCITS may not invest more than 10% of its assets in transferable securities and money market instruments other than those to which the previous sentence refers [294]. An investment company may purchase property that is indispensable to the "direct pursuit of its business" [295]. An UCITS may not obtain precious metals or certificates that represent these [296]. Investment companies and unit trusts may hold "ancillary liquid assets"[112] [297].

---

[107] Article 14(5) of the UCITS Directive empowers Member States to allow investment companies situated in their territories that advertise 80% of their units through one or more stock exchanges to dispense with depositaries, subject to conditions specified therein.

[108] See fn 79, for the definition of 'money market instruments' in Article 1(9) of the UCITS Directive.

[109] See the first sentence of the second paragraph of this subsection for the definition of 'UCITS' in Article 1(2) of the UCITS Directive, which gives this description.

[110] The UCITS Directive does not define 'credit institutions.' See fn 39, for the definition of this term that the September 2007 version of the MiFID applies. Both this definition, and the one in Article 4(1) of the BCD (original version), include not only banks but also electronic money institutions.

[111] See fn 13, for a description of the term 'derivative.'

[112] The UCITS Directive does not define the phrase 'ancillary liquid assets'. It might mean the daily cash that is sufficient to be able to promptly purchase assets for the portfolio.

The investment/management company is to use a risk-management process that enables it to measure and monitor at any time the risk positions and their contribution to the portfolio's risk profile; it is to employ a process for the independent and accurate evaluation of OTC derivative instruments [298]. Each UCITS is to ensure that its "global exposure"[113] in relation to derivative instruments is no more than the total net value of its portfolio [299]. Without prejudice to the provisions in this or the previous paragraph, neither an investment company nor a depositary or a management company that acts on behalf of a unit trust may provide loans on behalf of, or act as a guarantor for, any third party [300].

An UCITS may not invest more than 5% of its assets in transferable securities or money market instruments that the same entity issues[114]; it may not invest in excess of 20% of its assets in deposits held with the same institution [301]. The risk exposure to the UCITS' counterparty in an OTC derivative transaction is not to be in excess of 10% of the UCITS' assets if the counterparty is a credit institution, and 5% of its assets otherwise [302]. Notwithstanding these individual limits, an UCITS may not invest more than 20% of its assets in any combination of investments in transferable securities or money market instruments that are issued by, deposits held with, and exposures which arise from OTC derivative transactions with, a single entity [303]. The limits above in this paragraph are not to be combined; investments in transferable securities or money market instruments issued by the same institution, or in deposits or derivative instruments held with this entity, are not to exceed 35% in total of the UCITS' assets[115] [304]. By way of derogation from the previous sentence, "and without prejudice to Article 68(3) of the Treaty,"[116] the Member States may authorise UCITS to invest some or all of their assets in various transferable securities and money market instruments that a Member State, its local authorities, a third country or a public international organisation (to which at least one Member State belongs) issue or guarantee, provided that they believe unitholders to be protected as well as those in UCITS which observe the limits contained in Article 22 of the UCITS Directive and that UCITS hold securities from more than 5 different issues with no issue accounting for more than 30% of the total assets of the relevant fund [305].

---

[113] The exposure is computed by taking into consideration the current value of the underlying assets, future market movements, the counterparty risk, and the time that is available to close down the positions (UCITS Directive (as amended to 19/03/08), Article 21(3)).

[114] Any Member State may raise this limit to a maximum of 35%, if a Member State, its local authorities, a third country or a public international body to which at least one Member State belongs, issues or guarantees the transferable securities or money market instruments (UCITS Directive (as amended to 19/03/08), Article 22(3)).

[115] Companies that are included in the same group in accordance with recognised international accounting standards or for the purposes of consolidated accounts, are considered to be a single entity for the calculation of the limits that Article 22 of the UCITS Directive contains; any Member State may permit cumulative investment in transferable securities and money market instruments within the same group up to a maximum of 20% (UCITS Directive (as amended to 19/03/08), Article 22(5)).

[116] In 2008, 'the Treaty' in force was the Treaty Establishing the European Community. Article 68(3) of that Treaty was subsequently repealed, and therefore does not appear in the TFEU. It stated: "The Council, the Commission or a Member State may request the Court of Justice to give a ruling on a question of interpretation of this title [Title IV: Visa, Asylum, Immigration and Other Policies Related to the Free Movement of Persons] or of acts of the institutions of the Community based on this title. The ruling given by the Court of Justice in response to such a request shall not apply to judgments of courts or tribunals of the Member States which have become *res judicata*". As this provision concerned the free movement of persons, which is not relevant to the UCITS Directive, Article 23(1) of that Directive, in referring to 'Article 68(3) of the Treaty', may have meant the earlier Treaty, i.e., the EEC Treaty. This is confirmed by i) the fact that the consolidated UCITS Directive as at 19/03/08 does not show changes to Article 23(1) since the original provision of December 1985 – other than the insertion of "and money market instruments" from an amendment of 2002, and ii) Article 68(3) of the EEC Treaty concerned loans that are intended to finance a Member State.

Without prejudice to the limits that Article 25 of the UCITS Directive states[117], Member States may increase the 5% limit to up to 20% for investment in shares and/or debt securities that the same entity issues – if the written objective of the UCITS' investment policy is to replicate the composition of a specified stock or debt securities index which the competent authority recognizes,[118] on the following basis: its composition is adequately diversified, the index represents a suitable benchmark for the market to which it refers, and the index is published in a suitable way [306]. Member States may raise this limit to a maximum of 35%, for a single issuer, if this "proves to be justified by exceptional market conditions" in specified regulated markets in which identifiable securities "are highly dominant." [307].

An UCITS may purchase the units of UCITS and/or other collective investment undertakings that satisfy the description in Article 1(2) of the UCITS Directive,[119] as long as no more than 10% of its assets are invested in units of one collective investment undertaking[120] [308]. Investments that are made in collective investment undertakings other than UCITS are not to exceed, in total, 30% of the acquiring UCITS' assets [309].

The prospectus is to show the classes of assets into which an UCITS is authorised to invest. If transactions in financial derivative instruments are permitted, then the prospectus is to contain a statement as to whether these operations may be conducted for the purpose of hedging or with the aim of satisfying investment objectives, and the possible outcome of the use of financial derivative instruments on the UCITS' risk profile [310].

An investment company or a management company which acts in association with the unit trusts that it manages and which are within the ambit of the UCITS Directive, may not purchase any shares that carry voting rights which would enable it to exert "significant influence" over the management of an issuing entity [311]. A unit trust or an investment company may not acquire more than 10% of the non-voting shares, debt securities or money market instruments of any single issuer, or more than 25% of the units of any UCITS and/or other collective investment undertaking within the description in Article 1(2) of the UCITS Directive[121] [312].

Section VI of the UCITS Directive contains provisions that regulate information to be supplied to unitholders. An investment company and, for each of the common funds and unit trusts that it manages, a management company, is to publish a prospectus, a simplified prospectus, an annual report for every financial year and a half-yearly report that covers the first 6 months of that year[122] [313].

Both the simplified and the full prospectuses are to include the information that is required for investors to be able to make an informed judgment of the investment which is being proposed to them and, in particular, of the risks attached to it – including a clear explanation of the fund's risk profile [314]. The full prospectus is to contain at least the information in Schedule A of Annex I to the UCITS Directive[123], in so far as this information

---

[117] Article 25(2) of the UCITS Directive contains these limits; see below in this subsection.
[118] This is called a 'tracker fund', as the value of its units 'tracks' that of the market index to which it refers.
[119] See fn 109.
[120] Member States may increase this limit to a maximum of 20% (UCITS Directive (as amended to 19/03/08), Article 24(1)).
[121] See fn 109.
[122] The annual report is to be published within 4 months, and the half-yearly report within 2 months, of the end of the period to which each relates (UCITS Directive (as amended to 19/03/08), Article 27(2)).
[123] Schedule A of Annex I to the UCITS Directive contains a table that lists comparable information for a unit trust, a management company and an investment company – such as item 1.2, which is the date that the unit trust

is absent from the fund rules or investment company's incorporation documents that are to "form an integral part of" this prospectus and be annexed to it [315]. "The essential elements of" the full and the simplified prospectuses are to be regularly updated[124] [316]. If an UCITS markets its units in a Member State other than that in which it is located, then it must disseminate in that other Member State the full and simplified prospectuses, the annual and half-yearly reports, and the other information to which this paragraph refers[125] [317].

UCITS are to send their full and simplified prospectuses, any amendments to these, and their annual and half-yearly reports, to the competent authority [318]. The auditor's review for the annual report must be attached to that document [319].

The simplified prospectus is to be offered free of charge to subscribers to the fund, before the contract is agreed [320]. The annual and half-yearly reports are to be given to unitholders on request [321]. These reports must be available to the public as approved by the competent authority and as specified in the simplified and full prospectuses [322].

Section VII of the UCITS Directive states UCITS' general obligations. Neither an investment company nor a depositary or management company that acts on behalf of a unit trust, may borrow[126] [323]. However, a Member State may authorise an UCITS to borrow up to 10% of its assets (if it belongs to an investment company) or of the value of the fund (if it is a unit trust), as long as this borrowing is temporary [324]. It may also authorise an UCITS to borrow up to 10% of its assets, if it belongs to an investment company, if the borrowing is to facilitate the purchase of immovable property that is "is essential for the direct pursuit of its business"[127] [325].

An UCITS is to repurchase or redeem the units held by any unitholder, at his/her request [326]. In exceptional circumstances, an UCITS may, in accordance with the law, the fund rules or the investment company's incorporation documents, "temporarily suspend" the redemption or repurchase of its units – as long as suspension is warranted, given the unitholders' interests [327]. Member States may permit their competent authorities to require the suspension of the redemption or repurchase of its units, in the interests of the public or of the unitholders [328].

The rules for the valuation of assets and for computing the sale or issue price and the redemption or repurchase price of an UCITS' units is to be stated in the law, the fund rules or the investment company's documents of incorporation [329]. The distribution or reinvestment

---

was established, the date of incorporation of the management company and the date of incorporation of the investment company, respectively. Schedule A also lists other items of information – such as item 2.2, which is the main activity of the depositary.

[124] The UCITS Directive does not define what it means by 'the essential elements of' the prospectuses.

[125] If an UCITS proposes to advertise its units in a Member State other than the one in which it is located, then it must inform the competent authority of that other Member State accordingly; it must also send this authority a certification by the competent authority (of the Member State in which it is situated?) that it satisfies the conditions which the UCITS Directive imposes, its incorporation documents or fund rules, its simplified and full prospectuses, its most recent annual report and any later half-yearly report, and details of the arrangements made for the marketing of its units in the other Member State; a management company or an investment company may start to markets in that other Member State 2 months after this communication, unless that Member State's competent authority establishes within this period that the arrangements made for the marketing of units breach the rules in force in that Member State (UCITS Directive (as amended to 19/03/08), Articles 46, 44(1) and 45). The bracketed phrase containing the question mark is not stated in these provisions, but is added for clarity.

[126] An UCITS may enter into a back-to-back loan with a counterparty in another country, in order to acquire an agreed amount of that state's currency in return for its own (UCITS Directive (as amended to 19/03/08), Article 36(1)).

[127] The 2 borrowings must total to no more than 15% of the borrower's assets (UCITS Directive (as amended to 19/03/08), Article 36(2)(b)).

of an investment company's or a unit trust's income is to be carried out in accordance with the instructions from those sources [330].

An UCITS unit may only be issued, once the net issue price is paid into the UCITS' assets within the normal time period [331]. The law or the fund rules must state the remuneration and the expenditure that a management company is empowered to charge to a unit trust, and the method for calculating this payment; the law, or the company's incorporation documents, is to lay down "the nature of the cost" that an investment company is to bear [332].

Section IX of the UCITS Directive comments on the supervision of UCITS. The authority of the Member State in which an UCITS is located and, if different, in which the UCITS markets its units, is to be able to oversee that undertaking [333]. These entities are to be granted all of the powers that are necessary to perform this supervision [334]. They are to work closely together in order to conduct their task; for this purpose, they are to communicate to each other all of the information that is required [335].

Each Member State is to require all persons who work, or who have worked, for its competent authority, as well as experts and auditors whom the competent authority instructs, to be bound by the duty of professional secrecy; no confidential information which these persons receive whilst carrying out their functions may be disclosed to any person or authority, other than in aggregate or summary form such that depositaries, management companies and UCITS are unable to be identified individually[128] [336]. This is not to prevent Member States' competent authorities from exchanging information in accordance with Directives that apply to UCITS' or to "undertakings contributing towards their business activity"[129]; these data are to be subject to the duty of professional secrecy [337]. Competent authorities that receive confidential information under the provisions described above in this paragraph may only use it "in the course of their duties" (a) to ensure that the conditions which govern the initiation of UCITS' business "or of undertakings contributing towards their business activity"[130] are satisfied, and to promote the oversight of the conduct of this business, internal control mechanisms, and accounting and administrative procedures, (b) to introduce sanctions, (c) in administrative appeals against competent authorities' decisions, or (d) in court proceedings that are commenced under Article 51(2) of the UCITS Directive[131] [338]. These provisions shall not prevent information exchange within a Member State if there are at least 2 competent authorities there, and (within or between Member States) amongst competent authorities and (a) entities that are publicly responsible for the supervision of financial organisations and markets, (b) organisations which are concerned with the bankruptcy or the liquidation of UCITS "and of undertakings contributing towards their business activity"[132], (c) persons who are responsible for the performance of statutory audits of financial institutions' accounts, in the performance of their functions of supervision, or the divulgation to "bodies which administer compensation schemes" of information that is required for them to be able to perform their functions [339]. Member States may make co-operation agreements that provide for exchange of information with third countries'

---

[128] This is without prejudice to the application of the criminal law (UCITS Directive (as amended to 19/03/08), Article 50(2)).

[129] The UCITS Directive does not define the quoted phrase.

[130] See fn 129.

[131] See below in this subsection, for Article 51(2) of the UCITS Directive.

[132] See fn 129.

competent authorities and with other specified entities within those countries, only if the information disclosed "is subject to guarantees of professional secrecy at least equivalent to those" to which Article 50 of the UCITS Directive refers; this information exchange is to "be intended for the performance of the supervisory task" of these entities [340]. Notwithstanding the above provisions, Member States may authorise the exchange of information between competent authorities and the entities that are legally responsible for the detection and investigation of transgressions of company law [341]. If, through the founding of branches or the provision of cross-border services, a management company operates in at least one host Member State, then the competent authorities of all of these Member States are to work closely together, supplying each other on request with all of the information about the ownership and management of this company which "is likely to facilitate [its] supervision," and all data that may assist in its monitoring [342].

Competent authorities must provide reasons for any decision to refuse to grant authorisation, and for "any negative decision taken on implementation of the general measures adopted in application of [the UCITS]. Directive," and are to notify applicants of these [343]. Member States are to require decisions taken in relation to an UCITS pursuant to rules transposing the UCITS Directive, to be accompanied by "the right to apply to the courts"[133] [344].

BANKING LEGISLATION

Voluminous though the securities' legislation was, even before and at the time of the GFC – as the previous section shows, the banking legislation was also extensive. Why should this be? After all, in the latter case, there is not so much emphasis on different types of financial instrument as in the former, and market-related issues are of lesser concern.

Much of the detail in the banking legislation immediately before the GFC accompanied the need for the prudential supervision of banks and the enactment of the Basel II Framework. Accordingly, there are extensive requirements in the BCD and the CRD. The BCD also considers the authorisation and passporting requirements for banks.

Authorisation[134]

Member States are to require credit institutions[135] to acquire authorisation before starting their activities; "without prejudice to Articles 7 to 12" of the BCD, they are to specify the

---

[133] Although this provision is silent as to the identity of the courts to which it is referring, these are likely to be the civil courts of the particular Member State that is transposing the UCITS Directive.

[134] 'Authorisation' is an instrument that is issued by the competent authority by which the right to conduct the business of a credit institution is provided (BCD (original version), Article 4(2)). 'Credit institution' means an entity whose business is to receive repayable funds from the public and to provide credits for its own account, or an electronic money institution under Directive 2000/46/EC of the European Parliament and of the Council of 18 September 2000 on the taking up, pursuit of and prudential supervision of the business of electronic money institutions (BCD (original version), Article 4(1)).

[135] See fn 134, for the definition of 'credit institution' that the original version of the BCD applies.

requirements for this authorisation and to inform the Commission of these[136] [345]. Member States are to require "a programme of operations" to accompany applications for authorisation, which is to contain the credit institution's proposed classes of business and "structural organisation" [346]. Member States are not to require the application for authorisation to be assessed in the light of the market's economic needs [347].

The competent authority is not to provide authorisation if the credit institution does not have separate own funds or if its initial capital is less than 5 million Euros[137] [348]. Member States may grant authorisation to specific classes of credit institutions the initial capital of which is smaller than this amount, as long as that capital is at least 1 million Euros, the Member States inform the Commission of their reasons for taking this option, and the name of each credit institution that lacks an initial capital of at least 5 million Euros is "annotated to that effect" in the list containing the name of each credit institution to which authorisation has been given [349]. A credit institution's own funds[138] is not to fall below the quantity of initial capital that was required for its authorisation to be granted [350].

The competent authority is to grant an authorisation to the applicant credit institution only if there are 2 or more persons who "effectively direct" this credit institution's business and who are of "sufficiently good repute" and possess " sufficient experience" to perform their obligations[139] [351]. Each Member State is to require any credit institution that is a legal person and which has a registered office according to its national law, to situate its head office in the same Member State as its registered office, and any other credit institution to

---

[136] Articles 7-12 of the BCD contain its authorisation requirements. Article 6 of this Directive empowers each Member State to include requirements beyond these. Thus, the authorisation section of the BCD (i.e., Title II, which is entitled 'Requirements for Access to the Taking Up and Pursuit of the Business of Credit Institutions') pursues a 'minimum harmonisation' approach, rather than one of 'maximum harmonisation' – see fn 83 and accompanying text.

[137] 'Initial capital' comprises paid-up subscribed capital, including share premium accounts and excluding cumulative preference shares, and reserves – including profits and losses brought forward pursuant to the application of the profit or loss for the financial year; 'subscribed capital' consists of all items that national law considers to be equity capital (BCD (original version), Articles 9(1) and 57(a)-(b); Directive 86/635/EC (as amended to 16/08/06), Article 22).

[138] 'Own funds' comprise the following items: subscribed capital and reserves (see fn 137); funds for general banking risks (BCD (original version), Article 57(c)) – which is to "include those amounts which a credit institution decides to put aside to cover such risks where that is required by the particular risks associated with banking" (Directive 86/635/EC (as amended to 16/08/06), Article 38(1)); revaluation reserves (BCD (original version), Article 57(d)); value adjustments (BCD (original version), Article 57(e)); other items (BCD (original version), Article 57(f)) – which include (i) perpetual cumulative preference shares (BCD (original version), Article 63(2)), (ii) instruments of indefinite duration – subject to 5 conditions (BCD (original version), Article 63(2)), and (iii) items that are "freely available to the credit institutions to cover normal banking risks where revenue or capital losses have not yet been identified" (BCD (original version), Article 63(1)(a)), divulged in internal accounting records (BCD (original version), Article 63(1)(b)), and their amount determined by the credit institution's management and confirmed by independent auditors (BCD (original version), Article 63(1)(c)); the commitments of the members of credit institutions that are established as co-operative societies (BCD (original version), Article 57(g)) – these are those societies' uncalled capital and the legal commitments of the societies' members to make additional non-refundable payments if the credit institution makes a loss (BCD (original version), Article 64(1)); "the joint and several commitments of the borrowers of certain institutions organised as funds" (BCD (original version), Article 57(g)); fixed-term cumulative preference shares – subject to one condition (BCD (original version), Articles 57(h) and 64(3)); and subordinated loan capital – subject to 5 conditions (BCD (original version), Articles 57(h) and 64(3)). Article 57(i)-(r) specify deductions from 'own funds'. The application of Article 57 of the BCD in the calculation of 'own funds' is subject to the computational rules that Article 66 of the BCD lays down.

[139] None of these quoted terms are defined, which leaves an element of discretion to the competent authority as to whether they are satisfied under the particular circumstances.

locate its head office in the Member State that granted its authorisation and in which it conducts its business [352].

The competent authority is not to grant authorisation for the initiation of a credit institution's business unless it has been notified of the names of the members or shareholders that have qualifying holdings[140] in that company, and the amounts of these holdings [353]. The competent authority is not to grant authorisation if, taking into consideration "the need to ensure the sound and prudent management of" the credit institution, it is unhappy as to the "suitability"[141] of the latter's members or shareholders [354].

The competent authority is only to grant authorisation to the applicant credit institution, if the former is able to effectively exercise its supervisory functions in spite of any close links[142] between the latter and other persons. The competent authority is not to provide authorisation if the rules of a third country that govern at least one person with whom the credit institution has close links, or problems with the enforcement of those rules, preclude its supervisory powers from being effectively exercised. Credit institutions are to supply the competent authority with the information that it requires in order to monitor the former's continuous observance with the conditions to which this paragraph refers [355].

The competent authority is to provide reasons whenever it refuses to grant an authorisation [356]. It is also to give reasons if it withdraws an authorisation[143], notifying this to the Commission – which is then able to amend its list of authorised credit institutions [357].

Before granting authorisation to a credit institution, the competent authority is to consult the competent authority of another Member State that supervises an investment firm, an insurance company or another credit institution, in cases in which (i) the credit institution to be authorised is a subsidiary of, or a subsidiary of the parent company of, a credit institution, an investment firm or an insurance company which is authorised in another Member State, or (ii) the credit institution to be authorised is controlled by the person who controls a credit institution, an investment firm or an insurance company that is authorised in another Member State[144] [358]. In particular, these authorities are to consult each other when evaluating the appropriateness of the shareholders and the reputation and experience of directors who are concerned with the management of another company in the same group as the applicant credit institution [359].

---

[140] 'Qualifying holding' means a holding in an entity that represents at least 10% of the voting rights or of the capital of that undertaking, and which makes it possible to exert a "significant influence" over the company's management (BCD (original version), Article 4(11)). The BCD does not define 'significant influence'.

[141] The BCD does not define 'suitability'.

[142] 'Close links' is a situation in which at least 2 persons are connected by (a) ownership, "direct or by way of control," of at least 20% of the capital or voting rights in a company, (b) control, or (c) the fact that both or all are permanently connected to a third person by means of "a control relationship" (BCD (original version), Article 4(46)). 'Control' is the relationship between a parent company and its subsidiary, or a similar relationship between any person and an undertaking (BCD (original version), Article 4(9)). The BCD does not define 'control relationship'.

[143] Article 18(1) of the BCD provides 5 grounds on which the competent authority may revoke an authorisation that it has granted to a credit institution .

[144] Consultation is also required between different authorities within the same Member State, e.g., between an authority that has authorised an investment firm and one that is responsible for authorizing its subsidiary credit institution – if these authorities are distinct (BCD (original version), Article 15(2)).

The home Member State's[145] competent authority is to require each credit institution to possess effective arrangements for its governance, which are to include a clear organisational structure with consistent, transparent and well-defined lines of responsibility, effectual processes for the identification, management, monitoring and reporting of risks, and satisfactory mechanisms for internal control – including robust accounting and administrative procedures [360]. These arrangements, processes and mechanisms are to be both comprehensive and proportionate to the complexity, nature and scale of the credit institution's operations[146] [361].

Passporting

Member States are to provide that credit institutions founded and authorised in another Member State, and financial institutions[147] from another Member State, may carry out those activities in Annex I[148] to the BCD which they are authorised to conduct [362]. A financial institution may only provide services to another Member State if the following conditions are satisfied: (i) it is either the subsidiary of a credit institution or the jointly-owned subsidiary of at least 2 credit institutions, (ii) the memorandum and articles of association of the parent credit institution(s) allow the supplying of these services, (iii) the parent undertaking(s) are to be authorised as credit institution(s) in the Member State whose law governs the relevant financial institution, (iv) the activities in question are to be carried out within the territory of that Member State, (v) the parent undertakings are to hold at least 90% of the voting rights that attach to shares in the financial institution's capital, (vi) the parent undertaking(s) are to satisfy the competent authority that they prudently manage the financial institution, (vii) the parent undertaking(s) are to have declared – with the agreement of the home Member State's competent authority – that they jointly and severally guarantee the commitments that the financial institution enters into, and (viii) the financial institution shall be "effectively included ... in the consolidated supervision of the parent undertaking[(s)]." [363]. The home

---

[145] 'Home Member State' refers to the Member State in which a credit institution has been authorised in accordance with Articles 6-9 and 11-14 of the BCD (BCD (original version), Article 4(7)).

[146] The technical criteria in Annex V to the BCD are to be considered. Annex V is entitled 'Technical Criteria Concerning the Organisation and Treatment of Risks'. It contains 10 titles, which comprise governance, treatment of risks, and 8 risk types. There is guidance under each title. For example, Title 7 'Market Risk' contains the following point: "Policies and processes for the measurement and management of all material sources and effects of market risks shall be implemented".

[147] 'Financial institution' means an entity other than a credit institution, the main activity of which is to acquire holdings or to conduct at least one of the activities that Annex I to the BCD lists as points 2-12. See fn 148, for Annex I to the BCD. Thus, financial institutions are not empowered to accept deposits (i.e., point 1). The provisions of this paragraph of the text apply to a financial institution's subsidiaries, in a similar way to that in which they apply to financial institutions (BCD (original version), Article 24(3)).

[148] Annex I to the BCD is entitled 'List of Activities Subject to Mutual Recognition'. The activities, in the order of points given, are as follows: 1. Acceptance of repayable funds; 2. Lending; 3. Financial leasing; 4. Money transmission services; 5. Issuing and administering means of payment; 6. Guarantees and commitments; 7. Trading for own account, or for the accounts of customers, in money market instruments, foreign exchange, futures, options, exchange and interest-rate derivatives, or transferable securities; 8. Participation in securities' issues and the supplying of services related to these; 9. Advice to companies; 10. Money broking; 11. Portfolio management and advice; 12. Safekeeping and administration of securities; 13. Credit reference services; 14. Safe custody services; 'Investment services' and 'Ancillary services' in Sections A and B of Annex I to the MiFID, respectively, are subject to mutual recognition under the BCD, if they refer to 'financial instruments' for which Section C of Annex I to the MiFID provides (BCD (original version), Annex I). See fns 18, 25 and 19 for Sections A, B and C of Annex I to the MiFID, respectively.

Member State's competent authority is to verify compliance with these conditions, and to provide a certificate of compliance to the financial institution – which is to accompany the notification that is supplied to that authority when the right of establishment and the free movement of services are to be exercised for the first time[149] [364].

A credit institution that wishes to found a branch within the territory of another Member State is to notify its home Member State's competent authorities [365]. Member States are to require each credit institution that would like to establish such a branch, to supply the following information when effecting this notification: the name of the Member State where it plans to open a branch, a programme of operations that sets out the types of business to be conducted there and the branch's structural organisation, the address in the host Member State[150] from which documents may be acquired, and the names of the branch's managers [366]. Unless the home Member State's competent authority has "reason to doubt the adequacy of" the credit institution's financial circumstances or administrative structure, taking the planned activities into consideration, it is to communicate the information to the host Member State's competent authority within 3 months of receipt and to inform the credit institution that it has done so; the latter authority is also to communicate the amount of own funds and the sum of capital requirements of the credit institution that Article 75 of the BCD lays down[151] [367]. If the home Member State's competent authority refuses to forward the information to the host Member State's competent authority, it is to provide reasons for this refusal to the credit institution within 3 months of receipt of all of those data; this refusal, or a non-reply, is to be subject to a right to apply to the home Member State's courts [368]. Host Member States are not to require authorisation or endowment capital for branches of credit institutions that are authorised in other Member States [369]. Nevertheless, within 2 months of receiving the information from the home Member State's competent authority, the host Member State's competent authority is to prepare for the credit institution's supervision in accordance with the provisions in the next paragraph and, if necessary, state the conditions according to which, "in the interests of the general good," the branch's activities may be conducted in the host Member State [370]. On receipt of a communication from that Member State's competent authority, or in the event of expiry of the 2-month period without receipt of this communication, the branch may be founded and may start its activities [371].

This paragraph summarises the powers of the host Member State's competent authorities. Host Member States may, for statistical purposes, require all credit institutions that have branches within their territories to report periodically on the activities there of those branches to their competent authorities [372]. If the host Member State's competent authority discovers that a credit institution with a branch or supplying services within its territory is transgressing laws of that State which transpose provisions of the BCD and which involve this authority's powers, then the authority is to require the credit institution to terminate "that irregular

---

[149] Articles 25(1) and 28(1) of the BCD refer to a credit institution establishing a branch or conducting its activities, respectively, in another Member State. They do not refer to a financial institution. Nevertheless, Article 24(1) of the BCD permits a financial institution to do these things – subject to the conditions stated in that Article and referred to in the text. Thus, the notification that the text refers to is likely to be provided by a financial institution to its home Member State's competent authority, rather than by its parent credit institution.

[150] 'Host Member State' means the Member State in which a credit institution supplies services or in which it has established a branch (BCD (original version), Article 4(8)).

[151] Article 75 of the BCD instructs Member States to require credit institutions to possess own funds that are continuously at least the sum of specified capital requirements for credit, dilution, position, settlement, counterparty foreign-exchange, commodities and operational risks.

situation" [373]. If the credit institution does not "take the necessary steps," then this competent authority is to notify the home Member State's competent authority, which is to promptly "take all appropriate measures" in order to ensure that the credit institution terminates "that irregular situation" – and is to inform the former authority of these actions [374]. If, despite these measures or because they prove to be insufficient or are unavailable in the host Member State, the credit institution continues to contravene those laws, then that Member State may, after informing the home Member State's competent authority, "take appropriate measures" in order to preclude or to penalize further breaches and, if necessary, to prevent the credit institution from commencing further transactions there [375]. The provisions above in this paragraph are not to affect any host Member State's power "to take appropriate measures" to preclude or to penalize transgressions that are committed within its domain and which contravene laws that they have enacted "in the interests of the general good" [376]. Any of these measures that involve penalties or restrictions on the exercise of the free movement of services are to be justified and notified to the credit institution, and are to be subject to a right of appeal to the courts of the Member State in which the relevant measure was taken [377]. Before following the disciplinary procedure stated above, the host Member State's competent authority may, in emergencies, take any precautionary measures that are necessary to protect the interests of persons to whom the services are supplied, and shall swiftly inform the competent authorities of the other Member States involved; the Commission may, after consulting the competent authorities of the relevant Member States, determine that the host Member State shall abolish or amend these measures [378]. Each host Member State may exercise the powers that the BCD confers on it "by taking appropriate measures" to preclude or to penalize contraventions that are committed within its jurisdiction [379]. If a credit institution's authorisation is withdrawn, then the host Member State's competent authority is to be notified and is to "take appropriate measures" in order to stop that entity from commencing further transactions within its domain, and to protect depositors' interests [380].

Any credit institution that wishes to apply the free movement of services, by conducting its activities within the territory of another Member State for the first time, is to notify the competent authority of its home Member State of the activities on the list in Annex I to the BCD that it would like to perform in the host Member State[152] [381]. The home Member State's competent authority shall, within one month of receipt of this notification, send it to the host Member State's competent authority[153] [382].

Prudential Supervision and Capital Adequacy

Title V of the BCD, which is entitled 'Principles and Technical Instruments for Prudential Supervision and Disclosure', considers the principles of prudential supervision for credit institutions, and also capital adequacy requirements for these undertakings – following the Basel II Framework. This subsection also includes capital adequacy requirements for investment firms under the CRD; this material appears here rather than as a subsection in the

---

[152] See fn 148, for Annex I to the BCD.
[153] Article 28 of the BCD does not specify the moment at which the credit institution may start to provide services in the host Member State. It is submitted that this will be the time at which the host Member State's competent authority receives the notification from the competent authority of the credit institution's home Member State.

section entitled 'Securities Legislation' – which is above in this chapter – because the CRD provides some integrated coverage of credit institutions and investment firms.

The competent authority of the credit institution's home Member State is responsible for its prudential supervision [383]. In co-operation with the home Member State's competent authority, host Member States are "pending further coordination"[154] to retain responsibility for the supervision of the liquidity of the credit institution's branches [384].

Each Member State is to require all individuals who work, or have worked, for its competent authority, and experts or auditors who act on behalf of this authority, to be limited by the duty of professional secrecy; confidential information that these persons receive as they perform their functions may be not be disclosed to anyone, except in aggregate or summary form such that particular credit institutions cannot be identified [385]. Competent authorities that receive confidential information are only to use it whilst carrying out their duties, and solely for the following purposes: (a) to check that the conditions which govern the taking-up of credit institutions' business are satisfied and to ease monitoring of the conduct of this business, (b) to impose sanctions; (c) in an administrative appeal against a competent authority's decision, or (d) in court proceedings that are taken pursuant to Article 55 of the BCD[155] "or to special provisions provided for in this in other Directives adopted in the field of credit institutions"[156] [386]. Member States may enter into co-operation agreements that provide for the exchange of information, with competent authorities of third countries or with entities within third countries with the characteristics of the Member States' undertakings described in the paragraph below, only if the information divulged "is subject to guarantees of professional secrecy" which are "at least equivalent to those" to which the first sentence of the current paragraph refers; this exchange of information is to be intended for performance of the supervisory task of those authorities or entities[157] [387].

The provisions of the paragraph above are not to prevent the exchange of information, within a Member State – if there are at least 2 competent authorities within that country – or amongst Member States, between competent authorities and the following entities, as long as conditions of professional secrecy as stated in the first sentence of the aforementioned paragraph apply to the data received: (a) authorities that are charged with the public duty of overseeing financial organisations and insurance firms, and those which are responsible for supervising financial markets, (b) entities that are concerned with the bankruptcy and the liquidation of credit institutions, (c) persons who are responsible for conducting statutory audits of the accounts of credit institutions, and (d) undertakings that administer deposit guarantee schemes [388]. Notwithstanding the provisions of the paragraph above, each

---

[154] The 'pending further coordination' phrase is to ensure that each host Member State oversees the liquidity of the branches of any bank located there, until the home Member State is able to supervise as a whole this credit institution and its structure of branches.

[155] Member States are to ensure that decisions taken in relation to a credit institution, which are pursuant to rules that transpose the BCD, "may be subject to the right to apply to the courts" (BCD (original version), Article 55). The BCD uses the wording 'may be subject to', rather than 'are subject to'. It is submitted that the former phrase is used in order to reflect the need for the applicant to have standing to appeal against the relevant decision. Although Article 55 of the BCD does not identify the courts to which it is referring, these are likely to be the civil courts of the specific Member State that is transposing this Directive.

[156] The quoted phrase is unclear. It is submitted that the drafters omitted the word 'and', which should appear thus: "in this [and] and in other Directives," in Article 45(d) of the BCD.

[157] If the information originates in another Member State, it may only be divulged with the express agreement of the competent authority that has disclosed it, and, if appropriate, exclusively for the purpose for which this authority granted its agreement (BCD (original version), Articles 46, 48(1)(c) and 48(2)(c)).

Member State may authorise the exchange of information between its competent authority in respect of the supervision of credit institutions and (a) the authority that is responsible for overseeing the entities which are involved in the bankruptcy and the liquidation of these institutions, (b) the authority that is responsible for overseeing persons who are charged with conducting statutory audits of the accounts of investment firms, credit institutions, insurance firms and other financial organisations, and (c) in order to strengthen the stability of the financial system, the authority which is legally responsible for the discovery and investigation of contraventions of company law, provided that the information is for the performance of the required supervisory task and is subject to the obligation of professional secrecy which the first sentence of the aforesaid paragraph specifies[158] [389]. The provisions of the current and immediately preceding paragraph are neither to preclude competent authorities from sending information to monetary authorities and (if suitable) to other public authorities that are responsible for the supervision of payment systems, nor to prevent these monetary and payment authorities from transmitting to the competent authorities data that the latter may require for the purposes of (a) to (d) in the paragraph above; information received in this context is to be subject to the duty of professional secrecy to which the first sentence to the aforementioned paragraph refers [390]. Notwithstanding the provisions of that paragraph, Member States may, "by virtue of provisions laid down by law", authorise the divulgation of "certain information to other departments of their central government administrations responsible for legislation on the supervision of" investment firms, credit and financial institutions, and insurance companies, and to inspectors who act on behalf of these departments; these data may only be disclosed "where necessary and for reasons of prudential control"[159] [391]. The provisions of the current and immediately paragraph are not to preclude a Member State's competent authority from communicating the information to which the latter paragraph refers to a clearing house (or similar entity), if that authority considers it to be necessary to transmit this information in order to ensure the appropriate functioning of the entity in respect of (potential) defaults by participants in the market [392].

Credit institutions are to individually observe the duties that Articles 22[160] and 75, and Title V Chapter 2[161] Section 5 (entitled 'Large exposures'), of the BCD lay down [393]. Each credit institution which is neither a subsidiary in the Member State in which it is authorised and supervised, nor a parent company, nor included in the consolidation pursuant to Article 73 of the BCD[162], is required to individually fulfil the obligations that Articles 120 and 123,

---

[158] See fn 157.

[159] This provision of the BCD is opaque. It is submitted that its meaning is as follows. 'In spite of the obligation of professional secrecy, each Member State may introduce legislation that empowers its competent authority to pass information to other central government departments that supervise firms in the financial sector, and to inspectors who act on behalf of these divisions, if it considers this to be necessary for effective prudential oversight of the firms that it supervises.'

[160] See the last paragraph of the subsection entitled 'Authorisation', above in this section, for Article 22 of the BCD.

[161] Title V Chapter 2 of the BCD is entitled 'Technical instruments of prudential supervision', and contains Articles 56-122.

[162] Article 73 of the BCD lays down the following grounds for excluding from the consolidation a credit or financial institution that is a subsidiary: (a) the firm is located in a third country in which there are "legal impediments to" information transfer, (b) the competent authority which is responsible for the consolidated supervision considers that the company "is of negligible interest only with respect to the objectives of monitoring credit institutions," and "in any event" if the balance-sheet total of that organisation is less than the lower of 10 million Euros and 1% of the parent entity's balance-sheet total, and (c) if, in that competent authority's opinion, "the consolidation of the financial situation of the undertaking concerned would be inappropriate or misleading" with regard to "the objectives of the supervision of credit institutions."

and Chapter 5 (entitled 'Disclosure by credit institutions'), of the BCD contain [394]. The next 2 paragraphs are to consider these items, in turn.

Without prejudice to Article 136 of the BCD[163], Member States are to require credit institutions to possess own funds[164] that are continuously at least equal to the sum of the following capital requirements: (a) for credit and dilution risks – "8% of the total of their risk-weighted exposure amounts", computed in accordance with Section 3 (entitled 'Minimum own funds requirements for credit risk'), (b) with reference to their trading-book business – for position, counterparty and settlement risks, and for large exposures that exceed the limits which Articles 111 to 117 of the BCD specify (in so far as these limits are authorised to be exceeded) – the capital requirements that are determined in concurrence with Article 18 and Chapter V Section 4 (entitled 'Monitoring and control of large exposures') of the CRD, (c) as regards all of their business activities – for foreign-exchange and commodities risks – the capital requirements which are computed in accordance with Article 18 of the CRD, and (d) with respect to all of their business activities – for operational risk – the capital requirements that are calculated in accordance with Title V Chapter 2[165] Section 4 (entitled 'Minimum own funds requirements for operational risk') of the BCD [395]. In respect of point (a), each credit institution is either to apply the Standardised Approach for which Article 78 to 83 of the BCD provides, or (if the competent authority of its home Member State allows it to do so – a decision that the authority explicitly takes on an individual basis) the Internal Ratings Approach for which Articles 84 to 89 of the BCD provides, in order to compute its risk-weighted exposure [396]. With regard to points (b) and (c), credit institutions and investment firms are always to possess own funds that are at least equal to the sum of the capital requirements for their trading-book business – which are to be computed in accordance with the methods and options that Articles 28 to 32[166] and Annexes I[167], II[168], VI[169] and (as applicable) V[170] specify, and the capital requirements for all of their business activities – which are to be calculated in concurrence with the methods and options which Annexes III[171], IV[172] and (as applicable) V lay down [397]. In respect of point (d), competent authorities are to require credit institutions to possess funds against operational risk in accordance with the Basic Indicator Approach, the Standardised Approach or Advanced Measurement Approaches; the last of these requires approval from the competent authority of a credit

---

[163] Article 136(1) of the BCD directs each competent authority to require any credit institution that does not satisfy the capital requirements of the BCD, to promptly take the actions or steps that are necessary to remedy the situation. These include requiring credit institutions to hold own funds that are above the minimum level that Article 75 of the BCD lays down (BCD (original version), Article 136(1)(a)). The competent authority is to impose on credit institutions a specific own funds requirement that exceeds the minimum level that Article 75 of the BCD specifies, if they do not satisfy the requirements that Articles 22, 109 and 123 of the BCD lay down, or if these funds (and the arrangements, mechanisms, processes and strategies that the credit institutions implement) do not "ensure a sound management and coverage of their risks" (BCD (original version), Article 124(3)) – if the exclusive application of other measures is unlikely to improve sufficiently these arrangements, mechanisms, processes and strategies within a suitable period of time (BCD (original version), Article 136(2)).

[164] See fn 138, for the definition of 'own funds'.

[165] See fn 161.

[166] These Articles, in conjunction with Title V Chapter 2 Section 5 of the BCD, concern the monitoring and control of large exposures of credit institutions and investment firms (CRD (original version), Article 28(1)).

[167] Annex I to the CRD is entitled 'Calculating Capital Requirements for Position Risk'.

[168] Annex II to the CRD is entitled 'Calculating Capital Requirements for Settlement and Counterparty Risk'.

[169] Annex VI to the CRD is entitled 'Calculating Capital Requirements for Large Exposures'.

[170] Annex V to the CRD is entitled 'Use of Internal Models to Calculate Capital Requirements'.

[171] Annex III to the CRD is entitled 'Calculating Capital Requirements for Foreign-Exchange Risk'.

[172] Annex IV to the CRD is entitled 'Calculating Capital Requirements for Commodities Risk'.

institution's home Member State for that firm's use of its models to compute its own funds requirement in respect of operational risk[173] [398].

Each credit institution that is neither a parent undertaking, nor a subsidiary, nor included in the consolidation, must fulfil the following requirements. It is not to have a qualifying holding[174] that is in excess of 15% of its own funds, in an entity which is neither a credit institution, nor a financial institution, nor a firm that conducts activities which are relevant or ancillary to banking – such as factoring, leasing, or the management of unit trusts or data processing services [399]. The total amount of the credit institution's holdings in these firms is not to exceed 60% of its own funds [400]. These limits may only be exceeded "in exceptional circumstances", under which the competent authority is to require the credit institution either to raise the level of its own funds "or to take other equivalent measures"[175] [401]. The credit institution is to have in place effective, sound and complete processes and strategies, in order to assess and continuously maintain the amounts, distribution and types of internal capital that it considers to be sufficient to cover the level and nature of the risks to which it is, or may be, subject; these processes and strategies are to be regularly reviewed, in order to make sure that they remain both comprehensive and proportionate to the nature, complexity and scale of the credit institution's activities [402]. For the purposes of the CRD, credit institutions are to publicly disclose the information that Part 2 of Annex XII to the CRD lays down, subject to provisions that Article 146 of this Directive contains[176] [403]. These disclosure requirements are extensive, and include, for instance, the following items: (i) the credit institution's risk management policies and objectives for each separate class of risk, including the processes and strategies to manage those risks, the organisation and structure of the risk management function, the nature and scope of risk measurement and reporting systems, the policies for mitigating and hedging risk, and the strategies and processes for monitoring the effectiveness of these mitigants and hedges on an on-going basis; (ii) the credit institution's exposure to credit and dilution risks, including the definitions for accounting purposes of 'impaired' and 'past due', a description of the methods and approaches that are used to determine provisions and value adjustments, the total amount of

---

[173] Part 1 of Annex X to the BCD, entitled 'Operational Risk: Basic Indicator Approach', lays down the calculation for the credit institution's operational risk using this method (BCD (original version), Article 103). Part 2 of Annex X to the BCD, entitled 'Operational Risk: Standardised Approach', specifies the determination of the credit institution's operational risk using this technique, in accordance with the guidance that Article 104 of the BCD provides. Part 3 of Annex X to the BCD, entitled 'Operational Risk: Advanced Measurement Approaches', contains the qualifying criteria for the application of these methods (BCD (original version), Article 105(2)). Part 4 of Annex X to the BCD, entitled 'Operational Risk: Combined use of different methodologies', specifies the circumstances under which the credit institution may use a combination of these Approaches (BCD (original version), Article 102(4)). Without prejudice to this combined use, a credit institution is to demonstrate a good reason to change from an Advanced Measurement Approach to the Basic Indicator Approach or to the Standardised Approach, and to switch from the Standardised Approach to the Basic Indicator Approach; the competent authority must approve this change (BCD (original version), Article 102(2)-(3)).

[174] See fn 140, for the definition of 'qualifying holding' within the BCD.

[175] Whilst Article 120 of the BCD does not specify what these 'equivalent measures' are, it is submitted that these may be the measures that Article 136(1) of the BCD lays down, namely: (i) requiring the reinforcement of the arrangements, mechanisms, processes and strategies that the credit institution has implemented to comply with Articles 22 and 123 of the BCD, (ii) requiring the credit institution to apply a particular provisioning policy or treatment of assets, (iii) limiting or restricting the business, network or operations of the credit institution, and (iv) requiring a lowering in the risk that is inherent in the credit institution's activities, products and systems. See the next sentence in the text, for Article 123 of the BCD. See the last paragraph of the subsection 'Authorisation', above in this section, for Article 22 of the BCD.

[176] See below in this paragraph, for Article 146 of the CRD.

exposures, the average amount of exposures over the relevant period divided into different types of exposure categories, the geographic distribution of the exposures, the distribution of the exposures by counterparty or industry type, the residual maturity breakdown of all of the exposures, by significant counterparty or industry type – (1) the amount of the impaired exposures and the past due exposures, supplied separately, (2) provisions and values adjustments, and (3) charges for these latter items during the period, the amount of the impaired exposures and the past due exposures – provided separately and divided into significant geographical areas, the reconciliation of changes in the provisions and the value adjustments for impaired expenses, and value adjustments and recoveries that are directly recorded in the income statement [404]. The credit institution must disclose the information that Part 3 of Annex XII to the CRD specifies, in order for the competent authority to permit the former to use the particular methodology to which that data corresponds [405]. For example, if the credit institution uses an Advanced Measurement Approach in order to compute its own funds requirements for operational risk, then it is to divulge a description of how it uses insurance in order to mitigate this risk [406]. Credit institutions are to "adopt a formal policy" in order to comply with the above disclosure requirements, and to "have policies" for evaluating the suitability of their disclosures – including their frequency and their verification [407]. They should, if requested to do so, explain their rating decisions to corporate applicants for loans [408]. Credit institutions may omit at least one of the disclosures that Annex XII Part 2 lists, if the information divulged is "not … regarded as material," i.e., if its misstatement or omission would not influence or change "the assessment or decision of a user" who relies on those data in order to take "economic decisions." [409]. Credit institutions may leave out one or more of the disclosures that Annex XII Parts 2 and 3 list, if these items include information that "is regarded as proprietary or confidential," i.e., if sharing the data with the public would undermine the credit institution's competitive position, or if there are obligations to the credit institution's customers that bind it to confidentiality[177] [410]. Credit institutions are to publish the disclosures at least annually, and "as soon as practicable." [411]. They are also to determine whether these are to be published on a more frequent basis, taking into account pertinent characteristics of their business – such as participation in different financial sectors, international markets and payment, settlement and clearing systems, scope of activities, and scale of operations [412]. Each Member State is to empower its competent authority to require credit institutions to make at least one of the disclosures to which Annex XII Parts 2 and 3 refer, publish one or more of the disclosures more often than annually, use specified locations and media for divulgation, and utilize particular means of verification for the disclosures that are outside the scope of statutory audit [413].

---

[177] In these cases, the credit institution is to divulge the fact that the specific information is not disclosed and the reason for withholding those data; it is to publish "more general information about the subject matter of the disclosure requirement" – provided that this knowledge is considered to be neither proprietary nor confidential (BCD (original version), Article 146(3)).

Reorganisation and Winding Up

Directive 2001/24/EC on the reorganisation and winding up of credit institutions lays down measures on these matters that apply to credit institutions[178], their branches[179] within Member States, and branches of a credit institution whose head office is outside the European Community[180] if this entity has branches in 2 or more Member States [414]. The home Member State's[181] administrative or judicial authorities[182] are alone to be empowered to determine the implementation of reorganisation measures[183] in a credit institution, including branches founded in other Member States [415]. The reorganisation measures are to be applied in agreement with the rules that are applicable in the home Member State, unless Directive 2001/24/EC provides otherwise; they are to be completely effective in harmony with that Member State's legislation throughout the Community without any additional formalities [416]. The home Member State's administrative or judicial authorities are to promptly inform the host Member State's[184] competent authorities[185] of their decision to take up any reorganisation measure, including its practical consequences, via the home Member State's competent authorities [417]. If the host Member State's administrative or judicial authorities consider it to be necessary to implement within their jurisdiction at least one reorganisation measure, then they are to notify the home Member State's competent authorities accordingly, through the host Member State's competent authorities [418]. Reorganisation measures are to be fully effective against creditors, unless the home Member State's laws or its administrative or judicial authorities specify otherwise [419]. The administrative or judicial authorities of the host Member State of a branch of a credit institution whose head office is outside the European Community is to swiftly inform the competent authorities of the other Member States in which that firm has established branches, of their decision to introduce any reorganisation measure, including its practical effects, through that Member State's competent authorities [420].

---

[178] For the purpose of Directive 2001/24/EC, 'credit institution' is defined in Article 1(1) of Directive 2000/12/EC (Directive 2001/24/EC (original version), Article 1(1)). See fn 39, for this definition.

[179] For the purpose of Directive 2001/24/EC, 'branch' is defined in Article 1(3) of Directive 2001/24/EC (Directive 2001/24/EC (original version), Articles 1(1) and 2). 'Branch' means a place of business that is a legally-dependent element of a credit institution, and which directly conducts some or all of the transactions that are "inherent in the business of credit institutions" (Directive 2000/12/EC (as amended to 09/03/06), Article 1(3)).

[180] The 'European Community' became the 'European Union' when the Treaty of Lisbon entered into force on 1st December 2009 – hence the reference to 'European Community' in the legislation adopted prior to the GFC. Directive 2001/24/EC is not labelled a 'Text with EEA relevance'.

[181] 'Home Member State' means the Member State in which the credit institution was authorised (Directive 2001/24/EC (original version), Article 2; Directive 2000/12/EC (as amended to 09/03/06), Article 1(6)).

[182] 'Administrative or judicial authorities' means the Member States' administrative or judicial authorities that are competent for the purposes of winding-up proceedings or reorganisation measures (Directive 2001/24/EC (original version), Article 2). See fns 183 and 186, for the definitions of 'reorganisation measures' and 'winding-up proceedings', respectively.

[183] 'Reorganisation measures' means measures that are intended to maintain or restore the financial circumstances of a credit institution, and which might affect the pre-existing rights of third parties (Directive 2001/24/EC (original version), Article 2).

[184] ' ' means the Member State in which a credit institution supplies services or has a branch (Directive 2001/24/EC (original version), Article 2; Directive 2000/12/EC (as amended to 09/03/06), Article 1(7)).

[185] 'Competent authorities' means the national authorities that are legally empowered to supervise credit institutions (Directive 2001/24/EC (original version), Article 2; Directive 2000/12/EC (as amended to 09/03/06), Article 1(4)).

This paragraph considers winding-up proceedings.[186] The home Member State's administrative or judicial authorities are to be exclusively empowered to determine the commencement of winding-up proceedings concerning a credit institution, including branches set up in other Member States; a decision to begin winding-up proceedings is to be recognised within the domain of all other Member States, and shall be effective there as soon as it applies in the home Member State [421]. The home Member State's administrative or judicial authorities are to promptly notify the host Member State's competent authorities of their decision to commence winding-up proceedings, including their practical consequences, via the home Member State's competent authorities [422]. A credit institution is to be wound up in agreement with the rules that its home Member State applies, to the extent that Directive 2001/24/EC does not provide differently [423]. The home Member State's law shall determine, in particular: the goods to which administration applies; the treatment of goods that the credit institution acquires after winding-up proceedings are opened; the respective powers of the liquidator[187] and the credit institution; the conditions under which set-offs may be applied; the effects of winding-up proceedings on currently operative contracts to which the credit institution is a party, and on proceedings that individual creditors bring; the claims that are to be brought against the credit institution; the treatment of claims that arise after winding-up proceedings are started; the rules that govern the lodging, verification and admission of claims, the distribution of the proceeds from the realization of assets, the ranking of claims, and the rights of creditors who have achieved partial satisfaction of their claims after the commencement of insolvency proceedings through a property right or via a set-off; the conditions for, the effects of, and creditors' rights following the closure of winding-up proceedings; the parties who are to incur the costs of these proceedings; and the rules that relate to the unenforceability, voidability and voidness of the proceedings[188] [424]. A credit institution's governing bodies are to consult its home Member State's competent authorities, before they take a decision as to whether or not to liquidate it voluntarily [425]. The voluntary liquidation of a credit institution is to prevent neither the commencement of winding-up proceedings nor the adoption of a reorganisation measure [426]. If winding-up proceedings are to be started in relation to a credit institution in the absence of, or following the foundering of, reorganisation measures, then that firm's authorisation is to be withdrawn[189] [427]. This withdrawal of authorisation is not to preclude the person(s) who are entrusted with the winding up from conducting some of the credit institution's activities, insofar as this is necessary or suitable for the purposes of liquidation[190] [428]. As soon as

---

[186] 'Winding-up proceedings' means collective proceedings that are commenced and monitored by the administrative or judicial authorities of a Member State, with the objective of realizing assets under the supervision of these authorities (Directive 2001/24/EC (original version), Article 2).

[187] 'Liquidator' means a person or body whom the administrative or judicial authorities appoint, in order to administer winding-up proceedings (Directive 2001/24/EC (original version), Article 2).

[188] The rules of the credit institution's home Member State is not to determine the rules which concern the unenforceability, voidability and voidness of legal acts that are detrimental to its creditors as a whole, if the beneficiary of those acts proves that each act is "subject to the law of a Member State other than the home Member State," and that this law precludes any ways of challenging the act in the current instance (Directive 2001/24/EC (original version), Article 30(1)).

[189] The host Member State's competent authorities are to be notified of this withdrawal, and are to take suitable measures in order to prevent the credit institution from initiating further transactions there and to protect depositors' interests (Directive 2001/24/EC (original version), Article 12(1); Directive 2000/12/EC (as amended to 09/03/06), Article 22(9)).

[190] The home Member State may require these activities to be conducted with the consent of, and under the superintendence of, its competent authorities (Directive 2001/24/EC (original version), Article 12(2)).

winding-up proceedings are started, the liquidator or the home Member State's administrative or judicial authority shall swiftly and individually inform known creditors who have their domiciles, head offices or normal places of residence in other Member States, except in cases in which the home Member State's legislation "does not require lodgement of the claim with a view to its recognition"[191] [429]. Any creditor whose domicile, head office or normal place of residence is in a Member State other than the home Member State shall be entitled to lodge claims, or to submit comments in relation to claims [430]. The claims of all of these creditors shall be treated alike, and given the same ranking as claims of an equivalent nature that may be lodged by creditors with their domiciles, head offices or normal places of residence in the home Member State [431]. Liquidators are to regularly inform creditors of progress in the winding up [432].

If a credit institution whose head office is outside the European Community is wound up, then its branches therein are affected. Accordingly, the administrative or judicial authorities of the host Member State of the branch of such a firm is to promptly notify the competent authorities of the other host Member States in which it has established branches, of their decision to commence winding-up proceedings[192], including the practical consequences of those proceedings, via the competent authorities of the first aforementioned host Member State [433]. These administrative or judicial authorities are to notify the competent authorities of the other host Member States that winding-up proceedings have been started, and that the credit institution's authorisation has been withdrawn [434]. All persons who are required to disclose or receive information in association with the consultation or information procedures which provisions above in this subsection lay down, are to be bound by the duty of professional secrecy [435].

This paragraph concerns provisions of Directive 2001/24/EC's which apply to both reorganisation measures and winding-up proceedings. The effects of a reorganisation measure or the commencement of winding-up proceedings on (a) an employment contract are to be governed exclusively by the law of the Member State which applies to that agreement, (b) a contract that confers the right to acquire or use immovable property – are to be ruled solely by the law of the Member State within the territory of which these assets are located[193], and (c) rights in respect of immovable property, an aircraft or a ship subject to record in a public register – are to be governed exclusively by the law of the Member State under whose authority the register is maintained [436]. The adoption of reorganisation measures, or the initiation of winding-up proceedings, is not to affect the property rights of creditors or third parties, in respect of assets that belong to the credit institution which are located within the territory of another Member State at the time at which the reorganisation measures are taken

---

[191] The quoted phrase is unclear. It is submitted that the phrase means that, if there is no national provision at law for the court to refuse to admit the winding-up proceedings, then there is no obligation for creditors to be formally informed of the action – once it has commenced.

[192] Article 9(1) of Directive 2001/24/EC provides that the administrative or judicial authorities of a credit institution's home Member State is exclusively empowered to decide as to whether to commence winding-up proceedings in respect of that firm – see the second sentence of the preceding paragraph of the text. Yet Article 19(1) of the Directive empowers a *host* Member State's administrative or judicial authorities to do this in respect of a credit institution whose registered office is in a third country. It is submitted that Article 19(1) is beyond the jurisdiction of the EU, unless the initiation of winding-up proceedings is agreed with the competent authority of the country in which the credit institution is registered, before the action is commenced.

[193] That law is to determine whether the property is immovable or movable (Directive 2001/24/EC (original version), Article 20(b)).

or the winding-up proceedings are started[194] [437]. The assumption of reorganisation measures, or the commencement of winding-up proceedings, which concern a credit institution that is buying an asset, is not to affect those rights of the seller that are based on a reservation of title clause, if the asset is located within the territory of a Member State other than that in which the measures were taken or the proceedings were initiated, at the time that those measures were assumed or those proceedings were started [438]. Furthermore, the adoption of reorganisation measures or the commencement of winding-up proceedings, which relate to a credit institution that is selling an asset – after delivery of this item, is neither to provide grounds for terminating or rescinding the sale of the asset nor to stop the purchaser from acquiring title to it, if it is situated as the previous sentence describes [439]. The assumption of reorganisation measures or the opening of winding-up proceedings is not to affect the rights of creditors to require the set-off of their claims against those of the credit institution, if the law that applies to the claims of the latter allows this set-off [440]. The provisions that the previous 4 sentences contain are not to prevent actions for the unenforceability, voidability or voidness of winding-up proceedings [441]. The enforcement of rights, the existence of transfer of which requires their recording in an account, a centralised deposit system or a register that is located in a Member State, is to be governed by the law of that country[195] [442]. Netting agreements are to be solely governed by the law of the contract that applies to them [443]. Liquidators and administrators[196] are to be entitled to exercise within the lands of all Member States, every power that they are authorised to use in the home Member State's territory; they may appoint persons to help them or, as appropriate, to represent them during the course of the reorganisation measure or winding-up proceedings [444]. In exercising his/her powers, a liquidator or administrator is to observe the law of the Member State within the realm of which he/she wishes to act; these may include neither the right to judge legal proceedings, nor the use of force [445]. If, by an act that is taken after the adoption of a reorganisation measure or the commencement of winding-up proceedings, a credit institution sells an immovable asset, a ship or aircraft that is registered in a public register, or instruments (or rights in these instruments) the existence or transfer of which assumes that they are recorded in an account, a centralised deposit system or a register that is situated in a Member State, then the validity of this act is to be governed by the law of the Member State within the domain of which the immovable asset is located or under the authority of which the account, centralised deposit system or register is maintained [446].

---

[194] These property rights mean, in particular, (a) the right to relinquish assets and "to obtain satisfaction from the proceeds of or income from" them – especially via a mortgage or a lien, (b) the sole right for a claim to be satisfied – especially a right that is guaranteed by assignment of the claim or by a lien with regard to the claim, (c) the right to require restitution by, or to demand the assets from, a person who possesses or uses the assets against the wishes of the party who is entitled to possess or use them, and (d) a right to the beneficial use of the assets that arises from the property itself (Directive 2001/24/EC (original version), Article 21(2)).

[195] Notwithstanding this rule, repurchase agreements, and transactions which are conducted "in the context of a regulated market" are to be exclusively governed by the law of the contract that applies to them (Directive 2001/24/EC (original version), Articles 26 and 27).

[196] 'Administrator' means any person or body whom the administrative or judicial authorities appoint, in order to apply reorganisation measures (Directive 2001/24/EC (original version), Article 2).

Payment Services

The PSD was enacted in order "to establish at Community level a modern and coherent legal framework for payment services" [447]. The previous system, under which national law regulated the payment services market alongside a partial Community framework, was considered to cause confusion and legal uncertainty [448].

The Directive provides for the authorisation of payment institutions[197] to supply payment services[198] [449]. In addition, credit institutions[199] and other specified organisations[200] are empowered to provide payment services, without requiring further authorisation under the PSD [450]. Payment service providers[201] are expected to hold specified minimum amounts of initial capital[202] and own funds[203], as an authorisation requirement. An authorised payment institution may supply payment services in another Member State[204] under the free movement of services or right of establishment, provided that the host Member State's[205] competent authorities receive the payment institution's name and address, the names of the branch's managers (right of establishment only), the branch's organisational structure (right of establishment only), and the particular payment services which the payment institution wishes

---

[197] 'Payment institution' means a legal person that is authorised in accordance with Article 10 of the PSD to supply and carry out payment services throughout the Community (PSD (original version), Article 4(4)).

[198] 'Payment service' means any of the following business activities: the operation of a payment account including services enabling the placement of cash on, and/or the withdrawal of cash from, this account; the execution of payment transactions, the acquisition and/or issuance of payment instruments; money remittance (PSD (original version), Article 4(3) and Annex). 'Payment instrument' means any collection of procedures and/or "personalised device(s)" that are agreed between the payment service provider and the payment service user, and which are employed by the latter in order to initiate a payment order (PSD (original version), Article 4(23)).

[199] 'Credit institution' within the PSD means an organisation whose business is to receive repayable funds from the public and to supply credits for its own account, (PSD (original version), Article 1(1)(a); BCD (original version), Article 4(1)(a)).

[200] These 'other specified organisations' are electronic money institutions, post office giro institutions, the European Central Bank, national central banks, Member States, and the regional and local authorities of those countries (PSD (original version), Article 1(1)).

[201] 'Payment service provider' means payment institution, credit institution, the entities to which fn 200 refers, and – at the discretion of Member States or their competent authorities – persons whose payment transactions over the last year did not exceed a monthly average of 3 million Euros and who (or whose managers) have not been convicted of financial crimes (PSD (original version), Articles 4(9), 1(1) and 26(1)).

[202] 'Initial capital' consists of paid-up subscribed capital – including share premium accounts and excluding cumulative preference shares, and reserves – including profits and losses brought forward pursuant to the application of the profit or loss for the financial year; 'subscribed capital' comprises all items that domestic law considers to be equity capital (PSD (original version), Article 6; BCD (original version), Article 57(a)-(b); Directive 86/635/EC (as amended to 16/08/06), Article 22). If the payment institution provides only money remittance services, then its initial capital is to be at least 20,000 Euros; if it provides any other payment service, then its initial capital is to be 125,000 Euros or more – subject to one exception (in which case initial capital is to be at least 50,000 Euros) (PSD (original version), Article 6)).

[203] The PSD's definition of 'own funds' is that which the BCD provides (PSD (original version), Article 7(1)); see fn 138, for this definition. The payment institution's own funds must remain above the lower of the amount stated in Article 6 of the PSD and that prescribed by competent authorities' choice of one of the methods that Article 8 of the PSD lays down (PSD (original version), Articles 7(1) and 8(1)). See fn 202, for Article 6 of the PSD.

[204] As the PSD is labelled a 'Text with EEA relevance,' 'Member State' means a Contracting Party to the EEA Agreement, i.e., one of the following countries: any Member State of the EU, Iceland, Liechtenstein and Norway.

[205] 'Host Member State' means the Member State, other than the home Member State, in which a payment service provider has a branch or an agent, or supplies payment services (PSD (original version), Article 4(2)).

to provide in the host Member State's territory, from the home Member State's[206] competent authorities [451].

The PSD provides for informational requirements in respect of single payment transactions that are not covered by a framework contract[207], which the payer's and the payee's payment service provider must supply to the payer[208] and the payee[209], respectively, at each stage in the payment transaction[210]. The Directive also states informational requirements that the payment service provider must impart to the payment service user[211], prior to the point at which the latter is bound by a framework contract or offer [452]. These data are to include specified items on the payment service provider, the use of the payment service, charges, exchange rates and interest rates, safeguards and corrective measures, changes in and termination of the framework contract, and redress [453]. The payer's and payee's payment service provider are each expected to supply to the payer and payee, respectively, specified data concerning each individual payment transaction[212]. Nevertheless, due to the presence of the framework contract and its informational requirements, there is no provision for the payee's payment service provider to furnish information to the payee before the payment transaction takes place; furthermore, the payer's payment service provider is only required to supply the payee with the specified information for that moment at the request of the payer[213] [454].

Member States are to ensure that a payment transaction is authorised only if the payer has provided consent to carry out the payment transaction [455]. They shall make sure that, in the event of an unauthorised payment transaction, the payer's payment service provider immediately refunds the amount of the unauthorised payment transaction to the payer and, if applicable, restores the debited payment account to the state in which it would have been if the unauthorised payment transaction had not happened [456].

Nevertheless, the payer is liable for these losses if he/she incurred them by acting fraudulently, or by failing to satisfy one of specified obligations of the payment service user[214] with intent or with gross negligence[215] [457].

---

[206] 'Home Member State' means the Member State in which the payment service provider's registered office (or, in its absence, the payment service provider's head office) is located (PSD (original version), Article 4(1)).

[207] 'Framework contract' means a payment service contract that governs the future accomplishment of individual and successive payment transactions, and which may contain the requirement and conditions for establishing a payment account (PSD (original version), Article 4(12)). 'Payment account' means an account that is held in the name of at least one payment service user, and which is used for the fulfilment of payment transactions (PSD (original version), Article 4(14)).

[208] 'Payer' means a person who has a payment account and permits a payment order to be made from this account, or if there is no payment account, a person who makes a payment order (PSD (original version), Article 4(7)).

[209] 'Payee' means a person who is the intended recipient of funds from a payment transaction (PSD (original version), Article 4(8)).

[210] Articles 35-39 of the PSD specify this information.

[211] 'Payment service user' means a person who makes use of a payment service, either as payer or payee, or as both. (PSD (original version), Article 4(10)).

[212] Articles 46-48 of the PSD specify this information.

[213] This information comprises the charges that the payer is to pay (including a breakdown of their amounts, if this is applicable) and the maximum execution time (PSD (original version) Article 46).

[214] A payment service user that is entitled to employ a payment instrument is to be required to: (a) utilize the instrument in accordance with its terms of issue and use, and (b) promptly inform the payment service provider (or an entity that the latter specifies) on becoming aware of the loss, misappropriation, theft or unauthorised use of the payment instrument (PSD (original version), Article 56(1)). The payer is not to bear any financial loss that results from the use of the lost, misappropriated or stolen payment instrument after notification in concurrence with Article 56(1)(b) of the PSD, except if he/she has behaved fraudulently (PSD (original version), Article 61(4)).

Electronic Money

Directive 2000/46/EC on the taking up, pursuit and prudential supervision of the business of electronic money institutions was enacted in order to provide measures that co-ordinate and harmonise those rules of Member States which concern the initiation, performance and prudential superintendence of electronic money institutions' business [458]. 'Electronic money' is monetary value that is represented by a claim on the issuer which is stored on an electronic device, issued on the receipt of funds of an amount that is at least the monetary value issued, and accepted as a means of payment by firms other than the issuer [459]. Whilst this provision is difficult to understand, the corresponding Recital provides clarification. It states that electronic money is "an electronic surrogate for coins and banknotes" that is stored on computer memory, a chip card or another electronic device, and which is intended to effect "electronic payments of limited amounts" [460]. The next Recital explains that the approach the Directive adopts

> is appropriate to achieve only the essential harmonisation necessary and sufficient to secure the mutual recognition of authorisation and prudential supervision of electronic money institutions[216], making possible the granting of a single licence recognised throughout the Community and designed to ensure bearer confidence and the application of the principle of home Member State prudential supervision [461].

Thus, Directive 2000/46/EC was enacted in order to extend the conditions that are applicable to banks, to organisations that solely issue and administer electronic money[217], thereby furthering the internal market in financial services.

A bearer of electronic money may request the issuer to redeem it at par value in cash or by transfer to an account, at minimal charge [462]. Electronic money institutions are to have an initial capital[218], and own funds[219] on an on-going basis, of at least 1 million Euros [463]. Furthermore, they are to continuously possess own funds that are at least 2% of the higher of the average of the preceding 6 months' total amount, and the current quantity, of their financial liabilities that concern electronic money which is in issue [464]. Electronic money

---

[215] In cases in which the payer has neither acted fraudulently nor intentionally failed to meet one of his/her specified obligations as payment service user, Member States may reduce the payer's liability, taking into consideration the payment instrument's personalised security features and the circumstances under which it was lost, misappropriated or stolen (PSD (original version), Article 61(3)).

[216] 'Electronic money institution' means a legal person that is not a firm whose business is to receive repayable funds from the public and to provide credits for its own account (i.e., a bank), which issues electronic money as a means of payment (Directive 2000/46/EC, Article 3(a); Directive 2000/12/EC (as amended to 09/03/06), Article 1(1)).

[217] Other than the issuance of electronic money, electronic money institutions' business is limited to (i) the provision of associated services, such as the administration of electronic money by the performance of ancillary functions that are related to its issuance, (ii) the issuance and administration of other means of payment (excluding the granting of credit), and (iii) the storing of data on the electronic device on behalf of other entities (Directive 2000/46/EC, Article 1(5)).

[218] See fn 137, for the definition of 'initial capital'. The definition in Article 4(1) of Directive 2000/46/EC refers to Article 34(2)(1)-(2) of Directive 2000/12/EC rather than to Article 57(a)-(b) of the BCD, but without significant effect on this definition.

[219] See fn 138, for the definition of 'own funds'. The definition in Article 4(1) of Directive 2000/46/EC refers to Directive 2000/12/EC, rather than to Article 57 of the BCD. Article 34 of Directive 2000/12/EC contains the components of 'own funds' under that Directive – the immediate predecessor of the BCD – but with little effect on the definition.

institutions are to possess liquid investments[220] which amount to at least those financial liabilities [465]. Electronic money institutions are to operate "sound and prudent" procedures for accounting, administration and management and "adequate" mechanisms for internal control, which are to "respond" to the risks to which the firm is exposed [466]. There are a waivers of the application of "some or all of the provisions of" Directive 2000/46/EC, and of the whole of the relevant banking Directive[221], for small electronic money institutions and for specified limitations as to who can accept as payment electronic money that the firm issues [467].

Financial Collateral Arrangements

Directive 2002/47/EC on financial collateral arrangements was adopted to create a regime throughout the European Community for the provision of cash[222] and securities as collateral under security interest[223] and title transfer[224] structures, in order to contribute to the efficiency and integration of the financial market and to financial stability in the Community – thereby assisting the free movement of services and of capital in the single market for financial services [468]. Member States are not to require the formation, the perfection, the validity, the enforceability or the admissibility in evidence of a financial collateral arrangement[225], or the supply of financial collateral under such an arrangement, to depend upon "the performance of any formal act" [469]. The financial collateral is to comprise cash or financial instruments [470]. Both the collateral taker and the collateral provider must be a public authority, a central bank, the European Central Bank, the Bank for International Settlements, a multilateral development bank, the IMF, the European Investment Bank, a credit institution, an investment firm, a financial institution, an insurance company, an UCITS, a management company (as defined in the UCITS Directive), a central counterparty, a settlement agent or a clearing house[226] [471].

---

[220] Article 5(1) of Directive 2000/46/EC specifies liquid investments in accordance with Directive 2000/12/EC. Assets are to be valued at the lower of cost and market value (Directive 200/46/EC (original version), Article 5(5)).

[221] Article 8 of Directive 2000/46/EC refers to Directive 2000/12/EC; nevertheless, the 'relevant banking Directive' is the BCD from the date on which the latter entered into force – 20th July 2006 (BCD (original version), Article 159).

[222] 'Cash' means money that is credited to an account in any currency, or similar claims for the repayment of money – such as money market deposits (Directive 2002/47/EC (original version), Article 2(1)(d)).

[223] 'Security financial collateral arrangement' means an arrangement under which a provider of collateral supplies financial collateral in the form of security to, or in favour of, a collateral taker, and the ownership of the financial collateral remains with the collateral provider (Directive 2002/47/EC (original version), Article 2(1)(c)).

[224] 'Title transfer financial collateral arrangement' means an arrangement under which a supplier of collateral transfers full ownership of financial collateral to a collateral taker, in order to cover the carrying out of 'relevant financial obligations' (Directive 2002/47/EC (original version), Article 2(1)(b)). 'Relevant financial obligations' are the duties that are secured by a financial collateral arrangement, and which provide a right to cash settlement and/or delivery of financial instruments (Directive 2002/47/EC (original version), Article 2(1)(f)).

[225] 'Financial collateral arrangement' means a title transfer financial collateral arrangement or a security financial collateral arrangement (Directive 2002/47/EC (original version), Article 2(1)(a)).

[226] One of these parties may be another type of legal person, an unincorporated firm or an unincorporated partnership, as long as the other is an entity that is listed in the text (Directive 2002/47/EC (original version), Article 1(2)(e)). Member States may exclude from the scope of Directive 2002/47/EC, collateral arrangements in which one of the parties is a person whom Article 1(2)(e) mentions, (Directive 2002/47/EC (original version), Article 1(3)).

Member States are to ensure that, on the occurrence of an enforcement event[227], the collateral taker is able to realize any financial collateral that is supplied under, and subject to the terms agreed in, a security financial collateral arrangement, in the following ways: (a) financial instruments[228] – by appropriation or sale and by setting of their value against, or applying their value in release of, the relevant financial obligations, and (b) cash – by setting off the amount against, or applying it in discharging, the relevant financial obligations [472]. Appropriation may only take place if the parties have agreed to this, and to the valuation of the financial instruments, in the security financial collateral arrangement [473]. Subject to the terms agreed in the security financial collateral agreement, these ways of realizing the financial collateral are not to require that (a) prior notice of the intention to realize must have been provided, (b) the terms of realization be approved by any court or person, (c) the realization be conducted in any prescribed manner, (d) any additional time period must have passed [474].

If, and to the extent that, the terms of a security financial collateral arrangement so provide, Member States are to ensure that the collateral taker is entitled to exercise a right of use in respect of the financial collateral which is provided under this arrangement [475]. A 'right of use' means the collateral taker's right to use the financial collateral that is provided under a security financial collateral arrangement as its owner, in concurrence with the terms of this arrangement [476]. If a collateral taker exercises a right of use, then he/she thereby incurs an obligation to transfer equivalent collateral[229] to replace the original financial collateral, by the due date for the discharge of the relevant financial obligations that the security financial collateral arrangement covers; alternatively, on the due date for the fulfilment of these obligations, the collateral taker is to either (i) transfer equivalent collateral, or (ii) to the extent (if any) that the security financial collateral arrangement's terms provide, set off the equivalent collateral's value against, or apply it to discharge, the relevant financial obligations [477]. If there is an enforcement event whilst an obligation to transfer equivalent collateral under the security financial collateral arrangement remains outstanding, then this duty may be subject to a close-out netting provision [478]. Member States are to ensure that a title transfer financial collateral arrangement may take effect pursuant to its terms; if there is an enforcement event whilst any duty of the collateral taker to transfer equivalent collateral

---

[227] 'Enforcement event' means an event of default (or a similar event) that the parties agree, on the occurrence of which the collateral taker has the right to release or appropriate financial collateral, or a close-out netting provision comes into force (Directive 2002/47/EC (original version), Article 2(1)(l)). 'Close-out netting provision' means a provision of a financial collateral arrangement, or of an agreement of which a financial collateral arrangement is a component, or, in the absence of such a provision, any statutory rule by which, when an enforcement event occurs: (i) the parties' duties are accelerated so as to be due at once and expressed as an obligation to pay an amount that represents their estimated current value, or are terminated and replaced by an obligation to pay this amount, and/or (ii) an account is taken of the amount due from each person to the other with regard to these duties, and a net sum equal to the balance of the account is payable by the party from whom the greater amount is due to the other person (Directive 2002/47/EC (original version), Article 2(1)(n)).

[228] 'Financial instruments' means shares in companies, other securities that are "equivalent" to these, debt instruments that are negotiable on the capital market, and any other traded securities that provide the right to acquire the above or which generate a cash settlement – excluding instruments of payment but including money market instruments, units in collective investment undertakings, and claims that relate to, or rights in (or with regard to), any of the aforementioned items (Directive 2002/47/EC (original version), Article 2(1)(e)).

[229] 'Equivalent collateral' means in relation to (i) cash – a payment in the same currency of the same amount, and (ii) financial instruments – financial instruments of the same issuer or debtor which are part of the same issue or class and of the same nominal amount, description and currency, or, if a financial collateral arrangement enables the transfer of other assets after any event takes place that concerns or affects financial instruments provided as financial collateral, these other assets (Directive 2002/47/EC (original version), Article 2(1)(i)).

under a transfer collateral arrangement remains outstanding, then this obligation may be subject to a close-out netting provision [479]. They are to make sure that any close-out netting provision may take effect according to its terms, notwithstanding (a) the initiation or continuation of reorganisation measures or winding-up proceedings in respect of the collateral taker and/or the collateral provider, and/or (b) any disposition of rights that the close-out netting provision grants [480].

Supplementary Supervision

The Commission introduced Directive 2002/87/EC on the supplementary supervision of credit institutions, insurance undertakings and investment firms in a financial conglomerate, to address lacunae in the sectoral legislation within the internal market for financial services and "additional prudential risks," in order to make sure that there are "sound supervisory arrangements" in respect of financial groups that operate across these sectors [481]. 'Sector' and 'sectoral' refer to investment firms, credit institutions or insurance companies [482]. Directive 2002/87/EC stresses the importance of "transparency of rules and exchange of information" with the financial regulatory authorities of third countries, in respect of financial conglomerates whose parent company is located outside the Community but which has subsidiary investment firms, banks and/or insurance companies whose head offices are situated therein [483]. Recital 14 of the Directive 'clears the ground' for this co-operation, as follows.

> Equivalent and appropriate supplementary supervisory arrangements can only be assumed to exist if the third-country supervisory authorities have agreed to cooperate with the competent authorities concerned on the means and objectives of exercising supplementary supervision of the regulated entities of a financial conglomerate [484].

Thus, Directive 2002/87/EC contains rules for supplementary supervision of regulated entities[230] that have been authorised under the securities, banking and insurance legislation and which are part of a financial conglomerate.

A 'financial conglomerate' is a group[231] that satisfies the following conditions: (a) a regulated entity authorised under the sectoral legislation is at the group's head, or one or more of the subsidiaries[232] are regulated entities, (b) if a regulated entity is at the group's head, then

---

[230] 'Regulated entity' means a credit institution, an insurance company or an investment firm (Directive 2002/87/EC (as amended to 24/03/05), Article 2(4)).

[231] 'Group' means a collection of undertakings, comprising a parent undertaking, its subsidiaries, and the companies in which the parent company or any of its subsidiaries hold a participation, exercise a dominant influence, and/or control a majority of the voting rights and/or appointments to office through the exercise of these rights, and/or which the latter manage on a unified basis (Directive 2002/87/EC (as amended to 24/03/05), Article 2(12); Directive 83/349/EC (as amended to 20/12/06), Articles 12(1) and 1). 'Participation' means the direct or indirect ownership of at least 20% of the capital or voting rights of a company, or a right in the capital of other companies, which, by generating a lasting connection with those firms, is intended to contribute to the participating entity's activities (Directive 2002/87/EC (as amended to 24/03/05), Article 2(11); Directive 78/660/EC (as amended to 20/12/06), Article 17).

[232] 'Subsidiary undertaking' means a company in which another undertaking holds a majority of the shareholders' or the members' voting rights, is a shareholder or member and has the right to appoint or remove a majority of its directors, effectively exercises a dominant influence over it (in the competent authorities' opinion), and/or controls a majority of the voting rights and/or appointments to office through the exercise of these rights, and/or

it is a parent undertaking[233] of, or an entity that holds a participation[234] in, a firm within the financial sector[235], or an organisation that is connected to another within the broad meaning of parent-subsidiary relationship that Directive 83/349/EEC provides[236], (c) if the group is not headed by a regulated entity, then the group's activities are mainly to take place within the financial sector[237], (d) one or more of the entities within the group is within the insurance sector, and at least one of these firms is within the banking or investment services sector, and (e) the aggregated and/or consolidated activities of the entities within the insurance sector, and within the banking and investment services sector, are both significant[238] [485].

which the other undertaking manages on a unified basis (Directive 2002/87/EC (as amended to 24/03/05), Article 2(10); Directive 83/349/EC (as amended to 20/12/06), Article 1).

[233] 'Parent undertaking' means a firm that has the relationship to a subsidiary undertaking that is described for 'another undertaking' in fn 232 (Directive 2002/87/EC (as amended to 24/03/05), Article 2(9); Directive 83/349/EC (as amended to 20/12/06), Article 1).

[234] See fn 231, for the definition of 'participation'.

[235] 'Financial sector' means a sector that comprises at least one of the following entities: (a) a credit institution, a financial institution as Article 1(5) of Directive 2000/12/EC specifies, or an ancillary banking services undertaking as Article 1(23) of Directive 2000/12/EC provides – 'the banking sector', (b) an insurance undertaking, a reinsurance undertaking, or an insurance holding company as Article 1(i) of Directive 98/78/EC on the supplementary supervision of insurance and reinsurance undertakings in an insurance or reinsurance group specifies – 'the insurance sector', (c) an investment firm, or a financial institution as Article 2(7) of Council Directive 93/6/EEC on the capital adequacy of investment firms and credit institutions provides – 'the investment services sector', and (d) a mixed financial holding company (Directive 2002/87/EC (as amended to 24/03/05), Article 2(8)). A 'financial institution' is a firm other than a credit institution, the main function of which is to acquire holdings or to conduct at least one of the following activities: lending, financial leasing, money transmission services, the issuance and administration of means of payment, guarantees and commitments, advice on corporate business strategy and financial structure, services that concern acquisitions and mergers, money broking, portfolio management and advice, safeguarding and administration of securities, and trading for the accounts of customers or for own account in money market instruments, foreign exchange, financial futures and options, exchange and interest-rate instruments, and transferable securities (Directive 2000/12/EC (as amended to 09/03/06), Article 1(5) and Annex I). 'Ancillary banking services undertaking' is an entity whose main activity comprises the ownership or management of property, the management of data-processing services, or any similar activity that is ancillary to the principal activity of at least one credit institution (Directive 2000/12/EC (as amended to 09/03/06), Article 1(23)). 'Insurance holding company' means a parent undertaking whose main activity is to hold participations in subsidiary undertakings, in circumstances in which those subsidiary undertakings are solely or mainly: insurance and/or reinsurance companies that are authorised to provide (re)insurance services within the Community, or insurance and/or reinsurance firms from outside the Community as long as a least one of these is an insurance and/or reinsurance undertaking which is authorised to supply (re)insurance services within the Community and is not a mixed financial holding company (Directive 98/78/EC (as amended to 09/12/05), Articles 1(i) and 1(a)-(c)). 'Mixed financial holding company' means a parent undertaking (except for a regulated entity), which, together with its subsidiaries – one or more of which are regulated entities with their head offices within the Community – and other entities, make up a financial conglomerate (Directive 2002/87/EC (as amended to 24/03/05), Article 2(15)). 'Financial institution' under Council Directive 93/6/EEC has the same meaning as 'financial institution' under Directive 2000/12/EC (Directive 93/6/EEC (as amended to 24/03/05), Article 2(7); Council Directive 92/30/EEC on the supervision of credit institutions on a consolidated basis, Article 1; Second Council Directive 89/646/EEC on the coordination of laws, regulations and administrative provisions relating to the taking up and pursuit of the business of credit institutions and amending Directive 77/780/EEC, Annex). As Article 67 of Directive 2000/12/EC repealed Directives 92/30/EEC and 89/646/EEC, Article 2(7) of Directive 93/6/EEC should have been amended to refer to Article 1(5) of Directive 2000/12/EC rather than to Article 1 of Directive 92/30/EEC.

[236] Article 2(14)(c) of Directive 2002/87/EC refers to Article 12(1) of Directive 83/349/EEC, which, in turn, refers to Article 1 of the latter Directive. See fn 232, for the definition of 'subsidiary undertaking' that Article 1 of Directive 83/349/EEC provides.

[237] For the purposes of determining whether the group's activities take place within the financial sector, the ratio of the balance sheet total of the financial sector entities within the group to the balance sheet total of the whole group is to exceed 40% (Directive 2002/87/EC (as amended to 24/03/05), Articles 2(14)(c) and 3(1)).

[238] For the purposes of ascertaining whether activities are 'significant', for each of the insurance sector and the banking and investment services sector the average of the ratio of the balance sheet total of the group's companies within that sector to the balance sheet total of the group's financial sector entities, and the ratio of the

Competent authorities that have authorised regulated entities are to identify any group that is within the scope of Directive 2002/87/EC[239]; for this purpose, competent authorities that have authorised regulated entities within the group are to co-operate closely, as necessary[240] [486]. Without prejudice to the provisions on supervision that the sectoral rules contain, Member States are to provide for the supervision of regulated entities to the extent, and in the way, that Directive 2002/87/EC provides [487]. The following regulated entities are to be subject to supplementary supervision at the level of the financial conglomerate: (a) those that head a financial conglomerate, (b) those whose parent undertaking is a mixed financial holding company that has its head office within the European Community, and (c) those that are connected with another entity in the financial sector by one holding a majority of the members' or shareholders' rights in, having the right to appoint or remove a majority of the directors of and being a member of or a shareholder in, having the right to exercise a dominant influence over and being a member of or a shareholder in, appointing a majority of the members of the administrative, management or supervisory bodies of – solely as a consequence of the exercise of its voting rights – and being a member of or a shareholder in, controlling alone – pursuant to an agreement with other members of or shareholders in the other entity – a majority of members' or shareholders' voting rights in and being a member of or a shareholder in, having the power to exercise (or exerting) control or dominant influence over, and/or uniformly managing or being managed by, the other entity[241] [488]. If a regulated entity does not fulfil the requirements that the previous sentence contains, and if its parent undertaking is a regulated entity or a mixed financial holding company that has its head office outside the Community, then the former is to be subject to the specific supplementary supervision for which Article 18 of Directive 2002/87/EC provides[242] [489].

---

solvency requirements of the group's firms within that insurance or banking/investment services sector to the total solvency requirements of the group's financial sector entities, should both be greater than 10% (Directive 2002/87/EC (as amended to 24/03/05), Article 3(2)). Cross-sectoral activities are also to "be presumed to be significant," if the balance sheet total of the group's smallest financial sector exceeds 6 million Euros (Directive 2002/87/EC (as amended to 24/03/05), Article 3(3)). For the purposes of Directive 2002/87/EC, the smallest financial sector within a financial conglomerate is the sector with the lowest average, and the "most important financial sector" in the conglomerate is the sector with the highest average; for the purposes of computing the average, and for the measurement of the smallest and the most important financial sectors, the banking sector and the investment services sector are to be considered together (Directive 2002/87/EC (as amended to 24/03/05), Article 3(2)).

[239] This identification is to be done on the basis of Articles 2, 3 and 5 of Directive 2002/87/EC (Directive 2002/87/EC (as amended to 24/03/05), Article 4(1)).

[240] If a competent authority considers that a regulated entity which it has authorised, is a member of a group that may be a financial conglomerate which has not already been identified in accordance with Directive 2002/87/EC, then the competent authority is to notify the other competent authorities concerned (Directive 2002/87/EC (as amended to 24/03/05), Article 4(1).

[241] If a financial conglomerate is a subgroup of another financial conglomerate which satisfies these requirements, then Member States may only apply supplementary supervision to the regulated entities within the latter group; any reference that Directive 2002/87/EC makes to the terms 'financial conglomerate' and 'group' will refer to that latter group (Directive 2002/87/EC (as amended to 24/03/05), Article 5(2)).

[242] Competent authorities are to verify whether the regulated entities, the parent undertaking of which has its head office outside the European Community, are subject to supervision by a competent authority in a third country which is equivalent to that supplied by the provisions of Directive 2002/87/EC which concern the supplementary supervision of regulated entities (Directive 2002/87/EC (as amended to 24/03/05), Article 18(1)). If this equivalent supervision is absent, then Member States are to either apply the supplementary supervision for which Directive 2002/87/EC provides, or permit their competent authorities to apply other methods that ensure suitable supplementary supervision of the regulated entities in a financial conglomerate (Directive 2002/87/EC (as amended to 24/03/05), Article 18(2)-(3)).

In order to ensure appropriate supervision of the regulated entities in a financial conglomerate, a co-ordinator is to be appointed from amongst the competent authorities of the relevant Member States, and is to take responsibility for the co-ordination and exercise of supplementary supervision [490]. The co-ordinator's tasks are to include: (a) co-ordination of the collection and the dissemination of essential or pertinent information, including the spreading of data that is important for a competent authority's supervision according to sectoral rules, (b) supervisory overview and assessment of a financial conglomerate's financial circumstances, (c) evaluation of compliance with the rules on capital adequacy, risk concentration and intra-group transactions that Articles 6, 7 and 8, respectively, of Directive 2002/87/EC lay down, (d) assessment of the internal control systems, organisation and structure of the financial conglomerate, as set out in Article 9 of the Directive, (e) planning and co-ordination of supervisory activities in co-operation with the other relevant competent authorities, and (f) other decisions, measures and tasks that Directive 2002/87/EC assigns to the co-ordinator, or which derive from this Directive's application [491].

Member States are to require companies in a financial conglomerate to make sure that own funds "are available at the level of the financial conglomerate" which are always equal to or greater than the capital adequacy requirements that are computed in accordance with Annex I to Directive 2002/87/EC, and that regulated entities have "adequate" policies for capital adequacy at that group level[243] [492]. Annex I lays down 3 methods according to which the calculation of the supplementary capital requirements of the regulated entities in a financial conglomerate is to be performed [493]. The co-ordinator is to determine, after consulting the other relevant competent authorities and the particular financial conglomerate, which method the financial conglomerate should apply[244] [494]. The methods are the 'Accounting consolidation', 'Deduction and aggregation' and 'Book value/Requirement deduction' techniques, the first of which is based on the financial conglomerate's consolidated accounts and the others of which use the accounts of each of the group's constituent companies [495]. Member States are to require regulated entities or mixed financial holding companies to report regularly, and at least annually, to the co-ordinator "any significant risk concentration at the level of the financial conglomerate," and "all significant intra-group transactions of regulated entities within" that conglomerate, in accordance with the rules that Articles 7-8 and Annex II to Directive 2002/87/EC lay down [496]. Annex II requires the co-ordinator, having consulted the other relevant competent authorities, to

---

[243] The co-ordinator is to supervise these capital adequacy requirements, and, in particular, ensure that the following entities are included within the ambit of supplementary supervision in accordance with Annex I to Directive 2002/87/EC: credit institutions, financial institutions, ancillary banking service undertakings, insurance and reinsurance companies, insurance holding companies, investment firms and mixed financial holding companies (Directive 2002/87/EC (as amended to 24/03/05), Article 6(2)-(3)).

[244] Competent authorities may permit a combination of all, or of any 2, of the 3 methods (Directive 2002/87/EC (as amended to 24/03/05), Annex I, Title II, Method 4: Combination of methods 1, 2 and 3). A Member State may require the computation to be conducted according to one particular method, if a financial conglomerate is headed by a regulated entity that has been authorised in that country; in other instances, Member States are to authorise the application of any of the 3 methods, other than in situations in which the relevant competent authorities are situated in the same Member State – in which case that country may require one of the methods to be applied (Directive 2002/87/EC (as amended to 24/03/05), Annex I, Paragraph 3). It is submitted that this exception applies if the supervised entities are located in one Member State, but are not all supervised by the same entity – as, for example, in a situation in which a financial conglomerate wholly placed in the United Kingdom includes a bank – which the Prudential Regulation Authority and the Financial Conduct Authority both supervise, and an investment firm whose only service is the provision of investment advice – which the Financial Conduct Authority oversees.

identify the types of risks and transactions that companies in a particular financial conglomerate are to report, in accordance with Articles 7(2) and 8(2) of Directive 2002/87/EC; in doing this, the competent authorities are to take into consideration the financial conglomerate's group and risk management structure, and are to define suitable thresholds based on technical provisions in order to identify intra-group transactions and risk concentrations that are significant and are therefore to be reported in accordance with Articles 7 and 8 of the Directive [497]. To the extent that the co-ordinator has defined these thresholds, an intra-group transaction is to be presumed to be significant, if it amounts to 5% or more of the total requirements for capital adequacy "at the level of a financial conglomerate" – the regulated entity is to submit the required information to the co-ordinator; these transactions are to be overseen by the co-ordinator [498].

Member States are to require regulated entities to operate "adequate" internal control mechanisms and risk management processes "at the level of the financial conglomerate." [499]. The risk management processes are to include (a) "sound" management and governance, (b) "adequate capital adequacy policies," and (c) "adequate procedures" in order to make sure that systems for monitoring risk are integrated effectively into the organisation, and that all measures are taken to ensure consistency in respect of the systems introduced across the undertakings within the scope of supplementary supervision – so that risks are able to be monitored, measured and controlled at that level [500]. The internal control mechanisms are to include (a) "adequate" mechanisms in respect of capital adequacy, in order to identify and measure risks that are "material" and to "appropriately" apply own funds to risks, and (b) "sound" accounting and reporting procedures, in order to identify, monitor, measure and control the concentration of risks and the intra-group transactions [501]. Member States are to ensure that, in all firms that are within the bounds of supplementary supervision, there are "adequate" procedures for internal control in respect of the generation of information that is relevant to this supervision [502]. The co-ordinator is to superintend all of these internal control mechanisms and risk management processes [503].

The co-ordinator for the financial conglomerate and the other competent authorities which are responsible for the supervision of that group's regulated entities are to co-operate closely with each other, and are to supply each other with any information that is indispensable or pertinent to the exercise of their supervisory tasks under Directive 2002/87/EC and the sectoral rules [504]. This co-operation is to provide for at least the collection and exchange of information in respect of the following items: (a) identification of the group structure of all significant entities within the financial conglomerate, and of the competent authorities of the group's regulated entities, (b) the strategic policies of the financial conglomerate, (c) the conglomerate's financial circumstances – especially its capital adequacy, intra-group transactions, profitability and concentration of risks, (d) the conglomerate's shareholders and managers, (e) the internal control systems, organisation and risk management "at financial conglomerate level," (f) procedures for the collection and the verification of information from the companies in the financial conglomerate, (g) unfavourable developments in those firms that may "seriously affect" the group's regulated entities, and (h) exceptional measures and substantial sanctions that competent authorities have imposed in accordance with Directive 2002/87/EC or the sectoral rules [505]. Furthermore, the relevant competent authorities are to consult each other in respect of the following items before they take any decision, in instances in which this decision is important to the supervisory duties of other competent authorities: (a) changes in the organisational, management or ownership structure of a financial conglomerate that the competent authorities are required to approve, and (b) exceptional measures or significant sanctions that the competent authorities have taken[245] [506]. Information that is received within the system of supplementary supervision is to be subject to the obligations of professional secrecy and confidentiality that the sectoral rules lay down [507].

Member States are to require that the directors of a mixed financial holding company have "sufficient experience" and "are of sufficiently good repute" to undertake their duties [508]. These countries are to ensure that there are no legal obstacles within their jurisdiction that prevent persons within the scope of supplementary supervision from exchanging with each other any information which would be relevant for the purposes of this supervision [509]. They are to provide that their competent authorities have access to any information from a financial conglomerate's constituent entities that would be pertinent to supplementary supervision [510].

If the financial conglomerate's regulated entities breach the requirements of Articles 6 to 9 of Directive 2002/87/EC[246] or endanger its solvency, or if the concentration of risks or the intra-group transactions threaten the financial position of the regulated entities, then the co-ordinator (in respect of the mixed financial holding company) and the competent authorities (with regard to the regulated entities) are to take "the necessary measures" to righten the situation as soon as possible; these authorities (including the co-ordinator) are to harmonise their supervisory actions [511]. Following further convergence of sectoral rules, Member States are to empower their competent authorities to take any supervisory measure that is necessary in order to prevent or to contend with the evasion of sectoral rules by a financial conglomerate's regulated entities [512]. They are to ensure that sanctions which are directed towards stopping contraventions, or the causes of these transgressions, may be placed on mixed financial holding companies which, or their managers who, breach rules that are enacted pursuant to Directive 2002/87/EC[247] [513].

Distance Marketing of Consumer Financial Services

Directive 2002/65/EC concerning the distance marketing of consumer financial services is intended to contribute towards achieving "a high level of consumer protection," provide consumers with non-discriminatory access "to the widest possible range of financial services available in the Community," and enable them to be able to contract with suppliers that are founded in other Member States – all with the aim of furthering the internal market [514]. The objective of Directive 2002/65/EC is to approximate the rules of the Member States that consider the distance marketing of consumer financial services [515].

---

[245] A competent authority may decide not to consult, if this consultation may put at risk the effectiveness of the relevant decision(s) or if the decision is urgent; in this case, the competent authority is to swiftly notify all of the other competent authorities (Directive 2002/87/EC (as amended to 24/03/05), Article 12(2)).

[246] These are the Directive's provisions on capital adequacy, concentration of risks, intra-group transactions, internal control mechanisms and the risk management process. See above in this subsection, for Articles 6-9 of Directive 2002/87/EC.

[247] Competent authorities are to "co-operate closely," in order to make sure that these sanctions "produce the desired results" (Directive 2002/87/EC (as amended to 24/03/05), Article 17(2)).

A 'distance contract' is one that concerns financial services[248] whose offer, negotiation and agreement is conducted remotely, and which a supplier[249] and a consumer[250] conclude within the framework of "an organised distance sales or service-provision scheme" that the supplier runs – making sole use of at least one means of distance communication[251] up to the point at which the contract is concluded [516]. The supplier is to provide the consumer with the following information, "in good time before" the latter is bound by the distance contract or offer: (1) *data concerning the supplier*: the supplier's identity, main business and geographical address; the identity and geographical address of any representative of the supplier that is founded in the consumer's Member State of residence; the identity, capacity vis-à-vis the consumer, and geographical address of any professional (other than the supplier) with whom the consumer is dealing; the trade register (if any) in which the supplier is entered and his/her registration number; the particulars of the relevant supervisory authority in cases in which an authorisation scheme governs the supplier's activity; (2) *data concerning the financial service*: the main characteristics of the financial service; the total price that the consumer is to pay to the supplier for this service, or, if the supplier is unable to specify an exact price, the basis for the computation of the price that enables the consumer to verify the amount charged; as relevant, notice which indicates that the financial service is related to instruments that involve "special risks" which correspond to their particular features or the operations to be carried out, or whose price depends upon fluctuations in the financial markets that are beyond the supplier's control; notice of the possible existence of other costs and/or taxes that the supplier does not pay or impose; any limitations of the time for which the data are valid; the arrangements for performance and for payment; any specific additional cost to the consumer of utilizing the means of distance communication (3) *data concerning the distance contract*: the presence or absence of a right of withdrawal in accordance with Article 6 of Directive 2002/65/EC[252], and, if this exists, its duration and the conditions for exercising it – including the sum that the consumer may be required to pay in accordance with Article 7(1) of Directive 2002/65/EC[253], as well as the consequences for the consumer of

---

[248] 'Financial service' means a banking, credit insurance, investment, payment or personal pension service (Directive 2002/65/EC (as amended to 05/12/07), Article 2(b)).

[249] 'Supplier' means any person who, acting in his/her professional or commercial capacity, contractually provides services that are subject to distance contracts (Directive 2002/65/EC (as amended to 05/12/07), Article 2(c)).

[250] 'Consumer' means any natural person who, in distance contracts which Directive 2002/65/EC covers, is acting for purposes that are beyond the limits of his/her business, trade or profession (Directive 2002/65/EC (as amended to 05/12/07), Article 2(d)).

[251] 'Means of distance communication' refers to any means that, without the concurrent physical presence of the supplier and the consumer, may be used for the distance marketing of a service between them (Directive 2002/65/EC (as amended to 05/12/07), Article 2(e)).

[252] Member States are to ensure that the consumer is to be provided with a period of 14 calendar days, to be able to withdraw from the distance contract without giving any reason and without penalty; the period for withdrawal shall start from the later of the day on which the distance contract is concluded and the day on which the consumer receives the contractual terms and conditions and the prior information (Directive 2002/65/EC (as amended to 05/12/07), Article 6(1)). The right of withdrawal is not to apply to financial services whose price varies with fluctuations in the financial market that the supplier is unable to control, insurance policies of less than one month's duration, and contracts whose performance both parties have completed – at the consumer's express request – before the latter exercises his/her right to withdraw (Directive 2002/65/EC (as amended to 05/12/07), Article 6(2)).

[253] If the consumer exercises his/her rights of withdrawal under Article 6(1) of Directive 2002/65/EC, he/she may only be required to pay for the service that the supplier actually provides in accordance with the distance contract; the sum payable is not to exceed an amount that is proportionate to the extent of the service already supplied in comparison with the contract's full coverage, and may not be such that it could be construed as a penalty (Directive 2002/65/EC (as amended to 05/12/07), Article 7(1)).

ignoring that right; the minimum duration of the distance contract (if the services are to be performed indefinitely or recurrently); information on the parties' rights (if any) to terminate the contract early or unilaterally, including any penalties that the contract imposes under these circumstances; instructions for the exercise of the right of withdrawal, including the address to which the consumer's notification of withdrawal should be sent; the Member State(s) whose laws the supplier uses in order to establish relations with the consumer before the conclusion of the contract; any clause in the contract as to the law that applies to it and/or the competent court; the language(s) that the supplier and the contract are to use; (4) *data concerning redress*: whether the consumer has access to an out-of-court complaint and redress mechanism and, if so, the methods for pursuing this; the presence of compensation arrangements that Directives 94/19/EC[254] and 97/9/EC[255] do not cover [517]. If the supplier is to communicate the pre-contractual information to the consumer by telephone, then the former must make his/her identity and the commercial purpose of the telephone call "explicitly clear" to the consumer at the start of the conversation; subject to the consumer's express agreement, only the following information needs to be provided: the identity of the person who is speaking to the consumer and the former's connection to the supplier; a description of the financial service's main characteristics, the total price that the consumer is to pay to the supplier for the service, or, if an exact price cannot be stated, the basis for the computation of the price that enables the consumer to verify the sum charged; notice of the possible existence of other costs and/or taxes that the supplier does not pay or impose; the presence or absence of a right of withdrawal in accordance with Article 6 of Directive 2002/65/EC[256], and, if this exists, its duration and the conditions for exercising it – including the amount that the consumer may be required to pay in accordance with Article 7(1) of Directive 2002/65/EC[257] [518]. Until further harmonisation is forthcoming, Member States may maintain or introduce stricter provisions on prior information requirements than those listed above in this paragraph, if these rules comply with Community law [519]. The supplier is to communicate to the consumer all of the contractual terms and conditions and the prior information on a durable medium[258] that the consumer may access, "in good time before" the latter is bound by the distance contract or offer [520]. Whilst the contract is on-going, the consumer is entitled to request and receive all of these data on paper [521]. The supplier may only use automated calling systems and fax machines as means of distance communication with the consumer's prior consent[259] [522].

---

[254] This is Directive 94/19/EC of the European Parliament and of the Council of 30 May 1994 on deposit-guarantee schemes; see the next subsection, entitled 'Deposit guarantee and investor compensation schemes'.

[255] This is Directive 97/9/EC of the European Parliament and of the Council of 3 March 1997 on investor-compensation schemes; see the next subsection, entitled 'Deposit guarantee and investor compensation schemes'.

[256] See fn 252, for Article 6(1)-(2) of Directive 2002/65/EC.

[257] See fn 253, for Article 7(1) of Directive 2002/65/EC. The supplier is to inform the consumer that the remaining information is available on request, and of the nature of these data; he/she must provide the full information to the consumer on fulfilling his/her obligations under Article 5 of Directive 2002/65/EC (Directive 2002/65/EC (as amended to 05/12/07), Article 3(3)).

[258] 'Durable medium' means any instrument which enables the consumer to store information that is addressed to him/her in a way which is accessible for future reference, for a period of time that is sufficient "for the purposes of the information" and which permits the data stored to be reproduced without change (Directive 2002/65/EC (as amended to 05/12/07), Article 2(f)).

[259] For other means of distance communication, Member States are either to require the consent of the relevant consumer(s) to be obtained, or to allow the use of these means if the consumer has not explicitly objected (Directive 2002/65/EC (as amended to 05/12/07), Article 10(2)).

Member States are to "provide for appropriate sanctions" which are "effective, proportionate and dissuasive," if the supplier breaches national provisions that are adopted pursuant to Directive 2002/65/EC[260] [523]. Consumers may not waive the rights that Directive 2002/65/EC confers on them [524]. Member States are to take the measures which are necessary to ensure that the consumer retains the protection which Directive 2002/65/EC provides, if the law of a third country is selected as the law that governs the contract – in instances in which the agreement "has a close link"[261] with at least one Member State's territory [525].

Member States are to ensure that there are "adequate and effective means" to secure compliance with Directive 2002/65/EC, "in the interests of consumers" [526]. These means are to include national provisions whereby at least one or the following entities may take action before the courts or the "competent administrative bodies," in order to ensure that the rules which transpose Directive 2002/65/EC are applied: public institutions or person who represent them, consumer organisations and professional organisations [527]. Member States are to take the necessary measures to make sure that "operators and suppliers of means of distance communication"[262] terminate practices which a judicial, administrative or supervisory decision notified to them has declared to contravene Directive 2002/65/EC, under circumstances in which those operators or suppliers are able to do so [528]. Member States are to further the establishment or the development of "adequate and effective" procedures for alternative dispute resolution in respect of financial services that are supplied at a distance, and are to encourage the relevant tribunals to co-operate in the settlement of cross-border disputes which concern these services [529].

Deposit Guarantee and Investor Compensation Schemes

Although investor compensation schemes concern investment firms, and, therefore, fall within the ambit of the securities legislation[263], they are covered in the current subsection with deposit guarantee schemes as their regulatory Directives – at the time of the commencement of the GFC – took similar approaches. Both Directive 94/19/EC on deposit-guarantee schemes and Directive 97/9/EC on investor-compensation schemes provide for a harmonised minimum level of protection, but not for maximum harmonisation – i.e., the same level of deposit guarantee or investment compensation across the Community[264] [530]. Furthermore, both provide a minimum protection of 20,000 Euros[265] [531].

Deposit guarantee schemes are considered in this paragraph, and investor compensation schemes in the next. Each Member State is to ensure that, within its territory, at least one deposit guarantee scheme is introduced and recognised officially; all authorised credit

---

[260] In particular, Member States may provide as a sanction that the consumer may cancel the contract free of charge, at any time, without penalty (Directive 2002/65/EC (as amended to 05/12/07), Article 11).

[261] Directive 2002/65/EC does not define 'close link'. This phrase is unlikely to mean the same as 'close links', as defined in fns 27, 93 and 142 for the MiFID, the UCITS Directive and the BCD, respectively.

[262] 'Operator or supplier of a means of distance communication' means any person whose business, trade or profession involves making at least one means of distance communication available to suppliers (Directive 2002/65/EC (as amended to 05/12/07), Article 2(g)).

[263] See above in this chapter, for the section entitled 'Securities Legislation'.

[264] See fn 83 and accompanying text, for an explanation of 'maximum harmonisation'.

[265] Both Directives refer to 'ECU' rather than to Euros. 'ECU' is the abbreviation for the European Currency Unit, which was the predecessor of the Euro.

institutions must be members of this scheme, as a condition for taking deposits[266] [532]. If a credit institution[267] does not comply with its duties as a member of a deposit guarantee scheme, then the latter is to inform the competent authority that issued the former's authorisation, and, in co-operation with the guarantee scheme, this authority is to "take all appropriate measures" to ensure that the credit institution performs its obligations [533]. If those measures do not secure the credit institution's compliance, then the guarantee scheme may, with the competent authority's express consent, provide at least one year's notice of its intention to exclude the credit institution from membership of the scheme (if national law permits this); if, when the notice period expires, the credit institution has not undertaken its duties, then the guarantee scheme may (with the competent authority's express consent) "proceed to exclusion." [534]. If national law allows, and with the competent authority's express consent, a credit institution that is excluded from a deposit guarantee scheme may continue to take deposits if, prior to its exclusion, it made alternative guarantee arrangements which ensure that depositors will benefit from "a level and scope of protection at least equivalent to" the one that the officially recognised scheme offers [535]. If a credit institution whose exclusion from a deposit guarantee scheme has been proposed, is unable to make alternative arrangements that ensure these benefits, then the competent authority is to revoke the credit institution's authorisation [536]. Officially recognised deposit guarantee schemes are to cover depositors at branches that credit institutions establish in other Member States[268] [537]. If the level and/or the scope of the cover that the host Member State's deposit guarantee scheme offers exceeds the level and/or the scope of the cover that the credit institution's home Member State provides, then the former country is to ensure the presence of an officially recognised deposit guarantee scheme within its territory which a branch may choose to join, in order to supplement the guarantee that its depositors enjoy by virtue of its membership of the home Member State's guarantee scheme [538]. If a branch that is granted this voluntary membership breaches the obligations which it is required to fulfil as a member of the deposit guarantee scheme, then the latter is to inform the competent authority that granted the credit institutions' authorisation and, in co-operation with the guarantee scheme, that authority is to "take all appropriate measures" in order to make sure that the branch complies with these duties; if the measures taken do not secure the branch's compliance with those obligations, then "after an appropriate period of notice" of one year or more, the deposit guarantee scheme may (with that competent authority's consent) exclude the branch[269] [539].

---

[266] A 'deposit' is a credit balance that results from funds which are kept in an account, or from temporary situations that derive from normal banking transactions, and which a credit institution is to repay under the applicable legal and contractual conditions; it also includes debt as evidenced by a certificate that a credit institution issues (i.e., a certificate of deposit) (Directive 94/19/EC (as amended to 24/03/05), Article 1(1)). A Member State may exempt a credit institution from its obligation to be a member of a deposit guarantee scheme, if this firm belongs to a system that protects it and, in particular, ensures its solvency and its liquidity, thereby guaranteeing protection for depositors which is at least equivalent to that which a deposit guarantee scheme provides, and which satisfies 4 further conditions (Directive 94/19/EC (as amended to 24/03/05), Article 3(1)).

[267] 'Credit institution' means a firm the business of which is to receive repayable funds from the public and to provide credits for its own account (Directive 94/19/EC (as amended to 24/03/05), Article 1(4)).

[268] 'Branch' means a place of business that is a legally-dependent part of a credit institution and which directly performs at least some of the operations that are inherent in the business of these firms; any number of branches that a credit institution sets up in a Member State other than that in which it has its head office, are to be considered a single branch (Directive 94/19/EC (as amended to 24/03/05), Article 1(5)).

[269] Deposits that are made before the date of the branch's exclusion shall continue to be covered by the voluntary scheme until the dates on which they are due; the branch's depositors are to be informed of the withdrawal of the supplementary cover of their deposits (Directive 94/19/EC (as amended to 24/03/05), Article 4(4)). Article 4(4)

Deposits held when the authorisation of a credit institution is withdrawn are to continue to be covered that firm's (former) deposit guarantee scheme [540]. Member States are to check that branches founded by a credit institution whose head office is outside the European Community, have deposit guarantees in place that are "equivalent to" those which Directive 94/19/EC prescribes; if this is not the case, then Member States may, subject to Article 9(1) of Directive 77/780/EEC[270], require these branches to join deposit guarantee schemes that operate within their territories [541]. The credit institution is to supply depositors (and potential depositors) at those branches with "all relevant information" about the guarantee arrangements that cover their deposits[271] [542]. Deposit guarantee schemes are to state that each depositor's aggregate deposits are to be covered to at least 20,000 Euros[272], if his/her deposits are unavailable [543]. Member States may provide for any of the deposits that Annex II to Directive 94/19/EC lists[273], to be excluded from guarantee or to be given a lower level of guarantee [544]. Furthermore, Member States may retain or introduce provisions that offer a higher or more comprehensive cover for deposits, and may "on social considerations"[274] cover some types of deposits in full (regardless of their amount) [545]. These countries may restrict the deposit guarantee to a specified percentage of deposits, which must be at least 90% of aggregate deposits until the amount due under the guarantee reaches 20,000 Euros [546]. Member States are to ensure that each depositor is able to take action against the deposit guarantee scheme, in respect of his/her right to compensation[275] [547]. The amount of the deposit guarantee scheme's guarantee is to apply to the aggregate deposits placed with the same credit institution – irrespective of the currency, the number of deposits and their location within the European Community[276] [548]. Member States are to ensure that each credit institution publishes the information that is necessary for depositors (and potential depositors) to identify the deposit guarantee scheme of which the bank and its branches within the European Community are members, or any alternative arrangement made under

---

does not state who is to inform the branch's depositors as to the withdrawal of their supplementary cover; this is more likely to be the branch than the host Member State's deposit guarantee scheme from which the branch has been excluded.

[270] Article 9(1) of the First Council Directive 77/780/EEC of 12 December 1977 on the coordination of laws, regulations and administrative provisions relating to the taking up and pursuit of the business of credit institutions is as follows: "Member States shall not apply to branches of credit institutions having their head office outside the Community, when commencing or carrying on their business, provisions which result in more favourable treatment than that accorded to branches of credit institutions having their head office in the Community." Article 67(1) of Directive 2000/12/EC repealed Directive 77/780/EEC. Article 158(1) of the BCD repealed Directive 2000/12/EC. Article 24(1) of Directive 2000/12/EC and Article 38(1) of the BCD are identical to Article 9(1) of Directive 77/780/EEC.

[271] This information is to be made available in the official language(s) of the Member State in which the branch is founded, and is to be presented clearly and understandably (Directive 94/19/EC (as amended to 24/03/05), Article 6(3)).

[272] See fn 265.

[273] These deposits include, for instance, those by government, central administrative, provincial, regional, local and municipal authorities, insurance companies, collective investment undertakings and pension funds (Directive 94/19/EC (as amended by 24/03/05), Annex I, Points 2-6).

[274] Directive 94/19/EC does not provide guidance as to what these social considerations might be.

[275] Directive 94/19/EC does not specify the form of this action. The likely option is a facility to file a case before the relevant national civil court; an arbitration scheme is an alternative.

[276] This idea is perplexing, as it is an incentive to wealthy depositors to invest their funds in a number of banks within the European Community. Maybe this is an objective of the Commission, in order to keep funds within the region. An arguable alternative would be to introduce a maximum deposit guarantee per depositor, regardless of the bank(s) in which he/she invests within the Community.

Article 3(1)[277] or Article 3(4)[278] of Directive 94/19/EC; the firm is to notify depositors of the deposit guarantee scheme's provisions, including the amount and the scope of the guarantee that it offers, the conditions for compensation and the formalities to be undertaken in order to obtain this recompense [549]. Deposit guarantee schemes must be able to pay depositors' claims within 3 months of the date on which either (i) the competent authority has decided that the relevant credit institution is unable to repay their deposits within the foreseeable future, for reasons that directly concern the latter's financial situation, or (ii) a judicial authority has made a ruling for those reasons (before the event in (i)), "which has the effect of suspending depositors' ability to make claims against" the credit institution[279] [550].

Each Member State is to ensure that, within its territory, at least one investor compensation scheme is introduced and recognised officially; subject to 2 exceptions[280], an investment firm[281] that is authorised within that country must belong to an investor

---

[277] See fn 266, for alternative arrangements to which Article 3(1) of Directive 94/19/EC applies.

[278] See above in this paragraph, for the alternative deposit guarantee arrangements to which Article 3(4) of Directive 94/19/EC refers.

[279] "In wholly exceptional circumstances and in special cases," a deposit guarantee scheme may apply to the competent authority for an extension of this 3-month time limit for no more than 3 further months; at the guarantee scheme's request, the competent authority may grant up to 2 further extensions of no more than 3 months each (Directive 94/19/EC (as amended to 24/03/05), Article 10(2)).

[280] These exceptions are as follows. 1) A Member State may exempt a credit institution to which Directive 97/9/EC applies from its duty to belong to an investor compensation scheme, if that entity is already exempt under Article 3(1) of Directive 94/19/EC from its obligation to join a deposit guarantee scheme, as long as the protection and information provided to depositors are given to investors on the same terms, and investors therefore are given cover that is "at least equivalent to" the security that an investor compensation scheme affords (Directive 97/9/EC (original version), Article 2(1)); see fn 266, for the exemption that Article 3(1) of Directive 94/19/EC contains. 2) If the Member State's national law allows, and with the express consent of the competent authority that issued the investment firm's authorisation, this organisation may continue to supply investment services despite being excluded from an investor compensation scheme if, prior to its exclusion, it made alternative arrangements for the compensation of investors which ensure that they "enjoy cover that is at least equivalent to" the protection that the officially recognised scheme provides and possesses characteristics that are "equivalent to" the latter (Directive 97/9/EC (original version), Article 5(3)).

[281] 'Investment firm' means an investment firm as Article 1(2) of Directive 93/22/EEC states, or authorised as a credit institution in accordance with Council Directives 77/780/EEC and 89/646/EEC, the authorisation of which covers at least one of the investment services that Section A of the Annex to Directive 93/22/EEC lists (Directive 97/9/EC (original version), Article 1(1)). At the time of writing, Directive 97/9/EC is in force, without amendment. Nevertheless, by the start of the GFC – i.e., in 2007, the BCD was in force, and Article 158(1) of the BCD had repealed Directive 2000/12/EC – Article 67(1) of which had repealed Directives 77/780/EEC and 89/646/EEC (see fns 221 and 270). Furthermore, whilst the MiFID was in force at the start of the GFC, that Directive repealed Directive 93/22/EEC with effect from 1st November 2007 (MiFID (as amended and corrected to 22/02/14), Articles 69 and 72). Thus, the last consolidated version of Directive 93/22/EC can be used for the definition of 'investment firm' and for the list of investment services. However, the original version of the BCD should be used for the definition of 'credit institution' – see fn 134 – although the definition in Article 4(1) of the BCD differs from that in Article 1 of Directive 77/780/EEC (to which Article 1(1) of Directive 89/646/EEC refers) in that the latter does not include electronic money institutions within its definition of 'credit institution'. Nevertheless, the definition of 'credit institution' in part (a) of Article 4(1) of the original version of the BCD is identical to that in Article 1 of Directive 77/780/EEC, and is this: "an undertaking whose business is to receive deposits or other repayable funds from the public and to grant credit for its own account." An 'investment firm' is "any legal person the regular occupation of business of which is the provision of investment services for third parties on a professional basis" (Directive 93/22/EEC (as amended to 11/02/03), Article 1(2)). The 'investment services' are reception and transmission on investors' behalf of orders in relation to financial instruments, execution of these orders "other than for own account," management of portfolios of investments that include financial instruments, and underwriting in respect of issues of any of those instruments and/or the placement of these issues (Directive 93/22/EEC (as amended to 11/02/03), Annex, Section A). The 'financial instruments' comprise interest-rate, currency and equity swaps, transferable securities, money market instruments, futures contracts, forward interest-rate agreements, and options to acquire or to relinquish any of these listed items (Directive 93/22/EEC (as amended to 11/02/03), Annex, Section B).

compensation scheme in order to conduct investment business[282] there [551]. An investor compensation scheme is to provide cover for investors[283] if either (i) the competent authority has determined that an investment firm[284] currently appears, for reasons that are directly concerned with its financial circumstances, to be unable to satisfy its obligations that arise from investors' claims and has no imminent expectation of being able to do so, or, if earlier, (ii) a judicial authority has made a ruling, for those reasons, "which has the effect of suspending" the ability of investors to be able to make claims against the investment firm; the compensation scheme is to supply cover for claims that arise from an investment firm's inability to (i) repay money that is owed, or belongs, to investors and is held on their behalf in association with investment business, or (ii) return to investors any instruments[285] that investors own and which is held, managed or administered on their behalf in association with investment business[286] [552]. In respect of these claims, Member States are to ensure that investor compensation schemes provide for cover for each investor of at least 20,000 Euros[287] [553]. A Member State may exclude from cover, or reduce the level of protection for, the investors that Annex I to Directive 94/19/EC lists[288] [554]. It may limit cover to a specified percentage of the claim of an investor, as long as this guarantee equals or exceeds 90% of the claim in situations in which the amount due under the compensation scheme is less than 20,000 Euros [555]. Member States may retain or adopt provisions that give greater, or more comprehensive, cover to investors[289] [556]. If an investment firm which is required to belong to a compensation scheme does not satisfy its obligations as a member of that scheme, then the latter is to inform the competent authority which issued the former's authorisation; the competent authority, in co-operation with the compensation scheme, is to "take all measures appropriate to ensure that the investment firm meets is obligations." [557]. If these actions do not secure the investment firm's compliance, then the compensation scheme may, if national law allows a member to be excluded and with the competent authority's express consent, give at least one year's notice of its intention to shut out the investment firm from membership of the scheme – which is to provide cover in respect of investment business in that period; if, on expiry of the notice period, the investment firm has not fulfilled its duties, then the scheme

---

[282] 'Investment business' means any investment service as defined in Article 1(1) of Directive 93/22/EEC and the service to which point 1 of Section C of the Annex to Directive 93/22/EEC refers (Directive 97/9/EC (original version), Article 1(4)). 'Investment service' in Article 1(1) of Directive 93/22/EEC means any of the services that Section A of the Annex to that Directive lists, relating to any of the instruments that Section B of this Annex contains. See fn 281, for a list of these investment services and financial instruments. The service in point 1 of Section C of the Annex to Directive 93/22/EEC is safekeeping and administration in relation one or more of those financial instruments.

[283] 'Investor' means a person who has entrusted money or instruments to an investment firm in association with investment business (Directive 97/9/EC (original version), Article 1(4)).

[284] The English copy of Article 2(2) of Directive 97/9/EC reads "instrument firm," which is probably a mistake – it should read "investment firm." This is supported by the French version of Article 2(2) of Directive 97/9/EC, which reads "une entreprise d'investissement," i.e., an investment firm.

[285] 'Instruments' means the instruments that Section B of the Annex to Directive 93/22/EEC lists (Directive 93/22/EEC (as amended to 11/02/03), Article 1(3)). See fn 281, for a list of these financial instruments.

[286] Any claim under Article 2(2) of Directive 97/9/EC on a credit institution which, in a particular Member State, would be subject to both this Directive and Directive 94/19/EC, is to be directed by that country as it considers to be appropriate to a scheme under one or the other of those Directives; no claim is to be eligible for compensation more than once (Directive 97/9/EC (original version), Article 2(3)).

[287] See fn 265.

[288] The investors include, for instance, supranational institutions, and government, central administrative, provincial, regional, local and municipal authorities (Directive 97/9/EC (original version), Annex I, Points 2-3).

[289] Thus, as stated above in the first paragraph of this subsection, Directive 97/9/EC does not provide for maximum harmonisation in respect of cover for investor compensation.

may exclude the former from membership – having obtained the competent authority's express consent to exclude it [558]. As long as domestic law allows this, and with the competent authority's express consent, an investment firm excluded from a compensation scheme may continue to supply services, if, prior to its exclusion, it made alternative compensation arrangements which ensure that investors will receive cover which "is at least equivalent to" the protection that the officially recognised scheme offers and has features that are equivalent to those of the latter [559]. If an investment firm whose exclusion from a compensation scheme has been proposed, is unable to make alternative arrangements which reach these standards of equivalence, then the competent authority is to withdraw the firm's authorisation[290] [560]. A Member State's officially recognised investor compensation schemes are also to cover investors at branches that are established in that country by investment firms from other Member States; if the level and/or the scope of the cover offered by the host Member State's investor compensation scheme exceeds the level and/or the scope of the protection which the investment firm's home Member State provides, then the host Member State is to ensure that an officially recognised scheme is present in its territory which a branch may voluntarily join in order to supplement the cover that the home Member State's compensation scheme grants to the branch's investors[291] [561]. If a branch that has opted to join a scheme in the host Member State does not fulfil its obligations as a member of that arrangement, then the competent authority which issued its authorisation is to be informed and, in co-operation with the scheme, is "to take all measures necessary to ensure that the branch meets the aforementioned obligations"; if these actions do not ensure that the branch performs those duties, then, after a notice period of at least one year, the scheme may, with the competent authority's consent, exclude the branch[292] [562]. The cover is to apply to the investor's aggregate claim on an investment firm – regardless of the currency, the number of accounts and the place at which they are situated within the European Community; Member States may provide that funds, but not financial instruments, in the currencies of third countries are to be excluded from cover or subject to reduced protection [563]. The compensation scheme is to "take appropriate measures" in order to notify investors of the determination or the ruling to which Article 2(2) of Directive 97/9/EC refers[293], and (if required) to compensate them promptly; it may state a period during which investors are to submit their claims, which must be no more than 5 months from the date of the determination or the ruling or from the day on which this is published [564]. The scheme is to be able swiftly pay an investors claim – at the latest within 3 months from the moment at which its

---

[290] After an investment firm's authorisation has been revoked, the compensation scheme is to continue to supply cover in respect of investment business that is transacted up to the moment of withdrawal (Directive 97/9/EC (original version), Article 6).

[291] Member States are to ensure the application of "objective and generally applied conditions" in respect of branches' membership of every investor compensation scheme; admission is to depend upon a branch satisfying the relevant membership requirements, including especially the payment of all charges (Directive 97/9/EC (original version), Article 7(1)). Annex II to Directive 97/7/EC lays down guiding principles that Member States are to follow in their implementation of Article 7(1) of Directive 97/9/EC, which include (for instance) that the home Member State's investment scheme is to retain all rights to impose its objective and generally applied rules on investment firms which are members of the scheme (Directive 97/9/EC (original version), Article 7(1) and Annex II, Point (a)).

[292] The host Member State's compensation scheme is to continue to cover investment business that takes place before the date of the branch's exclusion from the scheme; investors are to be notified of the date upon which the withdrawal of the supplementary cover takes effect (Directive 97/9/EC (original version), Article 7(2)).

[293] See above in this paragraph, for Article 2(2) of Directive 97/9/EC.

eligibility and amount are established[294] [565]. Member States are to ensure that every investment firm "takes appropriate measures" to release to actual and potential investors the information that is necessary for them to identify the compensation scheme of which the firm and its branches within the European Community are members, or any alternative arrangement for which Article 2(1) or Article 5(3) of Directive 97/9/EC provides[295]; the firm is to notify investors of the compensation scheme's provisions, include the amount and the scope of the protection that the scheme offers, and any rules that the Member States lay down pursuant to Article 2(3) of Directive 97/9/EC[296] [566]. Member States are to introduce rules that restrict the use of this information in advertising, in order to prevent such usage from affecting investor confidence or financial stability [567]. Each Member State is to check whether branches that an investment firm whose head office is outside the European Community has founded, possess cover that is equivalent to that which Directive 97/9/EC prescribes; if this protection is not in place, then the Member State (subject to Article 5 of Directive 93/22/EC[297]) may require these branches to join investor compensation schemes that operate within its territory [568]. An investment firm whose head office is outside the European Community is to provide actual and potential investors at its branches with all information of relevance to the compensation arrangements that cover their investments [569]. Member States are to ensure that each investor is able to claim against the compensation scheme, in respect of the money that the latter owes to him/her[298] [570].

Settlement Finality

The purposes of Directive 98/26/EC on settlement finality in payment and securities settlement systems are (i) to reduce systemic and legal risks in association with the operation of securities settlement systems and payment systems, especially in circumstances in which there are close connections between these – as with real time gross settlement systems and payment systems that use multilateral netting, and (ii) to contribute to the efficient functioning of cross-border payment and securities settlement arrangements within the European Community, which reinforces the free movement of capital in the internal market [571]. In particular, the lowering of systemic risk requires settlement to be final and collateral

---

[294] "In wholly exceptional circumstances and in special cases," an investor compensation scheme may apply to the competent authority to extend the time limit for no more than 3 further months (Directive 97/9/EC (original version), Article 9(3)). Unlike deposit guarantee schemes (see fn 279), investor compensation schemes are not given the option to apply for additional extensions to the time limit.

[295] See fn 280, for alternative arrangements to an investor compensation scheme (under Articles 2(1) and 5(3) of Directive 97/9/EC).

[296] See fn 286, for Article 2(3) of Directive 97/9/EC. Information is to be provided, on request, as to the conditions that govern compensation, and the formalities to be completed in order to acquire this payment (Directive 97/9/EC (original version), Article 10(1)). The equivalent information in respect of compensation under deposit guarantee schemes is to be provided without the need for depositors to request it; see the previous paragraph in this subsection of the text.

[297] Member States are not to apply to branches of investment firms that are registered outside the European Community, provisions which result in treatment that is more favourable than that given to branches of investment firms with registered offices in Member States (Directive 93/22/EC (as amended to 11/02/03), Article 5).

[298] Directive 97/9/EC does not specify the form of this action – similarly to the right of claim that Directive 94/19/EC grants to depositors (see fn 275 and accompanying text).

security to be enforced [572]. Transfer orders and their netting are to be legally enforceable in all Member States, and are to be binding on third parties [573].

Directive 98/26/EC applies to (a) any system[299] that the law of a Member State governs, and which functions in any currency or currencies (which the system converts from one to another), (b) any participant[300] in this system, and (c) collateral security[301] that is supplied in association with participation in the system or with central banking operations in the Member States [574]. Transfer orders[302] and netting[303] are to be legally enforceable and binding upon

---

[299] 'System' means a formal arrangement between at least 3 participants with common rules and standardised arrangements for the execution of transfer orders between these participants, which is governed by the law of a Member State in which the head office of at least one of the participants is situated, and is designated as a system and notified to the Commission by the Member State whose law applies, once that country is satisfied that the system's rules are adequate (Directive 98/26/EC (original version), Article 2(a)). Furthermore, Member States may choose under Article 2(a) of Directive 98/26/EC to include two similar categories of arrangement as 'systems'.

[300] A 'participant' is an institution, a central counterparty, a settlement agent or a clearing house; the system's rules may allow the same participant to act as a central counterparty, a settlement agent or a clearing house, or to conduct all or part of these duties (Directive 98/26/EC (original version), Article 2(f)). 'Institution' means a credit institution as the first indent of Article 1 of Directive 77/780/EEC defines (see fn 281), an investment firm as Article 1(2) of Directive 93/22/EEC defines (see fn 281) – excluding the list of entities that Article 2(2)(a)-(k) of Directive 93/22/EEC sets out (insurance companies; reinsurance undertakings; firms that supply investment services to their own group only and/or exclusively administer employee participation schemes; persons who provide an investment service "in an incidental manner in the course of" a regulated professional activity; Member States' central banks and "other national bodies performing similar functions"; entities that manage the public debt; firms which do not hold clients' funds or securities and whose only investment service is the reception and transmission of orders in units of collective investment undertakings and in transferable securities to investment firms, credit institutions, branches of investment firms and credit institutions in third countries, "investment companies with fixed capital" the securities of which are listed or traded on a regulated market in a Member State and collective investment undertakings, the activities of which are governed domestically by rules or by a code of ethics; collective investment undertakings; "persons whose main business is trading in commodities" and who supply investment services solely "to the extent necessary" for this business; firms whose only investment services are dealing for their own account on financial futures or options markets, or which deal for the accounts of other members of these markets or set prices for them – and whose commitments to these persons are guaranteed by clearing members of these markets; associations which Danish pension funds set up with the sole objective of managing the assets of pension funds which are members of those associations (Directive 93/22/EEC (as amended to 11/02/03), Article 2(2)(a)-(k)), public authorities, entities that are "publicly guaranteed," or any credit institution or investment firm (as defined above in this sentence) whose head office is outside the European Community, which participates in a system (see fn 299) and which is responsible for carrying out the financial obligations that arise from transfer orders within this system (Directive 98/26/EC (original version), Article 2(b)). 'Central counterparty' means an entity that is interposed between the institutions in a system, and which acts as the sole counterparty of these institutions in respect of their transfer orders (Directive 98/26/EC (original version), Article 2(c)). 'Settlement agent' means an entity that provides institutions and/or a central counterparty with settlement accounts through which transfer orders within these systems are settled, and which extends credit (as necessary) to these institutions and/or central counterparties for the purposes of settlement (Directive 98/26/EC (original version), Article 2(d)). 'Clearing house' means an entity that is responsible for the computation of the net positions of institutions, a central counterparty and/or a settlement agent (Directive 98/26/EC (original version), Article 2(e)).

[301] 'Collateral security' means all assets that can be realized and which are supplied (i) under a pledge, a repurchase (or similar) agreement, or otherwise, for the purpose of securing obligations and rights that may arise in association with a system, or (ii) to Member States' central banks or the European Central Bank (Directive 98/26/EC (original version), Article 2(m)).

[302] 'Transfer order' means (i) a participant's instruction to place a sum of money at a recipient's disposal by way of a book entry on the accounts of a central bank, a credit institution or a settlement agent, (ii) an instruction that results in the assumption or the discharge of a payment obligation (as the system's rules define the latter), or (iii) a participant's instruction to transfer the title to, or an interest in, a security or securities (Directive 98/26/EC (original version), Article 2(i)).

[303] 'Netting' means the conversion into one net claim or net obligation, of claims and obligations that result from transfer orders which a participant or participants either issue to, or receive from, at least one other participant,

third parties, as long as the transfer orders were entered into a system before the moment at which any insolvency proceedings[304] were opened[305] [575]. No law, regulation, rule or practice on the setting aside of transactions and contracts concluded before this moment, shall lead to the unwinding of any netting [576]. Neither a participant in a system, nor a third party, may withdraw a transfer order, subsequent to the point in time defined in that system's rules [577].

Insolvency proceedings are not to have retroactive effects on a participant's rights and obligations that arise from, or connect to, its participation in a system, earlier than the moment of opening of these proceedings [578]. If insolvency proceedings are commenced against a participant in a system, then the rights and obligations which arise from, or connect to, its participation, are to be determined by the law that governs the system [579].

The rights of a participant to collateral security that is provided to it in association with a system, and of the Member States' central banks and the European Central Bank to collateral security that is supplied to them, are not to be affected by insolvency proceedings against the participant or the counterparty to these banks, which provided the collateral security; this collateral security may be realized in order to satisfy those rights [580]. If securities[306] are provided as collateral security to participants and/or Member States' central banks or the European Central Bank, and those entities' rights in respect of these securities is legally recorded on an account, a register or a centralised deposit system that is situated in a Member State, then the law of that country is to govern the determination of the rights of such entities as holders of collateral security in relation to the securities [581].

COMMENTS

As the contents of the 2 previous sections show, the European Community's securities and banking legislation immediately prior to the GFC is extensive and detailed. Nevertheless, the individual legal instruments are discrete, and do not tend to create a unified system for European financial regulation. There are common features across the legislation – for example, several instruments contain similar requirements in respect of the obligation of professional secrecy. However, the Directives tend to address their individual concerns – for instance, the MiFID to regulate at least some of the trades that take place in fora other than regulated markets, the TD to further the quality and consistency of information that is

---

with the result that only a net claim is demanded or a net obligation owed (Directive 98/26/EC (original version), Article 2(k)).

[304] 'Insolvency proceedings' means "any collective measure" for which the law of a Member State or of a third country provides, either to reorganise the participant or to wind it up, in cases in which this measure involves the suspension of, or the imposition of limitations on, payments or transfers (Directive 98/26/EC (original version), Article 2(j)).

[305] Transfer orders that are entered into a system after the moment at which insolvency proceedings are commenced, and which are executed on the day of the opening of these proceedings, are to be legally enforceable and binding upon third parties only if, subsequent to the time of settlement, the central counterparty, the clearing house or the settlement agent can prove that they were neither aware, nor should have been cognisant, of the commencement of these proceedings (Directive 98/26/EC (original version), Article 3(1)). For the purposes of Directive 98/26/EC, the moment of opening of insolvency proceedings is the point at which the relevant administrative or judicial authority hands down its decision (Directive 98/26/EC (original version), Article 6(1)).

[306] 'Securities' means all of the instruments to which Section B of the Annex to Directive 93/22/EEC refers (Directive 98/26/EC (original version), Article 2(h)). See fn 281, for a list of these (financial) instruments.

provided to investors in respect of listed securities, the BCD to improve the prudential supervision of banks in the light of the Basel II Framework, and Directive 98/26/EC to increase legal certainty and reduce risk in payment and settlement systems. Therefore, in 2006 or 2007, there is a developing European financial regulatory framework, but with a fair way to go before the sector is comprehensively and integrally supervised. This is the state of business which the GFC interrupted in 2007.

Next, a few features of the Directives should be noted. The MiFID does not regulate all trades; those in financial instruments that are neither conducted on a regulated market nor on an MTF, and are not of a type that are admitted to trading on a regulated market (which are brought within the regime for systematic internalisers) – such as OTC derivatives – are outside the scope of this Directive. Passporting requirements under the MiFID are excellent, with coverage for regulated markets and MTFs which is consistent with that for investment firms.

The TD's information disclosure requirements are detailed. The focus on half-yearly condensed statements and quarterly management reports is good in that it assists investors to observe on-going activity within the companies whose securities they hold.

The UCITS Directive neither includes close-ended investment funds nor all variants of open-ended investment funds. Thus, at the start of the GFC, there were investment funds that were not regulated at European Community level. Nevertheless, this is a difficult area over which to legislate effectively – and the Directive does this fairly well. In particular, the requirements for information under the UCITS Directive are extensive – these include full and simplified prospectuses, an annual report for each financial year, and a half-yearly report for the first 6 months of each financial year, for an investment company and for each of the unit trusts and common funds that a management company organises.

Whilst the BCD and the CRD (to a lesser extent) implement the requirements of the Basel II Framework, disclosure for banks under Title V (Principles and Technical Instruments for Prudential Supervision and Disclosure) Chapter 5 (Disclosure by credit institutions) and Annex XII Part 2 of the BCD, is more detailed than that laid down by Pillar III of the Basel II Framework. Furthermore, the professional secrecy obligations that the BCD introduces are extensive. The detailed nature of the Basel Agreements, and the widespread enactment of these by countries, leads to an important academic point: should a minimum harmonisation or a maximum harmonisation approach be taken to the enactment and implementation of the content of the Basel Agreements? Whilst minimum harmonisation ensures the presence of the contents of the Basel regulations within national laws, maximum harmonisation is better than minimum harmonisation in the sense that it ensures a greater degree of convergence over this area of law – but is insensitive to national differences, for instance, in bank structures, approaches to the funding of companies and political superintendence of banks.

The PSD is thorough and broad – it considers the authorisation of payment institutions, and the liability of the payer's payment service provider and the payer in the event of an unauthorised payment transaction, as well as payment procedures. Furthermore, it includes both debit card and (3 and 4 party) credit card transactions.

Directive 2000/46/EC is less comprehensive in respect of passporting requirements than other Directives, such as the MiFID and the BCD. As explained in the relevant subsection[307], this Directive advances only essential harmonisation for electronic money institutions,

---

[307] This is the subsection entitled 'Electronic money,' in the section 'Banking Legislation,' above in this chapter.

thereby furthering the internal market in financial services. The recent introduction of electronic money, in comparison with cash and bank deposits, may be a factor in explaining the cautious approach of Directive 2000/46/EC.

Directive 2002/87/EC includes detailed definitions, especially that in respect of 'financial conglomerate.' Furthermore, this Directive contains extensive provisions for supplementary supervision in respect of group-wide funds and risk management, intra-group transactions and internal processes across the conglomerate. It provides for the superintendence of groups beyond the strict requirements of sectoral supervision – including the attempted evasion of sectoral rules. Due to the ability of a conglomerate to move resources from one company to another within its structure, possibly in order to take advantage of perceived inconsistencies in regulation across the group – a practice called 'regulatory arbitrage,' consistent and sensitive supervision at the level of the conglomerate is essential to effective regulation.

Directives 94/19/EC and 97/9/EC provide for the same level of cover for deposit guarantee and investor compensation (20,000 Euros), are minimum harmonisation Directives, and have further similarities – such as the informational requirements that the former applies to banks and the latter to investment firms. The consistency between these 2 Directives demonstrates the presence of a level of supervisory integration which is greater than that shown by the pre-GFC financial legislation in general.

Directive 98/26/EC is an ordered, sensible legislative instrument. For instance, it raises legal certainty by providing for transfer orders and netting arrangements to be completed and enforceable before the commencement of insolvency proceedings.

CONCLUSION

Having established the legislative position of the European Community (now the EU) prior to the GFC, it is necessary to investigate how this legal structure has changed. The response to the crisis from within the EU is within the context of the global framework of codes, guidance and templates. Therefore the next chapter considers the international response to the crisis. In 2010, the EU introduced a new architecture for the supervision of financial institutions within its territories. Since the post-GFC legislation depends upon the functioning of this architecture, Chapter 3 describes how it works. In Chapter 4, aspects of the current legislation are considered – in the light of the law immediately before the crisis, as described in chapter 1. Finally, in Chapter 5, a few thoughts are shared – based upon the plans that the Commission has laid for the Eurozone for the next 9 years, and comments that it has made in relation to the Economic and Monetary Union.

REFERENCES

[1]   European Commission (1985). Completing the internal market, COM(85) 310 final, 14/ 06/85. http://europa.eu/documents/comm/white_papers/pdf/com1985_0310_f_en.pdf.
[2]   European Communities (1986). The Single European Act, Luxembourg, 17/02/86.

[3]   European Commission (1999). Financial S€rvices: Implementing the framework for financial markets: Action Plan, COM(1999)232, 11/05/99. http://ec.europa.eu/ internal_market/finances/docs/actionplan/index/action_en.pdf.

[4]   European Commission (1999). Financial S€rvices: Implementing the framework for financial markets: Action Plan, pp.13-14 and 30.

[5]   European Securities and Markets Authority (2015), Commission des opérations de bourse – Press Release: The Creation of the Forum of European Securities Commissions (FESCO), FD1047, 09/12/97. http://www.esma.europa.eu/ system/files/FD1047.pdf.

[6]   *European Commission (2001). Final Report of the Committee of Wise Men on the Regulation of European Securities Markets*, Brussels, 15/02/01. http://ec.europa.eu/ finance/securities/docs/lamfalussy/wisemen/final-report-wise-men_en.pdf.

[7]   *European Commission (2001). Final Report of the Committee of Wise Men on the Regulation of European Securities Markets*, p.19.

[8]   *European Commission (2001). Final Report of the Committee of Wise Men on the Regulation of European Securities Markets*, pp.28-29 and 36.

[9]   *European Commission (2001). Final Report of the Committee of Wise Men on the Regulation of European Securities Markets*, pp.6 and 37.

[10]   *European Commission (2001). Final Report of the Committee of Wise Men on the Regulation of European Securities Markets*, pp.6 and 40.

[11]   *Official Journal of the European Union* (2004). Directive 2004/39/EC of the European Parliament and of the Council of 21 April 2004 on markets in financial instruments amending Council Directives 85/611/EEC and 93/6/EEC and Directive 2000/12/EC of the European Parliament and of the Council and repealing Council Directive 93/22/EEC, L145/1-L145/44, as amended and corrected.

[12]   *Official Journal of the European Union* (2006). Commission Directive 2006/73/EC of 10 August 2006 implementing Directive 2004/39/EC of the European Parliament and of the Council as regards organisational requirements and operating conditions for investment firms and defined terms for the purposes of that Directive, L241/26-L241/58.

[13]   *Official Journal of the European Union* (2006). Commission Directive 2006/73/EC, Preamble.

[14]   European Commission (2008). Lamfalussy League Table – Transposition of Lamfalussy Directives: State of play as at 19/12/2008, p.1. http://ec.europa.eu/finance/ securities/docs/transposition/table_en.pdf.

[15]   *Official Journal of the European Union* (2003). Directive 2003/6/EC of the European Parliament and of the Council of 28 January 2003 on insider dealing and market manipulation (market abuse), L96/16-L96/25, as amended.

[16]   *Official Journal of the European Union* (2003). Directive 2003/71/EC of the European Parliament and of the Council of 4 November 2003 on the prospectus to be published when securities are offered to the public or admitted to trading and amending Directive 2001/34/EC, L345/64-L345/89, as amended.

[17]   *Official Journal of the European Union* (2004). Directive 2004/109/EC of the European Parliament and of the Council of 15 December 2004 on the harmonisation of transparency requirements in relation to information about issuers whose securities are

admitted to trading on a regulated market and amending Directive 2001/34/EC, L390/38-L390/57, as amended.

[18] *European Commission (2015).* Consultation Document: Review of the Prospectus Directive, Brussels, 18/02/15. http://ec.europa.eu/finance/consultations/2015/prospectus-directive/docs/consultation-document_en.pdf.

[19] *Official Journal of the European Union* (2004), Commission Regulation (EC) No 809/2004 of 29 April 2004 implementing Directive 2003/71/EC of the European Parliament and of the Council as regards information contained in prospectuses as well as the format, incorporation by reference and publication of such prospectuses and dissemination of advertisements, L149/1-L149/126, as amended.

[20] *Official Journal of the European Communities* (2001). Commission Decision 2001/528/EC of 6 June 2001 establishing the European Securities Committee, L191/45-L191/46, Article 1.

[21] *Official Journal of the European Communities* (2001). Commission Decision 2001/527/EC of 6 June 2001 establishing the Committee of European Securities Regulators, L191/43-L191/44, Article 1.

[22] *Official Journal of the European Union* (2004). Commission Decision 2004/5/EC of 5 November 2003 establishing the Committee of European Banking Supervisors, L3/28-L3/29, Article 2.

[23] *Official Journal of the European Union* (2004). Commission Decision 2004/6/EC of 5 November 2003 establishing the Committee on European Insurance and Occupational Pensions Supervisors, L3/30-L3/31, Article 2.

[24] *Official Journal of the European Union* (2004). Commission Decision 2004/5/EC, Article 1.

[25] *Official Journal of the European Union* (2004). Commission Decision 2004/6/EC, Article 1.

[26] *Official Journal of the European Union* (2004). Commission Decision of 5 November 2003 amending Decision 2001/527/EC establishing the Committee of European Securities Regulators, L3/32, Article 1(1).

[27] *Official Journal of the European Communities* (1987). Council Decision 87/373/EEC of 13 July 1987 laying down the procedures for the exercise of implementing powers conferred on the Commission, L97/33-L97/35, Article 1.

[28] *Official Journal of the European Communities* (1999). Council Decision 1999/468/EC of 28 June 1999 laying down the procedures for the exercise of implementing powers conferred on the Commission, L184/23-L184/26, Article 1.

[29] *Official Journal of the European Communities* (1999). Council Decision 1999/468/EC, Article 3.

[30] *Official Journal of the European Communities* (1999). Council Decision 1999/468/EC, Article 4.

[31] *Official Journal of the European Communities* (1999). Council Decision 1999/468/EC, Article 5.

[32] *Official Journal of the European Communities* (1999). Council Decision 1999/468/EC, Article 6.

[33] *Official Journal of the European Union* (2006). Council Decision 2006/512/EC of 17 July 2006 amending Decision 1999/468/EC laying down the procedures for the exercise

of implementing powers conferred upon the Commission, L200/11-L200/13, Article 1(7).

[34] *Official Journal of the European Union* (2011). Regulation (EU) No 182/2011 of the European Parliament and of the Council of 16 February 2011 laying down the rules and general principles concerning mechanisms for control by Member States of the Commission's exercise of implementing powers, L55/13-L55/18, Recitals 5-8 and Articles 3-5 and 16.

[35] *Official Journal of the European Communities* (1987). Council Decision 87/373/EEC, Article 2.

[36] *Official Journal of the European Communities* (1999). Council Decision 1999/468/EEC, Articles 3-5.

[37] *Official Journal of the European Union* (2006). Council Decision 2006/512/EC, Article 1(7).

[38] *Official Journal of the European Union* (2011). Regulation (EU) No 182/2011, Article 3(2).

[39] *Official Journal of the European Communities* (1987), Council Decision 87/373/EEC, Preamble.

[40] *European Commission (2001)*. Press release: Financial services: Commission proposes Directive on insider dealing and market manipulation, IP/01/758, Brussels, 30/05/01, pp.1-2. http://europa.eu/rapid/press-release_IP-01-758_en.htm?locale=en.

[41] *European Commission (2001)*. The Market Abuse Directive – Frequently Asked Questions, MEMO/01/203, Brussels, 30/05/01, p.1. http://europa.eu/rapid/press-release_MEMO-01-203_en.htm?locale=en.

[42] *Official Journal of the European Union* (2003). Directive 2003/6/EC of the European Parliament and of the Council of 28 January 2003 on insider dealing and market manipulation (market abuse), L96/16-L96/25, original version, Recitals 1 and 2.

[43] *Official Journal of the European Union* (2003). Directive 2003/6/EC (original version), Article 2(1).

[44] *Official Journal of the European Union* (2003). Directive 2003/6/EC (original version), Article 1(1).

[45] *Official Journal of the European Union* (2003). Directive 2003/6/EC (original version), Article 1(1).

[46] *Official Journal of the European Union* (2003). Directive 2003/6/EC (original version), Article 1(3).

[47] *Official Journal of the European Union* (2003). Directive 2003/6/EC (original version), Article 5.

[48] *Official Journal of the European Union* (2003). Directive 2003/6/EC (original version), Article 1(2)(a).

[49] *Official Journal of the European Union* (2003). Directive 2003/6/EC (original version), Article 1(2)(b).

[50] *Official Journal of the European Union* (2003). Directive 2003/6/EC (original version), Article 1(2)(c).

[51] *Official Journal of the European Union* (2003). Directive 2003/6/EC (original version), Articles 8 and 17(2).

[52] *Official Journal of the European Communities* (1999). Council Decision 1999/468/EC, Article 5.

[53] *Official Journal of the European Union* (2003), Directive 2003/6/EC (original version), Article 14(1).

[54] *European Commission (2001).* Press release: Financial services: Commission proposes Directive on insider dealing and market manipulation, p.2.

[55] *European Commission (2001).* Proposed Directive on Prospectuses – Frequently Asked Questions, MEMO/01/204, Brussels, 30/05/01, p.1. http://europa.eu/rapid/press-release_MEMO-01-204_en.htm?locale=en.

[56] *European Commission (2001).* The Proposed Prospectus Directive: Frequently asked questions, MARKT F2/HGD/NDB D(2001), Brussels, 28/09/01, p.2. http://ec.europa.eu/internal_market/securities/docs/prospectus/2001-09-faq_en.pdf.

[57] Official Journal of the European Union (2003). Directive 2003/71/EC of the European Parliament and of the Council of 4 November 2003 on the prospectus to be published when securities are offered to the public or admitted to trading and amending Directive 2001/34/EC, L345/64-L345/89, original version, Article 3(1).

[58] *Official Journal of the European Union* (2003). Directive 2003/71/EC (original version), Article 3(2).

[59] *Official Journal of the European Union* (2003). Directive 2003/71/EC (original version), Article 3(3).

[60] *Official Journal of the European Union* (2003). Directive 2003/71/EC (original version), Article 5(1).

[61] *Official Journal of the European Union* (2003). Directive 2003/71/EC (original version), Article 8(2).

[62] *Official Journal of the European Union* (2003). Directive 2003/71/EC (original version), Article 5(2).

[63] *Official Journal of the European Union* (2003). Directive 2003/71/EC (original version), Article 6(2).

[64] *Official Journal of the European Union* (2003). Directive 2003/71/EC (original version), Article 8(1)(a).

[65] *Official Journal of the European Union* (2003). Directive 2003/71/EC (original version), Article 8(1)(b).

[66] *Official Journal of the European Union* (2003). Directive 2003/71/EC (original version), Article 9(1).

[67] *Official Journal of the European Union* (2003). Directive 2003/71/EC (original version), Article 16(1).

[68] *Official Journal of the European Union* (2003). Directive 2003/71/EC (original version), Articles 10(1) and 10(3).

[69] *Official Journal of the European Union* (2003). Directive 2003/71/EC (original version), Article 13(1).

[70] *Official Journal of the European Union* (2003). Directive 2003/71/EC (original version), Article 25(1).

[71] European Commission (2002). Press release: Investment services: proposed new Directive would protect investors and help investment firms operate EU-wide, IP/02/1706, Brussels, 19/11/02, p.1. http://europa.eu/rapid/press-release_IP-02-1706_en.htm?locale=en.

[72] European Commission (2002). Proposal for Directive on investment services and regulated markets – frequently asked questions, MEMO/02/257, Brussels, 19/11/02, p.1. http://europa.eu/rapid/press-release_MEMO-02-257_en.htm?locale=en.

[73] European Commission (2004), Press release: Investment Services: final adoption of Directive is boost for investment firms and their clients, IP/04/546, Brussels, 27/04/04, p.1. http://europa.eu/rapid/press-release_IP-04-546_en.htm?locale=en.

[74] *Official Journal of the European Union* (2004). Directive 2004/39/EC of the European Parliament and of the Council of 21 April 2004 on markets in financial instruments amending Council Directives 85/611/EEC and 93/6/EEC and Directive 2000/12/EC of the European Parliament and of the Council and repealing Council Directive 93/22/EEC, L145/1-L145/44, as amended to 21/09/07, Article 5(1)-(2).

[75] *Official Journal of the European Union* (2004). Directive 2004/39/EC (as amended to 21/09/07), Article 6(1).

[76] *Official Journal of the European Union* (2004). Directive 2004/39/EC (as amended to 21/09/07), Article 6(3).

[77] *Official Journal of the European Union* (2004). Directive 2004/39/EC (as amended to 21/09/07), Article 5(4).

[78] *Official Journal of the European Union* (2004). Directive 2004/39/EC (as amended to 21/09/07), Article 7(2).

[79] *Official Journal of the European Union* (2004). Directive 2004/39/EC (as amended to 21/09/07), Article 9(3).

[80] *Official Journal of the European Union* (2004). Directive 2004/39/EC (as amended to 21/09/07), Article 10(1).

[81] *Official Journal of the European Union* (2004). Directive 2004/39/EC (as amended to 21/09/07), Article 10(2).

[82] *Official Journal of the European Union* (2004). Directive 2004/39/EC (as amended to 21/09/07), Article 11.

[83] *Official Journal of the European Union* (2004). Directive 2004/39/EC (as amended to 21/09/07), Article 12.

[84] *Official Journal of the European Union* (2004). Directive 2004/39/EC (as amended to 21/09/07), Articles 13(1) and 13(5).

[85] *Official Journal of the European Union* (2004). Directive 2004/39/EC (as amended to 21/09/07), Article 14(2).

[86] *Official Journal of the European Union* (2004). Directive 2004/39/EC (as amended to 21/09/07), Article 16(1).

[87] *Official Journal of the European Union* (2004). Directive 2004/39/EC (as amended to 21/09/07), Article 16(2).

[88] *Official Journal of the European Union* (2004). Directive 2004/39/EC (as amended to 21/09/07), Article 17(1).

[89] *Official Journal of the European Union* (2004). Directive 2004/39/EC (as amended to 21/09/07), Article 18(1).

[90] *Official Journal of the European Union* (2004). Directive 2004/39/EC (as amended to 21/09/07), Article 18(2).

[91] *Official Journal of the European Union* (2004). Directive 2004/39/EC (as amended to 21/09/07), Article 19(1).

[92]   *Official Journal of the European Union* (2004). Directive 2004/39/EC (as amended to 21/09/07), Article 19(8).

[93]   *Official Journal of the European Union* (2004). Directive 2004/39/EC (as amended to 21/09/07), Article 21(1).

[94]   *Official Journal of the European Union* (2004). Directive 2004/39/EC (as amended to 21/09/07), Article 21(2).

[95]   *Official Journal of the European Union* (2004). Directive 2004/39/EC (as amended to 21/09/07), Article 22(1).

[96]   *Official Journal of the European Union* (2004). Directive 2004/39/EC (as amended to 21/09/07), Article 24(1).

[97]   *Official Journal of the European Union* (2004). Directive 2004/39/EC (as amended to 21/09/07), Article 24(2).

[98]   *Official Journal of the European Union* (2004). Directive 2004/39/EC (as amended to 21/09/07), Article 25(1).

[99]   *Official Journal of the European Union* (2004). Directive 2004/39/EC (as amended to 21/09/07), Article 25(2).

[100] *Official Journal of the European Union* (2004). Directive 2004/39/EC (as amended to 21/09/07), Article 25(3).

[101] *Official Journal of the European Union* (2004). Directive 2004/39/EC (as amended to 21/09/07), Article 25(4).

[102] *Official Journal of the European Union* (2004). Directive 2004/39/EC (as amended to 21/09/07), Article 26(1).

[103] *Official Journal of the European Union* (2004). Directive 2004/39/EC (as amended to 21/09/07), Article 26(1)-(2).

[104] *Official Journal of the European Union* (2004). Directive 2004/39/EC (as amended to 21/09/07), Article 26(2).

[105] *Official Journal of the European Union* (2004). Directive 2004/39/EC (as amended to 21/09/07), Article 27(1).

[106] *Official Journal of the European Union* (2004). Directive 2004/39/EC (as amended to 21/09/07), Article 27(5).

[107] *Official Journal of the European Union* (2004). Directive 2004/39/EC (as amended to 21/09/07), Article 28(1).

[108] *Official Journal of the European Union* (2004). Directive 2004/39/EC (as amended to 21/09/07), Article 29(1).

[109] *Official Journal of the European Union* (2004). Directive 2004/39/EC (as amended to 21/09/07), Article 30(1).

[110] *Official Journal of the European Union* (2004). Directive 2004/39/EC (as amended to 21/09/07), Article 31(1).

[111] *Official Journal of the European Union* (2004). Directive 2004/39/EC (as amended to 21/09/07), Article 31(2).

[112] *Official Journal of the European Union* (2004). Directive 2004/39/EC (as amended to 21/09/07), Article 31(3).

[113] *Official Journal of the European Union* (2004). Directive 2004/39/EC (as amended to 21/09/07), Article 31(5).

[114] *Official Journal of the European Union* (2004). Directive 2004/39/EC (as amended to 21/09/07), Article 31(6).

[115] *Official Journal of the European Union* (2004). Directive 2004/39/EC (as amended to 21/09/07), Article 32(1).

[116] *Official Journal of the European Union* (2004). Directive 2004/39/EC (as amended to 21/09/07), Article 32(7).

[117] *Official Journal of the European Union* (2004). Directive 2004/39/EC (as amended to 21/09/07), Article 32(2).

[118] *Official Journal of the European Union* (2004). Directive 2004/39/EC (as amended to 21/09/07), Article 32(3).

[119] *Official Journal of the European Union* (2004). Directive 2004/39/EC (as amended to 21/09/07), Article 32(4).

[120] *Official Journal of the European Union* (2004). Directive 2004/39/EC (as amended to 21/09/07), Article 32(5).

[121] *Official Journal of the European Union* (2004). Directive 2004/39/EC (as amended to 21/09/07), Article 32(6).

[122] *Official Journal of the European Union* (2004). Directive 2004/39/EC (as amended to 21/09/07), Article 33(1).

[123] *Official Journal of the European Union* (2004). Directive 2004/39/EC (as amended to 21/09/07), Article 33(2).

[124] *Official Journal of the European Union* (2004). Directive 2004/39/EC (as amended to 21/09/07), Article 34(1).

[125] *Official Journal of the European Union* (2004). Directive 2004/39/EC (as amended to 21/09/07), Article 35(1).

[126] *Official Journal of the European Union* (2004). Directive 2004/39/EC (as amended to 21/09/07), Article 36(1).

[127] *Official Journal of the European Union* (2004). Directive 2004/39/EC (as amended to 21/09/07), Article 36(2).

[128] *Official Journal of the European Union* (2004). Directive 2004/39/EC (as amended to 21/09/07), Article 37(1).

[129] *Official Journal of the European Union* (2004). Directive 2004/39/EC (as amended to 21/09/07), Article 38(1).

[130] *Official Journal of the European Union* (2004). Directive 2004/39/EC (as amended to 21/09/07), Article 38(2).

[131] *Official Journal of the European Union* (2004). Directive 2004/39/EC (as amended to 21/09/07), Article 39.

[132] *Official Journal of the European Union* (2004). Directive 2004/39/EC (as amended to 21/09/07), Article 40(1)-(2).

[133] *Official Journal of the European Union* (2004). Directive 2004/39/EC (as amended to 21/09/07), Article 42(1).

[134] *Official Journal of the European Union* (2004). Directive 2004/39/EC (as amended to 21/09/07), Article 43(1).

[135] *Official Journal of the European Union* (2004). Directive 2004/39/EC (as amended to 21/09/07), Article 43(1)-(2).

[136] *Official Journal of the European Union* (2004). Directive 2004/39/EC (as amended to 21/09/07), Article 43(2).

[137] *Official Journal of the European Union* (2004). Directive 2004/39/EC (as amended to 21/09/07), Article 44(1).

[138] *Official Journal of the European Union* (2004). Directive 2004/39/EC (as amended to 21/09/07), Article 45(1).

[139] *Official Journal of the European Union* (2004). Directive 2004/39/EC (as amended to 21/09/07), Article 42(6).

[140] *Official Journal of the European Union* (2004). Directive 2004/39/EC (as amended to 21/09/07), Article 42(7).

[141] *Official Journal of the European Union* (2004). Directive 2004/39/EC (as amended to 21/09/07), Article 46(1).

[142] *Official Journal of the European Union* (2004). Directive 2004/39/EC (as amended to 21/09/07), Article 50(1).

[143] *Official Journal of the European Union* (2004). Directive 2004/39/EC (as amended to 21/09/07), Article 50(2).

[144] *Official Journal of the European Union* (2004). Directive 2004/39/EC (as amended to 21/09/07), Article 51(1).

[145] *Official Journal of the European Union* (2004). Directive 2004/39/EC (as amended to 21/09/07), Article 52(1).

[146] *Official Journal of the European Union* (2004). Directive 2004/39/EC (as amended to 21/09/07), Article 54(1).

[147] *Official Journal of the European Union* (2004). Directive 2004/39/EC (as amended to 21/09/07), Article 54(3).

[148] *Official Journal of the European Union* (2004). Directive 2004/39/EC (as amended to 21/09/07), Article 56(1).

[149] *Official Journal of the European Union* (2004). Directive 2004/39/EC (as amended to 21/09/07), Article 57(1).

[150] *Official Journal of the European Union* (2004). Directive 2004/39/EC (as amended to 21/09/07), Article 60(1)-(2).

[151] *Official Journal of the European Union* (2004). Directive 2004/39/EC (as amended to 21/09/07), Article 60(3).

[152] *Official Journal of the European Union* (2004). Directive 2004/39/EC (as amended to 21/09/07), Article 62(4).

[153] *Official Journal of the European Union* (2004). Directive 2004/39/EC (as amended to 21/09/07), Article 62(1).

[154] *Official Journal of the European Union* (2004). Directive 2004/39/EC (as amended to 21/09/07), Article 62(2).

[155] *Official Journal of the European Union* (2004). Directive 2004/39/EC (as amended to 21/09/07), Article 62(3).

[156] *Official Journal of the European Union* (2004). Directive 2004/39/EC (as amended to 21/09/07), Article 63(1).

[157] *Official Journal of the European Union* (2004). Directive 2004/39/EC (as amended to 21/09/07), Article 63(2).

[158] *Official Journal of the European Union* (2004). Directive 2004/39/EC (as amended to 21/09/07), Article 70.

[159] *Official Journal of the European Communities* (2001). Directive 2001/34/EC of the European Parliament and of the Council of 28 May 2001 on the admission of securities to official stock exchange listing and on information to be published on those securities, L184/1-L184/66, as amended to 24/03/05, Recital 1.

[160] *Official Journal of the European Communities* (2001). Directive 2001/34/EC (as amended to 24/03/05), Article 111(1).

[161] *Official Journal of the European Communities* (2001). Directive 2001/34/EC (as amended to 24/03/05), Article 5.

[162] *Official Journal of the European Communities* (2001). Directive 2001/34/EC (as amended to 24/03/05), Article 6.

[163] *Official Journal of the European Communities* (2001). Directive 2001/34/EC (as amended to 24/03/05), Article 8(1).

[164] *Official Journal of the European Communities* (2001). Directive 2001/34/EC (as amended to 24/03/05), Article 8(2).

[165] *Official Journal of the European Communities* (2001). Directive 2001/34/EC (as amended to 24/03/05), Articles 8(3) and 9.

[166] *Official Journal of the European Communities* (2001). Directive 2001/34/EC (as amended to 24/03/05), Article 12.

[167] *Official Journal of the European Communities* (2001). Directive 2001/34/EC (as amended to 24/03/05), Article 11(2).

[168] *Official Journal of the European Communities* (2001). Directive 2001/34/EC (as amended to 24/03/05), Article 14.

[169] *Official Journal of the European Communities* (2001). Directive 2001/34/EC (as amended to 24/03/05), Article 16(1).

[170] *Official Journal of the European Communities* (2001). Directive 2001/34/EC (as amended to 24/03/05), Article 18(1).

[171] *Official Journal of the European Communities* (2001). Directive 2001/34/EC (as amended to 24/03/05), Article 18(2).

[172] *Official Journal of the European Communities* (2001). Directive 2001/34/EC (as amended to 24/03/05), Article 19(1).

[173] *Official Journal of the European Communities* (2001). Directive 2001/34/EC (as amended to 24/03/05), Article 42.

[174] *Official Journal of the European Communities* (2001). Directive 2001/34/EC (as amended to 24/03/05), Article 43(1).

[175] *Official Journal of the European Communities* (2001). Directive 2001/34/EC (as amended to 24/03/05), Article 43(2).

[176] *Official Journal of the European Communities* (2001). Directive 2001/34/EC (as amended to 24/03/05), Article 43(4).

[177] *Official Journal of the European Communities* (2001). Directive 2001/34/EC (as amended to 24/03/05), Article 44.

[178] *Official Journal of the European Communities* (2001). Directive 2001/34/EC (as amended to 24/03/05), Article 45.

[179] *Official Journal of the European Communities* (2001). Directive 2001/34/EC (as amended to 24/03/05), Article 46(1).

[180] *Official Journal of the European Communities* (2001). Directive 2001/34/EC (as amended to 24/03/05), Article 47.

[181] *Official Journal of the European Communities* (2001). Directive 2001/34/EC (as amended to 24/03/05), Article 48(1).

[182] *Official Journal of the European Communities* (2001). Directive 2001/34/EC (as amended to 24/03/05), Article 48(4).

[183] *Official Journal of the European Communities* (2001). Directive 2001/34/EC (as amended to 24/03/05), Article 48(5).

[184] *Official Journal of the European Communities* (2001). Directive 2001/34/EC (as amended to 24/03/05), Article 49(1).

[185] *Official Journal of the European Communities* (2001). Directive 2001/34/EC (as amended to 24/03/05), Article 64.

[186] *Official Journal of the European Communities* (2001). Directive 2001/34/EC (as amended to 24/03/05), Article 53.

[187] *Official Journal of the European Communities* (2001). Directive 2001/34/EC (as amended to 24/03/05), Article 54(2).

[188] *Official Journal of the European Communities* (2001). Directive 2001/34/EC (as amended to 24/03/05), Article 55(1).

[189] *Official Journal of the European Communities* (2001). Directive 2001/34/EC (as amended to 24/03/05), Article 58(1).

[190] *Official Journal of the European Communities* (2001). Directive 2001/34/EC (as amended to 24/03/05), Article 58(2).

[191] *Official Journal of the European Communities* (2001). Directive 2001/34/EC (as amended to 24/03/05), Article 59(1).

[192] *Official Journal of the European Communities* (2001). Directive 2001/34/EC (as amended to 24/03/05), Article 59(2).

[193] *Official Journal of the European Communities* (2001). Directive 2001/34/EC (as amended to 24/03/05), Article 60.

[194] *Official Journal of the European Communities* (2001). Directive 2001/34/EC (as amended to 24/03/05), Article 61.

[195] *Official Journal of the European Communities* (2001). Directive 2001/34/EC (as amended to 24/03/05), Article 62.

[196] *Official Journal of the European Communities* (2001). Directive 2001/34/EC (as amended to 24/03/05), Article 106.

[197] *Official Journal of the European Communities* (2001). Directive 2001/34/EC (as amended to 24/03/05), Article 107(1).

[198] *Official Journal of the European Communities* (2001). Directive 2001/34/EC (as amended to 24/03/05), Article 107(2).

[199] European Commission (2003). Press release: Securities markets: Commission proposes Directive to increase investor protection and transparency, IP/03/436, Brussels, 26/03/03, p.1. http://europa.eu/rapid/press-release_IP-03-436_en.htm?locale=en.

[200] European Commission (2004). Press release: Financial services: final adoption of Transparency Directive will help investors and boost trust in markets, IP/04/1508, Brussels, 17/12/04, p.1. http://europa.eu/rapid/press-release_IP-04-1508_en.htm?locale=en.

[201] *Official Journal of the European Union* (2004). Directive 2004/109/EC of the European Parliament and of the Council of 15 December 2004 on the harmonisation of transparency requirements in relation to information about issuers whose securities are admitted to trading on a regulated market and amending Directive 2001/34/EC, L390/38-L390/57, original version, Article 1(1).

[202] *Official Journal of the European Union* (2004). Directive 2004/109/EC (original version), Article 1(2).

[203] *Official Journal of the European Union* (2004). Directive 2004/109/EC (original version), Article 3.

[204] *Official Journal of the European Union* (2004). Directive 2004/109/EC (original version), Recitals 7-8.

[205] *Official Journal of the European Union* (2004). Directive 2004/109/EC (original version), Article 4(1).

[206] *Official Journal of the European Union* (2004). Directive 2004/109/EC (original version), Article 4(2).

[207] *Official Journal of the European Union* (2004). Directive 2004/109/EC (original version), Article 4(4).

[208] *Official Journal of the European Union* (2004). Directive 2004/109/EC (original version), Article 5(1).

[209] *Official Journal of the European Union* (2004). Directive 2004/109/EC (original version), Articles 5(2) and 5(4).

[210] *Official Journal of the European Union* (2004). Directive 2004/109/EC (original version), Article 5(3).

[211] *Official Journal of the European Union* (2007). Commission Directive 2007/14/EC of 8 March 2007 laying down detailed rules for the implementation of certain provisions of Directive 2004/109/EC on the harmonisation of transparency requirements in relation to information about issuers whose securities are admitted to trading on a regulated market, L69/27-L69/36, original version, Article 3(2).

[212] *Official Journal of the European Union* (2007). Commission Directive 2007/14/EC (original version), Article 3(3).

[213] *Official Journal of the European Union* (2004). Directive 2004/109/EC (original version), Article 5(5).

[214] *Official Journal of the European Union* (2004). Directive 2004/109/EC (original version), Article 6(1).

[215] *Official Journal of the European Union* (2004). Directive 2004/109/EC (original version), Article 6(2).

[216] *Official Journal of the European Union* (2004). Directive 2004/109/EC (original version), Article 7.

[217] *Official Journal of the European Union* (2004). Directive 2004/109/EC (original version), Article 8(1).

[218] *Official Journal of the European Union* (2004). Directive 2004/109/EC (original version), Article 9(1).

[219] *Official Journal of the European Union* (2004). Directive 2004/109/EC (original version), Article 9(5).

[220] *Official Journal of the European Union* (2004). Directive 2004/109/EC (original version), Article 12(1).

[221] *Official Journal of the European Union* (2004). Directive 2004/109/EC (original version), Article 12(2)(a).

[222] *Official Journal of the European Union* (2007). Commission Directive 2007/14/EC (original version), Article 9.

[223] *Official Journal of the European Union* (2004). Directive 2004/109/EC (original version), Article 13(1).

[224] *Official Journal of the European Union* (2007). Commission Directive 2007/14/EC (original version), Article 11(1).

[225] *Official Journal of the European Union* (2004). Directive 2004/109/EC (original version), Article 16(1).

[226] *Official Journal of the European Union* (2004). Directive 2004/109/EC (original version), Article 16(2).

[227] *Official Journal of the European Union* (2004). Directive 2004/109/EC (original version), Article 16(3).

[228] *Official Journal of the European Union* (2004). Directive 2004/109/EC (original version), Article 17(1).

[229] *Official Journal of the European Union* (2004). Directive 2004/109/EC (original version), Article 17(2).

[230] *Official Journal of the European Union* (2004). Directive 2004/109/EC (original version), Article 18(1).

[231] *Official Journal of the European Union* (2004). Directive 2004/109/EC (original version), Article 18(2).

[232] *Official Journal of the European Union* (2004). Directive 2004/109/EC (original version), Article 23(1).

[233] *Official Journal of the European Union* (2007). Commission Directive 2007/14/EC (original version), Article 16.

[234] *Official Journal of the European Union* (2004). Directive 2004/109/EC (original version), Article 23(2).

[235] *Official Journal of the European Union* (2004). Directive 2004/109/EC (original version), Article 24(4).

[236] *Official Journal of the European Union* (2004). Directive 2004/109/EC (original version), Article 25(1).

[237] *Official Journal of the European Union* (2004). Directive 2004/109/EC (original version), Article 25(3).

[238] *Official Journal of the European Union* (2004). Directive 2004/109/EC (original version), Article 25(2).

[239] *Official Journal of the European Union* (2004). Directive 2004/109/EC (original version), Article 25(4).

[240] *Official Journal of the European Communities* (1985). Council Directive 85/611/EEC of 20 December 1985 on the coordination of laws, regulations and administrative provisions relating to undertakings for collective investment in transferable securities (UCITS), L375/3-L375/17, original version, Recital 2.

[241] *Official Journal of the European Communities* (1985). Council Directive 85/611/EEC (original version), Recital 3.

[242] *Official Journal of the European Communities* (1985). Council Directive 85/611/EEC of 20 December 1985 on the coordination of laws, regulations and administrative provisions relating to undertakings for collective investment in transferable securities (UCITS), L375/3-L375/17, as amended to 19/03/08, Article 1(2).

[243] *Official Journal of the European Communities* (1985). Council Directive 85/611/EEC (as amended to 19/03/08), Article 1(5).

[244] *Official Journal of the European Communities* (1985). Council Directive 85/611/EEC (as amended to 19/03/08), Article 2(1).

[245] *Official Journal of the European Communities* (1985). Council Directive 85/611/EEC (as amended to 19/03/08), Article 1(7).

[246] *Official Journal of the European Communities* (1985). Council Directive 85/611/EEC (as amended to 19/03/08), Article 4(1).

[247] *Official Journal of the European Communities* (1985). Council Directive 85/611/EEC (as amended to 19/03/08), Article 4(2).

[248] *Official Journal of the European Communities* (1985). Council Directive 85/611/EEC (as amended to 19/03/08), Article 4(3).

[249] *Official Journal of the European Communities* (1985). Council Directive 85/611/EEC (as amended to 19/03/08), Article 4(3).

[250] *Official Journal of the European Communities* (1985). Council Directive 85/611/EEC (as amended to 19/03/08), Article 4(3a).

[251] *Official Journal of the European Communities* (1985). Council Directive 85/611/EEC (as amended to 19/03/08), Article 5(1).

[252] *Official Journal of the European Communities* (1985). Council Directive 85/611/EEC (as amended to 19/03/08), Article 5(2) and Annex II.

[253] *Official Journal of the European Communities* (1985). Council Directive 85/611/EEC (as amended to 19/03/08), Article 5(3).

[254] *Official Journal of the European Communities* (1985). Council Directive 85/611/EEC (as amended to 19/03/08), Article 5a(1).

[255] *Official Journal of the European Communities* (1985). Council Directive 85/611/EEC (as amended to 19/03/08), Article 5a(2).

[256] *Official Journal of the European Communities* (1985). Council Directive 85/611/EEC (as amended to 19/03/08), Article 5b(1).

[257] *Official Journal of the European Communities* (1985). Council Directive 85/611/EEC (as amended to 19/03/08), Article 5b(3).

[258] *Official Journal of the European Communities* (1985). Council Directive 85/611/EEC (as amended to 19/03/08), Article 5d(1).

[259] *Official Journal of the European Communities* (1985). Council Directive 85/611/EEC (as amended to 19/03/08), Article 5d(2).

[260] *Official Journal of the European Communities* (1985). Council Directive 85/611/EEC (as amended to 19/03/08), Article 5f(1).

[261] *Official Journal of the European Communities* (1985). Council Directive 85/611/EEC (as amended to 19/03/08), Article 5h.

[262] *Official Journal of the European Communities* (1985). Council Directive 85/611/EEC (as amended to 19/03/08), Article 6(1).

[263] *Official Journal of the European Communities* (1985). Council Directive 85/611/EEC (as amended to 19/03/08), Article 6(2).

[264] *Official Journal of the European Communities* (1985). Council Directive 85/611/EEC (as amended to 19/03/08), Article 6a(1).

[265] *Official Journal of the European Communities* (1985). Council Directive 85/611/EEC (as amended to 19/03/08), Article 6a(2).

[266] *Official Journal of the European Communities* (1985). Council Directive 85/611/EEC (as amended to 19/03/08), Article 6a(3).

[267] *Official Journal of the European Communities* (1985). Council Directive 85/611/EEC (as amended to 19/03/08), Article 6a(4).

[268] *Official Journal of the European Communities* (1985). Council Directive 85/611/EEC (as amended to 19/03/08), Article 6a(5).

[269] *Official Journal of the European Communities* (1985). Council Directive 85/611/EEC (as amended to 19/03/08), Article 6b(1).

[270] *Official Journal of the European Communities* (1985). Council Directive 85/611/EEC (as amended to 19/03/08), Article 6b(2).

[271] *Official Journal of the European Communities* (1985). Council Directive 85/611/EEC (as amended to 19/03/08), Article 6b(3).

[272] *Official Journal of the European Communities* (1985). Council Directive 85/611/EEC (as amended to 19/03/08), Article 6c(2).

[273] *Official Journal of the European Communities* (1985). Council Directive 85/611/EEC (as amended to 19/03/08), Article 6c(3).

[274] *Official Journal of the European Communities* (1985). Council Directive 85/611/EEC (as amended to 19/03/08), Article 6c(4).

[275] *Official Journal of the European Communities* (1985). Council Directive 85/611/EEC (as amended to 19/03/08), Article 6c(5).

[276] *Official Journal of the European Communities* (1985). Council Directive 85/611/EEC (as amended to 19/03/08), Article 6c(8).

[277] *Official Journal of the European Communities* (1985). Council Directive 85/611/EEC (as amended to 19/03/08), Article 6c(6).

[278] *Official Journal of the European Communities* (1985). Council Directive 85/611/EEC (as amended to 19/03/08), Article 6c(7).

[279] *Official Journal of the European Communities* (1985). Council Directive 85/611/EEC (as amended to 19/03/08), Article 12.

[280] *Official Journal of the European Communities* (1985). Council Directive 85/611/EEC (as amended to 19/03/08), Articles 13 and 1(2).

[281] *Official Journal of the European Communities* (1985). Council Directive 85/611/EEC (as amended to 19/03/08), Article 13a(1).

[282] *Official Journal of the European Communities* (1985). Council Directive 85/611/EEC (as amended to 19/03/08), Articles 13b and 5h.

[283] *Official Journal of the European Communities* (1985). Council Directive 85/611/EEC (as amended to 19/03/08), Article 13b.

[284] *Official Journal of the European Communities* (1985). Council Directive 85/611/EEC (as amended to 19/03/08), Article 13c.

[285] *Official Journal of the European Communities* (1985). Council Directive 85/611/EEC (as amended to 19/03/08), Articles 7(1) and 14(1).

[286] *Official Journal of the European Communities* (1985). Council Directive 85/611/EEC (as amended to 19/03/08), Articles 7(3) and 14(3).

[287] *Official Journal of the European Communities* (1985). Council Directive 85/611/EEC (as amended to 19/03/08), Article 14(4).

[288] *Official Journal of the European Communities* (1985). Council Directive 85/611/EEC (as amended to 19/03/08), Articles 8(1) and 15(1).

[289] *Official Journal of the European Communities* (1985). Council Directive 85/611/EEC (as amended to 19/03/08), Articles 8(2) and 15(2).

[290] *Official Journal of the European Communities* (1985). Council Directive 85/611/EEC (as amended to 19/03/08), Articles 9 and 16.

[291] *Official Journal of the European Communities* (1985). Council Directive 85/611/EEC (as amended to 19/03/08), Articles 10(1) and 17(1).

[292] *Official Journal of the European Communities* (1985). Council Directive 85/611/EEC (as amended to 19/03/08), Articles 10(2) and 17(2).

[293] *Official Journal of the European Communities* (1985). Council Directive 85/611/EEC (as amended to 19/03/08), Article 19(1).

[294] *Official Journal of the European Communities* (1985). Council Directive 85/611/EEC (as amended to 19/03/08), Article 19(2)(a).

[295] *Official Journal of the European Communities* (1985). Council Directive 85/611/EEC (as amended to 19/03/08), Article 19(2)(c).

[296] *Official Journal of the European Communities* (1985). Council Directive 85/611/EEC (as amended to 19/03/08), Article 19(2)(d).

[297] *Official Journal of the European Communities* (1985). Council Directive 85/611/EEC (as amended to 19/03/08), Article 19(4).

[298] *Official Journal of the European Communities* (1985). Council Directive 85/611/EEC (as amended to 19/03/08), Article 21(1).

[299] *Official Journal of the European Communities* (1985). Council Directive 85/611/EEC (as amended to 19/03/08), Article 21(3).

[300] *Official Journal of the European Communities* (1985). Council Directive 85/611/EEC (as amended to 19/03/08), Article 41(1).

[301] *Official Journal of the European Communities* (1985). Council Directive 85/611/EEC (as amended to 19/03/08), Article 22(1).

[302] *Official Journal of the European Communities* (1985). Council Directive 85/611/EEC (as amended to 19/03/08), Article 22(1).

[303] *Official Journal of the European Communities* (1985). Council Directive 85/611/EEC (as amended to 19/03/08), Article 22(2).

[304] *Official Journal of the European Communities* (1985). Council Directive 85/611/EEC (as amended to 19/03/08), Article 22(5).

[305] *Official Journal of the European Communities* (1985). Council Directive 85/611/EEC (as amended to 19/03/08), Article 23(1)

[306] *Official Journal of the European Communities* (1985). Council Directive 85/611/EEC (as amended to 19/03/08), Article 22a(1).

[307] *Official Journal of the European Communities* (1985). Council Directive 85/611/EEC (as amended to 19/03/08), Article 22a(2).

[308] *Official Journal of the European Communities* (1985). Council Directive 85/611/EEC (as amended to 19/03/08), Article 24(1).

[309] *Official Journal of the European Communities* (1985). Council Directive 85/611/EEC (as amended to 19/03/08), Article 24(2).

[310] *Official Journal of the European Communities* (1985). Council Directive 85/611/EEC (as amended to 19/03/08), Article 24a(1).

[311] *Official Journal of the European Communities* (1985). Council Directive 85/611/EEC (as amended to 19/03/08), Article 25(1).

[312] *Official Journal of the European Communities* (1985). Council Directive 85/611/EEC (as amended to 19/03/08), Article 25(2).

[313] *Official Journal of the European Communities* (1985). Council Directive 85/611/EEC (as amended to 19/03/08), Article 27(1).

[314] *Official Journal of the European Communities* (1985). Council Directive 85/611/EEC (as amended to 19/03/08), Article 28(1).

[315] *Official Journal of the European Communities* (1985). Council Directive 85/611/EEC (as amended to 19/03/08), Articles 28(2) and 29(1).

[316] *Official Journal of the European Communities* (1985). Council Directive 85/611/EEC (as amended to 19/03/08), Article 30.

[317] *Official Journal of the European Communities* (1985). Council Directive 85/611/EEC (as amended to 19/03/08), Article 47.

[318] *Official Journal of the European Communities* (1985). Council Directive 85/611/EEC (as amended to 19/03/08), Article 32.

[319] *Official Journal of the European Communities* (1985). Council Directive 85/611/EEC (as amended to 19/03/08), Article 31.

[320] *Official Journal of the European Communities* (1985). Council Directive 85/611/EEC (as amended to 19/03/08), Article 33(1).

[321] *Official Journal of the European Communities* (1985). Council Directive 85/611/EEC (as amended to 19/03/08), Article 33(2).

[322] *Official Journal of the European Communities* (1985). Council Directive 85/611/EEC (as amended to 19/03/08), Article 33(3).

[323] *Official Journal of the European Communities* (1985). Council Directive 85/611/EEC (as amended to 19/03/08), Article 36(1).

[324] *Official Journal of the European Communities* (1985). Council Directive 85/611/EEC (as amended to 19/03/08), Article 36(2)(a).

[325] *Official Journal of the European Communities* (1985). Council Directive 85/611/EEC (as amended to 19/03/08), Article 36(2)(b).

[326] *Official Journal of the European Communities* (1985). Council Directive 85/611/EEC (as amended to 19/03/08), Article 37(1).

[327] *Official Journal of the European Communities* (1985). Council Directive 85/611/EEC (as amended to 19/03/08), Article 37(2)(a).

[328] *Official Journal of the European Communities* (1985). Council Directive 85/611/EEC (as amended to 19/03/08), Article 37(2)(b).

[329] *Official Journal of the European Communities* (1985). Council Directive 85/611/EEC (as amended to 19/03/08), Article 38.

[330] *Official Journal of the European Communities* (1985). Council Directive 85/611/EEC (as amended to 19/03/08), Article 39.

[331] *Official Journal of the European Communities* (1985). Council Directive 85/611/EEC (as amended to 19/03/08), Article 40.

[332] *Official Journal of the European Communities* (1985). Council Directive 85/611/EEC (as amended to 19/03/08), Article 43.

[333] *Official Journal of the European Communities* (1985). Council Directive 85/611/EEC (as amended to 19/03/08), Article 49(3).

[334] *Official Journal of the European Communities* (1985). Council Directive 85/611/EEC (as amended to 19/03/08), Article 49(4).

[335] *Official Journal of the European Communities* (1985). Council Directive 85/611/EEC (as amended to 19/03/08), Article 50(1).

[336] *Official Journal of the European Communities* (1985). Council Directive 85/611/EEC (as amended to 19/03/08), Article 50(2).

[337] *Official Journal of the European Communities* (1985). Council Directive 85/611/EEC (as amended to 19/03/08), Article 50(3).

[338] *Official Journal of the European Communities* (1985). Council Directive 85/611/EEC (as amended to 19/03/08), Article 50(5).

[339] *Official Journal of the European Communities* (1985). Council Directive 85/611/EEC (as amended to 19/03/08), Article 50(6).

[340] *Official Journal of the European Communities* (1985). Council Directive 85/611/EEC (as amended to 19/03/08), Article 50(4).

[341] *Official Journal of the European Communities* (1985). Council Directive 85/611/EEC (as amended to 19/03/08), Article 50(8).

[342] *Official Journal of the European Communities* (1985). Council Directive 85/611/EEC (as amended to 19/03/08), Article 52a(1).

[343] *Official Journal of the European Communities* (1985). Council Directive 85/611/EEC (as amended to 19/03/08), Article 51(1).

[344] *Official Journal of the European Communities* (1985). Council Directive 85/611/EEC (as amended to 19/03/08), Article 51(2).

[345] *Official Journal of the European Union* (2006). Directive 2006/48/EC of the European Parliament and of the Council of 14 June 2006 relating to the taking up and pursuit of the business of credit institutions (recast), L177/1-L177/200, original version, Article 6.

[346] *Official Journal of the European Union* (2006). Directive 2006/48/EC (original version), Article 7.

[347] *Official Journal of the European Union* (2006). Directive 2006/48/EC (original version), Article 8.

[348] *Official Journal of the European Union* (2006). Directive 2006/48/EC (original version), Article 9(1).

[349] *Official Journal of the European Union* (2006). Directive 2006/48/EC (original version), Articles 9(2) and 14.

[350] *Official Journal of the European Union* (2006). Directive 2006/48/EC (original version), Article 10(1).

[351] *Official Journal of the European Union* (2006). Directive 2006/48/EC (original version), Article 11(1).

[352] *Official Journal of the European Union* (2006). Directive 2006/48/EC (original version), Article 11(2).

[353] *Official Journal of the European Union* (2006). Directive 2006/48/EC (original version), Article 12(1).

[354] *Official Journal of the European Union* (2006). Directive 2006/48/EC (original version), Article 12(2).

[355] *Official Journal of the European Union* (2006). Directive 2006/48/EC (original version), Article 12(3).

[356] *Official Journal of the European Union* (2006). Directive 2006/48/EC (original version), Article 13.

[357] *Official Journal of the European Union* (2006). Directive 2006/48/EC (original version), Articles 18(2) and 14.

[358] *Official Journal of the European Union* (2006). Directive 2006/48/EC (original version), Article 15(1)-(2).

[359] *Official Journal of the European Union* (2006). Directive 2006/48/EC (original version), Article 15(3).

[360] *Official Journal of the European Union* (2006). Directive 2006/48/EC (original version), Article 22(1).

[361] *Official Journal of the European Union* (2006). Directive 2006/48/EC (original version), Article 22(2).

[362] *Official Journal of the European Union* (2006). Directive 2006/48/EC (original version), Articles 23 and 24(1).

[363] *Official Journal of the European Union* (2006). Directive 2006/48/EC (original version), Article 24(1).

[364] *Official Journal of the European Union* (2006). Directive 2006/48/EC (original version), Articles 24(1), 25(1) and 28(1).

[365] *Official Journal of the European Union* (2006). Directive 2006/48/EC (original version), Article 25(1).

[366] *Official Journal of the European Union* (2006). Directive 2006/48/EC (original version), Article 25(2).

[367] *Official Journal of the European Union* (2006). Directive 2006/48/EC (original version), Article 25(3).

[368] *Official Journal of the European Union* (2006). Directive 2006/48/EC (original version), Article 25(4).

[369] *Official Journal of the European Union* (2006). Directive 2006/48/EC (original version), Article 16.

[370] *Official Journal of the European Union* (2006). Directive 2006/48/EC (original version), Article 26(1).

[371] *Official Journal of the European Union* (2006). Directive 2006/48/EC (original version), Article 26(2).

[372] *Official Journal of the European Union* (2006). Directive 2006/48/EC (original version), Article 29.

[373] *Official Journal of the European Union* (2006). Directive 2006/48/EC (original version), Article 30(1).

[374] *Official Journal of the European Union* (2006). Directive 2006/48/EC (original version), Article 30(2).

[375] *Official Journal of the European Union* (2006). Directive 2006/48/EC (original version), Article 30(3).

[376] *Official Journal of the European Union* (2006). Directive 2006/48/EC (original version), Article 31.

[377] *Official Journal of the European Union* (2006). Directive 2006/48/EC (original version), Article 32.

[378] *Official Journal of the European Union* (2006). Directive 2006/48/EC (original version), Article 33.

[379] *Official Journal of the European Union* (2006). Directive 2006/48/EC (original version), Article 34.

[380] *Official Journal of the European Union* (2006). Directive 2006/48/EC (original version), Article 35.

[381] *Official Journal of the European Union* (2006). Directive 2006/48/EC (original version), Article 28(1).

[382] *Official Journal of the European Union* (2006). Directive 2006/48/EC (original version), Article 28(2).

[383] *Official Journal of the European Union* (2006). Directive 2006/48/EC (original version), Article 40(1).

[384] *Official Journal of the European Union* (2006). Directive 2006/48/EC (original version), Article 41(1).

[385] *Official Journal of the European Union* (2006). Directive 2006/48/EC (original version), Article 44(1).

[386] *Official Journal of the European Union* (2006). Directive 2006/48/EC (original version), Article 45.

[387] *Official Journal of the European Union* (2006). Directive 2006/48/EC (original version), Article 46.

[388] *Official Journal of the European Union* (2006). Directive 2006/48/EC (original version), Article 47.

[389] *Official Journal of the European Union* (2006). Directive 2006/48/EC (original version), Article 48.

[390] *Official Journal of the European Union* (2006). Directive 2006/48/EC (original version), Article 49.

[391] *Official Journal of the European Union* (2006). Directive 2006/48/EC (original version), Article 50.

[392] *Official Journal of the European Union* (2006). Directive 2006/48/EC (original version), Article 52.

[393] *Official Journal of the European Union* (2006). Directive 2006/48/EC (original version), Article 68(1).

[394] *Official Journal of the European Union* (2006). Directive 2006/48/EC (original version), Article 68(2).

[395] *Official Journal of the European Union* (2006). Directive 2006/48/EC (original version), Article 75.

[396] *Official Journal of the European Union* (2006). Directive 2006/48/EC (original version), Articles 76 and 84(1).

[397] *Official Journal of the European Union* (2006). Directive 2006/49/EC of the European Parliament and of the Council of 14 June 2006 on the capital adequacy of investment firms and credit institutions (recast), L177/201-L177/255, original version, Articles 18(1) and 3(1)(c).

[398] *Official Journal of the European Union* (2006). Directive 2006/48/EC (original version), Articles 102(1), 103, 104(1) and 105(1).

[399] *Official Journal of the European Union* (2006). Directive 2006/48/EC (original version), Article 120(1).

[400] *Official Journal of the European Union* (2006). Directive 2006/48/EC (original version), Article 120(2).

[401] *Official Journal of the European Union* (2006). Directive 2006/48/EC (original version), Article 120(3).

[402] *Official Journal of the European Union* (2006). Directive 2006/48/EC (original version), Article 123.

[403] *Official Journal of the European Union* (2006). Directive 2006/48/EC (original version), Article 145(1).

[404] *Official Journal of the European Union* (2006). Directive 2006/48/EC (original version), Annex XII Part 2, Points 1 and 6.

[405] *Official Journal of the European Union* (2006). Directive 2006/48/EC (original version), Article 145(2).

[406] *Official Journal of the European Union* (2006). Directive 2006/48/EC (original version), Annex XII Part 3, Point 3, and Article 105(1).

[407] *Official Journal of the European Union* (2006). Directive 2006/48/EC (original version), Article 145(3).

[408] *Official Journal of the European Union* (2006). Directive 2006/48/EC (original version), Article 145(4).

[409] *Official Journal of the European Union* (2006). Directive 2006/48/EC (original version), Article 146(1), and Annex XII Part 1, Point 1.

[410] *Official Journal of the European Union* (2006). Directive 2006/48/EC (original version), Article 146(2), and Annex XII Part I, Points 2 and 3.

[411] *Official Journal of the European Union* (2006). Directive 2006/48/EC (original version), Article 147(1).

[412] *Official Journal of the European Union* (2006). Directive 2006/48/EC (original version), Article 147(2), and Annex XII Part I, Point 4.

[413] *Official Journal of the European Union* (2006). Directive 2006/48/EC (original version), Article 149.

[414] *Official Journal of the European Communities* (2001). Directive 2001/24/EC of the European Parliament and of the Council of 4 April 2001 on the reorganisation and winding up of credit institutions, L125/15-L125/23, original version, Article 1.

[415] *Official Journal of the European Communities* (2001). Directive 2001/24/EC (original version), Article 3(1).

[416] *Official Journal of the European Communities* (2001). Directive 2001/24/EC (original version), Article 3(2).

[417] *Official Journal of the European Communities* (2001). Directive 2001/24/EC (original version), Article 4.

[418] *Official Journal of the European Communities* (2001). Directive 2001/24/EC (original version), Article 5.

[419] *Official Journal of the European Communities* (2001). Directive 2001/24/EC (original version), Article 6(5).

[420] *Official Journal of the European Communities* (2001). Directive 2001/24/EC (original version), Article 8(1).

[421] *Official Journal of the European Communities* (2001). Directive 2001/24/EC (original version), Article 9(1).

[422] *Official Journal of the European Communities* (2001). Directive 2001/24/EC (original version), Article 9(2).

[423] *Official Journal of the European Communities* (2001). Directive 2001/24/EC (original version), Article 10(1).

[424] *Official Journal of the European Communities* (2001). Directive 2001/24/EC (original version), Article 10(2).

[425] *Official Journal of the European Communities* (2001). Directive 2001/24/EC (original version), Article 11(1).

[426] *Official Journal of the European Communities* (2001). Directive 2001/24/EC (original version), Article 11(2).

[427] *Official Journal of the European Communities* (2001). Directive 2001/24/EC (original version), Article 12(1).

[428] *Official Journal of the European Communities* (2001). Directive 2001/24/EC (original version), Article 12(2).

[429] *Official Journal of the European Communities* (2001). Directive 2001/24/EC (original version), Article 14(1).

[430] *Official Journal of the European Communities* (2001). Directive 2001/24/EC (original version), Article 16(1).

[431] *Official Journal of the European Communities* (2001). Directive 2001/24/EC (original version), Article 16(2).

[432] *Official Journal of the European Communities* (2001). Directive 2001/24/EC (original version), Article 18.

[433] *Official Journal of the European Communities* (2001). Directive 2001/24/EC (original version), Article 19(1).

[434] *Official Journal of the European Communities* (2001). Directive 2001/24/EC (original version), Article 19(2).

[435] *Official Journal of the European Communities* (2001). Directive 2001/24/EC (original version), Article 33; *Official Journal of the European Communities* (2000). Directive 2000/12/EC of the European Parliament and of the Council of 20 March 2000 relating to the taking up and pursuit of the business of credit institutions, L126/1-L126/59, as amended to 09/03/06, Article 30(1).

[436] *Official Journal of the European Communities* (2001). Directive 2001/24/EC (original version), Article 20.

[437] *Official Journal of the European Communities* (2001). Directive 2001/24/EC (original version), Article 21(1).

[438] *Official Journal of the European Communities* (2001). Directive 2001/24/EC (original version), Article 22(1).

[439] *Official Journal of the European Communities* (2001). Directive 2001/24/EC (original version), Article 22(2).

[440] *Official Journal of the European Communities* (2001). Directive 2001/24/EC (original version), Article 23(1).

[441] *Official Journal of the European Communities* (2001). Directive 2001/24/EC (original version), Articles 21(4), 22(3), 23(2) and 10(2)(l).

[442] *Official Journal of the European Communities* (2001). Directive 2001/24/EC (original version), Article 24.

[443] *Official Journal of the European Communities* (2001). Directive 2001/24/EC (original version), Article 25.

[444] *Official Journal of the European Communities* (2001). Directive 2001/24/EC (original version), Article 28(2).

[445] *Official Journal of the European Communities* (2001). Directive 2001/24/EC (original version), Article 28(3).

[446] *Official Journal of the European Communities* (2001). Directive 2001/24/EC (original version), Article 31.

[447] *Official Journal of the European Union* (2007). Directive 2007/64/EC of the European Parliament and of the Council of 13 November 2007 on payment services in the internal market amending Directives 97/7/EC, 2002/65/EC, 2005/60/EC and 2006/48/EC and repealing Directive 97/5/EC, L319/1-L319/36, original version, Recital 4.

[448] *Official Journal of the European Union* (2007). Directive 2007/64/EC (original version), Recitals 2 and 3.

[449] *Official Journal of the European Union* (2007). Directive 2007/64/EC (original version), Recital 10, and Articles 5 and 10(1).

[450] *Official Journal of the European Union* (2007). Directive 2007/64/EC (original version), Recital 8, and Article 1(1).

[451] *Official Journal of the European Union* (2007). Directive 2007/64/EC (original version), Article 25(1).

[452] *Official Journal of the European Union* (2007). Directive 2007/64/EC (original version), Article 41(1).

[453] *Official Journal of the European Union* (2007). Directive 2007/64/EC (original version), Article 42.

[454] *Official Journal of the European Union* (2007). Directive 2007/64/EC (original version), Article 46.

[455] *Official Journal of the European Union* (2007). Directive 2007/64/EC (original version), Article 54(1).

[456] *Official Journal of the European Union* (2007). Directive 2007/64/EC (original version), Article 60(1).

[457] *Official Journal of the European Union* (2007). Directive 2007/64/EC (original version), Article 61(2).

[458] *Official Journal of the European Communities* (2000). Directive 2000/46/EC of the European Parliament and of the Council of 18 September 2000 on the taking up, pursuit and prudential supervision of the business of electronic money institutions, L275/39-L275/43, Recital 2.

[459] *Official Journal of the European Communities* (2000). Directive 2000/46/EC, Article 1(3)(b).

[460] *Official Journal of the European Communities* (2000). Directive 2000/46/EC, Recital 3.

[461] *Official Journal of the European Communities* (2000). Directive 2000/46/EC, Recital 4.

[462] *Official Journal of the European Communities* (2000). Directive 2000/46/EC, Article 3(1).

[463] *Official Journal of the European Communities* (2000). Directive 2000/46/EC, Article 4(1).

[464] *Official Journal of the European Communities* (2000). Directive 2000/46/EC, Article 4(2).

[465] *Official Journal of the European Communities* (2000). Directive 2000/46/EC, Article 5(1).

[466] *Official Journal of the European Communities* (2000). Directive 2000/46/EC, Article 7.

[467] *Official Journal of the European Communities* (2000). Directive 2000/46/EC, Article 8.

[468] *Official Journal of the European Communities* (2002). Directive 2002/47/EC of the European Parliament and of the Council of 6 June 2002 on financial collateral arrangements, L168/43-L168/50, original version, Recital 3.

[469] *Official Journal of the European Communities* (2002). Directive 2002/47/EC (original version), Article 3(1).

[470] *Official Journal of the European Communities* (2002). Directive 2002/47/EC (original version), Article 1(4)(a).

[471] *Official Journal of the European Communities* (2002). Directive 2002/47/EC (original version), Article 1(2)(a)-(d).

[472] *Official Journal of the European Communities* (2002). Directive 2002/47/EC (original version), Article 4(1).

[473] *Official Journal of the European Communities* (2002). Directive 2002/47/EC (original version), Article 4(2).

[474] *Official Journal of the European Communities* (2002). Directive 2002/47/EC (original version), Article 4(4).

[475] *Official Journal of the European Communities* (2002). Directive 2002/47/EC (original version), Article 5(1).

[476] *Official Journal of the European Communities* (2002). Directive 2002/47/EC (original version), Article 2(1)(m).

[477] *Official Journal of the European Communities* (2002). Directive 2002/47/EC (original version), Article 5(2).

[478] *Official Journal of the European Communities* (2002). Directive 2002/47/EC (original version), Article 5(5).

[479] *Official Journal of the European Communities* (2002). Directive 2002/47/EC (original version), Article 6.

[480] *Official Journal of the European Communities* (2002). Directive 2002/47/EC (original version), Article 7(1).

[481] *Official Journal of the European Union* (2003). Directive 2002/87/EC of the European Parliament and of the Council of 16 December 2002 on the supplementary supervision of credit institutions, insurance undertakings and investment firms in a financial conglomerate and amending Council Directives 73/239/EEC, 79/267/EEC, 92/49/EEC, 92/96/EEC, 93/6/EEC and 93/22/EEC, and Directives 98/78/EC and 2000/12/EC of the European Parliament and of the Council, L35/1-L35/27, as amended to 24/03/05, Recital 3.

[482] *Official Journal of the European Union* (2003). Directive 2002/87/EC (as amended to 24/03/05), Recitals 1 and 2.

[483] *Official Journal of the European Union* (2003). Directive 2002/87/EC (as amended to 24/03/05), Recital 13.

[484] *Official Journal of the European Union* (2003). Directive 2002/87/EC (as amended to 24/03/05), Recital 14.

[485] *Official Journal of the European Union* (2003). Directive 2002/87/EC (as amended to 24/03/05), Article 2(14).

[486] *Official Journal of the European Union* (2003). Directive 2002/87/EC (as amended to 24/03/05), Article 4(1).

[487] *Official Journal of the European Union* (2003). Directive 2002/87/EC (as amended to 24/03/05), Article 5(2); *Official Journal of the European Communities* (1983). Seventh Council Directive 83/349/EEC of 13 June 1983 based on the Article 54(3)(g) of the Treaty on consolidated accounts, L193/1-L193/17, as amended to 21/12/06, Articles 12(1) and 1.

[488] *Official Journal of the European Union* (2003). Directive 2002/87/EC (as amended to 24/03/05), Article 5(2).

[489] *Official Journal of the European Union* (2003). Directive 2002/87/EC (as amended to 24/03/05), Article 5(3).

[490] *Official Journal of the European Union* (2003). Directive 2002/87/EC (as amended to 24/03/05), Article 10(1).

[491] *Official Journal of the European Union* (2003). Directive 2002/87/EC (as amended to 24/03/05), Article 11(1).

[492] *Official Journal of the European Union* (2003). Directive 2002/87/EC (as amended to 24/03/05), Article 6(2).

[493] *Official Journal of the European Union* (2003). Directive 2002/87/EC (as amended to 24/03/05), Annex I, Paragraph 1.

[494] *Official Journal of the European Union* (2003). Directive 2002/87/EC (as amended to 24/03/05), Annex I, Paragraph 2.

[495] *Official Journal of the European Union* (2003). Directive 2002/87/EC (as amended to 24/03/05), Annex I, Title II.

[496] *Official Journal of the European Union* (2003). Directive 2002/87/EC (as amended to 24/03/05), Articles 7(2) and 8(2).

[497] *Official Journal of the European Union* (2003). Directive 2002/87/EC (as amended to 24/03/05), Annex II.

[498] *Official Journal of the European Union* (2003). Directive 2002/87/EC (as amended to 24/03/05), Article 8(2).

[499] *Official Journal of the European Union* (2003). Directive 2002/87/EC (as amended to 24/03/05), Article 9(1).

[500] *Official Journal of the European Union* (2003). Directive 2002/87/EC (as amended to 24/03/05), Article 9(2).

[501] *Official Journal of the European Union* (2003). Directive 2002/87/EC (as amended to 24/03/05), Article 9(3).

[502] *Official Journal of the European Union* (2003). Directive 2002/87/EC (as amended to 24/03/05), Article 9(4).

[503] *Official Journal of the European Union* (2003). Directive 2002/87/EC (as amended to 24/03/05), Article 9(5).

[504] *Official Journal of the European Union* (2003). Directive 2002/87/EC (as amended to 24/03/05), Article 12(1).

[505] *Official Journal of the European Union* (2003). Directive 2002/87/EC (as amended to 24/03/05), Article 12(1)(a)-(h).

[506] *Official Journal of the European Union* (2003). Directive 2002/87/EC (as amended to 24/03/05), Article 12(2),

[507] *Official Journal of the European Union* (2003). Directive 2002/87/EC (as amended to 24/03/05), Article 12(4).

[508] *Official Journal of the European Union* (2003). Directive 2002/87/EC (as amended to 24/03/05), Article 13.

[509] *Official Journal of the European Union* (2003). Directive 2002/87/EC (as amended to 24/03/05), Article 14(1).

[510] *Official Journal of the European Union* (2003). Directive 2002/87/EC (as amended to 24/03/05), Article 14(2).

[511] *Official Journal of the European Union* (2003). Directive 2002/87/EC (as amended to 24/03/05), Article 16.

[512] *Official Journal of the European Union* (2003). Directive 2002/87/EC (as amended to 24/03/05), Article 17(1).

[513] *Official Journal of the European Union* (2003). Directive 2002/87/EC (as amended to 24/03/05), Article 17(2).

[514] *Official Journal of the European Communities* (2002). Directive 2002/65/EC of the European Parliament and of the Council of 23 September 2002 concerning the distance marketing of consumer financial services and amending Council Directive 90/619/EEC and Directives 97/7/EC and 98/27/EC, L271/16-L271/24, as amended to 05/12/07, Recitals 1, 3 and 4.

[515] *Official Journal of the European Communities* (2002). Directive 2002/65/EC (as amended to 05/12/07), Article 1(1).

[516] *Official Journal of the European Communities* (2002). Directive 2002/65/EC (as amended to 05/12/07), Recital 15 and Article 2(a).

[517] *Official Journal of the European Communities* (2002). Directive 2002/65/EC (as amended to 05/12/07), Article 3(1).

[518] *Official Journal of the European Communities* (2002). Directive 2002/65/EC (as amended to 05/12/07), Article 3(3).

[519] *Official Journal of the European Communities* (2002). Directive 2002/65/EC (as amended to 05/12/07), Article 4(2).

[520] *Official Journal of the European Communities* (2002). Directive 2002/65/EC (as amended to 05/12/07), Article 5(1).

[521] *Official Journal of the European Communities* (2002). Directive 2002/65/EC (as amended to 05/12/07), Article 5(3).

[522] *Official Journal of the European Communities* (2002). Directive 2002/65/EC (as amended to 05/12/07), Article 10(1).

[523] *Official Journal of the European Communities* (2002). Directive 2002/65/EC (as amended to 05/12/07), Article 11.

[524] *Official Journal of the European Communities* (2002). Directive 2002/65/EC (as amended to 05/12/07), Article 12(1).

[525] *Official Journal of the European Communities* (2002). Directive 2002/65/EC (as amended to 05/12/07), Article 12(2).

[526] *Official Journal of the European Communities* (2002). Directive 2002/65/EC (as amended to 05/12/07), Article 13(1).

[527] *Official Journal of the European Communities* (2002). Directive 2002/65/EC (as amended to 05/12/07), Article 13(2).

[528] *Official Journal of the European Communities* (2002). Directive 2002/65/EC (as amended to 05/12/07), Article 13(3).

[529] *Official Journal of the European Communities* (2002). Directive 2002/65/EC (as amended to 05/12/07), Article 14.

[530] *Official Journal of the European Communities* (1994). Directive 94/19/EC of the European Parliament and of the Council of 30 May 1994 on deposit-guarantee schemes, L135/5-L135/14, as amended to 24/03/05, Recitals 8 and 16-17; *Official Journal of the European Communities* (1997). Directive 97/9/EC of the European Parliament and of

the Council of 3 March 1997 on investor-compensation schemes, L84/22-L84/31, original version, Recitals 4-5.

[531] *Official Journal of the European Communities* (1994). Directive 94/19/EC (as amended to 24/03/05), Recital 16 and Article 7(1); *Official Journal of the European Communities* (1997), Directive 97/9/EC (original version), Recitals 11-12 and Article 4(1).

[532] *Official Journal of the European Communities* (1994). Directive 94/19/EC (as amended to 24/03/05), Article 3(1).

[533] *Official Journal of the European Communities* (1994). Directive 94/19/EC (as amended to 24/03/05), Article 3(2).

[534] *Official Journal of the European Communities* (1994). Directive 94/19/EC (as amended to 24/03/05), Article 3(3).

[535] *Official Journal of the European Communities* (1994). Directive 94/19/EC (as amended to 24/03/05), Article 3(4).

[536] *Official Journal of the European Communities* (1994). Directive 94/19/EC (as amended to 24/03/05), Article 3(5).

[537] *Official Journal of the European Communities* (1994). Directive 94/19/EC (as amended to 24/03/05), Article 4(1).

[538] *Official Journal of the European Communities* (1994). Directive 94/19/EC (as amended to 24/03/05), Article 4(2).

[539] *Official Journal of the European Communities* (1994). Directive 94/19/EC (as amended to 24/03/05), Article 4(4).

[540] *Official Journal of the European Communities* (1994). Directive 94/19/EC (as amended to 24/03/05), Article 5.

[541] *Official Journal of the European Communities* (1994). Directive 94/19/EC (as amended to 24/03/05), Article 6(1).

[542] *Official Journal of the European Communities* (1994). Directive 94/19/EC (as amended to 24/03/05), Article 6(2).

[543] *Official Journal of the European Communities* (1994). Directive 94/19/EC (as amended to 24/03/05), Article 7(1).

[544] *Official Journal of the European Communities* (1994). Directive 94/19/EC (as amended to 24/03/05), Article 7(2).

[545] *Official Journal of the European Communities* (1994). Directive 94/19/EC (as amended to 24/03/05), Article 7(3).

[546] *Official Journal of the European Communities* (1994). Directive 94/19/EC (as amended to 24/03/05), Articles 7(4) and 7(1).

[547] *Official Journal of the European Communities* (1994). Directive 94/19/EC (as amended to 24/03/05), Article 7(6).

[548] *Official Journal of the European Communities* (1994). Directive 94/19/EC (as amended to 24/03/05), Article 8(1).

[549] *Official Journal of the European Communities* (1994). Directive 94/19/EC (as amended to 24/03/05), Article 9(1).

[550] *Official Journal of the European Communities* (1994). Directive 94/19/EC (as amended to 24/03/05), Articles 10(1) and 1(3).

[551] *Official Journal of the European Communities* (1997). Directive 97/9/EC (original version), Article 2(1).

[552] *Official Journal of the European Communities* (1997). Directive 97/9/EC (original version), Article 2(2).

[553] *Official Journal of the European Communities* (1997). Directive 97/9/EC (original version), Article 4(1).

[554] *Official Journal of the European Communities* (1997). Directive 97/9/EC (original version), Article 4(2).

[555] *Official Journal of the European Communities* (1997). Directive 97/9/EC (original version), Article 4(4).

[556] *Official Journal of the European Communities* (1997). Directive 97/9/EC (original version), Article 4(3).

[557] *Official Journal of the European Communities* (1997). Directive 97/9/EC (original version), Article 5(1).

[558] *Official Journal of the European Communities* (1997). Directive 97/9/EC (original version), Article 5(2).

[559] *Official Journal of the European Communities* (1997). Directive 97/9/EC (original version), Article 5(3).

[560] *Official Journal of the European Communities* (1997). Directive 97/9/EC (original version), Article 5(4).

[561] *Official Journal of the European Communities* (1997). Directive 97/9/EC (original version), Article 7(1).

[562] *Official Journal of the European Communities* (1997). Directive 97/9/EC (original version), Article 7(2).

[563] *Official Journal of the European Communities* (1997). Directive 97/9/EC (original version), Article 8(1).

[564] *Official Journal of the European Communities* (1997). Directive 97/9/EC (original version), Article 9(1).

[565] *Official Journal of the European Communities* (1997). Directive 97/9/EC (original version), Article 9(2).

[566] *Official Journal of the European Communities* (1997). Directive 97/9/EC (original version), Article 10(1).

[567] *Official Journal of the European Communities* (1997). Directive 97/9/EC (original version), Article 10(3).

[568] *Official Journal of the European Communities* (1997). Directive 97/9/EC (original version), Article 11(1).

[569] *Official Journal of the European Communities* (1997). Directive 97/9/EC (original version), Article 11(2).

[570] *Official Journal of the European Communities* (1997). Directive 97/9/EC (original version), Article 13.

[571] *Official Journal of the European Communities* (1998). Directive 98/26/EC of the European Parliament and of the Council of 19 May 1998 on settlement finality in payment and securities settlement systems, L166/45-L166/50, original version, Recitals 1-3.

[572] *Official Journal of the European Communities* (1998). Directive 98/26/EC (original version), Recital 9.

[573] *Official Journal of the European Communities* (1998). Directive 98/26/EC (original version), Recital 11.

[574] *Official Journal of the European Communities* (1998). Directive 98/26/EC (original version), Article 1.

[575] *Official Journal of the European Communities* (1998). Directive 98/26/EC (original version), Article 3(1).

[576] *Official Journal of the European Communities* (1998). Directive 98/26/EC (original version), Article 3(2).

[577] *Official Journal of the European Communities* (1998). Directive 98/26/EC (original version), Article 5.

[578] *Official Journal of the European Communities* (1998). Directive 98/26/EC (original version), Article 7.

[579] *Official Journal of the European Communities* (1998). Directive 98/26/EC (original version), Article 8.

[580] *Official Journal of the European Communities* (1998). Directive 98/26/EC (original version), Article 9(1).

[581] *Official Journal of the European Communities* (1998). Directive 98/26/EC (original version), Article 9(2).

Chapter Two

THE INTERNATIONAL RESPONSE TO THE GFC

ABSTRACT

In November 2008, the first summit of the Leaders of the G20 took place in Washington D.C., in order to address the effects of the GFC in a co-ordinated manner. Pursuant to Dr. Tietmeyer's report of February 2009, the G20 upgraded the FSF to the FSB, and put the latter in charge of co-ordinating the financial regulatory aspect of the global response to the crisis. During that year, G20 Leaders' summits were held in London and Pittsburgh. At the latter, it was decided that the G20 was to be the main international forum for economic co-operation. Following the G20's lead, the FSB and the international standard-setting institutions have published new principles and rules, which jurisdictions are putting into effect and whose implementation the FSB is monitoring. Over the area of bank recovery and resolution, the EU has partly enacted the FSB's Key Attributes of Effective Resolution Regimes. The worldwide organisations will need to decide whether it is sufficient for jurisdictions to adopt the spirit of international standards, or whether the latter will need to enact and to implement the letter of them as well. This second option will change the nature of international financial regulation, which to date has been a combination of global soft law and national hard law. That mix has provided certainty and flexibility, at both worldwide and national levels. For this good result to continue, trust between the international organisations and the domestic authorities, and between the latter and regulated firms, will need to be maintained.

Keywords: international, G20, summit, FSB, financial, standard, implement, resolution

INTRODUCTION

The international response to the GFC has been from within the ambit of the G20, which has overseen financial sector reform in the wake of the crisis. The FSB is responsible for co-ordinating these changes, both alone and in co-operation with other worldwide organisations such as the IMF and the IOSCO. This chapter looks at the development of the G20 and of the FSB, and considers how these have shaped changes in the sector consequential to the GFC. It then describes how post-crisis developments in EU law fit into this framework.

THE DEVELOPMENT OF THE G20

The G20 developed in the late 1990s, in response to the need to include larger developing countries in an informal peer-to-peer discussion, in respect of the pursuit of financial stability in the light of the Asian debt crisis of this period. The Americas, Africa, Asia, Europe and Oceania were to be represented in the new organisation in relatively equal measure, although South Africa was to be the sole African representative[308], and European countries outside 'the big four'[309] were to be represented by the country that held the Presidency of the EU and by the European Central Bank. In the period before the GFC, delegations for each country were limited to the finance minister, the governor of the central bank, and one deputy. The IMF, the World Bank, the International Monetary and Financial Committee of the IMF and the Development Committee[310] were also represented, in order to keep the G20 within the framework of the Bretton Woods Institutions[311] [1].

The GFC brought about an increase in the profile of the G20's role such that, from November 2008 onwards, some of the meetings included the leaders of each of the countries. These meetings are referred to as G20 summits. The Declaration from the first summit – the Summit on Financial Markets and the World Economy held in Washington D.C. on 14th and 15th November 2008 – lays down their purpose in the following words [2].

> We, the Leaders of the Group of Twenty, held an initial meeting in Washington on November 15, 2008, amid serious challenges to the world economy and financial markets. We are determined to enhance our cooperation and work together to restore global growth and achieve needed reforms in the world's financial systems.
>
> Over the past months our countries have taken urgent and exceptional measures to support the global economy and stabilize financial markets. These efforts must continue. At the same time, we must lay the foundation for reform to help to ensure that a global crisis, such as this one, does not happen again. Our work will be guided by a shared belief that market principles, open trade and investment regimes, and effectively regulated financial markets foster the dynamism, innovation, and entrepreneurship that are essential for economic growth, employment and poverty reduction.

Thus, the work of, and pursuant to, the G20 summits is not limited to the introduction of reforms and the restoration of economic growth across the world. The last sentence indicates that, once growth has been restored, there is an on-going supervisory role for the G20 to attempt to ensure continuity of benign economic conditions, extending beyond the remit of financial sector superintendence.

---

[308] Australia was to be the only representative from Oceania, which is the smallest and least populous of these 5 continents. Representation for the 6th continent, Antarctica, was not discussed.

[309] 'The big four' comprises the most populous countries of Europe and the European members of the G7, i.e., France, Germany, Italy and the United Kingdom.

[310] The Development Committee's full title is the Joint Ministerial Committee of the Boards of Governors of the World Bank and the International Monetary Fund on the Transfer of Real Resources to Developing Countries.

[311] The Bretton Woods Institutions are the IMF and the World Bank. At the Bretton Woods Conference of July 1944, participants created the IMF, the International Bank for Reconstruction and Development – the initial (and a continuing) component of the World Bank, and the International Trade Organization – which did not come into effect.

THE DEVELOPMENT OF THE FSB

In October 1998, the G7 Finance Ministers and Central Bank Governors asked Dr. Hans Tietmeyer, then the President of the Deutsche Bundesbank, to recommend any new arrangements and structures that may be required in respect of co-operation and co-ordination between the international financial regulators and supervisors, given the need to further global financial stability and to oversee national financial sectors and their regimes. Dr. Tietmeyer recommended (amongst other things) that the G7 should convene a Financial Stability Forum, in order to examine matters and vulnerabilities that affect the international financial system, and to identify and superintend the actions that are required to address these. Representation would include high-level representatives from the finance ministry, central bank and senior supervisory authority from each of the participating countries – initially to be the members of the G7, 2 representatives from each of the IMF, the International Bank for Reconstruction and Development, the BCBS, the IOSCO and the International Association of Insurance Supervisors, and one representative from each of the BIS, the OECD, the Committee on Payment and Settlement Systems and the Committee on the Global Financial System [3].

After the G7's swift endorsement of Dr. Tietmeyer's recommendation in February 1999, the FSF was convened for the first time in April of that year in Washington D.C. [4]. At the initial G20 summit[312], delegates recommended an urgent expansion of the FSF to include "a broader membership of emerging economies" [5]. At the next G20 summit[313], participants agreed to found a new Financial Stability Board to succeed the FSF, which was to have "a broadened mandate to promote financial stability" and to include a greater membership than that of the FSF [6, 7]. The FSB was to: (i) examine vulnerabilities that affect the financial system, and identify and superintend action needed to address these, (ii) further co-ordination and information exchange between authorities that are responsible for financial stability[314], (iii) monitor and advise on developments in the market and their implications for regulatory policy, (iv) advise on, and monitor, best practice in fulfilling regulatory standards, (v) undertake joint strategic reviews on the work of the international organisations which set standards[315], in order to ensure that this is timely, co-ordinated, prioritised and addressing regulatory gaps, (vi) set guidelines for, and support the founding and the operation of, and participation in, supervisory colleges, (vii) support contingency planning for crisis management involving more than one jurisdiction, and (viii) collaborate with the IMF in carrying out early warning exercises to identify and report on the accumulation of macroeconomic and financial risks and the actions that should be taken to address these [8]. Thus, the FSB is 'ringmaster' of the post-GFC standard-setting system, which reports to (and works with) the G20, in co-ordination with the other international financial institutions and with regional and national supervisory authorities that are responsible for financial stability.

---

[312] See the previous section, entitled 'The Development of the G20', for information concerning this summit.
[313] The 2nd G20 summit was held in London on 2nd April 2009.
[314] Although the report does not specify this, it is submitted that these include regional and national organisations, such as the EBA and the United Kingdom's Prudential Regulation Authority.
[315] It is submitted that these organisations are, in particular, the BCBS, the IOSCO and the International Association of Insurance Supervisors.

PROGRESS IN THE G20/FSB SYSTEM FROM NOVEMBER 2008

It is submitted that the Declaration from the first G20 summit and its annexed Action Plan are surprisingly detailed documents, given that the GFC was still on-going at the point at which these were published. The policymakers understood the crisis to be one of macroeconomic as well as financial effect, resulting in "severe market disruption" [9]. Having taken action "to stimulate our economies, provide liquidity, strengthen the capital of financial institutions, protect savings and deposits, address regulatory deficiencies and unfreeze credit markets," [10] the governments of G20 members needed to introduce measures to "stabilize financial markets and support economic growth," as, in particular "[e]conomic momentum is slowing substantially in major economies and the global outlook has weakened" [11]. Thus, "a broader policy response is needed, based on closer macroeconomic cooperation, to restore growth, avoid negative spillovers and support emerging market economies and developing countries"; G20 governments were to: (i) take necessary further actions "to stabilize the financial system," (ii) exercise supportive monetary policy, as suitable for national conditions, (iii) encourage domestic demand through appropriate fiscal policy, (iv) assist developing countries and emerging market economies to access finance and stress the IMF's role in responding to the GFC, (v) stimulate multilateral development banks to utilize their full capacity in order to support the development agenda, and (vi) ensure that those banks and the IMF are equipped with adequate resources in order to continue to act to overcome the GFC [12].

It is fortunate that the G20 responded to the GFC by promptly holding summit meetings, by perceiving the issue as a one of macroeconomic as well as financial proportions to which a co-ordinated response was required, and by involving both governments and several multinational institutions as players in this response. It is submitted that this is an unparalleled level of international co-operation for constructive objectives – at least in peacetime. Consequently, the G20 governments and other participating policymakers deserve credit for the approach that they have together taken. Notwithstanding this, it is the response over the financial regulatory area that is of concern in this section, and it is to this that the remainder of it will turn.

The G20 recognised that, whilst states are primarily responsible for financial regulation, greater worldwide co-operation amongst regulators and the raising of international standards and their consistent implementation is required – in order to address unfavourable cross-border, regional and global developments which affect international financial stability [13]. Accordingly, G20 governments declared their commitment to the following principles for reform: (i) strengthening transparency and accountability, (ii) enhancing sound regulation, (iii) promoting integrity in financial markets, (iv) reinforcing international co-operation, and (v) reforming international financial institutions [14]. The Action Plan contains a work plan to implement these principles [15]. These are considered in the next 5 subsections.

Strengthening Transparency and Accountability

Actions to be taken by 31ˢᵗ March 2009 comprised requirements for "key global accounting standards bodies"[316] to intensify guidance for the valuation of securities, address accounting and disclosure standards for off-balance sheet companies and trusts, enhance the disclosure to market participations of information concerning "complex financial instruments," and improve their governance, and for firms in the private sector that have developed practices for hedge funds and/or private capital pools to accelerate proposals for a group of unified best practices. In the medium term, these accounting standards bodies were to work thoroughly towards the creation of one "high-quality global standard," and co-ordinate continuously with regulators, supervisors and the private sector to ensure the application and enforcement of excellent accounting standards, whilst financial institutions should disclose their risks and losses on a continuing basis that is "consistent with international practice" [16].

Enhancing Sound Regulation

The following actions were to be taken by 31ˢᵗ March 2009. Regulators were to: (i) make recommendations to mitigate pro-cyclicality, (ii) take actions to ensure that credit rating agencies satisfy IOSCO standards, avoid conflicts of interest, disclose more information to issuers and to investors, and differentiate ratings for complex financial instruments, (iii) develop guidance to enhance the risk management practices of banks in line with international best practice, (iv) encourage financial institutions to implement stronger policies for good risk management, and (v) create and implement procedures to ensure that financial firms effect policies which improve their management of liquidity risk. Regulators and supervisors were to: (i) increase efforts to lower the systemic risks of credit default swaps and OTC derivatives transactions, (ii) require market participants to support exchange-traded or electronic-trading platforms for credit default swaps, (iii) improve the market transparency of OTC derivatives, and (iv) ensure that the infrastructure for OTC derivatives is such that it is able to support increasing trade in these instruments. The IOSCO should review the adoption by credit rating agencies of the standards and methods for surveilling compliance. Authorities were to make sure that financial institutions kept sufficient capital in quantities that are necessary to maintain confidence. The BCBS was to set out higher capital requirements for the structured finance activities of banks, and assist firms to develop new stress testing models (as appropriate). Supervisors were to ensure that financial institutions introduce processes that provide for thorough and timely measurement of risk concentrations and substantial counterparty risk positions across regions and products. Financial firms were to re-examine their risk management models in order "to guard against stress" and to report on this to their supervisors, and were to establish (as necessary) incentives to further stability and reward long-term goals. Banks were to exert due diligence and effectual risk management over structured products [17].

---

[316] These organisations include the International Accounting Standards Board, the United States of America's Financial Accounting Standards Board, the United Kingdom's Accounting Standards Board, and Accounting Standards Boards of other major jurisdictions.

The following actions were to be taken in the medium term. All G20 members were to agree to compile a Financial Sector Assessment Program report and to support transparent evaluation of national regulatory systems, in order to ensure that each member's regulatory structure "is compatible with a modern and increasingly globalized financial system." "The appropriate bodies" of G20 members were to provide a report on regulation in the securities, banking and insurance sectors and recommend required improvements, and to review the ambit of financial regulation. Regional and national authorities were to appraise their bankruptcy laws and resolution regimes in the light of recent events, in order to ensure that these allow an orderly wind-down of cross-border financial institutions. Credit rating agencies that give public ratings were to be registered. Central banks and supervisors were to advance robust and internationally convergent approaches for central bank liquidity operations for, and liquidity supervision of, cross-border banks. International standard-setting organisations were to ensure that policymakers are able to respond quickly to innovation in, and evolution of, financial products and markets. Authorities were to monitor large changes in the price of assets and the implications of these for the financial system and the macro-economy [18].

Promoting Integrity in Financial Markets

By 31st March 2009, regional and national authorities were to: (i) work together, in order to enhance regulatory co-operation at international and regional levels between countries, (ii) further the sharing of information about cross-border and domestic threats to market stability and ensure that regional or national legal provisions are able to address these difficulties, (iii) review the rules of business conduct in order to protect investors and markets, (iv) increase their cross-border co-operation, in order to protect the international financial system from unlawful conduct, and (v) introduce (as necessary) suitable sanctions for misconduct. In the medium term, regional and national authorities were to implement measures that protect the worldwide financial system from jurisdictions that may shelter illegal financial activity, the Financial Action Task Force was to persist in its work against terrorist financing and money laundering, and taxation authorities were to continue to further information exchange [19].

Reinforcing International Co-Operation

By 31st March 2009, supervisors were to co-operate to found supervisory colleges for all large cross-border financial institutions, each significant global bank was to meet regularly with its supervisory college in order to discuss its activities and risk assessment, and regulators were to take all actions necessary to improve arrangements for cross-border crisis management. In the medium term, authorities were to assemble information on areas in which convergence in regulatory practices is progressing, is in need of faster progress, or shows potential for progress, and were to make sure that temporary measures to restore confidence and stability are minimally disruptive and are removed in a timely, co-ordinated and well-sequenced way [20].

Reinforcing International Financial Institutions

In addition to the recommendation for the FSF to adopt emerging market economies as members[317], the following actions were planned for the period to 31st March 2009: the IMF and the FSF were to increase their collaboration – enhancing attempts to improve integration of regulatory and supervisory responses into the macroprudential policy framework and carry out early warning exercises, the IMF was to lead in learning from the GFC, the resources of the IMF and multilateral development banks were to be reviewed, the international financial institutions were to adapt their lending instruments to satisfy the needs of their members and revise their lending role in the light of the GFC, ways were to be investigated to restore the access of developing countries and emerging market economies to credit and to resume private capital flows that are crucial for sustainable growth and development, and multilateral development banks were to ensure that arrangements are in place to support (as necessary) countries with sound policies and a good record in cases in which serious disruptions in the market have limited those states' access to the financing that they require in order to pursue countercyclical fiscal policies. In the medium term, the Bretton Woods Institutions[318] were to be thoroughly reformed so that they are able to reasonably reflect shifting economic weights in the world economy and be more responsive to challenges in the future[319], the IMF was to carry out rigorous, fair surveillance reviews of all countries and integrate these with the joint IMF/World Bank Financial Sector Assessment Programs, and advanced economies and international organisations were to provide programs for capacity-building for developing countries and emerging market economies on the enactment and implementation of significant new regulations that observe international standards [21].

2009

The Leaders' Statement from the G20's London Summit in April 2009 includes sections entitled 'Restoring growth and jobs', 'Strengthening financial supervision and regulation', 'Strengthening our global financial institutions', 'Resisting protectionism and promoting global trade and investment', and 'Ensuring a fair and sustainable recovery for all'. As it is the second of these titles that is of most relevance, this is to be considered further here. In addition to establishment of the FSB[320], the G20 agreed to: (i) modify its regulatory systems

---

[317] See the previous section, entitled 'The Development of the FSB', for this recommendation.

[318] See fn 311.

[319] In particular, emerging market economies and developing countries were to have more say in the Bretton Woods Institutions (G20 (2008), Declaration Summit on Financial Markets and the World Economy, Action Plan, p.5). In December 2010, the IMF's Board of Governors completed the 14th General Review of Quotas, which doubled IMF quotas, moved more than 6% of quota shares from over-represented member countries to under-represented countries, shifted more than 6% of quota shares to emerging market and developing countries, and realigned quota shares – Brazil, China, India and Russia are within the 10 largest shareholders in the Fund; the 15th General Review of Quotas is due for completion in December 2015 (International Monetary Fund (2015), International Monetary Fund Factsheet: IMF Quotas, p.3, <http://www.imf.org/external/np/exr/facts/pdf/quotas.pdf>). Furthermore, the World Bank is enhancing the shareholdings, voting power, and representation on the Board of Governors, of developing and transition countries (World Bank (2009), Development Committee: Enhancing Voice and Participation of Developing and Transition Countries in the World Bank Group: Update and Proposals for Discussion, <http://siteresources.worldbank.org/DEVCOMMINT/Documentation/22335196/DC2009-0011(E)Voice.pdf>).

[320] This is described in the previous section, entitled 'The Development of the FSB'.

to enable its authorities to identify and consider macroprudential risks, (ii) extend supervision and regulation to all systemically important financial markets, institutions and instruments, (iii) support and implement the FSF's new principles on remuneration and compensation, (iv) back the corporate social responsibility of all firms and sustainable compensation schemes, (v) act to improve the quantity, quality and international consistency of capital in the banking system – once recovery is assured[321], (vi) stand ready to impose sanctions to protect its financial systems and public finances, in respect of "non-cooperative jurisdictions" – which include tax havens, (vii) request the accounting standard setters to urgently work with regulators and supervisors, in order to improve standards on provisions and valuation and to publish one set of high-quality worldwide accounting standards, and (viii) extend regulatory superintendence and registration to credit rating agencies, in order to ensure that these entities satisfy the international code of good practice [22].

In addition to producing a progress report against each of the actions set out in the previous G20 summit's Action Plan[322], the G20 Leaders published a document entitled 'Declaration on Strengthening the Financial System', aspects of which this paragraph surveys. The functions that the Declaration lays out for the FSB have been stated[323]. For international co-operation, the Leaders have agreed to: (i) complete the founding of supervisory colleges for substantial cross-border firms by June 2009, (ii) promptly implement the FSF principles for cross-border crisis management, (iii) back continuing attempts by the FSB, the IMF, the World Bank and the BCBS to create an international framework for cross-jurisdictional bank resolution arrangements, and (iv) the FSB and the IMF together starting an Early Warning Exercise at their Spring Meetings in 2009 [23]. The G20 Leaders have agreed to enhance international frameworks for prudential regulation, in the following ways: (i) the worldwide standard for the minimum level of capital should remain unchanged until recovery is assured; (ii) capital buffers above the required minimum levels should be allowed to reduce, in order to promote lending in deteriorating economic circumstances; (iii) as soon as recovery is assured, prudential regulatory standards should be upgraded, capital buffers should be raised and the quality of capital should be strengthened; (iv) guidelines for harmonisation of the definition of 'capital' should be published by the end of 2009; (v) the BCBS should review minimum levels of capital and evolve recommendations in 2010; (vi) the FSB, the BCBS and the Committee on the Global Financial System, together with accounting standard setters, should implement the recommendations to mitigate procyclicality; (vii) risk-based capital requirements are to be supplemented with a simple, clear measure that is not based on risk, is internationally comparable, takes off-balance sheet exposures into consideration, and helps to contain the accumulation of leverage within the banking system; (viii) "the BCBS and authorities" are to progress work in respect of "improving incentives for risk management of securitisation" by 2010; (ix) all G20 countries are to progressively adopt the Basel II Framework; (x) the BCBS and domestic authorities are to advance and agree, by 2010, a worldwide framework for advancing greater liquidity

---

[321] The document states: "In future, regulation must prevent excessive leverage and require buffers of resources to be built up in good times." (G20 (2009), London Summit – Leaders' Statement, p.5). This statement contains the seeds of aspects of the Basel III Framework.

[322] The previous 5 subsections contain the detail of the Action Plan.

[323] See the previous section, entitled 'The Development of the FSB'.

buffers at financial institutions[324] [24]. In respect of the extension of supervision and regulation to all systemically important financial markets, institutions and instruments[325], these should be "subject to an appropriate degree of regulation and oversight"; in particular: (i) G20 Leaders are to change their regulatory systems to ensure that authorities are able to take macroprudential risks into account throughout the financial system, in order to restrict the accumulation of systemic risk – the FSB is to work with the BIS and with "international standard setters" to develop macroprudential tools and to compile a report by the autumn of 2009; (ii) large, complex financial institutions require especially careful superintendence, as these are systemically important; (iii) the Leaders are to make sure that their states' national regulators have the powers to collect relevant information on all significant financial markets, institutions and instruments, in order to evaluate the potential for their serious stress or collapse to contribute to systemic risk; (iv) the FSB and the IMF are to publish guidelines for domestic authorities to assess whether a financial market, institution or instrument is "systemically important" by the next meeting of G20 Finance Ministers and Central Bank Governors; (v) hedge funds or their managers are to be registered, and will be required to divulge "appropriate information" to regulators or supervisors on a continuing basis that is necessary for evaluation of the systemic risks that they pose; (vi) the FSB is to evolve mechanisms for co-operation and information sharing between relevant authorities, in order to make sure that effective supervision is maintained in instances in which a fund is situated in a different jurisdiction to that of its manager; (vii) supervisors are to require institutions that have hedge funds as their counterparties to "have effective risk management"; (viii) G20 Leaders are to further the standardisation and robustness of markets for credit derivatives, and request this industry to draw up an action plan on standardisation by the autumn of 2009; (ix) the industry is to review and adapt the limits of the regulatory framework frequently, in order to keep up with developments in the financial system and to further consistent approaches and good practices at the international level [25]. G20 Leaders have endorsed the FSF's principles on pay and compensation in major financial institutions, in order to make sure that compensation structures are consistent with the long-term objectives of firms and with sensible risk-taking; the BCBS is to integrate these principles into its risk management guidance by the autumn of 2009 [26]. The Declaration makes the following comments in respect of taxation: (i) countries are to adopt the international standard for information exchange that the G20 endorsed in 2004 and which is reflected in the United Nations Model Tax Convention; (ii) the G20 Leaders are prepared to take agreed action against those states that fail to satisfy international standards in respect of "tax transparency"; to this end, the Leaders have agreed to develop a set of effective counter-measures for countries to review, such as: (a) increased disclosure requirements for financial firms and taxpayers to report transactions that involve "non-cooperative jurisdictions," (b) withholding taxes[326] with regard to various payments, (c) refusing to grant deductions for taxation purposes in respect of expense payments to persons who reside in a "non-cooperative jurisdiction," (d) reviewing the national policy in respect of double taxation avoidance agreements, (e) requesting

---

[324] These requirements for prudential regulation are precursory to the Basel III Framework, whose initial documentation the BCBS published in December 2010. The majority of the requirements relate directly to aspects of that Framework – for instance, requirement (vii) maps to the leverage ratio.

[325] See point (ii) in the previous paragraph.

[326] A 'withholding tax' is a tax that is imposed on a source of income by the government of the jurisdiction in which that income arises, the equivalent sum of which may later be recovered by the taxpayer in the jurisdiction in which he/she resides.

international institutions and regional development banks to appraise their investment policies, and (f) giving additional weight to the principles of information exchange and "tax transparency" whilst designing bilateral aid programs; (iii) the Leaders are committed to publishing proposals, by the end of 2009, to facilitate the acquisition by developing countries of "the benefits of a new cooperative tax environment"; (iv) the G20 leaders are committed to greater observance of international prudential regulatory and supervisory standards; the IMF and the FSB, in collaboration with "international standard-setters," are to provide an evaluation of implementation of these standards by "relevant jurisdictions," and the FSB is to develop a set of measures to further adherence to prudential standards and co-operation with governments; (v) the Financial Action Task Force should revise and re-energise the review process for examining compliance by jurisdictions with anti-money laundering and counter-financing of terrorism benchmarks [27]. In respect of accounting standards, the Leaders have: (i) agreed that the setters of accounting standards are to "improve" those for the valuation of financial instruments – based on the latter's liquidity and the period for which they are held, whilst re-affirming "the framework of fair value accounting," (ii) welcomed the FSF's recommendations on procyclicality which address accounting matters, and (iii) agreed that accounting standard setters are to act by the end of 2009 to simplify accounting standards for financial instruments, strengthen the recognition in the accounts of loan-loss provisions by incorporating a greater range of credit information, improve these standards for provisions, off-balance sheet exposures and uncertainty relating to valuation, achieve consistency and clarity in the international application of valuation norms, significantly progress towards one set of high-quality worldwide accounting standards, and increase stakeholders' involvement in the setting of these standards through the International Accounting Standards Board's constitutional review [28]. In respect of credit rating agencies, the G20 Leaders have agreed that: (i) all agencies whose credit ratings are utilized "for regulatory purposes" are to be registered and supervised; the "regulatory oversight regime" is to be established by the end of 2009, and be compatible with the IOSCO Code of Conduct Fundamentals; (ii) domestic authorities are to enforce compliance with that regime, and to require changes to an agency's procedures and practices for managing conflicts of interest and assuring the quality and the transparency of the credit rating process; (iii) agencies are to differentiate credit ratings for structured products; (iv) agencies are to fully divulge the track record of their ratings, and the assumptions and the data that support the ratings process; (v) the "oversight framework" is to be consistent across territories, with "appropriate sharing of information" between the IOSCO and the various domestic authorities; (vi) the BCBS is to progress its review on the function of external ratings in prudential regulation [29].

The Leaders' Statement from the G20's Pittsburgh Summit in September 2009 claimed that the measures reported in the London Summit in April of that year had stopped and reversed the GFC – a significant achievement, if history regards this to be true.

We meet in the midst of a critical transition from crisis to recovery to turn the page on an era of irresponsibility and to adopt a set of policies, regulations and reforms to meet the needs of the 21st century global economy. When we last gathered in April, we confronted the greatest challenge to the world economy in our generation. Global output was contracting at [a] pace not seen since the 1930s. Trade was plummeting. Jobs were disappearing rapidly. Our people worried that the world was on the edge of a depression. At that time, our countries agreed to do everything necessary to ensure recovery, to repair our financial systems and to maintain the global flow of capital. It worked. Our forceful response helped to stop the dangerous, sharp decline in global activity and stabilize financial markets. Industrial output is now rising in nearly all our economies. International trade is starting to recover. Our financial institutions are raising needed capital, financial markets are showing a willingness to invest and lend, and confidence has improved [30].

So, was this 'mission accomplished'? No, because the mission was to change.

Today, we designated the G-20 as the premier forum for our international economic cooperation. We have asked our representatives to report back at our next meeting with recommendations on how to maximize the effectiveness of our cooperation. We have agreed to have a G-20 Summit in Canada in June 2010, and in Korea in November 2010. We expect to meet annually thereafter, and will meet in France in 2011 [31].

Thus, the financial regulatory actions announced at the G20 summits from Pittsburgh onwards are to be primarily considered in the light of to the extent to which they are progressive, rather than the degree to which they contribute to restoration from the GFC. The Pittsburgh agenda in this area is as follows.

We committed to act together to raise capital standards, to implement strong international compensation standards aimed at ending practices that lead to excessive risk-taking, to improve the over-the-counter derivatives market and to create more powerful tools to hold large global firms to account for the risks they take. … [32].

The G20 Leaders asked their Finance Ministers and Central Bank Governors to agree upon an international framework for reform in the following areas: building high-quality capital and mitigating procyclicality, altering compensation practices in order to support financial stability, improving the markets for OTC derivatives, and addressing cross-border resolution and systematically important financial institutions (by the end of 2010) [33]. The next 4 paragraphs are to consider each of these, in turn.

The Leaders committed to developing by the end of 2010 internationally agreed rules to raise the quantity and the quality of bank capital and to reduce excessive leverage. The rules were to be gradually introduced, with the objective of implementation by the end of 2012. National adoption of these capital requirements, countercyclical capital buffers, higher capital requirements for high-risk products and off-balance sheet transactions, as components of the Basel II Framework, together with tighter requirements for liquidity risk and "forward-looking provisioning," will lower incentives for banks to run excessive risks and form a financial system that is better prepared to withstand unfavourable shocks. The Leaders back the introduction of a leverage ratio as a supplemental measure to the risk-based Basel II Framework. To ensure comparability, this ratio's details were to be harmonised internationally, adjusting in full for accounting differences between jurisdictions. "All major G-20 financial centers" were to adopt the Basel II Framework by 2011[327] [34].

---

[327] This paragraph reveals a further nudge by the authorities towards the introduction of the Basel III Framework. It is not clear what is meant by 'all major G-20 centers' – although interpretation of this phrase is rendered academic by the fact that all except one of the members of the G20 "have completed their regulatory adoption"

The G20 Leaders endorsed the standards of the FSB that are intended to align compensation with the generation of value in the long run, including by: (i) forbidding bonuses that are guaranteed over many years[328], (ii) requiring much of variable compensation to be deferred, linked to performance, subject to suitable clawback and vested in equity or quasi-equity instruments – provided that these are aligned with value creation in the long term and "the time horizon of risk," (iii) ensuring that compensation for employees whose work materially affects the firm's exposure to risk, align with performance and risk, (iv) clarifying the compensation structures and policies of firms through disclosure requirements, (v) restricting variable compensation as a percentage of total net revenues, if the former is inconsistent with the preservation of a secure capital base, and (vi) making sure that compensation committees are able to be independent. Supervisors were to be responsible for: (i) reviewing the compensation structures and policies of firms with a view to "institutional and systemic risk" and, if it is necessary to counteract additional risks, apply remedial measures – such as greater capital requirements – to those organisations that do not implement good compensation policies and practices, and (ii) modifying (as far as is necessary) compensation structures in respect of firms that go bankrupt or "require extraordinary public intervention." The Leaders requested firms to implement these sound compensation practices forthwith, and required the FSB to monitor the implementation of the latter's compensation standards and propose additional measures (as needed) by March 2010 [35].

The Leaders required all standardised OTC derivative contracts to be traded on exchanges or electronic trading platforms – in so far as this is appropriate, and to be cleared by central counterparties, both by the end of 2012. These contracts were to be reported to trade repositories. Contracts that are not cleared centrally were to be subject to increased capital requirements. The FSB was to regularly examine implementation – and whether this is sufficient to make markets for financial derivatives more transparent, mitigate systemic risk, and preclude market abuse [36].

The Leaders required "systemically important financial firms" to evolve "contingency and resolution plans" that are "internationally-consistent" and specific to the particular organisation which is developing those plans[329]. "Our authorities" were to establish frameworks and tools for the effectual resolution of financial groups, to help to mitigate the disruption of bankruptcies of financial firms and lower moral hazard in the future. Prudential standards for "systemically important institutions" were to be "commensurate with the costs of their failure"[330]. The FSB was to put forward "possible measures" by 31st October 2010,

---

of Basel II (Basel Committee on Banking Supervision (2015), Ninth progress report on adoption of the Basel regulatory framework: October 2015, p.2, <http://www.bis.org/bcbs/publ/d338.pdf>).

[328] The Leaders' Statement refers to "multi-year guaranteed bonuses." The minimum of 'multi-year' may be as little as 2 years, but a literal interpretation of this phrase is 'many years'.

[329] The concept of 'systemically important' is integral to the GFC, and is difficult to define precisely. Central to this concept is the idea that the actions of an institution of such designation will substantially affect 'the system'. For instance, if a bank with this characteristic goes into liquidation, then this would present a severe risk to collapse of the financial system as a whole and a significant adverse effect on the economy.

[330] It is submitted that it is difficult in practice to link prudential standards to costs of failure, in pecuniary terms. Reasons for this include the following (i) 'failure' has financial and social implications across the sector that may spread into other parts of the economy, which will be difficult to estimate in monetary value, (ii) it is difficult to calibrate the benefits of 'prudential standards' – the phrase might mean the capital and liquidity requirements that are to be imposed under the terms of a particular model – however, although this is quantifiable, it would be a narrow definition of the term 'prudential standards'. The high-level guidance should be clarified to read, for instance, 'Prudential standards for institutions whose performance significantly affects, or may significantly

which include supervision of greater intensity and "specific additional capital, liquidity, and other prudential requirements" [37].

Other commitments that the G20 Leaders made at Pittsburgh in respect of the international financial regulatory system include: (i) for international accounting bodies to work harder to publish one set of high-quality, worldwide accounting standards and "complete their convergence project by June 2011"; (ii) to be ready to apply countermeasures to tax havens from March 2010; (iii) to request the Financial Action Task Force to issue a list of high-risk jurisdictions (in respect of terrorist financing and money laundering) by February 2010; (iv) to call upon the FSB to report progress in respect of errant states' compliance with international co-operation and information exchange in November 2009, and to commence a peer review process by February 2010; (v) to require the IMF to prepare a report for the next G20 summit in respect of countries' views as to how the financial sector could fairly and substantially contribute towards payment for any burdens that are associated with government interventions to restore the banking system to good condition [38]. This summit was to take place in Toronto, in June 2010.

2010

In the Declaration from the Toronto Summit, G20 Leaders pledged to collaborate to accomplish the commitments to reform the financial sector that they had made at the Washington, London and Pittsburgh Summits, within the agreed timeframes [39]. They declared that their agenda for reform rested on the following 4 pillars: a strong regulatory framework, effective supervision, restructuring/resolution of financial institutions, and clear international assessment and peer review [40]. The following 4 paragraphs describe each of these, in turn.

The Leaders stated that important progress had been made on reforms that will substantially increase the resilience of the banking system: the quantity of capital is to be "significantly higher," and the quantity of capital is to be much improved in order to strengthen the ability of banks to absorb losses [41]. They supported: (i) reaching agreement at the next G20 summit on the new capital framework, which would raise capital requirements by requiring each bank to hold in Tier 1 capital an increasing share of common equity (as a percentage of risk-weighted assets) that enables them to withstand stresses of a size associated with the GFC, and (ii) changing to a "globally consistent and transparent set of conservative deductions" that are "generally applied at the level of common equity ... over a suitable globally-consistent transition period" [42]. The Leaders specified that all members of the G20 are to adopt the new standards, which are to be gradually brought in over a timeframe that is compatible with sustained recovery and which minimises market disruption, with the objective of implementation by the end of 2012, and a "transition horizon" which relates to the macroeconomic impact assessment of the FSB and the BCBS[331] [43]. They reiterated their

---

affect, that of the financial sector, the economy as a whole, and/or any significant part of the economy, should be set at a level that is higher than that for institutions of otherwise similar characteristics that do not show this tendency.' The use of the word 'significant' and the phrase 'otherwise similar characteristics', makes these qualities measurable statistically – at least in theory.

[331] Implementation of these arrangements, now known as the 'Basel III Framework,' is currently taking place, with 'all systems go' projected for 1st January 2019. The Ninth progress report on the adoption of the Basel III

earlier agreement to reinforce the financial market infrastructure by quickening the implementation of strong measures to improve clarity and regulatory superintendence of credit rating agencies, hedge funds and OTC derivatives, in a manner that is fair and "internationally consistent." [44].

The G20 Leaders stated that they are committed to the Core Principles of Effective Banking Supervision that the BCBS has published. They instructed the FSB (in discussion with the IMF) to report to the G20 Finance Ministers and Central Bank Governors in October 2010 on recommendations to enhance "oversight and supervision," relating in particular to the capacity, mandate and resourcing of supervisors and specific powers that should be adopted in order to identify and manage risks proactively [45].

The Leaders declared their commitment to the design and implementation of a system in which they possess the tools and powers to restructure or resolve "all types of financial institutions in crisis," without taxpayers paying for this; national resolution tools and powers are to be implemented in a way that maintains financial stability[332] [46]. They agreed that resolution regimes should display the following features: a "[p]roper allocation of losses" in order to mitigate moral hazard and "protect taxpayers," continuity of crucial financial services, market credibility of the resolution regime, minimisation of the spread of the problems, prior planning for organised resolution and the transfer of contractual relationships, and effectual co-operation and information exchange nationally and between jurisdictions in the event of the bankruptcy of a cross-border institution [47]. The Leaders welcomed the FSB's interim report on lowering "the moral hazard risks" to which "systemically important financial institutions" give rise, and recognised that action must be taken to address these risks; the FSB was to consider and evolve recommendations as to the policy to effectively address difficulties that are connected with, and resolve, these institutions by the next G20 summit – which should include more thorough supervision and the contemplation of financial mechanisms and instruments "to encourage market discipline." [48]. They welcomed the significant progress that had been made concerning the development of supervisory colleges and groups for crisis management in respect of the substantial financial entities that the FSB

Framework provides the progress towards implementation of 18 jurisdictions outside the EU (Argentina, Australia, Brazil, Canada, China, Hong Kong, India, Indonesia, Japan, the Republic of Korea, Mexico, Russia, Saudi Arabia, Singapore, South Africa, Switzerland, Turkey and the United States of America), the EU as a whole, and 9 states within the EU (Belgium, France, Germany, Italy, Luxembourg, the Netherlands, Spain, Sweden and the United Kingdom); the report supplies a numerical rank from 1 (draft regulation not published) through 2 (draft regulation published) and 3 (final rule published) to 4 (final rule in force) for each jurisdiction for several components of the Basel III Framework – definition of capital, capital conservation buffer, countercyclical buffer, capital requirements for equity investments in funds, the new standardised approach for measuring counterparty credit risk, securitisation framework, capital requirements for bank exposures to central counterparties, liquidity coverage ratio, disclosure requirements in respect of the liquidity coverage ratio, net stable funding ratio, disclosure requirements in respect of the net stable funding ratio, leverage ratio, disclosure requirements in respect of the leverage ratio, requirements for global systemically important banks, requirements for domestic systemically important banks, Pillar 3 disclosure requirements, and large exposures; Saudi Arabia displays an impressive set of numbers – its rank in respect of each of the above components, respectively, is as follows: 4, 3, 2, 3, 3, 2, 2, 4, 4, 4, 3, 4, 4, 3, 3, 2, 4 (Basel Committee on Banking Supervision (2015), Ninth progress report on adoption of the Basel regulatory framework: October 2015, pp.4-30).

[332] The G20 Leaders are committed to implement the BCBS's 10 recommendations to address the difficulties that arise in the resolution of a cross-border bank, which its Cross-border Bank Resolution Group released for publication in March 2010; "in this regard," the Leaders declared their support for changes to domestic resolution and insolvency laws and processes, as far as is needed to furnish the relevant national authorities with the capacity to co-operate and to co-ordinate cross-border actions on resolution (G20 (2010), The G-20 Toronto Summit: Declaration, Annex II, Paragraph 16, p.17).

has identified, and committed to continue to co-operate in order to generate firm-specific, speedy resolution plans for these institutions by the end of 2010 [49].

The G20 Leaders "pledged to support" clear, sound, independent international assessment and peer review of their financial systems via the IMF/World Bank Financial Sector Assessment Programs and the FSB's peer review procedure [50]. The Leaders reaffirmed the FSB's leading role in: (i) the elaboration of regulatory and supervisory policies and standards for the international financial sector, (ii) the co-ordination of actions amongst standard-setting organisations, (iii) the securing of accountability for the agenda of reforms by carrying out country and thematic peer reviews, and (iv) the fostering of a level playing field through consistent implementation across jurisdictions and sectors[333]; "to that end," they encouraged the FSB to consider ways of strengthening its capacity, in order to maintain pace with the need to satisfy "growing demands." [51]. The Leaders required the FSB to formalize and extend its activities beyond the G20, in order to reflect the financial system's "global nature." [52]. They "fully support[ed]." the FSB's thematic peer reviews as a method for nurturing consistent cross-country implementation of regulatory and financial policies, and for examining the effectiveness of these policies in accomplishing their intended results [53]. The Leaders expressed their approval in respect of "the significant progress in" the program of country reviews that the FSB conducts [54]. They specified that they "are addressing non-cooperative jurisdictions," on the basis of clear, coherent and thorough assessment with regard to tax havens, the observance of prudential standards, and the combatting of terrorist financing and money laundering [55].

In the Declaration from the Seoul Summit in November 2010, the G20 Leaders reported the delivery of (amongst other things) central components "of a new financial regulatory framework," measures to regulate and resolve "systemically important financial institutions," and more effectual superintendence. They stated the following [56].

> This new framework, complemented by other achievements in *the Seoul Summit Document*, will ensure a more resilient financial system by reining in the past excesses of the financial sector and better serving the needs of our economies.

The section named "Financial Sector Reforms" within *the Seoul Summit Document* is subdivided into parts entitled "Transformed financial system to address the root causes of the crisis," "Implementation and international assessment, including peer review," and "Future work: issues that warrant more attention" [57]. The next 3 paragraphs address these titles, in turn.

The G20 Leaders endorsed the forthcoming Basel III Framework, and stated that it would be transposed into the national laws and regulations of G20 member countries, with its implementation commencing on 1st January 2013 and being completed by 1st January 2019. They made the following comments [58].

> The new standards will markedly reduce banks' incentive to take excessive risks, lower the likelihood and severity of future crises, and enable banks to withstand – without extraordinary government support – stresses of a magnitude associated with the

---

[333] This sentence summarises the central function of the FSB in the international financial system. The next section, entitled 'G20/FSB Guidance and EU Law', provides examples as to how this works through, in the post-GFC EU regulations.

recent financial crisis. This will result in a banking system that can better support stable economic growth[334].

The Leaders approved the policy framework, procedures and timelines that the FSB proposed in order to lower the moral hazard risks that "systemically important financial institutions" pose and tackle the 'too-big-to-fail' difficulty[335]; they stated that this necessitates "a multi-pronged framework" that combines: (i) a resolution system and other measures, to make sure that every financial institution is able to be resolved safely, swiftly and without destabilising the financial system – thereby exposing taxpayers to the risk of loss, (ii) a requirement that "systemically important financial institutions," especially those which are "globally systemic"[336], should have a greater capacity for the absorbance of losses than other banks do – to reflect the higher risk that bankruptcy of the former pose to the worldwide financial system, (iii) more thorough supervision, (iv) a sound centre to the infrastructure of the financial markets, in order to reduce the risk of individual bankruptcies of companies operating thereon from spreading, and (v) "other supplementary prudential and other requirements" that domestic authorities determine – which may include, as appropriate, levies, liquidity surcharges, structural measures and tighter restrictions on large exposures to risk [59]. The Leaders agreed that global systemically important financial institutions were to "be subject to a sustained process of mandatory international recovery and resolution planning," and decided to carry out stringent risk assessment on these entities via international supervisory colleges, and to negotiate crisis co-operation agreements that are particular to each of those organisations within crisis management groups; the FSB was to conduct regular peer reviews "on the effectiveness and consistency of national policy measures" for such entities [60]. They called upon the FSB to specify the qualities required for resolution regimes to be effective – by 2011 – building upon the BCBS's suggestions for cross-border resolution and its planned review of these, and endorsed the FSB's policy recommendations on raising the concentration and effectiveness of supervision [61].

Recognising different starting points amongst their countries, the G20 Leaders considered it to be essential for them to "fully implement" the new principles and standards in a manner that "ensures a level playing field" and keeps away from market fragmentation, protectionism

---

[334] It is submitted that this belief has not been tested yet. There are counter-arguments to the Basel III Framework, such as that it has not been sufficiently demonstrated that the structure for obligatory capital requirements against credit and other risks is an optimal method for regulating excessive risk-taking in banks, that the capital requirements are too high to enable sufficient flexibility in the normal course of banking business, and that imposing highly detailed and specialised rules on economies with different legal, social and structural backgrounds may be unsustainable and/or against their long-term interests. It is also submitted that, further to the Leaders' reference to 'stable economic growth', the Framework may improve stability but may tend to stifle growth. In addition, there are costs to banks for imposing high levels of supervisory and reporting requirements on them on a continuing basis. It is a sensible scheme to require G20 members to phase the requirements in over a 6-year period, as their national supervisors and their banks have time to adapt to the increasing regulatory load; furthermore, there is time to accumulate data for the performance of banks over this period, which may provide useful feedback on the appropriateness of the Framework.

[335] In essence, major financial institutions may be deemed to be 'too big to fail' because, if they become bankrupt, this would have significant adverse consequences for the financial sector and for the wider economy; therefore, governments may choose to subsidise these organisations, which means that taxpayers pay to keep them afloat. For further information, see Stern, H. G., & Feldman, R. J. (2009), Too Big to Fail: The Hazards of Bank Bailouts (paperback edition). Washington D.C.: Brookings Institution Press.

[336] See fn 329, for an explanation of the concept of 'systemically important'. If the institution is 'globally systemic', in contrast to 'domestically systemic', then its failure is likely to adversely affect the economy beyond the borders of the country in which it is registered – as well as the national system.

and regulatory arbitrage [62]. Whilst, at the domestic level, these principles and standards were to be incorporated into pertinent policies and legislation, at the worldwide level international assessment and peer review procedures were to be "substantially enhanced" in order to ensure that the principles and standards are implemented consistently across states – and to identify areas for additional improvement in them; the IMF/World Bank Financial Sector Assessment Programs and the FSB's peer reviews were recognised as valuable to this consistent implementation [63]. Requesting the FSB to regularly monitor progress, the Leaders: (i) "firmly recommitted" to make efforts to enhance the regulation and the supervision of credit rating agencies, hedge funds and OTC derivatives – in a way that is "internationally consistent" and fair, (ii) "reaffirmed" the criticality of "fully implementing" the FSF/FSB Principles for Sound Compensation Practices, and (iii) endorsed the FSB's recommendations for adoption of the market reforms in respect of OTC derivatives; they welcomed continuing research by the IOSCO and the Committee on Payment and Settlement Systems on central counterparty standards, and approved the FSB's Principles for Reducing Reliance on CRA[337] Ratings [64]. The Leaders called upon the International Accounting Standards Board and the United States of America's Financial Accounting Standards Board to finish their accounting standards convergence project by the end of 2011, and encouraged the former to increase further the involvement of stakeholders (including emerging market economies) in the process of setting the worldwide standards [65]. The G20 Leaders repeated their commitment to stopping "non-cooperative jurisdictions" from presenting risks to the global financial system, and welcomed the on-going work by the FSB, the Global Forum on Tax Transparency and Exchange of Information, and the Financial Action Task Force [66]. The Leaders: (i) reaffirmed the FSB's role, at the worldwide level, in co-ordinating the tasks of domestic financial authorities and international standard setting entities in evolving and furthering the implementation of effectual policies for the financial sector, in the interests of global financial stability, (ii) asked the FSB to accelerate for review by Finance Ministers and Central Bank Governors its proposals to enhance its capacity, governance and resources in order to keep up with increasing demands, (iii) welcomed the FSB's outreach to emerging market economies, (iv) backed the establishment of consultative groups within the regions, and (v) welcomed the FSB's report concerning progress in the adoption of G20 recommendations for enhancing financial stability, and anticipated another progress report at the next summit [67].

The G20 Leaders stated that the following items justified further attention: (i) in order to manage systemic risks in the financial sector on a continuing basis, the FSB, the IMF and the BIS were to further research macroprudential policy frameworks – including tools to mitigate the effect of excessive capital flows; (ii) the FSB, the IMF and the World Bank were asked to report on financial stability matters that are of specific concern to emerging market and developing economies; (iii) the FSB was called upon to work in co-operation with other international standard setting entities to develop recommendations in order to strengthen the regulation and supervision of the shadow banking system[338], by the middle of 2011; (iv) the

---

[337] 'CRA' is an abbreviation for 'credit rating agency'. The abbreviated form is on the title page of the FSB's document, which it published on 27th October 2010 and which can be accessed at http://www. financialstabilityboard.org/wp-content/uploads/r_101027.pdf?page_moved=1.

[338] 'Shadow banking's is a difficult term to define. The concept describes transactions that might, by their substance, be undertaken by a bank but which are not, and transactions that are conducted by a bank that are unregulated or under-regulated. It is submitted that the aim of G20 Leaders was (and is) for there to be a

IOSCO's taskforce on commodities futures markets was requested to report to the FSB for consideration of the next steps in its work; (v) the IOSCO was called on to evolve by June 2011, and report to the FSB, recommendations to further the integrity and efficiency of markets, in order to mitigate the risks that "the latest technological developments" pose to the financial system; (vi) the FSB was requested to work with the OECD and other worldwide organisations on the exploration of options to promote the protection of consumer finance via "informed choice" – such as disclosure, education and transparency, and to report on this to the G20 Leaders at the next summit [68]. This meeting was to be held in Cannes, in November 2011.

2011

The Cannes Summit showed a broadening economic agenda, and the commencement of engagement groups within the umbrella of the G20 – initially B20 (B = Business) and L20 (L = Labour)[339], to be expanded by the end of 2015 to include C20 (Civil Society), T20 (T = Think (Tank)), W20 (W = Women) and Y20 (Y = Youth)[340]. In respect of international financial regulation, the Declaration from the Cannes Summit contains a section entitled "Implementing and deepening Financial sector reforms" in which the G20 Leaders stated a determination to satisfy a commitment that they made at the Washington Summit – to make sure that every financial market, instrument and participant is regulated or supervised "as appropriate to their circumstances in an internationally constituent and non-discriminatory way." [69]. This title's 5 subsections: "Meeting our commitments notably on banks, OTC derivatives, compensation practices and credit rating agencies, and intensifying our monitoring to track deficiencies," "Addressing the too big to fail issue," "Filling in the gaps in the regulation and supervision of the financial sector," "Tackling tax havens and non-cooperative jurisdictions" and "Strengthening the FSB capacity resources and governance," are described in the next paragraphs [70].

The G20 Leaders called upon jurisdictions to fulfil their commitment to "fully and consistently" implement the Basel II Framework and the Basel II.5 additional requirements on markets and securitisation by the end of 2011, and the Basel III Framework by 1st January 2019 [71]. They: (i) endorsed the FSB progress report on the implementation of the reforms for OTC derivatives, (ii) requested the IOSCO and the Committee on Payment and Settlement Systems to work with the FSB to progress research on identifying data that could be supplied to and by trade repositories, and to publish principles or guidance on the access of regulators and supervisors to data which trade repositories hold, (iii) required the BCBS, the IOSCO and "other relevant organizations" to generate, for consultation, standards on payments associated with OTC derivatives that are not cleared centrally – by June 2012, and (iv) called on the FSB to continue to report upon progress towards satisfying the G20 Leaders' commitments on

---

consistent level of regulation of all types of financial transaction, regardless of the counterparties to those deals. This is easier said than done.

[339] These 2 groups convened less formally prior to the Cannes Summit, under different names.

[340] It is submitted that these engagement groups could meet under the aegis of the United Nations, as this is the official international organisation for the determination of non-specialist issues. It is arguable that the United Nations should be carefully reformed and expanded to include the discussions which might take place at the G20 and/or its engagement groups, thereby putting these items on an official basis and providing the opportunity for most countries in the world (i.e., the United Nations membership) to contribute to them.

OTC derivatives [72]. The Leaders requested the FSB to undertake a continuing monitoring and reporting to the public on compensation practices, which is focused on deficiencies and impediments to complete implementation of the FSF/FSB Principles for Sound Compensation Practices, and conduct an on-going process for dealing with complaints – in order to address the "level-playing field concerns" of each organisation [73]. They called upon central banks, market participants, standard setters and supervisors to implement the FSB Principles for Reducing Reliance on CRA[341] Ratings, and to desist from practices that mechanistically rely on external credit ratings [74]. In order to intensify their monitoring of financial regulatory reforms, report on progress and track shortages, the Leaders endorsed the FSB's co-ordination framework for the monitoring of implementation, and committed to take all actions that are needed to progress in the areas in which deficiencies had been noted [75].

In order to ensure that no financial institution is 'too big to fail'[342] and that taxpayers are not charged for the costs of resolution, the G20 Leaders approved the FSB's comprehensive policy framework – which comprises a new global standard for resolution regimes, more effective and thorough supervision, requirements for resolution planning and for co-operation and recovery across borders, and (from 2016) additional specifications for absorbing losses for banks that are classified to be "global systemically important financial institutions." [76]. In addition, the Leaders: (i) asked the FSB, in discussion with the BCBS, to publish a progress report by April 2012 on the possible ways of efficiently extending the framework concerning "global systemically important financial institutions" to "domestic systemically important banks," (ii) requested the International Association of Insurance Supervisors to continue to work on a common framework for the superintendence of "internationally active insurance groups," (iii) called upon the IOSCO and the Committee on Payment and Settlement Systems to continue their research into "systemically important market infrastructures," and (iv) turned to the FSB, in deliberation with the IOSCO, to prepare methodologies to pinpoint "systemically important non-bank financial entities," by the end of 2012 [77].

In order to preclude possibilities for regulatory arbitrage and the accumulation of systemic risk, the G20 Leaders agreed to fortify the regulation and the supervision of the shadow banking system[343], and endorsed the FSB's initial 11 recommendations and work plan for the further development of these [78]. For the purpose of ensuring that the markets enable savings and investments to be allocated efficiently, the Leaders: (i) committed to implementing the IOSCO's initial recommendations on the efficiency and integrity of markets, and requested further work by the middle of 2012, (ii) called on the IOSCO to examine the functioning of credit default swap markets and the role of these in the determination of prices of the underlying assets, by the next G20 summit, (iii) supported the establishment of a global legal entity identifier, which uniquely specifies each party to a financial transaction, and (iv) asked the FSB to spearhead the co-ordination of work amongst regulators to prepare recommendations for the most suitable governance framework for a global legal entity identifier, by the next G20 summit [79]. The G20 Leaders: (i) welcomed the G20 study group report on commodities, (ii) endorsed the IOSCO's Final Report on the Principles for the Regulation and Supervision of Commodity Derivative Markets, and (iii)

---

[341] See fn 337.
[342] See fn 335.
[343] See fn 338.

called on the IOSCO to report on the implementation of these, by the end of 2012 [80]. They: (i) approved the FSB's Report on Consumer Finance Protection – including its enclosed High-level Principles on Financial Consumer Protection, which the OECD prepared[344], (ii) committed to "the full application" of the Principles within their territories, and (iii) asked the FSB, the OECD and "other relevant" organisations to report on the progress of the implementation of the Principles, and to publish further guidelines (if necessary) [81]. The Leaders: (i) endorsed the report by the FSB, the IMF and the World Bank on issues of specific interest to emerging market and developing economies, (ii) requested international organisations to take the concerns of these countries into account in planning new worldwide financial standards and policies, in instances in which this is appropriate, (iii) called upon the International Accounting Standards Board and the United States of America's Financial Accounting Standards Board to complete their accounting standards convergence project, and (iv) anticipated the completion of proposals to reform the governance framework of the International Accounting Standards Board [82].

The G20 Leaders: (i) asked the Global Forum on Transparency and Exchange of Information for Tax Purposes to complete the first round of its peer reviews of the legal framework of each jurisdiction for information exchange for the purposes of taxation, and to bring forward its peer reviews for the implementation of the international standards of transparency and exchange of information for taxation purposes by the end of 2012[345], (ii) urged all countries to take the actions required to remedy the deficiencies that were identified during their peer reviews, (iii) encouraged national regulators "to continue their work in the Global Forum," in order to ascertain ways to improve comprehensive exchange of information for taxation purposes, and (iv) encouraged more countries to ratify the Multilateral Convention on Mutual Administrative Assistance in Tax Matters[346], (v) with regard to prudential regulation, urged the 2 "non-cooperative jurisdictions" to take the measures that the FSB requests in order to respect "internationally agreed information exchange and cooperation standards," and (vi) encouraged all jurisdictions to fortify their anti-money laundering and counter-financing of terrorism systems, working together with the Financial Action Task Force [83]. In addition, they encouraged all jurisdictions to observe the international standards in the taxation, prudential and anti-money laundering and counter-financing of terrorism areas, and turned to the Financial Action Task Force and the OECD to work to ensure correct use of the corporate legal form [84].

Noting that the FSB had fulfilled a crucial role in furthering development and implementation of financial regulation, the G20 Leaders agreed to increase the FSB's capacity, governance and resources – in order to enable it keep up with this growing function.

---

[344] The Principles were prepared under the management of the OECD's Task Force on Financial Consumer Protection of the Committee on Financial Markets, and are in Annex J (pages 41-45) of the FSB's Report – which can be accessed at http://www.financialstabilityboard.org/wp-content/uploads/r_111026a.pdf.

[345] The peer reviews for jurisdictions are available on the OECD's website, at http://www.oecd-ilibrary.org/taxation/global-forum-on-transparency-and-exchange-of-information-for-tax-purposes-peer-reviews_2219469x; on 22nd October 2015, peer reviews had been submitted for many jurisdictions for both Phase 1 (Legal and Regulatory Framework) and Phase 2 (Implementation of the Standard in Practice) of the process.

[346] This Convention was created jointly by the OECD and the Council of Europe in 1988; it was amended by Protocol in 2010, to respond to the G20's call at its London Summit to bring it into alignment with the international standard on the exchange of information on request, and to make it available to all countries; on 1st June 2011, the amended Convention was opened for signature (Organisation for Economic Co-operation and Development (2015), Convention on Mutual Administrative Assistance in Tax Matters, <http://www.oecd.org/ctp/exchange-of-tax-information/conventiononmutualadministrativeassistanceintaxmatters.htm>).

The proposed changes were: (i) the placement of the FSB on an enduring institutional footing, with legal personality and a higher degree of financial autonomy, (ii) the reorganisation of the FSB's steering committee to include the executive part of the governments of the G20 Chair, the bigger financial systems, and the centres and geographical reasons that were unrepresented – in a way that is balanced and compatible with the FSB's Charter, and (iii) the strengthening of the FSB's role of co-ordination of the development of policy and the monitoring of implementation of the new regulations, in relation to other standard setting entities [85].

2012

The G20 summit in June 2012 was held in Mexico's Los Cabos municipality, which is located at the tip of the Baja California Peninsula. The Declaration from the Los Cabos Summit includes, amongst other things, a section entitled "Reforming the financial sector and fostering financial inclusion," elements of which the paragraphs below describe [86].

The G20 Leaders: (i) welcomed the FSB's progress report on advancing the G20 commitments to financial stability and its "enhanced monitoring" of national implementation of the changes, (ii) declared their dedication to "the timely, full and consistent implementation of agreed policies," so that financial crises may be prevented and "a stable and integrated global financial system" furthered, and (iii) promised to take all actions that are required to progress in the areas in which problems in the development of policy or in implementation had been noted [87]. Jurisdictions were required to introduce the necessary regulations to satisfy the G20 commitment to the clearing of OTC derivative contracts via central counterparties, by the end of 2012[347] [88]. The Leaders: (i) welcomed the BCBS's consultative proposals to fundamentally review the market risk aspects of the Basel Framework, (ii) welcomed progress on the development of principles for the identification of, and measures of policy for, "domestically systemically important banks," (iii) requested the FSB, in discussion with the International Association of Insurance Supervisors, to finish their work on the identification of, and policy measures for, "global systemic important insurers," by April 2013, (iv) anticipated the FSB's preparation, in consultation with the IOSCO, of methodologies to identify "other systemically important non-bank financial entities," by the end of 2012, (v) asked the International Association of Insurance Supervisors to continue in its development of a common framework for the superintendence of "international active insurance groups," by the end of 2013, (vi) encouraged actions that would increase clarity and competition amongst credit rating agencies, (vii) supported on-going work to achieve convergence to one set of high-quality accounting standards, and (viii) welcomed the IOSCO's Report entitled 'The Credit Default Swap Market'[348] [89].

The Leaders endorsed the FSB's recommendations in respect of the framework for the creation of a global legal entity identifier system, declared the system's launch by March 2013, and encouraged its worldwide adoption in order to assist authorities and market participants to pinpoint and manage financial risks [90]. They welcomed the FSB's study –

---

[347] The G20 Leaders made this commitment at the Pittsburgh Summit; see the subsection entitled '2009', above in this section.
[348] The IOSCO published this report in June 2012 – just in time for the Los Cabos Summit. It can be accessed at https://www.iosco.org/library/pubdocs/pdf/IOSCOPD385.pdf.

prepared with the IMF and the World Bank – to identify unintended outcomes of the "agreed financial regulatory reforms" for developing countries and emerging market economies, and encouraged the FSB to continue to monitor and report on, and all relevant participants to discuss, this issue – in order "to address material unintended consequences as appropriate" without detriment to their commitment to adopt those reforms [91]. The Leaders endorsed the recommendations, and the revised FSB Charter, for putting the FSB on a lasting institutional basis, and called for complete implementation of these recommendations by the next G20 summit [92].

In the taxation area, the G20 Leaders repeated their commitment to improve clarity and thorough exchange of information, commended the progress which the Global Forum on Transparency and Exchange of Information for Tax Purposes had reported, and urged all states to observe the international standard and implement the recommendations that the peer reviews had identified [93]. They supported the renewal of the Financial Action Task Force's mandate, approved the adoption of its revised standards and anticipated the implementation of these [94]. The Leaders: (i) welcomed the progress that the Global Partnership for Financial Inclusion had made in the implementation of the 5 recommendations in its 2011 report[349], and called on this organisation "to continue working towards their full implementation," (ii) endorsed the G20 Basic Set of Financial Inclusion Indicators that the Global Partnership for

---

[349] These recommendations are as follows: 1) encourage states to commit to further implementation of the 9 Principles for Innovative Financial Inclusion; 2) call upon the main standard setting entities to jointly explore the complementarities amongst their work and that of the Global Partnership for Financial Inclusion; 3) launch the SME Finance forum as a place to promote SME finance, welcome the SME Finance Policy Guide and acknowledge access to finance for business owned by women and agricultural SMEs as crucial for new jobs and sustainable growth; 4) welcome the progress made in fulfilling the G20's commitment to developing a finance framework that encourages capital for winning proposals from the SME Finance Challenge and for pursuing successful SME financing models on a larger scale, and 5) request the IMF to improve its collection of data on the provision of goods and services, and urge countries to develop and utilize data sources which are relevant to the measurement and monitoring of "policy success" (Global Partnership for Financial Inclusion (2011), GPFI Report to the Leaders: G20 Leaders Summit, Cannes, November 5th 2011, p.12, <http://www.gpfi.org/sites/default/files/documents/GPFI%20report%20to%20G-20.pdf>). The Principles for Innovative Financial Inclusion are as follows: "1. *Leadership*: Cultivate a broad-based government commitment to financial inclusion to help alleviate poverty. 2. *Diversity*: Implement policy approaches that promote competition and provide market-based incentives for delivery of sustainable financial access and usage of a broad range of affordable services (savings, credit, payments and transfers, insurance) as well as a diversity of service providers. 3. *Innovation*: Promote technological and institutional innovation as a means to expand financial system access and usage, including by addressing infrastructure weaknesses. 4. *Protection*: Encourage a comprehensive approach to consumer protection that recognises the roles of government, providers and consumers. 5. *Empowerment*: Develop financial literacy and financial capability. 6. *Cooperation*: Create an institutional environment with clear lines of accountability and co-ordination within government; and also encourage partnerships and direct consultation across government, business and other stakeholders. 7. *Knowledge*: Utilize improved data to make evidenced based policy, measure progress, and consider an incremental "test and learn" approach acceptable to both regulator and service provider. 8. *Proportionality*: Build a policy and regulatory framework that is proportionate with the risks involved in such innovative products and services and is based on an understanding of the gaps and barriers in existing regulation. 9. *Framework*: Consider the following in the regulatory framework, reflecting international standards, national circumstances and support for a competitive landscape: an appropriate flexible risk-based Anti-Money Laundering and Combating the Financing of Terrorism (AML/CFT) regime; conditions for the use of agents as a customer interface; a clear regulatory regime for electronically stored value; and market-based incentives to achieve the long-term goal of broad interoperability and interconnection." (G20 (2010), Innovative Financial Inclusion: Principles and Report on Innovative Financial Inclusion from the Access through Innovation Sub-Group of the G20 Financial Inclusion Experts Group, 25 May 2010, p.VII, <http://www.gpfi.org/sites/default/files/documents/Principles%20and%20Report%20on%20Innovative%20Financial%20Inclusion_0.pdf>).

Financial Inclusion had developed[350], (iii) recognised the crucial role of SMEs in economic development and the reduction of poverty, (iv) welcomed the initiation of the SME Finance Compact, which concerns the financing of SMEs in developing countries, (v) welcomed the pending conference of the Global Partnership for Financial Inclusion, on financial inclusion and standard setting entities, as a way of aiding the formation of "an enabling regulatory environment," and (vi) backed the continuing effort to establish a subgroup of the Global Partnership for Financial Inclusion, which is to focus on matters of financial literacy and consumer protection [95]. They acknowledged the work of states that are committed to domestic co-ordination strategies and platforms for financial inclusion under the G20 Financial Inclusion Peer Learning Program, encouraged attempts to further effectual implementation of the Principles for Innovative Financial Inclusion[351], and welcomed the inauguration of the Mexico Financial Inclusion Challenge: Innovative Solutions for Unlocking Access – which is to research innovations that address obstacles to financial inclusion via the creation of affordable, comprehensive, secure and valuable financial services [96].

The G20 Leaders: (i) approved the OECD/International Network on Financial Education High Level Principles on National Strategies for Financial Education, (ii) called upon these 2 organisations and the World Bank, in co-ordination with the Global Partnership of Financial Inclusion, to produce additional tools to advance financial education, (iii) acknowledged the need for women and young people to obtain access to financial education and services, and (iv) requested all 4 of these organisations to identify difficulties that these persons may encounter – and to report on this by the next G20 summit [97]. They endorsed the G20/OECD Task Force on Financial Consumer Protection's Action Plan for the development of effective methods to support the implementation of the High Level Principles on Financial Consumer Protection, and anticipate an update on this matter by the next G20 summit – which is to be held in St. Petersburg, in September 2013 [98].

2013

The Declaration from the St. Petersburg Summit includes a section that is entitled "Financial Regulation," which is divided into the following subtitles: "Achievements to date and a road ahead," "Towards a financial system that supports strong, sustainable and balanced economic growth," "Building resilient financial institutions and ending "too-big-to-fail"," "Promoting transparent, continuously functioning financial markets," "Addressing risks

---

[350] The Financial Inclusion Indicators are: 1) the percentage of adults who hold an account at a "formal financial institution," 2) the number of depositors or deposit accounts per 1,000 adults, 3) the percentage of adults with one or more current loans from a regulated financial institution, 4) the number of borrowers or current loans per 1,000 adults, 5) the percentage of SMEs which hold an account at a "formal financial institution," 6) the number of SMEs with deposit accounts as a percentage of the total number of deposit accounts, or the number of depositors that are SMEs as a percentage of the total number of depositors, 7) the percentage of SMEs with a current loan or credit line, 8) the number of SMEs with current loans or the number of current loans to SMEs, as a percentage of the total number of current loans, and 9) the number of branches of a financial institution per 100,000 adults (Global Partnership for Financial Inclusion (2012), The G20 Basic Set of Financial Inclusion Indicators, <http://www.gpfi.org/sites/default/files/G20%20Basic%20Set%20of%20Financial%20Inclusion%20Indicators.pdf>).

[351] See fn 349, for the G20's Principles of Innovative Financial Inclusion.

posed by the shadow banking," and "Tackling money laundering and terrorism financing"[352] [99]. Each of the following paragraphs describes the G20 Leaders' comments on these, in turn.

The G20 Leaders claimed to "have made substantial progress in implementing internationally consistent reforms to [their]. financial systems" since 2008, citing the Basel III Framework, the OTC derivatives' reforms, the legislation for "globally systemically important banks and insurers," the new resolution regime, and progression "in addressing potential systemic risks to financial stability" that arise from shadow banking, and making the following assertion [100].

> The international coordination and commitment to the implementation of these reforms is unprecedented.

Whilst one understands and appreciates their confidence, it should be left to history to determine the truth of this statement. It is submitted that more time is required from the few years since the end of the GFC, before firm conclusions can be drawn as to the development and implementation of the measures – and to the extent of their success.

The Leaders declared that they were advancing reforms in financial regulation which were aimed at lowering systemic risk and moral hazard, and nurturing a financial system which is stable and which underpins "sustainable and balanced economic growth." [101]. They expressed a determination to follow the agenda for financial reform through to its completion in a way that does not fragment the worldwide financial system, and committed to continuing to co-operate on all matters of financial regulation and to monitoring and gauging the effect of the reforms on that system's robustness, and on economic growth, stability and the availability of funds for investment in the long term [102].

The G20 Leaders welcomed the BCBS's work on assessing the consistency of the rules of jurisdictions with the Basel III Framework, its updated progress report on the implementation of that Framework, and the "recent BCBS report on the regulatory consistency of risk-weighted assets"[353]; they anticipated the BCBS's work "to improve the comparability of regulatory capital ratios," and expected the BCBS to complete its proposals on the net stable funding ratio and "the internationally harmonized leverage ratio" according to agreed procedures and schedules [103]. The Leaders: (i) welcomed the FSB's report on the progress that had been made, together with planned actions, towards terminating the 'too big to fail' problem[354], (ii) renewed their commitment to fully implementing the FSB's Key Attributes of Effective Resolution Regimes for Financial Institutions[355], in respect of all parts

---

[352] Unlike in the Declaration from the Los Cabos Summit, the issues relating to consumer protection, exchange of information for taxation purposes, financial education and financial inclusion appear in separate sections in the Declaration from the St. Petersburg Summit to those concerning international financial regulation.

[353] The G20 Leaders may have been referring to the report of the BCBS's Regulatory Consistency Assessment Programme, entitled "Analysis of risk-weighted assets for credit risk in the banking book," which is dated July 2013 and is available at http://www.bis.org/publ/bcbs256.pdf. The BCBS had also compiled, in January/February 2013, a report entitled "Regulatory consistency assessment programme (RCAP) – Analysis of risk-weighted assets for market risk," which is available at http://www.bis.org/publ/bcbs240.pdf.

[354] See fn 335, for an explanation of the concept of 'too big to fail'.

[355] This document, which the FSB published in October 2011, is available at http://www.financialstabilityboard.org/wp-content/uploads/r_111104cc.pdf?page_moved=1. The FSB issued a revised version of its Key Attributes of Effective Resolution Regimes for Financial Institutions on 15th October 2014, which is available at http://www.financialstabilityboard.org/wp-content/uploads/r_141015.pdf.

of the financial sector which may "cause systemic problems," (iii) promised to take the necessary steps to clear the way for the cross-border resolution of financial institutions, (iv) reaffirmed their commitment to making sure that supervisors have "strong mandates," sufficient resources and "independence to act," (v) turned to the FSB, in discussion with standard setting organisations, to generate proposals, by the end of 2014, on the capacity of "global systemically important financial institutions" to absorb losses in the event of bankruptcy, and (vi) called upon the FSB, in co-operation with the IMF and the OECD, to "assess cross-border consistencies and global financial stability implications" of "structural banking reforms" – taking into account the circumstances of individual states, and to report on this matter at the next G20 summit [104]. They welcomed the publication of the International Association of Insurance Supervisors' list of "global systemically important insurers," to which "enhanced group-wide supervision" and "resolution planning" were to apply, and anticipated the finalization of a simple group-wide capital requirement by the next G20 summit [105]. The Leaders requested the FSB, in discussion with the IOSCO and other standard setting organisations, to develop methodologies for the identification of "global systemically important non-bank non-insurance financial institutions," by the end of 2013 [106].

The G20 Leaders: (i) welcomed the FSB's report on progress in respect of OTC derivatives reforms, and the recent regulatory understandings on cross-border issues that relate to these reforms – anticipating the swift implementation of the latter, and (ii) called upon regulators, in co-operation with the FSB and the OTC Derivatives Regulators Group, to announce their timeline for determination of the remaining matters relating to regulatory arbitrage and to cross-border regimes that overlap [107]. They: (i) called on standard setting entities and domestic authorities to quicken progress in reducing reliance on credit rating agencies, (ii) urged additional actions to enhance clarity and competition amongst those agencies, (iii) anticipated the IOSCO's review of its Code of Conduct for such entities, (iv) supported the founding of the FSB's Official Sector Steering Group to co-ordinate research on the reforms that should be made in respect of financial benchmarks, (v) approved the IOSCO's Principles for Financial Benchmarks[356], and (vi) anticipated the necessary reform of the benchmarks that are used internationally in the financial markets and the banking industry, in accordance with the Principles for Financial Benchmarks [108]. The Leaders welcomed the FSB's progress report on the implementation of the FSF/FSB Principles for Sound Compensation Practices and of the FSB's Implementation Standards for these Principles[357], reaffirmed their commitment to ensuring that the Principles and the Standards are effected consistently, and requested the FSB to continue to monitor this matter [109]. They urged the International Accounting Standards Board and the United States of America's Financial Accounting Standards Board to finish their work on the main outstanding projects for accomplishing one set of high-quality accounting standards – by the end of 2013, and

---

[356] These were published by the IOSCO in July 2013, and are available at https://www.iosco.org/library/pubdocs/pdf/IOSCOPD415.pdf.

[357] Thus, jurisdictions are implementing implementation standards! The document to which the G20 Leaders refer is entitled "Implementing the FSB Principles for Sound Compensation Practices and their Implementation Standards: Second progress report," was published by the FSB on 26th August 2013, and is available at http://www.financialstabilityboard.org/wp-content/uploads/r130826.pdf.

encouraged efforts – including those of the Enhanced Disclosure Task Force[358] – to enable financial institutions to divulge more information concerning their risk profiles [110].

The G20 Leaders welcomed the progress made in the development of policy recommendations for the regulation and supervision of the shadow banking system. They agreed on a schedule of work on this matter [111].

The Leaders (i) backed the identification and the monitoring of jurisdictions with anti-money laundering and counter-financing of terrorism deficits, whilst recognizing states' good progress in satisfying the standards of the Financial Action Task Force, (ii) committed to taking actions to ensure that G20 countries fulfil those standards in respect of the identification of the beneficial owners of legal arrangements, and (iii) stated that they would ensure that information pursuant to the application of these standards is available in a timely way to pertinent authorities, in accordance with legal requirements for confidentiality [112]. They stated that the next G20 summit would take place in Brisbane, in November 2014 [113].

Brisbane and Antalya Summits; The FSB's Work in Progress

The focus of the Brisbane Summit was on growth and job creation, with financial sector reform making a small contribution to the G20 Leaders' Communiqué. The Leaders: (i) welcomed the FSB's proposal requiring "global systemically important banks" to hold additional capital that would shield taxpayers in the event of the failure of the former, (ii) endorsed the updated plan for further work in respect of "the shadow banking framework," (iii) called upon regulatory authorities to progress further in promptly implementing the G20 reforms on OTC derivatives, (iv) welcomed the FSB's plans to monitor the implementation and effects of the reforms, and to report on its priorities, and (v) welcomed the progress made to enhance "the orderliness and predictability of" the process for restructuring sovereign debt [114].

On 4th February 2015, the Chairman of the FSB, Dr. Mark Carney[359] wrote a letter to G20 Finance Ministers and Central Bank Governors, setting out the FSB's agenda in the wake of the Brisbane Summit[360]. The FSB is to step up its monitoring of jurisdictional implementation of the reforms, with the publication of its first annual report, FSB peer reviews that cover 4 aspects of the new rules[361], an FSB report that makes recommendations for improvement in

---

[358] The Enhanced Disclosure Task Force's Report of October 2012 succinctly states 7 fundamental principles for the enhancement of risk disclosures, which are as follows: Disclosures should: 1) "be clear, balanced and understandable," 2) "be comprehensive and include all of the bank's key activities and risks," 3) "present relevant information," 4) "reflect how the bank manages its risks," 5) "be consistent over time," 6) "be comparable among banks," and 7) "be provided on a timely basis" (Financial Stability Board (2012), Enhancing the Risk Disclosures of Banks: Report of the Enhanced Disclosure Task Force, 29 October 2012, p.6, <http://www.financialstabilityboard.org/wp-content/uploads/r_121029.pdf?page_moved=1>). The Report provides 32 recommendations for enhanced risk disclosures and, in Appendices A and B respectively, contains model formats for recommended disclosures and examples of good practice with regard to current disclosures by banks.

[359] Dr. Carney is currently the Governor of the Bank of England, having been a Deputy Governor, and later, the Governor, of the Bank of Canada.

[360] This letter is entitled "Financial Reforms – Finishing the Post-Crisis Agenda and Moving Forward," and is available at http://www.financialstabilityboard.org/wp-content/uploads/FSB-Chair-letter-to-G20-February-2015.pdf.

[361] These are as follows: the implementation of the G20's policy framework for "other shadow banking entities," effectual frameworks for the supervision of "global systemically important banks," the resolution and recovery

respect of "the resolvability of global systemically important banks," 2 IOSCO peer reviews[362], and the BCBS's continuing thorough reviews of the implementation in each jurisdiction of the Basel III Framework [115]. Dr. Carney noted "the slow and uneven implementation" of the reforms on OTC derivatives; the bar charts show tardy progress on 3 of the 4 planned reforms – the reporting of transactions to trade repositories being the exception [116]. Even though "much of the capital framework" for Basel III is in place, improvements are required with regard to "the consistency and comparability of capital ratios," and the BCBS is to continue to pursue agreement in respect of "the appropriate standard for the leverage ratio." [117].

In respect of point (i) above from the Brisbane Summit, the FSB settled the main issues concerning its proposed "international standard for total loss-absorbing capacity of global systemically important banks" at its plenary meeting in September 2015 [118, 119]. On 5th October 2015, the International Association of Insurance Supervisors published a document entitled "Higher Loss Absorbency Requirement for Global Systemically Important Insurers (G-SIIs)"[363], and is to revise this standard before its implementation in 2019, in order to include further work on the assessment methodology for these entities and on "insurance capital requirements." [120]. The FSB is co-ordinating research on guidelines for the resolution of central counterparties, an objective of which is to make certain that these entities are not 'too big to fail' [121, 122].

In order to help to ensure that the work to introduce comprehensive transaction reporting for OTC derivatives is effective in providing an overview of systemic risks and lowering the opaqueness of OTC derivative markets, the FSB is to publish a report that identifies obstructions to the aggregation, the reporting, and the sharing of important information concerning trades; this document will include an agreed timetable for addressing those difficulties – and the FSB is to inform the Antalya Summit as to specific countries in which action is needed on this matter [123]. The FSB asked the IOSCO and the Committee on Payments and Market Infrastructures to present, for consultation, guidance on the design of a worldwide Unique Transaction Identifier and Unique Product Identifier, in order to improve consistency in the reporting of trades[364] [124].

The FSB has published work programmes to address risks connected to: (i) the management of assets, and market liquidity (in collaboration with the IOSCO), and (ii) misconduct in financial institutions [125]. Furthermore, in response to the request of G20 Finance Ministers and Central Bank Governors in April 2015 to review the implications of climate change for the financial sector, the FSB has identified 3 types of risks from this source: physical risks – direct effect on property or disruption to trading, liability risks – the

---

planning requirements for, and the resolution powers of, banks; the effectiveness of the reporting of transactions in OTC derivatives to trade repositories (Financial Stability Board (2015), Letter from the Chairman of the Financial Stability Board to G20 Finance Ministers and Central Bank Governors: Financial Reforms – Finishing the Post-Crisis Agenda and Moving Forward, 4 February 2015, p.1).

[362] The IOSCO peer reviews are to cover "the timeliness of the implementation of reforms to money market funds and the alignment of incentives in securitisation" (Financial Stability Board (2015), Financial Reforms – Finishing the Post-Crisis Agenda and Moving Forward, 4 February 2015, p.1).

[363] This document is available from the International Association of Insurance Supervisors' website, at http://www.iaisweb.org/index.cfm?event=openFile&nodeId=57131.

[364] In August 2015, the IOSCO and the Committee on Payments and Market Infrastructures published a document entitled "Consultative report: Harmonisation of the Unique Transaction Identifier," which can be accessed from the website of the BIS at http://www.bis.org/cpmi/publ/d131.pdf, and from that of the IOSCO at http://www.iosco.org/library/pubdocs/pdf/IOSCOPD500.pdf.

risk of parties who have incurred damage seeking compensation, and transition risks –
financial risks that arise from the change "to a lower carbon economy" [126].

The Leaders' Declaration from the Antalya Summit covers a broad range of issues, with
global economic growth, international trade and the spread of wealth being matters that the
Turkish Presidency of the G20 has emphasized. Paragraphs 13 and 14 of the Declaration
contain comments on the financial sector reforms, as follows.

> Strengthening the resilience of financial institutions and enhancing stability of the
> financial system are crucial to sustaining growth and development. To enhance the
> resilience of the global financial system, we have completed further core elements of the
> financial reform agenda. In particular, as a key step towards ending too-big-to-fail, we
> have finalized the common international standard on loss-absorbing-capacity (TLAC) for
> global systemically important banks. We also agreed to the first version of higher loss
> absorbency requirements for global systemically important insurers [127].
>
> Critical work remains to build a stronger and more resilient financial system. In
> particular, we look forward to further work on central counterparty resilience, recovery
> planning and resolvability and ask the FSB to report back to us by our next meeting. We
> will continue to monitor and, if necessary, address emerging risks and vulnerabilities in
> the financial system, many of which may arise outside the banking sector. In this regard,
> we will further strengthen oversight and regulation of shadow banking to ensure
> resilience of market-based finance, in a manner appropriate to the systemic risks posed.
> We look forward to further progress in assessing and addressing, as appropriate, the
> decline in correspondent banking services. We will expedite our efforts to make further
> progress in implementing over-the-counter (OTC) derivatives' reforms, including by
> encouraging jurisdictions to defer to each other, when it is justified in line with the St.
> Petersburg Declaration. Going forward, we are committed to full and consistent
> implementation of the global financial regulatory framework in line with the agreed
> timelines, and will continue to monitor and address uneven implementation across
> jurisdictions. We welcome the FSB's first annual report on the implementation of
> reforms and their effects. We will continue to review the robustness of the global
> regulatory framework and to monitor and assess the implementation and effects of
> reforms and their continued consistency with our overall objectives, including by
> addressing any material unintended consequences, particularly for emerging markets and
> developing economies (EMDEs) [128].

In November 2015, the FSB published several reports and reviews; the G20 Leaders
mention some of the issues that these items cover, in the above passage. Of particular interest
are the documents entitled 'To G20 Leaders: Financial Reforms – Achieving and Sustaining
Resilience for All' and 'Implementation and effects of the G20 financial regulatory reforms',
to which the next 2 paragraphs, respectively, refer [129, 130].

In its letter to G20 Leaders, the FSB states that: (i) the implementation of the changes
"has substantially strengthened the resilience of the global system," (ii) it has finalized the
tools that are required "to end "Too Big To Fail" in the banking sector," (iii) the G20 is to
"remain vigilant to new risks and vulnerabilities," and (iv) it is emphasizing the effect of
reforms on developing countries and emerging market economies [131]. The FSB reports a
high level of enactment of Basel III capital and liquidity rules in its 24 jurisdictions[365], and

---

[365] These countries are Argentina, Australia, Brazil, Canada, China, France, Germany, Hong Kong SAR, India,
Indonesia, Italy, Japan, the Republic of Korea, Mexico, the Netherlands, Russia, Saudi Arabia, Singapore, South

the successful application of these standards by "internationally active banks"; it notes that, whilst all global systemically important banks have recovery plans and crisis management groups in place, plans for the resolution of these institutions require further work [132]. The FSB observes that the reforms for OTC derivatives are behind schedule, and specifies that: (i) 12 FSB jurisdictions have introduced central clearing frameworks which apply to more than 90% of their market, (ii) most FSB members "are in the early stages of adopting" margin requirements for non-centrally cleared derivatives, (iii) issues persist in respect of the quality and completeness of the data from the reporting of trades in OTC derivatives to trade repositories – which restricts the ability of the authorities to access, use and aggregate these items, and (iv) there are gaps and inconsistencies in requirements across jurisdictions – which may lead to fragmentation or to possibilities for regulatory arbitrage [133]. The tools are now available, including "a robust international standard for the total loss absorbing capacity (TLAC) that global systemically important banks need for orderly resolution without risks to public funds," for authorities to ensure that banks are not 'too big to fail'; these reforms seek to (i) remove "the implicit public subsidy" that international banks enjoy, (ii) ensure that shareholders and creditors (rather than taxpayers) bear the costs of bank failure, (iii) further "a level playing field for globally systemic banks," and (iv) give confidence to host countries that they will not be adversely affected by the insolvency of a global bank [134]. The FSB and the IOSCO have collaborated to identify risks that are connected to the management of assets and market liquidity; in 2016, they will continue work "on potential structural vulnerabilities and policy options to mitigate them." [135]. Worldwide banks have withdrawn their correspondent banking services from some countries, which may cause the local banks that are affected by this to lose their access to the global financial system; the FSB, the World Bank, the FATF and the Committee on Payment and Settlement Systems are to work together to (i) continue to assess "the dimensions and implications of the issue," (ii) clarify "regulatory expectations" in respect of correspondent banking and remittances, (iii) pursue "domestic capacity-building" in countries in which there are respondent banks that are affected by the withdrawal of correspondent banking services, and (iv) use technology in order "to improve the efficiency and effectiveness of customer due diligence" by both correspondent and respondent banks [136]. Whilst the G20 Leaders "ask the FSB to engage with public- and private- sector participants on how the financial sector can take account of climate change risks," [137] the FSB "recommend[s] to Leaders the establishment of an industry-led disclosure task force to develop recommendations for voluntary disclosures that effectively and efficiently meet the needs of investors and creditors." [138].

The FSB's Report to G20 Leaders entitled 'Implementation and effects of the G20 financial regulatory reforms' provides a rosy picture of the enactment and implementation of financial sector reforms by the FSB's constituent jurisdictions, especially with respect to the Basel III Framework and the FSF/FSB Principles for Sound Compensation Practices[366]. The FSB is not entirely satisfied with the speed of implementation of the OTC derivatives reforms in these countries, and is concerned that data in relation to cross-border trading in those

---

Africa, Spain, Switzerland, Turkey, the United Kingdom, and the United States of America (Financial Stability Board (2015), FSB Members, <http://www.financialstabilityboard.org/about/fsb-members/>). The FSB jurisdictions (including the EU) comprise the G20 Members, plus Hong Kong SAR, the Netherlands, Singapore, Spain and Switzerland (G20 (2015), G20 Members, <https://g20.org/about-g20/g20-members/>).

[366] The table on page 3 of the Report, which is entitled 'Implementation of reforms in priority areas by FSB jurisdictions', shows this in summary form.

instruments is not being shared between the relevant jurisdictions [139]. Resolution planning for banks whose failure may have a systemic effect is not fully in line with the FSB's Key Attributes of Effective Resolution Regimes for Financial Institutions[367] for the FSB jurisdictions outside Europe[368] – except for Canada, Japan, Mexico, Singapore and the United States of America [140]. The Report notes that the share of worldwide financial sector assets which are held by non-bank financial institutions has grown since 2008, whilst that of the banks has fallen – although remaining at over 40% [141]. This shift towards market-based finance illustrates the good sense of the G20 and the FSB, together with the International Association of Insurance Supervisors, the IOSCO and the Committee on Payment and Settlement Systems, to progress the identification and the regulation of global non-bank financial entities of systemic importance – thereby widening the scope of the management of possible sources of systemic risk[369].

Comment

The actions for financial reform that have taken place under the aegis of the G20 since 2008 are, on the whole, a constructive and welcome response to the GFC. Reforms concerning the banking sector, in particular, are comprehensive. The international financial institutions, whose actions the FSB has co-ordinated to date and continues to bring together, have worked hard on these matters – as has the FSB itself.

The key concern is that the measures put in place may stifle economic growth. The FSB points out that the banks have increased their buffers of capital mainly by retaining earnings and issuing shares, and that lending has not materially decreased [142]. This would indicate, other things being the same, that substantial levels of bank capital may be able to co-exist with a thriving real economy. However, it is possible that the need to maintain a high level of equity capital at all times may, in the long run, slow down the rate of bank lending. If growth is slowing in the real economy for reasons other than those originating in the financial sector, then governments are likely to require banks to maintain reasonable levels of lending. Banks may refuse to do this, if such a policy at the time has a substantial adverse effect upon their equity levels.

Thus, it is submitted that, in practice, there is a trade-off between financial stability[370] and economic growth – like the trade-off between inflation and unemployment that the Phillips

---

[367] See fn 355.

[368] The EU's legislation over this area is the BRRD, which "contains a comprehensive recovery and resolution regime for faulty banks and investment firms" (Baber, G. (2015), 'Deposit guarantee and bank recovery: Leads from the financial crisis?', *Company Lawyer*, 36(3), 83-85, at 85). In the United Kingdom, the Financial Services and Markets Act 2000 contains the necessary resolution powers, which are described in Baber, G. (2014b), 'The Prudential Regulation Authority: special measures for special times', *Company Lawyer*, 35(12), 353-360.

[369] The Report states: "The identification of G-SIFIs [global systemically important financial institutions] is underway. G-SIBs [global systemically important banks] and global systemically important insurers (G-SIIs) have been designated. A decision on the G-SII status of reinsurers has been postponed, pending further development of the assessment methodology. The assessment methodologies for non-bank non-insurer G-SIFIs will be finalized once the current FSB work on financial stability risks from asset management activities is completed," (Financial Stability Board (2015), Implementation and effects of the G20 financial regulatory reforms: Report of the Financial Stability Board to G20 Leaders, 9 November 2015, pp.9 and 30).

[370] This is likely to be the case if 'financial stability' is estimated by the amount of equity capital that financial institutions are required to hold. In practice, the latter is only one component of financial stability – low debt levels, for instance, being another.

curve shows. It may be possible, in practice, to 'shift' the trade-off curve between financial stability and economic growth – hopefully in the opposite direction to the adverse Phillips curve shift in the 1970s! It is possible that G20 macroeconomic policymakers are aware of this – hence the wish to couple global expansionary macroeconomic policy with the introduction of higher capital requirements for financial institutions and other tighter regulation for the sector. They would be aiming for a favourable move in any trade-off curve between financial stability and economic growth, so that the latter may be coupled with the former – especially in the long run.

Another factor that the G20, the FSB and international financial institutions need to consider in this context is the effect that the financial reforms have on developing countries – especially on those that are not members of the G20, the FSB or the BCBS. The IMF regularly reviews the economic and financial status of these states. Nevertheless, the considerable changes that the G20 has introduced may have substantial effects on developing countries; to the extent that these influences are adverse and are augmented by the maintenance of measures designed to further financial stability, the FSB may need to recommend a reduction in the pace of reform, and/or differential speeds of regulatory change in different parts of the financial sector. It is better for all states to progress forward slowly together than for a few countries to rush forward and the remainder to be left behind.

Another potential difficulty is that of overregulation. For instance, in respect of OTC derivatives, it is submitted that firms may consider it to be burdensome to promptly report every trade in an OTC derivative (or in any financial instrument) to a trade repositary. There are associated difficulties, such as that the data held by a trade repositary is entered incorrectly, deleted, misplaced, lost or stolen. Mitigating the risk of this is expensive and time-consuming. Cost-benefit analyses of the financial sector reforms might be helpful in assessing the extent to which these provisions are effective.

It is also noteworthy that the enactment of a rule does not guarantee the implementation of the practice that the former contains. Therefore, it is necessary for the authorities to continuously monitor the practices of the regulated entities – which is more difficult, time-consuming and expensive as the number and stringency of the rules increase. In the light of this, authorities have a responsibility to repeal, loosen or tighten, as appropriate, any specific regulation that is not adding value in terms of financial stability and/or economic growth. At best, this should be done at international level, in order to prevent the creation of possibilities for regulatory arbitrage between jurisdictions.

G20/FSB GUIDANCE AND EU LAW

The FSB and the BCBS monitor the extent to which their member jurisdictions have enacted the relevant standards – the Basel Accords in the case of the latter, and this, together with the compensation, OTC derivatives, resolution and shadow banking proposals in the case of the former[371]. The relevant table within the FSB's Report to the G20 Leaders shows

---

[371] The BCBS publishes progress reports on the adoption of the Basel Framework by its member jurisdictions. The latest of these the 9th progress report: see fns 327 and 331. The FSB monitors progress in the adoption of the post-GFC financial reforms by its member jurisdictions in its annual report to G20 Leaders. Pages 3 and 4 of the document entitled 'Implementation and effects of the G20 financial regulatory reforms: Report of the Financial Stability Board to G20 Leaders' provides a summary of this information, as at 31st October 2015. This document

that the bank resolution powers of transfer, bail-in and temporary stay are all available within the EU jurisdictions that are members of the FSB (France, Germany, Italy, the Netherlands, Spain and the United Kingdom), and that recovery and resolution planning are in place for "systemic banks" in these countries – although Italy only applies its resolution planning rules to global systemically important banks at present [143]. It is appropriate to investigate, using bank resolution as an example, how the guidance from the G20, the FSB and the BCBS has been adopted by the EU.

The Toronto Summit and the BCBS Recommendations

As stated above[372], at the Toronto Summit in June 2010 the G20 Leaders declared their commitment to the design and implementation of a robust system for the restructuring or the resolution of financial institutions, and to the implementation of the Recommendations of the BCBS's Cross-border Bank Resolution Group. These Recommendations are as follows.

1) Domestic authorities should be provided with suitable tools to address all types of financial institutions in trouble, in order to attain an orderly resolution that helps to minimise systemic risk, preserve financial stability, promote market efficiency, protect consumers and restrict moral hazard; examples of appropriate powers include those to transfer assets, business operations and liabilities to other entities, to found bridge financial institutions, and to resolve claims [144].

2) Each jurisdiction should establish a national framework, in order to co-ordinate the resolution of the legal entities of the financial groups within its territory [145].

3) Domestic authorities should pursue the convergence of national resolution measures towards those identified in Recommendations 1 and 2, in order to ease the co-ordinated resolution of financial institutions that operate in several jurisdictions [146].

4) Domestic authorities should consider the development of processes to facilitate the mutual recognition of resolution and crisis management across jurisdictions [147].

5) If domestic authorities consider that the group structures of financial institutions are too complex to allow orderly and cost-effective resolution, then they should consider the imposition of regulatory incentives on those entities that are designed to encourage simplification of the structures in a way that facilitates effectual resolution [148].

6) The contingency plans of "systemically important cross-border financial institutions and groups" are to provide a scheme to address a period of serious financial distress or instability – which is to maintain the business as a going concern, further the resilience of crucial functions, and ease the firm's or the group's swift resolution or winding-up (as necessary) [149].

7) The relevant home and host authorities should agree on arrangements that ensure the opportune disclosure and sharing of the necessary information, for both contingency

---

is available at http://www.financialstabilityboard.org/wp-content/uploads/Report-on-implementation-and-effects-of-reforms-final.pdf.

[372] See the subsection entitled '2010', in the section above entitled 'Progress in the G20/FSB System from November 2008'.

planning in normal conditions and crisis management and resolution during periods of stress [150].

8) Jurisdictions are to advance the use of techniques for risk mitigation that lower systemic risk and enhance the resilience of critical functions during a financial crisis or resolution; these methods include collateralization, enforceable netting contracts, and the separation of client positions [151].

9) Domestic resolution authorities are to be legally authorised to temporarily postpone immediate operation of early termination clauses in contracts, in order to complete a transfer of specified financial market contracts to a sound financial institution, a bridge financial institution, or another public undertaking; authorities should encourage industry groups, such as the International Swaps and Derivatives Association, to investigate the development of standardised contractual provisions which support these transfers in a way that lowers the risk of contagion in a crisis [152].

10) Domestic authorities are to consider, and include in their planning, principles or options for exit from public intervention, in order to reinstate market discipline and efficiency [153].

The Seoul Summit and the FSB's Key Attributes of Resolution Regimes

At the Seoul Summit in November 2010, the G20 Leaders reaffirmed the commitment that they made at the Toronto Summit for their jurisdictions to implement the Recommendations of the BCBS's Cross-border Bank Resolution Group[373] [154]. As stated above[374], they called upon the FSB to build on the BCBS's work and specify attributes of effectual resolution regimes by 2011. At the Cannes Summit in November 2011, the G20 Leaders welcomed, amongst other things, a new worldwide standard for resolution regimes[375]. This benchmark comprises the FSB's Key Attributes for Effective Resolution Regimes for Financial Institutions, which are the essential components that the FSB considers to be indispensable to a system of effective resolution[376] [155].

The Key Attributes specify 12 essential items that should be elements of the resolution regimes of all countries; these relate to: (i) scope; (ii) the resolution authority; (iii) resolution powers; (iv) set-off, netting, collateralisation and the segregation of client assets; (v) safeguards; (vi) the funding of firms in resolution; (vii) legal framework conditions for cross-border co-operation; (viii) crisis management groups; (ix) institution-specific cross-border co-operation arrangements; (x) resolvability assessments; (xi) recovery and resolution planning; (xii) access to information and information sharing [156]. A synopsis of these attributes follows.

---

[373] See the subsection entitled 'The Toronto Summit and the BCBS Recommendations', above in this section, for this commitment and for the Recommendations of the BCBS's Cross-border Bank Resolution Group.

[374] See the subsection entitled '2010', in the section above entitled 'Progress in the G20/FSB System from November 2008'.

[375] See the subsection entitled '2011', in the section above entitled 'Progress in the G20/FSB System from November 2008'.

[376] See fn 355, for the location of this document – which the FSB published in October 2011, and of its revised version – which the FSB issued on 15th October 2014.

1) *Scope*: Any financial institution that might "be systemically significant or critical" if it goes bankrupt, should be subject to a resolution regime that displays the FSB's Key Attributes – including holding companies, non-regulated operational firms within a financial group that are significant to its business, branches of foreign companies, and financial market infrastructures[377] [157].

2) *The resolution authority*: Each jurisdiction should designate an administrative authority that is, or administrative authorities which are, to be responsible for exercising the resolution powers over companies within the resolution regime's ambit [158]. The resolution authority should: (i) seek financial stability and ensure the continuance of "systemically important financial services," and of payment, settlement and clearing functions, (ii) protect depositors, investors and insurance policy holders, (iii) refrain from unnecessary breaking down of value, and attempt to minimise the costs of resolution and the losses to creditors, (iv) consider the potential effect of its resolution actions on financial stability in other countries, (v) be authorised to enter into agreements with resolution authorities of other states, (vi) be operationally independent, (vii) be subject to strict evaluation and accountability mechanisms to evaluate the effectiveness of resolution measures, (viii) possess the resources, the expertise and the functional capacity to put implementation measures into effect with regard to large, complex entities, (ix) be protected (together with its staff) against liability for actions taken and omissions made whilst carrying out their duties in good faith in the exercise of resolution powers, and (x) have ready access to firms, insofar as this is material "for the purposes of resolution planning and the preparation and implementation of resolution measures." [159].

3) *Resolution powers:* Resolution authorities should be empowered to: (i) remove and replace the directors and the senior management, and recover monies, (ii) appoint an administrator to manage the firm with a view to restoring it, or parts of its business, to sustainable, on-going viability, (iii) operate and resolve the firm – including powers to assign, continue and terminate contracts, buy or sell assets and write down debt, (iv) secure continuity of essential functions and services by requiring other companies within the same group to continue to provide these services to the entity in resolution, a successor or an acquiring organisation, ensuring that the entity in resolution is temporarily able to supply these services to a successor or an acquiring organisation, or obtaining the necessary services from unaffiliated third parties, (v) override the rights of shareholders of the company in resolution in order to allow measures to restructure and dispose of this entity's business or its assets and liabilities, (vi) transfer or sell assets, liabilities and legal rights and obligations to a solvent third party institution or a newly-founded bridge institution, (vii) establish at least one bridge institution on a temporary basis to take over and continue the performance of critical functions and on-going operations of the firm, (vii) found a separate vehicle (such a company or trust) for the management of assets, and transfer

---

[377] For the purposes of the FSB's Key Attributes of Resolution Regimes, a 'financial market infrastructure' is "a multilateral system among participating financial institutions, including the operator of the system, used for the purposes of recording, clearing, or settling payments, securities, derivatives or other financial transactions"; it includes central counterparties, central securities depositaries, securities settlement systems and trade repositories (Financial Stability Board (2011), Key Attributes of Effective Resolution Regimes for Financial Institutions, October 2011, fn 2, p.5).

to it non-performing loans and assets that are difficult to manage, (ix) conduct bail-in within resolution, in order to achieve (or help to achieve) continuity of essential operations, by recapitalizing the firm or, alternatively, by capitalising a newly-founded firm or bridge institution to which these functions were transferred after the unviable firm was terminated, (x) temporarily stay the exercise of rights to terminate a contract early, (xi) impose a moratorium in respect of payments to unsecured creditors (and clients) and a stay on the actions of creditors to collect property or money from the firm, whilst protecting the enforcement of permitted collateral and netting arrangements, and (xii) effect the closure and orderly liquidation of the whole, or part, of a firm that is failing [160]. Resolution authorities should be legally and operationally able to (i) apply resolution powers in combination or sequentially, (ii) apply different resolution powers to various parts of the firm's business, and (iii) commence a wind-down for those functions that the authorities consider not to be critical to the economy or the financial system [161]. In applying its resolution powers, the authority should exert its best efforts to avoid actions that may reasonably be expected to activate instability in other parts of the firm's group or in the financial system [162].

4) *Set-off, netting, collateralisation and the segregation of client assets:* The legal framework that governs collateralisation agreements, contractual netting, set-off rights and the segregation of client assets is to be "clear, transparent and enforceable during a crisis or resolution of firms," and is not to inhibit the effectual implementation of resolution measures [163]. "Subject to adequate safeguards," the onset of resolution and the exercise of resolution powers is not to trigger statutory or contractual rights of set-off, or constitute an event which entitles any of the firm's counterparties to accelerate or terminate its contract with the firm – as long as the substantive obligations under the contract continue to be carried out [164]. If contractual acceleration or early termination rights are nonetheless able to be exercised, then the resolution authority should be empowered to temporarily stay these rights – provided that they "arise by reason only of" the firm's entry into resolution or in association with the exercise of any resolution powers [165].

5) *Safeguards:* Resolution powers are to be exercised in a manner that observes the hierarchy of claims, whist providing flexibility to deviate from the general principle of equal treatment of creditors of the same class (with openness about the reasons for departures from that rule) – if this is necessary to contain the potential systemic effect of a firm's failure or to maximise value for the benefit of the creditors as a whole; equity should absorb losses before subordinated debt does, and the latter before senior debt does [166]. Creditors are to be entitled to compensation in cases in which they do not receive at least what they would have received in a winding-up of the firm under the relevant insolvency regime [167]. Officers of the entity under resolution should be legally protected for actions that they take in compliance with the resolution authority's decisions [168]. The legislation that establishes resolution regimes is not to provide for judicial actions that might constrain the implementation, or result in a reversal, of measures that resolution authorities have taken in good faith and within their legal powers; instead, this legislation should provide for redress through an award of compensation, if this is justified [169]. In order to maintain market confidence, jurisdictions should provide for resolution authorities to be able

to be flexible in permitting the firm to be temporarily exempt from divulgation requirements, or to postpone disclosures [170].

6) *The funding of firms in resolution:* Jurisdictions should ensure that resolution authorities do not need to rely on bail-out funds or public ownership in order to resolve firms [171]. If temporary sources of funding are required for the maintenance of critical functions for an orderly resolution, then the resolution authority or the entity that extends the temporary funding is to provide for the recovery of any losses that are incurred: (i) from shareholders and unsecured creditors – as long as the latter are no worse off than they would be in a winding-up of the firm under the relevant insolvency regime, or (ii) if necessary, from the financial system beyond the firm [172]. Jurisdictions should have in place privately-financed resolution funds or deposit insurance, or a funding mechanism for recovery from the financial sector of the costs of supplying temporary financing, in order to ease the resolution of the firm [173]. Any supply of temporary funding is to be subject to conditions that minimise the risk of moral hazard[378], and should include: (i) a statement that the provision of temporary funding is needed – in order to nurture financial stability, and will allow the implementation of a resolution option which is best able to satisfy the aims of an orderly resolution, and (ii) the allocation of losses to shareholders, and of residual costs (as appropriate) to unsecured and uninsured creditors and the financial sector [174]. As a final resort, and in order to preserve financial stability, jurisdictions may decide to empower the resolution authorities "to place the firm under temporary public ownership and control" so that it may continue to conduct essential functions – whilst attempting to arrange a permanent solution, such as a sale to, or a merger with, a commercial private sector purchaser[379]; if a state takes this decision, then it should provide for the recovery of any losses that it has incurred from unsecured creditors or (if necessary) the financial sector beyond the firm [175].

7) *Legal framework conditions for cross-border co-operation:* A resolution authority's statutory mandate should empower and encourage that entity to act to accomplish a co-operative outcome with foreign resolution authorities [176]. If a resolution authority takes discretionary national action, then it should consider the effect of this on financial stability in other countries [177]. The resolution authority is to be empowered to resolve local branches of foreign firms, and is to have the capacity to use these powers to support a resolution that a foreign home resolution authority carries out – for example, by ordering a transfer of property situated within its jurisdiction to a bridge institution that the latter authority has established; in the exceptional instances in which a host resolution authority exercises its discretion, it should notify and consult the home resolution authority beforehand [178]. Domestic laws and regulations are not to discriminate against creditors on the basis of the location of their claim, their nationality, or the country in which that claim is

---

[378] Moral hazard may arise in this context, because the providers of the temporary funding may not fully know what the resolution authority is doing, and, in particular, how the authority is allocating these funds and why.

[379] The United Kingdom Government directed the sale of the failing bank HBOS plc to Lloyds TSB Bank plc. This sale took place in January 2009. The Government held shares in both HBOS plc and Lloyds TSB Bank plc – which was renamed Lloyds Banking Group plc, and the shares of HBOS plc were converted to those of Lloyds Banking Group plc. At this point, the government owned 43 per cent of the Group's ordinary shares, which it has steadily sold. (Baber, G. (2014a), 'Legislative and regulatory responses to the global financial crisis from within the United Kingdom', *Journal of Financial Crime*, 21(2), 124-148, at 127).

payable; the treatment of creditors and their ranking in insolvency should be clear, transparent, and properly disclosed to all of them [179]. Countries are to provide for transparent, accelerated processes to effect foreign resolution measures – either by means of a mutual recognition process or by taking actions under the national resolution regime that support, and are consistent with, the measures that the foreign home resolution authority has taken; recognition or support of foreign measures should be conditional upon the fair treatment of creditors in the foreign resolution proceeding [180]. The resolution authority is to be empowered (subject to adequate confidentiality requirements and safeguards for sensitive data) to share information that relates to the group as a whole or to individual branches or subsidiaries, with relevant foreign resolution authorities – if sharing is required for recovery and resolution planning or for the implementation of a co-ordinated resolution [181]. Jurisdictions are to provide for statutory safeguards for the protection of information that that they receive from foreign resolution authorities [182].

8) *Crisis management groups:* Home and key host resolution authorities of all global systemically important financial institutions are to maintain crisis management groups, in order to enhance readiness for, and ease the management and the resolution of, a cross-border financial crisis that affects the firm; these groups should include central banks, finance ministries, resolution authorities, supervisory authorities, and the public entities that are responsible for guarantee schemes of relevant jurisdictions, and are to co-operate well with authorities in other countries [183].

9) *Institution-specific cross-border co-operation arrangements:* For all global systemically important financial institutions, there should be, at a minimum, institution-specific co-operation agreements between home and relevant host resolution authorities; these agreements should, amongst other things: (i) set out the objectives and processes for co-operation through crisis management groups, (ii) define the roles and responsibilities of the authorities before, and during, a crisis, (iii) set out the process for sharing information before, and during, a crisis – including sharing data with host resolution authorities that are not represented in the crisis management group, (iv) set out the processes for co-ordination in the development of the recovery and resolution plans for the firm, and for engagement with the latter, (v) lay down the processes for co-ordination amongst home and host resolution authorities as to the conduct of resolvability assessments, (vi) include agreed procedures for the home resolution authority to swiftly notify and consult host authorities, in cases in which there are substantial unfavourable developments which affect the firm – but before any measures of significance are taken, (vii) include agreed procedures for the host resolution authority to promptly notify and consult the home authority, in cases in which there are material unfavourable developments that affect the firm – but before significant measures are taken, (viii) supply a suitable amount of detail in respect of the cross-border implementation of each resolution measure, (ix) provide for high-level meetings between the home, and relevant host, resolution authorities to be held at least every year, in order to review the robustness of the resolution strategy for global systemically important financial institutions, and (x) provide for regular high-level reviews of the operational plans that implement the resolution strategies [184].

10) *Resolvability assessments:* Resolution authorities should regularly perform resolvability assessments that evaluate the feasibility and credibility of resolution strategies, in the light of the probable impact of the firm's failure on the financial system and the economy[380] [185]. In conducting these assessments, resolution authorities should examine, in particular: (i) the extent to which essential financial services, and payment, settlement and clearing functions, can continue to be carried out, (ii) the nature and the extent of intra-group risk exposures, and their effect on resolution – if they need to be unwound, (iii) the firm's capacity to deliver accurate, timely and sufficiently detailed information in order to assist its resolution, and (iv) the robustness of co-operation and information-sharing arrangements across borders [186]. The home resolution authority of a global systemic financial institution should carry out its group resolvability assessments; these evaluations should be co-ordinated within the entity's crisis management group, taking national assessments by host authorities into consideration [187]. Host resolution authorities that carry out resolvability assessments of subsidiaries that are situated in their jurisdiction, should co-ordinate as far as possible with the home authority which conducts the resolvability assessment for the whole group [188]. To improve the resolvability of a firm, supervisory authorities or resolution authorities should be empowered to require (if necessary) "the adoption of appropriate measures" – such as changes to the firm's business practices, organisation or structure, in order to lower the cost and complexity of resolution – taking into account the effect of these alterations on the integrity and stability of on-going business; to enable the continuity of systemically important functions, authorities are to assess whether to require these functions to be legally and operationally segregated in independent entities that are protected from difficulties elsewhere in the group [189].

11) *Recovery and resolution planning:* Jurisdictions should: (i) put in place a continuing process for recovery and resolution planning – which at least covers domestically-incorporated firms that may "be systemically significant or critical," in the event of their failure, (ii) require robust, credible recovery and resolution plans to be in place for all global systemically important financial institutions, and for any other company whose home resolution authority considers may have an effect on financial stability – if that organisation fails, and (iii) require the firm's senior management to be responsible for the provision of the necessary input to the resolution authorities for the evaluation of the recovery plans and the preparation of resolution plans [190]. Resolvability assessments should contribute to the recovery and resolution plan; this plan should consider the firm's particular circumstances, and is to reflect that entity's complexity, interconnectedness, extent of substitutability, nature and size[381] [191]. Supervisory and resolution authorities are to ensure that each firm for which a recovery and resolution plan is required, keeps a recovery plan which identifies options to restore financial viability and strength when the relevant firm is under

---

[380] A systemically important financial institution is 'resolvable', if it is feasible and credible for the resolution authorities to resolve that entity so as to shield its systemically important functions without substantial, widespread disruption and without requiring taxpayers to contribute (Financial Stability Board (2011), Key Attributes of Effective Resolution Regimes for Financial Institutions, October 2011, Annex II: Resolvability Assessments, Paragraph 1, p.27).

[381] Thus, the resolution plan is to be specific to the firm. Given the level of detail required to achieve this, it is essential that the plan is regularly updated, in order to change with the firm and its environment.

severe stress; recovery plans should include: (i) credible options to deal with a range of scenarios that include both firm-specific and market-wide stress, (ii) scenarios which address shortages of capital and "liquidity pressures," and (iii) processes to make sure that recovery options are promptly effected, in a range of situations of stress [192]. The resolution plan[382] is to include a resolution strategy, and an operational plan for the implementation of that strategy; the plan should identify, in particular: (i) the financial and economic functions whose continuity is crucial, (ii) appropriate resolution options to maintain those functions or to wind them down in an orderly way, (iii) data requirements in respect of the firm's business activities, structures and systemically important functions, (iv) potential obstacles to effective resolution, and actions to mitigate these difficulties, (v) actions to protect insurance policy holders and insured depositors, and to "ensure the rapid return of segregated client assets," and (vi) clear principles or options for the termination of the resolution process [193]. Jurisdictions should provide that firms are required to ensure the ability to maintain essential service-level agreements in situations of crisis and in resolution, and that the underlying contracts include terms which prevent them from being closed down as a result of "recovery or resolution events" and ease their transfer to a bridge institution or to a third party acquirer [194]. The home resolution authority should lead the evolution of the group resolution plan, in co-ordination with all members of the firm's crisis management group [195]. Host resolution authorities may maintain resolution plans for the firm's activities within their jurisdictions, co-operating with the home authority in order to ensure that each of these plans is as compatible as possible with the group resolution plan [196]. Supervisory authorities and resolution authorities are to ensure that recovery and resolution plans are regularly updated – at least once per year, and when there are material changes to a firm's structure or business – and routinely reviewed within the firm's crisis management group[383] [197]. The resolution strategy for each global systemic financial institution should be subject, at least once each year, to a high-level review by the home, and relevant host, resolution authorities; the operational plans to implement a resolution strategy are to be appraised, at least annually, by "appropriate senior officials" at those authorities [198]. If resolution authorities are dissatisfied with a firm's recovery and resolution plan, then they should require that entity to take "appropriate measures" in order to address the plan's weaknesses [199].

12) *Access to information and information sharing:* Jurisdictions are to ensure that there are no legal, policy or regulatory impediments to "the appropriate exchange of information" between central banks, finance ministries, public organisations that are responsible for guarantee schemes, resolution authorities and supervision authorities [200]. They should require firms to keep management information systems that are able to promptly provide data, at all times; this information should be available at both group and company levels [201].

---

[382] This plan is intended to ease the effective use of resolution powers, in order to secure systemically important functions – with the objective of making the resolution of any firm possible without serious disruption and without requiring taxpayers to contribute (Financial Stability Board (2011), Key Attributes of Effective Resolution Regimes for Financial Institutions, October 2011, Paragraph 11.6, p.17).

[383] See fn 381.

On 15th October 2014, the FSB published additional guidance, which provides further detail in respect of particular Key Attributes; this guidance concerns the sharing of information for the purposes of resolution, and sector-specific advice that sets out how these attributes should be applied for financial market infrastructures, insurance firms, and the protection of client assets during resolution [202]. The FSB did not make changes to the text of the 12 Key Attributes of October 2011 [203]. On 9th November 2015, it encouraged jurisdictions to swiftly implement both its Key Attributes and its Principles for Cross-border Effectiveness of Resolution Actions[384] [204].

The BRRD

The EU adopted the BRRD on 15th May 2014. The measures for transposing this Directive into the laws of Contracting Parties to the EEA Agreement[385] (henceforth, following the BRRD, referred to as 'Member States') came into force on 1st January 2015 [205]. As the dates of publication of the Basel Committee's Recommendations and the original version of the FSB's Key Attributes of Effective Resolution Regimes precede that of the adoption of the BRRD, it is reasonable to expect consistency between the Recommendations/Key Attributes and the provisions of the Directive. This subsection investigates the extent to which the BRRD incorporates the Recommendations and the Key Attributes, in order to illustrate whether EU law is consistent with the relevant international standards with regard to bank recovery and resolution.

The BRRD applies to: (i) credit institutions and investment firms that are established in the EEA[386]; [206]. (ii) financial institutions that are subsidiaries of financial holding companies, mixed financial holding companies, mixed-activity holding companies, parent financial holding companies in a Member State, Union parent financial holding companies, parent mixed financial holding companies in a Member State, and Union parent mixed financial holding companies[387]; [207]. (iii) all the types of company that are listed in point (ii); [208]. (iv) branches of credit institutions and investment firms that are founded outside the EEA, in accordance with the conditions that the BRRD lays down [209]. This is consistent with Key Attribute 1 of the FSB, although the Directive does not cover insurance companies and pension funds – which may be within the description in Key Attribute 1 of "any financial institution"[388]. The BCBS considers that resolution authorities are to be

---

[384] The FSB published the document entitled 'Principles for Cross-border Effectiveness of Resolution Actions' on 3rd November 2015. This item is available at http://www.financialstabilityboard.org/wp-content/uploads/Principles-for-Cross-border-Effectiveness-of-Resolution-Actions.pdf. The Principles contain statutory and contractual mechanisms that jurisdictions should consider including within their laws, in order "to provide cross-border effect to resolution actions in accordance with the Key Attributes" (Financial Stability Board (2015), Principles for Cross-border Effectiveness of Resolution Actions, 3 November 2015, p.5).

[385] The BRRD is labelled a 'Text with EEA relevance'.

[386] As the BRRD is a ''Text with EEA relevance', references to the "Union" within this Directive are deemed to be to the whole of the EEA – i.e., to Iceland, Liechtenstein and Norway, in addition to the 28 EU Member States.

[387] All of these terms (including 'financial institution' and 'subsidiary') are defined in Article 2(1) of the BRRD and Article 4(1) of the CRR. The detailed definitions are omitted here.

[388] See the subsection entitled 'The Seoul Summit and the FSB's Key Attributes of Resolution Regimes', above in this section, for FSB Key Attribute 1: Scope.

equipped with "suitable tools to address all types of financial institutions in trouble"[389], which may be a wider category of organisations than the entities to which Article 1(1) of the BRRD refers[390].

Each Member State is to specify "one or, exceptionally, more resolution authorities," which are empowered to exercise the resolution powers and use the resolution tools [210]. The resolution authority is to be a public administrative authority (or authorities), which is "entrusted with public administrative powers." [211]. These provisions are consistent with Key Attribute 2 of the FSB – although the 'exceptionally' term in the BRRD is not in the Key Attribute[391].

Member States are to ensure that each resolution authority "has the experience, resources and operational capacity to apply resolution actions," and that it may exercise its powers sufficiently swiftly and adaptably to be able to attain the objectives of the resolution [212]. This provision is compatible with BCBS Recommendation 1 – in which the achievement of an orderly resolution may be considered to be the objective of the resolution, although the Directive specifies required qualities of the resolution authority – which the Recommendation does not[392].

Member States are to ensure that the recovery plan includes all the information that Section A of the BRRD's Annex contains, and may require further data to be entered into this plan [213]. According to Section A, the recovery plan is to include the following information: (i) a summary of the plan's main elements and of the firm's "overall recovery capacity," (ii) a summary of the material changes to the company since the most recent recovery plan, (iii) a communication and disclosure plan, which outlines how the firm intents to manage any potentially adverse market reactions, (iv) "a range of capital and liquidity actions" that are required to preserve or restore the firm's "viability and financial position," (v) an estimate of how long each element of the plan will take to carry out, (vi) a detailed description of any substantial hindrance to the effective, prompt execution of the plan, (vii) identification of essential functions, (viii) a detailed description of the methods for determining the value and the marketability of the firm's main business lines, assets and operations, (ix) a detailed explanation of how recovery planning is integrated into the firm's corporate governance structure and of the policies and procedures for the plan's approval, and identification of the persons within the organisation who are responsible for the preparation and the implementation of the plan, (x) arrangements and actions to preserve or restore the firm's own funds, (xi) arrangements and measures to ensure that the firm has sufficient access to sources of funding to anticipate the occurrence of unforeseen events, an examination of collateral that is available, and an evaluation of the possibility of the transfer of liquidity between companies and business lines within the group, in order to ensure that the firm is able to continue to conduct its operations and fulfil its obligations as these become due, (xii) arrangements and measures to lower leverage and risk, (xiii) arrangements and actions to restructure liabilities, (xiv) arrangements and measures to reform business lines, (xv) arrangements and actions that are needed to support continuous access to the infrastructures

---

[389] See the subsection entitled 'The Toronto Summit and the BCBS Recommendations', above in this section, for BCBS Recommendation 1.
[390] See above in this paragraph, for Article 1(1) of the BRRD.
[391] See the subsection entitled 'The Seoul Summit and the FSB's Key Attributes of Resolution Regimes', above in this section, for FSB Key Attribute 2: The resolution authority.
[392] See the subsection entitled 'The Toronto Summit and the BCBS Recommendations', above in this section, for BCBS Recommendation 1.

of financial markets, (xvi) arrangements and measures that are required to sustain the continuous operation of the firm's operational processes, (xvii) preparatory arrangements to ease the sale of assets or business lines in a timeframe that is suitable for the restoration of financial health, (xviii) order management strategies or actions "to restore financial soundness," and the anticipated financial impact of these, (xix) preparatory measures that the firm has taken, or plans to take, in order to ease the implementation of the recovery plan, and (xx) a framework of indicators that identifies the points at which suitable actions to which the plan refers, may be taken [214]. These items are compatible with the recommended contents of recovery plans in Key Attribute 11 of the FSB – although it is possible that recovery plans which implement the information requirements of Section A of the BRRD's Annex will not fully cover the FSB's requirements[393].

The resolution authority, after consulting the competent authority and the resolution authorities of the countries in which any major branches are situated, is to construct a resolution plan for each credit institution and investment firm that is not part of a group[394] [215]. Resolution authorities may require firms to help them to draw up, and to update, the plans [216]. Member States are to ensure that resolution authorities are empowered to require firms to co-operate as much as is necessary in the construction of resolution plans, and supply them with all of the information that they need to draw up and carry out these plans; in particular, the resolution authorities are to be empowered to require the data that Section B of the Annex specifies [217]. According to Section B, resolution authorities may request banks and investment firms to supply (at least) the following information – for the purpose of constructing and maintaining resolution plans: (i) a detailed description of the firm's organisational structure, (ii) "identification of the direct holders," and of the percentage held by each of the firm's group companies of the voting and non-voting rights, (iii) the location of, country of incorporation of, and "key management associated with," every group company of the firm, (iv) "a mapping of" the firm's essential operations and its main business lines – including substantial liabilities and holdings of assets that relate to these operations and business lines – "by reference to legal persons," (v) a detailed description of the components of the liabilities of the firm and of each of its group companies, (vi) details of the firm's liabilities that are "eligible liabilities"[395], (vii) an identification of the processes that are necessary, in order to determine the persons to whom the firm has pledged – and those who hold – the collateral, and the state in which this collateral is situated, (viii) a description of the off-balance sheet risk exposures of the firm and its group companies – including a mapping to its essential operations and main business lines, (ix) the institution's substantial hedges – including a mapping to its group companies, (x) identification of the firm's main, and its

---

[393] See the subsection entitled 'The Seoul Summit and the FSB's Key Attributes of Resolution Regimes', above in this section, for FSB Key Attribute 11: Recovery and resolution planning.

[394] It is submitted that the legislators should insert a provision that requires the preparation of a revision plan for each credit institution and investment firm that belongs to a group, which is separate from, and in line with, the group resolution plan. The information requirements of Section B of the Annex to the BRRD includes references to legal entities, other than the particular credit institution or investment firm, which are part of that credit institution's or investment firm's group; see below in this paragraph, for these information requirements – in which those entities are referred to as "the firm's group companies." This information is also required for the group resolution plan – see the next paragraph.

[395] 'Eligible liabilities' are capital instruments and liabilities that are not Common Equity Tier 1, Additional Tier 1 or Tier 2 instruments of an entity to which the BRRD applies, which Article 44(2) of this Directive does not exclude from the ambit of the bail-in tool (BRRD, Article 2(1)(71)). For example, covered deposits are excluded (BRRD, Article 44(2)(a)).

"more critical," counterparties, and an analysis of the effect of the failure of those counterparties on the financial situation of the firm, (xi) each system on which the firm carries out a substantial number, or "value amount," of trades – including a mapping to the firm's group companies, essential operations and main business lines, (xii) each payment, settlement and clearing system of which the firm is a member – including a mapping to the firm's group companies, essential operations and main business lines, (xiii) a detailed list and description of the main management information systems – including a mapping to the firm's group companies, essential operations and main business lines, (xiv) an identification of the owners of these management information systems, service-level agreements that relate to those systems "and any software and systems or licences – including a mapping to the firm's group companies, essential operations and main business lines, (xv) "an identification and mapping of the legal persons and the interconnectedness and interdependence among the different legal persons," such as shared facilities, personnel and systems, (xvi) the competent authority and the resolution authority of each of the firm's group companies, (xvii) the director who is responsible for supplying the data that is needed to prepare the firm's resolution plan, and (if different) the directors/managers of the firm's group companies, essential operations and main business lines, (xviii) a description of the arrangements that the firm has in place, in order to ensure that, if resolution is required, the resolution authority will have all the information that it needs to be able to apply the resolution powers and tools, (xix) all of the agreements that the firm and its group companies have entered into with third parties, the termination of which may be set off by the resolution authority's decision to apply a resolution tool, and whether the consequences of this cessation may affect the resolution tool's application, and (xx) a description of sources of liquidity that may be available to support resolution, and (xxi) data on "booking practices," the encumbrance of assets, liquid assets, strategies for hedging, and activities that are not recorded on the face of the balance sheets of the firm or its group companies [218]. This detailed information is consistent with points (i), (ii), and (iii) of the resolution plan in Key Attribute 11 of the FSB; however points (iv), (v) and (vi) are not expressly covered in Section B of the BRRD's Annex[396].

Member States are to ensure that group-level resolution authorities, together with the resolution authorities of subsidiaries within the group and after consulting the resolution authorities of major branches, construct a group resolution plan [219]. The group resolution plan is to: (a) set out the resolution actions that are to be taken in respect of entities within the group, (b) assess the extent to which the resolution powers and tools might be applied and exercised in a co-ordinated manner to companies within the group that are founded within the EEA, and identify any potential obstacle to a co-ordinated resolution, (c) identify suitable arrangements for co-operation and co-ordination with the relevant authorities of those third countries in which group companies are located, (d) identify measures that are needed to facilitate group resolution – once the conditions for resolution have been satisfied, (e) set out any additional actions that the group-level resolution authority intends to take with regard to the resolution of the group, and (f) identify how group resolution measures could be funded [220]. Parent companies situated within the EEA are to submit the information that Article 11 of the BRRD may require, to the group-level resolution authority [221]. This information comprises all of the data that resolution authorities need in order to construct and carry out

---

[396] See the subsection entitled 'The Seoul Summit and the FSB's Key Attributes of Resolution Regimes', above in this section, for FSB Key Attribute 11: Recovery and resolution planning.

resolution plans, including those items specified in Section B of the BRRD's Annex[397]. The adoption of the group resolution plan is to be a joint decision of the group resolution authority and the resolution authorities of the group's constituent companies [222]. These provisions do not satisfy that part of Key Attribute 11 of the FSB which concerns group resolution plans – i.e., not all the members of the firm's crisis management group (if constituted in accordance with Key Attribute 8 of the FSB) are involved in the group resolution plan's development, and there is no comment as to whether host resolution authorities are to maintain resolution plans for the firm's activities within their jurisdictions (as Key Attribute 11 requires)[398].

Each resolution plan is to be reviewed, and updated as necessary, at least annually and after any substantial changes to the credit institution's or investment firm's business or financial position that may necessitate a revision [223]. Similarly, Member States are to ensure that group resolution plans are reviewed, and updated as appropriate, at least every year and after any change to the group's, or to a group company's, legal or organisational structure, business, or financial position that could materially affect, or require an alteration to, the plan [224]. These provisions are compliant with the relevant element of Key Attribute 11 of the FSB – although there is no mention of either a routine review of the resolution plan (or of the group resolution plan) by the firm's crisis management group, or of the regular update of recovery plans – as required by the crisis management group[399].

Analysis

Although the review in the previous subsection is not comprehensive, a sufficient number of provisions of the BRRD have been inspected for the application of the BCBS Recommendations and the Key Attributes of the FSB to show that, whilst EU legislators have placed some of these international guidelines into the Directive, other items within those guidelines have been partly applied or omitted. Furthermore, there are provisions within the BRRD that do not address issues that are contained in the Recommendations or the Key Attributes – for example, Articles 7 and 8 of the BRRD consider group recovery plans – a term that is omitted from both the BCBS's and the FSB's document.

This result raises issues as to the purpose of the international soft-law instruments, such as the FSB's Key Attributes of Resolution Regimes. If the G20, the FSB, the BCBS, the IOSCO and other international organisations expect jurisdictions to enact and implement international standards literally and/or specifically, then they would need to keep a close watch on both the content of national legislation and the practices of financial institutions that are required to comply with the rules. This may be costly, with regard to the time, the expertise and the resources – of the international standard-setters, the regional and national supervisory bodies, and the financial institutions.

By contrast, if the purpose of the international guidelines is to lay down principles to which jurisdictions should adhere, but with which they are not required to comply to the

---

[397] See the previous paragraph, for Section B of the Annex to the BRRD.

[398] See the subsection entitled 'The Seoul Summit and the FSB's Key Attributes of Resolution Regimes', above in this section, for FSB Key Attribute 11: Recovery and resolution planning, and for FSB Key Attribute 8: Crisis management groups.

[399] See the subsection entitled 'The Seoul Summit and the FSB's Key Attributes of Resolution Regimes', above in this section, for FSB Key Attribute 11: Recovery and resolution planning.

letter, then the superintendence of the adoption and implementation of these instruments will be less expensive than in the scenario described in the previous paragraph. Nonetheless, there is a risk that countries will deviate from adoption of aspects of the international guidelines, which may provide opportunities for regulatory arbitrage.

In this context, the central theme is thus. What is the future of international financial law to be? Is the model for the EU to be followed, for the purposes of regulatory uniformity? Or, alternatively, is a consensus approach to be pursued, which would allow for jurisdictions to display minor deviation in their laws and administrative provisions from international standards? If the former approach is preferred, then there are missing elements at present. There is no global court that has the authority to annul national provisions that do not comply with the standards of the FSB, the BCBS, and other international organisations. The jurisdiction of the International Court of Justice does not extend to cases of this type. In the EU model, the Court of Justice of the European Union nullifies national laws that are at variance with provisions of EU law[400]. Furthermore, it is currently accepted that these standards are soft-law instruments, i.e., states are expected to follow the spirit of the rules, but are not required to apply them literally.

If the latter approach is favoured, then the international authorities would need to monitor the supervision – and the practices – of financial institutions within their jurisdictions. I have previously argued in favour of soft law instruments at the international level, as follows [225].

This combination of "hard law" at national level and "soft law" at international level provides a good balance between certainty and flexibility. The certainty of hard law is required at national level, so that participants within the financial sector there are aware of their rights and obligations. Sufficient certainty is also provided at the international level, since the majority of countries who respect the international standards and guidelines implement broadly similar requirements.

Flexibility is provided at both regulatory levels, too. The FSB's Membership comprises the finance departments, national banks, and regulators from 24 developed and large developing countries, together with the international standard-setting bodies and other international organisations such as the IMF and the European Central Bank (ECB). This enables a thorough discussion to take place at the FSB, both at the level of the Plenary and also at that of the standing committees and working groups. At the national level, the soft law provides the legislators and regulators with room to consider the local business conditions within the financial sector.

To work well, this approach depends upon the maintenance of at least a reasonable level of trust between the international organisations and the national regulators, and also between the

---

[400] Article 260(1) of the TFEU states: "If the Court of Justice of the European Union finds that a Member State has failed to fulfil an obligation under the Treaties, the State shall be required to take the necessary measures to comply with the judgement of the Court". 'An obligation under the Treaties' includes the duty to comply with: (i) provisions of the TEU, of the TFEU, and of Regulations, (ii) directly effective provisions of Directives, (iii) Decisions – for their addressees, and (iv) EU case law. For example, in EU cases C367/98 *Commission v Portugal* [2002] ECR I-4731 and C463/00 *Commission v Spain* [2003] ECR I-4581, the European Court of Justice (as it then was) annulled provisions of Portuguese and Spanish law, respectively, as being contrary to Article 63 of the TFEU (formerly Article 56 of the Treaty Establishing the European Community, and, before this, Article 73b of the Treaty Establishing the European Community). The practice of the Court, especially since the landmark case of 120/78 *Rewe-Zentral v Bundesmonopolverwaltung für Branntwein* ('Cassis de Dijon') [1979] ECR 649, of striking out legal provisions of Member States that it considers to be incompatible with EU law, is called 'negative integration'.

latter and the financial institutions that they superintend. Furthermore, the FSF/FSB, the BCBS and the IOSCO have published many documents that contain international standards, especially since the GFC. Given the FSB's prolific output immediately prior to the Antalya Summit in November 2015, national legislatures and financial regulators will be busy over the coming years. There is a risk that this approach will lower levels of trust between international organisations and the domestic regulators, and between national legislators/supervisors and the firms that they oversee – as, in both cases, the latter holds the former responsible for the voluminous requirements. It is the responsibility of the international organisations, as the most senior participants in the financial regulatory system, to set and to maintain a tone that fosters a high level of trust. If they are able to do this, then the 'hard law/soft law' system is likely to continue to work well.

COMMENTS

The international agenda since the GFC has driven a considerable portion of the legislative response. As demonstrated above[401], the G20, the FSB, and several other international organisations have agreed, and published, standards on financial regulation and on other related areas, which their member jurisdictions are expected to adopt. The EU legislature has risen to the challenge, with a supply of new legislation – some of which are Regulations. This cross-hatches with the EU's pursuit of the internal market over the area of the provision of financial services, which it has pursued rigorously since the publication of the Financial Services Action Plan in 1999.

The GFC may have accelerated a trend towards the integration of financial law. In the 20th Century, regulation of the sector in the United Kingdom has changed from piecemeal and haphazard, through partial and segmented, to uniform – with the passing of the Financial Services and Markets Act 2000. However, the creation of novel legal structures, the introduction of new financial instruments and the pursuit of different methods and venues of trading, have led to increasing need for further financial legislation. In addition to this, the EU has been pursuing a harmonising approach to financial regulation, with regular consolidations of banking, securities and insurance laws. International moves towards the standardisation of financial law – described above in this chapter – have contributed to the trend towards integration. Since 2008, i.e., at the height of the GFC, more rules have emanated from all of these levels.

CONCLUSION

The G20 has promulgated a programme for financial sector reform for its jurisdictions, in the wake of the GFC. The FSB is responsible for co-ordinating the development and the implementation of these reforms. Whilst the changes are substantial – and contribute towards an integrated global financial regulatory system, it is too early to provide an accurate judgment as to the extent of their success.

---

[401] See the section entitled 'Progress in the G20/FSB System from November 2008'.

The co-ordinated, worldwide response to the GFC is impressively swift. Nonetheless, some doubts have been expressed in respect of the approach that the G20 and the international organisations have taken. The content of these reforms affects the substance of much of the post-crisis EU legislation. In the next chapter, the establishment and role of the EU's sectoral architecture is to be considered, as a necessary aspect of the development of the new rules.

REFERENCES

[1] G20 (2007). The Group of Twenty: a History, pp.8-27. http://www.g20.utoronto.ca/docs/g20history.pdf.

[2] G20 (2008). *Declaration Summit on Financial Markets and the World Economy*, Washington D.C., 15/11/08, Paragraphs 1-2, p.1. https://g20.org/wp-content/uploads/2014/12/Washington_Declaration_0.pdf.

[3] H. Tietmeyer (1999). International Cooperation and Coordination in the Area of Financial Market Supervision and Surveillance, Report by Hans Tietmeyer, President of the Deutsche Bundesbank, 11/02/99, pp.1-3 and 6-7. http://www.financialstabilityboard.org/wp-content/uploads/r_9902.pdf.

[4] Financial Stability Board (2015). Our History. http://www.financialstabilityboard.org/about/history/.

[5] G20 (2008). *Declaration Summit on Financial Markets and the World Economy*, Paragraph 9, p.3, and Action Plan, p.5.

[6] G20 (2009). London Summit – Leaders' Statement, London, 02/04/09, Paragraph 15, p.3. https://www.imf.org/external/np/sec/pr/2009/pdf/g20_040209.pdf.

[7] G20 (2009). Declaration on Strengthening the Financial System – London Summit, London, 02/04/09, p.1. www.g20.utoronto.ca/2009/2009ifi.pdf.

[8] G20 (2009). Declaration on Strengthening the Financial System – London Summit, p.1.

[9] G20 (2008). *Declaration Summit on Financial Markets and the World Economy*, Paragraphs 3-4, p.1.

[10] G20 (2008). *Declaration Summit on Financial Markets and the World Economy*, Paragraph 5, p.1.

[11] G20 (2008). *Declaration Summit on Financial Markets and the World Economy*, Paragraph 6, p.1.

[12] G20 (2008). *Declaration Summit on Financial Markets and the World Economy*, Paragraph 7, p.2.

[13] G20 (2008). *Declaration Summit on Financial Markets and the World Economy*, Paragraph 8, p.2.

[14] G20 (2008). *Declaration Summit on Financial Markets and the World Economy*, Paragraph 9, p.3.

[15] G20 (2008). *Declaration Summit on Financial Markets and the World Economy*, Action Plan, p.1.

[16] G20 (2008). *Declaration Summit on Financial Markets and the World Economy*, Action Plan, p.1.

[17] G20 (2008). *Declaration Summit on Financial Markets and the World Economy*, Action Plan, pp.2-3.

[18] G20 (2008). *Declaration Summit on Financial Markets and the World Economy*, Action Plan, pp.2-3.

[19] G20 (2008). *Declaration Summit on Financial Markets and the World Economy*, Action Plan, p.4.

[20] G20 (2008). *Declaration Summit on Financial Markets and the World Economy*, Action Plan, pp.4-5.

[21] G20 (2008). *Declaration Summit on Financial Markets and the World Economy*, Action Plan, p.5.

[22] G20 (2009). London Summit – Leaders' Statement, Paragraph 15, pp.3-4.

[23] G20 (2009). Declaration on Strengthening the Financial System – London Summit, p.2.

[24] G20 (2009). Declaration on Strengthening the Financial System – London Summit, pp.2-3.

[25] G20 (2009). Declaration on Strengthening the Financial System – London Summit, pp.3-4.

[26] G20 (2009). Declaration on Strengthening the Financial System – London Summit, p.4.

[27] G20 (2009). Declaration on Strengthening the Financial System – London Summit, pp.4-5.

[28] G20 (2009). Declaration on Strengthening the Financial System – London Summit, pp.5-6.

[29] G20 (2009). Declaration on Strengthening the Financial System – London Summit, p.6.

[30] G20 (2009). Leaders' Statement: The Pittsburgh Summit, 25/09/09, Paragraphs 1-6, p.1. https://g20.org/wp-content/uploads/2014/12/Pittsburgh_Declaration_0.pdf.

[31] G20 (2009). *Leaders' Statement: The Pittsburgh Summit*, Paragraph 50, p.19.

[32] G20 (2009). *Leaders' Statement: The Pittsburgh Summit*, Paragraph 17, p.2.

[33] G20 (2009). *Leaders' Statement: The Pittsburgh Summit*, Paragraph 13, pp.8-9.

[34] G20 (2009). *Leaders' Statement: The Pittsburgh Summit*, p.8.

[35] G20 (2009). *Leaders' Statement: The Pittsburgh Summit*, pp.8-9.

[36] G20 (2009). *Leaders' Statement: The Pittsburgh Summit*, p.9.

[37] G20 (2009). *Leaders' Statement: The Pittsburgh Summit*, p.9.

[38] G20 (2009). *Leaders' Statement: The Pittsburgh Summit*, Paragraphs 14-16, pp.9-10.

[39] G20 (2010). *The G-20 Toronto Summit: Declaration*, 27/06/10, Paragraph 16, p.4. http://www.g20.utoronto.ca/2010/g20_declaration_en.pdf.

[40] G20 (2010). *The G-20 Toronto Summit: Declaration*, Paragraphs, pp.17-18 and 20-22, pp.4-5.

[41] G20 (2010). *The G-20 Toronto Summit: Declaration*, Paragraph 18, p.4, and Annex II, Paragraph 6, pp.15-16.

[42] G20 (2010). *The G-20 Toronto Summit: Declaration*, Paragraph 18, p.4, and Annex II, Paragraph 7, p.16.

[43] G20 (2010). *The G-20 Toronto Summit: Declaration*, Paragraph 18, p.4, and Annex II, Paragraph 8, p.16.

[44] G20 (2010). *The G-20 Toronto Summit: Declaration*, Paragraph 19, p.4, and Annex II, Paragraph 26, p.19.

[45] G20 (2010). *The G-20 Toronto Summit: Declaration*, Paragraph 20, pp.4-5, and Annex II, Paragraph 15, p.17.

[46] G20 (2010). *The G-20 Toronto Summit: Declaration*, Paragraph 21, p.5, and Annex II, Paragraph 16, p.17.

[47] G20 (2010). *The G-20 Toronto Summit: Declaration*, Annex II, Paragraph 17, pp.17-18.

[48] G20 (2010). *The G-20 Toronto Summit: Declaration*, Annex II, Paragraph 18, p.18.

[49] G20 (2010). *The G-20 Toronto Summit: Declaration*, Annex II, Paragraphs 19-20, p.18.

[50] G20 (2010). *The G-20 Toronto Summit: Declaration*, Annex II, Paragraph 32, p.20.

[51] G20 (2010). *The G-20 Toronto Summit: Declaration*, Annex II, Paragraph 33, p.20.

[52] G20 (2010). *The G-20 Toronto Summit: Declaration*, Annex II, Paragraph 34, p.20.

[53] G20 (2010). *The G-20 Toronto Summit: Declaration*, Annex II, Paragraph 35, p.20.

[54] G20 (2010). *The G-20 Toronto Summit: Declaration*, Annex II, Paragraph 36, p.20.

[55] G20 (2010). *The G-20 Toronto Summit: Declaration*, Paragraph 22, p.5.

[56] G20 (2010). The G20 Seoul Summit: Leaders' Declaration, 12/11/10, Paragraph 9, p.2. https://g20.org/wp-content/uploads/2014/12/Seoul_Summit_Leaders_Declaration.pdf.

[57] G20 (2010). *The Seoul Summit Document*, pp.6-9. https://g20.org/wp-content/uploads/2014/12/Seoul_Summit_Document.pdf.

[58] G20 (2010). *The Seoul Summit Document*, Paragraph 29, p.7.

[59] G20 (2010). *The Seoul Summit Document*, Paragraph 30, p.7.

[60] G20 (2010). *The Seoul Summit Document*, Paragraph 31, pp.7-8.

[61] G20 (2010). *The Seoul Summit Document*, Paragraphs 32-33, p.8.

[62] G20 (2010). *The Seoul Summit Document*, Paragraph 34, p.8.

[63] G20 (2010). *The Seoul Summit Document*, Paragraph 36, p.8.

[64] G20 (2010). *The Seoul Summit Document*, Paragraph 37, p.8.

[65] G20 (2010). *The Seoul Summit Document*, Paragraph 38, p.9.

[66] G20 (2010). *The Seoul Summit Document*, Paragraph 39, p.9.

[67] G20 (2010). *The Seoul Summit Document*, Paragraph 40, p.9.

[68] G20 (2010). *The Seoul Summit Document*, Paragraph 41, pp.9-10.

[69] G20 (2011). *Cannes Summit final declaration* – Building our Common Future: Renewed Collective Action For the Benefit of All, 04/11/11, Paragraph 22, p.4. <https://g20.org/wp-content/uploads/2014/12/Declaration_eng_Cannes.pdf>

[70] G20 (2011). *Cannes Summit final declaration* – Building our Common Future: Renewed Collective Action For the Benefit of All, pp.5-8.

[71] G20 (2011). *Cannes Summit final declaration* – Building our Common Future: Renewed Collective Action For the Benefit of All, Paragraph 23, p.5.

[72] G20 (2011). *Cannes Summit final declaration* – Building our Common Future: Renewed Collective Action For the Benefit of All, Paragraph 24, p.5.

[73] G20 (2011). *Cannes Summit final declaration* – Building our Common Future: Renewed Collective Action For the Benefit of All, Paragraph 25, p.5.

[74] G20 (2011). *Cannes Summit final declaration* – Building our Common Future: Renewed Collective Action For the Benefit of All, Paragraph 26, p.5.

[75] G20 (2011). *Cannes Summit final declaration* – Building our Common Future: Renewed Collective Action For the Benefit of All, Paragraph 27, pp.5-6.

[76] G20 (2011). *Cannes Summit final declaration* – Building our Common Future: Renewed Collective Action For the Benefit of All, Paragraph 28, p.6.

[77] G20 (2011). *Cannes Summit final declaration* – Building our Common Future: Renewed Collective Action For the Benefit of All, Paragraph 29, p.6.

[78] G20 (2011). *Cannes Summit final declaration* – Building our Common Future: Renewed Collective Action For the Benefit of All, Paragraph 30, p.6.

[79] G20 (2011). *Cannes Summit final declaration* – Building our Common Future: Renewed Collective Action For the Benefit of All, Paragraph 31, pp.6-7.

[80] G20 (2011). *Cannes Summit final declaration* – Building our Common Future: Renewed Collective Action For the Benefit of All, Paragraph 32, p.7.

[81] G20 (2011). *Cannes Summit final declaration* – Building our Common Future: Renewed Collective Action For the Benefit of All, Paragraph 33, p.7.

[82] G20 (2011). *Cannes Summit final declaration* – Building our Common Future: Renewed Collective Action For the Benefit of All, Paragraph 34, p.7.

[83] G20 (2011). *Cannes Summit final declaration* – Building our Common Future: Renewed Collective Action For the Benefit of All, Paragraph 35, pp.7-8.

[84] G20 (2011). *Cannes Summit final declaration* – Building our Common Future: Renewed Collective Action For the Benefit of All, Paragraph 36, p.8.

[85] G20 (2011). *Cannes Summit final declaration* – Building our Common Future: Renewed Collective Action For the Benefit of All, Paragraphs 37-38, pp.8-9.

[86] G20 (2012). G2012 Los Cabos México: G20 Leaders Declaration, 19/06/12, p.6. <http://www.g20.utoronto.ca/2012/2012-0619-loscabos.pdf>

[87] G20 (2012). G2012 Los Cabos México: G20 Leaders Declaration, Paragraphs 36-37, p.6.

[88] G20 (2012). G2012 Los Cabos México: G20 Leaders Declaration, Paragraph 39, pp.6-7.

[89] G20 (2012). G2012 Los Cabos México: G20 Leaders Declaration, Paragraphs 40 and 42-43, p.7.

[90] G20 (2012). G2012 Los Cabos México: G20 Leaders Declaration, Paragraph 44, pp.7-8.

[91] G20 (2012). G2012 Los Cabos México: G20 Leaders Declaration, Paragraph 45, p.8.

[92] G20 (2012). G2012 Los Cabos México: G20 Leaders Declaration, Paragraph 46, p.8.

[93] G20 (2012). G2012 Los Cabos México: G20 Leaders Declaration, Paragraph 48, p.8.

[94] G20 (2012). G2012 Los Cabos México: G20 Leaders Declaration, Paragraph 49, p.8.

[95] G20 (2012). G2012 Los Cabos México: G20 Leaders Declaration, Paragraph 50,

[96] pp.8-9.

[97] G20 (2012). G2012 Los Cabos México: G20 Leaders Declaration, Paragraphs 51 and 54, p.9.

[98] G20 (2012). G2012 Los Cabos México: G20 Leaders Declaration, Paragraphs 52-53, p.9.

[99] G20 (2012). G2012 Los Cabos México: G20 Leaders Declaration, Paragraph 52, p.9.

[100] G20 (2013). *Russia G20: G20 Leaders' Declaration*, 06/09/13, p.2. <https://g20.org/wp-content/uploads/2014/12/Saint_Petersburg_Declaration_ENG_ 0.pdf>

[101] G20 (2013). *Russia G20: G20 Leaders' Declaration*, Paragraph 61, p.15.

[102] G20 (2013). *Russia G20: G20 Leaders' Declaration*, Paragraph 64, p.16.

[103] G20 (2013). *Russia G20: G20 Leaders' Declaration*, Paragraph 66, p.16.

[104] G20 (2013). *Russia G20: G20 Leaders' Declaration*, Paragraph 67, pp.16-17.

[105] G20 (2013). *Russia G20: G20 Leaders' Declaration*, Paragraph 68, p.17.

[106] G20 (2013). *Russia G20: G20 Leaders' Declaration*, Paragraph 69, p.17.

[107] G20 (2013). *Russia G20: G20 Leaders' Declaration*, Paragraph 70. p.17.

[108] G20 (2013). *Russia G20: G20 Leaders' Declaration*, Paragraph 71, p.17.

[109] G20 (2013). *Russia G20: G20 Leaders' Declaration*, Paragraph 72, p.18.

[110] G20 (2013). *Russia G20: G20 Leaders' Declaration*, Paragraph 73, p.18.

[111] G20 (2013). *Russia G20: G20 Leaders' Declaration*, Paragraph 74, p.18.

[112] G20 (2013). *Russia G20: G20 Leaders' Declaration*, Paragraph 76, p.18.

[113] G20 (2013). *Russia G20: G20 Leaders' Declaration*, Paragraph 77, pp.18-19.

[114] G20 (2013). *Russia G20: G20 Leaders' Declaration*, Paragraph 114, p.27.

[115] G20 (2014). G20 Australia 2014: G20 Leaders' Communiqué – Brisbane Summit, 16/11/14, Paragraph 12, p.2. https://g20.org/wp-content/uploads/2014/12/brisbane_g20_leaders_summit_communique1.pdf.

[116] Financial Stability Board (2015). Letter from the Chairman of the Financial Stability Board to G20 Finance Ministers and Central Bank Governors: Financial Reforms – Finishing the Post-Crisis Agenda and Moving Forward, 04/02/15, p.1. http://www.financialstabilityboard.org/wp-content/uploads/FSB-Chair-letter-to-G20-February-2015.pdf.

[117] Financial Stability Board (2015). Letter from the Chairman of the Financial Stability Board to G20 Finance Ministers and Central Bank Governors: Financial Reforms – Finishing the Post-Crisis Agenda and Moving Forward, p.2.

[118] Financial Stability Board (2015). Letter from the Chairman of the Financial Stability Board to G20 Finance Ministers and Central Bank Governors: Financial Reforms – Finishing the Post-Crisis Agenda and Moving Forward, p.3.

[119] Financial Stability Board (2015). Letter from the Chairman of the Financial Stability Board to G20 Finance Ministers and Central Bank Governors: Financial Reforms – Finishing the Post-Crisis Agenda and Moving Forward, p.3.

[120] Financial Stability Board (2015). Letter from the Chairman of the Financial Stability Board to G20 Finance Ministers and Central Bank Governors: Financial Reforms – Progress on the Work Plan for the Antalya Summit, 05/10/15, p.3. http://www.financialstabilityboard.org/wp-content/uploads/FSB-Chairs-letter-to-G20-Mins-and-Govs-5-October-2015.pdf.

[121] Financial Stability Board (2015). Letter from the Chairman of the Financial Stability Board to G20 Finance Ministers and Central Bank Governors: Financial Reforms – Progress on the Work Plan for the Antalya Summit, p.3.

[122] Financial Stability Board (2015). Letter from the Chairman of the Financial Stability Board to G20 Finance Ministers and Central Bank Governors: Financial Reforms – Finishing the Post-Crisis Agenda and Moving Forward, p.3.

[123] Financial Stability Board (2015). Letter from the Chairman of the Financial Stability Board to G20 Finance Ministers and Central Bank Governors: Financial Reforms – Progress on the Work Plan for the Antalya Summit, p.4.

[124] Financial Stability Board (2015). Letter from the Chairman of the Financial Stability Board to G20 Finance Ministers and Central Bank Governors: Financial Reforms – Progress on the Work Plan for the Antalya Summit, p.4.

[125] Financial Stability Board (2015). Letter from the Chairman of the Financial Stability Board to G20 Finance Ministers and Central Bank Governors: Financial Reforms – Finishing the Post-Crisis Agenda and Moving Forward, p.4.

[126] Financial Stability Board (2015). Letter from the Chairman of the Financial Stability Board to G20 Finance Ministers and Central Bank Governors: Financial Reforms – Progress on the Work Plan for the Antalya Summit, pp.4-5.

[127] Financial Stability Board (2015). Letter from the Chairman of the Financial Stability Board to G20 Finance Ministers and Central Bank Governors: Financial Reforms – Progress on the Work Plan for the Antalya Summit, p.5.

[128] G20 (2015). G20 Turkey 2015: G20 Leaders' Communiqué – Antalya Summit, 16/11/15, Paragraph 13, p.3. http://www.g20.utoronto.ca/2015/151116-communique.html.

[129] G20 (2015). G20 Turkey 2015: G20 Leaders' Communiqué – Antalya Summit, Paragraph 14, p.3.

[130] Financial Stability Board (2015). Letter from the Chairman of the Financial Stability Board to G20 Leaders: Financial Reforms – Achieving and Sustaining Resilience for All, 09/11/15. http://www.financialstabilityboard.org/wp-content/uploads/FSB-Chairs-letter-to-G20-Leaders-9-Nov.pdf.

[131] Financial Stability Board (2015). Implementation and effects of the G20 financial regulatory reforms: Report of the Financial Stability Board to G20 Leaders, 09/11/15. http://www.financialstabilityboard.org/wp-content/uploads/Report-on-implementation-and-effects-of-reforms-final.pdf.

[132] Financial Stability Board (2015). Letter from the Chairman of the Financial Stability Board to G20 Leaders: Financial Reforms – Achieving and Sustaining Resilience for All, pp.1-2.

[133] Financial Stability Board (2015). Letter from the Chairman of the Financial Stability Board to G20 Leaders: Financial Reforms – Achieving and Sustaining Resilience for All, p.2.

[134] Financial Stability Board (2015). Letter from the Chairman of the Financial Stability Board to G20 Leaders: Financial Reforms – Achieving and Sustaining Resilience for All, p.3.

[135] Financial Stability Board (2015). Letter from the Chairman of the Financial Stability Board to G20 Leaders: Financial Reforms – Achieving and Sustaining Resilience for All, p.4.

[136] Financial Stability Board (2015). Letter from the Chairman of the Financial Stability Board to G20 Leaders: Financial Reforms – Achieving and Sustaining Resilience for All, p.5.

[137] Financial Stability Board (2015). Letter from the Chairman of the Financial Stability Board to G20 Leaders: Financial Reforms – Achieving and Sustaining Resilience for All, p.6.

[138] G20 (2015). G20 Turkey 2015: G20 Leaders' Communiqué – Antalya Summit, p.11.

[139] Financial Stability Board (2015). Letter from the Chairman of the Financial Stability Board to G20 Leaders: Financial Reforms – Achieving and Sustaining Resilience for All, p.7.

[140] Financial Stability Board (2015). Implementation and effects of the G20 financial regulatory reforms: Report of the Financial Stability Board to G20 Leaders, pp.10 and 20.

[141] Financial Stability Board (2015). Implementation and effects of the G20 financial regulatory reforms: Report of the Financial Stability Board to G20 Leaders, pp.3-4.

[142] Financial Stability Board (2015). Implementation and effects of the G20 financial regulatory reforms: Report of the Financial Stability Board to G20 Leaders, p.19.

[143] Financial Stability Board (2015). Implementation and effects of the G20 financial regulatory reforms: Report of the Financial Stability Board to G20 Leaders, p.2.

[144] Financial Stability Board (2015). Implementation and effects of the G20 financial regulatory reforms: Report of the Financial Stability Board to G20 Leaders, pp.3-4.

[145] Basel Committee on Banking Supervision (2010). Report and Recommendations of the Cross-border Bank Resolution Group: March 2010, Recommendation 1, p.1. http://www.bis.org/publ/bcbs169.pdf.

[146] Basel Committee on Banking Supervision (2010). Report and Recommendations of the Cross-border Bank Resolution Group: March 2010, Recommendation 2, p.1.

[147] Basel Committee on Banking Supervision (2010). Report and Recommendations of the Cross-border Bank Resolution Group: March 2010, Recommendation 3, p.1.

[148] Basel Committee on Banking Supervision (2010). Report and Recommendations of the Cross-border Bank Resolution Group: March 2010, Recommendation 4, p.1.

[149] Basel Committee on Banking Supervision (2010). Report and Recommendations of the Cross-border Bank Resolution Group: March 2010, Recommendation 5, p.2.

[150] Basel Committee on Banking Supervision (2010). Report and Recommendations of the Cross-border Bank Resolution Group: March 2010, Recommendation 6, p.2.

[151] Basel Committee on Banking Supervision (2010). Report and Recommendations of the Cross-border Bank Resolution Group: March 2010, Recommendation 7, p.2.

[152] Basel Committee on Banking Supervision (2010). Report and Recommendations of the Cross-border Bank Resolution Group: March 2010, Recommendation 8, p.2.

[153] Basel Committee on Banking Supervision (2010). Report and Recommendations of the Cross-border Bank Resolution Group: March 2010, Recommendation 9, pp.2-3.

[154] Basel Committee on Banking Supervision (2010). Report and Recommendations of the Cross-border Bank Resolution Group: March 2010, Recommendation 10, p.3.

[155] G20 (2010). *The Seoul Summit Document*, Paragraph 32, p.8.

[156] *Financial Stability Board (2011).* Key Attributes of Effective Resolution Regimes for Financial Institutions, October 2011, p.1. <http://www.financialstabilityboard.org/wp-content/uploads/r_111104cc.pdf?page_moved=1>

[157] *Financial Stability Board (2011).* Key Attributes of Effective Resolution Regimes for Financial Institutions, October 2011, p.1.

[158] *Financial Stability Board (2011).* Key Attributes of Effective Resolution Regimes for Financial Institutions, October 2011, Paragraphs 1.1-1.2, p.5.

[159] *Financial Stability Board (2011).* Key Attributes of Effective Resolution Regimes for Financial Institutions, October 2011, Paragraph 2.1, pp.5-6.

[160] *Financial Stability Board (2011).* Key Attributes of Effective Resolution Regimes for Financial Institutions, October 2011, Paragraphs 2.3-2.7, p.6.

[161] *Financial Stability Board (2011).* Key Attributes of Effective Resolution Regimes for Financial Institutions, October 2011, Paragraphs 3.2-3.4, pp.7-8.

[162] *Financial Stability Board (2011).* Key Attributes of Effective Resolution Regimes for Financial Institutions, October 2011, Paragraph 3.8, p.10.

[163] *Financial Stability Board (2011).* Key Attributes of Effective Resolution Regimes for Financial Institutions, October 2011, Paragraph 3.9, p.10.

[164] *Financial Stability Board (2011)*. Key Attributes of Effective Resolution Regimes for Financial Institutions, October 2011, Paragraph 4.1, p.10.

[165] *Financial Stability Board (2011)*. Key Attributes of Effective Resolution Regimes for Financial Institutions, October 2011, Paragraph 4.2, p.10.

[166] *Financial Stability Board (2011)*. Key Attributes of Effective Resolution Regimes for Financial Institutions, October 2011, Paragraph 4.3, p.10.

[167] *Financial Stability Board (2011)*. Key Attributes of Effective Resolution Regimes for Financial Institutions, October 2011, Paragraph 5.1, p.11.

[168] *Financial Stability Board (2011)*. Key Attributes of Effective Resolution Regimes for Financial Institutions, October 2011, Paragraph 5.2, p.11.

[169] *Financial Stability Board (2011)*. Key Attributes of Effective Resolution Regimes for Financial Institutions, October 2011, Paragraph 5.3, p.11.

[170] *Financial Stability Board (2011)*. Key Attributes of Effective Resolution Regimes for Financial Institutions, October 2011, Paragraph 5.5, pp.11-12.

[171] *Financial Stability Board (2011)*. Key Attributes of Effective Resolution Regimes for Financial Institutions, October 2011, Paragraph 5.6, p.12.

[172] *Financial Stability Board (2011)*. Key Attributes of Effective Resolution Regimes for Financial Institutions, October 2011, Paragraph 6.1, p.12.

[173] *Financial Stability Board (2011)*. Key Attributes of Effective Resolution Regimes for Financial Institutions, October 2011, Paragraph 6.2, p.12.

[174] *Financial Stability Board (2011)*. Key Attributes of Effective Resolution Regimes for Financial Institutions, October 2011, Paragraph 6.3, p.12.

[175] *Financial Stability Board (2011)*. Key Attributes of Effective Resolution Regimes for Financial Institutions, October 2011, Paragraph 6.4, p.12.

[176] *Financial Stability Board (2011)*. Key Attributes of Effective Resolution Regimes for Financial Institutions, October 2011, Paragraph 6.5, p.12.

[177] *Financial Stability Board (2011)*. Key Attributes of Effective Resolution Regimes for Financial Institutions, October 2011, Paragraph 7.1, p.13.

[178] *Financial Stability Board (2011)*. Key Attributes of Effective Resolution Regimes for Financial Institutions, October 2011, Paragraph 7.2, p.13.

[179] *Financial Stability Board (2011)*. Key Attributes of Effective Resolution Regimes for Financial Institutions, October 2011, Paragraph 7.3, p.13.

[180] *Financial Stability Board (2011)*. Key Attributes of Effective Resolution Regimes for Financial Institutions, October 2011, Paragraph 7.4, p.13.

[181] *Financial Stability Board (2011)*. Key Attributes of Effective Resolution Regimes for Financial Institutions, October 2011, Paragraph 7.5, p.13.

[182] *Financial Stability Board (2011)*. Key Attributes of Effective Resolution Regimes for Financial Institutions, October 2011, Paragraph 7.6, pp.13-14.

[183] *Financial Stability Board (2011)*. Key Attributes of Effective Resolution Regimes for Financial Institutions, October 2011, Paragraph 7.7, p.14.

[184] *Financial Stability Board (2011)*. Key Attributes of Effective Resolution Regimes for Financial Institutions, October 2011, Paragraph 8.1, p.14.

[185] *Financial Stability Board (2011)*. Key Attributes of Effective Resolution Regimes for Financial Institutions, October 2011, Paragraph 9.1, pp.14-15.

[186] *Financial Stability Board (2011)*. Key Attributes of Effective Resolution Regimes for Financial Institutions, October 2011, Paragraph 10.1, p.15.

[187] *Financial Stability Board (2011).* Key Attributes of Effective Resolution Regimes for Financial Institutions, October 2011, Paragraph 10.2, pp.15-16.

[188] *Financial Stability Board (2011).* Key Attributes of Effective Resolution Regimes for Financial Institutions, October 2011, Paragraph 10.3, p.16.

[189] *Financial Stability Board (2011).* Key Attributes of Effective Resolution Regimes for Financial Institutions, October 2011, Paragraph 10.4, p.16.

[190] *Financial Stability Board (2011).* Key Attributes of Effective Resolution Regimes for Financial Institutions, October 2011, Paragraph 10.5, p.16.

[191] *Financial Stability Board (2011).* Key Attributes of Effective Resolution Regimes for Financial Institutions, October 2011, Paragraphs 11.1-11.2 and 11.4, p.16.

[192] *Financial Stability Board (2011).* Key Attributes of Effective Resolution Regimes for Financial Institutions, October 2011, Paragraph 11.3, p.16.

[193] *Financial Stability Board (2011).* Key Attributes of Effective Resolution Regimes for Financial Institutions, October 2011, Paragraph 11.5, p.17.

[194] *Financial Stability Board (2011).* Key Attributes of Effective Resolution Regimes for Financial Institutions, October 2011, Paragraph 11.6, p.17.

[195] *Financial Stability Board (2011).* Key Attributes of Effective Resolution Regimes for Financial Institutions, October 2011, Paragraph 11.7, p.17.

[196] *Financial Stability Board (2011).* Key Attributes of Effective Resolution Regimes for Financial Institutions, October 2011, Paragraph 11.8, p.17.

[197] *Financial Stability Board (2011).* Key Attributes of Effective Resolution Regimes for Financial Institutions, October 2011, Paragraph 11.9, pp.17-18.

[198] *Financial Stability Board (2011).* Key Attributes of Effective Resolution Regimes for Financial Institutions, October 2011, Paragraph 11.10, p.18.

[199] *Financial Stability Board (2011).* Key Attributes of Effective Resolution Regimes for Financial Institutions, October 2011, Paragraph 11.11, p.18.

[200] *Financial Stability Board (2011).* Key Attributes of Effective Resolution Regimes for Financial Institutions, October 2011, Paragraph 11.12, p.18.

[201] *Financial Stability Board (2011).* Key Attributes of Effective Resolution Regimes for Financial Institutions, October 2011, Paragraph 12.1, p.18.

[202] *Financial Stability Board (2011).* Key Attributes of Effective Resolution Regimes for Financial Institutions, October 2011, Paragraph 12.2, p.18.

[203] Financial Stability Board (2014). Key Attributes of Effective Resolution Regimes for Financial Institutions (updated), 15/10/14, p.1. http://www.financialstability board.org/wp-content/uploads/r_141015.pdf.

[204] Financial Stability Board (2014). Key Attributes of Effective Resolution Regimes for Financial Institutions (updated), p.2.

[205] Financial Stability Board (2015). Implementation and effects of the G20 financial regulatory reforms: Report of the Financial Stability Board to G20 Leaders, p.21.

[206] *Official Journal of the European Union* (2014). Directive 2014/59/EU of the European Parliament and of the Council of 15 May 2014 establishing a framework for the recovery and resolution of credit institutions and investment firms and amending Council Directive 82/891/EEC, and Directives 2001/24/EC, 2002/47/EC, 2004/25/EC, 2005/56/EC, 2007/36/EC, 2011/35/EU, 2012/30/EU and 2013/36/EU, and Regulations (EU) No 1093/2010 and (EU) No 648/2012, of the European Parliament and of the Council, L173/190-L173/348, Article 130(1).

[207] *Official Journal of the European Union* (2014). Directive 2014/59/EU, Articles 1(1)(a) and 2(1)(23).

[208] *Official Journal of the European Union* (2014). Directive 2014/59/EU, Article 1(1)(b).

[209] *Official Journal of the European Union* (2014). Directive 2014/59/EU, Article 1(1)(c)-(d).

[210] *Official Journal of the European Union* (2014). Directive 2014/59/EU, Article 1(1)(e).

[211] *Official Journal of the European Union* (2014). Directive 2014/59/EU, Article 3(1).

[212] *Official Journal of the European Union* (2014). Directive 2014/59/EU, Article 3(2).

[213] *Official Journal of the European Union* (2014). Directive 2014/59/EU, Article 3(8).

[214] *Official Journal of the European Union* (2014). Directive 2014/59/EU, Article 5(5).

[215] *Official Journal of the European Union* (2014). Directive 2014/59/EU, Annex, Section A.

[216] *Official Journal of the European Union* (2014). Directive 2014/59/EU, Article 10(1).

[217] *Official Journal of the European Union* (2014). Directive 2014/59/EU, Article 10(4).

[218] *Official Journal of the European Union* (2014). Directive 2014/59/EU, Article 11(1).

[219] *Official Journal of the European Union* (2014). Directive 2014/59/EU, Annex, Section B.

[220] *Official Journal of the European Union* (2014). Directive 2014/59/EU, Article 12(1).

[221] *Official Journal of the European Union* (2014). Directive 2014/59/EU, Article 12(3).

[222] *Official Journal of the European Union* (2014). Directive 2014/59/EU, Article 13(1).

[223] *Official Journal of the European Union* (2014). Directive 2014/59/EU, Article 13(4).

[224] *Official Journal of the European Union* (2014). Directive 2014/59/EU, Article 10(6).

[225] *Official Journal of the European Union* (2014). Directive 2014/59/EU, Article 13(3).

[226] Baber, G. (2012). International financial regulation: order or chaos?, *Company Lawyer*, 33(1), 17-18, at 17.

Chapter Three

THE EUROPEAN SECTORAL ARCHITECTURE

ABSTRACT

The de Larosière Report recommended the introduction of a European Systemic Risk Council and a European System of Financial Supervisors – which was to comprise authorities to replace the Committees of European Banking Supervisors, of European Insurance and Occupational Pensions Supervisors, and of European Securities Regulators. Pursuant to this, the European Systemic Risk Board, the EBA, the EIOPA and the ESMA were established – the latter 3 together comprising the ESAs and replacing the European Committees. Each ESA was founded to regulate a distinct part of the financial sector, as framed by primary legislation stated in each enabling Regulation. All 3 ESAs have the same objective, which concerns financial stability and effectiveness. The ESAs develop draft RTSs and draft ITSs on the basis of specifications in the relevant primary legislation, which the Commission may adopt as CDRs and CIRs. It is demonstrated that the draft RTS-to-CDR and draft ITS-to-CIR processes are efficient methods for producing secondary legislation. Nonetheless, this is insufficient to announce the success of the ESAs, which requires them to provide benefits in excess of their costs on a continuing basis. Council Regulation (EU) No 1024/2013 shows how the European Central Bank's supervisory role fits with the rule-making powers of the EBA. The former is required to comply with CDRs and CIRs that the EBA has developed. The foundation of the ESAs and the international response to the GFC have been the main agents for change with regard to the pre-GFC legislation. This should be reflected in the post-GFC rules.

Keywords: committee, Commission, RTS, CDR, ITS, CIR, ESA, EBA, EIOPA, ESMA

INTRODUCTION

In Chapter 1, it was stated that the establishment of the Committee of European Banking Supervisors and the Committee of European Insurance and Occupational Pensions Supervisors, and the extension of the scope of the Committee of European Securities Regulators to investment funds, were the seeds of the post-GFC European sectoral architecture, as, from 1st January 2004, there were committees in place to advise the Commission as to the content of secondary legislation in the fields of securities, banking and insurance[402]. Nonetheless, the EU institutions were concerned that "an appropriate framework" should be in place, in order to optimise the quality of the delegated legislation adopted through the Lamfalussy process [1]. Accordingly, in 2007, the Commission conducted a review of the Lamfalussy process, [2-4] concluding that the Committees' function at level 3 of the process[403] should be strengthened and that "changes to the legal framework will be considered concerning the decisions setting [the Committees] up and the definition of their role" [5]. Accordingly, the 3 Committees were re-established as "independent advisory group[s]" in their respective fields, with effect from 29th January 2009 [6-8].

The Committee of European Securities Regulators was to advise the Commission in respect of "the preparation of draft implementing measures in the field of securities." [9]. The Committee of European Banking Supervisors was to advise the Commission with regard to "the preparation of draft implementing measures in the field of banking activities and in the field of financial conglomerates." [10]. The Committee of European Insurance and Occupational Pensions Supervisors was to advise the Commission with reference to "the preparation of draft implementing measures in the fields of insurance, reinsurance, occupational pensions and financial conglomerates." [11]. In addition, each Committee was to "contribute to the common and uniform implementation of Community legislation by issuing guidelines, recommendations and standards, [12-14] to "enhance cooperation between national supervisory authorities" in its field, and to "foster the convergence of Member States' supervisory practices and approaches throughout the Community" [15-17]. Each Committee was to "contribute to the development of common supervisory practices" in its field, and "on a cross-sectoral basis in close cooperation with" the other 2 Committees [18-20]. Thus, the 2009 legislation organised and integrated the function of the Committees. Together, they were referred to as 'the Committees of Supervisors' [21-23].

THE DE LAROSIÈRE REPORT

In October 2008, the then President of the Commission, Mr. José Manuel Barroso, asked Mr. Jacques de Larosière to chair the High-Level Group on Financial Supervision in the EU, in order to advise on the future of European financial regulation and supervision [24]. Some of the recommendations of the Report, which was published on 25th February 2009, concerned changes to the EU's architecture for the sector. These included the following.

Recommendation 16: A new body called the European Systemic Risk Council (ESRC), to be chaired by the ECB [European Central Bank]. President, should be set up under the auspices and with the logical support of the ECB. The ESRC should be composed of the members of the General Council of the ECB, the chairpersons of CEBS [the Committee of European Banking Supervisors], CEIOPS [the Committee of European Insurance and Occupational Pensions Supervisors] and CESR [the Committee of

---

[402] See the section entitled 'European Supervisors for Banking and Insurance Activities', in Chapter 1.

[403] See the section entitled 'The Lamfalussy Process' in Chapter 1, for the function of the Committee of European Securities Regulators (and, from 24th November 2003 and 1st January 2004, respectively, the Committee of European Insurance and Occupational Pensions Supervisors and the Committee of European Banking Supervisors,) at level 3 of the Lamfalussy process (Commission Decision 2004/6/EC, Article 8; Commission Decision 2004/5/EC, Article 8).

European Securities Regulators] as well as representatives of the European Commission. … The ESRC should pool and analyse all information, relevant for financial stability, pertaining to macro-economic conditions and to macro-prudential developments in all the financial sectors. A proper flow of information between the ESRC and the micro-prudential supervisors must be ensured [25].

Recommendation 17: [A]n effective risk warning system shall be put in place under the auspices of the ESRC and of the Economic and Financial Committee (EFC). The ESRC should prioritise and issue macro-prudential risk warnings: there should be mandatory follow up and, where appropriate, action shall be taken by the relevant competent authorities in the EU. If the risks are of a serious nature, potentially having a negative impact on the financial sector or the economy as a whole, the ESRC shall inform the chairman of the EFC. The EFC, working with the Commission, will then implement a strategy ensuring that the risks are effectively addressed. If the risks identified relate to a global dysfunction of the monetary and financial system, the ESRC will warn the IMF, the FSF and the BIS in order to define appropriate action at both EU and global levels. If the ESRC judges that the response of a national supervisor to a priority risk warning is inadequate, it shall, after discussion with that supervisor, inform the chairman of the EFC, with a view to further action being taken against that supervisor [26].

Regulation (EU) No 1092/2010[404] includes some of these suggestions, with modifications. It establishes a European Systemic Risk Board, [27] whose first Chair is the President of the European Central Bank[405] [28]. Voting members of the Risk Board's General Board comprise the President and the Vice-President[406] of the European Central Bank, the governors of the central banks of each Member State, a Commissioner[407], the Chairpersons of the EBA[408], the EIOPA[409] and the ESMA[410], the Chair and the 2 Vice-Chairs of the Advisory Scientific Committee[411], and the Chair of the Advisory Technical Committee[412] [29]. The non-voting members of the General Board comprise one high-level representative from each Member State from the competent national supervisory authorities (depending on the issue to be discussed – unless these authorities have agreed upon a common representative), and the

---

[404] This is Regulation (EU) No 1092/2010 of the European Parliament and of the Council of 24 November 2010 on European Union macro-prudential oversight of the financial system and establishing a European Systemic Risk Board, which came into force on 16th December 2010 (Regulation (EU) No 1092/2010, Article 21).

[405] This is Dr. Mario Draghi (European Systemic Risk Board (2015), Permanent members of the ESRB General Board, p.1, <https://www.esrb.europa.eu/pub/pdf/other/Perm_memb_GB.pdf?4571846b1be15137940de88 b5ddadae4>).

[406] This is Dr. Vitor Constâncio (European Systemic Risk Board (2015), Permanent members of the ESRB General Board, p.5).

[407] This is Lord (Jonathan) Hill, the Commissioner for Financial Stability, Financial Services and Capital Markets Union (European Systemic Risk Board (2015), Permanent members of the ESRB General Board, p.6).

[408] This is Mr. Andrea Enria (European Systemic Risk Board (2015), Permanent members of the ESRB General Board, p.5).

[409] This is Mr. Gabriel Bernardino (European Systemic Risk Board (2015), Permanent members of the ESRB General Board, p.5).

[410] This is Dr. Steven Maijoor (European Systemic Risk Board (2015), Permanent members of the ESRB General Board, p.5).

[411] These are Drs. Philip Lane (Governor of the Central Bank of Ireland), Marco Pagano (Professor of Economics, University of Naples Federico II) and Javier Suárez (Professor of Finance, Center for Monetary and Financial Studies, Madrid) (European Systemic Risk Board (2015), Permanent members of the ESRB General Board, pp.1-2).

[412] This is Dr. Stefan Ingves (Governor of the Sveriges Riksbank (the central bank of Sweden)) (European Systemic Risk Board (2015), Permanent members of the ESRB General Board, p.2).

President of the Economic and Financial Committee[413] [30]. Thus, the national members of the General Board, and the representatives to the General Board from the Committees[414], are additional to Recommendation 16's suggested membership.

The European Systemic Risk Board is responsible for the macroprudential superintendence of the financial system within the EU, in order to contribute to the mitigation or the prevention of systemic risks to financial stability there which arise from developments in the system – and taking macroeconomic changes into account, so as to avoid times of extensive financial distress; in addition, the Risk Board contributes to the smooth operation of the internal market, thereby ensuring that the financial sector enduringly contributes to economic growth [31]. For these purposes, the Risk Board shall: (a) determine and/or collect and appraise all of "the relevant and necessary information," (b) identify and prioritise systemic risks, (c) issue warnings in cases in which it considers these risks to be material, (d) issue recommendations for actions to remedy the risks that it has identified, (e) address a confidential warning to the Council and provide the latter with an evaluation of the situation, in circumstances under which the Risk Board ascertains that an emergency situation may arise, in order to enable the Council to assess the need to take a decision addressed to the ESAs[415] that determines the presence of an emergency situation, (f) monitor the response to warnings and recommendations, (g) co-operate with the other parties to the European System of Financial Supervision[416] (as appropriate), supplying the ESAs with the data on systemic risks that are required for the carrying out of their tasks and (in particular) developing with the ESAs a common group of indicators to identify and to measure systemic risk, (h) participate (as appropriate) in the Joint Committee of the ESAs, (i) co-ordinate its actions with those of the FSB, the IMF and other international financial institutions – as well as the relevant organisations in third countries – on issues that are related to macroprudential supervision [32]. These provisions of Regulation (EU) No 1092/2010 are similar to the final sentence of Recommendation 16 and to Recommendation 17 – although the ESAs play a greater role than the de Larosière Report envisages and the Economic and Financial Committee a lesser part. That Committee's contribution to the European Systemic Risk Board is limited to the President of the former's presence on the latter's General Board[417] [33] and Steering Committee, [34]. The attendance of a representative of the former at the Advisory Technical Committee, [35] and the transmission of the Risk Board's warnings and recommendations to the Council and the preparation of the latter's discussion of these items[418] [36].

---

[413] This is Mr. Thomas Wieser (European Systemic Risk Board (2015), Permanent members of the ESRB General Board, p.4).

[414] Articles 12 and 13, respectively, of Regulation (EU) No 1092/2010, provide for the membership of Advisory Scientific Committee and the Advisory Technical Committee.

[415] The ESAs are the EBA, the EIOPA and the ESMA.

[416] The European System of Financial Supervision comprises the European Systemic Risk Board, the EBA, the EIOPA, the ESMA, the Joint Committee of the ESAs, and the competent/supervisory authorities of the Member States (Regulation (EU) No 1092/2010, Article 1(3)).

[417] See the previous paragraph. The attendance of the President of the Economic and Financial Committee reflects the role of Council and the finance ministries of the Member States in protecting financial stability and providing economic and financial supervision (Regulation (EU) No 1092/2010, Recital 25).

[418] Recital 19 of Regulation (EU) No 1092/2010 is as follows: "In order to increase and legitimacy, such warnings and recommendations should also be transmitted, subject to strict rules of confidentiality, to the Council and the Commission and, where addressed to one or more national supervisory authorities, to the ESAs. The deliberations of the Council should be prepared by the Economic and Financial Committee (EFC) in accordance with its role as defined in the TFEU. In order to prepare the Council's discussions and provide it with timely

The de Larosière Report's next recommendation concerns the upgrading of the EU supervisory structure. It is as follows.

Recommendation 18: A European System of Financial Supervisors (ESFS) should be set up. This ESFS should be a decentralized network: − existing national supervisors would continue to carry-out day-to-day supervision; − three new European Authorities would be set up, replacing CEBS [the Committee of European Banking Supervisors], CEIOPS [the Committee of European Insurance and Occupational Pensions Supervisors] and CESR [the Committee of European Securities Regulators]., with the role [to] coordinate the application of supervisory standards and guarantee strong cooperation between the national supervisors; − colleges of supervisors would be set up for all major cross-border institutions. The ESFS will need to be independent of the political authorities, but be accountable to them. It should rely on a common set of core harmonised rules and have access to high-quality information [37].

The changes were to be made in 2 stages. The first stage involved the fortification of the domestic supervisory authorities, in order to improve the quality of financial supervision within the EU [38]. Within that stage, the EU was also to harmonise financial regulations, sanctioning regimes and supervisory powers [39]. The convergence of these regulations was mainly to take place at level 3 of the Lamfalussy process, which would prepare the way for changes at levels 1 and 2[419]. The de Larosière Report explains the issue thus.

The European Institutions and the level 3 committees should initiate a determined and concerted effort to equip the EU financial sector with a consistent set of core rules by the beginning of 2013. A process should be set-up, whereby the key-differences in national legislation will be identified and removed [40]. These differences stem from exceptions, derogations, additions made at national level, or ambiguities contained in directives which have a material impact on the market, [which] are laxer than the minimum core standards [] or which may induce competition distortion or regulatory arbitrage[. Such differences] will be identified and removed. In its efforts to remove these differences, the European Commission should concentrate its first efforts on the main problems [41]. This process may not lead to identical rules in every case. However, the core harmonised rules should be sufficiently comprehensive. To that effect, the level 3 committees will examine the differences that exist and propose to the Commission new or further developments of level 1 and level 2 rules (e.g., harmonisation of the sanctions

---

policy advice, the ESRB [European Systemic Risk Board] should inform the EFC regularly and should send the texts of any warnings and recommendations as soon as they have been adopted". The Economic and Financial Committee was established "[i]n order to promote coordination of the policies of Member States to the full extent needed for the functioning of the internal market" (TFEU, Article 134(1)). The Economic and Financial Committee's duties are to: (i) prepare opinions for submission to the Council and/or the Commission, (ii) monitor, and regulatory report (to the Council and to the Commission) on, the economic and financial circumstances of the EU and of its Member States, (iii) contribute to the preparation of the Council's work to which specified provisions of the TFEU refer, and conduct other advisory and preparatory duties that the Council allocates to it, and (iv) examine, at least annually, the situation concerning the movement of capital and of payments, as these result from the application of the TFEU, the TEU and measures that the Council adopts (TFEU, Article 134(2)).

[419] Level 1 of the Lamfalussy process is the adoption of primary EU financial legislation. Level 2 is the passing of secondary EU financial legislation. Level 3 is the implementation of those rules. Level 4 is the monitoring of compliance with them. See the section entitled 'The Lamfalussy Process' in Chapter 1, for further information − especially on the fit between levels 1 and 2.

regimes, definition of core capital rules, harmonisation in the areas of short-selling, controls for security settlement systems) [42].

The developments contained in this passage prepare the way for the adoption of plentiful, post-GFC EU legislation. The preliminary removal of differences in the legal regimes of Member States facilitates the Commission's approach to these new rules, which is to introduce Regulations over areas in which it considers this to be possible[420].

In the second stage, the European System of Financial Supervision was founded. Recommendation 22 of the de Larosière Report states this, as follows.

> Recommendation 22: In the second stage (2011-2012), the EU should establish an integrated European System of Financial Supervision (ESFS). The level 3 Committees should be transformed into three European Authorities: a European Banking Authority, a European Insurance Authority and a European Securities Authority. The Authorities should be managed by a board comprised of the chairs of the national supervisory authorities. The chairpersons and director generals of the Authorities should be full-time independent professionals. The appointment of the chairpersons should be confirmed by the Commission, the European Parliament and the Council and should be valid for a period of 8 years. The Authorities should have their own autonomous budget, commensurate with their responsibilities. In addition to the competences currently exercised by the level 3 committees, the Authorities should have, *inter alia* [amongst other things]., the following key-competences: i) legally binding mediation between national supervisors; ii) adoption of binding supervisory standards; iii) adoption of binding technical decisions applicable to individual financial institutions; iv) oversight and coordination of colleges of supervisors; v) designation, where needed, of group supervisors; vi) licensing and supervision of specific EU-wide institutions (e.g., Credit Rating Agencies, and post-trading infrastructures); vii) binding cooperation with the ESRC to ensure adequate macro-prudential supervision. National supervisory authorities should continue to be fully responsible for the day-to-day supervision of firms [43].

Thus, the European System of Financial Supervision[421], [44-47] the EBA, [48] the EIOPA [49] and the ESMA [50] were duly established. The voting members of the EBA's Board of Supervisors are, for every Member State, "the head of the national public authority competent for the supervision of credit institutions" in that country[422] [51]. The voting

---

[420] For example, the MAR replaces the MAD, and the MiFIR (and MiFID II) will soon replace the MiFID.

[421] See fn 416, for the identities of the participants in the European System of Financial Supervision. This system's principal aims are to: i) ensure that rules which apply to the financial sector are implemented to the extent that is necessary to maintain financial stability, ii) engender confidence in the financial system, and iii) provide adequate safeguards for the users of financial services (Regulation (EU) No 1093/2010 of the European Parliament and of the Council of 24 November 2010 establishing a European Supervisory Authority (European Banking Authority), amending Decision No 716/2009/EC and repealing Commission Decision 2009/78/EC (original version), Article 2(1); Regulation (EU) No 1094/2010 of the European Parliament and of the Council of 24 November 2010 establishing a European Supervisory Authority (European Insurance and Occupational Pensions Authority), amending Decision No 716/2009/EC and repealing Commission Decision 2009/79/EC (original version), Article 2(1); Regulation (EU) No 1095/2010 of the European Parliament and of the Council of 24 November 2010 establishing a European Supervisory Authority (European Securities and Markets Authority), amending Decision No 716/2009/EC and repealing Commission Decision 2009/79/EC (original version), Article 2(1)).

[422] The non-voting members of the EBA's Board of Supervisors are its Chairperson, and one representative from each of the following: the Commission, the European Central Bank, the European Systemic Risk Board, the EIOPA and the ESMA (Regulation (EU) No 1093/2010 (original version), Article 40(1)).

members of the EIOPA's Board of Supervisors are, for each Member State, "the head of the national public authority competent for the supervision of financial institutions" there[423] [52]. The following people are the voting members on the ESMA's Board of Supervisors: for every Member State, "the head of the national public authority competent for the supervision of financial market participants" in that country[424] [53]. Thus, each ESA is managed by a Board of Supervisors that comprises the chairs of the relevant national supervisory authorities, in line with Recommendation 22.[425]

Each ESA is to be represented by a Chairperson[426] and to be managed by an Executive Director[427], both of whom are to be full-time independent professionals [54-56]. This is as recommended in the de Larosière Report.

Each ESA's Board of Supervisors is to appoint that authority's Chairperson, "on the basis of merit, skills, knowledge of financial institutions and markets, and of experience relevant to financial supervision and regulation"; the Parliament has up to one month after the appointment is made to be able to "object to the designation of the selected person" – having heard the candidate speak before expressing its disapproval[428] [57-59]. The Chairperson's term of office is 5 years [60-62]. This term may be extended once, subject to a satisfactory evaluation during the final 9 months of the Chairperson's first period and to the Parliament's confirmation of his/her reappointment [63-65]. These provisions differ from Recommendation 22, in that the latter proposed a longer term for the Chairperson of each ESA than former did, and that his/her appointment should be subject to confirmation by the Council and the Commission – as well as by the Parliament.

Each ESA's income is to comprise: (a) obligatory contributions from the relevant national financial regulatory authorities of the Member States, (b) a subsidy from the EU, and (c) any fees paid to the ESA "in the cases specified in the relevant instruments of [European]. Union law" [66-68]. The expenditure of each ESA is to include, at least, administrative, infrastructure, operational, professional training, remuneration and staff expenses [69-71]. Revenue and expenditure are to balance [72-74]. These provisions are in line with the Recommendation 22's statement that ESAs should have a budget to allocate as they choose, which is proportionate to their responsibilities.

---

[423] The non-voting members of the EIOPA's Board of Supervisors are its Chairperson, and one representative from each of the following: the Commission, the European Systemic Risk Board, the EBA and the ESMA (Regulation (EU) No 1094/2010 (original version), Article 40(1)).

[424] The non-voting members of the ESMA's Board of Supervisors are its Chairperson, and one representative from each of the following: the Commission, the European Systemic Risk Board, the EBA and the EIOPA (Regulation (EU) No 1095/2010 (original version), Article 40(1)).

[425] Article 4(1) of Regulation (EU) No 1093/2010 and Article 4(1) of Regulation (EU) No 1094/2010 contain different definitions of 'financial institution'. Article 4(1) of Regulation (EU) No 1095/2010 defines 'financial market participant', rather than 'financial institution'. These definitions are tailored to the subject matter of each Regulation – namely the supervision of banking, insurance/occupational pensions and financial instruments, respectively.

[426] See fns 408, 409 and 410, for the Chairpersons of the EBA, the EIOPA and the ESMA, respectively.

[427] Dr. Adam Farkas, Mr. Carlos Rebuelta and Ms. Verena Ross are the Executive Directors of the EBA, the EIOPA and the ESMA, respectively (European Banking Authority (2015), Top Management, <http://www.eba.europa.eu/about-us/organisation/top-management>; European Insurance and Occupational Pensions Authority (2015), EIOPA Organigram 2015, <https://eiopa.europa.eu/Publications/Administrative/EIOPA%20Organigram%202015%2011.pdf>; European Securities and Markets Authority (2015), Who is who, <https://www.esma.europa.eu/page/Whos-who>).

[428] The Regulations do not state whether or not the Board of Supervisors is obliged to deselect the Chairperson designate, if the Parliament expresses an objection to his/her appointment.

Each ESA is to: (a) contribute to the publication of "high-quality common regulatory and supervisory standards and practices," especially by giving opinions to the EU institutions and by developing draft RTSs and draft ITSs, guidelines and recommendations, (b) contribute to the consistent application of legally-binding EU Acts, especially by: "contributing to a common supervisory culture," ensuring consistent, efficacious and efficient application of EU legislation, ensuring that colleges of supervisors operate consistently, ensuring effective and consistent superintendence of financial institutions, mediating and resolving disputes between competent authorities, preventing regulatory arbitrage, and taking actions – particularly in emergency situations (c) encourage and ease the delegation of responsibilities and tasks among competent authorities, (d) work closely with the European Systemic Risk Board, (e) organise and carry out peer review analyses of competent authorities, in order to improve consistency in the outcomes from supervision, (f) monitor and examine developments in the market over the field of that ESA's competence, (g) conduct economic analyses of markets in order to assist in the discharge of the ESA's functions, (h) advance the protection of investors (the EBA and the ESMA) and/or depositors (the EBA), or insurance policyholders and pension scheme beneficiaries and members (the EIOPA), (i) contribute to the coherent and consistent operation of colleges of supervisors, the appraisal and measurement of systemic risk, and the evolution and co-ordination of recovery and resolution plans, (j) perform any other particular tasks that EU legislation specifies, (k) place on its website, and regularly update, data that relate to its area of activities, in order to ensure that the public is able to readily access this information, and (l) take over (as appropriate) all current and on-going tasks from the Committee of European Banking Supervisors (the EBA), the Committee of European Insurance and Occupational Pensions Supervisors (the EIOPA) or the Committee of European Securities Regulators (the ESMA) [75-77]. To accomplish these tasks, the ESA is to have the powers the relevant Regulation[429] sets out, especially to: (a) develop draft RTSs in the cases to which Article 10 of the relevant Regulation refers[430], (b) evolve draft ITSs in the cases to which Article 15 of the relevant Regulation refers[431], (c) issue guidelines and recommendations, (d) issue recommendations in particular cases, (e) take individual decisions that are addressed to national authorities in accordance with Articles 18(3) and 19(3) of the relevant Regulation[432], (f) in cases that concern EU law that is directly applicable[433], take

---

[429] The 'relevant Regulation' is Regulation (EU) No 1093/2010 for the EBA, Regulation (EU) No 1094/2010 for the EIOPA, and Regulation (EU) No 1095/2010 for the ESMA.

[430] See the subsection entitled 'RTSs and CDRs', in the section below entitled 'The ESAs and Delegated Legislation', for the procedure for the development of a draft RTS. See fn 429, for the meaning of "the relevant Regulation."

[431] See the subsection entitled 'ITSs and CIRs', in the section below entitled 'The ESAs and Delegated Legislation', for the procedure for the development of a draft ITS. See fn 429, for the meaning of "the relevant Regulation."

[432] If the Council has taken a decision, addressed to the EBA, the EIOPA or the ESMA, which declares the presence of an emergency situation for the purposes of the relevant Regulation, and in exceptional circumstances in which national authorities need to exercise co-ordinated action in order to respond to unfavourable developments that may seriously endanger the integrity and the orderly operation of financial markets or the stability of the financial system within the EU, the ESA may take individual decisions to address these developments by ensuring that domestic authorities, financial institutions (the EBA and the EIOPA) and financial markets (the ESMA) fulfil the requirements of the primary legislation on which those decisions are based (Regulation (EU) No 1093/2010 (original version), Article 18(2)-(3); Regulation (EU) No 1094/2010 (original version), Article 18(2)-(3); Regulation (EU) No 1095/2010 (original version), Article 18(2)-(3)). If national authorities do not reach an agreement within the conciliation phase of their dispute resolution in the event of a cross-border difference between them, then the ESA may take a decision that requires them to act in a specified way, or to refrain from action, in order to resolve the issue – with binding effects for those domestic authorities – in order to ensure observance of EU law (Regulation (EU) No 1093/2010 (original version), Article 19(2)-(3); Regulation

individual decisions which are addressed to financial institutions (the EBA and the EIOPA) or to financial market participants (the ESMA), in the instances to which Articles 17(6), 18(4) or 19(4) of the relevant Regulation refer[434], (g) issue opinions to the Commission, the Council or the Parliament, (h) collect the information that they require concerning financial institutions, (i) develop common methodologies for examining the impact of distribution processes and product characteristics on the financial position of "institutions"[435] (the EBA and the EIOPA) or of participants in financial markets (the ESMA), and (j) supply a database of registered financial institutions (the EBA and the EIOPA) or of financial market participants (the ESMA) [78-80].

These provisions are consistent with the key competences that Recommendation 22 of the de Larosière Report suggests for the ESAs. Furthermore, as recommended there, national supervisory authorities continue to be responsible for the daily oversight of the firms that are authorised within their jurisdictions.

Thus, although the resulting sectoral architecture is not identical to that which the de Larosière Report proposed, that structure is based upon, and consistent with, the Report's recommendations. The next section describes the scope of action of each of the ESAs.

(EU) No 1094/2010 (original version), Article 19(2)-(3); Regulation (EU) No 1095/2010 (original version), Article 19(2)-(3)). See fn 429, for the meaning of "the relevant Regulation."

[433] Regulations are directly applicable (TFEU, Article 288).

[434] If a national authority does not comply with the Commission's formal opinion in respect of a contravention of EU law within the period of time stated therein, and if it is necessary to remedy this non-compliance in a timely way in order to preserve or restore fair conditions for competition in the market or ensure the integrity and orderly operation of the financial system, then the ESA that issued the recommendation to set out the action which the domestic authority should take in order to observe EU law and on which the Commission's opinion is based, may take an individual decision addressed to a financial institution (the EBA and the EIOPA) or to a financial market participant (the EIOPA) – requiring the addressee to take the measures that are required for it to observe its obligations under EU law; the ESA's decision must to conform to the Commission's formal opinion (Regulation (EU) No 1093/2010 (original version), Articles 17(6) and 17(3)-(4); Regulation (EU) No 1094/2010 (original version), Articles 17(6) and 17(3)-(4); Regulation (EU) No 1095/2010 (original version), Article 17(6) and 17(3)-(4)). If a national authority does not observe the decision that the ESA takes under Article 18(3) of the relevant Regulation (see fn 432, for the adoption of that decision) within the period that this decision lays down, then the ESA may adopt an individual decision that is addressed to a financial institution (the EBA and the EIOPA) or to a financial market participant (the ESMA), which requires the addressee to take the action that is necessary for it to comply with its obligations under primary legislation; this only applies in situations in which a domestic authority does not apply the primary legislation – and delegated Acts that are adopted in accordance with it, or applies them in a manner that appears to be a clear contravention of those Acts, and where urgent remedying is required to restore the integrity and orderly operation of financial markets or the stability of the financial system within the EU (Regulation (EU) No 1093/2010 (original version), Article 18(4); Regulation (EU) No 1094/2010 (original version), Article 18(4); Regulation (EU) No 1095/2010 (original version), Article 18(4)). If a national authority does not observe the decision that the ESA takes under Article 19(3) of the relevant Regulation (see fn 432, for the adoption of that decision), then the ESA may take an individual decision that is addressed to a financial institution (the EBA and the EIOPA) or to a financial market participant (the ESMA), which requires the addressee to take the action required for it to abide by its obligations under EU law (Regulation (EU) No 1093/2010 (original version), Article 19(4); Regulation (EU) No 1094/2010 (original version), Article 19(4); Regulation (EU) No 1095/2010 (original version), Article 19(4)). See fn 429, for the meaning of "the relevant Regulation."

[435] Neither Regulation (EU) No 1093/2010 nor Regulation (EU) No 1094/2010 defines 'institution'. In the CRR, the term 'institution' means a credit institution or an investment firm (CRR (as amended to 17/01/15), Article 4(1)(3)).

DISTINGUISHING BETWEEN THE ESAs

In order to understand the role of the ESAs in respect of post-GFC legislation, it is helpful to consider how their enabling Regulations define the scope of the actions that these authorities may take. Whilst their names provide this information in summary, i.e., the EBA is concerned with the supervision of banking activities, the EIOPA with the superintendence of the provision of insurance and pensions, and the ESMA with the oversight of securities and other financial instruments that are traded on the markets, Article 1 of the relevant Regulation[436] gives precise guidance on this matter.

The EBA

Article 1(2) of Regulation (EU) No 1093/2010 states that the EBA is to act: (i) within the powers conferred on it by that Regulation, Directive 94/19/EC of the European Parliament and of the Council of 30 May 1994 on deposit-guarantee schemes[437], Regulation (EC) No 1781/2006 of the European Parliament and of the Council of 15 November 2006 on information on the payer accompanying transfers of funds[438], CRD IV and the CRR, and (ii) to the extent that the following Acts apply to credit institutions and financial institutions[439]

---

[436] See fn 429, for the meaning of "the relevant Regulation."

[437] This Directive was repealed by Directive 2014/49/EU of the European Parliament and of the Council of 16 April 2014 on deposit guarantee schemes (recast), "with effect from 4 July 2015" (Directive 2014/49/EU (as amended to 30/10/14), Article 21). The EU legislators should amend Article 1(2) of Regulation (EU) No 1093/2010 to reflect the replacement of Directive 94/19/EC by Directive 2014/49/EU.

[438] Regulation (EC) No 1781/2006 contains rules that concern information about the payer that is to accompany transfers of funds, in order to aid "the prevention, investigation and detection of money laundering and terrorist financing" (Regulation (EC) No 1781/2006 (as amended to 08/12/07), Article 1).

[439] For the purposes of Regulation (EU) No 1093/2010, 'financial institutions' means 'credit institutions' as defined in Article 4(1) of the BCD, 'investment firms' as defined in Article 3(1)(b) of the CRD, and 'financial conglomerates' as defined in Article 2(14) of Directive 2002/87/EC of the European Parliament and of the Council of 16 December 2002 on the supplementary supervision of credit institutions, insurance undertakings and investment firms in a financial conglomerate and amending Council Directives 73/239/EEC, 79/267/EEC, 92/49/EEC, 92/96/EEC, 93/6/EEC and 93/22/EEC, and Directives 98/78/EC and 2000/12/EC of the European Parliament and of the Council; with regard to Directive 2005/60/EC only, 'financial institutions' means 'credit institutions' and 'financial institutions' as defined in Article 3(1)-(2) of that Directive (Regulation (EU) No 1093/2010 (as amended to 30/07/14), Article 4(1)). 'Credit institution' means a firm the business of which is to receive repayable funds from the public and to provide credits for its own account (BCD (as amended to 24/04/12), Article 4(1)). This definition is the same as that in Article 4(1) of the CRR, which is the definition of 'credit institution' in force as applicable to banks – the BCD having been replaced by CRD IV and the CRR. 'Investment firms' means 'institutions' as defined in Article 4(1)(1) of the MiFID, excluding: (i) credit institutions, (ii) local firms (as defined in Article 3(1)(p) of the CRD), and firms that are only authorised to supply the service of investment advice and/or receive and transmit orders from investors without holding securities or money that belong to their clients and which, for that reason, may never become indebted to those customers (CRD (as amended to 15/12/10), Article 3(1)(b)). 'Local firm' means a firm that deals for: (i) its own account on markets in financial derivatives and on cash markets, for the exclusive purpose of hedging positions on derivatives markets, or (ii) the accounts of other members of those markets and being guaranteed by clearing members of such markets – in circumstances under which responsibility for ensuring the performance of contracts that the firm agrees is taken by the clearing members of those markets (CRD (as amended to 15/12/10), Article 3(1)(p)). Article 4(1)(1) of the MiFID defines the term 'investment firm' (rather than 'institutions' as Article 3(1)(b) of the CRD suggests), which means any legal person whose regular business or occupation is the supply of at least one investment service to third parties and/or the performance of at least one investment activity on a professional basis (MiFID (as amended to 22/02/14), Article 4(1)(1)). 'Investment services and activities' comprise: (1) the reception and the transmission of orders that relate to at least one financial instrument, (2) the carrying out of orders on behalf of clients, (3) dealing on own account, (4) portfolio

and the national authorities that supervise those firms, within the relevant sections of Directive 2002/65/EC of the European Parliament and of the Council of 23 September 2002 concerning the distance marketing of consumer financial services and amending Council Directive 90/619/EEC and Directives 97/7/EC and 98/27/EC, Directive 2005/60/EC of the European Parliament and of the Council of 20 October 2005 on the prevention of the use of the financial system for the purpose of money laundering and terrorist financing[440], Directive 2007/64/EC of the European Parliament and of the Council of 13 November 2007 on payment services in the internal market amending Directives 97/7/EC, 2002/65/EC, 2005/60/EC and 2006/48/EC and repealing Directive 97/5/EC, and Directive 2009/110/EC of the European Parliament and of the Council of 16 September 2009 on the taking up, pursuit and prudential supervision of the business of electronic money institutions amending Directives 2005/60/EC and 2006/48/EC and repealing Directive 2000/46/EC; that scope for action by the EBA is to include the guidance provided in Regulations, Directives and Decisions which are based on this primary legislation, and any further EU Act that "confers tasks on" the EBA [81]. The EBA "shall also act in the field of activities of credit institutions, financial conglomerates, investment firms, payment institutions and e-money institutions" in respect of matters that are "not directly covered" in the above Acts – including auditing, corporate governance and financial reporting, as long as these actions are "necessary to ensure the effective and consistent application of those [A]cts." [82].

The EBA's objective is "to protect the public interest by contributing to the short, medium and long-term financial stability and effectiveness of the financial system, for the [European]. Union economy, its citizens and businesses." [83]. The EBA is to contribute to: (a) improving the operation of the internal market, (b) ensuring the efficiency, integrity, orderly functioning, and transparency of financial markets, (c) enhancing the co-ordination of international supervision, (d) preventing regulatory arbitrage and advancing conditions for fair competition, (e) ensuring that "the taking of credit and other risks" is "appropriately regulated and supervised," and (f) enhancing the protection of clients [84]. For these purposes, the EBA is to: (i) contribute to the consistent, efficient and efficacious application of the Acts to which the paragraph above refers, (ii) nurture "supervisory convergence," (iii) supply opinions to the Commission, the Council and the Parliament, and (iv) perform

---

management, (5) investment advice, (6) the underwriting of financial instruments, (7) the placement of financial instruments, and (8) the operation of MTFs (MiFID (as amended to 22/02/14), Annex I, Section A). The definition of 'investment firm' in Article 3(1)(b) of the CRD is similar to, but not identical to, the definition of 'investment firm' in Article 4(1)(2) of the CRR. The latter supercedes the former, as the definition of 'investment firm' that is applicable in EU banking legislation. Therefore, Article 4(1) of Regulation (EU) No 1093/2010 should be amended to reflect this change. See the subsection 'Supplementary supervision', in the section entitled 'Banking legislation' in Chapter 1, for the definition of 'financial conglomerate' in Article 2(14) of Directive 2002/87/EC – as amended to 24/03/05. The definition of 'financial conglomerate' in Article 2(14) of Directive 2002/87/EC, as amended to 27/06/13, is similar, but not identical, to the definition of this term in the March 2005 consolidation of this Directive. Directive 2005/60/EC was repealed and replaced by Directive (EU) 2015/849 (see fn 440). Therefore, the part of Article 4(1) of Regulation (EU) No 1093/2010 that refers to the definitions of 'credit institution' and 'financial institution' in Directive 2005/60/EC should be updated to refer to the definitions of 'credit institution' and 'financial institution' of its successor – Directive (EU) 2015/849 – which are in paragraphs (1) and (2), respectively, of Article 3 of the latter. As the EU legislation to which those paragraphs refer – Regulation (EU) No 575/2013 (the CRR) and Directives 2009/138/EC (the Solvency II Directive), 2004/39/EC (the MiFID), and 2002/92/EC (the Insurance Mediation Directive) are all in force at the time of writing, this amendment would be straightforward to make.

[440] This Directive is to be repealed by Directive (EU) 2015/849, "with effect from 26 June 2017" (Directive (EU) 2015/849 (original version), Article 66). The EU legislators should amend Article 1(2) of Regulation (EU) No 1093/2010 to take into account the replacement of Directive 2005/60/EC by Directive (EU) 2015/849.

economic analyses of the markets in order to further the achievement of the EBA's objective[441] [85]. In the exercise of the tasks that Regulation (EU) No 1093/2010 confers upon the EBA, the latter is specifically to attend to any systemic risk that financial institutions present – whose bankruptcy may weaken the functioning of the financial system or of the real (i.e., non-monetary) part of the economy. When conducting its duties, the EBA is to act fairly, independently and objectively, in the interests of the EU as a whole [86].

The EIOPA

The EIOPA is to act: (i) within the powers that Regulation (EU) No 1094/2010 confers upon it, (ii) within the ambit of Directive 2009/138/EC of the European Parliament and of the Council of 25 November 2009 on the taking-up and pursuit of the business of Insurance and Reinsurance (Solvency II) (recast), except for Title IV of that Directive[442], (iii) within the scope of: (1) Council Directive 64/225/EEC of 25 February 1964 on the abolition of restrictions on freedom of establishment and freedom to provide services in respect of reinsurance and retrocession, (2) First Council Directive 73/239/EEC of 24 July 1973 on the coordination of laws, Regulations and administrative provisions relating to the taking-up and pursuit of the business of direct insurance other than life assurance, (3) Council Directive 73/240/EEC of 24 July 1973 abolishing restrictions on freedom of establishment in the business of direct insurance other than life assurance, (4) Council Directive 76/580/EEC of 29 June 1976 amending Directive 73/239 EEC on the co-ordination of laws, regulations and administrative provisions relating to the taking up and pursuit of the business of direct insurance other than life insurance, (5) Council Directive 78/473/EEC of 30 May 1978 on the coordination of laws, regulations and administrative provisions relating to Community co-insurance, (6) Council Directive 84/641/EEC of 10 December 1984 amending, particularly as regards tourist assistance, the First Directive (73/239/EEC) on the coordination of laws, regulations and administrative provisions relating to the taking-up and pursuit of the business of direct insurance other than life insurance, (7) Council Directive 87/344/EEC of 22 June 1987 on the coordination of laws, regulations and administrative provisions relating to legal expenses insurance, (8) Second Council Directive 88/357/EEC of 22 June 1988 on the coordination of laws, regulations and administrative provisions relating to direct insurance other than life assurance and laying down provisions to facilitate the effective exercise of freedom to provide services and amending Directive 73/239/EEC, (9) Council Directive 92/49/EEC of 18 June 1992 on the coordination of laws, regulations and administrative provisions relating to direct insurance other than life assurance and amending Directives 73/239/EEC and 88/357/EEC (third non-life insurance Directive), (10) Directive 98/78/EC of the European Parliament and of the Council of 27 October 1998 on the supplementary supervision of insurance undertakings in an insurance group, (11) Directive 2001/17/EC of the European Parliament and of the Council of 19 March 2001 on the reorganisation and winding-up of insurance undertakings, (12) Directive 2002/83/EC of the European Parliament and of the Council of 5 November 2002 concerning life assurance, and (13) Directive

---

[441] See above in this paragraph, for the EBA's objective.
[442] Title IV of Directive 2009/138/EC is entitled 'Reorganisation and winding-up of insurance undertakings'; it comprises Articles 267-296, inclusive.

2005/68/EC of the European Parliament and of the Council of 16 November 2005 on reinsurance and amending Council Directives 73/239/EEC, 92/49/EEC as well as Directives 98/78/EC and 2002/83/EC[443], (iv) within the ambit of Directive 2002/87/EC of the European Parliament and of the Council of 16 December 2002 on the supplementary supervision of credit institutions, insurance undertakings and investment firms in a financial conglomerate and amending Council Directives 73/239/EEC, 79/267/EEC, 92/49/EEC, 92/96/EEC, 93/6/EEC and 93/22/EEC, and Directives 98/78/EC and 2000/12/EC of the European Parliament and of the Council, Directive 2002/92/EC of the European Parliament and of the Council of 9 December 2002 on insurance mediation, and Directive 2003/41/EC of the European Parliament and of the Council of 3 June 2003 on the activities and supervision of institutions for occupational retirement provision, and (v) to the extent that those Acts apply to insurance companies, reinsurance undertakings, insurance intermediaries, and firms for occupational retirement provision, within the relevant sections of Directives 2002/65/EC and 2005/60/EC[444]; the EIOPA's scope for action is to include that provided by Regulations, Directives and Decisions which are based on the primary legislation listed above in this paragraph, and any further EU Act that "confers tasks on" the EIOPA [87]. The EIOPA is also to "act in the field of activities of" financial conglomerates and the entities listed in point (v) above, with regard to issues that are "not directly covered" in the Acts noted in this paragraph – including auditing, corporate governance and financial reporting, as long as such actions are "necessary to ensure the effective and consistent application of those [A]cts." [88].

The objective of the EIOPA is "to protect the public interest by contributing to the short, medium and long-term financial stability and effectiveness of the financial system, for the [European]. Union economy, its citizens and businesses" [89]. This objective is identical to that of the EBA[445].

Furthermore, the 6 items to which the EIOPA is to contribute are the same as those to which the EBA is to contribute[446], except for item (e) – in which the EIOPA is to contribute to making certain that "the taking of risks related to insurance, reinsurance and occupational pensions activities is appropriately regulated and supervised." [90]. The remaining provisions for the EIOPA are also identical to those for the EBA[447] – other than the following: (i) the Acts which the EIOPA is to apply are those listed above in the current subsection, rather than the Acts conferring powers upon the EBA[448], and (ii) Regulation (EU) 1094/2010 confers tasks upon the ESMA – rather than Regulation (EU) 1093/2010, which confers duties upon the EBA[449] [91].

---

443 These 13 Directives (i.e., Directives 64/225/EEC, 73/239/EEC, 73/240/EEC, 76/580/EEC, 78/473/EEC, 84/641/EEC, 87/344/EEC, 88/357/EEC, 92/49/EEC, 98/78/EC, 2001/17/EC, 2002/83/EC and 2005/68/EC) were repealed by Directive 2009/138/EC "with effect from 1 January 2016" (Directive 2009/138/EC (as amended to 25/07/14), Article 310). The EU legislators should amend Article 1(2) of Regulation (EU) No 1094/2010 to reflect these changes.

444 Directive 2005/60/EC is to be repealed by Directive (EU) 2015/849, "with effect from 26 June 2017" (Directive (EU) 2015/849 (original version), Article 66). The EU legislators should amend Article 1(2) of Regulation (EU) No 1094/2010 to take into account the replacement of Directive 2005/60/EC by Directive (EU) 2015/849.

445 See the last paragraph of the subsection entitled 'The EBA', above in this section, for the EBA's objective.

446 See the final paragraph of the subsection entitled 'The EBA', above in this section, for the 6 items to which the EBA is to contribute.

447 See the last paragraph of the subsection entitled 'The EBA', above in this section, for these provisions.

448 See the first paragraph of the subsection entitled 'The EBA', above in this section, for the Acts that confer powers upon the EBA.

449 See the final paragraph of the subsection entitled 'The EBA', above in this section, for this clause.

The ESMA

The ESMA is to act: (i) within the powers that Regulation (EU) No 1095/2010 confers upon it, (ii) within the ambit of the CRD – without prejudice to the EBA's competence in terms of prudential supervision[450], (iii) within the scope of Directive 97/9/EC of the European Parliament and of the Council of 3 March 1997 on investor-compensation schemes, Directive 98/26/EC of the European Parliament and of the Council of 19 May 1998 on settlement finality in payment and securities settlement systems, Directive 2001/34/EC of the European Parliament and of the Council of 28 May 2001 on the admission of securities to official stock exchange listing and on information to be published on those securities, Directive 2002/47/EC of the European Parliament and of the Council of 6 June 2002 on financial collateral arrangements, the MAD[451], the PD, the MiFID, the TD, the UCITS V Directive, the AIFM Directive, and Regulation (EC) No 1060/2009 of the European Parliament and of the Council of 16 September 2009 on credit rating agencies, and (iv) to the extent that these Acts apply to firms which provide investment services, collective investment undertakings that market their units or shares, and the competent authorities that supervise these firms and undertakings, within the relevant sections of Directives 2002/65/EC, 2002/87/EC and 2005/60/EC[452]; the ESMA's scope for action is to include that supplied by Regulations, Directives and Decisions which are based on the primary legislation that this paragraph specifies, and any further EU Act that "confers tasks on" the ESMA [92]. The ESMA is also to "act in the field of activities of market participants"[453] with respect to matters that the Acts listed above in this paragraph do not directly consider – including auditing, corporate governance and financial reporting, as long as these actions are "necessary to ensure the effective and consistent application of those [A]cts." [93].

As for the EBA[454] and the EIOPA[455], the ESMA's objective is "to protect the public interest by contributing to the short, medium and long-term financial stability and effectiveness of the financial system, for the [European]. Union economy, its citizens and businesses." [94]. The 6 items to which the ESMA is to contribute are identical to those to which the EBA[456] and the EIOPA[457] are to contribute, except for item (e) – in which the ESMA is to contribute to making sure that "the taking of investment and other risks" is

---

[450] The CRD was repealed by CRD IV, "with effect from 1 January 2014" (CRD IV (as amended to 12/06/14), Article 163). The EU legislators should amend Article 1(2) of Regulation (EU) No 1095/2010 to reflect the replacement of the CRD by CRD IV and the CRR.

[451] The MAR repeals the MAD, "with effect from 3 July 2016" (MAR (original version), Article 37). The EU legislators should amend Article 1(2) of Regulation (EU) No 1095/2010 to reflect the replacement of the CRD by the CRR and MAD II.

[452] Directive 2005/60/EC is to be repealed by Directive (EU) 2015/849, "with effect from 26 June 2017" (Directive (EU) 2015/849 (original version), Article 66). The EU legislators should amend Article 1(2) of Regulation (EU) No 1095/2010 to take into account the replacement of Directive 2005/60/EC by Directive (EU) 2015/849.

[453] For the purposes of Regulation (EU) No 1095/2010, 'financial market participant' means a "person in relation to whom" a requirement in one of the Acts listed in this paragraph, or in a domestic law that transposes this legislation, applies (Regulation (EU) No 1095/2010 (as amended to 22/05/14), Article 4(1)).

[454] See the last paragraph of the subsection entitled 'The EBA', above in this section, for the EBA's objective.

[455] See the second paragraph of the subsection entitled 'The EIOPA', above in this section, for the EIOPA's objective.

[456] See the final paragraph of the subsection entitled 'The EBA', above in this section, for the 6 items to which the EBA is to contribute.

[457] See the last paragraph of the subsection entitled 'The EIOPA', above in this section, for item (e) to which the EIOPA is to contribute. The other 5 items to which the EIOPA is to contribute are omitted from that subsection, as they are identical to those previously stated in respect of the EBA.

"appropriately regulated and supervised." [95]. The remaining rules for the ESMA are the same as those for the EBA[458] and the EIOPA[459], with 2 exceptions, as follows: (i) the Acts that the ESMA is to apply are those listed in the previous paragraph, rather than the Acts that confer powers upon the EBA or those which grant powers to the EIOPA, and (ii) in the exercise of the duties that Regulation (EU) 1095/2010 confers upon the ESMA, the latter is specifically to address any systemic risk that financial market participants present – rather than the systemic risk that financial institutions exhibit – as in the case of the EBA and the EIOPA [96].

Comment

The objective of all 3 of the ESAs is identical. Furthermore, the tasks to which they are committed are similar. Although the sources of authority of each ESA is different to those of the others, and the firms with which each is concerned correspond to its sources – for example, CRD IV and the CRR, which are items of banking legislation, are sources for the EBA, which is concerned with the supervision of banks – these ESAs together make a system that pursues financial stability and effectiveness. 'Effectiveness' in this context may mean the volume of financial business, especially across borders both within the EEA and between EEA States and third countries.

Do the benefits that the ESAs provide exceed the costs of establishing and administering them? As much of the supervision of firms that are located within any EEA State is performed by that country's regulatory authorities, it might be argued that the ESAs form an additional layer of administration within the EEA that generates red tape. Is it necessary to publish and patrol detailed secondary legislation and recommendations in order to further the internal market in financial services? The internal market falls within the area of shared competence between the EU and its Member States [97]. Therefore, the Member States are able to exercise their competence to the extent that the EU has not exercised, and to the extent that the EU has decided to stop exercising, its competence [98]. Yet the EU financial services legislation since the GFC is so extensive, and so dominated by Regulations (which are directly effective in the Member States) – including Commission Regulations pursuant to Technical Standards that the ESAs are producing, that the internal market with regard to financial services is approaching that of EU exclusive competence. When the TEU and the TFEU confer exclusive competence upon the EU in a particular area, then only the EU may legislate; the Member States may only legislate to the extent that the EU empowers them to do so, or for the implementation of EU Acts [99]. Whilst this might be justified in order to prevent or mitigate regulatory arbitrage between the financial supervisory regimes of the countries within the EEA, it amounts to integration by stealth. Furthermore, it may be expensive for taxpayers in Member States to set up the post-GFC EU financial services regime and to administer this. Decision-makers should keep these issues in mind, as they observe the enactment, implementation and implications of the post-GFC EU financial legislation take effect.

---

[458] See the final paragraph of the subsection entitled 'The EBA', above in this section, for these provisions.
[459] See the last paragraph of the subsection entitled 'The EIOPA', above in this section, for the equivalent of point (i) that applies to the EIOPA – which is also labelled "(i)."

The ESAs and Delegated Legislation

The primary legislation in financial services provides for the ESAs to publish draft RTSs and draft ITSs over specified areas, which the Commission then converts into secondary legislation – usually Regulations. The RTSs give detailed rules for regulated firms to follow. The ITSs state procedures and provide templates for data collection from those entities.

RTSs and CDRs

Articles 10 to 14 of the relevant Regulation[460] govern the procedure for the development and the publication of RTSs and CDRs. This method is as follows.

> Where the European Parliament and the Council delegate power to the Commission to adopt regulatory technical standards by means of delegated acts under Article 290 TFEU in order to ensure consistent harmonisation in the areas specifically set out in the legislative acts referred to in Article 1(2) [of the relevant Regulation, which for each ESA are listed in the previous section entitled 'Distinguishing Between the ESAs']., the Authority may develop draft regulatory technical standards. The Authority shall submit its draft standards to the Commission for endorsement [100-102].

Article 290(1) of the TFEU lays out the form of the delegation in the primary legislation.

> A legislative act may delegate to the Commission the power to adopt non-legislative[461] acts of general application to supplement or amend certain non-essential elements of the legislative act. The objectives, content, scope and duration of the delegation of power shall be explicitly defined in the legislative acts. The essential elements of an area shall be reserved for the legislative act and accordingly shall not be the subject of a delegation of power [103].

The clarity of these guidelines, whilst good, may be furthered by an example. The first subparagraph of Article 77(3) of CRD IV states the following.

> Competent authorities shall encourage institutions[462], taking into account their size, internal organisation, and the nature, scale and complexity of their activities, to develop internal specific risk assessment capacity and to increase use of internal models for calculating own funds requirements for specific risk of debt instruments in the trading book, together with internal models to calculate own funds requirements for default and migration risk *where their exposures to specific risk are material in absolute terms* and *where they have a large number of material positions in debt instruments of different issuers*[463] [104].

---

[460] See fn 429, for the meaning of "the relevant Regulation."

[461] Article 290 of the TFEU refers to primary EU legislation as 'legislative acts' and to secondary/delegated EU legislation as 'non-legislative acts'. Article 10(1) of the relevant Regulation refers to the latter as 'delegated acts'.

[462] For the purposes of CRD IV and the CRR, an 'institution' is an investment firm or a credit institution (CRD IV (as amended to 12/06/14), Article 3(1)(3); CRR (as amended to 17/01/15), Article 4(1)(3)).

[463] Emphasis added.

The first sentence of Article 77(1) of CRD IV is as follows.

> Competent authorities shall encourage institutions that are significant in terms of their size, internal organisation and the nature, scale and complexity of their activities to develop internal credit risk assessment capacity and to increase use of the internal ratings based approach for calculating own funds requirements for credit risk where their exposures are material in absolute terms and *where they have* at the same time *a large number of material counterparties*[464] [105].

Article 77(4) of CRD IV provides a particular mandate to the EBA to develop a draft RTS with respect to the italicised phrases in the above quotes from Articles 77(3) and 77(1) of CRD IV. Thus, in accordance with Article 290(1) of the TFEU, the content and scope of the delegated power are set out in the primary legislation. Furthermore, the area of delegation is specifically stated in CRD IV, in accordance with Article 10(1) of the relevant Regulation[465]. The EBA is to submit the draft RTS to the Commission by a specified date, which, for this item, is 1st January 2014. The Commission may then convert the RTS into a CDR, according to the procedure described below in this subsection.

> [The]. EBA shall develop draft regulatory technical standards to further define the notion 'exposures to specific risk which are material in absolute terms' referred to in the first subparagraph of paragraph 3 [of Article 77 of CRD IV] and the thresholds for large numbers of material counterparties and positions in debt instruments of different issuers [to which the first sentence of paragraph 1, and the first subparagraph of paragraph 3, respectively, of Article 77 of CRD IV, refer. The]. EBA shall submit those draft regulatory technical standards to the Commission by 1 January 2014. Power is delegated to the Commission to adopt the regulatory technical standards ... in accordance with Articles 10 to 14 of Regulation (EU) No 1093/2010 [106].

The resulting CRS is Commission Delegated Regulation (EU) No 530/2014 of 12 March 2014 supplementing Directive 2013/36/EU of the European Parliament and of the Council with regard to regulatory technical standards further defining material exposures and thresholds for internal approaches to specific risk in the trading book, which is considered below in this subsection. That CDR defines only 2 of the 3 phrases stated in Article 77(4) of CRD IV – it does not set the thresholds for a large number of material counterparties pursuant to Article 77(1) of CRD IV. Therefore, it is specifically concerned with the delegations in Article 77(4) of CRD IV which are pursuant to Article 77(3) of that Directive.

RTSs are to be technical, are not to imply the need for policy choices or strategic decisions. Their content is to be bound by the Acts on which they are based [107-109].

Before submitting draft RTSs to the Commission, the ESA is to consult the public and to evaluate the costs and benefits – unless these consultations and analyses are disproportionate in relation to the ambit and effect of the draft RTSs or the urgency of the issue. The ESA is also to request the opinion of the relevant stakeholder group[466] [110-112].

---

[464] Emphasis added.

[465] See fn 429, for the meaning of "the relevant Regulation."

[466] The 'relevant Stakeholder Group' is the Banking Stakeholder Group for the EBA, the Insurance and Reinsurance Stakeholder Group or the Occupational Pensions Stakeholder Group for the EIOPA, and the Securities and Markets Stakeholder Group for the ESMA (Regulation (EU) No 1093/2010 (as amended to 30/07/14), Articles

If the ESA submits a draft RTS to the Commission, the latter is to promptly forward it to the Council and the Parliament. The Commission may endorse the draft RTS in whole, in part, or with amendments, according to its view of what the interests of the EU require. Alternatively, it may reject the draft RTS. The Commission is to make this decision within 3 months of receiving the draft RTS [113-115].

If the Commission intends to endorse a draft RTS in part, with amendments, or not at all, then it is to return the draft RTS to the ESA, explaining the reasons for this decision. Within 6 weeks, the ESA may change the draft RTS "on the basis of the Commission's proposed amendments," and re-submit it to the latter as a formal opinion. The ESA is to send a copy of this opinion to the Council and the Parliament [116-118].

If the ESA has not submitted an amended draft RTS to the Commission within that 6-week period, or has submitted a draft RTS that is not changed in a manner that is "consistent with the Commission's proposed amendments," then the latter may either adopt the RTS with the changes that it considers to be relevant, or reject the RTS. The Commission must consult the ESA before modifying the content of a draft RTS – as set out above [119-121].

If the ESA has not submitted a draft RTS within the time limit that the primary legislation specifies, then the Commission request the draft RTS by a new deadline [122-124]. If the ESA does not submit a draft RTS by the latter target time, then the Commission may adopt the RTS by way of a delegated Act – without a draft from the ESA[467] [125-127].

RTSs are to be adopted as Regulations or Decisions. They are to be published in the *Official Journal of the European Union*, and are to "enter into force on the date stated therein." [128-130].

Commission Delegated Regulation (EU) No 530/2014 is used to illustrate aspects of this process. The CDR's Preamble is as follows.

> The European Commission, [h]aving regard to the Treaty on the Functioning of the European Union, [h]aving regard to Directive 2013/36/EU of the European Parliament and of the Council of 26 June 2013 on access to the activity of credit institutions and the prudential supervision of credit institutions and investment firms, amending Directive 2002/87/EC and repealing Directives 2006/48/EC and 2006/49/EC [i.e., CRD IV]., and in particular the third paragraph of Article 77(4) thereof … has adopted this Regulation. … [131].

The CDR recognises that the Commission's power to adopt it derives from the TFEU and CDR IV – in particular, the sentence in Article 77(4) of the latter commencing "Power is delegated to the Commission"[468]. Recitals 4 and 5 of the CDR describe aspects of its adoption, as follows.

> This Regulation is based on the draft regulatory standards submitted by the European Banking Authority to the Commission [132].

10(1) and 37(1); Regulation (EU) No 1094/2010 (as amended to 22/05/14), Articles 10(1) and 37(1); Regulation (EU) No 1095/2010 (as amended to 22/05/14), Articles 10(1) and 37(1)).

[467] Article 10(3) of the relevant Regulation contains the procedure by which the Commission may do this. See fn 429, for the meaning of "the relevant Regulation."

[468] This is the 3rd paragraph of Article 77(4) of CDR IV, and is the final sentence in the quote from that Article – see above in this subsection.

The European Banking Authority has conducted open public consultations on the draft regulatory technical standards on which this Regulation is based, analysed the potential related costs and benefits and requested the opinion of the Banking Stakeholder Group established in accordance with Article 37 of Regulation (EU) No 1093/2010 of the European Parliament and of the Council [133].

Thus, the EBA has complied with the procedure that Article 10(1) of Regulation (EU) No 1093/2010 lays down for that ESA's development of CDRs. The Commission adopted Commission Delegated Regulation (EU) No 530/2014 on 12th March 2014[469], which is within 3 months of the deadline for submission by the EBA of the draft RTS to the Commission[470]. It seems that both the EBA and the Commission were within their schedule. This is confirmed from identifying the date of submission of the draft RTS to the Commission, which is 16th December 2013 [134].

Recital 1 of Commission Delegated Regulation (EU) No 530/2014 defines the scope of application of the definition in Article 1 of the CDR, with reference to the limiting phrase 'debt instruments in the trading book' in Article 77(3) of CRD IV, to which the quote from Article 77(3) above in this subsection refers.

Article 77(3) of Directive 2013/36/EU refers solely to 'debt instruments', therefore equity instruments in the trading book should not be included in the assessment of materiality of specific risk [135].

Recital 2 of Commission Delegated Regulation (EU) No 530/2014 explains the basis for the definition used in Article 1 of the CDR, as follows.

The materiality in absolute terms of exposures to specific risk should be measured by applying the standardised rules for the calculation of net positions of debt instruments. That assessment should consider both long and short net positions calculated in accordance with Article 327(1) of Regulation (EU) No 575/2013 of the European Parliament and of the Council, after having given an allowance for hedges provided by credit derivatives in accordance with Articles 346 and 347 of Regulation (EU) No 575/2013 [136].

Article 327(1) of the CRR states that a credit institution or an investment firm's net long position or net short position is the sum of its net long or short position in respect of each category of its financial instruments, which is described by Articles 328 (interest rate futures and forwards), 329 (options and warrants) and 330 (swaps) of that Regulation.

The absolute value of the excess of an institution's long (short) positions over its short (long) positions in the same equity, debt and convertible issues and identical financial futures, options, warrants and covered warrants shall be its net position in each

---

[469] This is the date of the CDR, which is stated in the CDR's title. See above in this subsection, for the title of the CDR.

[470] This deadline is 1st January 2014; see above in this subsection.

of those different instruments. In calculating its net position, positions in derivative instruments shall be treated as laid down in Articles 328 to 330 [of the CRR]. ... [137].[471]

With Recitals 1 and 2 of Commission Delegated Regulation (EU) No 530/2014 having described how the definition in Article 1 is to be reached, the Article provides a simple numerical description, as follows.

> Definition of 'exposures to specific risk which are material in absolute terms' according to Article 77(4) of Directive 2013/36/EU
> An institution's exposure to specific risk of debt instruments shall be considered to be material in absolute terms where the sum of all net long and net short positions, as defined in Article 327 of Regulation (EU) No 575/2013, is greater than EUR 1 000 000 000 [138].

Thus, with the help of Recitals 1 and 2 of the CDR, Article 1 of the CDR provides the definition 'exposures to specific risk which are material in absolute terms' – as introduced in Article 77(3) of CRD IV, and as required by Article 77(4) of that Directive[472].

Article 2 of Commission Delegated Regulation (EU) No 530/2014 provides a definition of the phrase 'large number of material positions in debt instruments of different issuers', which is pursuant to Article 77(3)-(4) of CRD IV[473]. Recital 3 of this CDR contextualises that Article, as follows.

> The first subparagraph of Article 77(3) of Directive 2013/36/EU covering specific risk in the trading book refers to 'a large number of material positions in debt instruments of different issuers'. These rules therefore set out a materiality threshold for large numbers of material positions in debt instruments of different issuers, pursuant to Article 77(4) of that Directive [139].

Article 2 gives a numerical definition.

> Definition of 'large number of material positions in debt instruments of different issuers' according to Article 77(4) of Directive 2013/36/EU.
> An institution's specific risk portfolio shall be considered to comprise a large number of material positions in debt instruments of different issuers where the portfolio includes more than 100 positions, each of which is greater than EUR 2 500 000, whether those positions are net long or net short, as defined in Article 327 of Regulation (EU) No 575/2013 [140].

Thus, the EBA and the Commission worked through the draft RTS-to-CDR process in Article 10(1) of Regulation (EU) No 1093/2010, described above, to produce a CDR in a timely fashion, which fulfils its mandate in the primary legislation that delegates the power to those entities to develop and publish that secondary Regulation. From this description, the reader might conclude that the Council and the Parliament are only there to receive

---

[471] "All net positions, irrespective of their signs, shall be converted on a daily basis into the institution's reporting currency at the prevailing spot exchange rate before their aggregation" (CRR (as amended to 17/01/15), Article 327(3)).

[472] See above in this subsection, for quotes of the relevant parts of Article 77(3)-(4) of CRD IV.

[473] See fn 472.

documents. However, Articles 13 and 14 of the relevant Regulation[474] give these institutions an evaluative role in the draft RTS-to CDR procedure.

As soon as the Commission adopts any RTS, it is to simultaneously send it to the Council and the Parliament [141-143]. The Council and the Parliament may object to the RTS within 3 months from its date of receipt from the Commission. The Council or the Parliament may extend this period by 3 months. However, if the Commission adopts an ESA's draft RTS in whole without amending it, then the period during which the Council and the Parliament may object is one month from its date of receipt from the Commission. The Council or the Parliament may extend this time by one month, and, if so extended, by one further month [144-146].

Commission Delegated Regulation (EU) No 530/2014 was adopted by the Commission on 12th March 2014, and the consultation period for the Council and the Parliament ended on 12th May 2014 [147]. This is compatible with the following interpretation of the information in the previous paragraph. The Council and the Parliament received the RTS from the Commission on the date that the Commission adopted it as a CDR, which was 12th March 2014. The Commission had made no amendments to the draft RTS, as received from the EBA. Consequently, the Council and the Parliament had one month, i.e., until 12th April 2014, to be able to object to any of the CDR's contents. Either the Council or the Parliament extended this period by another month, i.e., until 12th May 2014. By that time, neither of these institutions had objected, and neither had requested a further month's extension.

If, on the expiry of the period, neither the Council nor the Parliament has objected to the RTS, then it is to be published in the *Official Journal of the European Union*, and to "enter into force on the date stated therein"; the RTS is to be published in *Official Journal of the European Union* and to come into force before that period expires, if both the Council and the Parliament have notified the Commission of their intention not to object [148-150]. Commission Delegated Regulation (EU) No 530/2014 was published in the *Official Journal of the European Union* on 20th May 2014, i.e., 8 days (and 6 working days) after the consultation period for the Council and the Parliament ended. It is submitted that neither the Council nor the Parliament notified the Commission that they did not object to this CDR prior to 12th May 2014, and that, as soon as this deadline had expired, the Commission queued the CDR for publication in the *Official Journal of the European Union*. Article 3 of Commission Delegated Regulation (EU) No 530/2014 stated that date for the CDR to come into force, as follows.

This Regulation shall enter into force on the twentieth day following that of its publication in the *Official Journal of the European Union* [151].

Accordingly, this CDR would have entered into force in all EEA States[475] on 9th June 2014. This is within a year of the adoption of the enabling primary legislation, CDR IV[476], which is efficient operation of the draft RTS-to-CDR process.

---

[474] See fn 429, for the meaning of "the relevant Regulation."

[475] As Commission Delegated Regulation (EU) No 530/2014 is labelled a 'Text with EEA relevance', it applies to all of the Contracting Parties to the EEA Agreement, i.e., the 28 EU Member States, Iceland, Liechtenstein and Norway.

[476] CDR IV was adopted on 26th June 2013, and published in the Official Journal of the European Union on the following day.

If either the Council or the Parliament objects to any RTS within the consultation period, then that RTS is not to become law. "In accordance with Article 296 TFEU"[477], the objector is to state its reasons for doing so [152-154].

If the Commission amends or rejects a draft RTS, then it is to inform the ESA, the Council and the Parliament of this, and must disclose its reasons for doing so [155-157]. "Where appropriate," the Council or the Parliament may invite the Chairperson of the ESA and the responsible Commissioner to a meeting, for these individuals to present and explain the differences in their views concerning the RTS [158-160].

Regulations (EU) No 1093/2010, (EU) No 1094/2010 and (EU) No 1095/2010 contain a procedure for each of the Council and the Parliament to revoke the power of the Commission to adopt RTSs. This power, "referred to in Article 10" of each of these Regulations, is conferred on the Commission for 4 years from 16th December 2010, and automatically extended for each subsequent 4-year period, unless the Council or the Parliament revokes it[478]. The Commission is to prepare a report concerning this power, at least 6 months before the 4-year period ends [161-163].

The Council or the Parliament may withdraw the Commission's power to adopt RTSs "at any time." [164-166]. If the Council (Parliament) has started an internal procedure for deciding whether to withdraw this power, then it is to "endeavour to inform" the Parliament (Council) and the Commission "within a reasonable time before the final decision is taken"[479] [167-169]. The decision of revocation shall: (i) terminate the delegation of the power that is specified therein, (ii) take effect at once, or at a later date that is specified in the decision, (iii) not affect the validity of RTSs in then in force, and (iv) be published in the *Official Journal of the European Union* [170-172].

---

[477] Article 296 of the TFEU states: "Legal acts shall state the reasons on which they are based." This Article does not refer to objections to prospective legal acts. Nevertheless, it is reasonable for the Council and the Parliament to express its reasons for objecting to a CDR, as this feedback would provide the Commission and the relevant ESA with guidance as to any future re-drafting of the RTS.

[478] The Council or the Parliament is to rescind the power of the Commission to adopt RTSs "in accordance with Article 14" (Regulation (EU) No 1093/2010, Article 11(1); Regulation (EU) No 1094/2010, Article 11(1); Regulation (EU) No 1095/2010, Article 11(1)). Article 14 of Regulation (EU) No 1093/2010, of Regulation (EU) No 1094/2010 and of Regulation (EU) No 1095/2010, concerns the Commission's amendment or rejection of draft RTSs. Article 12 of Regulation (EU) No 1093/2010, of Regulation (EU) No 1094/2010 and of Regulation (EU) No 1095/2010, contains the procedure for revocation of the Commission's power to adopt RTSs. It is therefore submitted that EU legislators should amend the phrase 'in accordance with Article 14', to read 'in accordance with Article 12'.

[479] The Council (Parliament) is to "indicat[e] the delegated power which could be subject to revocation" (Regulation (EU) No 1093/2010, Article 12(1); Regulation (EU) No 1094/2010, Article 12(1); Regulation (EU) No 1095/2010, Article 12(1)). This phrase, together with the reference to Article 14 noted previously (see fn 478) suggests that the Council or the Parliament may revoke delegations in the CRD IV and other enabling primary legislation on an individual basis. However, this is inconsistent with the reference in Article 11(1) of Regulation (EU) No 1093/2010, of Regulation (EU) No 1094/2010 and of Regulation (EU) No 1095/2010, to "[t]he power to adopt regulatory technical standards referred to in Article 10" – i.e., the Commission is either empowered by the Council and the Parliament to adopt RTSs under each of Regulations (EU) No, 1093/2010, (EU) No 1094/2010 and (EU) No 1095/2010, or it is not so empowered.

ITSs and CIRs

Article 15 of the relevant Regulation[480] contains the procedure for the development and the publication of ITSs and CIRs. This process is similar to that described in the section above for RTSs and CDRs – under Article 10 of the relevant Regulation.

The main differences between the rules for RTSs/CDRs and ITSs/CIRs are: (i) in the latter case, the relevant Regulation contains no rules for the Council and the Parliament that are equivalent to Article 13 of that Regulation – which applies to RTSs/CDRs, i.e., for ITSs/CIRs, the Council and the Parliament are merely passive recipients of documents; (ii) in the latter case, the relevant Regulation contains no provisions that are equivalent to Article 14 of the relevant Regulation – which applies to RTSs/CDRs, i.e., for ITSs/CIRs, the Commission is not explicitly required to provide reasons for rejecting or amending a draft ITS, and the Council and the Parliament are not directly authorised to hold a meeting in order to attempt to reconcile the differences between the responsible Commissioner and the Chairperson of the ESA that developed the draft ITS; (iii) in the latter case, the Council and the Parliament are not explicitly empowered to revoke the Commission's authority to adopt ITSs – which contrasts with the power of the Council and the Parliament to rescind the Commission's authority to adopt RTSs under Articles 11 and 12 of the relevant Regulation, and (iv) whilst Article 290(1) of the TFEU provides the authority for the Council and the Parliament to delegate power to the Commission to adopt RTSs, it is Article 291(2) of the TFEU that empowers the Commission to adopt ITSs – under the conditions specified therein. This Article is as follows.

> Where uniform conditions for implementing legally binding [European]. Union acts are needed, those acts shall confer implementing powers on the Commission ... [481] [173].

Article 15(1) of the relevant Regulation[482] refers to the Acts that grant the specific instances of delegation of powers in respect of each ESA.[483] This Article also defines the content of ITSs, as follows.

> The Authority may develop implementing technical standards, by means of implementing acts under[484] Article 291 TFEU, in the areas specifically set out in the legislative acts referred to in Article 1(2) [of the relevant Regulation]. Implementing technical standards shall be technical, shall not imply strategic decisions or policy choices and their content shall be to determine the conditions of application of those acts. ... [174-176].

An example of an ITS/CIR is considered, in the light of the above guidance. This is Commission Implementing Regulation (EU) No 620/2014 of 4 June 2014 laying down

---

[480] See fn 429, for the meaning of "the relevant Regulation."

[481] Article 291(4) of the TFEU states: "The word 'implementing' shall be inserted in the title of implementing acts.."

[482] See fn 429, for the meaning of "the relevant Regulation."

[483] These Acts are listed for Regulation (EU) No 1093/2010 in the subsection entitled 'The EBA', for Regulation (EU) No 1094/2010 in the subsection entitled 'The EIOPA', and for Regulation (EU) No 1095/2010 in the subsection entitled 'The ESMA', above in the section entitled 'Distinguishing Between the ESAs'.

[484] Whilst Article 15(1) of Regulation (EU) No 1094/2010 and Article 15(1) of Regulation 1095/2010 use the word "under," Article 15(1) of Regulation (EU) No 1093/2010 uses the phrase "pursuant to" in that word's stead.

implementing technical standards with regard to information exchange between competent authorities of home and host Member States, according to Directive 2013/36/EU of the European Parliament and of the Council.

The Preamble of this CIR identifies the primary legislation that gave rise to that Regulation. It is as follows.

> The European Commission, [h]aving regard to the Treaty on the Functioning of the European Union, [h]aving regard to Directive 2013/36/EU of the European Parliament and of the Council of 26 June 2013 on access to the activity of credit institutions and the prudential supervision of credit institutions and investment firms, amending Directive 2002/87/EC and repealing Directives 2006/48/EC and 2006/49/EC [i.e., CRD IV]., and in particular the third paragraph of Article 50(7) thereof ... has adopted this Regulation: ... [177].

As in the case of Commission Delegated Regulation (EU) No 530/2014, the CIR's last 2 Recitals show the EBA's procedural compliance with Regulation (EU) 1093/2010.

> This Regulation is based on the draft implementing standards submitted by the European Supervisory Authority (European Banking Authority) to the Commission [178].
> The EBA has conducted open public consultations on the draft implementing technical standards on which this Regulation is based, analysed the potential related costs and benefits and requested the opinion of the Banking Stakeholder Group established in accordance with Article 37 of Regulation (EU) No 1093/2010 of the European Parliament and of the Council [179].

Article 50(7) of CRD IV, the empowering provision, is as follows.

> [The]. EBA shall develop draft implementing technical standards to establish standard forms, templates and procedures for the information sharing requirements which are likely to facilitate the monitoring of institutions[485]. Power is delegated to the Commission to adopt the implementing technical standards ... in accordance with Articles 15 of Regulation (EU) No 1093/2010 [180].

The EBA was to submit the draft ITS to the Commission by 1st January 2014 [181]. The former duly did this – the date of submission being 16th December 2013; the Commission adopted the ITS on 4th June 2014 [182].

Article 50(1) of CRD IV provides information concerning the monitoring of institutions by the regulatory authorities of different EEA States[486]. This Article contextualises the mandate for the CIR in Article 50(7) of CRD IV, and is as follows.

> The competent authorities of the Member States concerned shall collaborate closely in order to supervise the activities of institutions operating, in particular through a branch, in one or more Member States other than that in which their head offices are situated. *They shall supply one another with* all information concerning the management and ownership of such institutions that is likely to facilitate their supervision and the

---

[485] Within CRD IV and the CRR, 'institutions' means credit institutions and investment firms; see fn 462.
[486] CRD IV is a 'Text with EEA relevance' – as is Commission Implementing Regulation (EU) No 620/2014.

examination of the conditions for their authorisation, and *all information likely to facilitate the monitoring of institutions, in particular with regard to liquidity, solvency, deposit guarantee*,[487] the limiting of large exposures [to risk]., other factors that may influence the systemic risk posed by the institution, administrative accounting procedures and internal control mechanisms [183].

As Article 7 and Annex II to Commission Implementing Regulation (EU) No 620/2014 concern information to be exchanged in situations of liquidity stress, Article 50(3) of the CRD is also relevant to the CIR, and is as follows.

> The competent authorities of the home Member State shall inform the competent authorities of all host Member States immediately where liquidity stress[488] occurs or can reasonably be expected to occur. That information shall also include details about the planning and implementation of a recovery plan and about any prudential supervision measures taken in that context [184].

Recital 1 of Commission Implementing Regulation (EU) No 620/2014 sets out the reasons for the CIR's particular legal provisions.

> In order to ensure efficient and timely cooperation between competent authorities of home and host Member States information exchange should be two-way, within the respective supervisory competences of those authorities. Standard forms, templates and operating procedures, including timelines, should therefore be established for the exchange of information during going concern situations and liquidity stress situations. Harmonised frequencies and maximum remittance dates for the information to be exchanged on a regular basis should also be established, providing for information to be exchanges on a bi-annual or annual basis. … [185].

The geographical scope of this CIR comprises credit institutions and investment firms whose head office is situated in an EEA State, and which have branches in, or provide cross-border services in, at least one other country within the EEA [186]. Annex I to the CIR contains 6 templates, as follows, which provide for the half-yearly and yearly information that competent authorities are to share in respect of branches and cross-border services [187].

Annex II to Commission Implementing Regulation (EU) No 620/2014 contains one template, which provides for information to be exchanged between national financial regulatory authorities in the event of a possible, probable or actual situation of liquidity stress [188]. Whilst the data to be inserted into these templates correspond to items of information

---

[487] Emphasis added. The first 3 items of particular information in respect of the monitoring of information in Article 50(1) of CRD IV are italicised, because these are specifically mentioned in Articles 2(2), 4(1)-(2), 4(5)(a), 4(5)(d), 4(6), and Annex I, of Commission Implementing Regulation (EU) No 620/2014. All of these items of particular information in Article 50(1) of CRD IV are relevant to Commission Delegated Regulation (EU) No 524/2014 of 12 March 2014 supplementing Directive 2013/36/EU of the European Parliament and of the Council with regard to regulatory technical standards specifying the information that competent authorities of home and host Member States supply to one another. That CDR was adopted pursuant to Article 50(6) of CRD IV, which is as follows: "[The] EBA shall develop draft regulatory technical standards to specify the information referred to this Article. Power is delegated to the Commission to adopt the regulatory technical standards … in accordance with Articles 10 to 14 of Regulation (EU) No 1093/2010.."

[488] Neither CRD IV nor the CRR defines 'liquidity stress'. This term describes a situation in which the bank or the investment firm is at risk of having insufficient cash to be able to meet its pending financial obligations.

in Commission Delegated Regulation (EU) No 524/2014[489], [189]. Commission Implementing Regulation (EU) No 620/2014 empowers a domestic financial regulatory authority to request information that does not need to be exchanged pursuant to the former [190]. The recipient national financial regulatory authority is obliged to comply with this request, unless the information sought is unavailable [191]. The authority seeking the information is to explain, in its request, how this data is likely to ease: (i) the superintendence or monitoring of a credit institution or an investment firm, (ii) the assessment of the conditions for the authorisation of a credit institution or an investment firm, or (iii) the preservation of financial stability [192].

Table 3.1. Templates provided in Annex I to CIR (EU) No 620/2014

Name of template	Title of template
Part 1: Bi-annual specific	Template for the information on liquidity and supervisory findings regarding individual institutions to be exchanged bi-annually with the competent authorities of a host Member State supervising a significant branch[490]
Part 2: Annual specific	Template for the information to be exchanged annually regarding the liquidity and solvency of individual institutions
Part 3: Annual – services	Template for the information to be exchanged regarding cross-border service providers
Part 4: Branch specific – from hosts	Template for the information to be exchanged regarding branches established in host Member States
Part 5: Annual generic – deposit-guarantee schemes	Template for the information to be exchanged concerning deposit-guarantee schemes
Part 6: Annual additional	Additional information to be exchanged concerning the management and ownership of individual institutions, their liquidity and funding policies, liquidity and funding contingency plans and preparations for emergency situations

Whilst the CIR states remittance dates by which for the information to be provided in the templates is to be supplied[491], a request for information that does not need to be exchanged pursuant to Commission Delegated Regulation (EU) No 620/2014 is to "specify a reasonable time by which the response must be provided, taking into account the nature and urgency of the request and information requested" [193]. The recipient financial regulatory authority is to "make every effort to respond by the time indicated in the request," promptly indicating a later date for supplying the information if it is unable to provide this data by the specified time [194].

---

[489] See fn 487, for the full title of Commission Delegated Regulation (EU) No 524/2014. Recital 8 of Commission Implementing Regulation (EU) No 620/2014 states: "Given the fact that the type of information to be exchanged between competent authorities is detailed in Commission Delegated Regulation (EU) No 524/2014, this Implementing Regulation should be considered the necessary corollary of Delegated Regulation (EU) No 524/2014.."

[490] Article 51 of CRD IV contains a procedure for the financial regulatory authority of a host Member State of a credit institution or an investment firm to make a request to the consolidating supervisor or the financial regulatory authority of the organisation's home Member State, for the branch in the former Member State "to be considered as significant" (CRD IV (as amended to 12/06/14), Article 51(1)).

[491] Article 2 of Commission Implementing Regulation (EU) No 620/2014 specifies the remittance dates for these data.

Comment

On the basis of the examples given above, the RTS/CDR and ITS/CIR systems work specifically, efficiently and clearly. The definitions in the CDR correspond precisely to those in the corresponding primary legislation. The CIR provides comprehensible templates, which national financial regulatory authorities should be able to complete with reasonable ease – given the available information.

Nonetheless, neither the example CDR nor the example CIR provide all of the items that the primary legislation empowers them so to do. In the former case, Commission Delegated Regulation (EU) No 530/2014 contains no definition of 'large number of material counterparties' pursuant to Articles 77(1) and 77(4) of CRD IV. This may be because Article 77(3) of CRD IV, but not Article 77(1) of that Directive, concerns debt instruments in the trading book – although Article 77(4) of CRD IV does not refer to the trading book. In the latter case, the templates in Annex I to Commission Implementing Regulation (EU) No 620/2014 do not provide for all of the particular items of information stated in the list in Article 50(1) of CRD IV. The EBA and the Commission may choose to develop and publish further delegated instruments in order to address these omissions. However, if they did, this would be beyond the deadlines stated in Articles 77(4) and 50(8) of CDR IV; in both instances, the EBA is to submit the draft standards to the Commission by 1st January 2014 [195].

Further to my earlier comment[492], the Council and the Parliament are less involved in the production of CDRs and, especially, CIRs, than they are in the enactment of primary legislation under the Ordinary Legislative Procedure in Article 294 of the TFEU. Although the Technical Standards tend to be detailed, there is much in the primary financial legislation that is similarly precise – such as the content of most of the CRR. In the latter case, the relevant divisions of the Council and the Parliament are expected to understand these detailed rules, and to adjust the provisions in instances in which they consider this to be necessary, and in the way in which they deem it to be appropriate. It is submitted that the same level of scrutiny should be extended to all EU legislation. Whilst the ESAs and the Commission are obliged to "conduct open public consultations" in respect of draft RTSs and draft ITSs, [196-198] the public do not have the right to submit modifications to draft standards; the Commission's adopted Technical Standards are final, subject only to a post-production scrutiny of CDRs (but not CIRs) by the Council and the Parliament. In comparison with the Ordinary Legislative Procedure, the process for developing CDRs and CIRs lacks democratic legitimacy.

The *status quo* may be defended against the point made in the previous paragraph by the argument that CDRs and, especially, CIRs, are operational rather than strategic – the primary legislation specifically provides for the Technical Standards, and, therefore, further 'democratic' scrutiny is unnecessary. It was observed above[493] that Commission Delegated Regulation (EU) No 530/2014 was developed and published efficiently. The draft RTS-to-CDR and the draft ITS-to-CIR processes are able to promptly deliver technical legal instruments. This is desirable in the financial sector – given the complexity of its instruments and markets, as the law should keep up with the pace of product development. Nonetheless,

---

[492] This is the subsection entitled 'Comment', in the section above entitled 'Distinguishing Between the ESAs'.
[493] See the subsection entitled 'RTS and CDRs', above in this section.

there is a risk that the ESAs, and the financial division of the Commission, might exert substantial costs on taxpayers in terms of emoluments, fixed assets and overhead expenses, whilst producing many detailed laws that are subject to little public scrutiny.

The EBA and the European Central Bank

Council Regulation (EU) No 1024/2013 of 15 October 2013 conferring specific tasks on the European Central Bank concerning policies relating to the prudential supervision of credit institutions, provides for the superintendence of banks within the Member States whose currency is the Euro by the European Central Bank. Whilst this role of the European Central Bank is different to the function of the EBA – which oversees all of the banks within the EEA (together with their national financial regulatory authorities), it may be helpful to ascertain the boundary between those responsibilities.

The EBA is to "act in accordance with Council Regulation (EU) No 1024/2013." [199]. That Regulation confers on the European Central Bank specified tasks that concern the prudential supervision of credit institutions[494], with the aim of contributing to the integrity and safety of those organisations and to financial stability within the EEA and each Member State[495] – and with complete duty of care and regard for the soundness and the unity of the internal market, founded on the equal treatment of credit institutions with the intention of preventing regulatory arbitrage [200]. Within the framework of the Single Supervisory Mechanism[496], the European Central Bank is to "be exclusively competent" to conduct the following tasks in respect all credit institutions that are founded in the participating Member States[497]: (a) to authorise each credit institution to provide financial services in its home Member State and to withdraw this licence, (b) for credit institutions that are founded in a participating Member State which would like to establish a branch or supply cross-border services in a non-participating Member State, to conduct the tasks that the home Member State's banking regulator has under the relevant EU Law, (c) to examine notifications of the acquisition and disposal of qualifying holdings[498] in credit institutions (although not in respect of bank resolutions), (d) to ensure observance of the laws[499] that place prudential requirements on credit institutions over the areas of large exposure limits, leverage, liquidity,

---

[494] A 'credit institution' is an organisation, the business of which is to accept repayable funds from the public and to provide credits for its own account (Council Regulation (EU) No 1024/2013, Article 2(3); CRR (as amended to 17/01/15), Article 4(1)(1)).

[495] Council Regulation (EU) No 1024/2013 is not labelled a 'Text with EEA relevance'. It, therefore does not apply to EEA States that are outside the EU, i.e., to Iceland, Liechtenstein or Norway.

[496] The European Central Bank is to conduct its tasks within a Single Supervisory Mechanism, which comprises the European Central Bank and the national banking regulator within each Member State whose currency is the Euro, and within every Member State whose currency is not the Euro that closely co-operates with the European Central Bank under Article 7 of Council Regulation (EU) No 1024/2013 (Council Regulation (EU) No 1024/2013, Articles 6(1), 2(9), 2(1) and 2(2)). These Member States are called 'participating Member States' (Council Regulation (EU) No 1024/2013, Article 2(1)).

[497] See fn 496, for the definition of 'participating Member States'.

[498] A 'qualifying holding' is a holding in a company that comprises at least 10% of its capital or voting rights, or which makes it possible to exert "a significant influence" on that firm's management (Council Regulation (EU) No 1024/2013, Article 2(8); CRR (as amended to 17/01/15), Article 4(1)(36)).

[499] 'The laws' in this context means EU law, national legislation that transposes Directives, and rules of Member States which exercise options that Regulations explicitly grant to those countries (Council Regulation (EU) No 1024/2013, Article 4(3)).

own funds requirements and securitisation, and those which concern the reporting and public disclosure of information on these issues, (e) to ensure compliance with the laws[500] that impose requirements on credit institutions to operate strong arrangements for their governance, (f) to conduct supervisory reviews – including, in co-ordination with the EBA, stress tests (as appropriate), in order to determine whether the arrangements, mechanisms, processes and strategies that credit institutions have put in place, and the own funds that these organisations hold, ensure a robust management and coverage of their risks and, on the basis of this supervisory review, to impose on credit institutions measures that EU law makes specifically available to national banking regulators, (g) to conduct consolidated supervision over the parent companies of credit institutions that are founded in one of the participating Member States, and to take part in consolidated supervision – including within colleges of supervisors – in relation to parent companies which are not established in a participating Member State, (h) to participate in supplementary supervision of a financial conglomerate[501] in respect of the credit institutions within that group, and to carry out the tasks of a co-ordinator in cases in which the European Central Bank is appointed as the co-ordinator for a financial conglomerate in accordance with the criteria that EU law sets out for this designation, and (i) to conduct supervisory tasks with regard to recovery plans and early intervention, in cases in which a credit institution does not satisfy, or is likely to contravene, the applicable prudential requirements[502] [201]. For credit institutions that are established in a non-participating Member State, which open a branch or provide cross-border services in a participating Member State, the European Central Bank is to conduct, within the scope of the functions that the previous sentence assigns to it, the tasks for which the national banking regulators are competent in accordance with relevant EU law [202].

In order to conduct the tasks that Regulation (EU) No 1024/2013 confers on it, with the aim of ensuring high supervisory standards, and in its application of the laws[503], the European Central Bank is to adopt guidelines and recommendations, and take decisions that are subject to, and which comply with, the relevant EU law [203]. In particular, the European Central Bank is to observe: (i) the RTSs and the ITSs that the EBA has developed and the Commission has adopted "in accordance with Article 10 to 15 of Regulation (EU) No 1093/2010," (ii) the guidelines and recommendations that the EBA issues under Article 16 of Regulation (EU) No 1093/2010, and (iii) the provisions of Regulation (EU) No 1093/2010 concerning the European supervisory handbook that the EBA has developed in conformity to that Regulation [204].

The European Central Bank may adopt Regulations to the extent that is required to specify and organise the arrangements for conducting the tasks which Regulation (EU) No

---

[500] See fn 499, for the meaning of 'the laws' in the context of the tasks conferred on the European Central Bank by Article 4(1) of Council Regulation (EU) No 1024/2013.

[501] For the purposes of Council Regulation (EU) No 1024/2013, 'financial conglomerate' means a financial conglomerate as Article 2(14) of Directive 2002/87/EC defines the term. See the subsection 'Supplementary supervision', in the section entitled 'Banking legislation' in Chapter 1, for the definition of 'financial conglomerate' in Article 2(14) of Directive 2002/87/EC, as amended to 24/03/05. The definition of 'financial conglomerate' in Article 2(14) of Directive 2002/87/EC, as amended to 27/06/13, is similar, although not identical, to the definition of that term in the March 2005 consolidation of Directive 2002/87/EC.

[502] In cases that relevant EU law specifies for national banking regulators, the European Central Bank is to conduct supervisory tasks which concern structural changes that credit institutions should make, in order to preclude "financial stress or failure" – excluding powers of resolution (Council Regulation (EU) No 1024/2013, Article 4(1)(i)).

[503] See fn 499, for the meaning of 'the laws' in Article 4(3) of Council Regulation (EU) No 1024/2013.

1024/2013 confers upon it [205]. Furthermore, it is to contribute as necessary to the EBA's development of draft RTSs or draft ITSs in agreement with Regulation (EU) No 1093/2010, or is to draw the EBA's attention to a possible need to submit draft standards to the Commission which amend RTSs or ITSs that are currently in force [206].

Thus, the European Central Bank is subject to the CDRs and the CIRs that are published pursuant to RTSs and ITSs which the EBA has developed, and to recommendations and guidelines that the ECB has produced. This makes sense, because the EBA is effectively acting as the senior national banking regulator in respect of the countries whose currency is the Euro, and with regard to other Member States that wish to participate in the Banking Union. Thus, like a domestic banking regulator in a non-participating Member State – such as the United Kingdom's Prudential Regulation Authority, the European Central Bank in its supervisory role (in contrast to its macroeconomic function) is subject to the rules and guidance of the EBA. Recital 32 of Regulation (EU) 1024/2013 clarifies the positions of the European Central Bank and the EBA, as follows.

> ... [The]. EBA is entrusted with developing draft technical standards and guidelines and recommendations ensuring supervisory convergence and consistency of supervisory outcomes within the [European]. Union. The ECB [European Central Bank] should not replace the exercise of those tasks by [the]. EBA, and should therefore exercise powers to adopt regulations in accordance with Article 132 of the Treaty on the Functioning of the European Union[504] and in compliance with Union acts adopted by the Commission on the basis of drafts developed by [the]. EBA and subject to Article 16 of Regulation (EU) No 1093/2010 [207].

Comments

On the basis of Recommendations in the de Larosière Report, the EU has established and conferred tasks upon the ESAs. Their role is deeper and wider than the function of the European Committees[505] that preceded them, and which were introduced in their original form in association with the development of the Lamfalussy process[506]. The objective of all 3 of the ESAs is "to protect the public interest by contributing to the short, medium and long-term financial stability and effectiveness of the financial system, for the [European]. Union economy, its citizens and businesses" [208-210]. Thus, the ESAs form a system for financial superintendence, with an emphasis on financial stability and effectiveness, the latter of which may mean the volume of cross-border business – as stated above[507].

---

[504] Article 132(1) of the TFEU states: "In order to carry out the tasks entrusted to the ESCB [the European System of Central Banks – which comprises the European Central Bank and national central bank of each of the 28 Member States], the European Central Bank shall, in accordance with the provisions of the Treaties [i.e., the TEU and the TFEU] and under the conditions laid down in the Statute of the ESCB and of the ECB [the European Central Bank] – make regulations to the extent necessary to implement [the specified Articles of the Statute of the ESCB and of the ECB], – take decisions necessary for carrying out the tasks entrusted to the ESCB under the Treaties and the Statute of the ESCB and of the ECB, [and] – make recommendations and deliver opinions.."

[505] These are the Committee of European Banking Supervisors, the Committee of European Insurance and Occupational Pensions Supervisors, and the Committee of European Securities Regulators.

[506] See the sections entitled 'The Lamfalussy Process' and 'European Supervisors for Banking and Insurance Activities', in Chapter 1, for the foundation of the European Committees in the financial sector.

[507] See the subsection entitled 'Comment', in the section above entitled 'Distinguishing Between the ESAs'.

'Financial stability' has been a strong theme since the GFC, which is epitomized by the expansion of the FSF into the FSB, as described in Chapter 2[508]. It was argued there, that a trade-off between financial stability and economic growth exists[509]. Financial effectiveness – an element of the objective of the ESAs[510] – is a narrower concept than economic growth. It may be possible to pursue financial stability and effectiveness successfully at the same time, which would please the staff at the ESAs and provide these regulators with a positive professional profile in the eyes of governments, financial firms and the public.

Together with the international response to the GFC, the establishment of the ESAs and their regulatory output is the other major agent of change in respect of the pre-crisis legislation. Those rules, as can be noted from reading Chapter 1, are lengthy and contain detailed provisions. Whilst the GFC was in the unknown future, I recall working my way through the MiFID, the BCD and the UCITS Directive, considering at that time that the Commission may have exceeded the optimum level of specificity in its generation of these laws. I also thought that it might 'respond big' to the effects of the crisis – as underlying change in the environment tends to cause the enactment of more laws and the repeal of fewer. An inspection of the Yellow and Orange Tax Handbooks in the early 1990s would reveal how much slimmer the Law of England and Wales on taxation was then than it is today – today's students of English revenue law must be walking dictionaries!

Thus, with the next part of the book moving onto the post-GFC rules, it is necessary to exercise caution due to the volume of these provisions – as well as their newness. This is recognised in the title of Chapter 4: 'Aspects of the legislation'. It would take a book of several volumes to discuss every component of the post-GFC EU legislation – no doubt resulting in a work of great scholarship, but also being out of date. This monograph focuses on elements of the new laws that correspond to items of the pre-GFC legislation which Chapter 1 considers, although fresh items are described as well – albeit to a lesser extent. The reader may like to note the degree of the involvement of the EBA and the ESMA in the post-GFC law – a development that would have been difficult to envisage before the financial crisis occurred.

CONCLUSION

5 years ago, the new EU financial regulatory architecture, comprising the European Systemic Risk Board, the EBA, the ESMA, the EIOPA and the national financial regulatory authorities, was launched, as the EU's structural response to the GFC. This chapter has investigated the creation of the architecture, considered the basis upon which the ESAs operate, and looked in depth at the rule-making powers of the ESAs and, in this context, the Commission. It has also considered how the EBA's rule-making function and the European Central Bank's supervisory role are delineated. It was observed, on the basis of the examples given, that the ESA-Commission system of delegated legislation is efficient. However, it was noted that, to be deemed a successful development, this system needs to persistently deliver

---

[508] See the section entitled 'The Development of the FSB', in Chapter 2, for the expansion of the FSF into the FSB.
[509] See the subsection entitled 'Comment', in the section entitled 'Progress in the G20/FSB System from November 2008', in Chapter 2.
[510] See the previous paragraph, for the objective of the ESAs.

benefits that exceed the costs of its creation and maintenance. Chapter 4 is to investigate elements of the legislation that the EU has enacted since the GFC.

REFERENCES

[1]   *Official Journal of the European Union* (2005). Directive 2005/1/EC of the European Parliament and of the Council of 9 March 2005 amending Council Directives 73/239/EEC, 85/611/EEC, 91/675/EEC, 92/49/EEC and 93/6/EEC and Directives 94/19/EC, 98/78/EC, 2000/12/EC, 2001/34/EC, 2002/83/EC and 2002/87/EC in order to establish a new organisational structure for financial services committees, L79/9-L79/17, Recital 12.

[2]   *Official Journal of the European Union* (2009). Commission Decision 2009/77/EC of 23 January 2009 establishing the Committee of European Securities Regulators, L25/18-L25/22, Recital 2.

[3]   *Official Journal of the European Union* (2009). Commission Decision 2009/78/EC of 23 January 2009 establishing the Committee of European Banking Supervisors, L25/23-L25/27, Recital 2.

[4]   *Official Journal of the European Union* (2009). Commission Decision 2009/79/EC of 23 January 2009 establishing the Committee of European Insurance and Occupational Pensions Supervisors, L25/28-L25/32, Recital 2.

[5]   European Commission (2007). Review of the Lamfalussy process – Strengthening supervisory convergence, COM(2007) 727 final, 20/11/07. http://eur-lex.europa.eu/legal-content/EN/TXT/HTML/?uri=URISERV:l32056&from=CS.

[6]   *Official Journal of the European Union* (2009). Commission Decision 2009/77/EC, Articles 1 and 17.

[7]   *Official Journal of the European Union* (2009). Commission Decision 2009/78/EC, Articles 1 and 17.

[8]   *Official Journal of the European Union* (2009). Commission Decision 2009/79/EC, Articles 1 and 17.

[9]   *Official Journal of the European Union* (2009). Commission Decision 2009/77/EC, Article 2.

[10]   *Official Journal of the European Union* (2009). Commission Decision 2009/78/EC, Article 2.

[11]   *Official Journal of the European Union* (2009). Commission Decision 2009/79/EC, Article 2.

[12]   *Official Journal of the European Union* (2009). Commission Decision 2009/77/EC, Article 3.

[13]   *Official Journal of the European Union* (2009). Commission Decision 2009/78/EC, Article 3.

[14]   *Official Journal of the European Union* (2009). Commission Decision 2009/79/EC, Article 3.

[15]   *Official Journal of the European Union* (2009). Commission Decision 2009/77/EC, Article 4.

[16] *Official Journal of the European Union* (2009). Commission Decision 2009/78/EC, Article 4.

[17] *Official Journal of the European Union* (2009). Commission Decision 2009/79/EC, Article 4.

[18] *Official Journal of the European Union* (2009). Commission Decision 2009/77/EC, Article 6(1).

[19] *Official Journal of the European Union* (2009). Commission Decision 2009/78/EC, Article 6(1).

[20] *Official Journal of the European Union* (2009). Commission Decision 2009/79/EC, Article 6(1).

[21] *Official Journal of the European Union* (2009). Commission Decision 2009/77/EC, Recital 3.

[22] *Official Journal of the European Union* (2009). Commission Decision 2009/78/EC, Recital 3.

[23] *Official Journal of the European Union* (2009). Commission Decision 2009/79/EC, Recital 3.

[24] European Commission (2009). The High-Level Group on Financial Supervision in the EU, Chaired by Jacques de Larosière: Report, 25/02/09, p.3.

[25] European Commission (2009). The High-Level Group on Financial Supervision in the EU, Chaired by Jacques de Larosière: Report, Recommendation 16, p.46.

[26] European Commission (2009). The High-Level Group on Financial Supervision in the EU, Chaired by Jacques de Larosière: Report, Recommendation 17, p.47.

[27] *Official Journal of the European Union* (2010). Regulation (EU) No 1092/2010 of the European Parliament and of the Council of 24 November 2010 on European Union macro-prudential oversight of the financial system and establishing a European Systemic Risk Board, L331/1-L331/11, Article 1(1).

[28] *Official Journal of the European Union* (2010). Regulation (EU) No 1092/2010, Article 5(1).

[29] *Official Journal of the European Union* (2010). Regulation (EU) No 1092/2010, Article 6(1).

[30] *Official Journal of the European Union* (2010). Regulation (EU) No 1092/2010, Article 6(2)-(3).

[31] *Official Journal of the European Union* (2010). Regulation (EU) No 1092/2010, Article 3(1).

[32] *Official Journal of the European Union* (2010). Regulation (EU) No 1092/2010, Article 3(2).

[33] *Official Journal of the European Union* (2010). Regulation (EU) No 1092/2010, Article 6(2)(b).

[34] *Official Journal of the European Union* (2010). Regulation (EU) No 1092/2010, Article 11(1)(h).

[35] *Official Journal of the European Union* (2010). Regulation (EU) No 1092/2010, Article 13(1)(g).

[36] *Official Journal of the European Union* (2010). Regulation (EU) No 1092/2010, Recital 19.

[37] European Commission (2009). The High-Level Group on Financial Supervision in the EU, Chaired by Jacques de Larosière: Report, Recommendation 18, p.48.

[38] European Commission (2009). The High-Level Group on Financial Supervision in the EU, Chaired by Jacques de Larosière: Report, Recommendation 19, p.50.

[39] European Commission (2009). The High-Level Group on Financial Supervision in the EU, Chaired by Jacques de Larosière: Report, Recommendation 20, p.51.

[40] European Commission (2009). The High-Level Group on Financial Supervision in the EU, Chaired by Jacques de Larosière: Report, Paragraph 198, p.50.

[41] European Commission (2009). The High-Level Group on Financial Supervision in the EU, Chaired by Jacques de Larosière: Report, Paragraph 199, p.51.

[42] European Commission (2009). The High-Level Group on Financial Supervision in the EU, Chaired by Jacques de Larosière: Report, Paragraph 200, p.53.

[43] European Commission (2009). The High-Level Group on Financial Supervision in the EU, Chaired by Jacques de Larosière: Report, Recommendation 22, pp.55-56.

[44] *Official Journal of the European Union* (2010). Regulation (EU) No 1092/2010, Article 1(2).

[45] *Official Journal of the European Union* (2010). Regulation (EU) No 1093/2010 of the European Parliament and of the Council of 24 November 2010 establishing a European Supervisory Authority (European Banking Authority), amending Decision No 716/2009/EC and repealing Commission Decision 2009/78/EC, L331/12-L331/47, original version, Article 2(1).

[46] *Official Journal of the European Union* (2010). Regulation (EU) No 1094/2010 of the European Parliament and of the Council of 24 November 2010 establishing a European Supervisory Authority (European Insurance and Occupational Pensions Authority), amending Decision No 716/2009/EC and repealing Commission Decision 2009/79/EC, L331/48-L331/83, original version, Article 2(1).

[47] *Official Journal of the European Union* (2010). Regulation (EU) No 1095/2010 of the European Parliament and of the Council of 24 November 2010 establishing a European Supervisory Authority (European Securities and Markets Authority) amending Decision No 716/2009/EC and repealing Commission Decision 2009/77/EC, L331/84-L331/119, original version, Article 2(1).

[48] *Official Journal of the European Union* (2010). Regulation (EU) No 1093/2010 (original version), Article 1(1).

[49] *Official Journal of the European Union* (2010). Regulation (EU) No 1094/2010 (original version), Article 1(1).

[50] *Official Journal of the European Union* (2010). Regulation (EU) No 1095/2010 (original version), Article 1(1).

[51] *Official Journal of the European Union* (2010). Regulation (EU) No 1093/2010 (original version), Article 40(1)(b).

[52] *Official Journal of the European Union* (2010). Regulation (EU) No 1094/2010 (original version), Article 40(1)(b).

[53] *Official Journal of the European Union* (2010). Regulation (EU) No 1095/2010 (original version), Article 40(1)(b).

[54] *Official Journal of the European Union* (2010). Regulation (EU) No 1093/2010 (original version), Articles 48(1) and 51(1).

[55] *Official Journal of the European Union* (2010). Regulation (EU) No 1094/2010 (original version), Articles 48(1) and 51(1).

[56] *Official Journal of the European Union* (2010). Regulation (EU) No 1095/2010 (original version), Articles 48(1) and 51(1).

[57] *Official Journal of the European Union* (2010). Regulation (EU) No 1093/2010 (original version), Article 48(2).

[58] *Official Journal of the European Union* (2010). Regulation (EU) No 1094/2010 (original version), Article 48(2).

[59] *Official Journal of the European Union* (2010). Regulation (EU) No 1095/2010 (original version), Article 48(2).

[60] *Official Journal of the European Union* (2010). Regulation (EU) No 1093/2010 (original version), Article 48(3).

[61] *Official Journal of the European Union* (2010). Regulation (EU) No 1094/2010 (original version), Article 48(3).

[62] *Official Journal of the European Union* (2010). Regulation (EU) No 1095/2010 (original version), Article 48(3).

[63] *Official Journal of the European Union* (2010). Regulation (EU) No 1093/2010 (original version), Article 48(3)-(4).

[64] *Official Journal of the European Union* (2010). Regulation (EU) No 1094/2010 (original version), Article 48(3)-(4).

[65] *Official Journal of the European Union* (2010). Regulation (EU) No 1095/2010 (original version), Article 48(3)-(4).

[66] *Official Journal of the European Union* (2010). Regulation (EU) No 1093/2010 (original version), Article 62(1).

[67] *Official Journal of the European Union* (2010). Regulation (EU) No 1094/2010 (original version), Article 62(1).

[68] *Official Journal of the European Union* (2010). Regulation (EU) No 1095/2010 (original version), Article 62(1).

[69] *Official Journal of the European Union* (2010). Regulation (EU) No 1093/2010 (original version), Article 62(2).

[70] *Official Journal of the European Union* (2010). Regulation (EU) No 1094/2010 (original version), Article 62(2).

[71] *Official Journal of the European Union* (2010). Regulation (EU) No 1095/2010 (original version), Article 62(2).

[72] *Official Journal of the European Union* (2010). Regulation (EU) No 1093/2010 (original version), Article 62(3).

[73] *Official Journal of the European Union* (2010). Regulation (EU) No 1094/2010 (original version), Article 62(3).

[74] *Official Journal of the European Union* (2010). Regulation (EU) No 1095/2010 (original version), Article 62(3).

[75] *Official Journal of the European Union* (2010). Regulation (EU) No 1093/2010 (original version), Article 8(1).

[76] *Official Journal of the European Union* (2010). Regulation (EU) No 1094/2010 (original version), Article 8(1).

[77] *Official Journal of the European Union* (2010). Regulation (EU) No 1095/2010 (original version), Article 8(1).

[78] *Official Journal of the European Union* (2010). Regulation (EU) No 1093/2010 (original version), Article 8(2).

[79] *Official Journal of the European Union* (2010). Regulation (EU) No 1094/2010 (original version), Article 8(2).

[80] *Official Journal of the European Union* (2010). Regulation (EU) No 1095/2010 (original version), Article 8(2).

[81] *Official Journal of the European Union* (2010). Regulation (EU) No 1093/2010 of the European Parliament and of the Council of 24 November 2010 establishing a European Supervisory Authority (European Banking Authority), amending Decision No 716/2009/EC and repealing Commission Decision 2009/78/EC, L331/12-L331/47, as amended to 30/07/14, Article 1(2).

[82] *Official Journal of the European Union* (2010). Regulation (EU) No 1093/2010 (as amended to 30/07/14), Article 1(3).

[83] *Official Journal of the European Union* (2010). Regulation (EU) No 1093/2010 (as amended to 30/07/14), Article 1(5).

[84] *Official Journal of the European Union* (2010). Regulation (EU) No 1093/2010 (as amended to 30/07/14), Article 1(5).

[85] *Official Journal of the European Union* (2010). Regulation (EU) No 1093/2010 (as amended to 30/07/14), Article 1(5).

[86] *Official Journal of the European Union* (2010). Regulation (EU) No 1093/2010 (as amended to 30/07/14), Article 1(5).

[87] *Official Journal of the European Union* (2010). Regulation (EU) No 1094/2010 of the European Parliament and of the Council of 24 November 2010 establishing a European Supervisory Authority (European Insurance and Occupational Pensions Authority), amending Decision No 716/2009/EC and repealing Commission Decision 2009/79/EC, L331/48-L331/83, as amended to 22/05/14, Article 1(2).

[88] *Official Journal of the European Union* (2010). Regulation (EU) No 1094/2010 (as amended to 22/05/14), Article 1(3).

[89] *Official Journal of the European Union* (2010). Regulation (EU) No 1094/2010 (as amended to 22/05/14), Article 1(6).

[90] *Official Journal of the European Union* (2010). Regulation (EU) No 1094/2010 (as amended to 22/05/14), Article 1(6).

[91] *Official Journal of the European Union* (2010). Regulation (EU) No 1094/2010 (as amended to 22/05/14), Article 1(6).

[92] *Official Journal of the European Union* (2010). Regulation (EU) No 1095/2010 of the European Parliament and of the Council of 24 November 2010 establishing a European Supervisory Authority (European Securities and Markets Authority) amending Decision No 716/2009/EC and repealing Commission Decision 2009/77/EC, L331/84-L331/119, as amended to 22/05/14, Article 1(2).

[93] *Official Journal of the European Union* (2010). Regulation (EU) No 1095/2010 (as amended to 22/05/14), Article 1(3).

[94] *Official Journal of the European Union* (2010). Regulation (EU) No 1095/2010 (as amended to 22/05/14), Article 1(5).

[95] *Official Journal of the European Union* (2010). Regulation (EU) No 1095/2010 (as amended to 22/05/14), Article 1(5).

[96] *Official Journal of the European Union* (2010). Regulation (EU) No 1095/2010 (as amended to 22/05/14), Article 1(5).

[97] *Official Journal of the European Union* (2012). Consolidated version of the Treaty on the Functioning of the European Union, C326/47-C326/199, Article 4(2)(a).

[98] *Official Journal of the European Union* (2012). Consolidated version of the Treaty on the Functioning of the European Union, Article 2(2).

[99] *Official Journal of the European Union* (2012). Consolidated version of the Treaty on the Functioning of the European Union, Article 2(1).

[100] *Official Journal of the European Union* (2010). Regulation (EU) No 1093/2010 (as amended to 30/07/14), Article 10(1).

[101] *Official Journal of the European Union* (2010). Regulation (EU) No 1094/2010 (as amended to 22/05/14), Article 10(1).

[102] *Official Journal of the European Union* (2010). Regulation (EU) No 1095/2010 (as amended to 22/05/14), Article 10(1).

[103] *Official Journal of the European Union* (2012). Consolidated version of the Treaty on the Functioning of the European Union, Article 290(1).

[104] *Official Journal of the European Union* (2013). Directive 2013/36/EU of the European Parliament and of the Council of 26 June 2013 on access to the activity of credit institutions and the prudential supervision of credit institutions and investment firms, amending Directive 2002/87/EC and repealing Directives 2006/48/EC and 2006/49/EC, L176/338-L176/436, as amended to 12/06/14, Article 77(3).

[105] *Official Journal of the European Union* (2013). Directive 2013/36/EU (as amended to 12/06/14), Article 77(1).

[106] *Official Journal of the European Union* (2013). Directive 2013/36/EU (as amended to 12/06/14), Article 77(4).

[107] *Official Journal of the European Union* (2010). Regulation (EU) No 1093/2010 (as amended to 30/07/14), Article 10(1).

[108] *Official Journal of the European Union* (2010). Regulation (EU) No 1094/2010 (as amended to 22/05/14), Article 10(1).

[109] *Official Journal of the European Union* (2010). Regulation (EU) No 1095/2010 (as amended to 22/05/14), Article 10(1).

[110] *Official Journal of the European Union* (2010). Regulation (EU) No 1093/2010 (as amended to 30/07/14), Article 10(1).

[111] *Official Journal of the European Union* (2010). Regulation (EU) No 1094/2010 (as amended to 22/05/14), Article 10(1).

[112] *Official Journal of the European Union* (2010). Regulation (EU) No 1095/2010 (as amended to 22/05/14), Article 10(1).

[113] *Official Journal of the European Union* (2010). Regulation (EU) No 1093/2010 (as amended to 30/07/14), Article 10(1).

[114] *Official Journal of the European Union* (2010). Regulation (EU) No 1094/2010 (as amended to 22/05/14), Article 10(1).

[115] *Official Journal of the European Union* (2010). Regulation (EU) No 1095/2010 (as amended to 22/05/14), Article 10(1).

[116] *Official Journal of the European Union* (2010). Regulation (EU) No 1093/2010 (as amended to 30/07/14), Article 10(1).

[117] *Official Journal of the European Union* (2010). Regulation (EU) No 1094/2010 (as amended to 22/05/14), Article 10(1).

[118] *Official Journal of the European Union* (2010). Regulation (EU) No 1095/2010 (as amended to 22/05/14), Article 10(1).

[119] *Official Journal of the European Union* (2010). Regulation (EU) No 1093/2010 (as amended to 30/07/14), Article 10(1).

[120] *Official Journal of the European Union* (2010). Regulation (EU) No 1094/2010 (as amended to 22/05/14), Article 10(1).

[121] *Official Journal of the European Union* (2010). Regulation (EU) No 1095/2010 (as amended to 22/05/14), Article 10(1).

[122] *Official Journal of the European Union* (2010). Regulation (EU) No 1093/2010 (as amended to 30/07/14), Article 10(2).

[123] *Official Journal of the European Union* (2010). Regulation (EU) No 1094/2010 (as amended to 22/05/14), Article 10(2).

[124] *Official Journal of the European Union* (2010). Regulation (EU) No 1095/2010 (as amended to 22/05/14), Article 10(2).

[125] *Official Journal of the European Union* (2010). Regulation (EU) No 1093/2010 (as amended to 30/07/14), Article 10(3).

[126] *Official Journal of the European Union* (2010). Regulation (EU) No 1094/2010 (as amended to 22/05/14), Article 10(3).

[127] *Official Journal of the European Union* (2010). Regulation (EU) No 1095/2010 (as amended to 22/05/14), Article 10(3).

[128] *Official Journal of the European Union* (2010). Regulation (EU) No 1093/2010 (as amended to 30/07/14), Article 10(4).

[129] *Official Journal of the European Union* (2010). Regulation (EU) No 1094/2010 (as amended to 22/05/14), Article 10(4).

[130] *Official Journal of the European Union* (2010). Regulation (EU) No 1095/2010 (as amended to 22/05/14), Article 10(4).

[131] *Official Journal of the European Union* (2014). Commission Delegated Regulation (EU) No 530/2014 of 12 March 2014 supplementing Directive 2013/36/EU of the European Parliament and of the Council with regard to regulatory technical standards further defining material exposures and thresholds for internal approaches to specific risk in the trading book, L148/50-L148/51, Preamble.

[132] *Official Journal of the European Union* (2014). Commission Delegated Regulation (EU) No 530/2014, Recital 4.

[133] *Official Journal of the European Union* (2014). Commission Delegated Regulation (EU) No 530/2014, Recital 5.

[134] *European Commission (2015).* Regulatory Technical Standards supplementing Regulation (EU) 575/2013 (CRR) and Directive 2013/36/EU (CRD): State of play, Brussels, 19/11/15, p.2. <http://ec.europa.eu/finance/bank/docs/regcapital/acts/overview-crr-crdiv-rts_en.pdf>

[135] *Official Journal of the European Union* (2014). Commission Delegated Regulation (EU) No 530/2014, Recital 1.

[136] *Official Journal of the European Union* (2014). Commission Delegated Regulation (EU) No 530/2014, Recital 2.

[137] *Official Journal of the European Union* (2013). Regulation (EU) No 575/2013 of the European Parliament and of the Council of 26 June 2013 on prudential requirements for

credit institutions and investment firms and amending Regulation (EU) No 648/2012, Article 327(1).

[138] *Official Journal of the European Union* (2014). Commission Delegated Regulation (EU) No 530/2014, Article 1.

[139] *Official Journal of the European Union* (2014). Commission Delegated Regulation (EU) No 530/2014, Recital 3.

[140] *Official Journal of the European Union* (2014). Commission Delegated Regulation (EU) No 530/2014, Article 2.

[141] *Official Journal of the European Union* (2010). Regulation (EU) No 1093/2010 (as amended to 30/07/14), Article 11(2).

[142] *Official Journal of the European Union* (2010). Regulation (EU) No 1094/2010 (as amended to 22/05/14), Article 11(2).

[143] *Official Journal of the European Union* (2010). Regulation (EU) No 1095/2010 (as amended to 22/05/14), Article 11(2).

[144] *Official Journal of the European Union* (2010). Regulation (EU) No 1093/2010 (as amended to 30/07/14), Article 13(1).

[145] *Official Journal of the European Union* (2010). Regulation (EU) No 1094/2010 (as amended to 22/05/14), Article 13(1).

[146] *Official Journal of the European Union* (2010). Regulation (EU) No 1095/2010 (as amended to 22/05/14), Article 13(1).

[147] *European Commission (2015).* Regulatory Technical Standards supplementing Regulation (EU) 575/2013 (CRR) and Directive 2013/36/EU (CRD): State of play, p.2.

[148] *Official Journal of the European Union* (2010). Regulation (EU) No 1093/2010 (as amended to 30/07/14), Article 13(2).

[149] *Official Journal of the European Union* (2010). Regulation (EU) No 1094/2010 (as amended to 22/05/14), Article 13(2).

[150] *Official Journal of the European Union* (2010). Regulation (EU) No 1095/2010 (as amended to 22/05/14), Article 13(2).

[151] *Official Journal of the European Union* (2014). Commission Delegated Regulation (EU) No 530/2014, Article 3.

[152] *Official Journal of the European Union* (2010). Regulation (EU) No 1093/2010 (as amended to 30/07/14), Article 13(3).

[153] *Official Journal of the European Union* (2010). Regulation (EU) No 1094/2010 (as amended to 22/05/14), Article 13(3).

[154] *Official Journal of the European Union* (2010). Regulation (EU) No 1095/2010 (as amended to 22/05/14), Article 13(3).

[155] *Official Journal of the European Union* (2010). Regulation (EU) No 1093/2010 (as amended to 30/07/14), Article 14(1).

[156] *Official Journal of the European Union* (2010). Regulation (EU) No 1094/2010 (as amended to 22/05/14), Article 14(1).

[157] *Official Journal of the European Union* (2010). Regulation (EU) No 1095/2010 (as amended to 22/05/14), Article 14(1).

[158] *Official Journal of the European Union* (2010). Regulation (EU) No 1093/2010 (as amended to 30/07/14), Article 14(2).

[159] *Official Journal of the European Union* (2010). Regulation (EU) No 1094/2010 (as amended to 22/05/14), Article 14(2).

[160] *Official Journal of the European Union* (2010). Regulation (EU) No 1095/2010 (as amended to 22/05/14), Article 14(2).

[161] *Official Journal of the European Union* (2010). Regulation (EU) No 1093/2010 (as amended to 30/07/14), Article 11(1).

[162] *Official Journal of the European Union* (2010). Regulation (EU) No 1094/2010 (as amended to 22/05/14), Article 11(1).

[163] *Official Journal of the European Union* (2010). Regulation (EU) No 1095/2010 (as amended to 22/05/14), Article 11(1).

[164] *Official Journal of the European Union* (2010). Regulation (EU) No 1093/2010 (as amended to 30/07/14), Article 12(1).

[165] *Official Journal of the European Union* (2010). Regulation (EU) No 1094/2010 (as amended to 22/05/14), Article 12(1).

[166] *Official Journal of the European Union* (2010). Regulation (EU) No 1095/2010 (as amended to 22/05/14), Article 12(1).

[167] *Official Journal of the European Union* (2010). Regulation (EU) No 1093/2010 (as amended to 30/07/14), Article 12(1).

[168] *Official Journal of the European Union* (2010). Regulation (EU) No 1094/2010 (as amended to 22/05/14), Article 12(1).

[169] *Official Journal of the European Union* (2010). Regulation (EU) No 1095/2010 (as amended to 22/05/14), Article 12(1).

[170] *Official Journal of the European Union* (2010). Regulation (EU) No 1093/2010 (as amended to 30/07/14), Article 12(2).

[171] *Official Journal of the European Union* (2010). Regulation (EU) No 1094/2010 (as amended to 22/05/14), Article 12(2).

[172] *Official Journal of the European Union* (2010). Regulation (EU) No 1095/2010 (as amended to 22/05/14), Article 12(2).

[173] *Official Journal of the European Union* (2010). Regulation (EU) No 1093/2010 (as amended to 30/07/14), Article 12(3).

[174] *Official Journal of the European Union* (2010). Regulation (EU) No 1094/2010 (as amended to 22/05/14), Article 12(3).

[175] *Official Journal of the European Union* (2010). Regulation (EU) No 1095/2010 (as amended to 22/05/14), Article 12(3).

[176] *Official Journal of the European Union* (2012). Consolidated version of the Treaty on the Functioning of the European Union, Article 291(2).

[177] *Official Journal of the European Union* (2010). Regulation (EU) No 1093/2010 (as amended to 30/07/14), Article 15(1).

[178] *Official Journal of the European Union* (2010). Regulation (EU) No 1094/2010 (as amended to 22/05/14), Article 15(1).

[179] *Official Journal of the European Union* (2010). Regulation (EU) No 1095/2010 (as amended to 22/05/14), Article 15(1).

[180] *Official Journal of the European Union* (2014). Commission Implementing Regulation (EU) No 620/2014 of 4 June 2014 laying down implementing technical standards with regard to information exchange between competent authorities of home and host Member States, according to Directive 2013/36/EU of the European Parliament and of the Council, L172/1-L172/25, Preamble.

[181] *Official Journal of the European Union* (2014). Commission Implementing Regulation (EU) No 620/2014, Recital 9.

[182] *Official Journal of the European Union* (2014). Commission Implementing Regulation (EU) No 620/2014, Recital 10.

[183] *Official Journal of the European Union* (2013). Directive 2013/36/EU (as amended to 12/06/14), Article 50(7).

[184] *Official Journal of the European Union* (2013). Directive 2013/36/EU (as amended to 12/06/14), Article 50(8).

[185] *European Commission (2015).* Implementing Technical Standards supplementing Regulation (EU) 575/2013 (CRR) and Directive 2013/36/EU (CRD): State of play, Brussels, 18/12/15, p.1. < http://ec.europa.eu/finance/bank/docs/regcapital/acts/overview-crr-crdiv-its_en.pdf>.

[186] *Official Journal of the European Union* (2013). Directive 2013/36/EU (as amended to 12/06/14), Article 50(1).

[187] *Official Journal of the European Union* (2013). Directive 2013/36/EU (as amended to 12/06/14), Article 50(3).

[188] *Official Journal of the European Union* (2014). Commission Implementing Regulation (EU) No 620/2014, Recital 1.

[189] *Official Journal of the European Union* (2014). Commission Implementing Regulation (EU) No 620/2014, Article 1.

[190] *Official Journal of the European Union* (2014). Commission Implementing Regulation (EU) No 620/2014, Annex I.

[191] *Official Journal of the European Union* (2014). Commission Implementing Regulation (EU) No 620/2014, Annex II.

[192] *Official Journal of the European Union* (2014). Commission Implementing Regulation (EU) No 620/2014, Article 1.

[193] *Official Journal of the European Union* (2014). Commission Implementing Regulation (EU) No 620/2014, Article 5(1).

[194] *Official Journal of the European Union* (2014). Commission Implementing Regulation (EU) No 620/2014, Article 5(3)-(4).

[195] *Official Journal of the European Union* (2014). Commission Implementing Regulation (EU) No 620/2014, Article 5(2).

[196] *Official Journal of the European Union* (2014). Commission Implementing Regulation (EU) No 620/2014, Article 5(2).

[197] *Official Journal of the European Union* (2014). Commission Implementing Regulation (EU) No 620/2014, Article 5(3).

[198] *Official Journal of the European Union* (2013). Directive 2013/36/EU (as amended to 12/06/14), Articles 50(8) and 77(4).

[199] *Official Journal of the European Union* (2010). Regulation (EU) No 1093/2010 (as amended to 30/07/14), Articles 10(1), 10(3), 15(1) and 15(3).

[200] *Official Journal of the European Union* (2010). Regulation (EU) No 1094/2010 (as amended to 22/05/14), Articles 10(1), 10(3), 15(1) and 15(3).

[201] *Official Journal of the European Union* (2010). Regulation (EU) No 1095/2010 (as amended to 22/05/14), Articles 10(1), 10(3), 15(1) and 15(3).

[202] *Official Journal of the European Union* (2010). Regulation (EU) No 1093/2010 (as amended to 30/07/14), Article 1(2).

[203] *Official Journal of the European Union* (2013). Council Regulation (EU) No 1024/2013 of 15 October 2013 conferring specific tasks on the European Central Bank concerning policies relating to the prudential supervision of credit institutions, L287/63-L287/69, Article 1.

[204] *Official Journal of the European Union* (2013). Council Regulation (EU) No 1024/2013, Article 4(1).

[205] *Official Journal of the European Union* (2013). Council Regulation (EU) No 1024/2013, Article 4(2).

[206] *Official Journal of the European Union* (2013). Council Regulation (EU) No 1024/2013, Article 4(3).

[207] *Official Journal of the European Union* (2013). Council Regulation (EU) No 1024/2013, Article 4(3).

[208] *Official Journal of the European Union* (2013). Council Regulation (EU) No 1024/2013, Article 4(3).

[209] *Official Journal of the European Union* (2013). Council Regulation (EU) No 1024/2013, Article 4(3).

[210] *Official Journal of the European Union* (2013). Council Regulation (EU) No 1024/2013, Recital 32.

[211] *Official Journal of the European Union* (2010). Regulation (EU) No 1093/2010 (as amended to 30/07/14), Article 1(5).

[212] *Official Journal of the European Union* (2010). Regulation (EU) No 1094/2010 (as amended to 22/05/14), Article 1(6).

[213] *Official Journal of the European Union* (2010). Regulation (EU) No 1095/2010 (as amended to 22/05/14), Article 1(5).

Chapter Four

ASPECTS OF THE LEGISLATION

ABSTRACT

This Chapter describes and assesses the Commission's plans for a CMU. It reports aspects of the banking and securities legislation that the EU has adopted since the GFC. In instances in which this is possible, the Chapter compares provisions of this legislation with their counterparts in the pre-GFC law as noted in Chapter 1. The current rules include instruments for which there are few amendments to the pre-GFC position, items that have been extensively altered, instruments that replace earlier legislation, and items which are new. The main changes since the start of the GFC are the co-ordinated international response to this crisis and the introduction of the ESAs, which have influenced the new legislation and modifications to the existing laws. In view of the considerable increase in the volume, scope and detail of these rules since the GFC, careful monitoring and editing is necessary in order to ensure that they fit the system that is being regulated. Whilst this increase is partly justified by the need to respond constructively to the events of the crisis, it is a bewildering outcome for practitioners in the sector – who need to make the post-GFC legislative structure work in their own circumstances. Constructive dialogue between the Commission, the ESAs, the national regulators and financial market participants is essential. The Commission and the ESAs, in particular, will need to listen carefully to the views from within the United Kingdom – as a country with experience and high levels of trade within the financial sector – if European finance is to become a world-leading entity in the long run.

Keywords: CMU, Commission, ESA, ESMA, EBA, securities, investment, banking

INTRODUCTION

The cartoon from today's copy of *The Times* newspaper is an adaptation of the popular children's fable entitled 'Jack and the Beanstalk,' in which Jack climbs a giant beanstalk to see what is located above the clouds. In the modified version, entitled 'Dave and the Beanstalk', the Prime Minister of the United Kingdom, the Right Honourable David Cameron MP, climbs beyond the clouds to observe a giant Chancellor of Germany, Dr. Angela Merkel, guarding a blue hen with the EU's stars on the side. The hen has laid 2 golden eggs, which are entitled 'Free movement' and 'Migrant benefits,' both of which Dr. Merkel holds. There are 3 characters at the base of the beanstalk, who are in the process of chopping it down [1].

This cartoon reaches to the heart of the on-going debate concerning Europe. How much sovereignty are countries prepared to accede to the EU, and what benefits can they expect in return for the transfer of these powers? In the case portrayed, the principles of the free movement of persons[511] and of non-discrimination based on racial or ethnic origin[512] are non-negotiable, which puts the Prime Minister in a potentially awkward spot concerning his re-negotiation of the United Kingdom's relationship with the EU. The growing influence of Germany[513] is shown, with the Chancellor of Germany being the protector of EU rights – rather than the President of the European Council[514], the President of the Parliament[515], or, as one might have expected[516], the President of the Commission[517].

The CMU is a major project for further EU integration, which is currently in the construction stage. Although legislative proposals for the CMU are (for the most part) not yet forthcoming, its significance warrants coverage in Chapter 4. The next section considers the development of the CMU and the principles upon which it is based.

THE CAPITAL MARKETS UNION

In July 2014, prior to becoming the President-elect of the Commission, Mr. Jean-Claude Juncker put forward 10 policy areas that the next Commission – if he was to be its leader – would address[518] [2]. The fourth of these, entitled 'A Deeper and Fairer Internal Market with a Strengthened Industrial Base,' [3] sets out a proposal for a CMU.

> Over time, I believe we should complement the new European rules for banks with a Capital Markets Union. To improve the financing of our economy, we should further develop and integrate capital markets. This would cut the cost of raising capital, notably for SMEs, and help reduce our very high dependence on bank funding. This would also increase the attractiveness of Europe as a place to invest [4].

---

[511] Article 26(2) of the TFEU contains the principle of the free movement of persons.

[512] Article 10 of the TFEU contains the principle of non-discrimination based on racial or ethnic origin.

[513] In the financial sector, the European Central Bank, the European Systemic Risk Board and the EIOPA are based in Frankfurt am Main. The EBA is situated in London. The ESMA is located in Paris.

[514] The current President of the European Council is Mr. Donald Tusk.

[515] The current President of the Parliament is Mr. Martin Schulz.

[516] The Commission is the 'guardian of the Treaties', and of the rights contained therein. Article 17(1) of the TEU states: "The Commission shall promote the general interest of the [European] Union and take appropriate initiatives to that end. It shall ensure the application of the Treaties, and of measures adopted by the institutions pursuant to them. ...."

[517] The current President of the Commission is Mr. Jean-Claude Juncker.

[518] These policy areas are as follows: 1. A new boost for jobs, growth and investment; 2. A connected digital single market; 3. A resilient energy union with a forward-looking climate change policy; 4. A deeper and fairer internal market with a strengthened industrial base; 5. A deeper and fairer Economic and Monetary Union; 6. A reasonable and balanced free trade agreement with the United States of America; 7. An area of justice and fundamental rights based on mutual trust; 8. Towards a new policy on migration; 9. A stronger global actor; 10. A Union of democratic change (Juncker, J.-C. (2014), A New Start for Europe: My Agenda for Jobs, Growth, Fairness and Democratic Change – Political Guidelines for the next European Commission, pp.5-12. <http://ec.europa.eu/priorities/docs/pg_en.pdf>).

In February 2015, the Commission published a Green Paper entitled 'Building a Capital Market Union,' which contained suggestions as to what might be done to achieve this, and proposed 32 questions, to which respondents from both within the EU and outside it were invited to reply by 13th May 2015 [5]. 430 replies were received; [6] the Commission published these in summary form, in a Feedback Statement on 30th September 2015. The essence of the Green Paper, which the Feedback Statement re-emphasizes, is as follows.

> In order to achieve the benefits of a fully integrated single market for capital, it is necessary to overcome challenges in particular in the following three key areas: - improving access to financing for all businesses across Europe (in particular SMEs) and investment projects such as infrastructure; - increasing and diversifying the sources of funding from investors in the EU and all over the world; - making markets work more effectively, linking investors to those who need funding more efficient and less costly, both within Member States and cross-border [7].

The Commission published a Staff Working Document simultaneously with its Green Paper, which identified obstacles to the development of the CMU[519]. This document distinguishes between the capital markets and the money markets, and defines the financial instruments that it considers to be elements of the former.

> The term "financial markets" is often used to refer to all sorts of markets in the financial sector, including ones that are not directly concerned with raising finance, such as commodity and foreign exchange markets. In the narrow sense, financial markets are formed by money markets and capital markets. The money markets are used for raising short-term finance … , whereas the capital markets are used for raising longer-term finance … . Funds borrowed from the money markets are typically used for general operating expenses to cover brief periods of illiquidity or short-term financing needs. … When a company borrows from the primary capital markets, the purpose is often to invest in additional physical capital goods, which will be used to help increase its future income. It can take many months or years before the investment generates sufficient return to pay back its cost. In this narrow sense, modern capital markets consist of: i. Debt and equity markets that intermediate between savers and those that need capital; ii. Derivatives markets that facilitate risk management, consisting of contracts such as futures, options, interest rate and foreign exchange swaps, typically associated with underlying debt and equity instruments; and iii. Securitisation and structured finance markets that improve funding access further by broadening the potential investor base [8].

The document identifies the following arrangements as being part of structured finance markets: collateralised debt, loan and mortgage obligations, asset-backed and mortgage-backed securities, and whole business securitisations[520]. It classifies obstacles to the adequate operation of capital markets, as follows.

---

[519] This document is entitled 'Commission Staff Working Document: Initial reflections on the obstacles to the development of deep and integrated EU capital markets, Accompanying the document 'Green Paper: Building a Capital Markets Union', and is available at http://ec.europa.eu/finance/consultations/2015/capital-markets-union/docs/staff-working-document_en.pdf.

[520] It is submitted that the Commission's inclusion of derivatives markets and structured finance arrangements in the description of 'capital markets' is broad, rather than, as it claims in the above quote, narrow. Some derivative instruments, such as interest rate forwards, are not directly associated with underlying debt or equity securities.

i. Underdeveloped or fragmented markets, due to regulatory and legal barriers, institutional shortcomings and other reasons; ii. Barriers on the demand side of the market in terms of access to finance, in particular as regards SMEs; iii. Constraints on the supply (i.e., investor) side of the market that limit the flow of savings into capital market instruments; iv. Market distortions or regulatory failures[521] that limit or impede direct financing of investments with a long-term horizon [9].

Each of these 4 categories is considered, in turn.

Underdeveloped or Fragmented Markets

Whilst the EU's economy (as measured by Gross Domestic Product) is "slightly larger" than that of the United States of America, the EU's public and private equity markets are smaller than those of the United States, as are the amounts of private placement of bonds and of public issuance of high-yield securities [10]. Furthermore, there is considerable variation in the maturity of the capital markets across Member States [11]. Obstacles to the development and the integration of capital markets include the following items.

1) *Endogenous constraints in reaching critical size.* The EU has more listed companies and more exchange traded-funds than the United States of America does, despite a smaller market capitalisation than the latter. The high concentration of asset managers in the EU may inhibit them in attaining a minimum critical size and in realizing economies of scale [12].

2) *Impaired availability of data on financial markets.* Financial markets need frequent and reliable data, in order to be liquid and efficient. Services for the supply of data to European markets are fragmented [13].

3) *Differences in regulation and supervisory enforcement.* Even though there has been substantial harmonisation of regulatory frameworks, the application of these structures does not converge. Furthermore, domestic provisions in areas that are not harmonised may impose barriers to capital movement. For example, supervisory fees that the competent authorities of host Member States charge to European funds may discourage those entities from providing services outside their home Member State [14].

4) *Diverse and fragmented legal frameworks for specific financial instruments.* These may be fragmented (e.g., covered bonds) or absent (e.g., crowdfunding[522]). There is limited standardisation – in respect of investor protection, for instance [15].

5) *Insufficiently harmonised or inadequate company law and corporate governance rules.* Company law and corporate governance are mainly regulated by domestic law. Whilst the diversity of approaches accommodates the particular needs of various

---

Furthermore, it is only the finance-raising part of structured finance arrangements – such as the bonds issued by the special purpose vehicle in the case of a classical securitisation, which contribute to the capital markets.

[521] Emphasis original.

[522] A few Member States have introduced laws to regulate crowdfunding – such as France, Italy and the United Kingdom (European Commission (2015), Commission Staff Working Document: Initial reflections on the obstacles to the development of deep and integrated EU capital markets, fn 56, p.27).

national markets, this can restrain cross-border investment and multi-state corporate functioning. Differences in provisions of company law hinder the establishment of companies as simultaneous going concerns in many Member States; furthermore, it may be slow and costly for companies to move from one Member State to another or to restructure across country boundaries. Efficient protection of minority shareholders betters corporate governance, and aids the appeal of companies to foreign investors. Competent and effective company boards of directors are important for attracting investment, as these guard the interests of investors [16].

6) *Non-harmonised conflict-of-law rules in respect of company law.* Currently, Member States regulate conflict-of-law rules in the field of company law. The divergence of these provisions leads to a situation in which a company may be simultaneously subject to the laws of several Member States [17].

7) *Insolvency laws and enforcement of contracts.* The absence or the inadequacy of rules in many Member States to enable the early restructuring of debt, the lack of laws to provide a second opportunity for entrepreneurs, and the length and the costs of insolvency proceedings in some Member States, discourage investors and lead to poor rates of recovery for creditors [18].

8) *Tax barriers.* The power to levy taxes and to set rates of taxation is mainly with national governments. Differences in taxation regimes across Member States can lead market participants to take decisions as to their location that are influenced by taxation considerations, which may result in "misallocations of capital" [19].

Barriers on the Demand Side

The following difficulties restrict the access of SMEs to funds – especially from the capital markets.

1. *Overdependence on bank finance.* The financial statements of SMEs are less informative than those of large companies, from the perspective of investors. In consequence, potential investors in SMEs face higher transaction costs and greater informational asymmetries than those in big firms. These difficulties for SMEs can be partly offset within longer bank lending relationships, in which banks gather a substantial history of information on each borrower that assists them in the evaluation of its creditworthiness [20].

2. *Lack of (credit) information for potential investors.* As banks usually hold the information on SMEs, the latter find it difficult to spread credit information to non-bank investors. More generally, there is insufficient business information about SMEs whose securities are listed or which seek a listing for them – in part because the suppliers of business information, and equity research analysts, are more likely to research large companies than to investigate SMEs [21].

3. *Underdeveloped market for risk capital.* Markets for risk capital are rudimentary in most Member States. The current fragmentation restricts the development of substantial supplies of potential risk capital. For example, venture capital financing for SMEs is insubstantial in most Member States. Reasons for this include high costs, informational difficulties, and the absence of a culture of equity investment. The

fragmentation of the market for venture capital "along national lines" restricts the supply of venture capital financing that is available to SMEs, because venture capital funds in some Member States struggle to reach "the critical mass" that they need in order to hold diversified investment portfolios [22].

4. *Barriers to the listing of the securities of SMEs.* The underwriting of debt and initial public offerings are characterized by the sizeable fixed costs that regulatory requirements and due diligence generate, which may be disproportionately burdensome for small companies. These expenses include the costs of divulging information that regulators or investors need, and of satisfying further requirements with regard to corporate governance. In respect of underwriting debt, there is the expense of commissioning an external credit rating [23].

Constraints on the Supply Side

Households tend to invest their savings in real estate, insurance policies and pension schemes and to hold deposits with banks, in preference to purchasing the units of mutual funds or directly holding shares and bonds [24]. The following may be contributory factors to the investment patterns of households in the EU.

1) *Lack of trust in financial markets and intermediaries.* The absence of an 'equity culture', and risk aversion on the part of households, mean that retail investors' shortage of trust in financial markets and intermediaries changes only slowly – and has been reinforced by the GFC. These investors' low levels of confidence in the providers of investment services impedes "the flow of savings into capital market instruments" [25].

2) *Lack of adequate financial expertise.* As most retail investors lack the specialised knowledge that is required in order to make investments in capital markets, many of them prefer to invest by means of "pooled vehicles" (such as investment funds, life assurance contracts and pension plans) which institutional investors manage – rather than by directly holding quoted securities [26].

3) *Household preference for investment in real estate.* Real assets constitute most of the gross total assets of households in the Eurozone[523]; the largest component is the households' main residence[524] [27].

4) *Technical barriers resulting in strong home bias.* Cross-border investment is adversely affected by language barriers and "fragmented legal frameworks" – including the rules that concern acquisitions and mergers, consumer protection, corporate governance, employment, insolvency, and investor protection [28].

---

[523] The 'Eurozone' is a collective term for the countries within the EU that use the Euro as their currency. At the date of writing (6th January 2016), these states are: Austria, Belgium, Cyprus, Estonia, Finland, France, Germany, Greece, Ireland, Italy, Latvia, Lithuania, Luxembourg, Malta, the Netherlands, Portugal, Slovakia, Slovenia and Spain.

[524] There is substantial variation in levels of ownership of real estate across the EU, as home ownership levels differ considerably between Member States (European Commission (2015), Commission Staff Working Document: Initial reflections on the obstacles to the development of deep and integrated EU capital markets, p.31).

Market Distortions and Regulatory Failures

1) *Constrained scale of pension funds.* Public pension plans tend to be established as pay-as-you-go schemes, under which there is no capital stock to guarantee the funding of current employees' future pension claims. Thus, that part of national savings represented by these schemes by-passes the capital market – which may reduce its size. If funded pensions (in either occupational or personal plans) are developed further, then this would increase the size of capital markets within the EU. Most private pension plans are funded – i.e., assets are purchased specifically to match the liabilities. To the extent that the latter are "covered by dedicated and legally separated assets," the savings that underlie those assets are allocated by means of the capital market [29].

2) *Short-termism and regulatory features drive inefficient asset allocation.* Institutional investors often do not apportion enough funds to long-term investment, especially those which have long-term liabilities – such as pension funds. This is explained mainly by the short-term investment horizon of those persons, and sometimes also by regulatory deficiencies – such as requirements in pension funds' investment mandates in some Member States to invest more than 50% of managed assets in sovereign bonds [30].

3) *Challenges associated with long-term and large-scale infrastructure investments.* A stable framework that has common rules, and which provides legal certainty, would help to ensure that projects are feasible [31].

Comments on the Concept of the CMU and on the Timing of Its Introduction

The idea of bringing investors and borrowers together in the same market is an ancient one, and is the basis for financial intermediation. Financial intermediaries manage the risk between the amounts that they owe to their creditors and the time at which these sums are payable, and the amounts due to them from their debtors and the time from which they may use those funds[525]. Financial markets and their traders make profits on this basis, charging margins between the price at which securities are bought and that at which they are sold. The proposed CMU is an application of this principle.

As at 6th January 2016, none of the 9 Member States whose currency is one other than the Euro[526] had joined the Single Supervisory Mechanism[527] [32]. Although most of these countries are required to do so, by virtue being within the Economic and Monetary Union under a provision of their Accession Treaties with the EU[528], it appears that they are in no hurry to participate.

---

[525] This concept is specifically applied to retail banking, at Baber, G. (2013), 'UK Banking and the Financial Crisis: What lessons have we learned?', *BPP Law School Opinion Piece*, April 2013, 1-10, at 1. This paper is available at www.bpp.com/delegate/r/content/bpp_publications_banking_crisis_apr_2013.pdf.

[526] These countries are: Bulgaria, Croatia, the Czech Republic, Denmark, Hungary, Poland, Romania, Sweden and the United Kingdom.

[527] See fn 496 in the section entitled 'The EBA and the European Central Bank' in Chapter 3, for a description of the Single Supervisory Mechanism.

[528] For example, Article 5 of the Act concerning the conditions of accession of the Republic of Croatia and the adjustments to the Treaty on European Union, the Treaty on the Functioning of the European Union and the

If, as claimed in the previous paragraph, the Single Supervisory Mechanism is in little demand from the Member States that have an element of choice as to whether, or when, to join it, then, if those same countries were presented with a choice as to whether, or when, to join the CMU, they are likely to show a similar reluctance to participate.

The essential difficulty is that these projects are being thrust upon countries at a rate at which it is difficult for them to keep up with developments. Why is it necessary to complete the CMU by 2019[529], given the myriad of procedural problems – some of which are described above in this section? One possible reason is that the current Commission term is due to end on 31st October of that year, giving this Commission the opportunity to guide the framework legislation for the project through to publication in the *Official Journal of the European Union*, before standing for re-appointment. However, Mr. Juncker's words on seeking appointment were[530]: "*Over time,*[531] I believe we should complement the new European rules for banks with a Capital Markets Union" [33]. It would be wise to take the full time that proves to be necessary in order to put the CMU safely, effectively and agreeably in place.

The Action Plan for Constructing the CMU

The Action Plan sets out measures that the Commission is to take, together with commentary. The simplest approach is to quote and to assess each of these proposals in turn.

> 1.1. Financing the start-up phase. … The Commission will assess national regimes and best practice and monitor the evolution of the crowdfunding sector. Following this assessment, the Commission will decide on the best means to enable the development of this new funding channel across the [European]. Union [34].

It is submitted that crowdfunding is not yet sufficiently established to be able to determine best practice. A preferable approach would be to collect primary data via interviews and/or questionnaires from providers and seekers of finance in respect of this sector, and to base any further proposed action on the outcomes of this research.

Treaty Establishing the European Atomic Energy Community, states: "Croatia shall participate in the Economic and Monetary Union from the date of accession as a Member State with a derogation within the meaning of Article 139 of the TFEU". Article 140 of the TFEU contains a procedure according to which Croatia, and the other Member States whose status is that of a participant in the Economic and Monetary Union with a derogation, can be admitted as full members of the Economic and Monetary Union – and the derogation be rescinded.

[529] The Green Paper states: "This Green Paper marks the beginning of a three month consultation. … The feed-back will help us to develop an action plan to put in place the building blocks for a fully functioning Capital Markets Union by 2019." (European Commission (2015), Green Paper: Building a Capital Markets Union, p.3, <http://ec.europa.eu/finance/consultations/2015/capital-markets-union/docs/green-paper_en.pdf>).   This statement is reinforced by the following paragraph in the Action Plan of 30th September 2015: "This Action Plan sets out the building blocks for putting a well-functioning and integrated Capital Markets Union, encompassing all Member States, into place by 2019. This is a long-term project but we will move quickly. The Commission will assess achievements and re-assess priorities in 2017." (European Commission (2015), Communication from the Commission to the European Parliament, the Council, the European Economic and Social Committee and the Committee of the Regions: Action Plan on Building a Capital Markets Union, p.6, <http://ec.europa.eu/finance/capital-markets-union/docs/building-cmu-action-plan_en.pdf>).

[530] See above in this section, for Mr. Juncker's proposal for the CMU, in his statement of July 2014.

[531] Emphasis added.

1.2. The early expansion phase. ... Complementing the financing provided to venture capital and SMEs under the Investment Plan[532], the Commission will take forward a comprehensive package of measures to support venture capital and risk capital financing in the EU. This will amend the EuVECA[533] and EuSEF[534] legislation and proposals for a range of pan-European venture capital funds-of-funds and multi-country funds, supported by the EU budget to mobilise private capital. This comprehensive package will also include the promotion of best practices on tax incentives [35].

This proposal is reasonable, with the legislation on European venture capital funds entailing simpler and more comprehensible authorisation and passporting requirements than those in the AIFM Directive.

1.3. Supporting SMEs seeking finance. ... The Commission will take forward a comprehensive strategy to overcome information barriers that prevent SMEs and prospective investors from identifying funding or investment opportunities through: – working with European banking federations and business organisations to structure the feedback given by banks declining SME credit applications; – working with the Enterprise Europe Network, to map existing local or national support and advisory capacities across the EU in order to promote best practices on assisting SMEs which could benefit from alternative funding options; building on work by the ECB and in Member States, investigate how to develop or support pan-European information systems that link up national systems to bring together finance-seeking SMEs and finance providers and take further action, as necessary [36].

This is constructive, provided that, as stated in the Action Plan, it is optional for SMEs to provide specified data to an information system [37] and that there are strict safeguards as to the use of the data by the subscribers to the system.

1.4. Loan-originating funds. ... The Commission will work with Member States and the ESAs to assess the need for a coordinated approach to loan origination by funds and the case for a future EU framework [38].

This approach may expose the unit-holders of institutional investors to higher risk of non-payment than they would be prepared to accept. Therefore, codes and laws should lay down strict criteria for these investors to make loans to firms. Those rules should also classify institutional investors into risk categories according to which types of firms they are authorised to lend.

---

[532] The 'Investment Plan' means the following document: European Commission (2014), Communication from the Commission to the European Parliament, the Council, the European Central Bank, the European Economic and Social Committee, the Committee of the Regions and the European Investment Bank: An Investment Plan for Europe, COM(2014) 903 final, which was published on 26th November 2014 and is available at http://ec.europa.eu/priorities/jobs-growth-investment/plan/docs/an-investment-plan-for-europe_com_2014_903_en.pdf.

[533] The 'EuVECA' legislation means Regulation (EU) No 345/2013 of the European Parliament and of the Council of 17 April 2013 on European venture capital funds.

[534] The 'EuSEF' legislation means Regulation (EU) No 346/2013 of the European Parliament and of the Council of 17 April 2013 on European social entrepreneurship funds.

2. Making it easier for companies to enter and raise capital on public markets ... The Commission will modernize the Prospectus Directive[535]. This will update when a prospectus is needed, streamline the information required and the approval process, and create a genuinely proportionate regime for SMEs to draw up a prospectus and access capital markets. The Commission will also explore how to support SMEs with the listing process through European advisory structures, such as, for example, the European Investment Advisory Hub [39].

The Commission will review the regulatory barriers to small firms for their admission to trading on public markets and work closely with the new SME Growth Markets under MiFID II to ensure that the regulatory environment for these incubator markets is fit for purpose [40].

The Commission will review the functioning of EU corporate bond markets, focusing on how market liquidity can be improved, the potential impact of regulatory reforms, market developments and voluntary standardisation of offer documentation [41].

As part of the broader work being taken forward on the Common Consolidated Corporate Tax Base (CCCTB)[536], where a new proposal will be prepared in 2016, the Commission will examine ways to address debt-equity bias [42].

The idea of reduced disclosure requirements for SMEs in respect of offers of their securities to the public is fine, in principle – the proposal from the Commission suggests that these firms are to disclose "a specific registration document and a specific securities note," the contents of which will be determined by the Commission in a delegated Act to be adopted for this purpose [43]. Nevertheless, it would be helpful if the Commission would indicate, prior to the adoption of the primary legislation, what information it is likely to recommend that SMEs are to include in these documents. It is submitted that most investors would consider the purchase of securities which an SME issues, to be a transaction of medium-to-high risk – which should therefore only be undertaken if there are substantial expected returns. The risk levels will rise further, if the information disclosed by the SME on the basis of which the offer of the securities to the public is launched, lacks facts that are crucial for the investors to be able to assess the issuing company and the securities.

The Commission's proposed review of debt-equity bias should not concentrate solely on the fact that the interest payable on debt instruments is deducted from company profits before

---

[535] See the subsection entitled 'The prospectus', in the section entitled 'Securities Legislation' in Chapter 1, for the original version of the Prospectus Directive (the PD – Directive 2003/71/EC), i.e., that in effect prior to the GFC.

[536] The Commission has re-launched the proposal on the Common Consolidated Corporate Tax Base, the consultation period for which closes today: 8th January 2016 (European Commission (2015), Re-launch of the Common Consolidated Tax Base (CCCTB), <http://ec.europa.eu/taxation_customs/common/ consultations/tax/relaunch_ccctb_en.htm>). This proposal is entitled 'Communication from the Commission to the European Parliament and the Council: A Fair and Efficient Corporate Tax System in the European Union: 5 Key Areas for Action', and is available at http://ec.europa.eu/taxation_customs/resources/documents/ taxation/company_tax/fairer_corporate_taxation/com_2015_302_en.pdf. One concern is the Commission's wish to make the Common Consolidated Corporate Tax Base mandatory, "at least for multinational enterprises" (European Commission (2015), Communication from the Commission to the European Parliament and the Council: A Fair and Efficient Corporate Tax System in the European Union, p.8). Although the TEU and the TFEU are silent on the issue – with the exception of Article 114(2) of the TFEU (which disapplies the EU's power under Article 114(1) of the TFEU to adopt measures to approximate national rules over the area of the internal market (see fn 587), if these are fiscal provisions), it is not unequivocally clear that the harmonisation of direct taxation is within the shared competence of the EU and the Member States. As this harmonisation would comprise standardising or approximating the tax base and/or the tax rates for direct taxes in Member States, care should be taken with regard to developments. Countries should be aware that these may include issues that affect their national sovereignty.

corporation tax, whilst the dividends payable on preference and equity shares are payable from the taxed profits. Ordinary shares have advantages over debt instruments, the greatest of which is that equity shareholders are the owners of the firm's net assets – whilst debtholders and preference shareholders have no residual claim over these resources[537].

> 3.1. Improving the investment environment through the regulatory framework. ... To facilitate the funding of infrastructure and sustainable long term investment in Europe, the Commission is presenting revised calibrations in Solvency II[538] to ensure that insurance companies are subject to a regulatory treatment which better reflects the risk of infrastructure and ELTIF[539] investments. The Commission will complete the review of the CRR and make changes to infrastructure calibrations, if appropriate [44].

This is a sensible suggestion. In order to improve clarity, it is submitted that the Commission should propose an 'Infrastructure Regulation' which contains the definition of the terms 'infrastructure' and 'infrastructure investment,' and which cross-references to the CRR, to Solvency II, and to any other Regulation or Directive governing financial services that involves long-term investment [45].

> 3.4. Call for evidence on existing regulatory framework. ... Building on the work of the European Parliament and international bodies ... , the Commission is today launching a call for evidence to evaluate the interactions between rules and the cumulative impact of the financial reform on the investment environment [46].

This is a constructive development. Much of the legislation is ineluctable, emerging from Brussels at a pace that would confound the hardiest of lawyers. Therefore, it would be useful if direct contact could be made with the Commission staff who are responsible for the specific items of legislation, in order to ask questions, share viewpoints and request clarification of particular issues and provisions. The 'Europe Direct' portal is excellent, but is not able to encompass all of the points that might reasonably be raised with regard to the Commission's legal proposals and other documents.

> 4.1. Retail investors. ... By the end of 2015, the Commission will publish a Green Paper on retail financial services and insurance that will seek views on how to increase choice, competition and the cross-border supply of retail financial products, as well as the impact of digitalisation on retail financial services [47].
> The Commission will undertake a comprehensive assessment of European markets for retail investment products, including distribution channels and investment advice, drawing on expert input. The assessment will identify ways to improve the policy framework and intermediation channels so that retail investors can access suitable products on cost-effective and fair terms. The assessment will examine how the policy

---

[537] In Baber G. (2012), 'Preferred stock: wisely named?', *Company Lawyer*, 33(5), 129-130, it is argued that preferred stock in English law has few advantages over equity shares from the holder's perspective, but is inferior to debt instruments from the holder's viewpoint in several respects. If the tax-deductibility of debt interest is removed, then debtholders would expect a higher return on their investment in order to compensate for the reduced priority of their claims on the issuing company – debt instruments would become more like preference shares.

[538] 'Solvency II' is an abbreviation for Directive 2009/138/EC of the European Parliament and of the Council of 25 November 2009 on the taking-up and pursuit of the business of Insurance and Reinsurance.

[539] 'ELTIF' is an abbreviation for 'European Long-Term Investment Funds'.

framework should evolve to benefit from the new possibilities offered by online based services and fintech [48].

The Commission will assess the case for a policy framework to establish a successful European market for simple, efficient and competitive personal pensions, and determine whether EU legislation is required to underpin this market [49].

The Green Paper has duly been published[540]. The proposed assessment of EU markets for retail investment products is a good idea; the Commission should disclose, as soon as is reasonably possible, how it intends to undertake this evaluation.

In respect of a European market for pensions, it would be desirable for the Commission to declare the characteristics of the pan-EU personal pension scheme that it plans to introduce. It is submitted that the Commission may wish to encourage the use of the capital markets in respect of this plan, which risks attracting resources away from existing pay-as-you-go schemes unless appropriate safeguards are put in place beforehand.

4.2. Institutional investors. ... The Commission will assess whether changes are warranted and, if so, prepare amendments which could be brought forward in the context of the Solvency II review. ... The Commission will gather evidence on the main barriers to the cross-border distribution of investment funds. This would include in particular disproportionate marketing requirements, fees, and other administrative arrangements imposed by host countries and the tax environment. Based on the evidence provided, the Commission will seek to eliminate key barriers, through legislative means if necessary [50].

This is fine, if the emphasis is on financial instruments that institutional investors might purchase with a view to long-term ownership. Cross-border barriers to investment should be eased away by consultation and persuasion; their removal should only be undertaken by means of legislation as a final resort.

5. Leveraging banking capacity to support the wider economy ... Credit Unions in certain Member States are already exempted from the CRD [Capital Requirements Directive]. Regulatory Framework. To ensure a level playing field, all Member States should be able to benefit from credit unions, which are subject to national regulatory safeguards commensurate with the risks that they incur. To this end, the Commission will explore the possibility for all Member States to authorise credit unions which operate outside the EU's capital requirements framework for banks [51].

The Commission is publishing today a proposal for an EU framework for simple, transparent and standardised (STS) securitisation, together with new prudential calibrations for banks in CRR. Equivalent calibrations for insurers through an amendment to the Solvency II Delegated Act to incorporate the STS criteria will follow as soon as the STS framework has been adopted [52].

The Commission is publishing today a consultation on the development of a pan-European framework for covered bonds, building on national regimes that work well without disrupting them and based on high-quality standards and best market practices. The consultation will also seek views on the use of similar structures to support SME loans [53].

---

[540] The Green Paper on retail financial services, COM(2015) 630 final, is available at http://eur-lex.europa.eu/legal-content/EN/TXT/PDF/?uri=CELEX:52015DC0630&from=EN.

It is submitted that there have been enough banking reforms in the wake of the GFC for further changes to be postponed. The securitisation proposals should be put on hold, at least until there has been a chance to undertake a comprehensive analysis of the effects of the post-crisis banking legislation. It may be advisable to formally review the operation of all methods of structured finance used since the GFC, with an emphasis on European markets.

6.1. Legal certainty and market infrastructure for cross-border investing. ... The Commission will take forward early targeted work on uncertainty surrounding securities ownership. On the basis of further consultation and impact assessment, the Commission will also propose uniform rules to determine with legal certainty which national law shall apply to third party effects of the assignment of claims [54].

To support more efficient and resilient post-trading systems and collateral markets, the Commission will undertake a broader review on progress in removing Giovannini barriers to cross-border clearing and settlement[541], following the implementation of recent legislation and market infrastructure developments [55].

It is crucial that the law applicable to cross-border securities transactions is able to be determined in a way that provides legal certainty to interested parties. Therefore, the Commission's work over this area is a welcome development.

It is reasonable to wait until the implementation of legislation that concerns the infrastructure of financial markets – such as the MiFIR[542] – before reviewing the extent to which barriers to cross-border transactions remain in place. The Giovannini Group's review

---

[541] This is a reference to obstacles to cross-border clearing and settlement that were identified by the Giovannini Group's Report on Cross-Border Clearing and Settlement Arrangements in the European Union. The Report was published in November 2001, and is available at http://www.ebf-fbe.eu/uploads/First%20Giovannini%20Report%20on%20Clearing%20&%20Settlement%20in%20the%20EU%20%282001%29.pdf. The Giovannini Group published a further document in April 2003, entitled Second Report on EU Clearing and Settlement Arrangements, which is available at http://ec.europa.eu/internal_ market/financial-markets/docs/clearing/second_giovannini_report_en.pdf. The Group identified 15 barriers to efficient cross-border clearing and settlement within the EU, 10 of which are classified as concerning differences in Member States in respect of market practice and/or technical requirements (category 'A'), 2 of which are listed as relating to national differences in taxation procedures (category 'B'), and 3 of which are classified as concerning matters of legal certainty (category 'C'); these obstacles are as follows: differences between Member States in information technology and interfaces between systems (A1), domestic restrictions on settlement and clearing that require several systems to be used (A2), differences in national rules which relate to beneficial ownership, corporate actions and custody (A3), the lack of intra-day settlement finality (A4), practical obstructions to remote access to domestic clearing and settlement systems (A5), differences in settlement periods between Member States (A6), differences in the operating hours of national systems and in domestic deadlines for settlement (A7), difference between Member States in securities' issuance practice (A8), domestic restrictions as to the location of securities (A9), limitations that Member States impose on the activity of market makers and primary dealers (A10), national regulations that disadvantage foreign intermediaries in their ability to offer relief from withholding tax at source (B1)(see fn 326 in the subsection entitled '2009', in the section entitled 'Progress in the G20/FSB System from November 2008' in Chapter 2, for a definition of 'withholding tax'), national requirements to collect transactions taxes through a functionality that is integrated into a local settlement system (B2), the absence of a pan-EU framework for the regulation of interests in securities (C1), domestic differences in the legal treatment of bilateral netting in respect of financial transactions (C2), and problems in the application of conflict of law rules (C3) (Giovannini Group (2001), Cross-Border Clearing and Settlement Arrangements in the European Union, pp.44-51 and 55-57).

[542] The MiFIR is due to come into force on 3rd January 2017 (MiFIR (as corrected to 15/10/15), Article 55.

of 2001 was thorough, in that it identified a large, diverse group of impediments to transnational settlement and clearing[543].

> 6.2. Removing national barriers to cross-border investment. ... The Commission, working with Member States, will map and work to resolve unjustified national barriers to the free movement of capital, stemming, amongst other things, from insufficient implementation or lack of convergence in interpretation of the single rulebook and from national law that are preventing a well-functioning Capital Markets Union and publish a report by the end of 2016 [56].
>
> The Commission will propose a legislative initiative on business insolvency, including early restructuring and second chance, drawing on the experience of the Recommendation[544]. The initiative will seek to address the most important barriers to the free flow of capital, building on national regimes that work well [57].
>
> To encourage Member States to adopt systems of relief-at-source from withholding taxes and to establish quick and standardised refund procedures, the Commission will promote best practice and develop a code of conduct with Member States on withholding tax relief principles. The Commission will also undertake a study on discriminatory tax obstacles to cross-border investment by life insurance companies and by pension funds and, where necessary, will initiate infringement procedures [58].

The idea of the Commission working with Member States to remove domestic barriers to cross-border investment is fine, in principle. However, much of what is actually done depends on the interpretation of the Commission's staff – or possibly that of the staff at the ESMA (if the Commission delegates this supervisory work to that ESA) – as to what national rules or practices are considered to be 'unjustified barriers to the free movement of capital,' There is a risk that this approach will be suppressive of the Member States, because the Commission – especially if backed by the Parliament – has the force or threat of law on which to rely in any disagreement with each Member State. Furthermore, it is noteworthy that the Court of Justice of the European Union has often declared a breach of the principle of free movement of capital[545], when the Commission has taken a Member State to the Court for an alleged contravention of this fundamental freedom.[546]

The Recommendation is clement to entrepreneurs. However, it is arguable that the points 30[547] and 31[548] within it are difficult to implement in practice, and that the idea of the second

---

[543] See fn 541, for the 15 barriers to efficient cross-border clearing and settlement that the Giovanni Group identified.

[544] This is Commission Recommendation of 12.3.2014 on a new approach to business failure and insolvency, C(2014) 1500 final, which is available at http://ec.europa.eu/justice/civil/files/c_2014_1500_en.pdf.

[545] Article 63(1) of the TFEU contains this principle, which is as follows: "Within the framework of the provisions set out in this Chapter, all restrictions on the movement of capital between Member States and between Member States and third countries shall be prohibited". 'This Chapter' refers to 'Chapter 4: Capital and Payments', in Title IV (entitled 'Free Movement of Persons, Services and Capital) of Part III (entitled 'Union Policies and Internal Actions') of the TFEU; it contains Articles 63-66 of this Treaty – which are, therefore, 'the provisions set out in this Chapter'. Article 63(2) of the TFEU contains a similar rule in respect of payments, which is as follows: "Within the framework of the provisions set out in this Chapter, all restrictions on payments between Member States and between Member States and third countries shall be prohibited.."

[546] The Court of Justice of the European Union interprets derogations from the free movement of capital narrowly (Baber, G. (2010), *The Impact of Legislation and Regulation on the Freedom of Movement of Capital in Estonia, Poland and Latvia*, pp.35 and 42; Baber, G. (2014), *The Free Movement of Capital and Financial Services: An Exposition?*, pp.27 and 42).

[547] Point 30 of the Commission Recommendation on a new approach to business failure and insolvency states: "The negative effects of bankruptcy on entrepreneurs should be limited in order to give them a second chance.

chance for entrepreneurs should therefore be shelved. It is submitted that the Commission should publish a draft Regulation for restructuring along the same lines as Council Regulation (EC) No 1346/2000 on insolvency proceedings; the two instruments could operate on a similar legal basis[549].

The development of a code of conduct on withholding tax principles is a good suggestion. This code should, initially, contain general principles – rather than detailed rules – and should be compatible with acceptable practice in respect of withholding taxes in major economies outside the EU.

> 6.3. Promoting financial stability and supervisory convergence. … The Commission will work with the FSB and ESAs alongside the European Systemic Risk Board (ESRB) to assess possible risks to financial stability arising from market-based finance. Further analytical work will be conducted, for example to better understand the issues of market liquidity and interconnectedness in the financial system, and to assess if additional macro-prudential instruments should be developed. The Commission will make any changes necessary to the macro-prudential framework in the context of the forthcoming ESRB review [59].
>
> The Commission will work with ESMA to develop and implement a strategy to strengthen supervisory convergence and to identify areas where a more integrated approach can improve the functioning of the single market for capital. The Commission will also work with ESMA to enhance the effectiveness of its thematic and country peer review decision-making. The Commission will publish a White Paper in 2016 on the governance and the financing of the ESAs. The CMU is a classic single market project for the benefit of all 28 Member States. To help capital markets deliver their full potential, the Commission will, through the Structural Reform Support Service, develop a strategy for providing technical assistance to Member States where needed to reinforce specific capacities of national capital markets [60].

These proposals are fine – in theory, and as long as, when they emerge from Brussels, they are subject to the principles of conferral[550], subsidiarity[551] and proportionality[552] that

---

> Entrepreneurs should be fully discharged of their debts which were [the] subject of a bankruptcy after no later than three years starting from: (a) in the case of a procedure ending with the liquidation of the debtor's assets, the date on which the court decided on the application to open bankruptcy proceedings; (b) in the case of a procedure which includes a repayment plan, the date on which implementation of the repayment plan started.."

[548] Point 31 of the Commission Recommendation on a new approach to business failure and insolvency states: "On the expiry of the discharge period, entrepreneurs should be discharged of their debts without the need in principle to re-apply to a court.."

[549] Article 4(1) of Council Regulation (EC) No 1346/2000 determines that, unless provisions of that Regulation state otherwise," the law applicable to insolvency proceedings and their effects shall be that of the Member State within the territory of which such proceedings are opened." Article 4(2) of Council Regulation (EC) No 1346/2000 holds that this applicable law "shall determine the conditions for the opening of those proceedings, their conduct and their closure," and specifies particular aspects of the insolvency proceedings which are to be governed by the applicable law, such as "the respective powers of the debtor and the liquidator" (Council Regulation (EC) No 1346/2000, Article 4(2)(c)). Subsequent Articles of the Regulation contain exceptions under which a law other than that of the main proceedings is to apply; for instance, Article 8 of Council Regulation (EC) No 1346/2000 states: "The effect of insolvency proceedings on a contract conferring the right to acquire or make use of immoveable property shall be governed solely by the law of the Member State within the territory of which the immoveable property is situated."

[550] Article 5(2) of the TEU states: "Under the principle of conferral, the [European] Union shall act only within the limits of the competences conferred upon it by the Member States in the Treaties [i.e., the TEU and the TFEU] to attain the objectives set out therein. Competences not conferred upon the Union in the Treaties remain with the Member States". Paragraphs 1-5 of Article 3 of the TEU contain the EU's objectives. Article 3(1) is the

Article 5 of the TEU lays down. However, this work should be taken at a steady pace, in order to fit systemic adjustments to the specific requirements for these.

It has not been established beyond reasonable doubt that 'the CMU is a classic single market project for the benefit of all 28 Member States' – the proposed level of integration is high, and may not be in the interests of all countries within the EEA[553]. Therefore, the Commission should demonstrate its case for the CMU on a cost-benefit basis – with a broader base for its accountability than the prevailing views within the Council and the Parliament.

What Do Others Write About the CMU?

The Commission's Economic Analysis that accompanies the Action Plan for the CMU, is remarkable for its complexity, its obscurity and its didactic approach[554]. The essence of this document comprises the 3 objectives of the CMU, which are as follows.

a. The CMU will broaden the sources of financing in Europe towards non-bank financing by giving a stronger role to capital markets. It will offer to borrowers and investors a broader set of financial instruments to meet their respective needs. b. The CMU will help [to] deepen the single market for financial services. Capital markets will benefit from size effects of the single market and become deeper, more liquid and more competitive, for the benefit of both borrowers and investors. c. The CMU will help [to] promote growth and financial stability[555]. By facilitating companies' access to finance, in particular SMEs, the CMU will support growth and jobs' creation. At the same time, by promoting more diversified funding channels to the economy, it will help [to] address possible risks stemming from the over-reliance on bank lending and intermediation in the financial system. By diversifying the risks, it will make the whole system more stable and help financial intermediaries [by?[556] OR which will then be?[557]] granting more funding to the economy [61].

---

most significant of these, because it is the EU's aim – which is "to promote peace, its values and the well-being of its peoples" (TFEU, Article 3(1)). Article 3(6) of the TEU declares: "The Union shall pursue its objectives by appropriate means commensurate with the competences which are conferred upon it in the Treaties.."

[551] Article 5(3) of the TEU states: "Under the principle of subsidiarity, in areas which do not fall within its exclusive competence, the [European] Union shall act only if and in so far as the objectives of the proposed action cannot be sufficiently achieved by the Member States, either at central level or at regional and local level, but can rather, by reason of the scale or effects of the proposed action, be better achieved at Union level. ...."

[552] Article 5(4) of the TEU states: "Under the principle of proportionality, the content and form of [European] Union action shall not exceed what is necessary to achieve the objectives of the Treaties. ...."

[553] It is likely that the legislation which sets up the CMU will apply to Iceland, Liechtenstein and Norway – in addition to the 28 Member States. If this is true, then these countries should be consulted before the CMU framework legislation is finalized.

[554] This document is entitled 'Commission Staff Working Document: Economic Analysis, Accompanying the document 'Communication for the Commission to the European Parliament, the Council, the European Economic and Social Committee and the Committee of the Regions – Action Plan on Building a Capital Markets Union', is referenced as SWD(2015) 183 final, and is available at http://ec.europa.eu/finance/capital-markets-union/docs/building-cmu-economic-analysis_en.pdf.

[555] Emphasis original.

[556] The logic for this statement may be that the additional investors who are attracted by the beneficial new EU rules that frame the CMU, will deposit some of their money with financial intermediaries (as well as directly in capital market instruments, such as listed equity shares). Another interpretation is that the additional investors demand the issue of further capital market instruments, which are then available to be purchased on the secondary capital markets by financial intermediaries.

The Economic Analysis mentions Mr. Hugo Dixon's[558] commentary of October 2014, entitled 'Unlocking Europe's capital market union' [62]. This paper's conclusion is striking.

> A genuine EU capital markets union would be a big prize. It would give the EU more ways of funding jobs and growth, help it to weather macroeconomic shocks, enable it to pursue more effective monetary policy and create more competitive financial markets. As a bonus, it would also cut the risks of Britain quitting the EU. Given the size of the prize, policy-makers should embark on an ambitious programme to make the capital markets union a reality. The guiding principles should be freeing up capital markets, ensuring their healthy development and respecting the subsidiarity principle. A top priority for the incoming Juncker Commission should be to produce a detailed action plan to create the capital markets union – and secure buy-in for it from the European Council and the Parliament in early 2015. The key building blocks should all be in place by the time the Commission leaves office in late 2019. The benefits will not all flow immediately. But over the coming decades, a capital markets union can make a significant contribution to improving the EU's economic prospects. Earlier Commissions were known variously for the single market, monetary union, enlargement and banking union. The Juncker Commission could go down in history as the creator of the capital markets union [63].

In addition, points made in Mr. Dixon's paper are consistent with elements of the Commission's CMU documentation – considered above in this section. It is submitted that his advice may have provided a significant input to the initial stages of the Commission's construction of the CMU.

Mr. Karel Lannoo's[559] paper of February 2015, which is entitled 'Which Union for Europe's Capital Markets,' states that Europe's capital markets are fragmented, in spite of a single currency and harmonising financial legislation that the EU has developed over many years [64]. He refers to the European Central Bank's price-based and quantity-based composite indicators from its April 2014 Financial Market Integration Report, stating that financial integration within the Eurozone on both measures has declined with the GFC and is at a similar level to that in 1999[560] [65]. Mr. Lannoo considers that a programme for CMU will be "very difficult to delineate," depending upon "the level of ambition and the objectives

---

[557] Alternatively, the logic for this statement might be that some financial intermediaries, such as venture capital funds, will provide additional financing to the economy as a result of attracting additional investors in accordance with the beneficial new EU rules that frame the CMU.

[558] In 2014, Mr. Dixon published a book entitled 'The In/Out Question: Why Britain should stay in the EU and fight to make it better', in which he argues a case for the United Kingdom's continuing membership of the EU. It is available at http://www.amazon.co.uk/gp/product/1496146670?keywords=Hugo%20Dixon%20the%20in% 2Fout%20question&qid=1452692955&ref_=sr_1_1&sr=8-1. Mr. Dixon is the Editor-at-large at Reuters News.

[559] Mr. Lannoo is the Chief Executive Officer at the Centre for European Policy Studies, and the General Manager of the European Capital Markets Institute – which is based at the Centre.

[560] Both the price-based and the quantity-based composite indicators of financial integration have risen during 2014, with the former – although not the latter – substantially below its peak level in 2005 (European Central Bank, Financial Integration in Europe: April 2015, Chart 1, p.5). The price-based composite indicator is "constructed from a selection of price-based indicators that cover the four main market segments: money, bond, equity and banking instruments" (European Central Bank, Financial Integration in Europe: April 2015, Statistical Annex, subsection 1.1, p.117). The quantity-based composite indicator is "constructed in a way similar to the one described above [i.e., in subsection 1.1 of the Statistical Annex] for the price-based composite indicator" (European Central Bank, Financial Integration in Europe: April 2015, Statistical Annex, subsection 1.2, p.119).

pursued" [66]. His commentary of July 2015, written with Messrs. Allan Polack[561] and Ole Staehr[562], argues for a pan-EU long-term savings product that is to be licensed by EIOPA (or another European supervisor), and has little time for the ELTIF Regulation – an agreement that "will to further fragmentation, which is just the opposite of the conditions needed for [illiquid] investments" [67]. Mr. Lannoo's later opinion piece – published on 2nd October 2015 in response to the Commission's release of the Action Plan[563] (which is dated 30th September 2015) – suggests that the prime difficulty to be addressed is the "overexposure of households to deposits, which do not find their way to the markets," and repeats the theme concerning long-term savings that his paper of July 2015 addressed: "The Action Plan is very timid at this stage on creating a new sizeable EU-wide savings product." [68]. He notes that financial portfolios of households in the United States of America contain more equity and units in investment funds than do those of their counterparts in the EU, but place a smaller percentage of savings in deposits than do the latter [69]. Thus, household savings within the EU are "not finding their way into more rewarding investments, which is caused by a variety of factors than cannot be easily changed" [70]. The paper concludes as follows.

> It is clear that a Capital Markets Union will not be created overnight. There are profound structural differences between EU member states, and even larger differences compared with the great benchmark, the US. To overcome these, and to live up to the expectations that have been raised, bold initiatives will be needed. This Action Plan has launched the debate with some concrete proposals and many ideas for further work. But it is only a start – more needs to be done [71].

Mr. Lannoo's submission of this work for comment to his colleagues at the European Capital Markets Institute, Drs. Cosmina Amariei[564] and Diego Valiante[565], encouraged the latter to swiftly publish a commentary on the Commission's Action Plan [72, 73]. Dr. Valiante affirms Mr. Lannoo's views, and goes even further along the road to integration.

> A truly pan-European Capital Markets Union will not be created overnight. Differences among EU member States and between the EU and the US are structural and require a bold response. This Action Plan[566] has launched the debate with few concrete proposals and many ideas for further work in several areas. The bright side of the CMU plan is certainly the attempt to unify efforts in a single plan and to exploit the political momentum surrounding the completion of the monetary union and the creation of a financial union. It also brings to the table important discussions that have been shelved in recent years, like harmonisation of tax collection and cross-border insolvency proceedings. But more needs to be done. This plan walks on a much thinner political support compared to the Banking Union proposals. The approach of the Action Plan assumes that wholesale investors or large companies can already access a well-functioning European capital market, but this is erroneous. EU equity markets, for example, are just a fraction of US equity markets and pan-European activity is for now

---

[561] Mr. Polack is the Chief Executive Officer of the Professional Footballers Association (PFA) Pension Scheme.
[562] Mr. Staehr is an Executive Adviser at Nordea Wealth Management.
[563] See the subsection entitled 'The Action Plan for constructing the CMU', above in this section, for the Commission's 'Action Plan on Building a Capital Markets Union'.
[564] Dr. Amariei is Research Assistant at the European Capital Markets Institute.
[565] Dr. Valiante is Head of Research at the European Capital Markets Institute, and Head of the Financial Markets and Institutions Research Unit at the Centre for European Policy Studies.
[566] See fn 563.

limited to the top liquid shares of domestic listings, with markets defined along national borders. ... Fostering cross-border capital flows through the creation of a common legal and financial architecture (with a focus on information flows and enforcement) will increase resilience, as it improves the quality of financial integration through more diversified financial flows, as well as efficiency for the benefit of small and big firms and investors alike. ... After the partial success to complete the single market for capital with the 1992 Single Market Programme and the 1999 Financial Services Action Plan, this may indeed offer the vision that will prevent the CMU from becoming another (failed) harmonisation attempt to restart financial integration [74].

Both of these commentators consider that the United States of America sets the standard for the EU in respect of activity on the capital markets. This also forms a part of the views of Dr. Orçun Kaya[567] who states: "With regard to stock markets, there is an enormous difference in size between the US and the EU," "stock and corporate bond markets in the EU are less than half the size of those in the US," and "Compared with the US, securitisation markets in Europe are small," and "Taken together with the low liquidity in corporate bond markets, the fact that euro-area corporate bond markets are much smaller than those in the US (or the UK, for that matter) may impede their effective and efficient functioning to finance non-financial corporations" [75].

Notwithstanding this, Dr. Kaya's paper contains a sensible, detailed and constructive reportage and analysis of the state of equity and bond markets, and of securitisation, within the Eurozone, and makes suggestions in respect of the CMU for each of these sectors.

Stock market financing is a cornerstone of corporate funding in Europe as well as in the US. Against the background of the recent slowdown or even partial reversal in cross-border financial holdings, the crucial question is: *"Could the CMU help advance stock market integration in the EU again and increase intra-European investments?*[568] Stock market integration and an expansion of intra-EU investments are strongly linked to the legal system in which issuers and investors are embedded. In this regard, the potential success of the CMU will depend upon its ability to overcome legal and regulatory barriers that govern European stock markets. A possible way to achieve this could be via a single set of rules for capital markets that harmonises company, securities and insolvency laws as well as tackling barriers in other cross-cutting areas such as taxation. And indeed one key objective of the CMU is to establish a single rulebook, a harmonised capital market regulatory framework [76].

The surge in [bond] issuance volumes [since the GFC, in France, Germany, Italy, Spain and the Netherlands,] underscores the major change which bond markets have been undergoing in recent years. Bond funding in many cases has become a notable alternative and cushioned the impact of the credit squeeze. Over time, outstanding debt market volumes in the euro area will probably grow further as the markets take on a bigger role (and bank lending a somewhat smaller one). Nevertheless, several factors are impeding this process as well as the further development of corporate bond markets in Europe, and the CMU could help to overcome them. First and foremost, to the extent that the CMU leads to a larger investor base for corporate bonds, it may help to lift issuance levels in Europe. Indeed, recent trends show that euro area corporations tap the debt capital markets as long as investor appetite creates favourable conditions for issuers. To preserve

---

[567] Dr. Kaya is Economist at the Banking, Financial Markets and Regulation Team of Deutsche Bank Research.
[568] Emphasis original.

these dynamics, the CMU could introduce measures to gradually (and at least partially) move more of the national pension schemes in Europe from the widespread "defined benefit" system (including public pay-as-you-go schemes) to a funded "defined contribution" system. With this transformation, pension savings could be channelled into capital markets that tend to offer higher rates of return in the longer term. ... The CMU could help institutional investors to widen their corporate bond portfolios by reducing a mechanistic reliance on ratings and by introducing more flexible measures. In addition, by increasing investor demand, these measures should lower the cost of issuing bonds in the long run and would also make bond issuance a more robust alternative to bank lending. ... [D]isclosure requirements in Europe are governed by five different sets of legislation ... which are not synchronized (this obviously creates a bottleneck for stock markets, too). The inefficiency with regard to disclosure is a significant administrative burden and induces non-negligible costs for firms that seek bond funding. ... As in the case of stock markets, the CMU is a good opportunity to harmonise these duplications and overlaps in disclosure regimes [77].

The CMU ... could revive securitisation markets in Europe by easing the regulatory treatment [under CRD IV and the CRR for banks, and under Solvency II[569] for insurance firms] that discourages institutional investors from buying these instruments. ... By introducing the concept of a "qualifying securitization," the CMU may contribute to the development and the sustainability of a stronger and safer securitisation market ... [C]oncerning the application of the STC criteria [Simple, Transparent and Comparable securitisations, which the BCBS and the IOSCO defined in July 2015]., the CMU should bring more clarification on points such as the ongoing monitoring and compliance of STC products, i.e., on the extent of information that needs to be updated throughout the life of the securitisation. The CMU could also help to simplify the overly prescriptive points and heavy regulatory terminology with regard to characteristics of the STC products. ... [T]he CMU should target measures for enhancing the European MBS [mortgage-backed securities] market ... . In order for SME lending to regain traction, a revival of the SME-ABS [asset-backed securities] market could also be helpful. ... To bring some standardisation and transparency into the SME loan landscape, a European credit risk database on SME loans could be beneficial. For the pooling and repackaging of SME loans, the credit risk database would also reduce the reliance on external ratings. ... [W]hen pursuing new frontiers such as a credit risk database, the CMU should include banks to draw on their risk management expertise and build on their client relations [78].

He endorses the Commission's CMU project, but with an encouragement to its creators to show dogged determination.

All in all, the CMU is an ambitious project with tremendous potential. That being said, the current discussion is overly abstract and lacks clear guidelines. Taking the steps we have mentioned would facilitate further growth in capital markets in Europe over time, enabling them to gradually strengthen their role compared to bank lending. However, without clearly defined measures and a roadmap as well as a prospective central implementing authority, uncertainty regarding the success of the CMU project will remain. Even in the optimal case with fully defined cornerstones, achieving a union for capital markets in Europe is going to be a long and rocky process. In this respect, the success of the CMU requires persistent dedication [79].

---

[569] See fn 538, for the definition of 'Solvency II'.

Further Comments on the CMU

Dr. Kaya's commentary illustrates that the Commission's wish for, and pursual of, a CMU offers opportunities for borrower-lender engagement – especially his ingenious scheme of stimulating lending to SMEs by attempting to revive the market for asset-backed securitisations, with its accompanying credit risk database for loans to SMEs. As the lack of due diligence in respect of the quality of securitised assets and their accompanying bonds was a determinant of the precipitation of the GFC, such a database would need to be established carefully and the accuracy of its data monitored continuously. In the light of the crisis, the Commission should exercise caution and care in its attempt to establish the framework for a thriving market for structured finance within the EU.

Dr. Kaya's paper draws attention to the market balance between the United Kingdom and the Eurozone – which is of particular interest to the author (who is British). In a table that reports EU centres for trading in financial instruments 'losing ground', he notes London as being the highest-ranked centre in the world in both 2007 and 2015 according to the Global Financial Centres Index, with the second European centre – Frankfurt – slipping from 6th in the world in 2007 to 14th in 2015 [80]. Another table records the London Stock Exchange Group as having the largest market capitalisation of any stock exchange (individually or as a group) in the world at the end of 2014 [81]. In 2014, corporate bonds outstanding as a percentage of Gross Domestic Product, were twice as high in the United Kingdom as in the Eurozone [82]. These figures demonstrate that the United Kingdom is the senior player within Europe with respect to capital markets – even though it is outside the Eurozone and, therefore, beyond the scope of the plans for further integration that the Commission (together with other EU institutions) has put forward in respect of that area – of which the CMU is a part[570]. From the United Kingdom's point of view, the issue is as follows: how is the country able to proceed with a CMU in which it is the major participant by virtue of the size of its markets, whilst a significant focus of the CMU is towards completing an Economic and Monetary Union of which the United Kingdom is not (and is unlikely to be) a part? With due respect to this Commission, the fact that the United Kingdom faces this predicament is a significant *faux pas*, for which the former bears the main responsibility – having put forward both the further integration plans for the Eurozone and the CMU proposals since it took office in November 2014. It would be sensible to carefully revisit the timing of these scheduled events.

The next 2 sections, entitled 'Securities Legislation' and 'Banking Legislation' respectively, consider aspects of the securities legislation and of the banking legislation that the EU has published since the GFC. In instances in which this is possible, a comparison is made with the EU legislation that was in force before the GFC – as stated in Chapter 1.

---

[570] Mr. Juncker proposed these plans, in co-ordination with Dr. Draghi and Messrs. Schulz, Tusk and Jeroen Dijsselbloem – the President of the Eurogroup (i.e., the meetings of the finance ministers of the countries within the Eurozone), in the European Commission's Report of June 2015, entitled 'Completing the Economic and Monetary Union.' This Report is known as the 'Five Presidents' Report,' and is available at http://ec.europa.eu/priorities/economic-monetary-union/docs/5-presidents-report_en.pdf.

SECURITIES LEGISLATION

Market Abuse

The MAR and MAD II entered into force on 2nd July 2014[571]. The MAD and its accompanying secondary legislation[572] are to be repealed from 3rd July 2016 [83]. Other than some provisions specified therein – which applied from the former date, the MAR is to apply from the latter time [84]. Member States are to transpose MAD II into national law by 3rd July 2016 [85]. Given the proximity of this date, the content of the MAR and of MAD II are considered in this subsection – in the light of the pre-GFC contents of the MAD as summarised in Chapter 1[573].

The EU considered that the MAD needed to be replaced in the light of "considerable changes to the financial landscape" which have resulted from "the legislative, market and technological developments" that have taken place since the MAD entered into force[574] [86]. It determined that there was "a need to establish a more uniform and stronger framework in order to preserve market integrity, to avoid potential regulatory arbitrage, to ensure accountability in the event of attempted manipulation, and to provide more legal certainty and less regulatory complexity for market participants" [87].

A person is not to: (a) participate, or to attempt to participate, in insider dealing, (b) recommend to, or persuade, another person to so participate, or (c) illegally divulge inside information [88]. For the purposes of the MAR, insider dealing takes place, if a person who possesses inside information uses it to acquire or dispose of financial instruments to which it relates, or cancels or amends an order that concerns a financial instrument to which that information relates – if the order was made before the relevant person possessed the inside information [89]. Offence (b) takes place, if the person who possesses inside information – on the basis of that information – (i) recommends that another person obtain or relinquish financial instruments to which it relates or induces this person to do so, or (ii) recommends that another person withdraw or amend an order that concerns a financial instrument to which the inside information relates or induces this person to do so [90]. The use of these recommendations or inducements amounts to insider dealing, if the person who uses a recommendation or an inducement knows, or ought to have known, that it is founded upon inside information [91]. Inside information comprises: (i) "information of a precise nature"

---

[571] The MAR and MAD II came into force on the 20th day after their publication in the *Official Journal of the European Union* (MAR, Article 39(1); MAD II, Article 14).

[572] This legislation comprises: (i) Commission Directive 2003/124/EC of 22 December 2003 implementing Directive 2003/6/EC of the European Parliament and of the Council as regards the definition and public disclosure of insider information and the definition of market manipulation, (ii) Commission Directive 2003/125/EC of 22 December 2003 implementing Directive 2003/6/EC of the European Parliament and of the Council as regards the fair presentation of investment recommendations and the disclosure of conflicts of interest, (iii) Commission Regulation (EC) No 2273/2003 of 22 December 2003 implementing Directive 2003/6/EC of the European Parliament and of the Council as regards exemptions for buy-back programmes and stabilisation of financial instruments, and (iv) Commission Directive 2004/72/EC of 29 April 2004 implementing Directive 2003/6/EC of the European Parliament and of the Council as regards accepted market practices, the definition of inside information in relation to derivatives on commodities, the drawing up of lists of insiders, the notification of managers' transactions and the notification of suspicious transactions.

[573] See the subsection entitled 'Market abuse', in the section entitled 'Securities Legislation' in Chapter 1, for a summary of the MAD.

[574] The MAD came into force on the day on which it was published in the *Official Journal of the European Union* (MAD, as amended to 15/12/10), Article 21), which was 12th April 2003.

that has not been made public, which relates to at least one issuer or financial instrument, and which, if it is to be published, would be likely to have a "significant effect" on the prices of those instruments or of related derivatives, (ii) in respect of commodity derivatives, "information of a precise nature" that has not been made public, which relates to at least one commodity derivative, and which, if it is to be published, would be likely to have a "significant effect" upon the prices of those derivatives or on "related spot commodity contracts," and – in circumstances under which this information is "reasonably expected to be disclosed" or is required to be divulged in accordance with the law, the rules of the exchange, the contract, custom or practice – on the relevant markets[575], (iii) with regard to emission allowances or auctioned products that are based on these, "information of a precise nature" that has not been made public, which relates to at least one of these instruments, and which, if it is to be published, would be likely to have a "significant effect" on the prices of these instruments or of related derivatives, and (iv) for persons who carry out orders that concern financial instruments, information "of a precise nature" that a customer conveys and which relates to his/her orders that are pending in respect of financial instruments, and which, if it is to be published, would be likely to have a "significant effect" on the prices of these financial instruments, of "related spot commodity contracts," or of related derivatives [92]. Information shall be considered to be "of a precise nature" if it points out a set of circumstances that exists or which may reasonably be expected to materialize, or if it is sufficiently specific to enable a conclusion to be made as to the possible effect of those circumstances on the relevant financial instrument [93]. The definition of 'inside information' in the MAR is consistent with that in the pre-GFC MAD[576], although the former is more precise than the latter – and includes an additional subheading for emission allowances. Although the MAD mentions 'insider dealing' in the title and in the Recitals, this term is not defined in any of its Articles. As the MAR carefully defines 'insider dealing' (in addition to 'inside information'), this offence is more comprehensive under the MAR than under the MAD.

A person is neither to engage in, nor to endeavour to engage in, market manipulation [94]. 'Market manipulation' includes: (a) any behaviour that (i) gives, or is likely to provide, false or misleading indications as to the price of, supply of, or demand for, a financial instrument, a "spot commodity contract" which is related to that instrument, or an auctioned product that is founded on emissions allowances, or (ii) secures, or is likely to secure, the price of at least one financial instrument, a "spot commodity contract" which is related to that instrument, or an auctioned product that is founded on emissions allowances, at an exceptional or artificial level – unless the person concerned demonstrates that his/her reasons for acting in this way are valid and that his/her conduct is in accordance "with an accepted

---

[575] The ESMA is to issue guidelines in order "to establish a non-exhaustive list of information that is reasonably expected or is required to be disclosed in accordance with legal or regulatory provisions in [European] Union or national law, market rules, contract, practice or custom, on the relevant commodity derivatives markets or spot markets as referred to in point (b) of paragraph 1" of Article 7 of the MAR (MAR, Article 7(5)). On 28th September 2015, the ESMA published a document entitled 'Final Report: Draft technical standards on the Market Abuse Regulation', which refers to Article 7(5) of the MAR but does not provide the guidelines that this provision requires. This item is available at https://www.esma.europa.eu/sites/default/files/library/2015/11/2015-esma-1455_-_final_report_mar_ts.pdf. The ESMA notes that it issues these guidelines, on its website at https://www.esma.europa.eu/regulation/trading/market-abuse; they are eagerly awaited.

[576] See the subsection entitled 'Market abuse', in the section entitled 'Securities Legislation' in Chapter 1, for the definition of 'inside information' in the original version of the MAD.

market practice"[577], (b) any conduct that affects, or is likely to influence, the price of at least one financial instrument, a "spot commodity contract" which is related to that instrument, or an auctioned product that is founded on emission allowances, which uses "a form of deception or contrivance," (c) the dissemination of information that gives, or is likely to provide, false or misleading signals as to the demand for, the price of, or the supply of, a financial instrument, "a related spot commodity contract" or an auctioned product that is founded on emission allowances, "at an abnormal or artificial level" – if the person who spread the information knew, or ought to have known, that it was false or misleading, and (d) the transmission of false or misleading information, or the provision of false or misleading inputs, with regard to a benchmark, in circumstances under which the person who sent the information or supplied the input knew, or ought to have known, that these data were false or misleading – or any other conduct that manipulates the computation of a benchmark [95]. The definition of 'market manipulation in the MAR is similar to that in the pre-GFC MAD[578], although it applies to additional items in the former case, and includes the manipulation of the calculation of a benchmark – which is absent from the definition in the MAD.

Member States are to equip their financial regulatory authorities with the power to impose suitable administrative measures in relation to specified breaches of the prohibitions that the MAR lays down – including the prohibitions on insider dealing and market manipulation [96]. This is similar to the equivalent provision in the pre-GFC MAD[579] – although the latter neither mentions the Member States' competent authorities nor specifically identifies the provisions of the MAD that contain the prohibitions. Whilst the MAD does not stretch to the inclusion of sanctions, MAD II introduces these using the authority conferred by Article 83(2) of the TFEU [97]. This Treaty provision is as follows.

> If the approximation of criminal laws and regulations of the Member States proves essential to ensure that the effective implementation of a [European]. Union policy in an area which has been subject to a harmonisation measure, directives may establish minimum rules with regard to the definition of criminal offences and sanctions in the area concerned. ... [98].

Thus, the EU must consider that the approximation of the criminal law in the Member States is vital for the implementation of its policy on market abuse – which has been subject to the harmonising measure of the MAD (and of its replacement – the MAR).

---

[577] A financial regulatory authority may declare "an accepted market practice," taking into consideration the following criteria: (a) whether the market practice provides for a material level of clarity to the market, (b) whether the market practice substantially safeguards the functioning of market forces and the proper interaction of supply and demand, (c) whether the market practice has a constructive effect on efficiency and liquidity within the market, (d) whether the market practice takes into consideration "the trading mechanism of the relevant market" and enables participants within the market to react fully and in a timely way to the circumstances of the new market that the practice generates, (e) whether the market practice does not generate risks to the soundness of related markets in the pertinent financial instruments within the EU, (f) the outcome of any investigation by an authority of the relevant market practice contravened rules that were put in place to prevent market abuse, and (g) the structural features of the market of concern (MAR, Article 13(2)).

[578] See the subsection entitled 'Market abuse', in the section entitled 'Securities Legislation' in Chapter 1, for the definition of 'market manipulation' in the original version of the MAD.

[579] See the subsection entitled 'Market abuse', in the section entitled 'Securities Legislation' in Chapter 1, for the general duty for Member States to determine and impose appropriate administrative penalties, in the original version of the MAD.

The definition of 'insider dealing' in MAD II is consistent with, although less detailed than, that in the MAR – being only the first clause in the latter[580]. Member States are to "take the necessary measures" to make sure that insider dealing, and recommending or inducing another person to participate in insider dealing, constitute criminal offences "at least in serious cases and when committed intentionally" [99]. The offence extends to instances of the possession and use of inside information. For instance, it applies to a person who has inside information as a result of[581]: (a) being a member of the financial instrument issuer's administrative, management or supervisory boards, (b) holding the issuer's capital, (c) having access to the data through the exercise of his/her duties, employment or profession, or (d) engaging in criminal activity[582] [100].

Member States are to "take the necessary measures" to make certain that illegal divulgation of inside information constitutes a criminal offence "at least in serious cases and when committed intentionally" [101]. For the purposes of MAD II, illicit disclosure of inside information occurs in circumstances under which a person possesses inside information and discloses those data to any other person – except if the divulgation is made in the normal course of duties, employment or a profession[583] [102].

Member States are to "take the necessary measures" to make sure that market manipulation constitutes a criminal offence "at least in serious cases and when committed intentionally" [103]. The offence of 'market manipulation' in MAD II is almost identical to that of 'market manipulation' in the MAR[584] – although the former (unlike the latter) does not apply to auctioned products that are based on emissions allowances, and the conveyance of false or misleading information or the provision of false or misleading inputs in respect of a benchmark amounts to 'market manipulation' for MAD II (but not for the MAR) if the person who sent the information or provided the input neither knew, nor ought to have known, that it was false or misleading[585] [104].

Member States are to "take the necessary measures" to make certain that aiding, abetting or inciting any of the criminal offences in MAD II – to which the above paragraphs refer – is "punishable as a criminal offence" [105]. They are also to "take the necessary measures" to

[580] For the purposes of MAD II, insider dealing takes place, if a person who possesses inside information uses it to acquire or dispose of financial instruments to which it relates (MAD II, Article 3(2)). See above in this subsection, for the definition of 'insider dealing' in the MAR.

[581] In addition to the specified persons, the offence of 'insider dealing' applies to any person who has acquired inside information under any other circumstances – if that person knows that the data are items of inside information (MAD II, Article 3(3)).

[582] This provision applies to participants in markets for emission allowances, as well as to issuers of financial instruments (MAD II, Article 3(3)). For the purposes of MAD II, 'issuer' means a legal entity that issues, or proposes to issue, financial instruments (MAD II, Article 2(14); MAR, Article 3(1)(21)). Although MAD II does not refer to 'emission allowance market participant', for the purposes of the MAR this term means a person who undertakes transactions – including the placing of orders to trade in emission allowances, auctioned products that are based on emissions allowances, or derivatives of emission allowances – subject to one exception (MAR, Article 3(1)(20)). This exception is a participant in a market for emission allowances in circumstances under which the installations or aviation facilities that it controls, owns or is responsible for, have had emissions that are equal to or below a minimum threshold of carbon dioxide equivalent in the previous year and, if they conduct combustion activities, have had a thermal input of below or equal to a minimum threshold (MAR, Article 17(2)).

[583] This offence applies to any person in the circumstances to which Article 3(3) of MAD II refers – i.e., those persons whom the last sentence of the previous paragraph in the text mentions, and those specified in fn 581 and in the first sentence of fn 582.

[584] See above in this subsection, for the definition of 'market manipulation' in the MAR.

[585] The offence of 'market manipulation' in MAD II omits this requirement for knowledge (MAD II, Article 5(2)(d)).

make sure that any attempt to commit the offences of 'insider dealing' or 'market manipulation' in MAD II, is "punishable as a criminal offence" [106]. Aiding, abetting or inciting a person to recommend or to induce another person to participate in insider dealing, is not to be criminalized [107] – which may be wise from the point of view of providing legal clarity for parliamentary draftsmen and judges.

Member States are to "take the necessary measures" to make certain that the offences described above are "punishable by effective, proportionate and dissuasive criminal penalties" [108]. They are also to "take the necessary measures" to make sure that legal persons can be held liable for these offences – if any of the latter are "committed for their benefit by any person" who has a "leading position" within the legal person that is based upon "a power of representation of," "an authority to take decisions on behalf of" or "an authority to exercise control within," the legal person [109]. Member States must "take the necessary measures" to make certain that legal persons may be held liable, in circumstances under which an absence of control or supervision by a person with a leading position within the legal person has made it possible for a person under the authority of the legal person to commit an offence to which the above paragraphs refer, for the latter's benefit [110]. They are also to "take the necessary measures" to make sure that a legal person that is held liable of one of the offences in MAD II is "subject to effective, proportionate and dissuasive sanctions," which are to include fines, and which may include: (a) "exclusion from entitlement to public benefit or aid," (b) suspension or exclusion from commercial practice, (c) placing under the supervision of a judge, (d) liquidation directed by a judge, (e) suspension or closure of the establishments that were used for the offence to be committed, and/or (f) other (unspecified) sanctions [111].

This combination of civil and criminal sanctions for market abuse is a significant 'ramping-up' of the regulatory response to these events, in comparison to the situation before the GFC. The EU replaced a Directive (i.e., the MAD) by a Regulation (i.e., the MAR) for the following reasons.

> In order to remove the remaining obstacles to trade and the significant distortions of competition resulting from divergences between national laws and to prevent any further obstacles to trade and significant distortions of competition from arising, it is necessary to adopt a Regulation establishing a more uniform interpretation of the [European]. Union market abuse framework, which more clearly defines rules applicable in all Member States. Shaping market abuse requirements in the form of a [R]egulation will ensure that those requirements are directly applicable. This should ensure uniform conditions by preventing diverging national requirements as a result of the transposition of a [D]irective. This Regulation will require that all persons follow the same rules in all [of] the Union. It will also reduce regulatory complexity and firms' compliance costs, especially for firms operating on a cross-border basis, and it will contribute to eliminating distortions of competition [112].

Thus, the passing of a Regulation, in place of a Directive, has a harmonising effect on the law of market abuse. Whilst it is unlikely that the EU will stretch its interpretation of either Article 67(3)[586] or Article 114(1)[587] of the TFEU so as to be able to pass a Regulation on

---

[586] Article 67(3) of the TFEU states: "The [European] Union shall endeavour to ensure a high level of security ... through the mutual recognition of judgements in criminal matters and, if necessary, through the approximation of criminal laws.."

criminal offences in relation to market abuse, the full convergence of the law within the EU over this area may be possible if there are only small changes to the TFEU – which could be made in order to improve the efficiency of operation of the markets therein. However, full convergence of the market abuse legislation is aligned with exclusive competence of the EU[588]. This is a greater degree of harmonisation that the TFEU provides for the internal market – which is an area of shared competence between the EU and the Member States[589] [113].

The MAR and MAD II classify aspects of market abuse as a civil law infringement and as a criminal offence, respectively – sometimes with overlap, as in the case of most instances of 'market manipulation' as defined in these instruments. The clearest way of distinguishing between a civil law breach of 'market manipulation' and a criminal offence of 'market manipulation' is in the standard of proof for it to be committed – the criminal standard being higher than the civil standard. However, both instruments are sparse in their consideration of this issue – the 'beyond all reasonable doubt' standard for the criminal offence being vaguely indicated by the referral in Recital 27 of MAD II to "the presumption of innocence" that Article 48 of the Charter of Fundamental Rights of the European Union provides[590], and the 'on the balance of probabilities' standard for the civil law transgression being implied by the consideration of a rebuttable presumption in Recital 25 of the MAR[591]. It would be most welcome, if the Commission decides to provide a clarification on this matter, or – better still – tables an amending Regulation that would insert a statement into each of the MAR and MAD II on the standard of proof to be applied to the contraventions of the law contained therein.

The Prospectus

On 30th November 2015, the Commission put forward a proposal for a Regulation to revise the PD[592], as "an important step to build the Capital Markets Union" [114]. The section

---

587 Article 114(1) of the TFEU states: "… The European Parliament and the Council shall, acting in accordance with the ordinary legislative procedure and after consulting the Economic and Social Committee, adopt the measures for the approximation of the provisions laid down by law, regulation or administrative action in Member States which have as their object the establishment and functioning of the internal market.."

588 If the TEU and the TFEU confer on the EU "exclusive competence in a specific area, [then] only the [European] Union may legislate and adopt legally binding acts, the Member States being able to do so themselves only if so empowered by the Union or for the implementation of Union acts" (TFEU, Article 2(1)).

589 If the TEU and the TFEU confer on the EU "a competence shared with the Member States in a specific area, then the [European] Union and the Member States may legislate and adopt legally binding acts in that area. The Member States may exercise their competence to the extent that the Union has not exercised its competence. The Member States shall again exercise their competence to the extent that the Union has decided to cease exercising its competence. (TFEU, Article 2(2)). See the subsection entitled 'Comment', in the section entitled 'Distinguishing Between the ESAs' in Chapter 3, for the author's view of the financial services legislation since the GFC, with regard to shared competence and exclusive competence.

590 Article 48(1) of the Charter of Fundamental Rights of the European Union states: "Everyone who has been charged shall be presumed innocent until innocent until proved guilty according to law.."

591 Recital 25 of the MAR is as follows: "Orders placed before a person possesses inside information should not be deemed to be insider dealing. However, where a person comes into possession of inside information, there should be a presumption that any subsequent change relating that information to orders placed before possession of such information, including the cancellation or amendment of an order, or an attempt to cancel or amend an order, constitutes insider dealing. That presumption could, however, be rebutted if the person establishes that he or she did not use the insider information when carrying out the transaction.."

592 This document is entitled 'Proposal for a Regulation of the European Parliament and of the Council on the prospectus to be published when securities are offered to the public or admitted to trading', and is available at

on the CMU[593] refers to this item. Its publication was pursuant to the Commission's release, on 18th February 2015 (simultaneously with the document entitled 'Green Paper: Building a Capital Markets Union'[594]), of a Consultation Document[595] that contains 51 questions on aspects of the PD – which was to be completed by 13th May 2015 [115].

At the date of writing, the law comprises the PD as amended to 22nd May 2014. In this subsection, the current version of the PD is compared with the pre-GFC (i.e., original) version as described in Chapter 1[596].

Whilst Member States are still to require the publication of a prospectus before the securities that it describes are offered to the public [116], the description of some of the categories of exemption from this requirement, has been altered since the GFC[597]. The duty to publish a prospectus does not apply to an offer of securities that is addressed only to qualified investors [117]. The definition of 'qualified investors' has changed since the GFC[598]. It has become more complex[599]. Furthermore, the obligation to publish a prospectus does not apply to an offer of securities: (i) that is addressed to fewer than 150 non-qualified investors (up from 100), (ii) which is addressed to investors who buy securities for a total sum of at least 100,000 Euros per investor per offer (up from 50,000 Euros per investor per offer), (iii) whose denomination per unit totals to at least 100,000 Euros (up from 50,000 Euros), and/or (iv) with a total amount in the EU of less than 100,000 – computed over one year (unchanged) [118]. Thus, the exemption threshold is lower for (i) and unchanged for (iv) – the 'small

---

http://eur-lex.europa.eu/resource.html?uri=cellar:036c16c7-9763-11e5-983e-01aa75ed71a1.0006.02/DOC_1&format=PDF.

[593] See the subsection entitled 'The Action Plan for constructing the CMU', in the section entitled 'The Capital Markets Union' above in this Chapter, for the proposed Regulation's reduced disclosure requirements for SMEs that would like to offer their securities to the public.

[594] See the initial paragraphs of the section entitled 'The Capital Markets Union', in this Chapter, for a description of this Green Paper.

[595] This item is entitled 'Consultation Document: Review of the Prospectus Directive', and is available at http://ec.europa.eu/finance/consultations/2015/prospectus-directive/docs/consultation-document_en.pdf.

[596] See the subsection entitled 'The prospectus', in the section entitled 'Securities Legislation' in Chapter 1, for a summary of the original version of the PD.

[597] Directive 2010/73/EU of the European Parliament and of the Council of 24 November 2010 amending Directives 2003/71/EC on the prospectus to be published when securities are offered to the public or admitted to trading and 2004/109/EC on the harmonisation of transparency requirements in relation to information about issuers whose securities are admitted to trading on a regulated market, introduced this change.

[598] Directive 2010/73/EU brought in this modification. See fn 17 in the subsection entitled 'The prospectus', in the section entitled 'Securities Legislation' in Chapter 1, for the definition of 'qualified investors' in the original version of the PD.

[599] For the purposes of the (post-GFC) PD, 'qualified investors' means the following: (i) entities that "are required to be authorised or regulated to operate in the financial markets," large firms that satisfy 2 of the following 3 criteria "on a company basis" – a balance sheet total of at least 20 million Euros, a net turnover of at least 40 million Euros, and own funds of at least 2 million Euros, governments, central banks, international organisations and "[o]ther institutional investors whose main activity is to invest in financial instruments" (PD (as amended to 22/05/14), Article 2(1)(e); MiFID (as amended to 22/02/14), Annex II, Section I, points 1-4); (ii) persons or firms who are, on request, treated as professional clients in accordance with Annex II to the MiFID (for which the investment firm must conduct a criteria-based assessment), or recognised as eligible counterparties in accordance with Article 24 of the MiFID ("investment firms, credit institutions, insurance companies, UCITS and their management companies, pension funds and their management companies, other financial institutions authorised or regulated under [EU] legislation or the national law of a Member State, undertakings exempted from the application of [the MiFID] under Article 2(1)(k)-(l) [of the MiFID], national governments and their corresponding offices including public bodies that deal with public debt, central banks and supranational organisations") unless those entities have requested that they are to be treated as non-professional clients (PD (as amended to 22/05/14), Article 2(1)(e); MiFID (as amended to 22/02/14), Article 24(2), and Annex II, Subsection II.1).

offers' exceptions, and higher for (ii) and (iii) – the 'large offers' exemptions, than in the pre-GFC legislation.

The requirement for Member States to ensure that all admissions of securities to trading on regulated markets within their territories are subject to the publishing of a prospectus, is unchanged [119]. However, a provision has been added to the PD that empowers the Commission to adopt delegated Acts "in order to take account of technological developments on financial markets, including inflation," which change the financial thresholds that the previous paragraph contains[600] [120]. If recent times are a guide, then the Commission will not need to worry about high inflation in the short run.

There have been 9 rounds of amendments to the PDR – 6 of them since the end of the GFC, in 2009[601]. Consequently, the information to be included in the prospectus for some securities has been revised. In particular, Commission Delegated Regulation (EU) No 486/2012[602] added Annexes XX to XXIX to the PDR, and Commission Delegated Regulation (EU) No 862/2012[603] inserted Annex XXX into the PDR – as well as introducing changes to several of its other Annexes [121].

The prospectus must include a summary for non-equity securities with a denomination of up to 100,000 Euros (up from 50,000 Euros in the pre-GFC legislation) – as well as for all equity instruments (unchanged) [122]. The summary's format and content are to provide (together with the prospectus) "appropriate information about essential elements of the securities," in order to assist investors in their consideration of whether or not to invest in these financial instruments [123]. The summary is to be drawn up in a common format, in order to ease its comparability with the summaries of similar securities, and its content is to communicate the key information concerning the relevant securities; the Commission is empowered to adopt delegated Acts which include measures that relate to the summary's format and to the content and the form of the essential information contained therein, by 1st July 2012, and to adopt CIRs pursuant to draft ITSs that the ESMA develops, in order to aid uniform application of these Acts and of the PD [124]. The Commission has done the former, which it included in Commission Delegated Regulation (EU) No 486/2012[604] [125]. These changes were thereby inserted into the PDR.

---

[600] Directive 2010/73/EU introduced this addition.

[601] At the time of writing, the Commission has adopted an RTS, which is with the Council and the Parliament in the consultation period for this RTS (see the subsection entitled 'RTSs and CDRs', in the section entitled 'The ESAs and Delegated Legislation in Chapter 3, for a description of the consultation period in relation to any RTS that the Commission has adopted), and which (amongst other things) amends the PDR by deleting Article 1(5)-(6) and Articles 29-34 (European Commission (2015), Commission Delegated Regulation (EU) .../... of 30.11.2015 supplementing Directive 2003/71/EC of the European Parliament and of the Council with regard to regulatory technical standards for approval and publication of the prospectus and dissemination of advertisements and amending Commission Regulation (EC) No 809/2004, Article 13, <http://ec.europa.eu/finance/securities/docs/prospectus/151130-delegated-regulation_en.pdf>). If these amendments remain in this CDR – once it is finalized and published in the *Official Journal of the European Union* – then there will have been 10 rounds of amendments to the PDR, 7 of which will have taken place since the end of the GFC.

[602] This is Commission Delegated Regulation (EU) No 486/2012 of 30 March 2012 amending Regulation (EC) No 809/2004 as regards the format and the content of the prospectus, the base prospectus, the summary and the final terms and as regards the disclosure requirements.

[603] This is Commission Delegated Regulation (EU) No 862/2012 of 4 June 2012 amending Regulation (EC) No 809/2004 as regards information on the consent to use the prospectus, information on underlying indexes and the requirement for a report prepared by independent accountants or auditors.

[604] See fn 602, for the full title of this CDR.

Member States are to make certain that no civil liability attaches to anyone solely on the basis of the summary – unless this is inaccurate, inconsistent or misleading when read in conjunction with the rest of the prospectus (unchanged from the pre-GFC rules), or unless the summary (when read together with the remaining parts of the prospectus) does not supply essential information to help investors to decide whether or not to purchase the securities (inserted since the GFC[605]) [126]. This change adds another head of civil liability to the persons who are responsible for the information that the prospectus provides [127]. However, as the main part of the prospectus is likely to supply essential information to aid investors in their consideration of whether or not to purchase the securities, the fact that the summary is to be read in conjunction with the rest of the prospectus means that a lack of pertinent information in the former may be insufficient to provide a ground for an action for civil liability in the law of any Member State.

As Article 10 of the PD has been deleted[606], there is no longer any obligation for issuers whose securities are admitted to trading on a regulated market to provide at least annually a document containing, or referring to, information that they have published or made available to the public over the preceding year[607]. Commission Delegated Regulation (EU) No 382/2014[608], which was issued pursuant to Article 16(3) of the PD – a paragraph inserted into the PD since the GFC[609] – "establishes technical standards specifying situations in which the publication of a supplement to the prospectus is mandatory" [128, 129]. For example, a supplement to the prospectus is to be published if: (i) the issuer is seeking admission to trading its securities on an additional regulated market in another Member State, or is intending to make an offer of its securities to the public in a Member State other than those countries for which the prospectus provides [130]., and/or (ii) the total nominal amount of the offering programme for the securities is raised [131].

The PD of today is fairly similar to the original (pre-GFC) version of this Directive, comprising some rules that are unchanged – such as the requirement for Member States to impose administrative sanctions for breach of the national provisions which transpose the PD[610], and others that have been deleted, modified or inserted – a selection of which are

---

[605] Directive 2010/73/EU added this requirement.

[606] Article 10 does not appear in the PD as amended to 22nd May 2014. In this consolidated version of the PD, there is no reference to the Directive which deleted that Article from the PD.

[607] Notwithstanding the absence of Article 10 from the PD as amended to 22nd May 2014, Recital 27 of the PD as amended to 22nd May 2014, is unchanged from that in the original version of the PD, and recommends a list to be compiled at least annually which contains this information. This Recital states: "… The issuers whose securities are admitted to trading on a regulated market are subject to an ongoing disclosure obligation … . Further to this obligation, issuers should, at least annually, list all relevant information published or made available to the public over the preceding 12 months, including information provided to the various reporting requirements laid down in other Community legislation. … To avoid excessive burdens for certain issuers, issuers of non-equity securities with high minimum denomination should not be required to meet this obligation." (PD (original version), Recital 27; PD (as amended to 22/05/14), Recital 27).

[608] This is Commission Delegated Regulation (EU) No 382/2014 of 7 March 2014 supplementing Directive 2003/71/EC of the European Parliament and of the Council with regard to regulatory technical standards for publication of supplements to the prospectus.

[609] Directive 2010/78/EU of the European Parliament and of the Council of 24 November 2010 amending Directives 98/26/EC, 2002/87/EC, 2003/6/EC, 2003/41/EC, 2003/71/EC, 2004/39/EC, 2004/109/EC., 2005/60/EC, 2006/48/EC, 2006/49/EC and 2009/65/EC in respect of the powers of the European Supervisory Authority (European Banking Authority), the European Supervisory Authority (European Insurance and Occupational Pensions Authority) and the European Supervisory Authority (European Securities and Markets Authority), added Article 16(3) to the PD.

[610] See the last paragraph of the subsection entitled 'The prospectus', in the section entitled 'Securities Legislation' in Chapter 1, for this requirement.

described in this subsection. Additions have been made to the PD – for the ESMA to propose draft RTSs and ITSs, and for the Commission to adopt CDRs and CIRs. A few of these Commission Regulations are in force.

Financial Instruments

There are substantial changes to the MiFID, which are contained in the MiFIR and in MiFID II. The author has described some of these alterations, in recent publications[611]. Therefore, they will not be considered further here.

The Official Listing of Securities

There have been no amendments to the CARD since the GFC. Therefore, the law is unchanged from that described in the corresponding subsection in Chapter 1[612].

Market Transparency Requirements for Listed Securities

The post-GFC TD continues to apply the 'home Member State principle,' which the original version of this Directive introduced[613] – although one exception to this rule has been recently added[614] [132]. The issuer of the listed securities is to publish its annual report within 4 months of the end of each financial year (unchanged from the pre-GFC rules), and is to

---

[611] The Financial Regulatory Update entitled 'From MiFID to MiFID II: A steady transition' in *Company Lawyer*, 33(10), 316-317 provides a summary of the changes that MiFID II and the MiFIR introduce, prior to the finalization of this legislation. The Chapter entitled 'The European Union's legislative response to the global financial crisis: A perspective taken from 2015' in J. Barnett (Ed.), *The Global Financial Crisis: Causes, Consequences and Impact on Economic Growth*, pp.89-158, contains a detailed account of a selection of the provisions of MiFID II and the MiFIR, and, in instances in which this is possible, compares these rules with the corresponding provisions of the MiFID; this account is in the section entitled 'Securities Sector: The Provision of Investment Services', at pp.96-130 of that publication.

[612] This is the subsection entitled 'The official listing of securities', in the section entitled 'Securities Legislation' in Chapter 1.

[613] See the 3rd paragraph of the subsection entitled 'Market transparency requirements for listed securities', in the section entitled 'Securities Legislation' in Chapter 1, for the 'home Member State principle'.

[614] This exception was added by Directive 2013/50/EU of the European Parliament and of the Council of 22 October 2013 amending Directive 2004/109/EC of the European Parliament and of the Council on the harmonisation of transparency requirements in relation to information about issuers whose securities are admitted to trading on a regulated market, Directive 2003/71/EC of the European Parliament and of the Council on the prospectus to be published when securities are offered to the public or admitted to trading and Commission Directive 2007/14/EC laying down detailed rules for the implementation of certain provisions of Directive 2004/109/EC. The exception states that the home Member State may not require an issuer of listed securities to publish periodic financial information more frequently than the annual and half-yearly financial reports (TD (as amended to 06/11/13), Article 3(1)). However, that country may disapply this exception if: (i) the additional periodic financial information does not amount to "a disproportionate financial burden" there, especially for any issuers that are SMEs, and (ii) the content of these data is proportionate to "the factors that contribute to investment decisions" by investors who are located there (TD (as amended to 06/11/13), Article 3(1a)).

ensure that this document remains available to the public for at least a decade (raised from 5 years)[615] [133].

The ESMA is to conduct a cost-benefit analysis, with a view to the EU introducing a system from 1st January 2020, according to which all annual financial reports would be prepared in one electronic reporting format [134]. The ESMA is to carry out "an adequate assessment of" alternative electronic reporting formats that might be used, and to perform "appropriate field tests" [135]. It is to develop draft RTSs to specify this format, and to submit these draft RTSs to the Commission by 31st December 2016, which the latter is empowered to adopt "in accordance with Articles 10 to 14 of Regulation (EU) No 1095/2010"[616] [136].

The issuer is to publish a half-yearly financial report that covers the first 6 months of the financial year – within 3 months of the end of this period (up from 2 months under the original (pre-GFC) version of the TD), and is to ensure that this report is available to the public for at least 10 years (increased from 5 years)[617] [137]. "[I]n order to take account of technical developments on financial markets," the Commission is to adopt measures to state the requirements, and to ensure the unvarying application, of Article 5 of the TD – which concerns half-yearly financial reports for issuers of listed securities[618] [138].

The requirement, in the original (pre-GFC) version of the TD, for an issuer whose shares are admitted to trading on a regulated market to publish an interim management report[619], has been replaced by a specialist provision for Member States to require issuers that are "active in the extracting or logging of primary forest industries" to prepare an annual report on payments that they make to governments[620] [139]. All of the above statements, other than the

---

[615] Directive 2013/50/EU introduced this change.

[616] See the subsection entitled 'RTSs and CDRs', in the section entitled 'The ESAs and Delegated Legislation' in Chapter 3, for the procedure for the development and the publication of RTSs and CDRs.

[617] Directive 2013/36/EU inserted these alterations into the TD.

[618] The Commission is to adopt these measures "in accordance with Article 27(2) or Article 27(2a), (2b) and (2c)" of the TD (TD (as amended to 06/11/13), Article 5(6)). Article 27(2) of the TD states: "Where reference is made to this paragraph, Articles 5 and 7 of Decision 1999/468/EC shall apply, having regard to the provisions of Article 8 thereof, provided that the implementing measures adopted in accordance with that procedure do not modify the essential provisions of this Directive. The period laid down in Article 5(6) of Decision 1999/468/EC shall be set at three months". Decision 1999/468/EC was repealed with effect from 1st March 2011 by Regulation (EU) No 182/2011 of the European Parliament and of the Council laying down the rules and general principles concerning mechanisms for control by Member States of the Commission's exercise of implementing powers (Regulation (EU) No 182/2011, Articles 12 and 16). This change clarified the procedure for the enactment of secondary legislation (in cases that involve neither ESAs, nor RTSs, nor ITSs) – see the section entitled 'A Pause to Consider: The Role of the Commission in the Enactment of Secondary Legislation', in Chapter 1. As Decision 1999/468/EC is no longer in force, the EU legislators should amend Article 27(2) of the TD to reflect the replacement of that Decision by Regulation (EU) No 182/2011. Article 27(2a) of the TD states: "The power to adopt the delegated acts referred to in [Article 5(6) and 12 other specified Articles of the TD] shall be conferred on the Commission for a period of 4 years from 4 January 2011. ... The delegation of power shall be automatically extended for periods of an identical duration, unless the European Parliament or the Council revokes it in accordance with Article 27a" of the TD. The Commission is to send the delegated Act to the Council and to the Parliament immediately after adopting it, each of which has a period of 3 months (extendible once) to be able to object to the delegated Act – giving its reasons for doing so (TD (as amended to 06/11/13), Articles 27(2b), 27(2c), 27b(1) and 27b(3)).

[619] See the 6th paragraph of the subsection entitled 'Market transparency requirements for listed securities', in the section entitled 'Securities Legislation' in Chapter 1, for this requirement – which Article 6 of the original version of the TD contained.

[620] Directive 2013/50/EU made this amendment to the TD. The 'voting rights held in the trading book' exception, which is contained in Article 9(6) of the TD, applied in the original version of the TD. Chapter 1 omits that provision. The 2013 amendment to Article 9(6) of the TD concerns the Directive referred to therein for the definition of 'trading book'. In the light of the comment in fn 623, it is noteworthy that the Directive to which

preceding sentence in this paragraph and the first sentence of the current subsection (entitled 'Market transparency requirements for listed securities'), do not apply to countries, their regional and local authorities, public international organisations to which one or more Member States belong, the European Central Bank, the European Financial Stability Facility – and any other mechanism which is established in order to maintain the financial stability of the Eurozone's Monetary Union by providing financial assistance on a temporary basis to countries within that area (this is an addition to the list in the pre-GFC TD), the central banks of Member States, and issuers "exclusively of debt securities admitted to trading on a regulated market" with a denomination of at least 100,000 Euros per unit (up from 50,000 Euros per unit)[621] [140].

2 exceptions have been added[622], to the requirement in Article 9(1) of the TD for Member States to require shareholders to notify changes in voting rights in shares that have been admitted to trading on a regulated market, if these cross at least one of the thresholds of 5%, 10%, 15%, 20%, 25%, 30%, 50% and 75% of the total number of shares of the issuer to which voting rights are attached – and/or those thresholds in respect of shares in the same class (if the issuer has issued more than one class of shares) and to which voting rights are attached [141]., as follows: (i) Article 9 of the TD is not to apply to voting rights that are held in the trading book, as described in Article 11 of the CRD[623], of a credit institution or an

---

Article 9(6) of the original version of the TD refers – Council Directive 93/6/EEC of 15 March 1993 on the capital adequacy of investment firms and credit institutions – was replaced by the CRD with effect from 20th July 2006 (CRD (as amended to 15/12/10), Articles 52 and 53).

[621] Directive 2013/50/EU introduced these 2 amendments to the TD. It also added a derogation to Article 8(1)(b) of the TD, which disapplies Articles 4 and 5 of the TD to issuers solely of debt securities with a denomination 50,000-100,000 Euros per unit that were admitted to trading on a regulated market before 31st December 2010, as long as the amounts payable in respect of these debt securities have not all been made (TD (as amended to 06/11/13), Article 8(4)).

[622] Directive 2013/50/EU made these changes to the TD – which also apply in respect of paragraphs 2 and 3 of Article 9 of the TD; these paragraphs are described in fn 73 in the subsection entitled 'Market transparency requirements for listed securities', in the section entitled 'Securities Legislation' in Chapter 1. The first of these 2 exceptions (i.e., that stated in point (i) in the text) applied in an optional form in the original version of the TD: "Home Member States … may provide that the voting rights held in the trading book … shall not be counted for the purpose of this Article …" (TD (original version), Article 9(6)).

[623] Article 11(1) of the CRD states: "The trading book of an institution shall consist of all positions in financial instruments and commodities held either with trading intent or in order to hedge other elements of the trading book and which are either free of any restrictive covenants on their tradability or able to be hedged". Article 11(2) of the CRD defines 'positions held with trading intent' as: "those held intentionally for short-term resale and/or with the intention of benefiting from actual or expected short-term price differences between buying and selling prices or from other price or interest rate variations." Thus, financial instruments and commodities may be held in the trading book for short-term speculative purposes, and, possibly, in order to benefit from longer-term variations in interest rates or in the prices of assets – not just differences between buying and selling prices. For the purposes of the CRD, 'institutions' means investment firms and credit institutions (CRD (as amended to 15/12/10), Article 3(1)(c)). CRD IV repealed the CRD (and the BCD), with effect from 1st January 2014 (CRD IV (as amended to 12/06/14), Article 163). Article 163 of CRD IV continues: "References to the repealed Directives shall be construed as references to this Directive and to Regulation (EU) No 575/2013 [i.e., the CRR] and shall be read in accordance with the correlation table set out in Annex II to this Directive and in Annex IV to Regulation (EU) No 575/2013". Article 11(1) of the CRD has been superseded by Article 102(1) of the CRR (CRR (as amended to 17/01/15), Annex IV). Neither Annex II to CRD IV, nor Annex IV to the CRR, gives a replacement provision for Article 11(2) of the CRD. Notwithstanding these observations, the definition of 'trading book' is not in Article 102 of the CRR – but in Article 4(1)(86) of the CRR, which is as follows: for the purposes of the CRR, "'trading book' means all positions in financial instruments and commodities held by an institution either with trading intent, or in order to hedge positions held with trading intent". As, in this instance, Annex IV to the CRR is not entirely accurate, the EU legislators are insufficiently careful in placing the equivalence statement in the second paragraph of Article 163 of CRD IV (see above in this footnote), with no or only partial updating of the references to the CRD in provisions of

investment firm, as long as (a) the voting rights that are held in the trading book are 5%[624] or less, and (b) the voting rights which are attached to shares that are held in the trading book are not used to interfere in the management of the issuer; [142]. (ii) Article 9 of the TD is not to apply to voting rights which are attached to shares that are acquired for stabilisation purposes in accordance with Commission Regulation (EC) No 2273/2003[625] – as long as the voting rights that are attached to those shares are not used to interfere with the management of the issuer [143]. These notification requirements apply to a person who holds financial instruments[626] which: (a) on maturity, provide the holder with either the right to acquire, or the discretion as to his/her right to obtain, shares that have already been issued to which voting rights are attached, of an issuer whose shares have been admitted to trading on a regulated market (modified from the pre-GFC legislation), and (b) are not included in point (a), but which are referenced to shares to which point (a) refers – and with "economic effect"

---

other Regulations and Directives (such as in Article 9(6) of the TD – see the text that accompanies this footnote). It is submitted that the Commission should regularly check all Regulations and Directives within the *acquis communautaire*, in order to ensure that, as far as is reasonably possible, all references to Articles of other Regulations and Directives are to legislative provisions that are currently in force. (See fn 1032 in the section entitled 'Recommended Alternative Strategies' in Chapter 5, for a definition of the *acquis communautaire*.)

[624] Article 9(6)(a) of the TD does not state what the total voting rights are, of which the 5% is a part. It is submitted that, in line with Article 9(1) of the TD, the 'total voting rights' comprise the voting rights of all of: (i) the issued shares, and (ii) the shares in the same class as those held in the trading book. Element (ii) would be made more complex, if the shares in the trading book to which voting rights are attached are of more than one class of shares. Furthermore, if the 'total voting rights' in (i) and (ii) are different – due to their being more than one class of issued shares, then the Court of Justice of the European Union would need to decide whether Article 9(6)(a) applies to the smaller total, i.e., that in (i), or to the larger total, i.e., that in (ii). The following guidance is provided in the CDR which the Commission adopted, pursuant to the draft RTS that the ESMA provided to specify the method of calculation of the '5% threshold' for paragraphs 5 and 6 of Article 9 of the TD (TD (as amended to 06/11/13), Article 9(6b)). Article 2 of this CDR – Commission Delegated Regulation (EU) 2015/761 of 17 December 2014 supplementing Directive 2004/109/EC of the European Parliament and of the Council with regard to certain regulatory technical standards on major holdings – states: "For the purpose of calculation of the 5% threshold referred to in Article 9(5) and (6) of Directive 2004/109/EC, holdings under Article 9, 10 and 13 of that Directive shall be aggregated". As neither Article 10 nor Article 13 of the TD refers to the issue raised in this footnote, the guidance in Commission Delegated Regulation (EU) 2015/761 does not address this difficulty in the interpretation of the 5% threshold of the 'total voting rights' in the trading book.

[625] This is Commission Regulation (EC) No 2273/2003 of 22 December 2003 implementing Directive 2003/6/EC of the European Parliament and of the Council as regards exemptions for buy-back programmes and stabilisation of financial instruments, which the MAR repeals from 3rd July 2016 (see fn 572, and accompanying text).

[626] For the purposes of this provision, 'financial instruments' means transferable securities, options, futures, swaps, forward rate agreements, contracts for differences, and any other agreements or contracts "with similar economic effects" that may be settled in cash or physically; the ESMA is to draw up and to regularly update a list of these financial instruments, taking into consideration "technical developments on financial markets" (TD (as amended to 06/11/13), Article 13(1b)). 'Securities' for the purposes of the TD means 'transferable securities' as defined in Article 4(1)(18) of the MiFID, i.e., those classes of securities that are negotiable on the capital market (other than instruments of payment), such as: (a) shares – and depositary receipts in respect of these, (b) securitised debt instruments – and depositary receipts in respect of these, and (c) any other securities that give the right to buy or sell any such transferable securities, or which give rise to a cash settlement that is determined by reference to commodities, currencies, interest rates or yields, transferable securities, "or other indices or measures"; the term 'securities' (for the purposes of the TD) excludes those classes of financial instruments that are usually traded on the money market, such as certificates of deposit, commercial paper and treasury bills, and which have a maturity of less than one year (TD (as amended to 06/11/13), Article 2(1)(a); MiFID (as amended and corrected to 22/02/14), Article 4(1)(18)-4(1)(19)). The definition in Article 2(1)(a) of the TD is that of 'securities', rather than that of 'transferable securities' – the latter being the term to which Article 13(1b) of the TD refers.

that is similar to that of the financial instruments to which that point refers (a post-GFC addition to the TD)[627] [144].

The requirements in Article 16 of the TD for issuers to publish modifications to the rights of shareholders and debtholders, remain unchanged from those in the original (pre-GFC) version of this Directive [145]. However, Directive 2013/50/EU has deleted Article 16(3) from the TD, which required issuers of securities that are admitted to trading on a regulated market to swiftly publish issues of new loans[628].

The permission that Article 23(1) of the TD grants to the home Member State's competent authority to exempt an issuer whose registered office is in a third country from requirements in Articles 4 to 7, 12(6) and 14 to 18 of the TD, is unchanged; a requirement has been added for the competent authority to notify the ESMA of any exemptions that it has granted[629] [146]. Articles 13 to 22 of the TDID continue to provide guidance as to the equivalence requirements for third countries; these remain the same as in the original (pre-GFC) version of the TDID, except for Article 16 of that Directive, which has been deleted[630] [147].

As in the pre-GFC legislation, each competent authority is to have all of the powers that are necessary for it to be equipped to carry out its functions [148]. Directive 2013/50/EU has added the following provisions to the TD: (i) without detriment to those powers, each competent authority is to be granted all investigative capacities that it needs in order to be able to perform its functions; it is to exercise these powers of enquiry in accordance with domestic law; [149]. (ii) competent authorities are to "exercise their sanctioning powers[631], in" conformity with the TD and with national law – directly, in co-operation with other authorities, by delegation to the latter, or by applying "to the competent judicial authorities" [150].

The provisions that concern professional secrecy, co-operation between competent authorities, and the exchange of confidential information, continue to apply as in the original (pre-GFC) version of Article 25 of the TD[632]. Directive 2013/50/EU added requirements for competent authorities to co-operate "in the exercise of their sanctioning and investigative powers" – in order to make certain that measures or sanctions "produce the desired results," and to co-ordinate their actions when addressing cross-border cases [151].

---

[627] The required notification is to include a breakdown by the type of financial instruments that are held under each of points (a) and (b), distinguishing between those which confer a right to a physical settlement and those that grant a right to a cash settlement (TD (as amended to 06/11/13), Article 13(1)).

[628] See the 9th paragraph of the subsection entitled 'Market transparency requirements for listed securities', in the section entitled 'Securities Legislation' in Chapter 1, for this requirement.

[629] Directive 2010/78/EU inserted this requirement into Article 23(1) of the TD.

[630] Directive 2013/50/EU removed Article 16 from the TDID. This Article contained the example given from the pre-GFC legislation – see the 12th paragraph of the subsection entitled 'Market transparency requirements for listed securities', in the section entitled 'Securities Legislation' in Chapter 1.

[631] The TD omits guidance as to the scope of the phrase 'sanctioning powers'. A broad interpretation of this phrase would encompass all of the powers that each Member State grants its competent authority in order to fulfil its tasks. A narrow interpretation of this phrase would comprise those powers that were granted for the purpose of law enforcement, such as the prohibition of trading on a regulated market in the event of a breach (or a suspected contravention) of the TD or of national law – as stated in Article 24(4)(e) of the TD.

[632] See the last paragraph of the subsection entitled 'Market transparency requirements for listed securities', in the section entitled 'Securities Legislation' in Chapter 1, for these provisions.

Article 25 of the TD has been augmented by the involvement of the European Systemic Risk Board and, especially, the ESMA – both of which have been founded since the GFC[633]. Any competent authority may refer to the ESMA a situation in which another competent authority has rejected, or ignored, the former's request to the latter for co-operation[634] [152]. The competent authorities are to co-operate with the ESMA for the purposes of the TD, and "in accordance with Regulation (EU) No 1095/2010"[635] [153]. They are to promptly supply the ESMA with all information that is necessary for it to carry out its obligations under the TD and under Regulation (EU) No 1095/2010, in conformity with Article 35[636] of the latter[637] [154].

Notwithstanding the duty of professional secrecy in Article 25(1) of the TD[638], competent authorities may exchange confidential information with, or send data to, the ESMA, the European Systemic Risk Board, and other competent authorities; this information is subject to the obligation of professional secrecy [155]. In addition to Member States (as in the original (pre-GFC) version of the GFC), the ESMA may make co-operation agreements for the exchange of information with entities of third countries whose legislation enables them to carry out any of the tasks that the TD allots to competent authorities; each Member State is to inform the ESMA, at the time that it concludes a co-operation agreement[639] [156].

Although the structure of the version of the TD currently in force is similar to that of the original (pre-GFC) version of this Directive, there are several additions and changes to the pre-GFC legislation. It is submitted that 2 determinants of these changes are the increasing

---

[633] Article 1(1) of Regulation (EU) No 1092/2010 of the European Parliament and of the Council of 24 November 2010 on European Union macro-prudential oversight of the financial system and establishing a European Systemic Risk Board, founded the European Systemic Risk Board. Article 1(1) of Regulation (EU) No 1095/2010 of the European Parliament and of the Council of 24 November 2010 establishing a European Supervisory Authority (European Securities and Markets Authority) amending Decision No 716/2009/EC and repealing Commission Decision 2009/77/EC, founded the ESMA. See the section entitled 'The de Larosière Report' in Chapter 3, for further information.

[634] Article 19 of Regulation (EU) No 1095/2010 contains a procedure for the ESMA to attempt to resolve disagreements between competent authorities in different Member States. In such a situation, the ESMA may act in accordance with the powers that Article 19 Regulation (EU) No 1095/2010 confers upon it (TD (as amended to 06/11/13), Article 13(1)).

[635] Regulation (EU) No 1095/2010 describes the powers and duties of the ESMA, and the ways in which it should act – in its exercise of the former and in its fulfilment of the latter.

[636] Article 35 of Regulation (EU) No 1095/2010 concerns the provision of information by competent authorities to the ESMA. Article 35(1) of Regulation (EU) No 1095/2010 states: "At the request of the Authority [i.e., the ESMA], the competent authorities of the Member States shall provide the Authority with all the necessary information to carry out the duties assigned to it by this Regulation, provided that they have legal access to the relevant information, and that the request for information is necessary in relation to the nature of the duty in question.."

[637] Directive 2010/78/EU inserted the provisions of this paragraph into Article 25 of the TD.

[638] Thus, the ESMA and the European Systemic Risk Board are 'within the inner circle' for the distribution of confidential information – which is subject to the duty of professional secrecy.

[639] The co-operation agreements that the ESMA and the Member States conclude with entities of third countries are to be "in accordance with Article 33 of Regulation (EU) No 1095/2010" (TD (as amended to 06/11/13), Article 25(4)). Article 33(1) of Regulation (EU) No 1095/2010 states: "Without prejudice to the respective competences of the Member States and the [European] Union institutions, the Authority [i.e., the ESMA] may develop contacts and enter into administrative arrangements with supervisory authorities, international organisations and the administrations of third countries. Those arrangements shall not create legal obligations in respect of the Union and its Member States nor shall they prevent Member States and their competent authorities from concluding bilateral or multilateral arrangements with those third countries.."

number and complexity of financial instruments, and the introduction of the post-GFC European sectoral architecture – especially the ESMA[640].

Rights of Shareholders in Listed Companies

Directive 2007/36/EC on the exercise of certain rights of shareholders[641] in listed companies entered into force on 3rd August 2007 [157]. It was amended by the BRRD, and does not apply to the use of resolution mechanisms, powers and tools for which Title IV of the latter Directive provides [158]. Directive 2007/36/EC contains requirements in respect of the exercise of shareholder rights that attach to voting shares, in connection with general meetings of companies whose registered office is in a Member State and whose shares have been admitted to trading on a regulated market[642] that is located, or operational, within a Member State [159]. This area is beyond the ambit of both the CARD[643] and the TD[644] [160]. The Member State which is competent to regulate issues that Directive 2007/36/EC considers, is that in which the company's registered office is situated [161].

The company is to ensure that "all shareholders who are in the same position with regard to participation and the exercise of voting rights" are treated equally [162]. Member States are to make certain that the company issues the convocation of a general meeting no later than on the 21st day before that of the meeting[645] [163]. They are to require the company to: (i) issue the convocation in a way that ensures quick, fair access to it, and (ii) use "such media as may reasonably be relied upon," in order to spread information to the public throughout the EU effectively[646] [164]. The company is to issue the convocation free-of-charge [165]. The convocation is to: (a) state the place and the time of, and the proposed agenda for, the general meeting, (b) include a clear, precise description of the procedures with which shareholders are to comply in order to able to participate in, and vote at, the general meeting, (c) specify (if

---

[640] Chapter 3 considers the evolution and the operation of the current European sectoral architecture – in particular the role of the ESAs in the development of secondary legislation.

[641] For the purposes of Directive 2007/36/EC, 'shareholder' means the person who "the applicable law" recognises as a shareholder (Directive 2007/36/EC (as amended to 12/06/14), Article 2(b)). 'The applicable law' means the law of the Member State in which the company's registered office is located (Directive 2007/36/EC (as amended to 12/06/14), Article 1(2)).

[642] For the purposes of Directive 2007/36/EC, 'regulated market' means "a multilateral system operated and/or managed by a market operator, which brings together or facilitates the bringing together of multiple third-party buying and selling interests in financial instruments – in the system and in accordance with its non-discretionary rules – in a way that results in a contract, in respect of the financial instruments admitted to trading under its rules and/or systems, and which is authorised and functions regularly and in accordance with the provisions of Title III [of the MiFID, which is entitled 'Regulated Markets']" (Directive 2007/36/EC (as amended to 12/06/14), Article 1(1); MiFID (as amended and corrected to 22/02/14), Article 4(1)(14)).

[643] See the subsection entitled 'The official listing of securities', above in this section, for the CARD.

[644] See the subsection entitled 'Market transparency requirements for listed securities', above in this section, for the TD.

[645] Article 5(1) of Directive 2007/36/EC specifies circumstances under which Member States may provide for the convocation of a general meeting that is not an annual general meeting to be issued no later than on 14th day before that of the meeting.

[646] Any Member State may choose not to apply these requirements to companies that are able to identify their shareholders' names and addresses from an up-to-date register of shareholders, as long as those firms are required to send the convocation to each of their registered shareholders (Directive 2007/36/EC (as amended to 12/06/14), Article 5(2)).

applicable) the record date[647], and explain that only those persons who are shareholders at that time are to be entitled to participate in, and vote at, the general meeting, (d) state how, and from where, the complete text of the documents and draft resolutions for the general meeting may be acquired, and (e) give the address of the website on which this information is to be made available [166]. Member States are to ensure that, for the 3 weeks running up to the general meeting[648], the company is to make available to its shareholders on its website (at least) the following information: (a) the convocation, (b) the total number of shares, and of voting rights, at the date of the general meeting, (c) the documents to be provided at the general meeting, (d) a draft resolution, and (e) if applicable, the forms to be used to vote by correspondence, and to vote by proxy, unless these forms are directly sent to each shareholder [167].

Member States are to ensure that shareholders are entitled to: (a) place items on the agenda for the general meeting, as long as each of these items is accompanied by a justification or a draft resolution to be adopted at that meeting,[649] and (b) propose draft resolutions for items included, or to be included, on the agenda for a general meeting [168]. If either of these rights is subject to the condition that the relevant shareholder(s) hold a minimum proportion of the company's share capital, then this proportion is not to exceed 5% [169].

Member States are to allow companies to offer to their shareholders any form of participation in the general meeting by electronic means, notably: (a) real-time transmission of that meeting, (b) real-time, 2-way communication, which enables shareholders to address the meeting from a remote location, and/or (c) a mechanism for casting votes, without the need to appoint a proxy who is physically present at the meeting [170]. Shareholder participation in the general meeting by electronic means may only be made subject to such constraints and requirements "as are necessary to ensure the identification of shareholders and the security of the electronic communication," and only to the extent that these are proportionate to the achievement of those objectives [171].

Each shareholder is to have the right to ask questions that are related to items on the agenda for the general meeting; the company is to answer these queries [172]. This right, and the duty to reply, are subject to the measures that Member States may take (or permit firms to take) in order to ensure that: (i) shareholders are identified, (ii) the preparation for, and the proceedings at, general meetings run smoothly, and (iii) the business interests and the confidentiality of organisations is protected [173].

---

[647] The 'record date' is the date on which a shareholder's rights to participate in, and vote at, a general meeting is to be decided with regard to the shares that he/she holds (Directive 2007/36/EC (as amended to 12/06/14), Article 7(2)). Each Member State is to make certain that one record date applies to all companies, which is not to be more than 30 days before the date of the general meeting to which it applies; it may set a record date for all companies that have issued bearer shares, and another record date for all firms which have issued registered shares – as long as a single record date applies to each organisation that has issued both kinds of shares (Directive 2007/36/EC (as amended to 12/06/14), Article 7(3)).

[648] If the convocation is legally issued later than on the 21st day before the general meeting (see fn 644), then the period for the specified information to be placed on the company's website is to "be shortened accordingly" (Directive 2007/36/EC (as amended to 12/06/14), Article 5(4)).

[649] Member States may provide that this right may only be exercised in respect of the annual general meeting – as long as shareholders are entitled to call, or to require the company to call, an extraordinary general meeting, the agenda for which includes (at least) all of the items that those shareholders request (Directive 2007/36/EC (as amended to 12/06/14), Article 6(1)).

Every shareholder is to be entitled to appoint any other person as a proxy, who is to have the same rights to participate in the proceedings at the general meeting as those to which the shareholder whom the proxy represents would be entitled [174]. The proxy is to vote in accordance with the appointing shareholder's instructions[650] [175]. A proxy may vote on behalf of more than one shareholder, in which case the applicable law[651] is to enable him/her to cast votes for one shareholder differently to those cast for another shareholder [176].

Member States are to permit shareholders to appoint a proxy, and companies to accept the notification of this nomination, by electronic means [177]. They are to ensure that each proxy is designated, and that this position is communicated to the firm, only in writing[652] [178]. Member States are to allow companies to offer their shareholders the opportunity to vote by correspondence, before the general meeting is held [179].

The company is to establish, for each resolution of the shareholders, at least the following information: (i) "the number of shares for which votes have been validly cast," (ii) the percentage of the share capital that these votes represent, (iii) the total number of votes that have been lawfully cast, (iv) the number of votes that have been cast in favour of, and in opposition to, each resolution, and (v) "the number of abstentions" [180]. Within a time period that the applicable law[653] is to determine – which is not to exceed 15 days following the general meeting, the company is to publish the voting results on its website [181].

These are sensible, uncontentious provisions, which clarify, simplify and update the procedure for voting at general meetings of companies whose shares are listed on a regulated market. The rules fill a gap that is between the CARD, the PD and the TD. For both of these reasons, they are a constructive addition to the EU's legislative base.

Central Securities Depositories

A trade in securities[654] is followed by post-trade processes, which include (for instance) confirmation of the details of that trade by a trading venue and/or clearing by a CCP – which

---

[650] Member States may require proxies to record the instructions for voting, and to confirm on request that these orders have been followed (Directive 2007/36/EC (as amended to 12/06/14), Article 10(4)).

[651] See fn 641, for the definition of 'the applicable law' for the purposes of Directive 2007/36/EC.

[652] These provisions also apply to the revocation of an appointment as a proxy (Directive 2007/36/EC (as amended to 12/06/14), Article 11(3)).

[653] See fn 641, for the definition of 'the applicable law' for the purposes of Directive 2007/36/EC.

[654] For the purposes of the CSDR, 'financial instruments' or 'securities' means financial instruments as defined in Article 4(1)(15) of MiFID II (CSDR, Article 2(1)(8)). 'Financial instrument' means those instruments that Section C of Annex I to MiFID II specifies (MiFID II (as amended to 28/08/14), Article 4(1)(15). The list of financial instruments in Section C of Annex I to MiFID II is as follows: (i) transferable securities (see fn 659, for the definition of 'transferable securities' for the purposes of the CSDR), (ii) money-market instruments, (iii) units in collective investment undertakings, (iv) derivative contracts that relate to currencies, interest rates or yields, securities, emission allowances, "other derivative instruments," financial indices, or financial measures, which may be settled in cash or physically, (v) derivative contracts that relate to commodities, which must be settled in cash, or which may be settled in cash at the choice of one of the parties, (vi) derivative contracts that relate to commodities, which can be settled physically – provided that they are traded on a regulated market, an MTF or an organised trading facility (with one exception), (vii) derivative contracts that relate to commodities, which can be settled physically that are absent from (vi), are not for commercial purposes, and "have the characteristics of other derivative financial instruments," (viii) derivative instruments that are "for the transfer of credit risk," (ix) financial contracts for differences, (x) derivative contracts that relate to official economic statistics, which must be settled in cash, or may be settled in cash at the choice of one of the parties, and other derivative contracts that relate to assets, indices, measures, obligations and rights that are not otherwise mentioned in Section C of Annex I to MiFID II, which "have the characteristics of other

leads to the settlement[655] of the trade, i.e., the delivery of securities to the purchaser and of funds to the seller [182]. A central securities depository[656] is an institution that operates a securities settlement system[657], and which ensures that the records of ownership of securities are maintained [183]. There are more than 30 central securities depositories in the EU, and 2 global central securities depositories – Euroclear Bank and Clearstream Banking Luxembourg – which specialise in transactions in international bonds [184].

The CSDR contains unvarying requirements for the settlement of transactions in financial instruments[658] within the EU, and rules on the organisation and behaviour of central securities depositories, in order to further orderly, secure and smooth settlement [185]. If a transaction in transferable securities[659] takes places at a trading venue, then these securities are to be recorded in book-entry form in a central securities depository on or before the intended settlement date[660], unless they have already been recorded in this way [186].

Without detriment to the requirement in the previous sentence, any issuer which is established in the EU that issues, or has issued, transferable securities that are admitted to trading, or are traded, on trading venues, is to arrange for these assets "to be represented in

---

derivative instruments," and (xi) emission allowances that comprise any units that are recognised for compliance with the requirements of Directive 2003/87/EC of 13 October 2003 establishing a scheme for greenhouse gas emission allowance trading within the Community and amending Council Directive 96/61/EC (MiFID II (as amended to 28/08/14), Annex I, Section C).

[655] For the purposes of the CSDR, 'settlement' means the completion of a transaction in securities, if this trade is concluded in order to discharge the obligations of the parties to it through the transfer of securities or cash, or both (CSDR, Article 2(1)(7)).

[656] For the purposes of the CSDR, 'central securities depository' (or 'CSD') means a legal person that operates a securities settlement system (a 'settlement service'), and which provides one or both of the following core services: (i) the initial recording of securities in a book-entry system (a 'notary service'), and (ii) the supply and maintenance of accounts for securities "at the top tier level" (a 'central maintenance service') (CSDR, Article 2(1)(1), and Annex, Section A).

[657] For the purposes of the CSDR, 'securities settlement system' means 'system' as described in the first, second and third indents of Article 2(a) of Directive 98/26/EC of the European Parliament and of the Council of 19 May 1998 on settlement finality in payment and securities settlement systems, which is not operated by a CCP whose activity comprises the carrying out of transfer orders (CSDR, Article 2(1)(10)). 'System' means a formal arrangement between at least 3 participants (excluding the system operator and any settlement agent, CCP, clearing house and indirect participants) with common rules and standardised procedures for the execution or clearing of transfer orders between the participants, which is governed by the law of a Member State that the participants have selected and in which one or more of them have their head office, and which is designated as a system and notified to the ESMA by the Member State whose law applies – after that country is satisfied that the rules of the system are satisfactory (Directive 98/26/EC (as amended to 28/08/14), Article 2(a)).

[658] See fn 654, for the definition of 'financial instruments' (for the purposes of the CSDR).

[659] For the purposes of the CSDR, 'transferable securities' means those categories of securities that are negotiable on the capital market (other than instruments of payment), such as: (a) shares – and depositary receipts in respect of these, (b) securitised debt instruments – and depositary receipts in respect of these, and (c) any other securities that grant the right to buy or sell any such transferable securities, or which give rise to a cash settlement that is determined by reference to commodities, currencies, interest rates or yields, transferable securities, "or other indices or measures" (CSDR, Article 2(1)(35); MiFID II (as amended to 28/08/14), Article 4(1)(44)). This definition of 'transferable securities' in MiFID II is the same as the definition of 'transferable securities' in the current version of the MiFID – which is stated fn 626. Whilst MiFID II is already in force, its transposing national legislation enters into force on 3rd July 2017 – which is the same day on which the MiFID is to be repealed (MiFID II (as amended to 28/08/14), Articles 93, 94 and 96).

[660] For the purposes of the CSDR, 'intended settlement date' means the date which is placed in the securities settlement system as the date of settlement, and on which the parties to a transaction in securities agree that settlement is to happen (CSDR, Article 2(1)(12)).

book-entry form as immobilisation[661] or subsequent to a direct issuance in dematerialised form[662]" [187].

A participant in a securities settlement system which settles transactions in that system, is to do this on the intended settlement date[663] [188]. In respect of transactions in transferable securities that are conducted on trading venues, the intended settlement date is to be no later than the second business day after the trading occurs[664] [189].

Settlement internalisers[665] are to report to the competent authority of their place of foundation, the total volume and value of all transactions in securities which they settle outside any securities settlement system [190]. That authority is to promptly communicate this information to the ESMA, and to notify the ESMA of any possible risk which may result "from that settlement activity" [191].

Without detriment to the superintendence by the members of the European System of Central Banks to which Article 12(1) of the CSDR refers[666], the competent authority of a central securities depository's home Member State[667] is to supervise that depository [192]. Each Member State is to designate the competent authority that is responsible for accomplishing the duties under the CSDR for the authorisation and the supervision of central securities depositories in its territory, and is to notify the ESMA thereof[668] [193]. The ESMA is to publish a list of all of the designated competent authorities on its website[669] [194]. The

---

[661] For the purposes of the CSDR, "'immobilisation' means the act of concentrating the location of physical securities in a [central securities depository,] in a way that enables subsequent transfers to be made by book entry" (CSDR, Article 2(1)(3)).

[662] For the purposes of the CSDR, 'dematerialised form' means the sole existence of financial instruments as book-entry records (CSDR, Article 2(1)(4)).

[663] Trading venues are to set up procedures that enable "relevant details" of these transactions to be confirmed on the date on which each trade has been carried out (CSDR, Article 6(1)).

[664] This requirement does not apply to: (i) transactions that are negotiated privately but carried out on a trading venue, (ii) transactions which are conducted bilaterally but reported to a trading venue, and (iii) the first transaction, if the relevant transferable securities are subject to initial recording in book-entry form, pursuant to the second sentence of the previous paragraph (CSDR, Article 5(2)).

[665] For the purposes of the CSDR, 'settlement internaliser' means any institution that carries out transfer orders on behalf of customers or on its own account, other than via a securities settlement system (CSDR, Article 2(1)(11)).

[666] The following authorities are to be concerned with the licensing and the superintendence of central securities depositories, in instances in which the CSDR refers to those authorities: (a) the authority which is responsible for the oversight of the securities system that the central securities depository operates in the Member State whose law applies to this system, (b) the central banks in the EU that issue "the most relevant currencies in which settlement takes place," and (c) if relevant, the central bank in the EU in whose books the cash component of a securities settlement system that the central securities depository operates, is settled (CSDR, Article 12(1)).

[667] For the purposes of the CSDR, 'home Member State' means the country in which a central securities depository is founded (CSDR, Article 2(1)(23)).

[668] If a Member State designates more than one competent authority, it is to determine their respective functions, and is to specify one authority to be responsible for co-operation with the competent authorities of other Member States, "the relevant authorities," the EBA and the ESMA – where the CSDR specifically refers to this authority (CSDR, Article 11(1)). The ESMA is to publish the names of "the relevant authorities" to which Article 12(1) of the CSDR refers, on its website (CSDR, Article 12(2)). It is submitted that, at the date of writing, the ESMA had not done this. See fn 666, for Article 12(1) of the CSDR. For the purposes of the CSDR, 'relevant authority' means any authority to which Article 12 of the CSDR refers (CSDR, Article 2(1)(18)).

[669] This information is available at https://www.esma.europa.eu/sites/default/files/library/competent authoritiesundercsdr.pdf. The United Kingdom has designated the Bank of England and the Prudential Regulation Authority as the competent authorities in its territory; the Bank of England is responsible for co-operation with the EBA, the ESMA and the competent authorities of other Member States (European Securities and Markets Authority (2015), Competent Authorities for Central Securities Depositories (CSDs)

competent authorities are to be granted the powers of supervision and investigation that are necessary for them to carry out their functions[670] [195].

Competent authorities, relevant authorities and the ESMA shall, promptly on request, supply each other with the information that is necessary in order to fulfil their duties under the CSDR [196]. These institutions, and other persons that receive confidential information whilst carrying out their functions under the CSDR, are only to use it "in the course of their duties" [197].

Competent authorities, relevant authorities and the ESMA are to "cooperate closely"; this co-operation is to include the exchange of "all relevant information for the application of" the CSDR[671] [198]. In the exercise of its general functions, each competent authority is to duly consider the potential effect of its decisions on the stability of the financial system in all of Member States that are affected by these resolutions – especially in those emergency situations to which the next sentence refers, given the information that is available to it [199]. Without detriment to the notification procedure that Article 6(3) of Directive 98/26/EC provides[672], competent authorities and relevant authorities are to immediately notify each other, the ESMA, and the European Systemic Risk Board, of any emergency situation that relates to a central securities depository [200].

Any legal person that is within the definition of 'central securities depository' is to acquire an authorisation from the competent authority of the Member State in which it is established, before starting its activities [201]. This permission is to specify the core services in Section A of the Annex to the CSDR[673], and the non-banking-type ancillary services in Section B of the Annex to the CSDR[674], which the central securities depository is licensed to supply [202]. A central securities depository is to continuously comply with the conditions that need to be satisfied for authorisation to be granted [203]. This depository, together with

---

designated in accordance with Article 11(1) of Regulation (EU) No 909/2014 (CSDR), p.29, <https://www.esma.europa.eu/sites/default/files/library/competentauthoritiesundercsdr.pdf>).

[670] This provision is too vague to be useful to Member States – especially in a Regulation, which is directly applicable. It is submitted that the CSDR should be modified to expressly grant the power to the ESMA to publish guidelines as to what these powers of supervision and investigation are to be.

[671] This co-operation is to include other public institutions, "where appropriate and relevant" (CSDR, Article 14(1)).

[672] A Member State in which insolvency proceedings are commenced is to swiftly inform other Member States, the ESMA and the European Systemic Risk Board of this decision (Directive 98/26/EC (as amended to 28/08/14), Article 6).

[673] See fn 146, for the core services of central securities depositories – which are a 'notary service', a 'central maintenance service' and a 'settlement service'.

[674] Section B of the Annex to the CSDR is entitled 'Non-banking-type ancillary services of CSDs that do not entail credit or liquidity risks', and permits the following services to be supplied: "Services provided by CSDs [central securities depositories] that contribute to enhancing the safety, efficiency and transparency of the securities markets, which may include but are not restricted to: 1. Services related to the settlement service, such as: (a) Organising a securities lending mechanism, as agent among participants of a securities settlement system; (b) Providing collateral management services, as agent for participants in a securities settlement system; (c) Settlement matching, instruction routing, trade confirmation, trade verification. 2. Services related to the notary and central maintenance services, such as: (a) Services related to shareholders' registers; (b) Supporting the processing of corporate actions, including tax, general meetings and information services; (c) New issue services, including allocation and management of ISIN [International Securities Identification Number] codes and similar codes; (d) Instruction routing and processing, fee collecting and processing and related reporting. 3. Establishing CSD links, providing, maintaining or operating securities accounts in relation to the settlement service, collateral management, other ancillary services. 4. Any other service, such as: (a) Providing general collateral management services as agent; (b) Providing regulatory reporting; (c) Providing information, data and statistics to market/census bureaus or other governmental or inter-governmental entities; (d) Providing IT [information technology] services". Taken together, these ancillary services cover a broad range of activities – especially those tasks that category 4 may include.

its independent auditors, is to promptly notify the competent authority of any material changes that affect its observance of the conditions for authorisation [204].

The applicant central securities depository is to submit an application for authorisation to the competent authority of its home Member State [205]. The application for authorisation is to be accompanied by all information which is necessary to enable this authority to satisfy itself that, at the time of the authorisation, the applicant has established all of the arrangements which are necessary for it to fulfil its obligations under the CSDR[675] [206]. Within 30 working days from its receipt of the application, the competent authority is to determine whether or not that application is complete; if it is incomplete, then the authority is to set a time limit by which the applicant is to supply additional information, and is to notify the latter when the application is deemed to be complete [207]. From the moment at which the competent authority considers the application to be complete, it is to send all information that is included in the application to the relevant authorities and to consult those authorities about the characteristics of the securities settlement system which the applicant operates; each relevant authority has 3 months from its receipt of that information to notify the competent authority of its views on this matter [208]. Before granting authorisation to the applicant central securities depository, the competent authority is to consult[676] the competent authority of the other Member State if the applicant is: (a) a subsidiary[677] of a central securities depository that is authorised in another Member State, (b) a subsidiary of the parent company of a central securities depository which is licensed in another Member State, and/or (c) controlled[678] by the same persons who control a different central securities depository that is authorised in another Member State [209]. Within 6 months from the submission of a complete application, the competent authority is to provide written notification to the applicant "with a fully reasoned decision [as to] whether the authorisation has been granted or refused"[679] [210].

---

[675] The application for authorisation is to include a programme of operations, which sets out the types of business that are planned and the central securities depository's "structural organisation" (CSDR, Article 17(2)).

[676] This 'consultation' is to include: (a) the "suitability" of the applicant's shareholders and those who exercise control over its management, and the experience and the reputation of the persons who "effectively direct" the applicant's business – if those shareholders, controllers and persons are common to the applicant and to a central securities depository that is authorised in another Member State, and (b) whether the relations between the applicant and the other central securities depository (which is authorised in another Member State) "do not affect" the former's ability to observe the requirements of the CSDR (CSDR, Articles 7 and 27(6)).

[677] For the purposes of the CSDR, 'subsidiary' means an undertaking: (i) which is controlled by another company – including any subsidiary undertaking of an ultimate parent company, (ii) that has a majority of its voting rights in the possession of another company, (iii) in which the right to appoint or to remove a majority of the members of its board of directors is in the possession of another company that is a shareholder or a member, (iv) over which another company that is a shareholder or a member in it "has the right to exercise a dominant influence" over it, (v) in which another company that is a shareholder or a member of it has exercised voting rights in it to appoint a majority of the members of its board of directors, in both the current financial year and the previous financial year, and/or (vi) in which another company that is a shareholder or member in it controls a majority of members' or shareholders' voting rights in that undertaking (CSDR, Article 2(1)(22); Directive 2013/34/EU of the European Parliament and of the Council of 26 June 2013 on the annual financial statements, consolidated financial statements and related reports of certain types of undertakings, amending Directive 2006/43/EC of the European Parliament and of the Council and repealing Council Directives 78/660/EEC and 83/349/EEC, Articles 2(10) and 22(1)-(2)).

[678] For the purposes of the CSDR, 'control' means the relationship between 2 companies "as described in Article 22 of Directive 2013/34/EU" (CSDR, Article 2(1)(21)). Points (ii) to (vi) inclusive in the definition of 'subsidiary' in fn 677, correspond to Article 22(1)-(2) of Directive 2013/34/EU. The first company is the subsidiary; the second company (i.e., the 'parent company') is the entity called 'another company' in fn 677.

[679] "[I]n close cooperation with members of the ESCB [the European System of Central Banks]," the ESMA is to: (i) publish draft RTSs to state the information that the applicant central securities depository is to supply to the

An authorised central securities depository may supply services to which the Annex refers[680] "within the territory of the [European]. Union," including through the establishment of a branch, as long as those services are within the authorisation [211]. If this depository intends to provide the 'notary service' and/or the 'central maintenance service'[681], in respect of financial instruments that are "constituted under the law of another Member State referred

---

competent authority in its application for authorisation, and (ii) develop draft ITSs "to establish standard forms, templates and procedures for the application for authorisation," and (iii) to submit these draft RTSs and draft ITSs to the Commission by 18th June 2015 (CSDR, Article 17(9)-(10)). The ESMA has published the draft RTS and the draft ITS; at the time of writing, the final version, i.e., the respective corresponding CDR and CIR, had not been published in the *Official Journal of the European Union*. The draft RTS and the draft ITS are in the document entitled 'Draft technical standards under CSDR: Annex II to the Final Report on the draft technical standards under the Regulation No 909/2014 of the European Parliament and of the Council of 23 July 2014 on improving securities settlement in the European Union and on central securities depositories and amending Directives 98/26/EC and 2014/65/EU and Regulation (EU) No 236/2012 (CSDR)', which is available at https://www.esma.europa.eu/sites/default/files/library/2015/11/2015-esma-1457_-_annex_ii_-_csdr_ts_on_csd_requirements_and_internalised_settlement.pdf, at pp.4-106 and 114-195, respectively; as the large number of pages in these standards would indicate, they cover additional delegations of power in the CSDR to those granted by Article 17 of that Regulation.

[680] These services comprise the 'core services of central securities depositories' in Section A of the Annex – which are the notary, central maintenance and settlement services (see fn 656, for a description of each of these services), the 'non-banking-type ancillary services of central securities depositories that do not entail credit or liquidity risks' in Section B of the Annex (see fn 674, for a list of services that are within this category), and the 'banking-type ancillary services' in Section C of the Annex, which are as follows: "Banking-type services directly related to core or ancillary services listed in Sections A and B, such as (a) Providing cash accounts to, and accepting deposits from, participants in a securities settlement system and holders of securities accounts, within the meaning of point 1 of Annex I to Directive 2013/36/EU [i.e., CRD IV]; (b) Providing cash credit for reimbursement no later than the following business day, cash lending to pre-finance corporate actions and lending securities to holders of securities accounts, within the meaning of point 2 of Annex I to Directive 2013/36/EU; (c) Payment services involving processing of cash and foreign exchange transactions, within the meaning of point 4 of Annex I to Directive 2013/36/EU; (d) Guarantees and commitments related to securities lending and borrowing, within the meaning of point 6 of Annex I to Directive 2013/36/EU; (e) Treasury activities involving foreign exchange and transferable securities related to managing participants' long balances, within the meaning of points 7(b) and (e) of Annex I to Directive 2013/36/EU." (CSDR, Annex, Section C). The points in Annex I to CRD IV, to which Section C of the Annex to the CSDR refers, are as follows: "1. Taking deposits and other repayable funds. 2. Lending including, *inter alia*: consumer credit, credit agreements relating to immovable property, factoring, with or without recourse, financing of commercial transactions (including forfaiting). ... 4. Payment services as defined in Article 4(3) of Directive 2007/64/EC [i.e., the PSD]. ... 6. Guarantees and commitments. ... 7. Trading for own account or for account of customers in any of the following: ... (b) foreign exchange; ... (e) transferable securities. ..." (CRD IV (as amended to 12/06/14), Annex I). Article 4(3) of the PSD defines 'payment service' as "any business activity" that is listed in that Directive's Annex. PSD II came into force on 12th January 2016 (PSD II, Article 116). However, the national measures that are necessary to comply with PSD II are only to be adopted and applied from 13th January 2018 (PSD II, Article 115(1)-(2)). Correspondingly, the PSD "is repealed with effect from 13 January 2018" (PSD II, Article 114). Thus, Article 4(3) of the PSD is a valid source of the definition of 'payment service' until the latter date. The Annex to the PSD contains the list of 'payment services' to which Article 4(3) of that Directive refers. These are as follows: "1. Services enabling cash to be placed on a payment account as well as all [of] the operations required for operating a payment account. 2. Services enabling cash withdrawals from a payment account as well as all [of] the operations required for operating a payment account. 3. Execution of payment transactions, including transfers of funds on a payment account with the user's payment service provider or with another payment service provider ... . 4. Execution of payment transactions where the funds are covered by a credit line for a payment service user ... . 5. Issuing and/or acquiring of payment instruments. 6. Money remittance. 7. Execution of payment transactions where the consent of the payer to execute a payment transaction is given by means of any telecommunication, digital or IT [information technology] device and the payment is made to the telecommunication, IT system or network operator, acting only as an intermediary between the payment service user and the supplier of the goods and services." (PSD, Annex).

[681] See fn 656, for a description of the 'notary service' and of the 'central maintenance' service'.

to in Article 49(1) [of the CSDR]."[682], or to found a branch in another Member State, then the following procedure is to apply [212]. The central securities depository is to send the following information to its home Member State's competent authority: (a) the name of the Member State in which it would like to operate (i.e., the host Member State[683]), (b) a programme of operations, which specifies the services that it intends to provide, (c) the currency (or currencies) that it wishes to process, (d) if it is to establish a branch, the latter's organisational structure and the names of the persons who will be responsible for managing that branch, and (e) if relevant, an evaluation of the measures that it intends to take, in order to permit its users to observe "the national law referred to in Article 49(1) [of the CSDR]"[684] [213]. Before 3 months have elapsed from the date of receipt of this information by the home Member State's competent authority, this authority is to send these data to the host Member State's competent authority, unless "it has reason to doubt the adequacy of the administrative structure or the financial situation of the" central securities depository that wishes to supply its services in the host Member State – taking into consideration the services which the latter would like to provide there[685] [214]. If the home Member State's competent authority decides, in conformity with the previous sentence, to withhold the information from the host Member State's competent authority, then, within 3 months of receiving those data, it is to provide reasons to the central securities depository for its refusal to send them [215]. The central securities depository may begin to supply the specified services in the host Member State, if: (a) it receives a communication from the host Member State's competent authority which states that the latter has received the information from the home Member State's competent authority, and, if relevant, that the home Member State's competent authority has approved the evaluation to which point (e) above refers, or (b) in the absence of its receipt of a communication from the host Member State's competent authority, after 3 months from the date of transmission of the information to that authority from the home Member State's competent authority[686] [216].

---

[682] Article 49(1) of the CSDR states: "An issuer shall have the right to arrange for its securities admitted to trading on regulated markets or MTFs or trading on trading venues to be recorded in any CSD [central securities depository] established in any Member State, subject to compliance by that CSD with conditions referred to in Article 23 [of the CSD (see the current paragraph in the text, for Article 23 of the CSDR)]. Without prejudice to the issuer's right referred to in the [previous sentence], the corporate or similar law of the Member State under which the securities are constituted shall continue to apply. ...." It is submitted that 'constituted' in this context means 'created' – i.e., in the case of corporate shares, the authorisation in the company's articles of association that permit the company to allot and to issue the relevant shares.

[683] For the purposes of the CSDR, 'host Member State' means the Member State in which a central securities depository establishes a branch or supplies "CSD services" – other than the home Member State (CSDR, Article 2(1)(24)).

[684] It is submitted that this national law is the law under which the relevant securities are constituted – see fn 682.

[685] The host Member State's competent authority is to promptly notify that Member State's relevant authorities of the information that it received from the host Member State's competent authority (CSDR, Article 23(4)). See fn 668, for the definition of 'relevant authority'.

[686] The central securities depository is to provide the information which the current paragraph in the text specifies to its home Member State's competent authority, if there is a change in the range of services that it would like to supply in the host Member State (CSDR, Article 23(3)). Article 23(7) of the CSDR states: "In the event of a change in any of the information communicated in accordance with [Article 23(3) of the CSDR], a CSD [central securities depository] shall give written notice of that change to the competent authority of the home Member State at least one month before implementing the change. The competent authority of the host Member State shall also be informed of that change without delay by the competent authority of the home Member State.."

The concept of the authorised central securities depository, which applies across the EEA[687], is an ingenious way of simplifying and unifying this complex area of securities law. The authorisation and passporting processes, described above, show similarities to those in the MiFID (or in MiFID II) – for instance the maximum permitted time period before forwarding, and the reason for refusing to forward, the information provided by the authorised central securities depository to the host Member State's competent authority are the same for the home Member State's competent authority in the CSDR[688] as they are for the home Member State's competent authority in the MiFID in the case in which the authorised investment firm establishes a branch in the host Member State[689]. Notwithstanding this, the CSDR is a substantial, directly applicable legal instrument, which is to be accompanied by CDRs and CIRs. Although these measures may precipitate the convergence of professional practice across EEA States, they are likely to bring about only limited simplification in the law.

OTC Derivatives, Central Counterparties and Trade Repositories

The author has considered the essence of the EMIR, and its development from the G20's commitment at the Pittsburgh Summit in 2009[690], in 2 Financial Regulatory Updates written in 2013[691]. Recital 5 of the EMIR confirms this commitment as the Regulation's origin, as follows.

> At the 26 September 2009 summit in Pittsburgh, G20 leaders agreed that all standardised OTC derivative contracts should be cleared through a central counterparty (CCP) by the end of 2012 and that OTC derivative contracts should be reported to trade repositories. In June 2010, G20 leaders in Toronto reaffirmed their commitment and also committed to accelerate the implementation of strong measures to improve transparency and regulatory oversight of OTC derivative contracts in an internationally consistent and non-discriminatory way [217].

It is submitted that the EMIR is framed in a surprising way. Recital 99 of this instrument is as follows [218].

> Since the objectives of this Regulation, namely to lay down uniform requirements for OTC derivative contracts and for the performance of activities of CCPs and trade

---

[687] The CSDR is labelled 'Text with EEA relevance'. Thus, 'Member State' within the CSDR means 'EEA State'.

[688] See the previous paragraph, for this time period and for the reason for the home Member State's competent authority, to refuse to forward the information.

[689] The 11th paragraph of the subsection entitled 'Financial instruments', in the section entitled 'Securities Legislation' in Chapter 1, gives the relevant provision (Article 32(3)) of the MiFID, which is unchanged from the original version of the MiFID through the version of that Directive which is in force at the time of writing, and into the equivalent provision of MiFID II – which is Article 35(3) of the latter Directive.

[690] See the subsection entitled '2009', in the section entitled 'Progress in the G20/FSB System from November 2008' in Chapter 2, for a synopsis of the G20's financial regulatory reforms at the point reached at its Pittsburgh Summit in September 2009. This section includes the development of G20 and FSB reforms in respect of OTC derivatives from the G20's Washington Summit in November 2008.

[691] These Financial Regulatory Updates are: Baber, G. (2013), 'The EMIR of Strasbourg: A three-year journey from Pittsburgh', *Company Lawyer*, 34(4), 117-119, and Baber, G. (2013), 'The EMIR of Strasbourg: changing the financial landscape of the EEA, *Company Lawyer*, 34(9), 285-286.

repositories, cannot be sufficiently achieved by the Member States and can therefore, by reason of the scale of the action, be better achieved at [European]. Union level, the Union may adopt measures, in accordance with the principle of subsidiary as set out in Article 5 of the Treaty on European Union. In accordance with the principle of proportionality, as set out in that Article, this Regulation does not go beyond what is necessary in order to achieve those objectives [218].

The EMIR is based on Article 114 of the TFEU [219]. Article 114(1) provides that "[t]he European Parliament and the Council shall acting in accordance with the ordinary legislative procedure[692] and after consulting the Economic and Social Committee, adopt the measures for the approximation of the provisions laid down by law, regulation or administrative action in Member States which have as their objective the establishment and functioning of the internal market." It is submitted that the objective 'to lay down uniform requirements' in Recital 99 of the EMIR is beyond the power granted in Article 114(1) of the TFEU for the Council and the Parliament 'to adopt measures for the approximation of the provisions laid down by law'. Furthermore, the ambition of the EMIR's objective in Recital 99 means that the principles of subsidiarity[693] and proportionality[694] can be pushed aside without due consideration of them.

It is further submitted that the concept of 'shared competence'[695] – which applies to the internal market [220]. – does not provide for the introduction of uniform requirements in Regulations. This practice is in line with 'exclusive competence'[696]; if the EU institutions wish to pursue this approach over the area of financial regulation, then the Treaties need to be changed accordingly[697].

The EMIR contains requirements for the clearing[698], the reporting, and the risk management of OTC derivative contracts[699], and "uniform requirements" for the activities of

---

[692] Article 294 of the TFEU contains the ordinary legislative procedure.

[693] Article 5(3) of the TEU states: "Under the principle of subsidiarity, in areas which do not fall within its exclusive competence, the [European] Union shall act only if and in so far as the objectives of the proposed action cannot be sufficiently achieved by the Member States, either at central level or at regional and local level, but can rather, by reason of the scale or effects of the proposed action, be better achieved at Union level. ...."

[694] Article 5(4) of the TEU declares: "Under the principle of proportionality, the content and form of [European] Union action shall not exceed what is necessary to achieve the objectives of the Treaties [i.e., the TEU and the TFEU]. ...."

[695] Article 2(2) of the TFEU declares: "When the Treaties confer on the [European] Union a competence shared with the Member States in a specific area, the Union and the Member States may legislate and adopt legally binding acts in that area. The Member States shall exercise their competence to the extent that the Union has not exercised its competence. The Member States shall again exercise their competence to the extent that the Union has decided to cease exercising its competence.."

[696] Article 2(1) of the TFEU states: "When the Treaties confer on the [European] Union exclusive competence in a specific area, only the Union may legislate and adopt legally binding acts, the Member States being able to do so themselves only if so empowered by the Union or for the implementation of Union acts.."

[697] A similar point is made with regard to the possibility of full convergence of the market abuse legislation: see the penultimate paragraph of the subsection entitled 'Market abuse', above in this section. This issue is raised in more general terms in respect of the output of Regulations since the GFC: see the subsection entitled 'Comment', in the section entitled 'Distinguishing Between the ESAs' in Chapter 3.

[698] For the purposes of the EMIR, 'clearing' means the procedure for "establishing positions," and for making certain that cash and/or financial instruments are available in order to cover the exposures that arise from those positions (EMIR (as amended to 23/12/15), Article 2(3)).

[699] For the purposes of the EMIR, 'derivative' or 'derivative contract' means a financial instrument as stated in points 4-10 of Section C of Annex I to the MiFID, as implemented by Articles 38-39 of Commission Regulation (EC) No 1287/2006 of 10 August 2006 implementing Directive 2004/39/EC of the European Parliament and of the Council as regards record-keeping obligations for investment firms, transaction reporting, market transparency, admission of financial instruments to trading, and defined terms for the purposes of that Directive (EMIR, Article 2(5)). Points 4, 5, 8 and 9 are the same in Section C of Annex I to

CCPs[700] and trade repositories[701] [221]. It applies "to CCPs and their and their clearing members, to financial counterparties[702] and to trade repositories," and "to non-financial counterparties[703] and trading venues where so provided" [222].

Counterparties are to clear all OTC derivative contracts that relate to a class of OTC derivatives which have been held to be "subject to the clearing obligation" in conformity with

---

the MiFID as in Section C of Annex I to MiFID II, which are listed as points (iv), (v), (viii) and (ix), respectively, in fn 654. Points 6, 7 and 10 in Section C of Annex I to the MiFID are as follows: "(6) Options, futures, swaps, and any other derivative contract relating to commodities that can be physically settled provided that they are traded on a regulated market and/or an MTF; (7) Options, futures, swaps, forwards and any other derivative contracts relating to commodities, that can be physically settled not otherwise mentioned in C.6 and not being for commercial purposes, which have the characteristics of other derivative instruments, having regard to whether, *inter alia*, they are cleared and settled through recognised clearing houses or are subject to regular margin calls; … (10) Options, futures, swaps, forward rate agreements and any other derivative contracts relating to climatic variables, freight rates, emission allowances or inflation rates or other official economic statistics that must be settled in cash or may be settled in cash at the option of one of the parties (otherwise than by reason of a default or other termination event), as well as any other derivative contracts relating to assets, rights, obligations, indices and measures not otherwise mentioned in this Section, which have the characteristics of other derivative financial instruments, having regard to whether, *inter alia*, they are traded on a regulated market or an MTF, are cleared and settled through recognised clearing houses or are subject to regular margin calls." (MiFID (as amended and corrected to 22/02/14), Annex I, Section C). Paragraphs 1, 2 and 4 of Article 38 of Commission Regulation (EC) No 1287/2006 lay down conditions for a derivative contract to be 'not being for commercial purposes, and having the characteristics of other derivative financial instruments', in point 7 of Section C of Annex I to the MiFID. Articles 38(3)-(4) and 39 of Commission Regulation (EC) No 1287/2006 provide guidance as to what derivative contracts are within point 10 of Section C of Annex I to the MiFID. For the purposes of the EMIR, 'OTC derivative' or 'OTC derivative contract' means a derivative contract, the completion of which does not take place on a regulated market within the meaning of Article 4(1)(14) of the MiFID, or on a market in a third country that is "considered to be equivalent to a regulated market" in conformity with Article 2a of the EMIR (EMIR (as amended to 23/12/15), Article 2(7)). "'Regulated market' means a multilateral system operated and/or managed by a market operator, which brings together or facilitates the bringing together of multiple third-party buying and selling interests in financial instruments – in the system and in accordance with its non-discretionary rules – in a way that results in a contract, in respect of the financial instruments admitted to trading under its rules and/or systems, and which is authorised and functions regularly and in accordance with the provisions of Title III" of the MiFID (MiFID (as amended and corrected to 22/02/14), Article 4(1)(14)). Title III of the MiFID is entitled 'Regulated Markets', and contains Articles 36-47 – which concern the authorisation of, the organisational requirements of, and other provisions that relate to, regulated markets. Article 2a(1) of the EMIR states: "For the purposes of Article 2(7) of [the EMIR], a third-country market shall be considered to be equivalent to a regulated market within the meaning of Article 4(1)(14) of Directive 2004/39/EC [i.e., the MiFID] where it complies with legally binding requirements which are equivalent to the requirements laid down in Title III of that Directive and it is subject to effective supervision and enforcement in that third country on an ongoing basis, as determined by the Commission in accordance with the procedure referred to in [Article 2a(2) of the EMIR]". Article 2a(2) of the EMIR declares: "The Commission may adopt implementing acts determining that a third-country market complies with legally binding requirements which are equivalent to the requirements laid down in Title III of Directive 2004/39/EC and it is subject to effective supervision and enforcement in that third country on an ongoing basis for the purposes of [Article 2a(1) of the EMIR]. ….."

[700] For the purposes of the EMIR, 'CCP' means a legal person which inserts itself between the counterparties to the contracts that are traded on financial markets, thus becoming the seller to every buyer and the buyer to every seller (EMIR (as amended to 23/12/15), Article 2(1)).

[701] For the purposes of the EMIR, 'trade repository' means a legal person which collects and maintains central records of derivatives (EMIR (as amended to 23/12/15), Article 2(2)).

[702] For the purposes of the EMIR, 'financial counterparty' means an authorised credit institution, investment firm, insurance company, life assurance undertaking, reinsurance company, UCITS, UCITS management company and "institution for occupational retirement provision," and an AIF that is "managed by AIFMs authorised or registered in accordance with [the AIFM Directive]" (EMIR (as amended to 23/12/15), Article 2(8)).

[703] For the purposes of the EMIR, 'non-financial counterparty' means an entity that is founded in the EEA (as the EMIR is labelled 'Text with EEA relevance') other than a CCP or a financial counterparty (EMIR (as amended to 23/12/15), Article 2(9)). See fn 700, for the definition of 'CCP'. See fn 702, for the definition of 'financial counterparty'.

Article 5(2) of the EMIR[704], if those contracts: (a) have been agreed between: (i) 2 financial counterparties, (ii) a financial counterparty and a non-financial counterparty that satisfies the conditions to which Article 10(1)(b) of the EMIR[705] refers, (iii) 2 non-financial counterparties

---

[704] If a competent authority "authorises a CCP to clear a class of OTC derivatives," in accordance with Articles 14 and 15 of the EMIR – which concern the authorisation of a CCP to supply clearing services and the addition to its services and/or activities, respectively – then it is to notify the ESMA of this authorisation (EMIR (as amended to 23/12/15), Article 5(1)). Article 6 of Commission Delegated Regulation (EU) No 149/2013 of 19 December 2012 supplementing Regulation (EU) No 648/2012 of the European Parliament and of the Council with regard to regulatory technical standards on indirect clearing arrangements, the clearing obligation, the public register, access to a trading venue, non-financial counterparties, and risk mitigation techniques for OTC derivative contracts not cleared by a CCP, specifies the data that the notification is to include – pursuant to Article 5(1) of the EMIR. These data include, for instance, the identification of the relevant class of OTC derivative contracts, and of the particular type of OTC derivative contracts within that class (Commission Delegated Regulation (EU) No 149/2013, Article 6(1)(a)-(b)). Within 6 months of receiving this notification, or of "accomplishing a procedure for recognition" of a CCP established in a third country (in accordance with Article 25 of the EMIR) – so that the CCP may supply clearing services within the EEA, the ESMA is to hold a public consultation and to consult the European Systemic Risk Board (and, if appropriate, the competent authorities of third countries), and then to evolve and submit to the Commission draft RTSs which specify: (a) the class of OTC derivatives that are "to be subject to the clearing obligation" to which Article 4 of the EMIR refers, (b) the date(s) "from which the clearing obligation takes effect," and (c) "the minimum remaining maturity of the OTC derivative contracts" to which Article 4(1)(b)(ii) of the EMIR refers (see point (b)(ii) in the text); the Commission is empowered to adopt these RTSs "in accordance with Articles 10 to 14 of Regulation (EU) No 1095/2010" (EMIR (as amended to 23/12/15), Article 5(2)). See the subsection entitled 'RTSs and CDRs', in the section entitled 'The ESAs and Delegated Legislation' in Chapter 3, for a description of the procedure in Articles 10-14 of Regulation (EU) No 1095/2010 for the development and the publication of RTSs and CDRs. At the date of writing, the ESMA had sent 3 draft RTSs that are pursuant to Article 5(2) of the EMIR to the Commission, one of which has successfully completed the procedure in Articles 10-14 of Regulation (EU) No 1095/2010 (European Securities and Markets Authority (2016), OTC derivatives and clearing obligation, <https://www.esma.europa.eu/regulation/post-trading/otc-derivatives-and-clearing-obligation>). This CDR is Commission Delegated Regulation (EU) 2015/2205 of 6 August 2015 supplementing Regulation (EU) No 648/2012 of the European Parliament and of the Council with regard to regulatory technical standards on the clearing obligation. The derivatives that are "subject to the clearing obligation" under Commission Delegated Regulation (EU) 2015/2205 comprise specified: (i) basis swaps in Euros, GBP, JPY and USD, (ii) fixed-to-floating interest-rate swaps in Euros, GBP, JPY and USD, (iii) forward rate agreements in Euros, GBP and USD, and (iv) overnight index swaps in Euros, GBP and USD (Commission Delegated Regulation (EU) 2015/2205, Article 1(1) and Annex).

[705] Article 10(1)(b) of the EMIR states: "Where a non-financial counterparty takes positions in OTC derivative contracts and those positions exceed the clearing threshold as specified under [Article 10(3) of the EMIR], that non-financial counterparty shall … (b) become subject to the clearing obligation for future contracts in accordance with Article 4 [of the EMIR] if the rolling average position over 30 working days exceeds the threshold …." Article 10(3) of the EMIR declares: "In calculating the positions referred to in [Article 10(1) of the EMIR], the non-financial counterparty shall include all [of] the OTC derivative contracts entered into by the non-financial counterparty or by other non-financial entitites within the group to which the non-financial counterparty belongs, which are not objectively measurable as reducing risks directly relating to the commercial activity or treasury financing activity of the non-financial counterparty or of that group." The other duties for a non-financial counterparty whose positions in OTC derivatives exceed the clearing threshold are to promptly inform the ESMA and the competent authority that the Member State concerned designates for this purpose, and "to clear all relevant future contracts within four months of becoming subject to the clearing obligation" (EMIR (as amended to 23/12/15), Articles 10(1)(a), 10(1)(c) and 10(5)). Article 10(4) of the EMIR empowers the ESMA to develop draft RTSs "after consulting the ESRB [European Systemic Risk Board] and other relevant authorities," which specify "criteria for establishing which OTC derivative contracts are objectively measurable as reducing risks directly relating to the commercial activity or treasury financing activity" to which Article 10(3) of the EMIR refers, and "values of the clearing thresholds." After carrying out a consultation of the public, the ESMA was to submit these draft RTSs to the Commission by 30th September 2012 – which was empowered to adopt them "in accordance with Articles 10 to 14 of Regulation (EU) No 1095/2010" (EMIR (as amended to 23/12/15), Article 10(4)). The subsection entitled 'RTSs and CDRs', in the section entitled 'The ESAs and Delegated Legislation' in Chapter 3, describes the procedure in Articles 10-14 of Regulation (EU) No 1095/2010 for the development and the publication of RTSs and CDRs. The final RTSs that implement Article 10(4) of the EMIR are in Articles 10 and 11 of Commission Delegated Regulation (EU) No 149/2013. Article 10 of Commission Delegated Regulation (EU) No 149/2013 states: "An

that fulfil those conditions, (iv) a financial counterparty – or a non-financial counterparty that satisfies those conditions – and an undertaking founded in a third country which "would be subject to the clearing obligation if it were established in the [EEA]," or (v) 2 entities that are founded in at least one third country, which "would be subject to the clearing obligation if they were established in the [EEA]," as long as the contract "has a direct, substantial and foreseeable effect within the [EEA] or where such an obligation is necessary or appropriate to prevent the evasion of any provisions of [the EMIR].," and (b) are entered into, or are novated[706], on or after: (i) "the date from which the clearing obligation takes effect," or (ii) "notification as referred to in Article 5(1) [of the EMIR[707],]. but before the date from which the clearing obligation takes effect if the contracts have a remaining maturity higher than the minimum remaining maturity determined by the Commission in accordance with Article 5(2)(c)[708]" [223]. Without detriment to methods for mitigating risks in Article 11 of the EMIR[709], OTC derivative contracts which are intra-group[710] transactions[711] are not to be

---

OTC derivative contract shall be objectively measurable as reducing risks directly relating to the commercial activity or treasury financing activity of the non-financial counterparty or of that group, when, by itself or in combination with other derivative contracts, directly or through closely correlated instruments, it meets *one* of the following criteria: (a) it covers the risks arising from the potential change in the value of assets, services, inputs, products, commodities or liabilities that the non-financial counterparty or its group owns, produces, manufactures, processes, provides, purchases, merchandises, leases, sells or incurs or reasonably anticipates owning, producing, manufacturing, processing, providing, purchasing, merchandising, leasing, selling or incurring in the normal course of its business; (b) it covers the risks arising from the potential indirect impact on the value of assets, services, inputs, products, commodities or liabilities referred to in point (a), resulting from fluctuation of interest rates, inflation rates, foreign exchange rates or credit risk; (c) it qualifies as a hedging contract pursuant to International Financial Reporting Standards (IFRS) adopted in accordance with Article 3 of Regulation (EC) No 1606/2002 of the European Parliament and of the Council [of 19 July 2002 on the application of international accounting standards]." (emphasis added). The values of the clearing thresholds "for the purposes of the clearing obligation" are: one billion Euros in gross notional value for OTC credit derivative contracts and OTC equity derivative contracts, and 3 billion Euros in gross notional value for OTC interest rate derivative contracts, OTC foreign exchange derivative contracts, OTC commodity derivative contracts and other OTC derivative contracts (Commission Delegated Regulation (EU) No 149/2013, Article 11). The ESMA is to consult the European Systemic Risk Board "and other relevant authorities," and then to "periodically review the thresholds" – proposing RTSs to alter these "where necessary" (EMIR (as amended to 23/12/15), Article 10(4)).

[706] This provision applies to "all types of trade novations," i.e., on each occasion on which a counterparty "steps into the trade" (European Securities and Markets Authority (2016), Questions and Answers: Implementation of the Regulation (EU) No 648/2012 on OTC derivatives, central counterparties and trade repositories (EMIR), p.33, <https://www.esma.europa.eu/sites/default/files/library/2016-293_qa_xvi_on_emir_implementation.pdf>).

[707] See fn 704, for Article 5(1) of the EMIR.

[708] See fn 704, for Article 5(2)(c) of the EMIR – which is point (c) in Article 5(2) in that footnote.

[709] These techniques apply to OTC derivative contracts that a CCP does not clear, and are as follows. The counterparties are to ensure that there are "appropriate" arrangements and procedures "in place to measure, monitor and mitigate operational risk and counterparty credit risk," which include at least: (a) the prompt confirmation of the particular OTC derivative contract's terms, and (b) auditable, formalised, resilient, robust processes, for the reconciliation of portfolios, the management of risks that are connected to these portfolios, the early identification and the settlement of disputes between the parties, and the monitoring of the value of OTC derivative contracts that are outstanding (EMIR (as amended to 23/12/15), Article 11(1)). Financial counterparties, and non-financial counterparties whose trade in OTC derivative contracts exceeds the clearing threshold (see fn 705, for the clearing threshold), are to mark-to-market the value of their outstanding OTC derivative contracts each day; if conditions in the market prevent this activity, then a prudent, reliable model is to be used for the daily valuation of OTC derivative contracts (EMIR (as amended to 23/12/15), Article 11(2)). Financial counterparties are to apply risk-management processes that require the accurate, punctual and "appropriately segregated exchange of collateral" in respect of OTC derivative contracts; non-financial counterparties whose trade in OTC derivative contracts exceeds the clearing threshold are to operate risk-management procedures that require such use of collateral, with regard to OTC derivative contracts that are entered into as soon as the clearing threshold is exceeded (EMIR (as amended to 23/12/15), Article 11(3)).

Paragraphs 5-10 of Article 11 of the EMIR contain exemptions from the requirement that Article 11(3) of that Regulation lays down. The counterparty to an intra-group transaction that has been exempted from the requirement in Article 11(3) of the EMIR, is to divulge information to the public about the exemption (EMIR (as amended to 23/12/15), Article 11(11)). Financial counterparties are to possess "an appropriate and proportionate amount of capital," in order to manage the risk that "appropriate exchange of collateral" does not cover (EMIR (as amended to 23/12/15), Article 11(4)). The obligations that Article 11(1)-(11) of the EMIR sets out, are to apply to OTC derivative contracts agreed between entities which are authorised in third countries "that would be subject to those obligations if they were established in the [EEA (as the EMIR is labelled 'Text with EEA relevance')], provided that those contracts have a direct, substantial and foreseeable effect within the [EEA] or where such obligation is necessary or appropriate to prevent the evasion of any provision of this Regulation" (EMIR (as amended to 23/12/15), Article 11(12)). Article 11(14)(a)-(b) of the EMIR empowers the ESMA to develop draft RTSs and to submit these to the Commission by 30th September 2012, and for the Commission to adopt them "in accordance with Articles 10 to 14 of Regulation (EU) No 1095/2010" (– the procedure that these Articles contain for the development and the publication of RTSs and CDRs is described in the subsection entitled 'RTSs and CDRs', in the section entitled 'The ESAs and Delegated Legislation' in Chapter 3), which specify "the procedures and arrangements" to which Article 11(1) of the EMIR refers and "the market conditions that prevent marking-to-market and the criteria for using marking-to-model" to which Article 11(2) of the EMIR refers. Articles 13, 14 and 15 of Commission Delegated Regulation (EU) No 149/2013 contain those procedures and arrangements, which are entitled 'Portfolio reconciliation', 'Portfolio compression' and 'Dispute resolution', respectively. The following market conditions prevent marking-to-market of an OTC derivative contract: (a) if the market is inactive, and/or (b) if the range of reasonable estimates of fair values is large, and the probabilities of these estimates are unable to be evaluated rationally (Commission Delegated Regulation (EU) No 149/2013, Article 16(1)). Article 16(2) of Commission Delegated Regulation (EU) No 149/2013 states: "A market for an OTC derivative contract shall be considered inactive when quoted prices are not readily and regularly available and those prices available do not reflect actual and regularly occurring market transactions on an arm's length basis". If counterparties use a model in order to determine the daily value of their OTC derivative contracts, then this model must: (a) incorporate all factors that counterparties would consider in order to set a price, (b) be compatible "with accepted economic methodologies for pricing financial instruments," (c) be "calibrated and tested for validity" using prices that are based upon "observable market data," (d) be "validated and monitored independently" – by a corporate division other than that which takes the risk, and (e) be "duly documented and approved by the board of directors" or by one of its committees, "as frequently as necessary" – at least once each year and after "any material change" (Commission Delegated Regulation (EU) No 149/2013, Article 17). The ESAs are to evolve common draft RTSs, which specify (amongst other things) the procedures for risk management that are required for observance of Article 11(3) of the EMIR (EMIR (as amended to 23/12/15), Article 11(15)(a)). The ESMA, the EBA and the EIOPA have jointly published a document entitled 'Second Consultation Paper: Draft Regulatory Technical Standards on risk-mitigation techniques for OTC-derivative contracts not cleared by a CCP under Article 11(15) of Regulation (EU) No 648/2012', which is available from the EBA's website at https://www.eba.europa.eu/documents/ 10180/1106136/JC-CP-2015-002+JC+CP+on+Risk+Management+Techniques+for+OTC+derivatives+.pdf, and which contains various draft Articles within the framework of a CDR: for instance Article 1 VM – Variation margin (on pp.31-32 of the document), which provides for collateral to be collected on a daily basis by counterparties to an OTC derivative contract in the form of variation margin, within 3 business days of the date of computation of that margin. These draft Articles are complex, and, at the time of writing, the final version of the CDR (to be published in the *Official Journal of the European Union*) is awaited.

710 For the purposes of the EMIR, "'group' means the group of undertakings consisting of a parent undertaking and its subsidiaries within the meaning of Articles 1 and 2 of [Seventh Council] Directive 83/349/EEC [of 13 June 1983 based on the Article 54(3)(g) of the Treaty on consolidated accounts] or the group of undertakings referred to in Article 3(1) and Article 80(7) and (8) of Directive 2006/48/EC [i.e., the CRD]" (EMIR (as amended to 23/12/15), Article 2(16)). For the purposes of the EMIR, "'parent undertaking' means a parent undertaking as described in Articles 1 and 2 of Directive 83/349/EEC" (EMIR (as amended to 23/12/15), Article 2(21)). For the purposes of the EMIR, "'subsidiary' means a subsidiary undertaking as described in Articles 1 and 2 of Directive 83/349/EEC, including a subsidiary of a subsidiary undertaking of an ultimate parent undertaking" (EMIR (as amended to 23/12/15), Article 2(21)). Directive 83/349/EEC is replaced by Directive 2013/34/EU, which entered into force on 19th July 2013 (Directive 2013/34/EU (as amended to 21/11/14), Articles 52 and 54). References to Directive 83/349/EEC in other EU legislation are to be "construed as references to [Directive 2013/34/EU]," and are to be "read in accordance with the correlation table in Annex VII" of Directive 2013/34/EU (Directive 2013/34/EU (as amended to 21/11/14), Article 52). Articles 1 and 2 of Directive 83/349/EEC correlate with Article 22(1)-(5) of Directive 2013/34/EU (Directive 2013/34/EU (as amended to 21/11/14), Annex VII). Thus, for the purposes of the EMIR, it is necessary to decipher the meaning of 'group', 'parent undertaking' and 'subsidiary' from the content of Articles 22(1)-(5)

of Directive 2013/34/EU, which are as follows. A Member State is to require any company that is governed by its domestic law to construct consolidated financial statements and a consolidated management report, if that entity (a 'parent undertaking'): (a) holds a majority of the members' or shareholders' voting rights in another company (a 'subsidiary undertaking'), (b) possesses the right to appoint or remove a majority of the board of directors of another company (a 'subsidiary undertaking') whilst being a member or a shareholder of that firm, (c) "has the right to exercise a dominant influence over" a company (a 'subsidiary undertaking') of which it is a member or a shareholder, or (d) is a member or a shareholder of a company (a 'subsidiary undertaking') and (i) a majority of the members of that subsidiary's board of directors "who have held office during the financial year, during the preceding financial year and up to the time when the consolidated financial statements are drawn up, have been appointed solely as a result of the exercise of its voting rights," or (ii) controls a majority of the members' or shareholders' voting rights in that subsidiary (Directive 2013/34/EU (as amended to 21/11/14), Article 22(1)). For the purposes of points (a), (b) and (d) in the previous sentence, "the voting rights and the rights of appointment and removal of any other subsidiary undertaking as well as those of any person acting in his own name but on behalf of the parent undertaking or of another subsidiary undertaking shall be added to those of the parent undertaking"; these rights are to be lessened by the rights that attach to shares which are held: (i) "on behalf of a person who is neither the parent undertaking nor a subsidiary of that parent undertaking," (ii) "by way of security," or (iii) in association with the allotment of loans in the normal course of business (Directive 2013/34/EU (as amended to 21/11/14), Article 22(3)-(4)). For the purposes of points (a) and (d) above, "the total of the shareholders' or members' voting rights in the subsidiary undertaking shall be reduced by the voting rights attaching to the shares held by that undertaking itself, by a subsidiary undertaking of that undertaking or by a person acting in his own name but on behalf of those undertakings" (Directive 2013/34/EU (as amended to 21/11/14), Article 22(5)). In addition to the cases to which Article 22(1) of Directive 2013/34/EU refers, each Member State may require any company that is governed by its domestic law to produce consolidated financial statements and a consolidated management report, if that entity (a 'parent undertaking'): (a) "has the power to exercise, or actually exercises, dominant influence or control over" a second company (a 'subsidiary undertaking'), or (b) together with another company (a 'subsidiary undertaking') is "managed on a unified basis by the parent undertaking" (Directive 2013/34/EU (as amended to 21/11/14), Article 22(2)). In addition to 'a group comprising a parent undertaking and its subsidiaries' as described above in this footnote, Article 2(16) of the EMIR also includes in the meaning of 'group' (for the purposes of that Regulation) the 'group of undertakings' to which Articles 3(1) and 80(7)-(8) of the CRD refer. The CRD was repealed "with effect from 1 January 2014"; references to the CRD are to "be construed as references to [CRD IV] and to [the CRR]" and are to "be read in accordance with the correlation table set out in Annex II to [CRD IV] and in Annex IV to [the CRR]" (CRD IV (as amended to 12/06/14), Article 163). Articles 3(1), 80(7) and 80(8) of the CRD correlate with Articles 10(1), 113(6) and 113(7) of the CRR, respectively (CRR (as amended to 17/01/15), Annex IV). Thus, in the definition of 'group' in Article 2(16) of the EMIR, 'the group of undertakings to which Articles 3(1) and 80(7)-(8) of the CRD refer' should read 'the group of undertakings to which Articles 10(1) and 113(6)-(7) of the CRR refer'. The most relevant pieces within those Articles of the CRR are as follows. National banking regulators "may ... waive the application of the requirements set out in Parts Two to Eight [of the CRR] to one or more *credit institutions situated in the same Member State* and which are *permanently affiliated to a central body which supervises them and which is established in the same Member State*, if the following conditions are met: (a) *the commitments of the central body and affiliated institutions are joint and several liabilities or the commitments of its affiliated institutions are entirely guaranteed by the central body*; (b) *the solvency and liquidity of the central body and of all of the affiliated institutions are monitored as a whole on the basis of the consolidated accounts of these institutions*, (c) *the management of the central body is empowered to issue instructions to the management of the affiliated institutions*" (CRR (as amended to 17/01/15), Article 10(1); emphasis added). A national banking regulator may permit *an institution (i.e., a credit institution or an investment firm)* to disapply Article 113(1) of the CRR (subject to one exception), "if the following conditions are fulfilled: (a) *the counterparty is an institution, a financial institution or an ancillary services undertaking* subject to appropriate prudential requirements; (b) *the counterparty is included in the same consolidation as the institution* on a full basis; (c) *the counterparty is subject to the same risk evaluation, measurement and control procedures* as the institution; (d) *the counterparty is established in the same Member State as the institution*; (e) *there is no* current or foreseen material practical or legal *impediment to the prompt transfer of own funds or repayment of liabilities from the counterparty to the institution*" (CRR (as amended to 17/01/15), Article 113(6); emphasis added). A national banking regulator may allow an *institution (i.e., a credit institution or an investment firm)* to disapply Article 113(1) of the CRR (subject to one exception) "*to exposures to counterparties with which the institution has entered into an institutional protection scheme that is a contractual or statutory liability arrangement which protects those institutions and in particular ensures their liquidity and solvency to avoid bankruptcy* where necessary. Competent authorities are empowered to grant permission if the following conditions are fulfilled: (a) *the requirements set out in points (a), (d) and (e) of [Article 113(6) of the CRR – see the previous sentence] are met*; ... (h) the institutional protection scheme shall be *based on a broad membership of credit institutions*

subject to the clearing obligation; this exemption only applies in each of the following situations: (a) if 2 counterparties established in the EEA that belong to the same group have given prior written notification to their respective competent authorities that they would like to use the exemption for the OTC derivative contracts which they conclude betwixt one another[712], and (b) if 2 counterparties, which are founded in a Member State[713] and in a third country, belong to the same group, and the counterparty that is established in the EEA has been authorised by its competent authority to apply the exemption within 30 days of being notified by that counterparty of the parties' wish to use the exemption – as long as the conditions that Article 3 of the EMIR[714] lays down are satisfied [224].

Counterparties and CCPs are to ensure that the details of each derivative contract[715] which they have agreed, and of any change to or termination of this contract, are reported to a trade repository that is registered in conformity with Article 55 of the EMIR[716] or recognised

---

of a predominantly homogenous business profile; …" (CRR (as amended to 17/01/15), Article 113(7); emphasis mine).

[711] Article 3(1) of the EMIR states: "In relation to a non-financial counterparty [see fn 703, for the definition of 'non-financial counterparty'], an intragroup transaction is an OTC derivative contract entered into with another counterparty which is part of the same group [see fn 710, for the definition of 'group'] provided that both counterparties are included in the same consolidation on a full basis and they are subject to an appropriate centralised risk evaluation, measurement and control procedures and that counterparty is established in the [EEA (as the EMIR is labelled 'Text with EEA relevance')] or, if it is established in a third country, the Commission has adopted an implementing act under Article 13(2) [of the EMIR] in respect of that third country". Article 3(2) of the EMIR declares: "In relation to a financial counterparty [see fn 702, for the definition of 'financial counterparty'], an intragroup transaction is any of the following: (a) an OTC derivative contract entered into with another counterparty which is part of the same group, provided that the following conditions are met: (i) the financial counterparty is established in the [EEA] or, if it is established in a third country, the Commission has adopted an implementing act under Article 13(2) [of the EMIR] in respect of that third country; (ii) the other counterparty is a financial counterparty, a financial holding company, a financial institution or an ancillary services undertaking subject to appropriate prudential requirements; (iii) both counterparties are included in the same consolidation on a full basis; and (iv) both counterparties are subject to appropriate centralised risk-evaluation, measurement and control procedures; (b) an OTC derivative contract entered into with another counterparty where both counterparties are part of the same institutional protection scheme, … provided that the condition set out in point (a)(ii) [above in this sentence] is met; (c) an OTC derivative contract entered into between credit institutions affiliated to the same central body or between [one] such credit institution and the central body … ; or (d) an OTC derivative contract entered into with a non-financial counterparty which is part of the same group provided that both counterparties are included in the same consolidation on a full basis and they are subject to an appropriate centralised risk evaluation, measurement and control procedures and that counterparty is established in the [EEA] or in a third-country jurisdiction for which the Commission has adopted an implementing act referred to in Article 13(2) [of the EMIR] in respect of that third country". Article 13(2) of the EMIR states: "The Commission may adopt implementing acts declaring that the legal, supervisory and enforcement arrangements of a third country: (a) are equivalent to the requirements laid down in [the EMIR] under Articles 4, 9, 10 and 11; (b) ensure protection of professional secrecy that is equivalent to that set out in [the EMIR]; and (c) are being effectively applied and enforced in an equitable and non-distortive manner so as to ensure effective supervision and enforcement in that third country. …."

[712] Within 30 days of receipt of the notification, the competent authorities may object to this exemption being used, if the transactions between the counterparties do not fulfil the conditions that Article 3 of the EMIR lays down (EMIR (as amended to 23/12/15), Article 4(2)(a)). See fn 711, for Article 3(1)-(2) of the EMIR.

[713] 'Member State' means 'EEA State', as the EMIR is labelled 'Text with EEA relevance'.

[714] See fn 711, for Article 3(1)-(2) of the EMIR.

[715] The definition of 'derivative contract' is broader than that of 'OTC derivative contract'; see fn 699, for the descriptions of these terms.

[716] A trade repository is to register with the ESMA (EMIR (as amended to 23/12/15), Article 55(1)). To be eligible to be registered under Article 55 of the EMIR, a trade repository is to be a legal person founded in the EEA which fulfils the requirements that Title VII of the EMIR lays down (EMIR (as amended to 23/12/15), Article 55(2)). Title VII of the EMIR is entitled 'Requirements for Trade Repositories'; it contains Articles 78-82 of the EMIR, which impose on each registered trade repository: (a) general requirements – such as to possess

in agreement with Article 77 of the EMIR[717]; these details are to be reported to the trade repository "no later than the working day following the conclusion, modification or termination of the contract" [225]. If a trade repository is unavailable to record the data concerning a derivative contract, then counterparties and CCPs are to ensure that these details are reported to the ESMA [226].

Member States are to introduce rules on penalties that apply to contraventions of the provisions in Title II of the EMIR – entitled 'Clearing, Reporting and Risk Management of OTC Derivatives'[718], which are to be "effective, proportionate and dissuasive" and to "include at least administrative fines" [227]. They are to communicate these rules to the Commission by 17th February 2013, and to swiftly inform the Commission of any amendment to them[719] [228].

The EMIR lays down organisational requirements for authorised CCPs. For instance, each CCP is to "have robust governance arrangements ..., effective processes to identify, manage, monitor and report the risks to which it is or might be exposed, and adequate internal control mechanisms" [229].

"robust governance arrangements ... which prevent any disclosure of confidential information" (EMIR (as amended to 23/12/15), Article 78(1)), (b) requirements for operational reliability – such as to "establish, implement and maintain an adequate business continuity policy and disaster recovery plan aiming at ensuring the maintenance of its functions, the timely recovery of operations and the fulfilment of the trade repository's obligations" (EMIR (as amended to 23/12/15), Article 79(2)), (c) requirements for safeguarding and recording information – such as "to take all reasonable steps to prevent any misuse of the information maintained in its systems" (EMIR (as amended to 23/12/15), Article 80(6)), and (d) requirements for transparency and data availability – such as to "regularly ... publish aggregate positions by class of derivatives on the contracts reported to it" (EMIR (as amended to 23/12/15), Article 81(1)). The registration of a trade repository is effective throughout the EEA (EMIR (as amended to 23/12/15), Article 55(3)). A registered trade repository is to observe the conditions for its registration at all times, and is to inform the ESMA of "any material changes to" these conditions (EMIR (as amended to 23/12/15), Article 55(4)).

[717] A trade repository that is founded in a third country may supply its services and activities to entities which are established in the EEA, only after the ESMA has recognised it in accordance with Article 77(2) of the EMIR (EMIR (as amended to 23/12/15), Article 77(1)). A trade repository to which Article 77(1) of the EMIR refers is to submit its application for recognition to the ESMA "together with all necessary information," which includes the data that are necessary to confirm that the trade repository is authorised and effectively supervised in a third country which: (a) the Commission has recognised (by means of an implementing act adopted under Article 75(1) of the EMIR) as possessing "an equivalent and enforceable regulatory and supervisory framework"; (b) has concluded an international agreement with the EU pursuant to Article 75(2) of the EMIR; and (c) has entered into co-operation arrangement in accordance with Article 75(3) of the EMIR, in order to ensure that the EU authorities (including the ESMA) have "immediate and continuous access to all [of] the necessary information"; within 180 working days of its receipt of a complete application, the ESMA is to inform the applicant trade repositary in writing as to whether or not it has granted recognition to the latter, giving reasons to support its decision – and is to publish on its website a list of the trade repositories to which it has granted recognition (EMIR (as amended to 23/12/15), Article 77(2)). It is submitted that, at the date of writing, this list is absent from the ESMA's website – as is the list of trade repositories that are authorised within the EEA to provide services there. The ESMA has published a document entitled 'List of third-country Central Counterparties recognised to offer services and activities in the Union' which is available at https://www.esma.europa.eu/sites/default/files/library/third-country_ccps_recognised_under_emir.pdf, and which shows that 16 CCPs have been recognised – 4 established in Hong Kong, 3 each founded in Canada and Singapore, 2 each established in Australia and Japan, and one each founded in Mexico and South Africa. The number of recognised third-country CCPs is equal to the number of CCPs that are authorised within the EEA (European Securities and Markets Authority (2015), List of Central Counterparties authorised to offer services and activities in the Union, pp.1-2, <https://www.esma.europa.eu/sites/default/files/library/ccps_authorised_under_emir.pdf>). Similar lists to these for CCPs are anticipated from the ESMA in respect of trade repositories.

[718] Title II of the EMIR comprises Articles 4-13 of that Regulation.

[719] Article 12 of the EMIR is in the form of a Directive, i.e., the 2 provisions in this paragraph are addressed to Member States.

The Regulation includes conduct of business rules for CCPs. For example, each CCP is to "act fairly and professionally in accordance with the best interests of [its] clearing members and clients and sound risk management" whilst supplying services to those members, [230] and to possess "accessible, transparent and fair rules for the prompt handling of complaints" [231].

The EMIR imposes prudential requirements on CCPs. Every CCP is to measure and to evaluate its credit and liquidity exposures to each of its clearing members – and to any CCP with which it has made "an interoperability arrangement," in or close to real time [232]. Each CCP is to "impose, call and collect margins to limit its credit exposures from its clearing members and ... from CCPs with which it has interoperability arrangements" [233]. To further restrain a CCP's credit exposures to its clearing members, each CCP is to maintain a default fund which is to cover losses that exceed those that the margin requirements meet – and which arise from the default of any of those clearing members[720] [234]. The CCP is to determine the minimum size of the contributions to the default fund, and the criteria to be used in order to compute the amount to be provided by every clearing member[721] [235]. Each CCP is to maintain additional financial resources to cover potential losses that are in excess of those to be met by the margin requirements and the default fund [236]. Furthermore, a CCP may require clearing members that have not defaulted to supply additional funds up to a limit, if another clearing member defaults [237]. In order that a CCP has continuous access to enough liquidity to supply its services and conduct its activities, it is to put in place the arrangements that are necessary to cover its need for liquidity, in case the funds at its disposal cannot be accessed immediately[722] [238]. A CCP is to accept "highly liquid collateral with minimal credit and market risk," in order to cover its initial and continuous "exposure to its clearing members"; a CCP may accept bank guarantees, in respect of non-financial counterparties[723] [239]. A CCP may accept the underlying asset of the derivative contract that gives rise to the CCP exposure, as collateral to meet its margin requirements – if this is "appropriate and sufficiently prudent" [240]. A CCP is to invest its funds "only in cash or in highly liquid financial instruments with minimal market and credit risk"; its investments must be capable of being accessed quickly "with minimal adverse price effect" [241]. "[W]here practical and available," a CCP is to use central bank money in order to settle its transactions;

---

[720] The CCP is to set a minimum amount above which the default fund is to remain at all times (EMIR (as amended to 23/12/15), Article 42(1)).

[721] The contribution that each member is to make to the default fund is to be proportional to its credit exposure (EMIR (as amended to 23/12/15), Article 42(2)).

[722] A clearing member, and the parent company and the subsidiaries of that member, are together to provide no more than one quarter of the credit lines that the CCP requires (EMIR (as amended to 23/12/15), Article 44(1)).

[723] Further to Article 46(3) of the EMIR: (i) Article 38 of Commission Delegated Regulation (EU) No 153/2013 of 19 December 2012 supplementing Regulation (EU) No 648/2012 of the European Parliament and of the Council with regard to regulatory technical standards on requirements for central counterparties, states that "highly liquid collateral in the form of cash" is to be denominated in a currency: (a) for which the CCP is able to show the competent authorities that it can "adequately manage the risk," and/or (b) in which the CCP clears transactions in OTC derivatives – up to a maximum of its "exposures in that currency"; (ii) Article 39 of Commission Delegated Regulation (EU) No 153/2013 permits financial instruments, bank guarantees and gold to be deemed to be highly liquid collateral, if they satisfy the requirements of Section 1, Section 2 and Section 3, respectively, of Annex I to that CDR. Each CCP is to mark its collateral to market "on a near to real time basis" as far as possible and, if not so, to show the competent authorities that it can "manage the risks" (Commission Delegated Regulation (EU) No 153/2013, Article 40).

if funds from this source are not used, then it is to take action to restrict the risks arising from settlement in cash [242].

The international origin of the main requirements for regulating transactions in OTC derivatives makes it imperative that the EMIR is comprehensive and effective – which explains to some extent the complexity of the Regulation and its associated CDRs and the plentiful provisions within it that apply to CCPs. The definitional and explanatory addendums to key provisions of the EMIR has necessitated the use of long footnotes for accuracy and completeness, which is expensive in words and research time. Consequently, a summary treatment is to be given to the remaining securities legislation and to the banking legislation – whilst maintaining the essence of these instruments as far as is reasonably possible.

Short Selling and Credit Default Swaps

The Commission proposed Regulation (EU) No 236/2012 of the European Parliament and of the Council of 14 March 2012 on short selling and certain aspects of credit default swaps, in order to address the following risks: (i) the lack of transparency concerning short selling prevents regulators from being able to promptly identify the development of short positions that may cause risks to market integrity or to financial stability, (ii) short selling may augment falls in the price of securities in distressed markets, which may precipitate systemic risks, and (iii) the risk of settlement failure if the short seller has not borrowed, or agreed to borrow, the relevant security – which might cause financial instability [243]. Purchasing credit default swaps without possessing a long position in underlying sovereign debt, or any assets, asset portfolios, financial contracts or financial obligations the value of which correlates with that of sovereign debt, is economically equivalent to taking a short position in the underlying debt instrument; the computation of a net short position in respect of sovereign debt should therefore include credit default swaps that relate "to the obligation of" an issuer of sovereign debt [244].

For the purpose of Regulation (EU) No 236/2012, 'short sale' means any sale of a share or of a debt instrument, which the seller does not own at the time he/she enters into the agreement to sell[724] [245]. For the purpose of Regulation (EU) No 236/2012, 'credit default swap' means "a derivative contract in which one party pays a fee to another party in return for a ... benefit[,] if there is a credit event concerning a reference entity, or any other default relating to that derivative contract which has a similar economic effect [246]. For the purposes of Regulation (EU) No 236/2012, a short position in relation to "issued share capital[725] or issued sovereign debt[726]" is: (a) a short sale of a share that a company has issued,

---

[724] A 'short sale' includes a sale of the above description in which the seller, when he/she enters into the agreement to sell, "has borrowed or agreed to borrow the share or [the] debt instrument for delivery at settlement"; it excludes: (i) "a sale by either party under a repurchase agreement where one party has agreed to sell the other a security at a specified price with a commitment from the other party to sell the security back at a later date at another specified price," (ii) "a transfer of securities under a securities lending agreement," or (iii) entry into a derivative contract in which "it is agreed to sell securities at a specified price at a future date" (Regulation (EU) No 236/2012 (as amended to 28/08/14), Article 2(1)(b)).

[725] For the purposes of Regulation (EU) No 236/2012, 'issued share capital' means the sum of ordinary and any preference shares that a company issues, excluding convertible debt securities (Regulation (EU) No 236/2012 (as amended to 28/08/14), Article 2(1)(h)).

[726] For the purpose of Regulation (EU) No 236/2012, 'issued sovereign debt' means the aggregate sovereign debt that a sovereign issuer has issued but not redeemed (Regulation (EU) No 236/2012 (as amended to 28/08/14),

or of a debt instrument that a sovereign issuer has issued, or (b) conducting a transaction that creates, or relates to, a financial instrument (other than one to which point (a) refers), if an effect of this deal is to bestow a financial advantage on the person who enters into it – in the event of a reduction in the value or price of the share or the debt instrument [247]. For the purposes of Regulation (EU) No 236/2012, a long position in respect of "issued share capital or issued sovereign debt" is: (a) holding a share that a company has issued, or a debt instrument that a sovereign issuer has issued, or (b) carrying out a transaction which creates, or relates to, a financial instrument (other than one to which point (a) refers), if an effect of that deal is to confer a financial advantage upon the person who enters into it – in the event of a rise in the value or price of the share or the debt instrument [248].

For the purposes of Regulation (EU) No 236/2012, a person has "an uncovered position in a sovereign credit default swap[727]," if this swap is not used to hedge against the risk of: (a) the issuer's default, if the person has a long position in sovereign debt of this issuer – "to which the sovereign credit default swap relates," or (b) a reduction in the sovereign debt's value, if the person possesses assets or bears liabilities – "a portfolio of assets or financial obligations the value of which is correlated to the value of the sovereign debt"[728] [249]. A person may only enter into a sovereign credit default swap transaction, if that deal does not result in "an uncovered position in a sovereign credit default swap" – as defined in the previous sentence [250]. A competent authority may suspend this restriction, if "it has objective grounds[729] for believing that its sovereign debt market is not functioning properly" and that the limitation might adversely affect the sovereign credit default swap market [251]. If it does this, then each person with "an uncovered position in a credit default swap" is to inform the competent authority in circumstances under which this position "reaches or falls below the relevant notification thresholds for the sovereign issuer"[730] [252].

Article 2(1)(g). For the purposes of Regulation (EU) No 236/2012, 'sovereign debt' means a debt instrument that a sovereign issuer issues (Regulation (EU) No 236/2012 (as amended to 28/08/14), Article 2(1)(f)). For the purposes of Regulation (EU) No 236/2012, 'sovereign issuer' means any of the following which issues debt instruments: (i) the EU, (ii) a Member State – including a department of the government, an agency, or a special purpose vehicle, of that country, (iii) a member of the federation of a federal Member State, (iv) "a special purpose vehicle for several member states," (v) "an international financial instrument established by two or more Member States which has the purpose of mobilising funding and provid[ing] financial assistance to the benefit of its members that are experiencing or threatened by severe financing problems," and (vi) the European Investment Bank (Regulation (EU) No 236/2012 (as amended to 28/08/14), Article 2(1)(d)).

[727] For the purpose of Regulation (EU) No 236/2012, 'sovereign credit default swap' means a credit default swap in respect of which a benefit is to be paid, if there is a credit event or default that relates to a sovereign issuer (Regulation (EU) No 236/2012 (as amended to 28/08/14), Article 2(1)(e)).

[728] Further to Article 4(2) of Regulation (EU) No 236/2012, Articles 14 and 15 of Commission Delegated Regulation (EU) No 918/2012 of 5 July 2012 supplementing Regulation (EU) No 236/2012 of the European Parliament and the Council on short selling and certain aspects of credit default swaps with regard to definitions, the calculation of net short positions, covered sovereign credit default swaps, notification thresholds, liquidity thresholds for suspending restrictions, significant falls in the value of financial instruments and adverse events, describe situations that are not uncovered positions in a sovereign credit default swap.

[729] These grounds are to be based upon at least the following indicators: (a) the interest rate on the sovereign debt is high or rising, (b) the interest rate spread on the sovereign debt is widening, relative "to the sovereign debt of other sovereign issuers," (c) sovereign credit default swap spreads are widening, relative "to the own curve and compared to other sovereign issuers," (d) the sovereign debt's price is slow to return to its equilibrium, following a large trade, (e) only small amounts of sovereign debt are available for trading (Regulation (EU) No 236/2012 (as amended to 28/08/14), Article 14(2)).

[730] Pursuant to Article 7(3) of Regulation (EU) No 236/2012, Article 21 of Commission Delegated Regulation (EU) No 918/2012 lays down notification thresholds for net short positions that relate to issued sovereign debt.

A person may only conclude a short sale of sovereign debt, if the person has: (a) borrowed this debt, (b) made an agreement to borrow the debt, or (c) an arrangement with a third party according to which the latter "has confirmed that the sovereign debt has been located or otherwise has a reasonable expectation that settlement can be effected when it is due"[731] [253]. A person who has a net position in respect of issued sovereign debt is to notify the competent authority, if this position "reaches or falls below the relevant notification thresholds for the sovereign issuer concerned"[732] [254].

A person may only make a short sale of a share that is admitted to trading on a trading venue[733], if that person has: (a) borrowed this share, (b) concluded an agreement to borrow the share, or (c)(i) an arrangement with a third party according to which the latter "has confirmed that the share has been located," and (ii) taken the necessary measures "to have a reasonable expectation that settlement can be effected when it is due"[734] [255]. A person who has a net short position with respect to the issued share capital of a company whose shares are admitted to trading on a trading venue, is to inform the relevant competent authority, if "the position reaches or falls below ... a percentage that equals 0.2% of the issued share capital of the company concerned and each 0.1% above that"[735] [256]. If the person has such a net short position, then it is to divulge details of this position to the public, if it "reaches or falls below ... a percentage that equals 0.5% of the issued share capital of the company concerned and each 0.1.% above that"[736] [257]. The provisions in this paragraph are not to apply to company shares that are admitted to trading on a trading venue in the EEA[737], if the main venue for the trading of these shares is situated in a third country [258].

The rules in the previous 3 paragraphs are not to apply to "transactions performed due to market making activities" [259]. The relevant (natural or legal) person is to given written

---

[731] These restrictions do not apply, if the transaction hedges a long position in debt instruments – the pricing of which correlates strongly with the pricing of the relevant sovereign debt (Regulation (EU) No 236/2012 (as amended to 28/08/14), Article 13(2)). Further to Articles 12(2) and 13(5) of Regulation (EU) No 236/2012, Article 5(1) of Commission Implementing Regulation (EU) No 827/2012 of 29 June 2012 laying down implementing technical standards with regard to the means for public disclosure of net position[s] in shares, the format of the information to be provided to the European Securities and Markets Authority in relation to net short positions, the types of agreements, arrangements and measures to adequately ensure that shares or sovereign debt instruments are available for settlement and the dates and period for the determination of the principal venue for a share according to Regulation (EU) No 236/2012 of the European Parliament and of the Council on short selling and certain aspects of credit default swaps, specifies the types of agreement to borrow the share or the sovereign debt (as appropriate) that are "legally binding for the duration of the short sale."

[732] See fn 730.

[733] For the purpose of Regulation (EU) No 236/2012, 'trading venue' means a 'regulated market' or a 'multilateral trading facility', as defined in Articles 4(1)(14) and 4(1)(15) of the MiFID, respectively (Regulation (EU) No 236/2012 (as amended to 28/08/14), Article 2(1)(l)).

[734] Further to Article 12(2) of Regulation (EU) No 236/2012, Article 6 of Commission Implementing Regulation (EU) No 827/2012 specifies the acceptable arrangements and measures (to which points (c)(i) and (ii) in the text, respectively, refer) with regard to short sales of a share that has been admitted to trading on a trading venue. See the final sentence of fn 731, for implementing measures in respect of agreements to borrow (to which point (b) in the text refers).

[735] The Commission is "empowered to adopt delegated acts" in order to change these percentages, taking "the development in financial markets" into consideration (Regulation (EU) No 236/2012 (as amended to 28/08/14), Article 5(4)).

[736] The Commission is "empowered to adopt delegated acts" in order to alter these thresholds, taking "the development in financial markets" into account (Regulation (EU) No 236/2012 (as amended to 28/08/14), Article 6(4)).

[737] As Regulation (EU) No 236/2012 is labelled 'Text with EEA relevance', references to 'Union' in this Regulation are to be read as references to 'EEA'.

notification to the competent authority of his/her/its home Member State, of his/her/its intended use of the exemption – at least 30 days in advance[738] [260].

If "the price of a financial instrument on a trading venue has fallen significantly" in one trading day, in comparison with the closing price on this venue on the previous day, then the competent authority of the home Member State for the venue is to "consider whether it is appropriate to prohibit or restrict natural or legal persons from engaging in short selling of the financial instrument on that trading venue," in order to stop a disorderly fall in that instrument's price [261]. The fall in value is to be at least 10% for a 'liquid share'[739], and an amount that the Commission is to specify for illiquid shares and other financial instruments[740] [262].

A competent authority may prohibit, or introduce conditions that concern any person who enters into: (i) a short sale, and/or (ii) another transaction that creates, or affects, a financial instrument – where one result of that deal is to bestow a financial advantage on this person in the event of a fall in the value or the price of another financial instrument, if (a) there are unfavourable events or developments which "constitute a serious threat to financial stability or to market confidence" in any Member State(s), and (b) the measure is required in order to address this threat, and will not "have a detrimental effect on the efficiency of financial markets that is disproportionate to its benefits"[741] [263]. Furthermore, a competent authority may limit the scope of persons to enter into transactions that involve sovereign credit default swaps, or restrict the value of the sovereign credit default swap positions that these persons are allowed to take, if (a) and (b) in the previous sentence apply[742] [264].

A competent authority is to publish on its website any decision to introduce or renew any measure(s) under the provisions in the previous 2 paragraphs, which specifies: (a) the measure(s) imposed, including their duration – and the financial instruments and the classes of transactions to which they apply, and (b) the reasons why that authority considers it to be necessary to introduce these measures, including supporting evidence [265]. A measure is to take effect at the moment that the notice is published, or at a time which the notice specifies – if later than its publication; the measure is only to be applied prospectively [266]. Any measure that is imposed under a rule in the previous paragraph is to be valid for an initial

---

[738] Paragraphs 3 and 4 of Article 17 of Regulation (EU) No 236.2012 provide 2 further exemptions, which are less comprehensive than that for market making in Article 17(1) of that Regulation.

[739] A 'liquid share' is as defined in Article 22 of Regulation (EC) No 1287/2006 (Regulation (EU) No 236/2012 (as amended to 28/08/14), Article 23(5)). A 'liquid share' (i.e., a share "considered to have a liquid market") is a share that "is traded daily," "with a free float" of at least 500 million Euros, and either (a) there are on average at least 500 transactions in the share each day, or (b) the share's average daily turnover is at least 2 million Euros (Regulation (EC) No 1287/2006, Article 22(1)).

[740] The Commission is to "adopt delegated acts," in order to determine "a significant fall in value for financial instruments other than liquid shares" – taking into consideration "the specificities of each class of financial instrument and the differences of volatility" (Regulation (EU) No 236/2012 (as amended to 28/08/14), Article 23(7)). Further to Article 23(7) of Regulation (EU) No 236/2012, Article 23 of Commission Delegated Regulation (EU) No 918/2012 lays down these values. For instance, "a significant fall in value for a money-market instrument" is a decrease of at least 1.5% in the price of a money market instrument during a single day of trading (Commission Delegated Regulation (EU) No 918/2012 (as amended to 23/01/15), Article 23(4)).

[741] This measure may apply to: (i) transactions that concern all financial instruments, financial instruments of a particular class, or a specific financial instrument, and/or (ii) "in circumstances or be subject to exceptions" which the competent authority specifies (Regulation (EU) No 236/2012 (as amended to 28/08/14), Article 20(3)).

[742] This measure may apply to: (i) sovereign credit default swap transactions of a particular class, or a specific credit default swap deal, and/or (ii) "in circumstances or be subject to exceptions" which the competent authority specifies (Regulation (EU) No 236/2012 (as amended to 28/08/14), Article 21(3)).

period of up to 3 months from the date of publication of the notice – which may be renewed for further periods of up to 3 months each, "if the grounds for taking the measure continue to apply" [267].

Member States are to "establish rules on penalties and administrative measures" that apply to breaches of Regulation (EU) No 236/2012, and are to "take all measures necessary to ensure that they are implemented"; those sanctions are to be "effective, proportionate and dissuasive" [268]. These countries are to inform the Commission and the ESMA of the sanctions that they have proposed, by 1st July 2012, and shall notify those institutions promptly of any subsequent amendments to the measures [269]. These provisions are addressed to Member States – i.e., they are in the form of a Directive, thereby mirroring Article 12 of the EMIR – which also concerns penalties[743].

Regulation (EU) No 236/2012 is a sensible piece of legislation – holding uncovered short positions in securities invokes settlement risk and, if extensive, the risk of financial instability. Furthermore, it is inherently unacceptable for a person to offer to sell an asset that is outside his/her/its ownership, possession or control.

Credit Rating Agencies

International guidance in respect of national (and regional) legal treatment of credit rating agencies in the wake of the GFC dates back to the Washington Summit of November 2008, in which the G20 recommended that these organisations were to meet IOSCO standards, avoid conflicts of interest, divulge more information to issuers and to investors, and differentiate ratings for complex financial instruments, and that credit rating agencies which provide public ratings were to be registered[744]. Regulation (EC) No 1060/2009 "lays down conditions for the issuing of credit ratings and rules on the organisation and conduct of credit rating agencies," in order to further the independence of those entities, avoid conflicts of interest and enhance the protection of consumers and investors[745] [270]. It applies to credit ratings which are issued by credit institutions that are registered within the EEA, and which are distributed to subscribers or publicly disclosed [271].

For the purposes of Regulation (EC) No 1060/2009, 'credit rating' means an opinion concerning the creditworthiness of an entity, a debt or a financial instrument, or of an issuer of a debt or a financial instrument, which is provided "using an established and defined ranking system of rating categories"[746] [272]. For the purposes of Regulation (EC) No

---

[743] See fn 719, for this point in respect of Article 12 of the EMIR.

[744] See the subsection entitled 'Enhancing sound regulation', in the section entitled 'Progress in the G20/FSB System from November 2008' in Chapter 2, for the G20's comments at the Washington Summit on credit rating agencies.

[745] Regulation (EC) No 1060/2009 "also lays down obligations for issuers, originators and sponsors established in the Union regarding structured finance instruments" (Regulation (EC) No 1060/2009 (as amended to 22/05/14), Article 1). The reference in Article 1 of Regulation (EC) No 1060/2009 to 'structured finance instruments' corresponds to the expression 'complex financial instruments' (see the previous sentence in the text). Thus, the EU institutions apply the international framework for the regulation of credit rating agencies, in their enactment of Regulation (EC) No 1060/2009. References to the 'Union' in Regulation (EC) No 1060/2009 are to be read as references to the EEA, as this Regulation is labelled 'Text with EEA relevance'.

[746] For example, Standard and Poor's Rating Services' long-term credit ratings run from the investment grade categories of AAA, AA+, AA, AA-, A+, A, A-, BBB+, BBB, BBB-, through the high-yield classes of BB+, BB, BB-, B+, B, B-, CCC+, CCC, CCC-, CC+, CC, CC-, C+, C, C-, to the rating for a default – D. Further

1060/2009, 'credit rating agency' means a legal person that issues "credit ratings on a professional basis" [273]. "Credit institutions, investment firms, insurance undertakings, reinsurance undertakings, institutions for occupational retirement provision, management companies, investment companies, alternative investment fund managers and central counterparties" are only to "use credit ratings for regulatory purposes," if these ratings are issued by credit rating agencies that are founded in the EEA and registered in conformity with Regulation (EC) No 1060/2009 [274]. These entities are to "make their own credit risk assessment," and are not to "solely or mechanistically rely on credit ratings" in order to evaluate the creditworthiness of an entity or a financial instrument [275].

A credit rating agency must be a legal person that is established in the EEA, in order to be eligible to apply for registration [276]. The registration is effective throughout the EEA, as soon as the ESMA's decision to register the credit rating agency has taken effect [277]. A registered credit rating agency is to continuously observe the conditions for initial registration, and is to promptly inform the ESMA of "any material changes to the conditions for initial registration" – which include the opening or shutting of a branch within the EEA [278]. The credit rating agency is to submit its application for registration to the ESMA, which is to contain information on the issues that Annex II to Regulation (EC) No 1060/2009 sets out[747] [279]. The ESMA is not to impose requirements on the credit rating agency for which Regulation (EC) No 1060/2009 does not provide [280]. The credit ratings relating to entitites that are founded, or financial instruments that originate, in third countries, and which are issued by a credit rating agency that is established in a third country, may be used in the EEA (without the need for endorsement under Article 4(3) of Regulation (EC) No 1060/2009[748]), as long as: (a) that agency is authorised/registered and supervised in the third country, (b) the Commission has taken "an equivalence decision" that complies with Article 5(6) of Regulation (EC) No 1060/2009[749], (c) the co-operation arrangements to which Article

---

detail on these ratings is available in Table 1 of the Standard and Poor's webpage that defines its credit ratings, i.e., at https://www.standardandpoors.com/en_US/web/guest/article/-/view/sourceId/504352. For the purposes of Regulation (EC) No 1060/2009, 'rating category' means a symbol for rating (such as those in the previous sentence), which is "used in a credit rating to provide a relative measure of risk to distinguish the different risk characteristics of the types of rated entities, issuers and financial instruments or other assets" (Regulation (EC) No 1060/2009 (as amended to 22/05/14), Article 3(1)(h)).

[747] The credit rating agency's application for registration is to include the following information: "1. Full name of the credit rating agency, address of the registered office within the [EEA] 2. Name and contact details of a contact person and of the compliance officer 3. Legal status 4. Class of credit ratings for which the credit rating agency is applying to be registered 5. Ownership structure 6. Organisational structure and corporate governance 7. Financial resources to perform credit rating activities 8. Staffing of credit rating agency and its expertise 9. Information regarding subsidiaries of credit rating agency 10. Description of the procedures and methodologies used to issue and review credit ratings 11. Policies and procedures to identify, manage and disclose any conflicts of interests 12. Information regarding rating analysts 13. Compensation and performance evaluation arrangements 14. Services other then credit rating activities, which the credit rating agency intends to provide 15. Programme of operations, including indications of where the main business activities are expected to be carried out, branches to be established, and setting out the type of business envisaged 16. Documents and detailed information related to the expected use of endorsement 17. Documents and detailed information related to the expected outsourcing arrangements including information on entities assuming outsourcing functions." (Regulation (EC) No 1060/2009 (as amended to 22/05/14), Annex II).

[748] Article 4(3) of Regulation (EC) No 1060/2009 lays down conditions with which credit rating activities that result in the issuing in a third country of a credit rating are to comply, for a credit rating agency founded in the EEA to be eligible to endorse that rating.

[749] If a third country's regulatory structure satisfies the 3 conditions specified therein, then Article 5(6) of Regulation (EC) No 1060/2009 empowers the Commission to take "an equivalence decision," which states: "the legal and supervisory framework of [the named] third country ensures that credit rating agencies authorised or registered in that third country comply with legally binding requirements which are equivalent to

5(7) of Regulation (EC) No 1060/2009 refers are operative[750], (d) the agency's credit ratings and credit rating activities are "not of systemic importance to the financial stability or integrity of the financial markets of" at least one Member State[751], and the agency is certified in conformity with Article 5(2) of Regulation (EC) No 1060/2009[752] [281].

A credit rating agency is to "take all necessary steps" in order to make certain that the issuing of a credit rating or of a rating outlook[753] is unaffected by any current or potential conflicts of interest or business relationship which involves that agency, its employees, its managers, its rating analysts[754], its shareholders, or any other individual "whose services are placed at the disposal or under the control[755] of the credit agency, or any person directly or indirectly linked to it by control"[756] [282]. A member or a shareholder of a credit rating agency, who holds 5% or more of the capital of, or the voting rights in, that agency – "or in a company which has the power to exercise control or a dominant influence over" the agency, is to be prohibited from: (a) holding at least 5% of any other credit rating agency's capital, (b) possessing the power or the right to exercise at least 5% of the voting rights in any other credit rating agency, (c) having the power or the right to appoint or to remove members of the board of directors of any other credit rating agency, (d) being a member of the board of directors of any other credit rating agency, and (e) having the power to exert, or exercising, "control or a dominant influence over any other credit rating agency"[757] [283].

A credit rating agency is to make sure that individuals "whose services are placed at its disposal or under its control and who are directly involved in credit rating activities have

---

the requirements resulting from this Regulation and which are subject to effective supervision and enforcement in that third country."

[750] The ESMA is to set up co-operation agreements with "the relevant supervisory authorities of third countries whose legal and supervisory frameworks" the Commission has considered to be equivalent to Regulation (EC) No 1060/2009, in conformity with Article 5(6) of Regulation (EC) No 1060/2009 (see fn 749); these agreements are to specify: (a) the process of information exchange between the ESMA and the third countries' supervisory authorities, and (b) the procedures for the co-ordination of activities of superintendence (Regulation (EC) No 1060/2009 (as amended to 22/05/14), Article 5(7)).

[751] As Regulation (EC) No 1060/2009 is labelled 'Text with EEA relevance', 'Member State' within this Regulation means 'EEA State'.

[752] The credit rating agency is to submit to the ESMA its application for certification, which must contain information on the issues that Annex II to Regulation (EC) No 1060/2009 sets out (Regulation (EC) No 1060/2009 (as amended to 22/05/14), Articles 5(2) and 15(1)). See fn 747, for Annex II to Regulation (EC) No 1060/2009.

[753] For the purposes of Regulation (EC) No 1060/2009, 'rating outlook' means an opinion concerning the probable direction of a credit rating (Regulation (EC) No 1060/2009 (as amended to 22/05/14), Article 3(1)(w)).

[754] For the purposes of Regulation (EC) No 1060/2009, 'rating analyst' means a person who undertakes analytical functions that are required for a credit rating to be issued (Regulation (EC) No 1060/2009 (as amended to 22/05/14), Article 3(1)(d)).

[755] For the purposes of Regulation (EC) No 1060/2009, 'control' means the relationship between a parent company and its subsidiary, or a close link between a (natural or legal) person and a company (Regulation (EC) No 1060/2009 (as amended to 22/05/14), Article 3(1)(j)).

[756] In order to ensure observance of this provision, the credit rating agency is to comply with the requirements that Sections A and B of Annex I to Regulation (EC) No 1060/2009 set out (Regulation (EC) No 1060/2009 (as amended to 22/05/14), Article 6(2)). Section A of Annex I to Regulation (EC) No 1060/2009 contains organisational requirements for independence and avoidance of conflicts of interests; for instance, point 3 of this Section states: "A credit rating agency shall establish adequate policies and procedures to ensure compliance with its obligations under this Regulation". Section B of Annex I to Regulation (EC) No 1060/2009 lays down organisational requirements for independence and avoidance of conflicts of interests; for instance, point 2 of that Section declares: "A credit rating agency shall disclose to the public the names of the rated entities or related third parties from which it receives more than 5% of its annual revenue.."

[757] This provision "does not apply to investments in other credit rating agencies belonging to the same group of credit rating agencies" (Regulation (EC) No 1060/2009 (as amended to 22/05/14), Article 6a(2)).

appropriate knowledge and experience" to be able to carry out their duties[758] [284]. It is to put "an appropriate gradual rotation mechanism" in place for each person within the agency who is concerned with credit ratings[759] [285]. The remuneration and the performance evaluation of employees who participate in the credit rating process or the rating outlook procedure, are not to depend upon the amount of revenue that the agency receives from its rated entitites or third parties which are related to them [286].

A credit rating agency is to divulge to the public the methodologies, descriptions of models, and the essential assumptions for rating, which it uses in its credit rating activities, as well as substantial changes in these items [287]. It is to use methodologies for credit rating that are "rigorous, systematic, continuous and subject to valuation based on historical experience" [288].

A credit rating agency is to monitor credit ratings, and to review its credit methodologies and ratings "on an ongoing basis and at least annually"; it is to set up internal arrangements in order to monitor the effect "of changes in macroeconomic or financial market conditions on credit ratings" [289]. Credit rating agencies are to review their sovereign ratings[760] at least semi-annually [290].

If an issuer, or a related third party[761] wishes to solicit a credit rating for a structured finance instrument[762], it is to appoint at least 2 credit rating agencies to supply credit ratings

---

[758] The credit rating agency is to ensure that these individuals fulfil the requirements that Section C of Annex I to Regulation (EC) No 1060/2009 lays down (Regulation (EC) No 1060/2009 (as amended to 22/05/14), Article 7(3)). Section C to Annex I to Regulation (EC) No 1060/2009 specifies rules that concern persons who are directly involved in credit rating activities, in order to promote their independence and to avoid conflicts of interests; for instance, point 4 of that Section states: "Persons referred to in point 1 [i.e., individuals whose services are put the disposal of, or under the control of, the credit rating agency, and who are directly involved in credit rating activities, and persons who are closely associated with those individuals] shall not solicit or accept money, gifts or favours from anyone with whom the credit rating agency does business.."

[759] Point 8 of Section C to Annex I to Regulation (EC) No 1060/2009 provides firm guidance as to this rotation mechanism, and is as follows: "For the purposes of Article 7(4) [of Regulation (EC) No 1060/2009 – i.e., the current provision in the text]: (a) credit rating agencies shall ensure that the lead rating analysts shall not be involved in credit rating activities related to the same rated entity or a related third party for a period exceeding four years; (b) credit rating agencies other than those appointed by an issuer or a related third party and all credit rating agencies issuing sovereign ratings shall ensure that: (i) the rating analysts shall not be involved in credit rating activities related to the same rated entity or a related third party for a period exceeding five years; (ii) the persons approving credit ratings shall not be involved in credit rating activities related to the same rated entity or a related third party for a period exceeding seven years. The persons referred to in points (a) and (b) of the [previous sentence] shall not be involved in credit rating activities related to the rated entity or a related third party referred to in those points within two years of the end of the periods set out in those points". See fn 763, for the definition of 'lead rating analyst'.

[760] For the purposes of Regulation (EC) No 1060/2009, 'sovereign rating' means a credit rating in cases in which: (i) the entity rated is a country, or a regional or local authority of a country; (ii) the issuer of the debt or financial instrument is a country, a regional or local authority of a country, or a special purpose vehicle of a country, regional authority or local authority; (iii) the issuer is an international financial institution that is founded by at least 2 Member States, whose purpose is to mobilise funding and to provide financial assistance to those of its members which are encountering, or are endangered by, grievous financing difficulties (Regulation (EC) No 1060/2009 (as amended to 22/05/14), Article 3(1)(v)).

[761] For the purposes of Regulation (EC) No 1060/2009, 'related third party' means a party which interacts with a credit rating agency on behalf of a rated entity – including any person who is connected to the latter by control (Regulation (EC) No 1060/2009 (as amended to 22/05/14), Article 3(1)(i)). See fn 755, for the definition of 'control'.

[762] For the purposes of Regulation (EC) No 1060/2009, 'structured finance instrument' means assets that result from a securitisation or scheme to which Article 4(36) of the CRD refers (Regulation (EC) No 1060/2009 (as amended to 22/05/14), Article 3(1)(l)). The CRD is repealed "with effect from 1 January 2014"; all references to that Directive are to be construed as references to CRD IV and to the CRR, and to be read in conformity with the correlation table in Annex II to CRD IV and in Annex IV to the CRR (CRD IV (as amended to

independently of each other [291]. The issuer or its related third party is to make sure that the designated credit rating agencies observe the following conditions: (a) they are not members of the same group of credit rating agencies, (b) they are neither members nor shareholders of any other credit rating agencies, (c) they have neither the power nor the right to exercise voting rights in any other credit rating agencies, (d) they have neither the power nor the right to appoint or to remove members of the board of directors of any other credit rating agency, (e) no member of their boards of directors is a member of the board of directors of any other credit rating agency, and (f) they do not exert, or have the power to apply, "control or a dominant influence over any" other credit rating agency [292].

A credit rating agency is to divulge any credit rating, rating outlook, and decision to cease its provision of a credit rating (including complete reasons for this decision), "on a non-selective basis and in a timely manner"[763] [293]. It is to "fully disclose to the public" and to promptly update, information concerning the issues that Part I of Section E of Annex I to Regulation (EC) No 1060/2009 sets out [294]. This Part is entitled 'General disclosures'; it requires the credit rating agency to divulge the following information: (i) the fact that the agency is registered in accordance with Regulation (EC) No 1060/2009, (ii) any actual and potential conflicts of interest that may affect the work of individuals who are involved in activities which relate to credit rating, (iii) a catalogue of its ancillary services, (iv) the agency's policy in respect of its publication of credit ratings and communications that relate to these, (v) "the general nature of" the agency's arrangements for being paid, (vi) the methodologies, models and vital assumptions that are used in the agency's credit rating activities, and major changes in these, (vii) any substantial change to the agency's procedures, resources or systems, and (viii) the agency's code of conduct [295].

A credit rating agency is to supply to the ESMA, by 31st March each year, the following information: (i) a listing of the fees charged to every customer for each of the latter's credit ratings and for any ancillary services, (ii) the agency's pricing policy, (iii) a catalogue of those clients "whose contribution to the growth rate in the generation of revenue of the credit rating agency in the previous financial year exceeded the growth rate in the total revenues of the credit rating agency in that year by a factor of more than 1.5 times" – as long as the agency's income from that customer exceeded 0.25% of the former's global revenues, and

---

12/06/14), Article 163). Article 4(36) of the CRD is superseded by Article 4(1)(61) of the CRR (CRR (as amended to 17/01/15), Annex IV). Article 4(1)(61) of the CRR states: "'securitisation' means a transaction or scheme, whereby the credit risk associated with an exposure or pool of exposures is tranched, having both of the following characteristics: (a) payments in the transaction or scheme are dependent upon the performance of the exposure or pool of exposures; (b) the subordination of tranches determines the distribution of losses during the ongoing life of the transaction or scheme;."

[763] The credit rating agency is to ensure that its credit ratings and rating outlooks comply with Section D of Annex I to Regulation (EC) No 1060/2009, and is to only present data that relate to those ratings (Regulation (EC) No 1060/2009 (as amended to 22/05/14), Article 10(2)). Section D of Annex I to Regulation (EC) No 1060/2009 is entitled 'Rules on the presentation of credit ratings and rating outlooks', and contains general duties, additional obligations with regard to credit ratings of structured finance instruments, and additional duties in respect of sovereign ratings; for instance, point 1 (a general obligation) of that Section declares: "A credit rating agency shall ensure that any credit rating and rating outlook states clearly and prominently the name and job title of the lead rating analyst in a given credit rating activity and the name and position of the person primarily responsible for approving the credit rating or rating outlook". For the purposes of Regulation (EC) No 1060/2009, 'lead rating analyst' means the individual with the main responsibility for the elaboration of a credit rating, or for communication with the issuer with regard to a specific credit rating or to the credit rating of a particular financial instrument, and (if relevant) for the preparation of recommendations to the rating committee in respect of that credit rating (Regulation (EC) No 1060/2009 (as amended to 22/05/14), Article 3(1)(e)).

(iv) a listing of the credit ratings that the agency issued during the year [296]. A registered or certified credit rating agency is to publish data on its past performance – in a central repository that the ESMA has established, and is to supply information to this repository on a standard form that the ESMA provides [297].

If, in fulfilling its obligations under Regulation (EC) No 1060/2009, the "ESMA finds that there are serious indications of the possible existence of facts liable to constitute one or more of the infringements listed in Annex III" to that Regulation[764], then the ESMA is to internally appoint an independent officer to examine the issue [298]. The investigating officer is to look into the alleged contraventions – taking into consideration any comments that are made by the persons who are "subject to investigation," and is to submit a complete file which contains his/her findings to the ESMA's Board of Supervisors; in order to conduct his/her activities, the investigating officer may require the provision of information under Article 23b of Regulation (EC) No 1060/2009[765], and to carry out investigations and on-site inspections in conformity with Articles 23c and 23d of Regulation (EC) No 1060/2009[766]; when using these powers, the investigating officer is to comply with Article 23a of Regulation (EC) No 1060/2009[767] [299]. Upon completion of his/her investigation, and before sending the file containing his/her findings to the ESMA's Board of Supervisors, the investigating officer is to provide the persons who are subject to investigation with the opportunity to be heard on the issues that are being investigated; he/she is to base his/her findings only on facts about which those persons have been given the chance to comment [300]. The persons who are subject to investigation are to be permitted access to this file, "subject to the legitimate interest of other persons in the protection of their business secrets"; this right of access is not to extend to confidential information that affects third parties [301].

---

[764] Part I of Annex III to Regulation (EC) No 1060/2009 is entitled 'Infringements related to conflicts of interest, organisational or operational requirements', and lists these contraventions; for example, point 1 of this Part states: "The credit rating agency infringes Article 4(3) [of Regulation (EC) No 1060/2009 (see fn 748)] by endorsing a credit rating issued in a third country without complying with the conditions set out in that paragraph, unless the reason for that infringement is outside the credit rating agency's knowledge or control". Part II of Annex III to Regulation (EC) No 1060/2009 is entitled 'Infringements related to obstacles to the supervisory activities', and lists those transgressions; for instance, point 4 of this Part declares: "The credit rating agency infringes Article 11(2) [of Regulation (EC) No 1060/2009 (see the final sentence in the previous paragraph in the text)] by not making available the required information or by not providing that information in the required format as referred to in that paragraph.."

[765] The ESMA may require credit rating agencies, persons who are "involved in credit rating activities," and persons who are "closely and substantially related or connected to credit rating agencies or credit rating activities," to supply "all information that is necessary in order to carry out its duties under [Regulation (EC) No 1060/2009]" (Regulation (EC) No 1060/2009 (as amended to 22/05/14), Article 23b(1)).

[766] In order to fulfil its obligations under Regulation (EC) No 1060/2009, the ESMA may carry out "all necessary investigations of persons" to whom Article 23b(1) of Regulation (EC) No 1060/2009 (see fn 765) refers; to this end, persons whom the ESMA authorises are empowered to: (a) examine material that is relevant to the performance of its tasks, (b) take, or acquire, certified copies of, or excerpts from, this material, (c) require any person to whom Article 23(b)(1) of Regulation (EC) No 1060/2009 refers to provide explanations on documents or facts that relate to the purpose and the subject matter of the inspection, and to record these, (d) interview any person who consents to be interviewed, in order to collect information that concerns the subject matter of an investigation, and (e) ask for "records of telephone and data traffic" (Regulation (EC) No 1060/2009 (as amended to 22/05/14), Article 23c(1)). In order to fulfil its tasks under Regulation (EC) No 1060/2009, the ESMA may carry out "all necessary on-site inspections at the business premises of the legal persons" to which Article 23b(1) refers (Regulation (EC) No 1060/2009 (as amended to 22/05/14), Article 23d(1)).

[767] The powers that Articles 23b, 23c and 23d of Regulation (EC) No 1060/2009 confer upon the ESMA (or any person whom the ESMA authorises) are not to be used to require information or documents to be disclosed that "are subject to legal privilege" (Regulation (EC) No 1060/2009 (as amended to 22/05/14), Article 23a).

On the basis of the file, and when "the persons concerned" request, "after having heard the persons subject to investigation in accordance with Articles 25 and 36c" of Regulation (EC) No 1060/2009[768], the ESMA's Board of Supervisors is to decide whether the latter persons have committed one or more of the transgressions that Annex III to Regulation (EC) No 1060/2009 lists[769], and, if so, is to "take a supervisory measure in accordance with Article 24" of that Regulation[770] and levy a fine in conformity with Article 36a of the Regulation[771] [302]. The investigating officer is not to become involved in the decision-making process of the ESMA's Board of Supervisors [303]. If the ESMA "finds that there are serious indications of the possible existence of facts liable to constitute criminal offences," then it is to refer issues for criminal prosecution to the relevant domestic authorities [304].

There are 40 registered credit rating agencies – these are resident in the EEA, and 4 certified credit rating agencies – 2 that are resident in the United States of America, one from Japan, and one from Mexico [305]. Thus, entities that require credit ratings have sufficient choice to be equipped to satisfy the requirements of Regulation (EC) No 1060/2009 to regularly change credit rating agencies and, in specified cases, to have more than one rating. Although extensive, this Regulation addresses concerns about credit rating agencies in the

---

[768] Article 25(1) of Regulation (EC) No 1060/2009 states: "Before taking any decision under Article 24(1) [of Regulation (EC) No 1060/2009 (see fn 770)], ESMA's Board of Supervisors shall give the persons subject to the proceedings the opportunity to be heard on ESMA's findings. ESMA's Board of Supervisors shall base its decisions only on findings on which the persons subject to the proceedings have had the opportunity to comment. The [previous 2 sentences] shall not apply if urgent action is needed in order to prevent significant and imminent damage to the financial system. In such a case ESMA's Board of Supervisors may adopt an interim decision and shall give the persons concerned the opportunity to be heard as soon as possible after taking its decision". Article 36c of Regulation (EC) No 1060/2009 declares: "Before taking any decision imposing a fine ... under Article 36a [of Regulation (EC) No 1060/2009 (see fn 771)], ESMA's Board of Supervisors shall base its decisions only on findings on which the persons subject to the proceedings have had the opportunity to comment.."

[769] See fn 764, for Annex III to Regulation (EC) No 1060/2009.

[770] Article 24(1) of Regulation (EC) No 1060/2009 states: "Where, in accordance with Article 23e(5) [of Regulation (EC) No 1060/2009 – i.e., the sentence in the text that corresponds to this footnote], ESMA's Board of Supervisors finds that a credit rating agency has committed one of the infringements listed in Annex III [to Regulation (EC) No 1060/2009 (see fn 764)], it shall take one or more of the following decisions: (a) withdraw the registration of the credit rating agency; (b) temporarily prohibit the credit rating agency from issuing credit ratings with effect throughout the [EEA], until the infringement has been brought to an end; (c) suspend the use, for regulatory purposes, of the credit ratings issued by the credit rating agency with effect throughout the [EEA], until the infringement has been brought to an end; (d) require the credit rating agency to bring the infringement to an end; (e) issue public notices". Article 24(2) of Regulation (EC) No 1060/2009 declares: "When taking the decisions referred to in [Article 24(1) of Regulation (EC) No 1060/2009], ESMA's Board of Supervisors shall take into account the nature and seriousness of the infringement, having regard to the following criteria: (a) the duration and frequency of the infringement; (b) whether the infringement has revealed serious or systemic weaknesses in the undertaking's procedures or in its management systems or internal controls; (c) whether financial crime was facilitated, occasioned or otherwise attributable to the infringement; (d) whether the infringement has been committed intentionally or negligently". The ESMA's Board of Supervisors is to inform the EBA and the EIOPA of the decisions to which Article 24(1)(a)-(c) of Regulation (EC) No 1060/2009 refers, before it takes those decisions (Regulation (EC) No 1060/2009 (as amended to 22/05/14), Article 24(3)).

[771] Article 36a(1) of Regulation (EC) No 1060/2009 states: "Where, in accordance with Article 23e(5) [of Regulation (EC) No 1060/2009 – i.e., the sentence in the text that corresponds to this footnote], ESMA's Board of Supervisors finds that a credit rating agency has, intentionally or negligently, committed one of the infringements listed in Annex III [to Regulation (EC) No 1060/2009 (see fn 764)], it shall adopt a decision imposing a fine in accordance with [Article 36a(2) of Regulation (EC) No 1060/2009]. An infringement by a credit rating agency shall be considered to have been committed intentionally if ESMA finds objective factors which demonstrate that the credit rating agency or its senior management acted deliberately to commit the infringement". Article 36a(2) of Regulation (EC) No 1060/2009 provides maximum and minimum amounts payable, in Euros, for the infringements to which the points in Annex III of that Regulation refer.

light of the GFC – such as the subjectivity of credit ratings, a lack of thorough preparation in allotting a credit rating to an entity or a financial instrument, and the shortage of competition and accountability in this field. The ESMA directly supervises credit rating agencies – rather than the normal model in which the relevant ESA oversees the national regulatory authorities, which supervise the financial firms providing the services. This reflects the particular importance that the EU institutions give to monitoring credit ratings across the EEA.

UCITS

In 2008, the Commission proposed to recast the UCITS Directive, in response to alleged inefficiencies; these included, in particular, oppressive notification in respect of cross-border distribution of UCITS, a simplified prospectus that "is too long, too complex, and which does not allow for useful comparisons," and the absence of an EU-wide framework to counter the "[p]roliferation of a high number of small funds" – with their high level of investment costs per investor [306]. The UCITS V Directive resulted. This was amended in 2014, in order to clarify the functions of UCITS depositaries and the scope of their liability for assets of investors that are lost, introduce regulation on the remuneration policies to be applied to the staff of UCITS management companies and third parties who materially affect the risk profile of the funds, and lay down minimum administrative sanctions to be available to supervisors in order to address breaches of the UCITS rules[772] [307]. The remainder of this subsection considers changes that the consolidated UCITS V Directive has made to provisions of the consolidated UCITS Directive that Chapter 1 describes.

The competent authority "of the UCITS home Member State[773]" is only to authorise an UCITS if: (a) it finds that the investment company does not observe "the preconditions laid down in Chapter V[774]," or (b) the management company is not licensed to manage UCITS in its home Member State [308]. This is an adaptation in terminology from the equivalent provision in the consolidated UCITS Directive[775], but with the same meaning. The UCITS V Directive includes the following new provision: the competent authority of the UCITS home Member State is to inform the management company or the investment company (if applicable), as to whether or not it has granted the authorisation of the UCITS – "within 2 months of the submission of a completed application" [309]. The authorisation requirements

---

[772] These changes to the UCITS V Directive are contained in Directive 2014/91/EU of the European Parliament and of the Council of 23 July 2014 amending Directives 2009/65/EC on the coordination of laws, regulations and administrative provisions relating to undertakings for collective investment in transferable securities (UCITS) as regards depositary functions, remuneration policies and sanctions. By 18th March 2016, Member States are to adopt, publish and apply the national "laws, regulations and administrative provisions [that are] necessary to comply with [Directive 2014/91/EU]" (Directive 2014/91/EU, Article 2(1)).

[773] For the purposes of the UCITS V Directive, "'UCITS home Member State' means the Member State in which the UCITS is authorised ..." (UCITS V Directive (as amended to 28/08/14), Article 2(1)(e)). As the UCITS V Directive is labelled 'Text with EEA relevance', 'Member State' within that Directive means 'EEA State'.

[774] Chapter V of the UCITS V Directive is entitled 'Obligations Regarding Investment Companies', and contains Articles 27-31 of that Directive.

[775] See the 4th paragraph of the subsection entitled 'UCITS', in the section entitled 'Securities Legislation' in Chapter 1, for the corresponding provision in the consolidated UCITS Directive.

for a management company are very similar in the UCITS V Directive to those in the consolidated UCITS Directive[776], as are the operating conditions[777].

Directive 2014/91/EU introduces new provisions into the UCITS V Directive in respect of remuneration policies and practices for management companies. Each Member State is to ensure that these policies and practices are "consistent with, and promote, sound and effective risk management" [310]. They are to apply to "those categories of staff ... whose professional activities have a material impact on the risk profiles of the management companies of the UCITS that they manage" [311]. In establishing their remuneration policies, management companies are to comply with 18 specified principles "in a way and to the extent that it is appropriate to their size, internal organisation and the nature, scope and complexity of their activities" [312]. For example, one of these principles requires each management company's remuneration policy to be "in line with the business strategy, objectives, values and interests of the management company and the UCITS that it manages and of the investors in such UCITS, and include measures to avoid conflicts of interest" [313]. Management companies which are "significant in terms of their size or of the size of the UCITS that they manage, their international organisation and the nature, scope and complexity of their activities" are to set up a remuneration committee (of their board of directors), which is to prepare decisions that concern remuneration that the board is to take[778] [314]. These rules are analogous to Articles 92 to 95 of CRD IV – which provide for remuneration policies and a remuneration committee in respect of banks and investment firms[779].

The UCITS V Directive introduces the following provision in respect of passporting. If an authorised management company plans only to market the units of the UCITS that it manages in a Member State other than the UCITS home Member State, without founding a branch and without proposing to provide any other services or to pursue any other activities, then this marketing is merely subject to the requirements of Chapter XI of the UCITS V Directive [315]. This chapter is entitled 'Obligations Concerning Information to be Provided to Investors'. Thus, in the most straightforward case of passporting, no additional administrative formalities are required.

The essence of the structure for management companies to provide services through a branch to another Member State, remains unchanged from that in the consolidated UCITS Directive[780]. However there are modifications – for instance, in addition to specifying the branch's planned services and activities and its organisational structure, the programme of operations for the new branch is to include a description of the arrangements and processes

---

[776] The drafters of the UCITS V Directive have replaced '*inter alia*' in the consolidated UCITS Directive with 'at least' (UCITS Directive (as amended to 19/03/08, Article 5a(1)(c); UCITS V Directive (as amended to 28/08/14), Article 7(1)(c)).

[777] See the 6th and 7th paragraphs of the subsection entitled 'UCITS', in the section entitled 'Securities Legislation' in Chapter 1, for management companies' authorisation requirements and operating conditions, respectively.

[778] The remuneration committee is to be established in a manner which "enables it to exercise competent and independent judgment on remuneration policies and practices and the incentives created for managing risk" (UCITS V Directive (as amended to 28/08/14), Article 14b(4)).

[779] The similarity between Article 14b(4) of the UCITS V Directive and Article 95 of CRD IV is striking. For example, compare the following provision with that in fn 778. The remuneration committee is to be constituted so "as to enable it to exercise competent and independent judgment on remuneration policies and practices and the incentives created for managing risk, capital and liquidity" (CRD IV (as amended to 12/06/14), Article 95(1)).

[780] See the 9th paragraph of the subsection entitled 'UCITS', in the section entitled 'Securities Legislation' in Chapter 1, for provisions on the establishment of a branch by a management company in another Member State under the consolidated UCITS Directive.

that the management company has set up to handle investor complaints [316]. Similarly, this change is made in respect of the programme of operations that the management company is to provide to its home Member State's competent authority, in order for that company to start business in the territory of another Member State using the free movement of services[781] [317]. The 'interests of the general good' phrase disappears from the provisions governing both forms of passporting for management companies.

Although Annex II of the consolidated UCITS V Directive – which specifies the component functions of collective portfolio management, is unchanged from Annex II of the consolidated UCITS Directive, the UCITS V Directive introduces a provision for the passporting of collective portfolio management –through either the foundation of a branch or the free movement of services[782]. These functions are investment management, marketing and administration[783] [318].

Unlike the consolidated UCITS Directive, the UCITS V Directive does not state that host Member States may require branches of foreign management companies to supply the same particulars as national management companies[784]. However, management companies are to ensure that the arrangements and the procedures to which Article 15 of the UCITS V Directive refers[785], enable the competent authority of the UCITS home Member State to acquire the information which is necessary for the monitoring of management companies' observance of the standards that the host Member State sets for them [319].

The consolidated UCITS V Directive specifies the actions that the host Member State's competent authority may take, if the management company continues to contravene the provisions which that country has enacted pursuant to the UCITS V Directive (or continues to refuse to supply to that authority the data which is necessary for the latter to monitor the management company's compliance with "the rules under the responsibility of the management company's host Member State that apply to them"), in spite of the measures that the home Member State's competent authority has applied; these actions are: (a) to "take appropriate measures" to prevent or to punish further contraventions, and insofar as is necessary, to stop the management company from commencing any further business within its territory, and (b) to refer the issue to the ESMA, which may exercise the powers that Article 19 of Regulation (EU) No 1095/2010 confers upon it[786] – in instances in which it considers "that the competent authority of the management company's home Member State has not acted adequately" [320]. The consolidated UCITS V Directive omits the provision in the consolidated UCITS Directive that permits a host Member State to take suitable measures

---

[781] See the 10th paragraph of the subsection entitled 'UCITS', in the section entitled 'Securities Legislation' in Chapter 1, for provisions on the free movement of services in respect of a management company under the consolidated UCITS Directive.

[782] This provision is Article 19 of the UCITS V Directive.

[783] 'Administration' comprises legal services, fund management accounting services, customer enquiries, valuation and pricing, regulatory compliance monitoring, maintenance of the register of unit-holders, the issue and redemption of units, contract settlements and the keeping of records (UCITS V Directive (as amended to 28/08/14), Annex II).

[784] See the 11th paragraph of the subsection entitled 'UCITS', in the section entitled 'Securities Legislation' in Chapter 1, for this statement.

[785] The second paragraph of Article 15 of the UCITS V Directive states: "Management companies shall also establish appropriate procedures and arrangements to make information available at the request of the public or the competent authorities of the UCITS home Member State.."

[786] Article 19 of Regulation (EU) No 1095/2010 is entitled 'Settlement of disagreements between competent authorities in cross-border situations', and contains a procedure for these differences to be resolved.

in order to prevent or to punish transgressions within its territory which contravene rules that are adopted in order to further the general good[787].

This paragraph concerns the authorisation and the operating conditions of investment companies. The UCITS V Directive adds the rule that an investment company's registered office is to be located in that firm's home Member State [321]. The authorisation conditions for an investment company which has not appointed a management company which is authorised under the UCITS V Directive, are unchanged from those in the consolidated UCITS Directive[788].

Directive 2014/91/EU has inserted into the UCITS V Directive revised, expanded obligations concerning the depositary[789]. An investment company and, for each of the common funds which that firm manages, a management company, is to ensure that a single depositary is designated "in accordance with" Chapter IV of the UCITS V Directive[790] [322]. This appointment is to be "evidenced by a written contract," which regulates the flow of information that is considered to be necessary for the depositary to carry out "its functions for the UCITS for which it has been appointed as depositary," as stated in the relevant rules [323]. The depositary's main functions are similar to those specified in the consolidated UCITS Directive[791]; the depositary is to: (a) make sure that the sale, issue, redemption, repurchase and cancellation of units of the UCITS are conducted in conformity with the applicable domestic law and "the fund rules or instruments of incorporation," (b) ensure that the value of the UCITS' units is computed in accordance with that law and those rules or instruments, (c) implement the management company's, or an investment company's, instructions – unless these are at variance with that law or those rules or instruments, (d) ensure that, in transactions which involve the UCITS' assets, any payment is remitted to that UCITS within the normal time limits, and (e) ensure that the UCITS' income is applied in conformity with that law and those rules or instruments [324]. In addition, the depositary is to make sure that the cash flows of the UCITS are monitored thoroughly, and, in particular, that all payments which investors have made on subscribing for units of the UCITS have been received, and that all of the UCITS' cash has been placed in cash accounts which are: (a) opened in the UCITS' name or in the name of the management company or the depositary that is acting on the UCITS' behalf, (b) opened at an entity to which Article 18(1)(a)-(c) of Directive 2006/73/EC[792] refers, and (c) maintained in conformity with the principles that

---

[787] See the 12th paragraph of the subsection entitled 'UCITS', in the section entitled 'Securities Legislation' in Chapter 1, for this provision, which is Article 6c(6) of the consolidated UCITS Directive.

[788] See the 3rd sentence of the 13th paragraph of the subsection entitled 'UCITS', in the section entitled 'Securities Legislation' in Chapter 1, for these authorisation conditions.

[789] See the 14th paragraph of the subsection entitled 'UCITS', in the section entitled 'Securities Legislation' in Chapter 1, for provisions in the consolidated UCITS Directive that concern the depositary.

[790] Chapter IV of the UCITS V Directive is entitled 'Obligations Regarding the Depositary', and contains Articles 22-26a of that Directive.

[791] See the 3rd sentence of the 14th paragraph of the subsection entitled 'UCITS', in the section entitled 'Securities Legislation' in Chapter 1, for these functions under the consolidated UCITS Directive.

[792] 'Directive 2006/73/EC' is Commission Directive 2006/73/EC of 10 August 2006 implementing Directive 2004/39/EC of the European Parliament and of the Council as regards organisational requirements and operating conditions for investment firms and defined terms for the purposes of that Directive. Article 18(1)(a) of Commission Directive 2006/73/EC refers to "a central bank." Article 18(1)(b) of Commission Directive 2006/73/EC refers to "a credit institution." Article 18(1)(c) of Commission Directive 2006/73/EC refers to "a bank authorised in a third country."

Article 16 of Directive 2006/73/EC[793] sets out[794] [325]. For financial instruments which "may be held in custody," the depositary is to: (i) "hold in custody" those financial instruments which "may be registered in financial instruments account" in the books of the depositary, and all financial instruments that can be physically conveyed to the depositary, and (ii) make sure that all financial instruments that can be registered in this account, are registered within segregated accounts in conformity with the principles that Article 16 of Directive 2006/73/EC lays down[795]; these accounts are to be opened in the name of the UCITS – or of the management company acting on the UCITS' behalf [326]. For other assets, the depositary is to: (i) verify the ownership of these assets by the UCITS, or by the management company that acts on the UCITS' behalf, and (ii) maintain, and keep up to date, a record of those assets which it is satisfied are owned by the UCITS, or by the management company acting on the UCITS' behalf [327]. The depositary is to regularly furnish the management company, or the investment company, with a comprehensive list of all the UCITS' assets [328]. The depositary must either have its registered office, or be founded, in the UCITS home Member State [329]. It must be the central bank of a Member State, a credit institution, or another entity that fulfils the capital adequacy requirements of the CRR and possesses own funds of least equal to the amount of initial capital that Article 28(2) of CRD IV specifies – in which it case it needs to satisfy 9 further specified requirements [330]. No company is to act as a depositary and a management company, or as a depositary and an investment company [331]. "In carrying out their respective functions," the depositary and the management/investment company are to "act honestly, fairly, professionally, independently and solely in the interest of the UCITS and the investors of the UCITS"; [332] this duty is more extensive than its predecessor in the consolidated UCITS Directive[796] – honesty, fairness and professionalism are additions.

Chapter VI of the UCITS V Directive, which is entitled 'Merger of UCITS' and contains Articles 37 to 48 of that Directive, contains new provisions – with no equivalent in the UCITS Directive. These rules facilitate domestic and cross-border mergers between UCITS, and between investment compartments of UCITS – "in order to improve the functioning of the internal market" [333].

---

[793] In order to protect clients' rights in respect of funds and financial instruments that they own, each Member State is to require investment firms to: (a) maintain accounts and records as necessary to enable them to promptly distinguish between assets held for one customer, assets held for any other client, and their own assets, (b) keep their accounts and records in a manner that ensures their accuracy, (c) regularly conduct reconciliations between their internal accounts and records, and those of any third parties which hold those assets, (d) take what action is necessary to ensure that any client financial instruments that a third party holds are separately identifiable from the financial instruments that the investment firm owns, and from financial instruments that the third party owns, (e) take what steps are necessary to ensure that any client funds that are placed in a central bank, a credit institution, a bank that is authorised in a third country, or a qualifying money market fund, are held in an account or accounts which are distinct from any accounts that are used to hold the investment firm's funds, and (f) introduce organisational arrangements that are sufficient to minimise the risk of the reduction or loss of client assets – or rights associated with those assets, as a consequence of misuse of the assets, fraud, inadequate maintenance of records, negligence, or poor administration (Commission Directive 2006/73/EC, Article 16(1)).

[794] If the cash accounts are opened in the name of the depositary that is acting on the UCITS' behalf, then none of the depositary's own cash, and no cash of the entity to which point (b) refers, are to be placed in these accounts (UCITS V Directive (as amended to 28/08/14), Article 22(4)).

[795] See fn 793, for these principles.

[796] See the final sentence of the 14th paragraph of the subsection entitled 'UCITS', in the section entitled 'Securities Legislation' in Chapter 1, for the equivalent provision in the UCITS Directive.

Chapter VII of the UCITS V Directive supersedes Section V of the UCITS Directive, in respect of the legal framework for the investment policies of UCITS[797]. The permissible investments of an UCITS – as listed in Article 50(1) of the UCITS V Directive – are unchanged from those described as the allowable investments of an investment company or a unit trust in Article 19(1) of the consolidated UCITS Directive[798]. The remaining provisions of Article 19 of the consolidated UCITS Directive[799] are also unchanged (although ordered differently) in Article 50(2)-(3) of the consolidated UCITS V Directive.

The consolidated UCITS V Directive adds to the rule on the investment/management company's risk-management process (which is unchanged from that in the consolidated UCITS Directive[800]), that the company must "not solely or mechanistically rely on credit ratings issued by credit rating agencies" [334]. The provision in the UCITS Directive which forbids investment companies, and depositaries and management companies that act on behalf of a unit trust, from supplying loans on behalf of, or acting as a guarantor for, any third party[801], remains in the UCITS V Directive – although "unit trust" is changed to "common fund" [335].

The investment limits for UCITS in the consolidated UCITS V Directive are unchanged from those in the consolidated UCITS Directive[802]. Whilst the UCITS Directive stated that a unit trust or an investment company may obtain no more than 10% of the non-voting shares, debt securities or money instruments of any single issuer, and no more than 25% of the units of any UCITS and/or other collective investment undertaking[803], the UCITS V Directive replaces 'a unit trust or an investment company' with 'an UCITS', and 'any UCITS and/or other collective investment undertaking' with 'any UCITS or other collective investment undertaking' – which is necessary, because combining 'and' with a single collective investment undertaking makes no sense [336].

An investment company and, for each common fund[804] that it manages, a management company, is no longer required to publish a simplified prospectus [337]. The prospectus is not only required to contain the information that Schedule A of Annex I to the UCITS V Directive provides – in so far as this information is absent from the fund rules or the company's documents of incorporation (which are to "form an integral part of" that

---

[797] If an UCITS consists of more than one investment compartment, then each compartment is to be treated as a separate UCITS for the purposes of Chapter VII of the UCITS V Directive (UCITS V Directive (as amended to 28/08/14), Article 49).

[798] See the 2nd sentence of the 15th paragraph of the subsection entitled 'UCITS', in the section entitled 'Securities Legislation' in Chapter 1, for the list of permissible investments of an investment company or a unit trust in Article 19(1) of the consolidated UCITS Directive. Paragraphs (e)(i), h(i) and h(iii) of Article 50(1) of the consolidated UCITS V Directive refer to 'Community' (i.e., the European Community) rather than to 'Union' (i.e., the EU), and should be updated to reflect the change in name from the former to the latter since 2009.

[799] See the 3rd, 4th, 5th and 6th sentences of the 15th paragraph of the subsection entitled 'UCITS', in the section entitled 'Securities Legislation' in Chapter 1, for these provisions.

[800] See the opening sentence of the 16th paragraph of the subsection entitled 'UCITS', in the section entitled 'Securities Legislation' in Chapter 1, for this rule.

[801] See the final sentence of the 16th paragraph of the subsection entitled 'UCITS', in the section entitled 'Securities Legislation' in Chapter 1, for this provision.

[802] See the 17th, 18th and 19th paragraphs of the subsection entitled 'UCITS', in the section entitled 'Securities Legislation' in Chapter 1, for these investment limits.

[803] See the final sentence of the 21st paragraph of the subsection entitled 'UCITS', in the section entitled 'Securities Legislation' in Chapter 1, for this provision.

[804] The reference to 'unit trusts' is deleted – see the final sentence of the 22nd paragraph of the subsection entitled 'UCITS', in the section entitled 'Securities Legislation' in Chapter 1.

prospectus and be annexed to it)[805], but also the following data – which is a requirement that Directive 2014/91/EU inserts into the UCITS V Directive: either (a) the details of the firm's current remuneration policy, or (b) a summary of the company's remuneration policy, and a statement which declares that the details of this policy are available at a specified website and that a paper copy will be provided upon request for no charge [338]. The UCITS V Directive requires the "essential elements of the prospectus" to be kept current [339] – as did the consolidated UCITS Directive[806]. Both the former and the latter state that each UCITS is to send its prospectus, any amendments to this document, and their annual and half-yearly reports, to the competent authority[807] – although the UCITS V Directive specifies that the authority is that "of the management company's home Member State" and that these documents are to be sent to this authority "on request" [340].

The rules on UCITS' general obligations in the consolidated UCITS V Directive are consistent with those in the consolidated UCITS Directive[808]. On the 4 occasions upon which the term 'the law' appears in the relevant text[809], it is twice replaced by 'the applicable national law', then once by 'the law of the UCITS home Member State', and then not replaced [341]. The term 'unit trust' is replaced by 'common fund' [342]. – except in the provision that refers to the distribution or reinvestment of an investment company's or a unit trust's income[810], in which case the UCITS V Directive refers to "the income of a UCITS" [343].

Section IX of the UCITS Directive is superseded by Chapter XII of the UCITS V Directive, which is entitled 'Provisions Concerning the Authorities Responsible for Authorisation and Supervision'[811]. The UCITS V Directive specifies the split of supervisory duties between competent authorities of different EEA States even more precisely than does

---

[805] See the 2nd sentence of the 23rd paragraph of the subsection entitled 'UCITS', in the section entitled 'Securities Legislation' in Chapter 1, for a similar statement – which refers to the Schedule A of Annex I to the UCITS Directive (rather to Schedule A of Annex I to the UCITS V Directive). The contents of Schedule A of Annex I to the consolidated UCITS V Directive are similar, but not identical, to those of Schedule A of Annex I to the consolidated UCITS Directive – for instance, point 2 of Schedule A of Annex I to the UCITS Directive states: "2. Information concerning the depositary: 2.1. Name or style, form in law, registered office and head office if different from the registered office; 2.2. Main activity.," whilst point 2 of Schedule A of Annex I to the consolidated UCITS V Directive requires more information about the depositary, as follows: "2. Information concerning the depositary: 2.1. the identity of the depositary of the UCITS and a description of its duties and of conflicts of interest that may arise; 2.2 a description of any safekeeping functions delegated by the depositary, the list of delegates and sub-delegates and any conflicts of interest that may arise from such a delegation; 2.3. a statement to the effect that up-to-date information regarding points 2.1 and 2.2 will be made available to investors on request.."

[806] See the 3rd sentence of the 23rd paragraph of the subsection entitled 'UCITS', in the section entitled 'Securities Legislation' in Chapter 1, for this requirement in the consolidated UCITS Directive – which applied to the simplified prospectus as well as to the main document.

[807] See the opening sentence of the 24th paragraph of the subsection entitled 'UCITS', in the section entitled 'Securities Legislation' in Chapter 1, for this provision.

[808] See the 26th, 27th, 28th and 29th paragraphs of the subsection entitled 'UCITS', in the section entitled 'Securities Legislation' in Chapter 1, for these rules.

[809] The 'relevant text' comprises the paragraphs to which fn 808 refers.

[810] See the final sentence of the 28th paragraph of the subsection entitled 'UCITS', in the section entitled 'Securities Legislation' in Chapter 1, for this provision.

[811] The provisions in the final 3 paragraphs of the subsection entitled 'UCITS', in the section entitled 'Securities Legislation' in Chapter 1, are from Section IX of the consolidated UCITS Directive. The title to Section IX of the UCITS Directive refers to "authorization," whilst that to Chapter VII of the UCITS Directive refers to "authorisation," showing a discreet spelling change in the English language. This also applies in respect of EU banking law: see Baber G. (2015), 'Banking law in the EU: has the law come of age?', *Company Lawyer*, 36(12), 369-370, at 369 – fns 10-11 and accompanying text.

its predecessor (i.e., the UCITS Directive) – the UCITS home Member State's authority is to "be competent to supervise the UCITS"; notwithstanding this, the UCITS host Member State's authority is to be "competent to supervise compliance with the provisions falling outside the field governed by this Directive and the requirements set out in Articles 92 and 94 [of the UCITS V Directive]."[812]. The UCITS V Directive is also more specific about the powers to be granted to the competent authorities than is its predecessor; they are to "be given all supervisory and investigatory powers that are necessary for the exercise of their functions" [344]., which are to include the power to: (a) access, and receive a copy of, all documents, (b) require any person to supply information, (c) conduct on-site inspections, (d) requisition data traffic records which are held by entities that the UCITS V Directive regulates, and those which a telecommunication operator holds "where there is a reasonable suspicion of an infringement and where such records may be relevant to an investigation into" contraventions of the UCITS V Directive, (e) require the termination of any practice which is contrary to the national laws that transpose the UCITS V Directive, (f) request assets to be frozen or confiscated, (g) request professional activity to be suspended, (h) require authorised depositaries, investment companies or management companies to supply information, (i) "adopt any type of measure to" make certain that those entities observe the requirements of the UCITS V Directive, (j) "in the interest of the unit-holders or of the public," require the issue, redemption or repurchase of units to be suspended, (k) revoke the authorisation of a depositary, a management company or an UCITS, (l) refer issues for prosecution under the criminal law, and (m) permit auditors or experts to conduct investigations or verifications [345].

Directive 2014/91/EU inserts new provisions into the UCITS V Directive on administrative sanctions, the essence of which is as follows. Without detriment to the supervisory powers of competent authorities[813] and the right of Member States to prescribe criminal sanctions, Member States are to lay down rules on "effective, proportionate and dissuasive" administrative measures to be applied to companies and persons for breaches of domestic provisions that transpose the UCITS V Directive, and are to take all steps which are necessary to ensure that those measures are implemented[814] [346]. In accordance with domestic law, Member States are to ensure that the administrative measures which are to be applied include: (i) a public statement that identifies the person who is responsible for the transgression, and "the nature of" that breach, (ii) an order which requires the person responsible to stop the illegal conduct and to refrain from repeating it, (iii) suspension or revocation of the management company's or the UCITS' authorisation, (iv) a ban against any individual "who is held responsible," from undertaking management functions in the management company, the investment company, or "other such companies," (v) a maximum

---

[812] Article 92 of the UCITS V Directive states: "UCITS shall, in accordance with the laws, regulations and administrative provisions in force in the Member State where their units are marketed, take the measures necessary to ensure that facilities are available in that Member State for making payments to unit-holders, repurchasing and redeeming units and making available the information which UCITS are required to provide". If an UCITS markets its units in at least one UCITS Member State, then it is to "provide to investors within the territory of such Member State all information and documents which it is required pursuant to Chapter IX [of the UCITS V Directive] to provide to investors in its home Member State …" (UCITS V Directive (as amended to 28/08/14), Article 94(1)).

[813] See the final sentence of the previous paragraph, for these supervisory powers.

[814] By 18th March 2016, Member States are to inform the Commission and the ESMA of the national rules that transpose Article 99(1) of the UCITS V Directive, and are to promptly notify those institutions of any subsequent amendments to those rules (UCITS V Directive (as amended to 28/08/14), Article 99(1)).

fine of at least 5 million Euros for legal and natural persons, or – for legal persons only – 10% of its "total annual turnover" according to the most recent accounts that its board of directors has approved, and (vi) as, as an alternative to point (v), a maximum fine "of at least twice the amount of the benefit derived from the infringement where that benefit can be determined" [347]. Each Member State may pass laws to empower its competent authority to impose additional classes of penalty, or to impose fines that exceed the amounts to which points (v) and (vi) in the previous sentence refer [348]. Member States are to ensure that, when determining the types of administrative measures and the level of fines, their competent authorities make certain that these "are effective, proportionate and dissuasive," taking into account (as appropriate): (a) the severity and the duration of the contravention, (b) the extent to which the relevant person is responsible for that breach, (c) that person's "financial strength," (d) the significance of the profits or losses made by that person, the harm done to other persons and, if applicable, the damage to the economy or "to the functioning of markets," (e) the extent to which the person responsible for the transgression co-operates with the relevant competent authority, (f) previous contraventions by that person, and (g) measures which that person has taken after the breach, in order to prevent its recurrence [349]. Competent authorities are to supply the ESMA each year with data concerning all measures that are imposed, and are to publish this information in an annual report [350].

The obligation of professional secrecy that the consolidated UCITS Directive lays down[815], is unchanged in the UCITS V Directive [351]. Directive 2010/78/EU inserts into the UCITS V Directive the provision that this obligation is not to prevent Member States' competent authorities from sending information to the ESMA in conformity with Regulation (EU) No 1095/2010, or to the European Systemic Risk Board – although those data are to be subject to the duty of professional secrecy [352]. The rule concerning the exchange of information between competent authorities within a Member State and between Member States[816] has been modified; the obligation of professional secrecy and the use of confidential information by the competent authorities that receive it, are not to prevent information exchange within a Member State or between Member States, if this exchange is to take place betwixt a competent authority and (a) entities that are publicly responsible for the supervision of financial organisations and markets, (b) organisations which are concerned with the bankruptcy or the liquidation of UCITS "and of undertakings contributing towards their business activity, or bodies involved in similar procedures," (c) persons who are responsible for the performance of statutory audits of financial institutions' accounts, (d) the ESAs and the European Systemic Risk Board[817] [353].

Whilst, under the UCITS Directive, Member States were to require decisions taken in relation to an UCITS pursuant to rules transposing that Directive to be accompanied by a

---

[815] See the opening sentence of the penultimate paragraph of the subsection entitled 'UCITS', in the section entitled 'Securities Legislation' in Chapter 1, for the obligation of professional secrecy in the consolidated UCITS Directive.

[816] See the 4th sentence of the penultimate paragraph of the subsection entitled 'UCITS', in the section entitled 'Securities Legislation' in Chapter 1, for this rule.

[817] In particular, the duty of professional secrecy and the use of confidential information by the competent authorities that receive it, are not to prevent the performance by these authorities of their supervisory functions, or the divulgation to entities that manage compensation schemes of information that is required for them to be able to perform their functions (UCITS V Directive (as amended to 28/08/14), Article 102(5)).

right to file a court case[818], Member States are to "provide that any decision taken under" rules transposing the UCITS V Directive is to be "properly reasoned and subject to a right to appeal in the courts" [354]. The UCITS V Directive adds the following requirement: Member States are to provide that public, consumer and/or professional organisations may, "in the interests of consumers and in accordance with national law, take action before the courts or competent administrative bodies" in order to make sure that the national rules transposing the UCITS V Directive are applied; to take this action, consumer organisations are to have "a legitimate interest in protecting consumers, and professional organisations are to have "a legitimate interest in protecting their members" [355].

The above paragraphs show that the consolidated UCITS V Directive contains substantial additions and changes from the March 2008 consolidation of its predecessor – the UCITS Directive. There are also discrete modifications to provisions of the earlier legal instrument. Some rules – such as the investment limits for UCITS – remain unaltered. The later instrument uses 'common fund' in place of 'unit trust', and tends to be more full and specific in its legislative style than its predecessor. Given that the UCITS Directive is dated 20th December 1985, was published in the *Official Journal of the European Communities* on 31st December 1985, and required the measures transposing it into national law to enter into force by 1st October 1989 [356]., it is submitted that the UCITS framework has worked well to be operative in 2016 – notwithstanding the unification of Germany, the introduction of the Euro, an increase in EU Membership of more than twofold, and the GFC.

Other Legislation Concerning Investment Funds

The AIFM Directive came into force on 21st July 2011 [357]. With the exception of Articles 35 and Articles 37 to 41 of this Directive – whose transposing legislation is to be adopted in accordance the date stated in a CDR, Member States were to adopt, publish and apply "provisions necessary to comply with [the AIFM Directive]." by 22nd July 2013 [358]. The AIFM Directive "aims to provide for an internal market for AIFMs and a harmonised and stringent regulatory and supervisory framework for the activities within the Union[819] of all AIFMs" – including those whose registered office is located in a third country [359]. Although AIFMs are not to manage UCITS on the basis of an authorisation for which the AIFM Directive provides, that Directive is to apply to AIFMs that manage all types of funds which are outside the scope of the UCITS V Directive – thereby offering "comprehensive and common arrangements for supervision" [360].

Regulation (EU) No 345/2013 of the European Parliament and of the Council of 17 April 2013 on European venture capital funds came into force on 22nd July 2013, with the exception of one provision[820] [361]. This Regulation fits in with the AIFM Directive – it entered into force on the same day as the national legislation transposing the latter, and it applies to funds with assets under management that are no more than 500 million Euros – which is the maximum exemption-from-authorisation threshold for AIFMs [362]. Thus, a small fund is

---

[818] See the final sentence of the subsection entitled 'UCITS', in the section entitled 'Securities Legislation' in Chapter 1, for this provision.

[819] As the AIFM Directive is labelled 'Text with EEA relevance', 'Union' within that Directive means 'EEA'.

[820] This provision is Article 9(5) of Regulation (EU) No 345/2013, which came into force on 15th May 2013 (Regulation (EU) No 345/2013, Article 28).

exempt from authorisation as an AIFM – but may seek recognition as a European venture capital fund under Regulation (EU) No 345/2013 (and thereby use the designation 'EuVECA') [363]., whilst a large fund must obtain authorisation as an AIFM under the AIFM Directive and its transposing legislation. The requirements to qualify as a European Venture Capital Fund under the former are onerous, but are less so than those "that relate to the authorisation and operation of an AIFM in accordance with" the latter [364]. The concept of a European Venture Capital Fund is a good one, especially in the light of the considerable investment that the EU is putting into financing for SMEs across the continent[821].

Regulation (EU) No 346/2013 of the European Parliament and of the Council of 17 April 2013 on European social entrepreneurship funds entered into force on 15th May 2013, but applied from 22nd July 2013 – with the exception of 4 provisions[822], which applied from the former date [365]. Thus, most of the rules in this Regulation applied from the same day as those in Regulation (EU) No 345/2013 and in the domestic regulation transposing the AIFM Directive – 22nd July 2013. Regulation (EU) 346/2013 lays down requirements for investments funds to qualify as a European Social Entrepreneurship Fund (and thereby use the designation 'EuSEF)' [366]. This Regulation accords with the AIFM Directive, because it applies to funds with assets under management that do not surpass 500 million Euros – i.e., the maximum limit for funds to be exempt from the authorisation requirements as an AIFM [367]. A 'qualifying social entrepreneurship fund' is an AIF which: (i) intends to invest 70% or more of its total "capital contributions and uncalled committed capital[823] in assets that are qualifying investments[824]," within a period that its rules lay down, (ii) uses 30% or less of its

---

[821] For further information about the EU's initiatives in respect of funding for SMEs, see Baber G. (2015), 'Venture capital in Europe: something ventured, something gained', *Company Lawyer*, 36(10), 310-313, at 310-311.

[822] These provisions are Articles 3(2), 9(5), 10(2) and 14(4) of Regulation (EU) No 346/2013 (Regulation (EU) No 345/2013, Article 29).

[823] For the purposes of Regulation (EU) No 346/2013, 'committed capital' means any commitment further to which an investor must, within the period that the social entrepreneurship fund's rules lays down, obtain an interest in, or make contributions of capital to, that fund (Regulation (EU) No 346/2013, Article 3(1)(j)).

[824] For the purposes of Regulation (EU) No 346/2013, 'qualifying investments' means: (i) equity or quasi-instruments which are issued by: (a) a qualifying portfolio undertaking, and which are directly obtained by the qualifying social entrepreneurship fund from the former, (b) "a qualifying portfolio undertaking in exchange for an equity security issued by the qualifying portfolio undertaking," or (c) "an undertaking of which the qualifying portfolio undertaking is a majority-owned subsidiary and which is acquired by the qualifying social entrepreneurship fund in exchange for an equity instrument issued by the qualifying portfolio undertaking," (ii) debt instruments that a qualifying portfolio undertaking issues, (iii) shares or units of at least one other qualifying social entrepreneurship fund – as long as those funds have not invested more than 10% of their total capital contributions and uncalled committed capital (see fn 823) in qualifying social entrepreneurship funds, (iv) loans that the qualifying social entrepreneurship fund grants to a qualifying portfolio undertaking, and (v) "any other type of participation in a qualifying portfolio undertaking" (Regulation (EU) No 346/2013, Article 3(1)(e)). For the purposes of Regulation (EU) No 346/2013, 'quasi-equity' means a financing instrument that combines equity and debt, where: (a) the return on the instrument is connected to the qualifying portfolio undertaking's profit or loss, and (b) the repayment of the instrument (if there is a default) is at least partly unsecured (Regulation (EU) No 346/2013, Article 3(1)(h)). For the purposes of Regulation (EU) No 346/2013, 'qualifying portfolio undertaking' means an undertaking which: (i) at the time of the qualifying social entrepreneurship fund's investment, is not admitted to trading on a regulated market or on an MTF, (ii) "has the achievement of measurable, positive social impacts as its primary objective in accordance with its ... rules or instruments of incorporation establishing the business," in situations in which it: (a) supplies goods or services "to vulnerable or marginalised, disadvantaged or excluded persons," (b) uses a method for the production or goods or services that reflects its social objective, or (c) provides financial support solely to social undertakings – as defined in (a) and (b), (iii) uses its profits mainly to achieve its primary social objective, in conformity with the "rules or instruments of incorporation establishing the business and with the predefined procedures and rules therein, which determine the circumstances in which profits are distributed to shareholders and owners to ensure that any such distribution of profits does not undermine its primary

total "capital contributions and uncalled committed capital for the acquisition of assets other than qualifying investments," and (iii) is founded in a Member State.[825][368]. Thus, as the Commission remarks, the 70% threshold for investing in social businesses is intended to achieve a balance between showing commitment to that sector whilst enabling the fund to diversify its risk by purchasing other assets [369].

The ELTIF Regulation came into force on 8th June 2015, and applied from 9th December 2015 [370]. It invites EU AIFs[826] to apply to be authorised as ELTIFs; this authorisation is only granted it if the applicant EU AIF's competent authority: (i) is satisfied that the EU AIF is able to fulfil all of the ELTIF Regulation's requirements, and (ii) has approved the application of an EU AIFM[827] that is authorised under the AIFM Directive, "to manage the ELTIF, the fund rules or instruments of incorporation, and the choice of the depositary" [371]. An ELTIF is to invest 70% or more of its capital in 'eligible investment assets' [372]., which comprise: (a) "equity[828] or quasi-equity[829] instruments" that have been issued by: (i) a qualifying portfolio undertaking[830], and obtained by the ELTIF from that undertaking or from

---

objective," (iv) "is managed in an accountable and transparent way," and (v) is founded in a Member State or in a third country, as long as the latter "is not listed as a Non-Cooperative Country and Territory by the Financial Action Task Force on Anti-Money Laundering and Terrorist Financing," and "has signed an agreement with the home Member State of the manager of a qualifying social entrepreneurship fund and with each other Member State in which the units or shares of the qualifying social entrepreneurship fund are intended to be marketed to ensure that the third country fully complies with the standards laid down in Article 26 of the OECD Model Tax Convention on Income and on Capital and ensures an effective exchange of information in tax matters, including any multilateral tax agreements" (Regulation (EU) No 346/2013, Article 3(1)(d)). As Regulation (EC) No 346/2013 is labelled 'Text with EEA relevance', 'Member State' within this Regulation means 'EEA State'.

[825] See the final sentence of fn 824, in respect of the term 'Member State'.

[826] For the purposes of the ELTIF Regulation, 'EU AIF' means an AIF that is: (i) "authorised or registered in Member State under the applicable national law," or (ii) "not authorised or registered in a Member State, but has its registered office and/or head office in a Member State" (ELTIF Regulation, Article 2(8); AIFM Directive, Article 4(1)(k)). As both the ELTIF Regulation and the AIFM Directive are labelled 'Text with EEA relevance', 'Member State' within these legislative instruments means 'EEA State'.

[827] For the purposes of the ELTIF Regulation, 'EU AIFM' means an AIFM whose registered office is located in a Member State (ELTIF Regulation, Article 2(9); AIFM Directive, Article 4(1)(l)).

[828] For the purposes of the ELTIF Regulation, "'equity' means ownership interest in a qualifying portfolio undertaking, represented by the shares or other forms of participation in the capital of the qualifying portfolio undertaking issued to its investors" (ELTIF Regulation, Article 2(4)).

[829] For the purposes of the ELTIF Regulation, 'quasi-equity' means "any type of financing instrument," in respect of which: (a) the return on the instrument is joined to the qualifying portfolio undertaking's profit or loss, and (b) the repayment of the instrument (if there is a default) is at least partly unsecured" (ELTIF Regulation, Article 2(5)). This definition of 'quasi-equity' is broader than the definition of 'quasi-equity' in Article 3(1)(h) of Regulation (EU) No 346/2013 (see the second sentence of fn 824), as, although the features of the instrument are the same in both definitions, the former includes all financing instruments with those characteristics – whereas the latter specifies that the financing instrument with such characteristics is to combine equity and debt.

[830] A 'qualifying portfolio undertaking' is a portfolio undertaking (except for a collective investment undertaking) that: (a) "is not a financial undertaking" – unless it "exclusively finances qualifying portfolio undertakings … or real assets" (see fn 831, for the definition of 'real asset'), (b) is an undertaking which is: (i) "not admitted to trading on a regulated market or on [an MTF]," or (ii) "admitted to trading on a regulated market or on [an MTF] and" simultaneously has a market capitalisation of 500 million Euros or less, and (c) is founded in a Member State or in a third country, as long as the latter: (i) "is not a high-risk and non-cooperative jurisdiction" as determined by the Financial Action Task Force, and "has signed an agreement with the home Member State of the manager of the ELTIF and with every other Member State in which the units or shares of the ELTIF are intended to be marketed to ensure that the third country fully complies with the standards laid down in Article 26 of the OECD Model Tax Convention on Income and on Capital and ensures an effective exchange of information in tax matters, including any multilateral tax agreements" (ELTIF Regulation, Article 11). For the purposes of the ELTIF Regulation, 'financial undertaking' means any of the following entities: a

a third party by way of the secondary market, (ii) "a qualifying portfolio undertaking in exchange for an equity or quasi-equity instrument" that the ELTIF has previously acquired from that entity or from a third party through the secondary market, or (iii) a company "of which the qualifying portfolio undertaking is a majority[-]owned subsidiary, in exchange for an equity or quasi-equity instrument acquired in accordance with points (i) or (ii) by the ELTIF" from that undertaking or from a third party by way of the secondary market, (b) debt instruments that a qualifying portfolio undertaking issues, (c) loans whose maturity is no longer than the ELTIF's life, which the ELTIF has granted to a qualifying portfolio undertaking, (d) shares or units of one or more other ELTIFs, European Venture Capital Funds and European Social Entrepreneurship Funds, as long as those funds have not "invested more than 10% of their capital in ELTIFs," and (e) holdings (directly or through qualifying portfolio undertakings) "of individual real assets[831]" that are worth 10 million Euros or more [373]. The other 30% of the capital of the ELTIF must either be invested in these 'eligible investment assets', or in 'assets' as described in Article 50(1) of the UCITS Directive [374]. In essence, these 'assets' comprise transferable securities and money market instruments that are traded on a regulated market, units of collective investment undertakings, deposits with banks which are repayable on demand or include the right to be withdrawn – which mature within one year, most categories of derivative contracts, and some further classes of money market instruments [375]. This limited selection of alternative assets provides opportunities for the ELTIF to diversify its risk, whilst (as the Commission notes [376].) preventing that fund from holding assets whose value is likely to be volatile.

The shares or units of an ELTIF may only be marketed in the EU[832], after the publication of a prospectus – and of a key information document in conformity with the PRIIPs Regulation [377]. Before a PRIIP may be offered to retail investors, the PRIIP manufacturer is to construct a key information document for that product [378]. This information includes the name of the PRIIP and of the PRIIP manufacturer, the latter's contact details and the identity of its competent authority, the date of the document, the PRIIP's "nature and main features," a short description of the PRIIP's risk-reward profile, a concise statement concerning the investor compensation or guarantee scheme (if any), the costs that are connected to an investment in the PRIIP, information concerning how and to a whom a retail investor may lodge a complaint, and additional documents to be supplied to the retail investor [379]. Even though an UCITS is to provide key investor information to its investors – which is to describe the "essential characteristics" of the UCITS [380]. – including its name, competent authority, investment objectives, investment policy, past performance, charges and risk-reward profile [381]., UCITS management companies, investment companies and advisers are to be subject to the requirements of the PRIIPs Regulation from 31st December

---

credit institution, an investment firm, an insurance company, a financial holding company, a mixed-activity holding company, an UCITS management company and an AIFM (ELTIF Regulation, Article 2(7)).

[831] For the purposes of the ELTIF Regulation, "'real asset' means an asset that has value due to its substance and properties and may provide returns, including infrastructure and other assets that give rise to economic or social benefit, such as education, counselling, research and development, and including commercial property or housing only where they are integral to, or an ancillary element of, a long-term investment project that contributes to the Union objective of smart, sustainable and inclusive growth" (ELTIF Regulation, Article 2(6)). It is submitted that this is an abstruse definition of the term 'real property', which is connected to social development as well as to profit margins. It may be difficult for Court of Justice of the European Union to define the precise scope of the term 'real asset', on the basis of this description.

[832] As the ELTIF Regulation is labelled 'Text with EEA relevance', 'Union' within that Regulation means 'EEA'.

2019 [382]. The PRIIPs Regulation entered into force on 29th December 2014, and will apply from 31st December 2016 [383].

Comment

In the years since the GFC, there has been a considerable increase in the number of provisions that regulate the securities sector. Many of these are in new legal instruments – such as the EMIR and the AIFM Directive. In addition, with the exception of the CARD, there have been changes in, and additions to, the pre-GFC legislative base – i.e., as the law was immediately preceding the crisis. In the instruments that have been modified, the structure tends to remain similar to the pre-GFC format, which shows continuity through and beyond the crisis.

All of the primary legal instruments regulating the securities sector before the crisis occurred were Directives. Several items of primary legislation introduced since the GFC are Regulations – such as the MAR, the CSDR and the ELTIF Regulation.

Thus, EU regulation of the securities sector is more comprehensive, detailed and harmonised than it was immediately prior to the GFC. Notwithstanding this, firms that operate in this sector may have difficulty in setting up the structures and procedures to apply the new rules – due to their volume, the cost of the changes, and uncertainty in the effect that they will have. In February 2016, the Commission proposed to defer the application of the national laws that transpose MiFID II, the date of repeal of the MiFID, and the date of application of the MiFIR, from 3rd January 2017 to 3rd January 2018 [384, 385] – together with other specified postponements of one year in these legal instruments and in related provisions of the MAR and of the CSDR – although not the dates from which those latter 2 Regulations apply. The Commission states that this extension is required to provide time for the national authorities and market participants to be able to set up the systems that are necessary to be able collect the large amount of data on trading venues and financial instruments which is required under MiFID II and the MiFIR [386].

BANKING LEGISLATION

There are volumes of legislation, and limited space and time. Consequently, a decision is required as to which legislative instruments should be included in this section. The author has reviewed CRD IV and the CRR elsewhere – in relation to the Basel III Framework which these laws implement, and before they were finalized[833]. More recently, a random sample of the CDRs and CIRs pursuant to CRD IV and the CRR were appraised – resulting in a positive endorsement of these secondary instruments [387].

As Chapter 1 considers provisions from the predecessors of CRD IV and the CRR – i.e., the BCD and the CRD – in the first 3 subsections of the 'Banking Legislation' section

---

[833] For these reviews, see Baber, G. (2012), 'Basel III Implementation and the European Union – an overview', *Company Lawyer*, 33(9), 271-272; Baber, G. (2012), Basel III Implementation and the European Union – the proposed Capital Requirements Directive (CRD IV), *Company Lawyer*, 33(11), 341-355; Baber, G. (2012), Basel III Implementation and the European Union – the proposed Capital Requirements Regulation, *Company Lawyer*, 33(12), 386-399.

contained therein[834], the post-GFC coverage of EU banking law in the current 'Banking Legislation' section works in reverse order through the corresponding pre-GFC subsections in Chapter 1. Thus, the first subsection below investigates changes in the legislation relating to settlement finality.

Settlement Finality

The application of Directive 98/26/EC is as in the original (pre-GFC) version of this Directive[835] – except for slight changes to the definition of 'system' and the inclusion of collateral security that is supplied in association with operations of the European Central Bank [388]. Whilst it remains true that insolvency proceedings are not to have retroactive effects on a participant's rights and obligations that arise from, or connect to, its participation in a system[836], the post-GFC version of Directive 98/26/EC defines the minimum scope of this statement; it is to apply (amongst other things) in respect of the rights and obligations of a participant in an interoperable system[837], and with regard to the rights and obligations of a system operator[838] of that system which is not a participant [389]. As in the original (pre-GFC) version of Directive 98/26/EC, the rights of holders of collateral security are not to be affected by insolvency proceedings[839]; in addition to the participant and the counterparty to Member States' central banks, the specified classes of insolvent entities for this provision to apply comprise "the system operator of an interoperable system which is not a participant" and any third party that supplied the collateral security [390]. The current (post-GFC) version of Directive 98/26/EC is consistent with the original version of this Directive, the main developments being the introduction and use of the terms 'interoperable system' and 'system operator' and the involvement of the ESMA – with which the competent authorities of Member States are required to co-operate and to supply "all the information that is necessary to carry out its duties" [391].

Deposit Guarantee and Investor Compensation Schemes

There have been no amendments to Directive 97/9/EC on investor-compensation schemes. In July 2010, the Commission proposed an update to this Directive, "to align Directive 97/9/EC with Directive 2004/39/EC [i.e., the MiFID] in order to ensure that the provision of all investment services and activities continue[s] to be adequately covered under

---

[834] These subsections are entitled 'Authorisation', 'Passporting' and 'Prudential supervision and capital adequacy'.

[835] See the opening sentence of the 2nd paragraph of the subsection entitled 'Settlement finality', in the section entitled 'Banking Legislation' in Chapter 1, for the application of the pre-GFC version of Directive 98/26/EC.

[836] See the opening sentence of the 3rd paragraph of the subsection entitled 'Settlement finality', in the section entitled 'Banking Legislation' in Chapter 1, for this provision.

[837] For the purposes of Directive 98/26/EC, 'interoperable systems' means at least 2 systems whose system operators have "entered into an arrangement with one another" which includes the carrying out of transfer orders across those systems (Directive 98/28/EC (as amended to 28/08/14), Article 2(o)). See fn 838, for the definition of 'system operator'.

[838] For the purposes of Directive 98/28/EC, 'system operator' means the entity (or entities) that are legally responsible for the functioning of a system (Directive 98/28/EC (as amended to 28/08/14), Article 2(p)).

[839] See the opening sentence of the final paragraph of the subsection entitled 'Settlement finality', in the section entitled 'Banking Legislation' in Chapter 1, for this statement.

schemes" – the MiFID "introduced a new list of investment services and activities"[840] [392]. The proposed update continues to take account of changes to Directive 94/19/EC on deposit-guarantee schemes[841] [393]. Amongst other things, the update plans to raise the level of cover that investor compensation schemes are to provide for each investor from 20,000 Euros to 50,000 Euros – the new limit would be a fixed amount across all EEA States[842] [394], and to provide for partial payment of at least one third of the investor's claim – if the final sum has not been paid within 9 months of the ruling that the compensation scheme is to reimburse this claim [395]. It is submitted that, as the proposed update has not been adopted as a Directive, the Commission should withdraw this draft legislation and introduce a possible recast of Directive 97/9/EC – after the MiFIR and the national rules transposing MiFID II come into force. The new proposal should be written to be in line with those legal instruments and with the recast Directive on deposit guarantee schemes, i.e., Directive 2014/49/EU. That Directive is to be considered in the remainder of this subsection, in the light of the rules on deposit guarantee schemes that applied immediately before the GFC.

The introduction and official recognition of deposit guarantee schemes under Directive 2014/49/EU are the same as under the pre-GFC version of its predecessor – Directive 94/19/EC as consolidated to 24th March 2005[843], except that: (i) the exemption is removed[844], (ii) a statement is added to the effect that the duty of Member States[845] to ensure that deposit guarantee schemes are introduced and officially recognised does not prevent cross-border mergers of deposit guarantee schemes or the foundation of these schemes across borders, and (iii) an institutional protection scheme "may be officially recognised as a" deposit guarantee scheme – if it satisfies the criteria that Article 113(7) of the CRR lays down[846] and complies with Directive 2014/49/EU [396].

The disciplinary measures concerning each credit institution's compliance with its duties as a member of the deposit guarantee scheme are unchanged[847], except for the deletion of the 'alternative guarantee arrangements' exception[848] [397].

---

[840] The list of "Investment services and activities" in Section A of Annex I to the MiFID covers more investment services than did the list of "Services" in Section A of the Annex to Council Directive 93/22/EEC of 10 May 1993 on investment services in the securities field (i.e., the MiFID's predecessor). In particular, the MiFID added investment advice and the operation of MTFs to the list of investment services (Directive 93/22/EEC (as amended to 11/02/03), Annex, Section A; MiFID (original version), Annex I, Section A).

[841] At the time at which the GFC began, Directives 94//19/EC and 97/9/EC took similar approaches – see the first paragraph of the subsection entitled 'Deposit guarantee and investor compensation schemes', in the section entitled 'Banking Legislation' in Chapter 1.

[842] This is a maximum harmonisation approach. See fn 83 and accompanying text in the subsection entitled 'UCITS', in the section entitled 'Securities Legislation' in Chapter 1, for an explanation of 'maximum harmonisation'.

[843] See the 2nd sentence of the 2nd paragraph of the subsection entitled 'Deposit guarantee and investor compensation schemes', in the section entitled 'Banking Legislation' in Chapter 1, for the introduction and official recognition of deposit guarantee schemes under Article 3(1) of Directive 94/19/EC.

[844] See the 2nd sentence of fn 266 in the subsection entitled 'Deposit guarantee and investor compensation schemes', in the section entitled 'Banking Legislation' in Chapter 1, for this exemption.

[845] As Directive 2014/49/EU is labelled 'Text with EEA relevance', 'Member State' means 'EEA State'.

[846] Article 113(7) of the CRR contains 9 criteria for institutional protection schemes, which include (for instance) that each scheme is to: (i) carry out its own risk review (CRR (as amended to 17/01/15), Article 113(7)(d)), and (ii) "be based on a broad membership of credit institutions of a predominantly homogenous business profile" (CRR (as amended to 17/01/15), Article 113(7)(h)).

[847] See the 3rd and 4th sentences of the 2nd paragraph of the subsection entitled 'Deposit guarantee and investor compensation schemes', in the section entitled 'Banking Legislation' in Chapter 1, for these disciplinary measures.

As under the Directive 94/19/EC[849], deposit guarantee schemes are to cover depositors at branches that credit institutions found in other Member States [398]. However, the subsequent provisions in that Directive which concern branches of deposit guarantee schemes and the host Member State's guarantee scheme[850], are absent from Directive 2014/49/EU. The latter adds new rules in this area; for instance, depositors at branches that are established by credit institutions in another Member State, are to be repaid by a deposit guarantee scheme in the host Member State – on behalf of, and in concurrence with the instructions of, the home Member State's depositor guarantee scheme [399]. Directive 2014/49/EU also omits the statement in its predecessor that deposits held when a credit institution's authorisation is revoked are to continue to be covered by that company's deposit guarantee scheme[851].

The 'equivalence' rule for branches of credit institutions founded in third countries, is the same in Directive 2014/49/EU as it was in Directive 94/19/EC[852] – except that 'Community' is changed to 'Union'[853], and the reference to 'Article 9(1) of Directive 77/780/EEC' is altered to 'Article 47(1) of Directive 2013/36/EU', i.e., CRD IV[854]; in performing the equivalence check, Member States are to verify that depositors receive the same level and degree of coverage that Directive 2014/49/EU lays down [400]. The obligation to supply depositors and potential depositors with "all relevant information" about the guarantee arrangements that cover their deposits[855], is present in Directive 2014/49/EU – which changes the obligor from the credit institution to the branch, and narrows the duty further by excluding from it every credit institution (whose head office is outside the EEA) that does not belong to a deposit guarantee scheme [401].

Directive 2014/49/EU requires the coverage level for the "aggregate deposits of each depositor" to be 100,000 Euros, "in the event of deposits being unavailable" [402]. This is up from 20,000 Euros in the pre-GFC consolidation of Directive 94/19/EC – although the coverage level of 100,000 Euros had already been established by a post-GFC amendment to

---

[848] See the 5th and 6th sentences of the 2nd paragraph of the subsection entitled 'Deposit guarantee and investor compensation schemes', in the section entitled 'Banking Legislation' in Chapter 1, for the 'alternative guarantee arrangements' exception.

[849] See the 7th sentence of the 2nd paragraph of the subsection entitled 'Deposit guarantee and investor compensation schemes', in the section entitled 'Banking Legislation' in Chapter 1, for this statement.

[850] See the 8th and 9th sentences of the 2nd paragraph of the subsection entitled 'Deposit guarantee and investor compensation schemes', in the section entitled 'Banking Legislation' in Chapter 1, for those provisions.

[851] See the 10th sentence of the 2nd paragraph of the subsection entitled 'Deposit guarantee and investor compensation schemes', in the section entitled 'Banking Legislation' in Chapter 1, for that statement.

[852] See the 11th sentence of the 2nd paragraph of the subsection entitled 'Deposit guarantee and investor compensation schemes', in the section entitled 'Banking Legislation' in Chapter 1, for this rule.

[853] As Directive 2014/49/EU is labelled 'Text with EEA relevance', references to 'Union' in that Directive are to be read as references to 'EEA'.

[854] Article 47(1) of CRD IV states: "Member States shall not apply to branches of credit institutions having their head office in a third country, when commencing or continuing to carry out their business, provisions which result in more favourable treatment than that accorded to branches of credit institutions having their head office in the [European] Union". This provision is almost identical in wording, and has the same meaning, as Article 99(1) of Directive 77/780/EEC – which is quoted in fn 270 in the subsection entitled 'Deposit guarantee and investor compensation schemes', in the section entitled 'Banking Legislation' in Chapter 1. The author recently observed continuity between Directive 77/780/EEC – which created the 'credit institution' – and its 'great-grandchild' CRD IV, with reference to the 'withdrawal of authorisation' provision in each of these Directives: see Baber G. (2015), 'Banking law in the EU: has the law come of age?', *Company Lawyer*, 36(12), 369-370.

[855] See the 12th sentence of the 2nd paragraph of the subsection entitled 'Deposit guarantee and investor compensation schemes', in the section entitled 'Banking Legislation' in Chapter 1, for this obligation.

that Directive[856]. That amendment also replaced the pre-GFC minimum harmonisation approach by one of maximum harmonisation[857], i.e., Member States are no longer permitted to provide a guarantee per depositor per bank[858] of more than the stated sum. The list of exclusions is modified from those in Annex I to Directive 94/19/EC – for instance, reference to deposits by 'government, central administrative, provincial, regional, local and municipal authorities is replaced in Directive 2014/49/EU with the collective term 'public authorities'[859]; furthermore, the list in the latter Directive "shall be excluded from any repayment" by a deposit guarantee scheme – i.e., that Directive removes the right of the Member State to be able to decide whether or not to: (i) exclude any of the specified deposits from guarantee or (ii) reduce the level of guarantee in respect of any of these items[860] [403]. This change has a further harmonising effect – as does the omission from Directive 2014/39/EU of the right of Member States to retain or to introduce provisions that offer a higher or more comprehensive cover for deposits[861].

Directive 2009/14/EC deleted the provision in Directive 94/19/EC that allowed Member States to limit the deposit guarantee to a specified percentage of deposits[862] [404]. Directive 2014/49/EU did not reintroduce this item. In the immediate wake of the GFC, the removal of this rule was sensible.

Reference to 'any alternative arrangement' is removed from the obligation of each credit institution to publish the information concerning the deposit guarantee scheme of which it, and its branches within the EEA, are members[863]; Member States are to ensure that credit institutions notify actual and potential depositors of items which the scheme excludes from its guarantee [405]. Annex I to Directive 2014/65/EU contains a template that provides information to depositors in respect of the protection of deposits; credit institutions must

---

[856] Article 1(3)(a) of Directive 2009/14/EC of the European Parliament and of the Council of 11 March 2009 amending Directive 94/19/EC on deposit-guarantee schemes as regards the coverage level and the payout delay, states: "[Article 7(1) of Directive 94/19/EC] shall be replaced by the following: 1. Member States shall ensure that the coverage for the aggregated deposits of each depositor shall be at least EUR 50 000 in the event of deposits being unavailable. 1a. By 31 December 2010, Member States shall ensure that the coverage for the aggregate deposits of each depositor shall be set at EUR 100 000 in the event of deposits being unavailable. ....."

[857] The rise of the deposit guarantee from 50,000 Euros to 100,000 Euros was accompanied by a change from a minimum harmonisation approach to one of maximum harmonisation: see fn 856. Fn 83 and its accompanying text in the subsection entitled 'UCITS', in the section entitled 'Securities Legislation' in Chapter 1, explain the term 'maximum harmonisation'.

[858] As previously – i.e., under Directive 94/19/EC (see the 18th sentence of the 2nd paragraph of the subsection entitled 'Deposit guarantee and investor compensation schemes', in the section entitled 'Banking Legislation' in Chapter 1), the deposit guarantee applies to the total deposits of the depositor placed with the same credit institution (Directive 2014/65/EU (as corrected to 30/12/14), Article 6(3)).

[859] See fn 273 in the subsection entitled 'Deposit guarantee and investor compensation schemes', in the section entitled 'Banking Legislation' in Chapter 1, for examples of the exclusions that Annex I to Directive 94/19/EC contains.

[860] See the 14th sentence of the 2nd paragraph of the subsection entitled 'Deposit guarantee and investor compensation schemes', in the section entitled 'Banking Legislation' in Chapter 1, for this right.

[861] See the 15th sentence of the 2nd paragraph of the subsection entitled 'Deposit guarantee and investor compensation schemes', in the section entitled 'Banking Legislation' in Chapter 1, for that right. Notwithstanding this, Directive 2014/65/EU allows some flexibility for Member States, in that they may maintain or introduce schemes that protect "old-age provision products and pensions," as long as these "offer comprehensive coverage for all products and situations relevant in this regard – including deposits (Directive 2014/65/EU (as corrected to 30/12/14), Article 6(3)).

[862] See the 16th sentence of the 2nd paragraph of the subsection entitled 'Deposit guarantee and investor compensation schemes', in the section entitled 'Banking Legislation' in Chapter 1, for this provision.

[863] See the penultimate sentence of the 2nd paragraph of the subsection entitled 'Deposit guarantee and investor compensation schemes', in the section entitled 'Banking Legislation' in Chapter 1, for this obligation.

supply the information on the template to depositors, before the latter sign a contract on deposit-taking, and at least annually thereafter (once the contract has been agreed) [406].

Directive 2009/14/EC reduced the deposit repayment period from 3 months to 20 days[864] [407]. Directive 2014/65/EU lowers this repayment period further – to 7 working days [408]. The latter reduction in the deposit repayment period is to be phased in; it is to be up to: (a) 20 working days until 31st December 2018, (b) 15 working days from 1st January 2019 until 31st December 2020, and (c) 10 working days from 1st January 2021 until 31st December 2023 [409]. Thus, the deposit repayment period in the years from 2024 onwards is approximately one tenth of the duration that it was prior to the GFC which, although excellent news for the holders of bank accounts, may present difficulties for deposit guarantee schemes to maintain at all times. More generally, Directive 2014/65/EU provides a tight, fairly harmonised regime for deposit protection, which is likely to be beneficial in reassuring retail depositors that their holdings are protected in the face of adverse economic conditions.

Distance Marketing of Consumer Financial Services

There have been no amendments to the Directive 2002/65/EC since December 2007. Therefore, the law is unchanged from that described in the corresponding subsection in Chapter 1[865].

Supplementary Supervision

Directive 2011/89/EU[866] has revised the definitions with Directive 2002/87/EC. 'Financial conglomerate' means a group or subgroup that is either headed by a regulated entity[867], or in which one or more of its subsidiaries is a regulated entity, and which fulfils the following conditions: (i) at least one of the entities within the group or subgroup is within the insurance sector, and one or more of the companies within the group or subgroup is within the banking or investment services sector, (ii) the aggregated and/or consolidated activities of the firms within the insurance sector, and within the banking and investment services sector, are both significant[868], and (iii)(a) if a regulated entity heads the group or subgroup, then that

---

[864] See the final sentence of the 2nd paragraph of the subsection entitled 'Deposit guarantee and investor compensation schemes', in the section entitled 'Banking Legislation' in Chapter 1, for rules in the pre-GFC version of Directive 94/19/EC that govern the deposit repayment period.

[865] This is the subsection entitled 'Distance marketing of consumer financial services', in the section entitled 'Banking Legislation' in Chapter 1.

[866] This is Directive 2011/89/EU of the European Parliament and of the Council of 16 November 2011 amending Directives 98/78/EC, 2002/87/EC, 2006/48/EC and 2009/138/EC as regards the supplementary supervision of financial entities in a financial conglomerate.

[867] For the purposes of Directive 2002/87/EC, 'regulated entity' means an investment firm, a credit institution, an insurance company, a reinsurance undertaking, an asset management company or an AIFM (Directive 2002/87/EC (as amended to 27/06/13), Article 2(4)). The last 3 firms in this list have been added to the definition of 'regulated entity' since the GFC: see fn 230 in the subsection entitled 'Supplementary supervision', in the section entitled 'Banking Legislation' in Chapter 1, for the definition of 'regulated entity' in the pre-GFC consolidated version of Directive 2002/87/EC.

[868] The current definition of 'significant' in Article 3(2)-(3) of Directive 2002/87/EC is unchanged from that in the pre-GFC definition of 'significant' in Article 3(2)-(3) of Directive 2002/87/EC: see fn 238 in the subsection entitled 'Supplementary supervision', in the section entitled 'Banking Legislation' in Chapter 1, for that

organisation is to be either a parent undertaking of a company within the financial sector, or a firm which holds a participation in a company within the financial sector, or a firm that is connected to another in the financial sector within the broad meaning of parent-subsidiary relationship that Article 22 of Directive 2013/34/EU provides[869], or (b) if the head of the group or subgroup is not a regulated entity, then the group's or subgroup's activities are chiefly to take place within the financial sector[870] [410].

The rules on the scope of supplementary provision in the current version of Directive 2002/87/EC are almost identical to those in the original and pre-GFC consolidated versions of that Directive[871]. The phrase 'within the European Community' becomes 'within the EU'[872], and 'outside the Community' becomes 'in a third country' [411]. The reference to 'Article 12(1) of Directive 83/349/EEC' remains in Directive 2002/87/EC, but should be changed to 'Article 22(7) of Directive 2013/34/EU' – as the latter has replaced the former[873] [412].

The co-ordinator's identity is to be published on the website of the Joint Committee of the ESAs[874] [413]. The tasks of the co-ordinator in respect of supplementary supervision are unchanged from those in the original and pre-GFC consolidated versions of Directive 2002/87/EC[875] [414].

Whilst Member States are still to require own funds to be "available at the level of the financial conglomerate" that are always equal to or greater than the capital adequacy requirements which are computed in conformity with Annex I to Directive 2002/87/EC[876]

---

definition. Notwithstanding this, Directive 2011/89/EU has modified the content of paragraphs 2 and 3 of, and added paragraph 3a to, Article 3 of Directive 2002/87/EC.

[869] Article 2(14)(a)(iii) of Directive 2002/87/EC refers to Article 12(1) of Directive 83/349/EEC. Directive 2013/34/EU has repealed Directive 83/349/EEC; references to the latter are to be construed as references to the former, and are to "be read in accordance with the correlation table in Annex VII" of Directive 2013/34/EU (Directive 2013/34/EU (as amended to 21/11/14), Article 52). Article 12(1) of Directive 83/349/EEC correlates with Article 22(7) of Directive 2013/34/EU (Directive 2013/34/EU (as amended to 21/11/14), Annex VII). Article 22(7) of Directive 2013/34/EU refers to Article 22(1)-(2) of Directive 2013/34/EU, which contains a broad definition of the parent-subsidiary relationship.

[870] The test for determining whether the group's activities take place within the financial sector is unchanged from the pre-GFC original and consolidated versions of Directive 2002/87/EC; see fn 237 in the subsection entitled 'Supplementary supervision', in the section entitled 'Banking Legislation' in Chapter 1, for this test.

[871] See the 3rd, 4th and 5th sentences of the 2nd paragraph of the subsection entitled 'Supplementary supervision', in the section entitled 'Banking Legislation' in Chapter 1, for those provisions.

[872] As Directive 2002/87/EC is not labelled 'Text with EEA relevance', 'Union' within this Directive means 'EU'.

[873] See fn 869, for information concerning the replacement of Article 12(1) of Directive 83/349/EEC by Article 22(1) of Directive 2013/34/EU.

[874] The Joint Committee of the ESAs does not have its own website. Information concerning the Joint Committee of the ESAs is available from the websites of the EBA – at http://www.eba.europa.eu/about-us/organisation/joint-committee, the EIOPA – at https://eiopa.europa.eu/about-eiopa/organisation/joint-committee, and the ESMA – at https://www.esma.europa.eu/sections/joint-committee. The Joint Committee of the ESAs publishes a 'List of Identified Financial Conglomerates' each year, which includes the identity of the co-ordinator in respect of each financial conglomerate. The most recently published list shows 78 financial conglomerates whose head of group is within the EEA, and 4 financial conglomerates whose head of group is in a third country (European Banking Authority (2015), Joint Committee: List of Identified Conglomerates as per 31 December 2014 figures, JC 2015 079, 19/10/15. <http://www.eba.europa.eu/documents/10180/1294818/JC+2015+079+%282015+list+of+identified+Financial+Conglomerates%29_Final.pdf>). Even though Directive 2002/87/EC is not labelled a 'Text with EEA relevance' (see fn 872), the Norwegian-based financial conglomerates DNB, Gjensidige, Jernbane-personalets, Storebrand and Eika Gruppen, and the Norwegian co-ordinator 'Finanstilsynet', are included in the EU/EEA listing (European Banking Authority (2015), Joint Committee: List of Identified Conglomerates as per 31 December 2014 figures, p.7).

[875] See the final sentence of the 3rd paragraph of the subsection entitled 'Supplementary supervision', in the section entitled 'Banking Legislation' in Chapter 1, for these tasks.

[876] See the opening sentence of the 4th paragraph of the subsection entitled 'Supplementary supervision', in the section entitled 'Banking Legislation' in Chapter 1, for this requirement.

[415]. Directive 2011/89/EU has deleted the 'Book value/Requirement' method from that Annex, and simplified the 'Combination method' to be an amalgamation of the 'Accounting consolidation' and the 'Deduction and aggregation' methods[877] [416]. The reporting requirements for regulated entities and mixed financial holding companies in respect of risk concentration and intra-group transactions are unchanged[878] – although Directive 2011/89/EU has added a new provision to each of Articles 7 and 8 of Directive 2002/87/EC, which requires the Joint Committee of the ESAs to "issue common guidelines aimed at the convergence of supervisory practices with regard to the application of supplementary supervision" to risk concentration as Article 7 of Directive 2002/87/EC lays down, and to intra-group transactions as Article 8 of Directive 2002/87/EC specifies, respectively[879] [417].

The provisions on internal control mechanisms and risk management processes in the original and pre-GFC consolidated versions of Directive 2002/87/EC, are unchanged in the current version of this Directive[880]. Notwithstanding this, Directive 2010/78/EU adds the following required risk management process to Directive 2002/87/EC: arrangements are to be established "to contribute to and develop, if required, adequate recovery and resolution arrangements and plans," and are to be periodically updated [418]. Directive 2011/89/EU adds the following reporting and disclosure requirements to Directive 2002/87/EC: Member States are to "require the regulated entities, at the level of the financial conglomerate, to" frequently supply their competent authority with data on, and publish annually, their "legal structure and governance and organisational structure" [419].

Directive 2010/78/EU adds the following provision to Directive 2002/87/EC: the Joint Committee of the ESAs is to "ensure coherent cross-sectional and cross-border supervision and compliance with [European]. Union legislation," within the ambit of Article 56 of Regulation (EU) No 1093/2010, Article 56 of Regulation (EU) No 1094/2010 and Article 56 of Regulation (EU) No 1095/2010 [420] – which empower the EBA, the EIOPA and the ESMA to "reach joint positions … with respect to the implementation of Directive 2002/87/EC" [421]. Directive 2011/89/EU inserts new requirements into Directive 2002/87/EC for Member States to require the co-ordinator to "ensure appropriate and regular stress testing of financial conglomerates" [422]., and for the Joint Committee of the ESAs and the European Systemic Risk Board to "develop supplementary parameters that capture the specific risks associated with financial conglomerates" in order to facilitate stress testing across the EU [423].

The rules for co-operation and exchange of information between competent authorities in the original and pre-GFC consolidated versions of Directive 2002/87/EC continue to apply in

---

[877] See the opening sentence of fn 244 in the subsection entitled 'Supplementary supervision', in the section entitled 'Banking Legislation' in Chapter 1, for the 'Combination of methods 1, 2 and 3' in the original and pre-GFC versions of Directive 2002/87/EC.

[878] See the final 3 sentences of the 4th paragraph of the subsection entitled 'Supplementary supervision', in the section entitled 'Banking Legislation' in Chapter 1, for these requirements.

[879] On 22nd December 2014, the Joint Committee of the ESAs published a document entitled 'Joint Guidelines on the convergence of supervisory practices relating to the consistency of supervisory coordination arrangements for financial conglomerates', which, in Title IV, provides for the supervisory assessment of financial conglomerates – including the assessment of risk concentration and intra-group transactions at pp.14-15 of that document. These Joint Guidelines are available at https://www.eba.europa.eu/documents/10180/936042/ JC+GL+2014+01+%28Joint+Guidelines+on+coordination+arrangements+for+financi....pdf.

[880] See the 5th paragraph of the subsection entitled 'Supplementary supervision', in the section entitled 'Banking Legislation' in Chapter 1, for these provisions.

the current version of the Directive[881] – except for one change[882], as follows: the collection and exchange of information applies not only to the identification of the group structure of all significant entities within the financial conglomerate (and of the competent authorities of the group's regulated entities)[883], but also to the wider category of "the group's legal structure and the governance and organisational structure, including all regulated entities, non-regulated subsidiaries and significant branches belonging to the financial conglomerate [and] the holders of qualifying holdings at the ultimate parent level" [424]. Furthermore, Directive 2010/78/EU has inserted a provision into Directive 2002/87/EC that permits the competent authorities to exchange with central banks, the European Central Bank, the European System of Central Banks and the European Systemic Risk Board, "such information as may be needed for the performance of their respective tasks, regarding regulated entities in a financial conglomerate, in line with the provisions laid down in the sectoral rules[884]" [425].

The competent authorities are to co-operate with the Joint Committee of the ESAs "for the purposes of" Directive 2002/87/EC "in accordance with Regulation (EU) No 1093/2010, Regulation (EU) No 1094/2010, and Regulation No 1095/2010"[885] [426]. The Joint Committee of the ESAs is to publish common guidelines as to how each competent authority is to carry out risk-based appraisals of financial conglomerates[886] [427].

The current provisions of Articles 13 and 14 of Directive 2002/87/EC are unchanged from those in the original and pre-GFC consolidated versions of that Directive[887], except for one addition[888]: Member States are to ensure that there are no legal obstacles within their jurisdiction that prevent persons within the ambit of supplementary supervision from exchanging information: (i) in conformity with Directive 2002/87/EC, and (ii) with the EBA in accordance with Article 35 of Regulation (EU) No 1093/2010, the EIOPA in conformity with Article 35 of Regulation (EU) No 1094/2010, and the ESMA in accordance with Article 35 of Regulation (EU) No 1095/2010[889] [428]. The rules in Articles 16 and 17 of Directive

---

[881] See the 6th paragraph of the subsection entitled 'Supplementary supervision', in the section entitled 'Banking Legislation' in Chapter 1, for these rules.

[882] Directive 2011/89/EU makes this modification to Directive 2002/87/EC.

[883] See point (a) in the 2nd sentence of the 6th paragraph of the subsection entitled 'Supplementary supervision', in the section entitled 'Banking Legislation' in Chapter 1, for this statement in the original and pre-GFC versions of Directive 2002/87/EC.

[884] For the purposes of Directive 2002/87/EC, 'sectoral rules' means EU legislation that concerns "the prudential supervision of regulated entities" (Directive 2002/87/EC (as amended to 27/06/13), Article 2(7)). See fn 867, for the definition of 'regulated entity'.

[885] Directive 2010/78/EU inserts this provision into Directive 2002/87/EC.

[886] Directive 2011/89/EU adds this rule to Directive 2002/87/EC.

[887] See the penultimate paragraph of the subsection entitled 'Supplementary supervision', in the section entitled 'Banking Legislation' in Chapter 1, for those provisions.

[888] Directive 2010/78/EU makes this addition to Directive 2002/87/EC.

[889] See fn 636, for Article 35 of Regulation (EU) No 1095/2010. Article 35 of Regulation (EU) No 1094/2010 is identical to Article 35 of Regulation (EU) No 1095/2010 – except that the term 'the Authority' refers to the ESMA in the latter Regulation, and to the EIOPA in the former. Article 35 of Regulation (EU) No 1093/2010 has been amended by Regulation (EU) No 1022/2013 of the European Parliament and of the Council of 22 October 2013 amending Regulation (EU) No 1093/2010 establishing a European Supervisory Authority (European Banking Authority) as regards the conferral of specific tasks on the European Central Bank pursuant to Council Regulation (EU) No 1024/2013. Article 35 in the original version of Regulation (EU) No 1093/2010 was identical to both Article 35 of Regulation (EU) No 1094/2010 and Article 35 of Regulation (EU) No 1095/2010 – except for the meaning of the term 'the Authority', which is the EBA in Regulation (EU) No 1093/2010.

2002/87/EC are also unchanged from those in the pre-GFC versions of this Directive[890] – except for an addition that empowers the Joint Committee of the ESAs to "develop guidelines for measures in relation to mixed financial holding companies" [429].

The largest change to the pre-GFC versions of Directive 2002/87/EC is the post-GFC involvement of the Joint Committee of the ESAs in the regulation of supplementary supervision. As each financial conglomerate includes entities from more than one of the banking, insurance and investment sectors, at least 2 of the ESAs will be involved in the supervision of that group. Thus, the co-ordinated superintendence and guidelines of all 3 ESAs is required for effective supervision at the level of the financial conglomerate. It is submitted that there is a possibility that this system will work well, despite the complexity in co-ordinating macro- and micro-oversight, and simultaneous supervision across the whole of the group.

Financial Collateral Arrangements

The provision in the original (pre-GFC) version of Directive 2002/47/EC, according to which Member States are not to require the formation, the perfection, the validity, the enforceability or the admissibility in evidence of a financial collateral arrangement, or the supply of financial collateral under this arrangement, to depend upon "the performance of any formal act," is unchanged in the current (post-GFC) version of that Directive[891] [430]. Directive 2009/44/EC[892] adds the rule that, if a credit claim[893] is supplied as financial collateral, then Member States are not to require the priority, the perfection, the validity, the enforceability or the admissibility in evidence of this collateral to depend upon "the performance of a formal act" – for instance the registration, or the notification, of the debtor of this credit claim[894] [431]. The financial collateral is to comprise cash, financial instruments or credit claims; only the latter is a post-GFC addition to Directive 2002/47/EC[895] [432]. The set of entities of which the collateral taker and the collateral provider must be members, is the same in the current version of Directive 2002/47/EC as in the original (pre-GFC) version[896] – other than updates in the reference number of Directives from which the definitions of some of these entities arise [433]. In addition to the collateral taker, on the occurrence of an enforcement event, being able to realize financial collateral that is supplied under a security

---

[890] See the final paragraph the subsection entitled 'Supplementary supervision', in the section entitled 'Banking Legislation' in Chapter 1, for these rules.

[891] See the 2nd sentence of the opening paragraph of the subsection entitled 'Financial collateral arrangements', in the section entitled 'Banking Legislation' in Chapter 1, for that provision.

[892] This is Directive 2009/44/EC of the European Parliament and of the Council of 4 May 2009 amending Directive 98/26/EC on settlement finality in payment and securities settlement systems and Directive 2002/47/EC on financial collateral arrangements as regards linked systems and credit claims.

[893] For the purposes of Directive 2002/47/EC, 'credit claims' means monetary claims that arise from an agreement in which a credit institution provides a loan (Directive 2002/47/EC (as amended to 12/06/14), Article 2(1)(o)).

[894] Article 3(1) of Directive 2002/47/EC declares: "Member States may require the performance of a formal act ... for the purposes of perfection, priority, enforceability or admissibility in evidence against the debtor or third parties". Directive 2009/44/EC adds this provision to Directive 2002/47/EC.

[895] See the 3rd sentence of the opening paragraph of the subsection entitled 'Financial collateral arrangements', in the section entitled 'Banking Legislation' in Chapter 1, for the pre-GFC version of this rule. Directive 2009/44/EC added the term 'credit claims' to that rule in Directive 2002/47/EC.

[896] See the final sentence of the opening paragraph of the subsection entitled 'Financial collateral arrangements', in the section entitled 'Banking Legislation' in Chapter 1, for a list of these entities.

financial collateral arrangement[897] as financial instruments and/or cash[898], since the GFC that person may also realize financial collateral as credit claims – by appropriation or sale and by setting of their value against, or applying their value in release of, the relevant financial obligations [434]. Appropriation may only take place if the parties have agreed to it, and to the valuation of the financial instruments and the credit claims, in the security financial collateral arrangement; [435]. Directive 2009/44/EC adds the phrase 'and the credit claims' to this provision, which is otherwise unchanged from the original version[899].

The laws on the right of use of financial collateral under security financial collateral arrangements in the current version of Directive 2002/47/EC, are identical to those in the original (pre-GFC) version of the Directive[900]. These rules are not to apply to credit claims [436]. There are no alterations to the pre-GFC rules with regard to the recognition of title transfer financial collateral arrangements[901], or of close-out netting provisions[902]. Directive 2002/47/EC applies "without prejudice to" the BRRD [437] – which the final subsection in this section considers. There is little difference between the original (pre-GFC) version of Directive 2002/47/EC and the current version of this Directive. The main change is the inclusion of credit claims within the scope of the Directive's definition of 'financial collateral,' which is supported by modifications to other provisions.

Electronic Money

The review that the Commission contracted to evaluate Directive 2000/46/EC[903] found amongst other things, that: (i) the e-money market had progressed more slowly than expected

---

[897] Directive 2009/44/EC has amended the definition of 'security financial collateral arrangement' in the original (pre-GFC) version of Directive 2002/47/EC (see fn 223 in the subsection entitled 'Financial collateral arrangements', in the section entitled 'Banking Legislation' in Chapter 1, for that definition) as follows – with changes in *italic text*: 'security financial collateral arrangement' means an arrangement under which a provider of collateral supplies financial collateral in the form of security to, or in favour of, a collateral taker, and the full *or qualified* ownership of, *or full entitlement to*, the financial collateral remains with the collateral provider (Directive 2002/47/EC (as amended to 12/06/14), Article 2(1)(c)).

[898] See the opening sentence of the 2nd paragraph of the subsection entitled 'Financial collateral arrangements', in the section entitled 'Banking Legislation' in Chapter 1, for this provision.

[899] See the 2nd sentence of the 2nd paragraph of the subsection entitled 'Financial collateral arrangements', in the section entitled 'Banking Legislation' in Chapter 1, for that provision in the original version of Directive 2002/47/EC.

[900] See the first 4 sentences of the final paragraph of the subsection entitled 'Financial collateral arrangements', in the section entitled 'Banking Legislation' in Chapter 1, for those laws.

[901] See the penultimate sentence of the final paragraph of the subsection entitled 'Financial collateral arrangements', in the section entitled 'Banking Legislation' in Chapter 1, for the rules in respect of the recognition of title transfer financial collateral arrangements. Directive 2009/44/EC has amended the definition of 'title financial collateral arrangement' in the original (pre-GFC) version of Directive 2002/47/EC (see fn 224 in the subsection entitled 'Financial collateral arrangements', in the section entitled 'Banking Legislation' in Chapter 1, for that definition) as follows – with additions in *italic text*: 'title financial collateral arrangement' means an arrangement under which a supplier of collateral transfers full ownership of, *or full entitlement to*, financial collateral to a collateral taker, in order to cover the carrying out of 'relevant financial obligations' (Directive 2002/47/EC (as amended to 12/06/14), Article 2(1)(b)). Fn 224 in Chapter 1 also contains the definition 'relevant financial obligations' – which is the same in the current version of Directive 2002/47/EC as in the original version of that Directive.

[902] See the final sentence of the subsection entitled 'Financial collateral arrangements', in the section entitled 'Banking Legislation' in Chapter 1, for the rules concerning the close-out netting provisions.

[903] This is Directive 2000/46/EC of the European Parliament and of the Council of 18 September 2000 on the taking up, pursuit and prudential supervision of the business of electronic money institutions.

and was far short of its potential, (ii) there were few active electronic money institutions in Member States, (iii) although the Directive had ensured that electronic money issuers were stable and sound, some of the requirements and restrictions on these issuers may have been excessive and aspects of the regulatory framework disproportionate to the risks presented by their activities, and (iv) the passporting regime for electronic money issuers eased cross-border activity, but was more cumbersome that the passporting regime that applied to banks [438]. The findings of this review encouraged the Commission to propose a new Directive for electronic money institutions [439]. Its rules were to "ensure a level playing field for all payment services providers" – including electronic money institutions [440]. The new legislation was (and is) Directive 2009/110/EC of the European Parliament and of the Council of 16 September 2009 on the taking up, pursuit and prudential supervision of the business of electronic money institutions amending Directives 2005/60/EC and 2006/48/EC and repealing Directive 2000/46/EC.

Directive 2009/110/EC introduces a clearer definition of 'electronic money' than that of its predecessor (Directive 2000/46/EC)[904], which is as follows:

> For the purposes of this Directive [i.e., Directive 2009/110/EC]., … 'electronic money' means electronically, including magnetically, stored monetary value as represented by a claim on the issuer which is issued on receipt of funds for the purpose of making payment transactions as defined in point 5 of Article 4 of Directive 2007/64/EC [i.e., the PSD[905]]., and which is accepted by a natural or legal person other than the electronic money issuer[.] [441].

The definition of 'electronic money institution' has also changed[906]; it is a legal person which has been granted authorisation to issue electronic money under Title II of Directive 2009/110/EC[907] [442]. Initial capital requirements for electronic money institutions are reduced from at least 1 million Euros in Directive 2000/46/EC[908] to "not less than 350,000 Euros" in Directive 2009/110/EC [443]. Each electronic money institution is to possess own funds which are the higher of 350,000 Euros and a calculation in Article 5 of Directive 2009/110/EC that depends upon: (i) whether or not the institution supplies payment services in accordance with Article 6(1)(a) of Directive 2009/110/EC[909], (ii) the amount of electronic

---

[904] See the 2nd sentence of the opening paragraph of the subsection entitled 'Electronic money', in the section entitled 'Banking Legislation' in Chapter 1, for the definition of 'electronic money' in Directive 2000/46/EC.

[905] Article 4(5) of the PSD states: "'payment transaction' means an act, initiated by the payer or by the payee, of placing, transferring or withdrawing funds, irrespective of any underlying obligations between the payer and the payee." The PSD "is repealed with effect from 13 January 2018" (PSD II, Article 114). With regard to the meaning of 'payment transaction', the replacement of the PSD by PSD II presents no difficulty, because the definition of that term in Article 4(5) of PSD II is identical to its definition in Article 4(5) of the PSD.

[906] See fn 216 in the subsection entitled 'Electronic money', in the section entitled 'Banking Legislation' in Chapter 1, for the definition of 'electronic money institution' in Directive 2000/46/EC.

[907] Title II of Directive 2009/110/EC is entitled 'Requirements for the taking up, pursuit and prudential supervision of the business of electronic money institutions', and comprises Articles 3-9 of this Directive.

[908] See the 2nd sentence of the final paragraph of of the subsection entitled 'Electronic money', in the section entitled 'Banking Legislation' in Chapter 1, for the initial capital requirement for electronic money institutions under Directive 2000/46/EC.

[909] Electronic money institutions may provide payment services that the Annex to the PSD lists (Directive 2009/110/EC, Article 6(1)). These payment services comprise: (i) the operation of a payment account including services enabling the placement of cash on, and/or the withdrawal of cash from, this account, (ii) the carrying out of payment transactions, (iii) the acquisition and/or issuance of payment instruments, and (iv) money remittance (PSD (as amended to 18/07/09), Annex). These services are identical to those listed in the

money that it has issued[910], (iii) the other activities that it undertakes in concurrence with Article 6(1) of the PSD[911], and (iv) a possible appraisal by the competent authority of the electronic money institution's risk management procedures, databases for losses associated with risk, and internal control processes – which may raise or lower its own funds requirements by up to 20% [444]. This 'own funds' calculation is an amalgam between the computation in Directive 2000/46/EC[912] – of which Method D in Directive 2009/110/EC is a modification[913] – and the calculation in Article 8(1) of the PSD – which corresponds to Methods A, B and C in Directive 2009/110/EC; furthermore, the competent authority's appraisal in point (iv) above is also available to the competent authority under the PSD, in association with any payment institution's choice of Method A, B or C for the computation of its 'own funds' requirement for the purposes of that Directive [445].

Member States[914] are to require each electronic money institution to safeguard money that it has received in exchange for electronic money that it has issued, in concurrence with Article 9(1)-(2) of the PSD [446]. Article 9(1) of the PSD states that Member States or competent authorities are to require each payment institution that simultaneously provides both payment services and other services[915] "to safeguard funds" received from its payment service users or via another payment service provider either: (a) by not mixing them with funds of any person "other than the payment service users on whose behalf the funds are held" and (b) by insulating them from the claims of the payment institution's other creditors, or (c) by covering them by a guarantee from an insurance undertaking or a bank, which is not from the same group as the payment institution, "for an amount equivalent to that which would have been segregated in the" guarantee's absence, which is payable if the payment institution does not satisfy its financial obligations [447]. Article 9(2) of the PSD applies the requirements of Article 9(1) of the PSD to that portion of the funds, which the payment

---

original version of the PSD: see the opening sentence of fn 198 in the subsection entitled 'Payment services', in the section entitled 'Banking Legislation' in Chapter 1.

[910] Article 5(3) of Directive 2009/110/EC states: "Method D: The own funds of an electronic money institution for the activity of issuing electronic money shall amount to at least 2% of the average outstanding electronic money". For the purposes of Directive 2009/110/EC, the 'average outstanding electronic money' is the mean total amount of financial liabilities that are connected with electronic money in issue at the end of each day over the preceding 6 months, computed on the first day of each month and applied for that month (Directive 2009/110/EC, Article 2(4)). Article 8(1) of the PSD contains Methods A, B and C – one of which the electronic money institution is to apply to payment services that it provides which are not connected to the issuance of electronic money (Directive 2009/110/EC, Article 5(2)).

[911] These' other activities' comprise: (i) the provision of credit, in relation to 3 specified payment services in the Annex to the PSD, and under 4 conditions that Article 16(3) of the PSD lists, (ii) the supply of operational services, and of ancillary services that are "closely related" to the provision of payment services and/or the issuance of electronic money, (iii) the functioning of 'payment systems' as Article 4(6) of the PSD defines, and (iv) "business activities other than the issuance of electronic money, having regard to the applicable Community [i.e., EU] and national law" (Directive 2009/110/EC, Article 6(1)(b)-(e)). Article 4(6) of the PSD defines 'payment system' as "a funds transfer system with formal and standardised arrangements and common rules for the processing, clearing and/or settlement of payment transactions." Electronic money institutions are not to take repayable funds from the public (Directive 2009/110/EC, Article 6(2)). Furthermore, Member States are to prohibit the granting of any time-related benefit – including interest – to any holder of electronic money (Directive 2009/110/EC, Article 12).

[912] See the 3rd sentence of the subsection entitled 'Electronic money', in the section entitled 'Banking Legislation' in Chapter 1, for the 'own funds' calculation in Directive 2000/46/EC.

[913] See fn 910, for Method D.

[914] Directive 2009/110/EC is labelled a 'Text with EEA relevance'. Therefore, 'Member State' within this Directive means 'EEA State'.

[915] Article 9(1) of the PSD refers to Article 16(1)(c) of the PSD, which specifies "business activities other than the provision of payment services, having regard to applicable Community [i.e., EU] and national law."

institution is to safeguard, which "is to be used for future payment transactions" – with the remainder "to be used for non-payment services" [448].

Directive 2009/110/EC is tied in with the PSD, which contrasts with Directive 2000/46/EC, whose provisions were unrelated to payment services. This change in emphasis may help to increase the number of electronic money issuers, and the amount of electronic money issued, within the EEA[916]. In particular, a credit institution that is authorised in accordance with CRD IV may provide payment services in concurrence with the provisions of the PSD and its national transposing legislation, and also issue electronic money in agreement with the rules in Directive 2009/110/EC and its domestic transposing law. Thus, there is a harmonising effect across the financial sector by the alignment of electronic money issuance with mainstream retail banking. This change may successfully address some of the criticisms that the Commission's review of Directive 2000/46/EC raised in respect of that Directive, which has now been repealed[917].

Payment Services

Whilst the PSD results in shorter execution times for, and greater clarity in, cross-border payment transactions and materially contributes towards accomplishing a single market for payment services, it does not substantially affect the entry of new payment service providers into the market, "technical innovations," and the efficiency of the provision of these services [449]. Furthermore: (i) "card, internet and mobile payments" are not integrated across the EEA[918], (ii) "many innovative payment products or services" are beyond the PSD's scope, and (iii) in some instances, the PSD's ambit has proved "to be too ambiguous, too general or simply outdated, taking into account market developments," which has "resulted in legal uncertainty, potential security risks in the payment chain and a lack of consumer protection in certain areas" [450].

Thus, "new rules should be established to close the regulatory gaps," whilst "providing more legal clarity and ensuring consistent application of the legislative framework" throughout the EEA [451]. PSD II "should aim to ensure continuity in the market, enabling existing and new service providers ... to offer their services within a clear and harmonised regulatory framework" [452]. Nevertheless, PSD II "does not substantially change the conditions for granting and maintaining authorisation as payment institutions" [453].

PSD II is accompanied by Regulation (EU) No 2015/751 of the European Parliament and of the Council of 29 April 2015 on interchange fees for card-based payment transactions, which "aims to accelerate the achievement of an effective integrated market for card-based payments" [454]. For the purposes of Regulation (EU) No 2015/751, an 'interchange fee' is a sum that is paid for each transaction between the issuer[919] and the acquirer[920] in respect of a

---

[916] Unlike Directive 2009/110/EC, Directive 2000/46/EC is not labelled a 'Text with EEA relevance'.

[917] Directive 2000/46/EC was "repealed with effect from 30 April 2011" (Directive 2009/110/EC, Article 21).

[918] The PSD and PSD II are both labelled 'Text with EEA relevance'. Therefore, 'Member State' within these Directives means 'EEA State'.

[919] For the purposes of Regulation (EU) No 2015/751, 'issuer' means a payment service provider which contracts to supply a payer with a payment instrument to commence and process the card-based payment transactions of that payer (Regulation (EU) No 2015/751, Article 2(2)). For the purposes of Regulation (EU) No 2015/751, 'payment instrument' means any set of procedures and/or personalised device(s) that the payment service user

card-based payment transaction[921] [455]. Payment service providers are only to offer or request an interchange fee per transaction of 0.2% or less of that transaction's value for any debit card transaction [456]., and of 0.3% or less of that transaction's value for any credit card transaction [457]. Member States may define a lower interchange fee cap per transaction than 0.2% for domestic debit card transactions[922] [458], and 0.3% for credit card transactions [459]. These levels of interchange fee cap "are based on an estimate of the fee at which a merchant would be indifferent between being paid by card and cash" [460]. The Commission explains why it is necessary to apply this cap, as follows [461].

> Cardholders are encouraged to use cards that generate higher fees, and card companies compete primarily to attract issuing banks by offering high(er) interchange fees. Hence, competition between payment card schemes actually leads to cost increases for retailers, which they pass on to all consumers through relatively higher retail prices, given that merchants find it difficult to refuse and/or to surcharge in particular the 'must-take' consumer debit and credit cards. Consumers paying with debit cards or in cash thus 'subsidise' the air miles of the users of expensive cards. New and innovative providers of mobile or online payment services cannot enter the market and (low fee) domestic operators cannot expand as banks expect at least the same (high) revenues from them as for normal card payments. As a result, consumers and merchants cannot benefit from seamless and efficient payment means and European companies are at a competitive disadvantage on the global stage [461].

Regulation (EU) No 2015/751 also lays down business rules for payment card schemes[923]. Payment card schemes and processing entities[924]: (a) are to "be independent in

---

and the payment service provider agree, and use in order to begin a payment order (Regulation (EU) No 2015/751, Article 2(19)).

[920] For the purposes of Regulation (EU) No 2015/751, 'acquirer' means a payment service provider that contracts with a payee to accept and to process card-based payment transactions, which results in a transfer of funds to that payee (Regulation (EU) No 2015/751, Article 2(1)).

[921] For the purposes of Regulation (EU) No 2015/751, 'card-based payment transaction' means a service that is founded on a payment card scheme's business rules and infrastructure, to make a payment transaction using any card, digital, information technology or telecommunication device or software – if this results in a credit or debit card transaction (Regulation (EU) No 2015/751, Article 2(7)). For the purposes of Regulation (EU) No 2015/751, 'payment card scheme' means one set of implementation guidelines, practices, rules and/or standards for the carrying out of card-based transactions, which is separated from any payment system or infrastructure that supports that scheme's functioning, and which includes any specific decision-making entity that is accountable for the scheme's operation (Regulation (EU) No 2015/751, Article 2(16)). For the purposes of Regulation (EU) No 2015/751, 'payment transaction' means an action of transferring funds between the payer and the payee, irrespective of any underlying duties between them (Regulation (EU) No 2015/751, Article 2(26)).

[922] Member States may permit payment service providers to combine this interchange fee cap per transaction for domestic debit card transactions with an interchange fee per transaction of up to 0.05 Euros, as long as the payment card scheme's aggregate interchange fees are no more than 0.2% of the total yearly transaction value of these transactions within each payment card scheme (Regulation (EU) No 2015/751, Article 3(2)(b)).

[923] Chapter III of Regulation (EU) No 2015/751 contains these rules, and comprises Articles 6-12 of that Regulation.

[924] For the purposes of Regulation 2015/751, "'processing entity' means any natural or legal person providing payment transaction processing services" (Regulation (EU) No 2015/751, Article 2(28)). For the purposes of Regulation (EU) No 2015/751, 'processing' means the carrying out of payment transaction processing services – i.e., the actions that are necessary in order to deal with a payment instruction between the issuer and the acquirer (Regulation (EU) No 2015/751, Article 2(27)).

terms of accounting, organisation and decision-making processes"[925], (b) are not to "present prices for payment card scheme and processing activities in a bundled manner," and are not to "cross-subsidise" these activities, and (c) are not to discriminate between their subsidiaries/shareholders and their contractual partners – especially by making the supply of any of the services that they offer conditional on any contractual partner's acceptance of any other service that they provide [462]. After the carrying out of an individual card-based payment transaction, the payee's payment service provider is to supply the following information to the payee: (a) the reference number of this transaction, (b) the amount of the transaction, and (c) the amount of any charges for the transaction – showing separately the merchant service charge and the interchange fee[926] [463]. Regulation (EU) No 2015/751 straightens out, and harmonises, aspects of the law in relation to the processing of card-based payment transactions. This is a welcome development, which is likely to reduce costs and improve competition in this area – although payment service providers may find and exploit loopholes in the law, so it will need regular review from the EBA and the Commission.

PSD II entered into force on 12th January 2016 [464]. Notwithstanding this, Member States are to adopt, publish and apply "the measures necessary to comply with" PSD II only from 13th January 2018 [465]. Consequently, the PSD is to be "repealed with effect from" the latter date [466]. At the date of writing, the PSD, its national transposing legislation, and PSD II, are all in force. As it is hoped that this book will be read beyond 13th January 2018, at which point PSD II and its domestic transposing legislation will be in force, it is PSD II – rather than the most recent consolidation of the PSD – which is to be compared with the original version of the PSD as reported in Chapter 1.

As under the PSD[927], payment service providers comprise payment institutions – which are authorised in accordance with PSD II[928], credit institutions, electronic money institutions, post office giro institutions, the European Central Bank, national central banks, Member States[929], and the regional and local authorities of those countries [467]. Branches within the

---

[925] The EBA may, after consulting an advisory panel that is established pursuant to Article 41 of Regulation (EU) No 1093/2010, develop draft RTSs which establish "the requirements to be complied with by payment card schemes and processing entities to ensure the application of" Article 7(1)(a) of Regulation (EU) No 2015/751 – i.e., point (a) in the text; these draft RTSs were to be sent to the Commission by 9th December 2015, which has power to adopt them "in accordance with Articles 10 to 14 of Regulation (EU) No 1093/2010" (Regulation (EU) No 2015/751, Article 7(6)). See the subsection entitled 'RTSs and CDRs', in the section entitled 'The ESAs and Delegated Legislation' in Chapter 3, for for a description of the procedure in Articles 10-14 of Regulation (EU) No 1093/2010 for the development and the publication of RTSs and CDRs. The EBA published this draft RTS on 8th December 2015, within a Consultation Paper upon which it invited responses to be returned by 8th March 2016 (European Banking Authority (2015), Consultation Paper: Draft Regulatory Technical Standards on separation of payment card schemes and processing entities under Article 7(6) of Regulation (EU) 2015/751, EBA/CP/2015/24, pp.1 and 3, <https://www.eba.europa.eu/documents/10180/1303831/EBA-CP-2015-24+%28CP+on+RTS+on+separation+under+IFR+%29.pdf>).

[926] If the payee gives "prior and explicit consent," this information "may be aggregated by brand, application, payment instrument categories and rates of interchange fees" that apply to the transaction (Regulation (EU) No 2015/751, Article 12(1)).

[927] See the opening 2 sentences of the 2nd paragraph of the subsection entitled 'Payment services', in the section entitled 'Banking Legislation' in Chapter 1, for these provisions in the original version of the PSD.

[928] For the purposes of PSD II, 'payment institution' means a legal person which has been granted authorisation in concurrence with Article 11 of PSD II, to supply and carry out payment services throughout the EEA (PSD II, Article 4(4)). As PSD II is labelled 'Text with EEA relevance', references to 'Union' in this Directive are to be read as references to 'EEA' – except if the word 'Union' is followed by the word 'law', in which case the phrase is to be read as 'EU law'.

[929] 'Member States' means 'EEA States' – see fn 918.

EEA of electronic money institutions whose head office is in a third country[930], and of credit institutions, are also included as payment service providers – which differs from the original version of the PSD [468].

The amount of initial capital that payment institutions are required to hold is the same under PSD II as under the PSD[931] – although the list of payment services in the Annex of the PSD has been modified in Annex I to PSD II[932] [469]. Each payment institution's own funds requirements are also unchanged[933].

The passporting requirements for an authorised payment institution under PSD II are consistent with those that the PSD specifies[934] – although PSD II introduces the following additional specifications that the institution must provide in order to establish a branch in a Member State other than its home Member State (i.e., under the right of establishment), "with regard to the payment service business in the host Member State": (i) a business plan – which is to include "a forecast budget calculation for the first 3 financial years which demonstrates that the applicant is able to employ the appropriate and proportionate systems and procedures to operate annually," and (ii) "a description of the applicant's governance arrangements and internal control mechanisms, including administrative, risk management and accounting procedures, which demonstrates that those governance arrangements, control mechanism and procedures are proportionate, appropriate, sound and adequate" [470]. It is submitted that this is a substantial amount of information – which renders the right of establishment a conditional passport. In addition, PSD II introduces new requirements as to: (i) the procedure for passporting payment services[935], (ii) the supervision of payment institutions that are passporting these services[936], and (iii) measures that the competent authority of the home Member State, or of the host Member State, may take – in instances of "a serious threat to the collective interests of the payments service users in the host Member State" [471]. or of actual

---

[930] The payment services that these branches provide must be connected to "the issuance of electronic money" (PSD II, Article 1(1)(b)).

[931] See fn 202 in the subsection entitled 'Payment services', in the section entitled 'Banking Legislation' in Chapter 1, for the amount of capital that payment institutions are required to hold under the PSD.

[932] Payment service no. 5 is modified from "Issuing and/or acquiring of payment instruments." in the PSD, to "Issuing of payment instruments and/or acquiring of payment transactions." in PSD II; payment service no. 7 is altered from "Execution of payment transactions where the consent of the payer to execute a payment transaction is given by means of any telecommunication, digital or IT device and the payment is made to the telecommunication, IT system or network operator, acting only as an intermediary between the payment service user and the supplier of the goods and services." in the PSD, to "Payment initiation services." in PSD II; PSD II introduces "Account information services." as payment service no. 8 (PSD (original version), Annex; PSD II, Annex I).

[933] See fn 203 in the subsection entitled 'Payment services', in the section entitled 'Banking Legislation' in Chapter 1, for the own funds requirements for payment institutions under the PSD. Article 8(2)(b) of the PSD, which refers to the scaling factor for payment service no. 7 in the Annex (which PSD II changes: see fn 932) – to be used in Methods B and C in Article 8(1) of that Directive for the calculation of a payment institution's own funds, does not appear in PSD II; moreover, Article 9(2) of PSD II, which supersedes Article 8(2) of the PSD, does not include a scaling factor for either replacement payment service no. 7 or new payment service no. 8 (see fn 932). It is submitted that these are minor modifications in respect of the computation of the own funds requirements for payment institutions – which is otherwise identical in the PSD and PSD II.

[934] See the final sentence of the 2nd paragraph of the subsection entitled 'Payment services', in the section entitled 'Banking Legislation' in Chapter 1, for the passporting requirements that the PSD specifies.

[935] Paragraphs 2-5 of Article 28 of PSD II contain these requirements.

[936] Article 29 of PSD II contains these requirements, which are much more comprehensive than their rudimentary equivalents in paragraphs 2-4 of Article 25 of the PSD.

non-compliance with specified parts of PSD II and/or its national transposing provisions[937] [472].

The informational requirements under PSD II in respect of single payment transaction are consistent with those under PSD[938], although additional information is required under PSD II. For example, a new Article 46 is inserted into PSD II, which is entitled 'Information for the payer and payee after the initiation of a payment order', and is as follows.

> In addition to the information and conditions specified in Article 45 [of PSD II]., where a payment order is initiated through a payment initiation service provider, the payment initiation service provider shall, immediately after initiation, provide or make available all of the following data to the payer and, where applicable, the payee: (a) confirmation of the successful initiation of the payment order with the payer's account servicing payment service provider; (b) a reference enabling the payer and the payee to identify the payment transaction and, where appropriate, the payee to identify the payer, and any information transferred with the payment transaction; (c) the amount of the payment transaction; (d) where applicable, the amount of any charges payable to the payment initiation service provider for the transaction, and where applicable a breakdown of the amounts of such charges [473].

There is no definition of 'payment initiation service provider' in the PSD,. For the purposes of PSD II, 'payment initiation service provider' is defined as "a payment service provider pursuing business activities as referred to in point (7) of Annex I" of PSD II [474]. As stated above[939], payment service no. 7 in Annex I of PSD II is entitled "Payment initiation services" [475]. This payment service is absent from the PSD, as PSD II changes the description of payment service no. 7[940].

The 30 definitions in Article 4 of the PSD have equivalent provisions in Article 4 of PSD II, whilst there are 18 new definitions in the latter [476]. The definition of 'payment initiation service provider'[941] is one of these new items. Another of these is the definition of 'account information service provider', which is described as "a payment service provider pursuing business activities as referred to in point (8) of Annex I" of PSD II [477]. As stated above[942], payment service no. 8 in Annex I of PSD II is entitled "Account information services" [478]. Whilst 'payment initiation service provider' appears in connection with single payment transactions but not with framework contracts, 'account information service provider' is absent from both[943]. Much of the detail concerning account information service providers is concentrated in Article 33 of PSD II, which exempts them from several of the authorisation requirements for payment institutions and from many of the operative provisions of the Directive [479]., and in Article 67 of PSD II, which concerns restrictions on the provision of

---

[937] Article 30 of PSD contains these requirements.

[938] See the opening sentence of the penultimate paragraph of the subsection entitled 'Payment services', in the section entitled 'Banking Legislation' in Chapter 1, for an outline of those requirements.

[939] See fn 932.

[940] Fn 932 provides the titles of payment service no. 7 in the PSD, and in PSD II.

[941] See the antepenultimate sentence in the previous paragraph, for the definition of 'payment initiation service provider' in PSD II.

[942] See fn 932.

[943] In PSD II, Chapter 2 of Title III (Articles 43-49) contains informational requirements for single payment transactions, and Chapter 3 of Title III (Articles 50-58) informational requirements for framework contracts.

account information services to payment service users[944] [480]. For example, the account information service provider is only to supply services for which the payment service user has given his/her/its explicit consent [481]., and is not to require "sensitive payment data" that is connected to the payment accounts[945] [482].

Thus, PSD II builds upon the authorisation, passporting and payment procedural structure of the PSD. It inserts additional requirements, and defines further categories of payment service provider. As the classes of payment service become better delineated, there may be further subdivisions in the precise regulatory requirements for different types of payment service, with the eventual outcome being a Payment Services Regulation supplemented by CDRs and CIRs that the Commission develops in association with the EBA.

Reorganisation and Winding Up

Directive 2001/24/EC has only been amended once – by the BRRD in 2014. Thence, other than these modifications, the law is unchanged from that described in the corresponding subsection in Chapter 1[946].

This subsection describes the amendments that the BRRD has introduced to Directive 2001/24/EC. The BRRD is considered in the next subsection.

Recital 119 of the BRRD introduces the rationale for its changes to Directive 2001/24/EC, as follows.

> Directive 2001/24/EC ... provides for the mutual recognition and enforcement in all Member States of decisions concerning the reorganisation or winding up of institutions having branches in Member States other than those in which they have their head offices. That [D]irective ensures that all assets and liabilities of the institution, regardless of the country in which they are situated, are dealt with in a single process in the home Member State and that creditors in the host Member States are treated in the same way as creditors in the home Member State. In order to achieve an effective resolution, Directive 2001/24/EC should apply in the event of use of the resolution tools both when those instruments are applied to institutions and when they are applied to other entities covered by the resolution regime. Directive 2001/24/EC should therefore be amended accordingly [483].

The above Recital refers to 'institutions,' which, for the purposes of the BRRD, comprise credit institutions and investment firms [484]. The scope of the original (pre-GFC) version of Directive 2001/24/EC applies to credit institutions and their branches, but not to investment

---

[944] For the purposes of PSD II, 'payment service user' means a (natural or legal) person who makes use of a payment service, either as payer or payee, or as both (PSD II, Article 4(10)). This definition is unchanged from that in Article 4(10) of the PSD – which is stated in fn 211 in the subsection entitled 'Payment services', in the section entitled 'Banking Legislation' in Chapter 1.

[945] For the purposes of PSD II, 'payment account' means an account that is held in the name of at least one payment service user, which is used to carry out payment transactions (PSD II, Article 4(12)).

[946] This is the subsection entitled 'Reorganisation and winding up', in the section entitled 'Banking Legislation' in Chapter 1.

firms or their branches[947]. Accordingly, the BRRD adds the following sentence to Directive 2001/24/EC, thereby broadening the latter's sphere of application.

This Directive [i.e., Directive 2001/24/EC] shall also apply to investment firms … and their branches located in Member States other than those in which they have their head offices [485, 486].

The above Recital states that Directive 2001/24/EC should apply when the BRRD's tools for resolution are "applied to other entities covered by the resolution regime." Therefore, the BRRD inserts the following provision into Directive 2001/24/EC.

In the event of application of the resolution tools and exercise of the resolution powers provided for in Directive 2014/59/EU [i.e., the BRRD]., this Directive [Directive 2001/24/EC] shall also apply to the financial institutions, firms and parent undertakings falling within the scope of Directive 2014/59/EU [487, 488].

The BRRD also adds the following sentences to Directive 2001/24/EC.

Articles 4 and 7 of this Directive [Directive 2001/24/EC] shall not apply where Article 83 of Directive 2014/59/EU [the BRRD] applies. Article 33 of this Directive [Directive 2001/24/EC] shall not apply where Article 84 of Directive 2014/59/EU applies [489, 490].

These provisions prioritise BRRD rules over laws on the same subject area in Directive 2001/24/EC, in situations in which the BRRD applies. For example, Article 33 of Directive 2001/24/EC requires all persons who are "required to receive or divulge information" in association with the procedures laid down in 6 specified Articles[948] of that Directive, to "be bound by professional secrecy, in accordance with the rules and conditions laid down in" the relevant banking legislation[949], other than "any judicial authorities to which existing national provisions apply" [491]. In instances in which the BRRD applies, the duty of professional

---

[947] See the opening sentence of the subsection entitled 'Reorganisation and winding up', in the section entitled 'Banking Legislation' in Chapter 1, for the scope of the original version of Directive 2001/24/EC.

[948] These are Articles 4, 5, 8, 9, 11 and 19 of Directive 2001/24/EC (Directive 2001/24/EC (as amended to 12/06/14), Article 33).

[949] This legislation is "Article 30 of Directive 2000/12/EC" (Directive 2001/24/EC (as amended to 12/06/14), Article 33). The BCD repealed Directive 2000/12/EC (BCD (original version), Article 158(1)). References to Directive 2000/12/EC are to "be construed as being made to this Directive [i.e., the BCD] and should be read in accordance with the correlation table in Annex XIV" of the BCD (BCD (original version), Article 158(2)). Article 30 of Directive 2000/12/EC correlates with Articles 44-52 of the BCD (BCD (original version), Annex XIV). CRD IV repealed the BCD (and the CRD) "with effect from 1 January 2014"; references to those "repealed Directives shall be construed as references to this Directive [i.e., CRD IV] and to Regulation (EU) No 575/2013 [i.e., the CRR] and shall be read in accordance with the correlation table set out in Annex II to this Directive and in Annex IV to Regulation (EU) No 575/2013" (CRD IV (as amended to 12/06/14), Article 163). Articles 44-52 of the BCD correlate with Articles 53(1)-(2), 54-58, 59(1) and 60-61 of CRD IV (CRD IV (as amended to 12/06/14), Annex II). These provisions of CRD IV concern professional secrecy, confidentiality and the disclosure, transmission and exchange of information. As it is unclear which of these provisions is to apply to Article 33 of Directive 2001/24/EC, the Commission should introduce an amendment to Directive 2001/24/EC to replace the phrase "Article 30 of Directive 2000/12/EC" in Article 33 of Directive 2001/24/EC, which should contain a reference to the provisions from CRD IV that it would like place in that phrase's stead.

secrecy under Article 33 of Directive 2001/24/EC and 'the relevant banking legislation'[950] is replaced by the duties of professional secrecy and confidentiality in Article 84(1)-(3) of the BRRD, subject to the derogations in paragraphs 4, 5 and 6 of that Article [492].

The BRRD inserts a revised list of definitions into Directive 2001/24/EC. Whilst the definitions of 'administrator', 'administrative or judicial authorities', 'liquidator' and 'winding-up proceedings' are the same in the current version of Directive 2001/24/EC to those in the original (pre-GFC) version of that Directive[951], the definitions of 'home Member State'[952], 'host Member State'[953], 'branch'[954], 'competent authorities'[955] and 'reorganisation measures'[956] have been modified to reflect the recent addition of investment firms and their branches to the scope of Directive 2001/24/EC[957] and the resolution tools and powers for which the BRRD provides [493, 494].

The original (pre-GFC) version of Directive 2001/24/EC stated that repurchase agreements (subject to one proviso[958]), and netting agreements, were to be exclusively governed by the law of the contract that applied to them[959]. Whilst these rules persist in the

---

[950] See fn 949.

[951] See fns 196, 182, 187 and 186 in the subsection entitled 'Reorganisation and winding up' in the section entitled 'Banking Legislation' in Chapter 1, for the definitions of 'administrator', 'administrative or judicial authorities', 'liquidator' and 'winding-up proceedings', respectively.

[952] For the purposes of Directive 2001/24/EC, 'home Member State' means the Member State in which a credit institution or an investment firm has been provided with authorisation (Directive 2001/24/EC (as amended to 12/06/14), Article 2; CRR (as amended to 17/01/15), Articles 4(1)(43) and 4(1)(3)). See fn 181 of the subsection entitled 'Reorganisation and winding up', in the section entitled 'Banking Legislation' in Chapter 1, for the definition of 'home Member State' in the original version of Directive 2001/24/EC.

[953] For the purposes of Directive 2001/24/EC, 'host Member State' means the Member State in which a credit institution or an investment firm supplies services or has a branch (Directive 2001/24/EC (as amended to 12/06/14), Article 2; CRR (as amended to 17/01/15), Articles 4(1)(44) and 4(1)(3)). See fn 184 of the subsection entitled 'Reorganisation and winding up', in the section entitled 'Banking Legislation' in Chapter 1, for the definition of 'host Member State' in the original version of Directive 2001/24/EC.

[954] For the purposes of Directive 2001/24/EC, 'branch' means a place of business that is a legally-dependent component of a credit institution or of an investment firm, and which directly executes some or all of the transactions which are "inherent in the business of" credit institutions and investment firms (Directive 2001/24/EC (as amended to 12/06/14), Article 2; CRR (as amended to 17/01/15), Articles 4(1)(17) and 4(1)(23)). See fn 179 of the subsection entitled 'Reorganisation and winding up', in the section entitled 'Banking Legislation' in Chapter 1, for the definition of 'branch' in the original version of Directive 2001/24/EC.

[955] For the purposes of Directive 2001/24/EC, 'competent authority' means: (i) a public entity that national law officially recognises, which that law empowers to supervise credit institutions and investment firms as part of the relevant Member State's functioning supervisory system, or (ii) a resolution authority that a Member State designates, which is empowered to administer the resolution tools and use the resolution powers specified in the BRRD – with respect to reorganisation measures that this authority takes in accordance with that Directive (Directive 2001/24/EC (as amended to 12/06/14), Article 2; CRR (as amended to 17/01/15), Articles 4(1)(40) and 4(1)(3)); BRRD, Articles 2(1)(18) and 3(1)). See fn 185 of the subsection entitled 'Reorganisation and winding up', in the section entitled 'Banking Legislation' in Chapter 1, for the definition of 'competent authorities' in the original version of Directive 2001/24/EC.

[956] For the purposes of Directive 2001/24/EC, 'reorganisation measures' means measures that are intended to maintain or restore the financial circumstances of a credit institution or of an investment firm, and which might affect the pre-existing rights of third parties – including the resolution tools and powers that the BRRD provides (Directive 2001/24/EC (as amended to 12/06/14), Article 2). See fn 183 of the subsection entitled 'Reorganisation and winding up', in the section entitled 'Banking Legislation' in Chapter 1, for the definition of 'reorganisation measures' in the original version of Directive 2001/24/EC.

[957] See above in this subsection, for the BRRD's insertion of a provision into Directive 2001/24/EC that extends the latter's scope to include investment firms and their branches.

[958] See the 8th sentence of the final paragraph of the subsection entitled 'Reorganisation and winding up', in the section entitled 'Banking Legislation' in Chapter 1, for this proviso.

[959] See the 9th sentence of, and fn 195 in, the final paragraph of the subsection entitled 'Reorganisation and winding up', in the section entitled 'Banking Legislation' in Chapter 1, for these statements.

current version of Directive 2001/24/EC, the BRRD has subordinated them to Articles 68 and 71 of that Directive [495, 496]., which respectively provide for the exclusion of specified contractual terms in early intervention and resolution as long as "the substantive obligations under the contract … continue to be performed" [497]., and for "resolution authorities to have the power to suspend the termination rights of any party to a contract with an institution under resolution … provided that the payment and delivery obligations and the provision of collateral continue to be performed" [498].

It is submitted that the fit between the relatively straightforward provisions of Directive 2001/24/EC and the complex rules of the BRRD – which was introduced after the GFC and is based on international standards[960] – is only partial. One reason for this is the ideological basis for the earlier legislative instrument, in comparison to the damage-limitation nature of the later one – due to the different circumstances. Compare the first 2 recitals of each of these Directives.

> In accordance with the objectives of the Treaty [Establishing the European Community]., the harmonious and balanced development of economic activities throughout the Community should be promoted through the elimination of any obstacles to the freedom of establishment and the freedom to provide services within the Community [499]. At the same time as those obstacles are eliminated, consideration should be given to the situation which might arise if a credit institution runs into difficulties, particularly where that institution has branches in other Member States [500].
>
> The financial crisis has shown that there is a significant lack of adequate tools at [European]. Union level to deal effectively with unsound or failing credit institutions and investment firms ('institutions'). Such tools are needed, in particular, to prevent insolvency or, when insolvency occurs, to minimise negative repercussions by preserving the systemically important functions of the institution concerned. During the crisis, those challenges were a major factor that forced Member States to save institutions using taxpayers' money. The objective of a credible recovery and resolution framework is to obviate the need for such action to the greatest extent possible [501]. The financial crisis was of systemic dimension in the sense that it affected the access to funding of a large proportion of credit institutions. To avoid failure, with consequences for the overall economy, such a crisis necessitates measures aiming to secure access to funding under equivalent conditions for all credit institutions that are otherwise solvent. Such measures involve liquidity support from central banks and guarantees from Member States for securities issued by solvent credit institutions [502].

The 'heavier regulatory atmosphere' that is now present in the wake of the GFC is likely to remain, and is something with which all participants in the financial sector need to, and will need to, work. More specifically, it remains to explore and to examine some of the measures that the BRRD has introduced – before the post-GFC legislation is considered as a whole.

---

[960] See the subsections entitled 'The BRRD' and 'Analysis', in the section entitled 'G20/FSB Guidance and EU Law' in Chapter 2, for an investigation as to the extent to which the BRRD is consistent with the Recommendations of the BCBS' Cross-border Banking Resolution Group and the FSB's Key Attributes for Effective Resolution Regimes.

Bank Recovery and Resolution

The BRRD contains rules and procedures that relate to the recovery and resolution of: (a) credit institutions and investment firms that are founded in the EEA[961], (b) financial institutions that are established in the EEA, which are subsidiaries of a credit institution, an investment firm or a company to which point (c) or (d) refer, and which is "covered by the supervision of the parent undertaking on a consolidated basis in accordance with Articles 6 to 17 of" the CRR, (c) financial holding companies, mixed financial holding companies and mixed-activity holding companies that are founded in the EEA, (d) parent financial holding companies in a Member State, Union parent financial holding companies, parent mixed financial holding companies in a Member State, and Union parent mixed financial holding companies, and branches of credit institutions and investment firms that are established in third countries in concurrence with the particular conditions that the BRRD lays down[962] [503]. Member States[963] are to ensure that each credit institution and investment firm, which is not a member of a group[964] that is "subject to consolidated supervision pursuant to Articles 111 and 112 of" CRD IV, constructs and maintains a recovery plan[965], which provides for the credit institution/investment firm "to restore its financial position following a significant deterioration of its financial situation" [504]. A competent authority[966] is to ensure that each credit institution and investment firm updates its recovery plan every year, and after alterations to "the legal or organisational structure," the business or the financial circumstances of the credit institution/investment firm that could substantially affect, or precipitate a change to, this plan[967] [505]. Section A of the Annex to the BRRD contains the

---

[961] As the BRRD is labelled 'Text with EEA relevance', references to 'Union' in this Directive are to be read as references to 'EEA'.

[962] For the purposes of the BRRD, definitions are provided as follows; (i) credit institution: Article 4(1)(1) of the CRR, excluding the entities to which Article 2(5) of CRD IV refers (BRRD, Article 2(1)(2)), (ii) investment firm: Article 4(1)(2) of the CRR, which "is subject to the initial capital requirement" to which Article 28(2) of the CRR refers (BRRD, Article 2(1)(3)), (iii) financial institution: Article 4(1)(26) of the CRR (BRRD, Article 2(1)(4)), (iv) subsidiary: Article 4(1)(16) of the CRR (BRRD, Article 2(1)(5)), (v) parent undertaking: Article 4(1)(15)(a) of the CRR (BRRD, Article 2(1)(6)), (vi) consolidated basis: "the basis of the consolidated situation," as Article 4(1)(47) of the CRR defines (BRRD, Article 2(1)(7)), (vii) financial holding company: Article 4(1)(20) of the CRR (BRRD, Article 2(1)(9)), (viii) mixed financial holding company: Article 4(1)(21) of the CRR (BRRD, Article 2(1)(10)), (ix) mixed-activity holding company: Article 4(1)(22) of the CRR (BRRD, Article 2(1)(11)), (x) parent financial holding company in a Member State: Article 4(1)(30) of the CRR (BRRD, Article 2(1)(12)), (xi) Union parent financial holding company: "an EU parent financial holding company" as Article 4(1)(31) of the CRR defines (BRRD, Article 2(1)(13)), (xii) parent mixed financial holding company in a Member State: Article 4(1)(32) of the CRR (BRRD, Article 2(1)(14)), (xiii) Union parent mixed financial holding company: "an EU parent mixed financial holding company" as Article 4(1)(33) of the CRR defines (BRRD, Article 2(1)(15)), and (xiv) branch: Article 4(1)(17) of the CRR (BRRD, Article 2(1)(17)); see fn 954, for the definition of 'branch' in Articles 4(1)(17) and 4(1)(23) of the CRR.

[963] As the BRRD is labelled 'Text with EEA relevance', 'Member State' within this Directive means 'EEA State'.

[964] For the purposes of the BRRD, a 'group' is "a parent undertaking and its subsidiaries" (BRRD, Article 2(1)(26)).

[965] For the purposes of the BRRD, 'recovery plan' means a recovery plan that is constructed and maintained in agreement with Article 5 of the BRRD (BRRD, Article 2(1)(32)).

[966] For the purposes of the BRRD, a 'competent authority' is a public entity that domestic law officially recognises, which that law empowers to oversee credit institutions and investment firms as part of the relevant Member State's operational supervisory system, including the European Central Bank in respect of tasks that Council Regulation (EU) No 1024/2013 confers upon it (BRRD, Article 2(1)(21); CRR (as amended to 17/01/15), Articles 4(1)(40) and 4(1)(3)). The section entitled 'The EBA and the European Central Bank' in Chapter 3 considers the interface between the EBA and the European Central Bank, as laid down in Council Regulation (EU) No 1024/2013.

[967] A competent authority may require credit institutions or investment firms to update their recovery plans more often than annually or after material changes (BRRD, Article 5(2)).

information that each recovery plan is to include – for instance, summaries of the main components of the plan, the overall capacity of the entity for recovery, and of substantial changes to it since the most recently-filed recovery plan[968] [506]. Member States are to require recovery plans to: (i) "include appropriate conditions and procedures," in order to ensure that actions for recovery are adopted in a timely way and that a broad range of recovery options are included, and (ii) consider different "scenarios of severe macroeconomic and financial stress" which are pertinent to the credit institution's or investment firm's particular circumstances [507]. Member States are to ensure that Union parent undertakings[969] construct a group recovery plan[970], and submit this to the consolidating supervisor[971]; this plan is to "identify measures that may be required to be implemented at the level of the Union parent undertaking and each individual subsidiary [508]. A competent authority may require a subsidiary to construct and submit a recovery plan on an individual basis, pursuant to a joint decision with the consolidating supervisor – or alone if there is no joint decision within 4 months of the consolidating supervisor sending the group recovery plan to the relevant competent authorities and resolution authorities[972] [509].

---

[968] Member States may require information which is additional to that specified in Section A of the Annex to the BRRD, to be placed in the recovery plans; these plans are also to include measures that the credit institution/investment firm might take, in circumstances under which the conditions for early intervention in Article 27 of the BRRD are fulfilled (BRRD, Article 5(5)). Article 27(1) of the BRRD contains both the conditions that are to be satisfied for a competent authority to apply early intervention measures, and a list of these measures; that authority may: (a) require the credit institution's/investment firm's board of directors to implement at least one of the measures or arrangements in the recovery plan, or to update the plan and apply one or more of the measures or arrangements in the updated plan, (b) require that entity's board of directors to enquire into the situation, identify measures to overcome recognised difficulties, and construct an action programme to solve these problems and a timetable for the implementation of that programme, (c) require the entity's board of directors to convene a meeting of its shareholders and to "require certain decisions to be considered for adoption by the shareholders," (d) require one or more directors or senior managers to be dismissed or replaced, if those persons are considered to be "unfit to perform their duties pursuant to Article 13 of Directive 2013/36/EU [i.e., CRD IV] or Article 9 of Directive 2014/65/EU [i.e., MiFID II]," (e) require the entity's board of directors to construct a plan "for negotiation on restructuring of debt with some or all of its creditors according to the recovery plan" (if applicable), (f) require alterations to the entity's business strategy, (g) require changes to the entity's "legal or operational structures," and (h) obtain through on-site inspections, and supply to the resolution authority, all of the information that is necessary for the resolution plan to be updated, and prepare for the entity's possible resolution and the valuation of its assets and liabilities "in accordance with Article 36" of the BRRD (BRRD, Article 27(1)).

[969] For the purposes of the BRRD, a 'Union parent undertaking' is a Union parent institution, a Union parent financial holding company (see point (xi) in fn 962), or a Union parent mixed financial holding company (see point (xiii) in fn 962). For the purposes of the BRRD, a 'Union parent institution' is "a parent institution in a Member State [defined in Articles 2(1)(49) of the BRRD and 4(1)(28) of the CRR] which is not a subsidiary [see point (iv) in fn 962] of another institution [i.e., a credit institution or an investment firm] authorised in any Member State, or of a financial holding company [see point (vii) in fn 962] or mixed financial holding company [see point (viii) in fn 962] set up in any Member State" (BRRD, Articles 2(1)(50) and 2(1)(23); CRR (as amended to 17/01/15), Article 4(1)(29)).

[970] For the purposes of the BRRD, 'group recovery plan' means a group recovery plan that is constructed and maintained in concurrence with Article 7 of the BRRD (BRRD, Article 2(1)(33)).

[971] For the purposes of the BRRD, a 'consolidating supervisor' is "a competent authority [see fn 966] responsible for the exercise of supervision on a consolidated basis of EU parent institutions [i.e., Union parent institutions – see fn 969] and of institutions [i.e., credit institutions and investment firms] controlled by EU parent financial holding companies [defined in Article 4(1)(31) of the CRR] or EU parent mixed financial holding companies [defined in Article 4(1)(33) of the CRR]" (BRRD, Articles 2(1)(37) and 2(1)(23); CRR (as amended to 17/01/15), Article 4(1)(41)).

[972] For the purposes of the BRRD, a 'resolution authority' is an authority that a Member State designates in concurrence with Article 3 of the BRRD (BRRD, Article 2(1)(18)). Article 3(1) of the BRRD states: "Each Member State shall designate one or, exceptionally, more resolution authorities that are empowered to apply the resolution tools and exercise the resolution powers [which the BRRD provides]". The resolution authority

'Resolution' means the use of a resolution tool, or an additional tool that a Member State confers upon its resolution authority in accordance with Article 37(9) of the BRRD, in order to accomplish at least one of the resolution objectives[973] to which Article 31(2) of the BRRD refers [510]. Resolution authorities are to consider the resolution objectives when using the resolution tools[974] and powers[975], and are to select "the tools and powers that best accomplish the objectives that "are relevant in the circumstances of the case" [511]. The resolution objectives are: (a) to ensure that "critical functions" continue, (b) to circumvent "a significant adverse effect on the financial system," (c) to "protect public funds," (d) to shield depositors and investors, and (e) to protect the funds and the assets of clients [512]. Member States are to ensure that a resolution authority takes a resolution action in relation to a credit institution that is founded in the EEA or an investment firm that is established there, only if all of the following conditions are satisfied: (a) the competent authority has determined that the credit institution/investment firm "is failing or is likely to fail," after it has consulted the resolution authority[976], (b) on consideration of the circumstances, "there is no reasonable prospect [that] any alternative private sector measures ... or supervisory action" (such as early intervention measures[977]) would stop the credit institution/investment firm from failing "within a reasonable timeframe," and (c) a resolution action is "necessary in the public interest," in accordance with Article 32(5) of the BRRD[978] [513].

Member States are to ensure that, when resolution authorities use the resolution tools and powers, they "take all appropriate measures to ensure that" the following principles apply to the resolution action: (a) the shareholders of the institution under resolution[979] carry the first losses, (b) creditors of the institution under resolution bear the next losses, in concurrence with the order of precedence of their claims in standard insolvency proceedings – unless the BRRD states otherwise, (c) the directors and the senior managers of the institution under resolution are replaced, except in instances in which their retention "is considered to be necessary to the achievement of the resolution objectives," (d) the board of directors and the senior managers of the institution under resolution are to give all the assistance that is necessary for the accomplishment of the resolution objectives, (e) "natural or legal persons are made liable, subject to Member State law, under civil or criminal law for their responsibility for the failure of the" credit institution/investment firm, (f) creditors within the same class are treated equitably, unless the BRRD provides otherwise, (g) no creditor is to

---

is to "be a public administrative authority or authorities trusted with public administrative powers" (BRRD, Article 3(2)).

[973] For the purposes of the BRRD, 'resolution objectives' means the objectives to which Article 31(2) of the BRRD refers (BRRD, Article 2(1)(36)). See the 3rd sentence of the current paragraph in the text, for these objectives.

[974] 'Resolution tool' means a resolution tool to which Article 37(3) of the BRRD refers (BRRD, Article 2(1)(19)).

[975] 'Resolution power' means a power to which Articles 63-72 of the BRRD refer (BRRD, Article 2(1)(20)).

[976] Member States may provide that the resolution authority may make this determination, after it has consulted the competent authority, as long as the resolution authority "has the necessary tools for making such a determination" (BRRD, Articles 32(2) and 32(1)(a)).

[977] See fn 968, for the BRRD's list of early intervention measures.

[978] A resolution action is to be considered to be "in the public interest," if it is essential to the accomplishment of, and proportionate to, at least one of the resolution objectives, and if the winding-up of the credit institution/investment firm in the usual way would not satisfy those objectives sufficiently (BRRD, Article 32(5)). See the preceding sentence of the current paragraph in the text, for the resolution objectives.

[979] For the purposes of the BRRD, an 'institution under resolution' is a credit institution, an investment firm, "a financial institution, a financial holding company, a mixed financial holding company, a mixed-activity holding company, a parent financial holding company in a Member State, a Union parent financial holding company, a parent mixed financial holding company in a Member State, or a Union parent mixed financial holding company, in respect of which a resolution action is taken" (BRRD, Articles 2(1)(83) and 2(1)(23)).

incur larger losses that would have been incurred, if the credit institution, investment firm, or entity to which points (b), (c) or (d) in the opening sentence of this subsection[980] refer, had been wound up under standard insolvency proceedings, in concurrence with the safeguards in Articles 73 to 75 of the BRRD[981], (h) "covered deposits[982] are fully protected," and (i) resolution action is taken in agreement with the safeguards that the BRRD contains [514]. The resolution tools are: (a) the sale of business tool[983], (b) the bridge institution tool[984], (c) the asset separation tool[985], and (d) the bail-in tool[986] [515].

The sale of business tool: Member States are to ensure that resolution authorities are to transfer to a buyer that is not a bridge institution[987]: (a) the equity that an institution under resolution has issued, and (b) all, or any, of the assets, liabilities or rights of an institution under resolution [516]. This transfer is to be "made on commercial terms," taking account of the circumstances, and in observance of "the Union State aid framework[988]" [517].

The bridge institution tool: Member States are to make certain that resolution authorities are empowered to transfer the following to a bridge institution: (a) the equity that one or more institutions under resolution have issued, and (b) all, or any, of the assets, liabilities or rights of one or more institutions under resolution [518]. The bridge institution is to be a legal person that satisfies the following requirements: (i) it is owned (wholly or partly) by one or more public authorities, (ii) it "is controlled by the resolution authority," and (iii) it is established in order to receive and to hold some or all of the equity that an institution under

---

[980] 'This subsection' is the subsection entitled 'Bank recovery and resolution'.

[981] For example, Article 74(1) of the BRRD states: "For the purposes of assessing whether shareholders and creditors would have received better treatment if the institution under resolution had entered into normal insolvency proceedings, ... Member States shall ensure that a valuation is carried out by an independent person as soon as possible after the resolution action or actions have been effected. ...."

[982] For the purposes of the BRRD, 'covered deposits' means that part of eligible deposits that is no greater than the coverage level that Article 6 of Directive 2014/49/EU lays down (BRRD, Article 2(1)(94); Directive 2014/49/EU (as corrected to 30/12/14), Article 2(1)(5)). 'Eligible deposits' are deposits that Article 5 of Directive 2014/49/EU does not exclude from protection (Directive 2014/49/EU, (as corrected to 30/12/14), Article 2(1)(4)). Examples of deposits that are excluded from repayment by a deposit guarantee scheme, are those by collective investment undertakings, by pension and retirement funds, and by public authorities (Directive 2014/49/EU (as corrected to 30/12/14), Article 5(1)(h)-(j)). The coverage level for eligible deposits is 100,000 Euros (Directive 2014/49/EU (as corrected to 30/12/14), Article 6(1)) – see the opening sentence of the 5th paragraph of the subsection entitled 'Deposit guarantee and investor compensation schemes', above in this section.

[983] For the purposes of the BRRD, "'sale of business tool' means the mechanism for effecting a transfer by a resolution authority of shares or other instruments of ownership issued by an institution under resolution, or assets, rights or liabilities, of an institution under resolution to a purchaser that is not a bridge institution, in accordance with Article 38" of the BRRD (BRRD, Articles 2(1)(58) and 2(1)(23)).

[984] For the purposes of the BRRD, "'bridge institution tool' means the mechanism for transferring shares or other instruments of ownership issued by an institution under resolution or assets, rights or liabilities of an institution under resolution to a bridge institution, in accordance with Article 40" of the BRRD (BRRD, Articles 2(1)(60) and 2(1)(23)). See fn 987, for the definition of 'bridge institution'.

[985] For the purposes of the BRRD, "'asset separation tool' means the mechanism for effecting a transfer by a resolution authority of assets, rights or liabilities of an institution under resolution to an asset management vehicle in accordance with Article 42" of the BRRD (BRRD, Articles 2(1)(55) and 2(1)(23)).

[986] For the purposes of the BRRD, "'bail-in tool' means the mechanism for effecting the exercise by a resolution authority of the write-down and conversion powers in relation to liabilities of an institution under resolution in accordance with Article 43" of the BRRD (BRRD, Articles 2(1)(57) and 2(1)(23)).

[987] For the purposes of the BRRD, a 'bridge institution' is a legal person that fulfils the requirements that Article 40(2) of the BRRD lays down (BRRD, Article 2(1)(59)). See the 2nd sentence of the next paragraph in the text, for these requirements.

[988] For the purposes of the BRRD, 'Union State aid framework' means the structure that Articles 107-109 of the TFEU establishes, and the regulations and all EU Acts – including communications guidelines and notices – that are made or adopted under Article 108(4) or Article 109 of the TFEU (BRRD, Article 2(1)(53)).

resolution has issued, or of the assets, liabilities and rights of at least one institution under resolution, with a view to preserving "access to critical functions" and to selling the credit institution, investment firm, or entity to which points (b), (c) or (d) in the opening sentence of this subsection[989] refer [519]. The resolution authority is to ensure that the total value of the liabilities that are transferred to the bridge institution is no more than the total values of the assets and the rights which are transferred from the institution under resolution or supplied by other sources [520].

The asset separation tool: Member States are to ensure that resolution authorities are empowered to transfer assets, liabilities or rights of an institution under resolution, or of a bridge institution, to one or more asset management vehicles[990] [521]. This vehicle is to be a legal person that fulfils the following requirements: (i) it is owned (wholly or partly) by one or more public authorities, (ii) it "is controlled by the resolution authority," and (iii) it is founded in order to receive and hold some or all of the assets, liabilities and rights of at least one institution under resolution, or of a bridge institution [522]. The asset management vehicle is to "manage the assets transferred to it," with the intention of "maximising their value through eventual sale or orderly wind down" [523].

The bail-in tool: Member States are to ensure that resolution authorities possess the resolution powers that Article 63(1) of BRRD specifies, "[i]n order to give effect to the bail-in tool" [524]. These powers are to: (a) "require any person to provide information required for the resolution authority to decide upon and prepare a resolution action," (b) take control of an institution under resolution, and use all the powers and rights that are conferred upon the owners and the board of directors of this entity, (c) transfer equity instruments that an institution under resolution has issued, (d) transfer assets, liabilities or rights of an institution under resolution to another entity, with the latter's consent, (e) reduce the main or outstanding amount that is due, with respect to eligible liabilities[991], of an institution under resolution, (f) convert an institution under resolution's eligible liabilities into equity instruments of that credit institution, investment firm, entity to which points (b), (c) or (d) in the opening sentence of this subsection[992] refer, a relevant parent institution[993], or a bridge institution to which assets, liabilities or rights of the credit institution, investment firm or entity to which points (b), (c) or (d) in the opening sentence of this subsection refer, are transferred, (g) cancel debt instruments[994] that an institution under resolution has issued "except for secured

---

[989] 'This subsection' is the subsection entitled 'Bank recovery and resolution'.

[990] For the purposes of the BRRD, an 'asset management vehicle' is a legal person that satisfies the requirements that Article 42(2) of the BRRD lays down (BRRD, Article 2(1)(56)). See the following sentence in the text, for those requirements.

[991] For the purposes of the BRRD, 'eligible liabilities' are the capital instruments and liabilities that do not qualify as Tier 1 or Tier 2 instruments of a credit institution, an investment firm, or an entity to which points (b), (c) or (d) in the opening sentence of this subsection refer, which Article 44(2) of the BRRD does not exclude from the bail-in tool's scope (BRRD, Article 2(1)(71) and 2(1)(23)). See the next sentence in the text, for Article 44(2) of the BRRD.

[992] 'This subsection' is the subsection entitled 'Bank recovery and resolution'.

[993] For the purposes of the BRRD, a 'relevant parent institution' is "a parent institution in a Member State, a Union parent institution, a financial holding company, a mixed financial holding company, a mixed-activity holding company, a parent financial holding company in a Member State, a Union parent financial holding company, a parent mixed financial holding company in a Member State, or a Union parent mixed financial holding company, in relation to which the bail-in tool is applied" (BRRD, Article 2(1)(79)).

[994] For the purposes of the BRRD, "'debt instruments' referred to in points (g) and (j) of Article 63(1) [of the BRRD – see points (g) and (j) in this sentence in the text] means bonds and other forms of transferable debt, instruments creating or acknowledging a debt, and instruments giving rights to acquire debt instruments" (BRRD, Article 2(1)(48)).

liabilities[995] subject to Article 44(2)" of the BRRD[996], (h) reduce the nominal amount of an institution under resolution's equity instruments, and to cancel these items, (i) require an institution under resolution or a relevant parent institution to issue new capital instruments, (j) alter or amend the maturity date of eligible liabilities that an institution under resolution has issued, or modify the amount of interest that is payable under these liabilities, "or the date on which the interest becomes payable" – other than "secured liabilities subject to Article 44(2)[997]" of the BRRD, (k) close out, and terminate, financial or derivatives contracts, in order to apply Article 49 of the BRRD[998], (l) dismiss or replace the board of directors and the senior managers of an institution under resolution, and (m) require the competent authority to appraise the purchaser of a qualifying holding in a timely way [525]. Resolution authorities are "not to exercise the write down or conversion powers[999] in relation to the following liabilities": (a) covered deposits, (b) secured liabilities, (c) any liability which arises from the holding by the credit institution, investment firm or entity to which points (b), (c) or (d) in the opening sentence of this subsection[1000] refer, of the assets or funds of clients – as long as these customers are "protected under the applicable insolvency or civil law," (d) any liability which arises through a fiduciary relationship between the credit institution, investment firm or entity to which points (b), (c) or (d) in the opening sentence of this subsection refer (as fiduciary) and a different person (as beneficiary) – as long as the "beneficiary is protected under the applicable insolvency or civil law," (e) liabilities to credit institutions and investment firms (other than to entities within the same group), which have an initial maturity of fewer than 7 days, (f) liabilities that have a remaining maturity of fewer than 7 days, which are "owed to systems or operators of systems designated according to Directive 98/26/EC[1001] or their participants and arising from the participation in such a system," and (g) liabilities to: (i) an employee, in respect of the fixed component of his/her remuneration, (ii) a commercial or trade creditor, which arise from the supply of goods or services to the credit institution, investment firm or entity to which points (b), (c) or (d) in the opening sentence of this subsection refer, and which are essential to that organisation's daily operations, (iii) "tax and social security authorities," as long as "those liabilities are preferred under the applicable law," or (iv) deposit guarantee schemes, which arise from contributions that are due under Directive 2014/49/EU[1002] [526].

---

[995] For the purposes of the BRRD, a 'secured liability' is a liability in respect of which the creditor's right "to payment or other form of performance is secured by a charge, pledge, or lien or collateral arrangements" (BRRD, Article 2(1)(67)).

[996] See the next sentence in the text, for Article 44(2) of the BRRD.

[997] See fn 996.

[998] Article 49 of the BRRD concerns the write-down and conversion powers of resolution authorities, in respect of liabilities that arise from derivatives. See fn 999, for the definition of 'write-down and conversion powers'.

[999] For the purposes of the BRRD, 'write down and conversion powers' are the powers to which Articles 59(2) and 63(1)(e)-(i) of the BRRD refer (BRRD, Article 2(1)(66)). Article 63(1)(e)-(i) of the BRRD corresponds to points (e) to (i) in the previous sentence in the text. Article 59(2) of the BRRD declares: "Member States shall ensure that the resolution authorities have the power to write down or convert relevant capital instruments into shares or other instruments of ownership of" credit institutions, investment firms, and entities to which points (b), (c) or (d) in the opening sentence of this subsection refer (BRRD, Article 59(2)).

[1000] 'This subsection' is the subsection entitled 'Bank recovery and resolution'.

[1001] See the subsection entitled 'Settlement finality', above in this section, for Directive 98/26/EC.

[1002] See the subsection entitled 'Deposit guarantee and investor compensation schemes', above in this section, for Directive 2014/49/EU.

The BRRD ensures that credit institutions and investment firms undertake active recovery planning[1003], and provides resolution authorities with a comprehensive set of resolution tools and powers that may be used in instances in which the entity's recovery becomes infeasible. Resolution of financial entities and their groups is an area that requires both skill and judgment, and it is difficult for the Directive and/or its transposing legislation to provide for this. Nevertheless, as these tools are to be available across the EEA, and for the most part within the world's major jurisdictions – due to the international basis of this legislation, it is submitted that the means are available for rescuing or resolving the majority of structures that enter into financial difficulties.

COMMENTS

The post-GFC banking and securities legislation includes instruments for which there are no or few amendments to the pre-GFC position (such as the CARD and Directive 2001/24/EC), items that have been extensively altered (such as the TD and Directive 2002/87/EC), instruments that replace earlier (pre-GFC) legislation (such as the UCITS V Directive and Directive 2009/110/EC), and items which are new (such as the EMIR and the BRRD). The main changes since the start of the GFC in 2007, are the co-ordinated international response to this crisis and the introduction of the ESAs, considered in Chapters 2 and 3 respectively, which have influenced the new legislation that has emerged and modifications to the existing laws. It is too early to comment on the extent to which the current EU framework of financial laws forms an integrated whole that furthers the internal market in financial services, as not all of the new legislation is in force. One risk is that some of the provisions are a reaction to the events of 2007 to 2009 and their effect on market participants since that time. Reactionary law-making would tend to lead to overregulation, because some of the provisions would not directly apply to the daily operation of financial markets and companies.

Is overregulation a response to the breakdown of order – of which the GFC is an example? If this is the case, do decision-makers have a responsibility to 'row-back' from overregulation, if and when it becomes clear that some of the laws are not necessary for the efficient and effective operation of the financial (or other) system? Careful monitoring of the current laws, and editing by appropriate additions, changes and deletions, is necessary to ensure that the rules fit the system that is being regulated.

In this process, it is advisable to progress steadily, in order to retain the co-operation of market participants and to ensure that changes are in the correct direction – in so far as it is possible to judge this. In the section entitled 'The Capital Markets Union,' above in this Chapter, it was argued that the Commission should drive the pace of change more steadily than its goal of completing the CMU by 2019. In the weeks since that section was written, the EU has experienced a low rate of economic growth, negative interest rates (in the Eurozone), further immigration, and a conference concerning the United Kingdom's position. None of these events are compatible with a rush to CMU. It is time to reflect, review, and consider

---

[1003] The BRRD also ensures that credit institutions and investment firms engage in resolution planning, as laid down in Articles 10-14 of this Directive.

what the priorities should be, both in respect of the provision of financial services across the EEA and more generally with regard to the EU's internal market.

The single market – together with its expansion on equivalence terms to service providers that are established in third countries – is an excellent conception, and one which has mainly worked well. Rather than the tendency to territorial fragmentation that appears to be emerging, it is wise that good conditions for intra- and intercontinental trade are maintained, as far as is reasonably possible. In particular, given this, and given the responsibility that we in the United Kingdom have towards the welfare of our continent, it is irresponsible for us to be pursuing an exit from the EU – even though Europe as a concept extends wider and deeper than the its legislative structure[1004]. Mr. Matthew Parris recently identified the issue of the United Kingdom's responsibility to Europe, in the following terms.

> Our breakaway [from the EU] would be a collapse for the whole. It would carry profound implications for more than the balance of power in the world: but for the battle of ideas and values, too: a battle which is turning critical, and for which the century ahead looks ever more likely to form the stage. With or without us the future of the European Union looks fragile. Without us I [would] predict disintegration. … Quitting now would be an abdication of responsibility. We should care about that [527].

What implications might this issue of the United Kingdom's responsibility to Europe have for the financial sector? With our experience and high levels of trade within this sector, we in the United Kingdom have a responsibility to ensure that the laws which emerge from Brussels – and from the ESAs in London, Paris and Frankfurt – are pertinent, workable, applicable, moderate and up-to-date. The work in Chapter 1 and this Chapter of the current monograph, and in the related Chapter for the book entitled *The Global Financial Crisis: Causes, Consequences and Impact on Economic Growth*[1005], has shown there to have been a considerable increase in the volume, scope and detail of EU securities and banking legislation since the GFC. Although this result is partly justified by the need to respond constructively to the events of the crisis, it is a bewildering outcome for practitioners in the sector – who need to make the post-GFC legislative structure operative in their own circumstances. Constructive dialogue between the Commission, the ESAs, the national regulators and financial market participants is essential. The Commission and the ESAs, in particular, will need to listen carefully to the views from within the United Kingdom, if European finance is to become a world-leading entity in the long run.

CONCLUSION

This Chapter has reported and examined the plans for the CMU and aspects of the post-GFC securities and banking legislation, in the light of the pre-GFC securities and banking legislation – which Chapter 1 describes. Much of the work in this chapter is on a comparative

---

[1004] Chapter 5 provides further comment on the concept of Europe and the EU, in relation to the Economic and Monetary Union.

[1005] This publication is Baber, G. (2015). "The European Union's legislative response to the global financial crisis: A perspective taken from 2015." In *The Global Financial Crisis: Causes, Consequences and Impact on Economic Growth*, edited by J. Barnett, 89-158. New York: Nova Science Publishers, Inc.

basis with the corresponding legal provisions from before the crisis. The development of the EU's financial sectoral architecture – considered in Chapter 3 – and its involvement in post-crisis regulation of this sector, means that the latter's legislative and regulatory basis will not return to its pre-crisis state. The extent to which the structural and legal expansion is appropriate to today's environment is not yet clear. Several, and possibly many, years of operation of the new regulatory framework are required, in order to provide the necessary data for an accurate judgment to be made. Nevertheless, considerable ground has been covered since the Financial Services Action Plan – with which this book started[1006]. The final Chapter discusses the Commission's proposals for the development of the Economic and Monetary Union.

REFERENCES

[1]   Morland, M. (2015). Times cartoons: Dave and the Beanstalk, *The Times*, 29/12/15, 71792, 27.

[2]   Juncker, J.-C. (2014). A New Start for Europe: My Agenda for Jobs, Growth, Fairness and Democratic Change – *Political Guidelines for the next European Commission*, Strasbourg, 15/07/14, pp.4-5. http://ec.europa.eu/priorities/docs/pg_en.pdf.

[3]   Juncker, J.-C. (2014). A New Start for Europe: My Agenda for Jobs, Growth, Fairness and Democratic Change – *Political Guidelines for the next European Commission*, p.7.

[4]   Juncker, J.-C. (2014). A New Start for Europe: My Agenda for Jobs, Growth, Fairness and Democratic Change – *Political Guidelines for the next European Commission*, p.8.

[5]   *European Commission (2015).* Green Paper: Building a Capital Markets Union, COM(2015) 63 final, Brussels, 18/02/15, pp.26-27. <http://ec.europa.eu/finance/consultations/2015/capital-markets-union/docs/green-paper_en.pdf>/.

[6]   *European Commission (2015).* Commission Staff Working Document: Feedback Statement on the Green Paper "Building a Capital Markets Union," Accompanying the document 'Communication for the Commission to the European Parliament, the Council, the European Economic and Social Committee and the Committee of the Regions – Action Plan on Building a Capital Markets Union', SWD(2015) 184 final, Brussels, 30/09/15, p.2. http://ec.europa.eu/finance/consultations/2015/capital-markets-union/docs/summary-of-responses_en.pdf.

[7]   *European Commission (2015). Green Paper: Building a Capital Markets Union*, p.13.

[8]   *European Commission (2015).* Commission Staff Working Document: Initial reflections on the obstacles to the development of deep and integrated EU capital markets, Accompanying the document 'Green Paper: Building a Capital Markets Union,' SWD(2015) 13, Brussels, 18/02/15, pp.4-5. http://ec.europa.eu/finance/consultations/2015/capital-markets-union/docs/staff-working-document_en.pdf.

[9]   *European Commission (2015).* Commission Staff Working Document: Initial reflections on the obstacles to the development of deep and integrated EU capital markets, p.10.

[1006] See the final paragraph of the section entitled 'Introduction' in Chapter 1, for the Financial Services Action Plan.

[10] *European Commission (2015)*. Commission Staff Working Document: Initial reflections on the obstacles to the development of deep and integrated EU capital markets, p.11.

[11] *European Commission (2015)*. Commission Staff Working Document: Initial reflections on the obstacles to the development of deep and integrated EU capital markets, p.11.

[12] *European Commission (2015)*. Commission Staff Working Document: Initial reflections on the obstacles to the development of deep and integrated EU capital markets, p.14.

[13] *European Commission (2015)*. Commission Staff Working Document: Initial reflections on the obstacles to the development of deep and integrated EU capital markets, p.14.

[14] *European Commission (2015)*. Commission Staff Working Document: Initial reflections on the obstacles to the development of deep and integrated EU capital markets, p.15.

[15] *European Commission (2015)*. Commission Staff Working Document: Initial reflections on the obstacles to the development of deep and integrated EU capital markets, pp.15-17.

[16] *European Commission (2015)*. Commission Staff Working Document: Initial reflections on the obstacles to the development of deep and integrated EU capital markets, pp.17-18.

[17] *European Commission (2015)*. Commission Staff Working Document: Initial reflections on the obstacles to the development of deep and integrated EU capital markets, p.19.

[18] *European Commission (2015)*. Commission Staff Working Document: Initial reflections on the obstacles to the development of deep and integrated EU capital markets, p.19.

[19] *European Commission (2015)*. Commission Staff Working Document: Initial reflections on the obstacles to the development of deep and integrated EU capital markets, p.21.

[20] *European Commission (2015)*. Commission Staff Working Document: Initial reflections on the obstacles to the development of deep and integrated EU capital markets, p.24.

[21] *European Commission (2015)*. Commission Staff Working Document: Initial reflections on the obstacles to the development of deep and integrated EU capital markets, p.25.

[22] *European Commission (2015)*. Commission Staff Working Document: Initial reflections on the obstacles to the development of deep and integrated EU capital markets, pp.26-27.

[23] *European Commission (2015)*. Commission Staff Working Document: Initial reflections on the obstacles to the development of deep and integrated EU capital markets, p.28.

[24] *European Commission (2015)*. Commission Staff Working Document: Initial reflections on the obstacles to the development of deep and integrated EU capital markets, p.28.

[25] *European Commission (2015).* Commission Staff Working Document: Initial reflections on the obstacles to the development of deep and integrated EU capital markets, p.29.

[26] *European Commission (2015).* Commission Staff Working Document: Initial reflections on the obstacles to the development of deep and integrated EU capital markets, p.30.

[27] *European Commission (2015).* Commission Staff Working Document: Initial reflections on the obstacles to the development of deep and integrated EU capital markets, p.30.

[28] *European Commission (2015).* Commission Staff Working Document: Initial reflections on the obstacles to the development of deep and integrated EU capital markets, p.31.

[29] *European Commission (2015).* Commission Staff Working Document: Initial reflections on the obstacles to the development of deep and integrated EU capital markets, p.32.

[30] *European Commission (2015).* Commission Staff Working Document: Initial reflections on the obstacles to the development of deep and integrated EU capital markets, p.33.

[31] *European Commission (2015).* Commission Staff Working Document: Initial reflections on the obstacles to the development of deep and integrated EU capital markets, p.35.

[32] European Central Bank (2016). ECB Banking Supervision: SSM priorities 2016, Frankfurt am Main, 06/01/16, p.3. https://www.bankingsupervision.europa.eu/ecb/pub/pdf/publication_supervisory_priorities_2016.en.pdf.

[33] Juncker, J.-C. (2014). A New Start for Europe: My Agenda for Jobs, Growth, Fairness and Democratic Change – Political Guidelines for the next European Commission, p.8.

[34] *European Commission (2015).* Communication from the Commission to the European Parliament, the Council, the European Economic and Social Committee and the Committee of the Regions – Action Plan on Building a Capital Markets Union, COM(2015) 468 final, Brussels, 30/09/15, p.7. http://ec.europa.eu/finance/capital-markets-union/docs/building-cmu-action-plan_en.pdf.

[35] *European Commission (2015).* Communication from the Commission to the European Parliament, the Council, the European Economic and Social Committee and the Committee of the Regions – Action Plan on Building a Capital Markets Union, pp.8-9.

[36] *European Commission (2015).* Communication from the Commission to the European Parliament, the Council, the European Economic and Social Committee and the Committee of the Regions – Action Plan on Building a Capital Markets Union, p.9-10.

[37] *European Commission (2015).* Communication from the Commission to the European Parliament, the Council, the European Economic and Social Committee and the Committee of the Regions – Action Plan on Building a Capital Markets Union, p.10.

[38] *European Commission (2015).* Communication from the Commission to the European Parliament, the Council, the European Economic and Social Committee and the Committee of the Regions – Action Plan on Building a Capital Markets Union, pp. 10-11.

[39] *European Commission (2015).* Communication from the Commission to the European Parliament, the Council, the European Economic and Social Committee and the Committee of the Regions – Action Plan on Building a Capital Markets Union, p.12.

[40] *European Commission (2015).* Communication from the Commission to the European Parliament, the Council, the European Economic and Social Committee and the Committee of the Regions – Action Plan on Building a Capital Markets Union, p.13.

[41] *European Commission (2015).* Communication from the Commission to the European Parliament, the Council, the European Economic and Social Committee and the Committee of the Regions – Action Plan on Building a Capital Markets Union, p.13.

[42] *European Commission (2015).* Communication from the Commission to the European Parliament, the Council, the European Economic and Social Committee and the Committee of the Regions – Action Plan on Building a Capital Markets Union, p.14.

[43] *European Commission (2015).* Proposal for a Regulation of the European Parliament and of the Council on the prospectus to be published when securities are offered to the public or admitted to trading, COM(2015) 583 final, Brussels, 30/11/15, Articles 15(1) and 15(3), p.53. <http://eur-lex.europa.eu/resource.html?uri=cellar:036c16c7-9763-11e5-983e-01aa75ed71a1.0006.02/DOC_1&format=PDF>

[44] *European Commission (2015).* Communication from the Commission to the European Parliament, the Council, the European Economic and Social Committee and the Committee of the Regions – Action Plan on Building a Capital Markets Union, pp. 15-16.

[45] *European Commission (2015).* Communication from the Commission to the European Parliament, the Council, the European Economic and Social Committee and the Committee of the Regions – Action Plan on Building a Capital Markets Union, p.15.

[46] *European Commission (2015).* Communication from the Commission to the European Parliament, the Council, the European Economic and Social Committee and the Committee of the Regions – Action Plan on Building a Capital Markets Union, p.17.

[47] *European Commission (2015).* Communication from the Commission to the European Parliament, the Council, the European Economic and Social Committee and the Committee of the Regions – Action Plan on Building a Capital Markets Union, p.18.

[48] *European Commission (2015).* Communication from the Commission to the European Parliament, the Council, the European Economic and Social Committee and the Committee of the Regions – Action Plan on Building a Capital Markets Union, p.19.

[49] *European Commission (2015).* Communication from the Commission to the European Parliament, the Council, the European Economic and Social Committee and the Committee of the Regions – Action Plan on Building a Capital Markets Union, p.19.

[50] *European Commission (2015).* Communication from the Commission to the European Parliament, the Council, the European Economic and Social Committee and the Committee of the Regions – Action Plan on Building a Capital Markets Union, p.20.

[51] *European Commission (2015).* Communication from the Commission to the European Parliament, the Council, the European Economic and Social Committee and the Committee of the Regions – Action Plan on Building a Capital Markets Union, p.21.

[52] *European Commission (2015).* Communication from the Commission to the European Parliament, the Council, the European Economic and Social Committee and the Committee of the Regions – Action Plan on Building a Capital Markets Union, p.22.

[53] *European Commission (2015).* Communication from the Commission to the European Parliament, the Council, the European Economic and Social Committee and the Committee of the Regions – Action Plan on Building a Capital Markets Union, p.22.

[54] *European Commission (2015).* Communication from the Commission to the European Parliament, the Council, the European Economic and Social Committee and the Committee of the Regions – Action Plan on Building a Capital Markets Union, p.23.

[55] *European Commission (2015).* Communication from the Commission to the European Parliament, the Council, the European Economic and Social Committee and the Committee of the Regions – Action Plan on Building a Capital Markets Union, p.24.

[56] *European Commission (2015).* Communication from the Commission to the European Parliament, the Council, the European Economic and Social Committee and the Committee of the Regions – Action Plan on Building a Capital Markets Union, p.24.

[57] *European Commission (2015).* Communication from the Commission to the European Parliament, the Council, the European Economic and Social Committee and the Committee of the Regions – Action Plan on Building a Capital Markets Union, p.25.

[58] *European Commission (2015).* Communication from the Commission to the European Parliament, the Council, the European Economic and Social Committee and the Committee of the Regions – Action Plan on Building a Capital Markets Union, p.25.

[59] *European Commission (2015).* Communication from the Commission to the European Parliament, the Council, the European Economic and Social Committee and the Committee of the Regions – Action Plan on Building a Capital Markets Union, p.26.

[60] *European Commission (2015).* Communication from the Commission to the European Parliament, the Council, the European Economic and Social Committee and the Committee of the Regions – Action Plan on Building a Capital Markets Union, p.27.

[61] *European Commission (2015).* Commission Staff Working Document: Economic Analysis, Accompanying the document 'Communication from the Commission to the European Parliament, the Council, the European Economic and Social Committee and the Committee of the Regions – Action Plan on Building a Capital Markets Union,' SWD(2015) 183 final, Brussels, 30/09/15, p.14. http://ec.europa.eu/finance/capital-markets-union/docs/building-cmu-economic-analysis_en.pdf.

[62] *European Commission (2015).* Commission Staff Working Document: Economic Analysis, pp.18 and 111.

[63] Dixon, H. (2014). Unlocking Europe's capital markets union, *Centre for European Reform*, October 2014, p.8.

[64] Lannoo, K. (2015). Which Union for Europe's Capital Markets?, *ECMI Policy Brief*, No.22/February 2015, p.1.

[65] Lannoo, K. (2015). Which Union for Europe's Capital Markets?, *ECMI Policy Brief*, No.22/February 2015, p.4.

[66] Lannoo, K. (2015). Which Union for Europe's Capital Markets?, *ECMI Policy Brief*, No.22/February 2015, p.5.

[67] Lannoo, K., Pollack, A., & Staehr, O. (2015). Keep capital markets union simple, *ECMI Commentary*, No.38/July 2015, pp.1-2.

[68] Lannoo, K. (2015). Detailed CMU Action Plan, but more (ambition) is required, *ECMI Commentary*, No.39/2 October 2015, p.2.

[69] Lannoo, K. (2015). Detailed CMU Action Plan, but more (ambition) is required, *ECMI Commentary*, No.39/2 October 2015, p.2.

[70] Lannoo, K. (2015). Detailed CMU Action Plan, but more (ambition) is required, *ECMI Commentary*, No.39/2 October 2015, p.1.

[71] Lannoo, K. (2015). Detailed CMU Action Plan, but more (ambition) is required, *ECMI Commentary*, No.39/2 October 2015, p.3.

[72] Lannoo, K. (2015). Detailed CMU Action Plan, but more (ambition) is required, *ECMI Commentary*, No.39/2 October 2015, p.1.

[73] Valiante, D. (2015). Light and shadows in Europe's new Action Plan for Capital Markets Union, *ECMI Commentary*, No.40/5 October 2015, p.1.

[74] Valiante, D. (2015). Light and shadows in Europe's new Action Plan for Capital Markets Union, *ECMI Commentary*, No.40/5 October 2015, p.4.

[75] Kaya, O. (2015). Capital Markets Union: An ambitious goal, but few quick wins, *Deutsche Bank Research: EU Monitor – Global financial markets*, 02/11/15, pp.1-2 and 10.

[76] Kaya, O. (2015). Capital Markets Union: An ambitious goal, but few quick wins, *Deutsche Bank Research: EU Monitor – Global financial markets*, 02/11/15, p.9.

[77] Kaya, O. (2015). Capital Markets Union: An ambitious goal, but few quick wins, *Deutsche Bank Research: EU Monitor – Global financial markets*, 02/11/15, pp.10-13.

[78] Kaya, O. (2015). Capital Markets Union: An ambitious goal, but few quick wins, *Deutsche Bank Research: EU Monitor – Global financial markets*, 02/11/15, pp.17-18.

[79] Kaya, O. (2015). Capital Markets Union: An ambitious goal, but few quick wins, *Deutsche Bank Research: EU Monitor – Global financial markets*, 02/11/15, p.19.

[80] Kaya, O. (2015). Capital Markets Union: An ambitious goal, but few quick wins, *Deutsche Bank Research: EU Monitor – Global financial markets*, 02/11/15, Table 10, p.6.

[81] Kaya, O. (2015). Capital Markets Union: An ambitious goal, but few quick wins, *Deutsche Bank Research: EU Monitor – Global financial markets*, 02/11/15, Table 11, p.7.

[82] Kaya, O. (2015). Capital Markets Union: An ambitious goal, but few quick wins, *Deutsche Bank Research: EU Monitor – Global financial markets*, 02/11/15, Table 16, p.10.

[83] *Official Journal of the European Union* (2014). Regulation (EU) No 596/2014 of the European Parliament and of the Council of 16 April 2014 on market abuse (market abuse regulation) and repealing Directive 2003/6/EC of the European Parliament and of the Council and Commission Directives 2003/124/EC, 2003/125/EC and 2004/72/EC, L173/1-L173/61, Article 37.

[84] *Official Journal of the European Union* (2014). Regulation (EU) No 596/2014, Article 29(4).

[85] *Official Journal of the European Union* (2014). Regulation (EU) No 596/2014, Article 13(1).

[86] *Official Journal of the European Union* (2014). Regulation (EU) No 596/2014, Recital 3.

[87] *Official Journal of the European Union* (2014). Regulation (EU) No 596/2014, Recital 4.

[88] *Official Journal of the European Union* (2014). Regulation (EU) No 596/2014, Article 14.

[89] *Official Journal of the European Union* (2014). Regulation (EU) No 596/2014, Article 8(1).

[90] *Official Journal of the European Union* (2014). Regulation (EU) No 596/2014, Article 8(2).

[91] *Official Journal of the European Union* (2014). Regulation (EU) No 596/2014, Article 8(3).

[92] *Official Journal of the European Union* (2014). Regulation (EU) No 596/2014, Article 7(1).

[93] *Official Journal of the European Union* (2014). Regulation (EU) No 596/2014, Article 7(2).

[94] *Official Journal of the European Union* (2014). Regulation (EU) No 596/2014, Article 15.

[95] *Official Journal of the European Union* (2014). Regulation (EU) No 596/2014, Article 12(1).

[96] *Official Journal of the European Union* (2014). Regulation (EU) No 596/2014, Article 30(1)(a).

[97] *Official Journal of the European Union* (2014). Directive 2014/57/EU of the European Parliament and of the Council of 16 April 2014 on criminal sanctions for market abuse (market abuse directive), L173/179-L173/189, Preamble.

[98] *Official Journal of the European Union* (2012). Consolidated version of the Treaty on the Functioning of the European Union, C326/47-C326/199, Article 83(2).

[99] *Official Journal of the European Union* (2014). Directive 2014/57/EU, Article 3(1).

[100] *Official Journal of the European Union* (2014). Directive 2014/57/EU, Article 3(3).

[101] *Official Journal of the European Union* (2014). Directive 2014/57/EU, Article 4(1).

[102] *Official Journal of the European Union* (2014). Directive 2014/57/EU, Article 4(2).

[103] *Official Journal of the European Union* (2014). Directive 2014/57/EU, Article 5(1).

[104] *Official Journal of the European Union* (2014). Directive 2014/57/EU, Article 5(2).

[105] *Official Journal of the European Union* (2014). Directive 2014/57/EU, Article 6(1).

[106] *Official Journal of the European Union* (2014). Directive 2014/57/EU, Article 6(2).

[107] *Official Journal of the European Union* (2014). Directive 2014/57/EU, Article 6(1).

[108] *Official Journal of the European Union* (2014). Directive 2014/57/EU, Article 7(1).

[109] *Official Journal of the European Union* (2014). Directive 2014/57/EU, Article 8(1).

[110] *Official Journal of the European Union* (2014). Directive 2014/57/EU, Article 8(2).

[111] *Official Journal of the European Union* (2014). Directive 2014/57/EU, Article 9.

[112] *Official Journal of the European Union* (2014). Regulation (EU) No 596/2014, Recital 5.

[113] *Official Journal of the European Union* (2012). Consolidated version of the Treaty on the Functioning of the European Union, Article 4(2)(a).

[114] *European Commission (2015)*. Proposal for a Regulation of the European Parliament and of the Council on the prospectus to be published when securities are offered to the public or admitted to trading, p.2.

[115] *European Commission (2015)*. Consultation Document: Review of the Prospectus Directive,   Brussels,   18/02/15,   p.1. <http://ec.europa.eu/finance/consultations/2015/prospectus-directive/docs/consultation-document_en.pdf>

[116] *Official Journal of the European Union* (2003). Directive 2003/71/EC of the European Parliament and of the Council of 4 November 2003 on the prospectus to be published when securities are offered to the public or admitted to trading and amending Directive 2001/34/EC, L345/64-L345/89, as amended to 22/05/14, Article 3(1).

[117] *Official Journal of the European Union* (2003). Directive 2003/71/EC (as amended to 22/05/14), Article 3(2)(a).

[118] *Official Journal of the European Union* (2003). Directive 2003/71/EC (as amended to 22/05/14), Article 3(2)(b)-(e).

[119] *Official Journal of the European Union* (2003). Directive 2003/71/EC (as amended to 22/05/14), Article 3(3).

[120] *Official Journal of the European Union* (2003). Directive 2003/71/EC (as amended to 22/05/14), Article 3(4).

[121] *Official Journal of the European Union* (2004). Commission Regulation (EC) No 809/2004 of 29 April 2004 implementing Directive 2003/71/EC of the European Parliament and of the Council as regards information contained in prospectuses as well as the format, incorporation by reference and publication of such prospectuses and dissemination of advertisements, L149/1-L149/126, as amended to 25/09/15, Annexes I-XXX.

[122] *Official Journal of the European Union* (2003). Directive 2003/71/EC (as amended to 22/05/14), Article 5(2).

[123] *Official Journal of the European Union* (2003). Directive 2003/71/EC (as amended to 22/05/14), Article 5(2).

[124] *Official Journal of the European Union* (2003). Directive 2003/71/EC (as amended to 22/05/14), Articles 5(2) and 5(5).

[125] *Official Journal of the European Union* (2012). Commission Delegated Regulation (EU) No 486/2012 of 20 March 2012 amending Regulation (EC) No 809/2004 as regards the format and the content of the prospectus, the base prospectus, the summary and the final terms and as regards the disclosure requirements, L150/1-L150/65, Articles 1(10) and 1(12).

[126] *Official Journal of the European Union* (2003). Directive 2003/71/EC (as amended to 22/05/14), Article 6(2).

[127] *Official Journal of the European Union* (2003). Directive 2003/71/EC (as amended to 22/05/14), Article 6(2).

[128] *Official Journal of the European Union* (2003). Directive 2003/71/EC (as amended to 22/05/14), Article 16(3).

[129] *Official Journal of the European Union* (2014). Commission Delegated Regulation (EU) No 382/2014 of 7 March 2014 supplementing Directive 2003/71/EC of the European Parliament and of the Council with regard to regulatory technical standards for publication of supplements to the prospectus, L111/36-L111/39, Article 1.

[130] *Official Journal of the European Union* (2014). Commission Delegated Regulation (EU) No 382/2014, Article 2(f).

[131] *Official Journal of the European Union* (2014). Commission Delegated Regulation (EU) No 382/2014, Article 2(h).

[132] *Official Journal of the European Union* (2004). Directive 2004/109/EC of the European Parliament and of the Council of 15 December 2004 on the harmonisation of transparency requirements in relation to information about issuers whose securities are

admitted to trading on a regulated market and amending Directive 2001/34/EC, L390/38-L390/57, as amended to 06/11/13, Article 3.

[133] *Official Journal of the European Union* (2004). Directive 2004/109/EC (as amended to 06/11/13), Article 4(1).

[134] *Official Journal of the European Union* (2004). Directive 2004/109/EC (as amended to 06/11/13), Article 4(7).

[135] *Official Journal of the European Union* (2004). Directive 2004/109/EC (as amended to 06/11/13), Article 4(7).

[136] *Official Journal of the European Union* (2004). Directive 2004/109/EC (as amended to 06/11/13), Article 4(7).

[137] *Official Journal of the European Union* (2004). Directive 2004/109/EC (as amended to 06/11/13), Article 5(1).

[138] *Official Journal of the European Union* (2004). Directive 2004/109/EC (as amended to 06/11/13), Article 5(6).

[139] *Official Journal of the European Union* (2004). Directive 2004/109/EC (as amended to 06/11/13), Article 6.

[140] *Official Journal of the European Union* (2004). Directive 2004/109/EC (as amended to 06/11/13), Article 8(1).

[141] *Official Journal of the European Union* (2004). Directive 2004/109/EC (as amended to 06/11/13), Article 9(1).

[142] *Official Journal of the European Union* (2004). Directive 2004/109/EC (as amended to 06/11/13), Article 9(6).

[143] *Official Journal of the European Union* (2004). Directive 2004/109/EC (as amended to 06/11/13), Article 9(6a).

[144] *Official Journal of the European Union* (2004). Directive 2004/109/EC (as amended to 06/11/13), Article 13(1).

[145] *Official Journal of the European Union* (2004). Directive 2004/109/EC (as amended to 06/11/13), Article 16(1)-(2).

[146] *Official Journal of the European Union* (2004). Directive 2004/109/EC (as amended to 06/11/13), Article 23(1).

[147] *Official Journal of the European Union* (2007). Commission Directive 2007/14/EC of 8 March 2007 laying down detailed rules for the implementation of certain provisions of Directive 2004/109/EC on the harmonisation of transparency requirements in relation to information about issuers whose securities are admitted to trading on a regulated market, L69/27-L69/36, as amended to 06/11/13, Articles 13-22.

[148] *Official Journal of the European Union* (2004). Directive 2004/109/EC (as amended to 06/11/13), Article 24(4).

[149] *Official Journal of the European Union* (2004). Directive 2004/109/EC (as amended to 06/11/13), Article 24(4a).

[150] *Official Journal of the European Union* (2004). Directive 2004/109/EC (as amended to 06/11/13), Article 24(4b).

[151] *Official Journal of the European Union* (2004). Directive 2004/109/EC (as amended to 06/11/13), Article 25(2).

[152] *Official Journal of the European Union* (2004). Directive 2004/109/EC (as amended to 06/11/13), Article 25(2a).

[153] *Official Journal of the European Union* (2004). Directive 2004/109/EC (as amended to 06/11/13), Article 25(2b).

[154] *Official Journal of the European Union* (2004). Directive 2004/109/EC (as amended to 06/11/13), Article 25(2c).

[155] *Official Journal of the European Union* (2004). Directive 2004/109/EC (as amended to 06/11/13), Article 25(3).

[156] *Official Journal of the European Union* (2004). Directive 2004/109/EC (as amended to 06/11/13), Article 25(4).

[157] *Official Journal of the European Union* (2007). Directive 2007/36/EC of the European Parliament and of the Council of 11 July 2007 on the exercise of certain rights of shareholders in listed companies, L184/17-L184/24, as amended to 12/06/14, Article 16.

[158] *Official Journal of the European Union* (2007). Directive 2007/36/EC (as amended to 12/06/14), Article 1(4).

[159] *Official Journal of the European Union* (2007). Directive 2007/36/EC (as amended to 12/06/14), Article 1(1).

[160] *Official Journal of the European Union* (2007). Directive 2007/36/EC (as amended to 12/06/14), Recital 4.

[161] *Official Journal of the European Union* (2007). Directive 2007/36/EC (as amended to 12/06/14), Article 1(2).

[162] *Official Journal of the European Union* (2007). Directive 2007/36/EC (as amended to 12/06/14), Article 4.

[163] *Official Journal of the European Union* (2007). Directive 2007/36/EC (as amended to 12/06/14), Article 5(1).

[164] *Official Journal of the European Union* (2007). Directive 2007/36/EC (as amended to 12/06/14), Article 5(2).

[165] *Official Journal of the European Union* (2007). Directive 2007/36/EC (as amended to 12/06/14), Article 5(2).

[166] *Official Journal of the European Union* (2007). Directive 2007/36/EC (as amended to 12/06/14), Article 5(3).

[167] *Official Journal of the European Union* (2007). Directive 2007/36/EC (as amended to 12/06/14), Article 5(4).

[168] *Official Journal of the European Union* (2007). Directive 2007/36/EC (as amended to 12/06/14), Article 6(1).

[169] *Official Journal of the European Union* (2007). Directive 2007/36/EC (as amended to 12/06/14), Article 6(2).

[170] *Official Journal of the European Union* (2007). Directive 2007/36/EC (as amended to 12/06/14), Article 8(1).

[171] *Official Journal of the European Union* (2007). Directive 2007/36/EC (as amended to 12/06/14), Article 8(2).

[172] *Official Journal of the European Union* (2007). Directive 2007/36/EC (as amended to 12/06/14), Article 9(1).

[173] *Official Journal of the European Union* (2007). Directive 2007/36/EC (as amended to 12/06/14), Article 9(2).

[174] *Official Journal of the European Union* (2007). Directive 2007/36/EC (as amended to 12/06/14), Article 10(1).

[175] *Official Journal of the European Union* (2007). Directive 2007/36/EC (as amended to 12/06/14), Article 10(4).

[176] *Official Journal of the European Union* (2007). Directive 2007/36/EC (as amended to 12/06/14), Article 10(5).

[177] *Official Journal of the European Union* (2007). Directive 2007/36/EC (as amended to 12/06/14), Article 11(1).

[178] *Official Journal of the European Union* (2007). Directive 2007/36/EC (as amended to 12/06/14), Article 11(2).

[179] *Official Journal of the European Union* (2007). Directive 2007/36/EC (as amended to 12/06/14), Article 12.

[180] *Official Journal of the European Union* (2007). Directive 2007/36/EC (as amended to 12/06/14), Article 14(1).

[181] *Official Journal of the European Union* (2007). Directive 2007/36/EC (as amended to 12/06/14), Article 14(2).

[182] European Commission (2014). Regulation on securities settlement and on Central Securities Depositories in the EU ('CSD Regulation') – Frequently Asked Questions, MEMO/14/312, Brussels, 16/04/14, Point 2, p.1. http://europa.eu/rapid/press-release_MEMO-14-312_en.htm?locale=en.

[183] European Commission (2014). Regulation on securities settlement and on Central Securities Depositories in the EU ('CSD Regulation') – Frequently Asked Questions, Point 3, p.1.

[184] European Commission (2014). Regulation on securities settlement and on Central Securities Depositories in the EU ('CSD Regulation') – Frequently Asked Questions, Point 5, p.2.

[185] *Official Journal of the European Union* (2014). Regulation (EU) No 909/2014 of the European Parliament and of the Council of 23 July 2014 on improving securities settlement in the European Union and on central securities depositories and amending Directives 98/26/EC and 2014/65/EU and Regulation (EU) No 236/2012, L257/1-L257/72, Article 1(1).

[186] *Official Journal of the European Union* (2014). Regulation (EU) No 909/2014, Article 3(2).

[187] *Official Journal of the European Union* (2014). Regulation (EU) No 909/2014, Article 3(1).

[188] *Official Journal of the European Union* (2014). Regulation (EU) No 909/2014, Article 5(1).

[189] *Official Journal of the European Union* (2014). Regulation (EU) No 909/2014, Article 5(2).

[190] *Official Journal of the European Union* (2014). Regulation (EU) No 909/2014, Article 9(1).

[191] *Official Journal of the European Union* (2014). Regulation (EU) No 909/2014, Article 9(1).

[192] *Official Journal of the European Union* (2014). Regulation (EU) No 909/2014, Article 10.

[193] *Official Journal of the European Union* (2014). Regulation (EU) No 909/2014, Article 11(1).

[194] *Official Journal of the European Union* (2014). Regulation (EU) No 909/2014, Article 11(2).

[195] *Official Journal of the European Union* (2014). Regulation (EU) No 909/2014, Article 11(3).

[196] *Official Journal of the European Union* (2014). Regulation (EU) No 909/2014, Article 13(1).

[197] *Official Journal of the European Union* (2014). Regulation (EU) No 909/2014, Article 13(2).

[198] *Official Journal of the European Union* (2014). Regulation (EU) No 909/2014, Article 14(1).

[199] *Official Journal of the European Union* (2014). Regulation (EU) No 909/2014, Article 14(2).

[200] *Official Journal of the European Union* (2014). Regulation (EU) No 909/2014, Article 15.

[201] *Official Journal of the European Union* (2014). Regulation (EU) No 909/2014, Article 16(1).

[202] *Official Journal of the European Union* (2014). Regulation (EU) No 909/2014, Article 16(2).

[203] *Official Journal of the European Union* (2014). Regulation (EU) No 909/2014, Article 16(3).

[204] *Official Journal of the European Union* (2014). Regulation (EU) No 909/2014, Article 16(4).

[205] *Official Journal of the European Union* (2014). Regulation (EU) No 909/2014, Article 17(1).

[206] *Official Journal of the European Union* (2014). Regulation (EU) No 909/2014, Article 17(2).

[207] *Official Journal of the European Union* (2014). Regulation (EU) No 909/2014, Article 17(3).

[208] *Official Journal of the European Union* (2014). Regulation (EU) No 909/2014, Article 17(4).

[209] *Official Journal of the European Union* (2014). Regulation (EU) No 909/2014, Article 17(6).

[210] *Official Journal of the European Union* (2014). Regulation (EU) No 909/2014, Article 17(8).

[211] *Official Journal of the European Union* (2014). Regulation (EU) No 909/2014, Article 23(1).

[212] *Official Journal of the European Union* (2014). Regulation (EU) No 909/2014, Article 23(2).

[213] *Official Journal of the European Union* (2014). Regulation (EU) No 909/2014, Article 23(3).

[214] *Official Journal of the European Union* (2014). Regulation (EU) No 909/2014, Article 23(4).

[215] *Official Journal of the European Union* (2014). Regulation (EU) No 909/2014, Article 23(5).

[216] *Official Journal of the European Union* (2014). Regulation (EU) No 909/2014, Article 23(6).

[217] *Official Journal of the European Union* (2012). Regulation (EU) No 648/2012 of the European Parliament and of the Council of 4 July 2012 on OTC derivatives, central counterparties and trade repositories, L201/1-L201/59, as amended to 23/12/15, Recital 5.

[218] *Official Journal of the European Union* (2012). Regulation (EU) No 648/2012 (as amended to 23/12/15), Recital 99.

[219] *Official Journal of the European Union* (2012). Regulation (EU) No 648/2012 (as amended to 23/12/15), Preamble.

[220] *Official Journal of the European Union* (2012). Consolidated version of the Treaty on the Functioning of the European Union, Article 4(2)(a).

[221] *Official Journal of the European Union* (2012). Regulation (EU) No 648/2012 (as amended to 23/12/15), Article 1(1).

[222] *Official Journal of the European Union* (2012). Regulation (EU) No 648/2012 (as amended to 23/12/15), Article 1(2).

[223] *Official Journal of the European Union* (2012). Regulation (EU) No 648/2012 (as amended to 23/12/15), Article 4(1).

[224] *Official Journal of the European Union* (2012). Regulation (EU) No 648/2012 (as amended to 23/12/15), Article 4(2).

[225] *Official Journal of the European Union* (2012). Regulation (EU) No 648/2012 (as amended to 23/12/15), Article 9(1).

[226] *Official Journal of the European Union* (2012). Regulation (EU) No 648/2012 (as amended to 23/12/15), Article 9(3).

[227] *Official Journal of the European Union* (2012). Regulation (EU) No 648/2012 (as amended to 23/12/15), Article 12(1).

[228] *Official Journal of the European Union* (2012). Regulation (EU) No 648/2012 (as amended to 23/12/15), Article 12(2).

[229] *Official Journal of the European Union* (2012). Regulation (EU) No 648/2012 (as amended to 23/12/15), Article 26(1).

[230] *Official Journal of the European Union* (2012). Regulation (EU) No 648/2012 (as amended to 23/12/15), Article 36(1).

[231] *Official Journal of the European Union* (2012). Regulation (EU) No 648/2012 (as amended to 23/12/15), Article 36(2).

[232] *Official Journal of the European Union* (2012). Regulation (EU) No 648/2012 (as amended to 23/12/15), Article 40.

[233] *Official Journal of the European Union* (2012). Regulation (EU) No 648/2012 (as amended to 23/12/15), Article 41(1).

[234] *Official Journal of the European Union* (2012). Regulation (EU) No 648/2012 (as amended to 23/12/15), Article 42(1).

[235] *Official Journal of the European Union* (2012). Regulation (EU) No 648/2012 (as amended to 23/12/15), Article 42(2).

[236] *Official Journal of the European Union* (2012). Regulation (EU) No 648/2012 (as amended to 23/12/15), Article 43(1).

[237] *Official Journal of the European Union* (2012). Regulation (EU) No 648/2012 (as amended to 23/12/15), Article 43(3).

[238] *Official Journal of the European Union* (2012). Regulation (EU) No 648/2012 (as amended to 23/12/15), Article 44(1).

[239] *Official Journal of the European Union* (2012). Regulation (EU) No 648/2012 (as amended to 23/12/15), Article 46(1).

[240] *Official Journal of the European Union* (2012). Regulation (EU) No 648/2012 (as amended to 23/12/15), Article 46(2).

[241] *Official Journal of the European Union* (2012). Regulation (EU) No 648/2012 (as amended to 23/12/15), Article 47(1).

[242] *Official Journal of the European Union* (2012). Regulation (EU) No 648/2012 (as amended to 23/12/15), Article 50(1).

[243] European Commission (2011). Regulation on Short Selling and Credit Default Swaps – Frequently Asked Questions, MEMO/11/713, Brussels, 19/10/11, pp.2-3. http://europa.eu/rapid/press-release_MEMO-11-713_en.htm?locale=en.

[244] *Official Journal of the European Union* (2012). Regulation (EU) No 236/2012 of the European Parliament and of the Council of 14 March 2012 on short selling and certain aspects of credit default swaps, L86/1-L86/24, as amended to 28/08/14, Recital 14.

[245] *Official Journal of the European Union* (2012). Regulation (EU) No 236/2012 (as amended to 28/08/14), Article 2(1)(b).

[246] *Official Journal of the European Union* (2012). Regulation (EU) No 236/2012 (as amended to 28/08/14), Article 2(1)(c).

[247] *Official Journal of the European Union* (2012). Regulation (EU) No 236/2012 (as amended to 28/08/14), Article 3(1).

[248] *Official Journal of the European Union* (2012). Regulation (EU) No 236/2012 (as amended to 28/08/14), Article 3(2).

[249] *Official Journal of the European Union* (2012). Regulation (EU) No 236/2012 (as amended to 28/08/14), Article 4(1).

[250] *Official Journal of the European Union* (2012). Regulation (EU) No 236/2012 (as amended to 28/08/14), Article 14(1).

[251] *Official Journal of the European Union* (2012). Regulation (EU) No 236/2012 (as amended to 28/08/14), Article 14(2).

[252] *Official Journal of the European Union* (2012). Regulation (EU) No 236/2012 (as amended to 28/08/14), Article 8.

[253] *Official Journal of the European Union* (2012). Regulation (EU) No 236/2012 (as amended to 28/08/14), Article 13(1).

[254] *Official Journal of the European Union* (2012). Regulation (EU) No 236/2012 (as amended to 28/08/14), Article 7(1).

[255] *Official Journal of the European Union* (2012). Regulation (EU) No 236/2012 (as amended to 28/08/14), Article 12(1).

[256] *Official Journal of the European Union* (2012). Regulation (EU) No 236/2012 (as amended to 28/08/14), Article 5(1)-(2).

[257] *Official Journal of the European Union* (2012). Regulation (EU) No 236/2012 (as amended to 28/08/14), Article 6(1)-(2).

[258] *Official Journal of the European Union* (2012). Regulation (EU) No 236/2012 (as amended to 28/08/14), Article 16(1).

[259] *Official Journal of the European Union* (2012). Regulation (EU) No 236/2012 (as amended to 28/08/14), Article 17(1).

[260] *Official Journal of the European Union* (2012). Regulation (EU) No 236/2012 (as amended to 28/08/14), Article 17(5).

[261] *Official Journal of the European Union* (2012). Regulation (EU) No 236/2012 (as amended to 28/08/14), Article 23(1).

[262] *Official Journal of the European Union* (2012). Regulation (EU) No 236/2012 (as amended to 28/08/14), Article 23(5).

[263] *Official Journal of the European Union* (2012). Regulation (EU) No 236/2012 (as amended to 28/08/14), Article 20(1)-(2).

[264] *Official Journal of the European Union* (2012). Regulation (EU) No 236/2012 (as amended to 28/08/14), Article 21(1)-(2).

[265] *Official Journal of the European Union* (2012). Regulation (EU) No 236/2012 (as amended to 28/08/14), Article 25(1)-(2).

[266] *Official Journal of the European Union* (2012). Regulation (EU) No 236/2012 (as amended to 28/08/14), Article 25(3).

[267] *Official Journal of the European Union* (2012). Regulation (EU) No 236/2012 (as amended to 28/08/14), Article 24.

[268] *Official Journal of the European Union* (2012). Regulation (EU) No 236/2012 (as amended to 28/08/14), Article 41.

[269] *Official Journal of the European Union* (2012). Regulation (EU) No 236/2012 (as amended to 28/08/14), Article 41.

[270] *Official Journal of the European Union* (2009). Regulation (EC) No 1060/2009 of the European Parliament and of the Council of 16 September 2009 on credit rating agencies, L302/1-L302/31, as amended to 22/05/14, Article 1.

[271] *Official Journal of the European Union* (2009). Regulation (EC) No 1060/2009 (as amended to 22/05/14), Article 2(1).

[272] *Official Journal of the European Union* (2009). Regulation (EC) No 1060/2009 (as amended to 22/05/14), Article 3(1)(a).

[273] *Official Journal of the European Union* (2009). Regulation (EC) No 1060/2009 (as amended to 22/05/14), Article 3(1)(b).

[274] *Official Journal of the European Union* (2009). Regulation (EC) No 1060/2009 (as amended to 22/05/14), Article 4(1).

[275] *Official Journal of the European Union* (2009). Regulation (EC) No 1060/2009 (as amended to 22/05/14), Article 5a(1).

[276] *Official Journal of the European Union* (2009). Regulation (EC) No 1060/2009 (as amended to 22/05/14), Article 14(1).

[277] *Official Journal of the European Union* (2009). Regulation (EC) No 1060/2009 (as amended to 22/05/14), Article 14(2).

[278] *Official Journal of the European Union* (2009). Regulation (EC) No 1060/2009 (as amended to 22/05/14), Article 14(3).

[279] *Official Journal of the European Union* (2009). Regulation (EC) No 1060/2009 (as amended to 22/05/14), Article 15(1).

[280] *Official Journal of the European Union* (2009). Regulation (EC) No 1060/2009 (as amended to 22/05/14), Article 14(5).

[281] *Official Journal of the European Union* (2009). Regulation (EC) No 1060/2009 (as amended to 22/05/14), Article 5(1).

[282] *Official Journal of the European Union* (2009). Regulation (EC) No 1060/2009 (as amended to 22/05/14), Article 6(1).

[283] *Official Journal of the European Union* (2009). Regulation (EC) No 1060/2009 (as amended to 22/05/14), Article 6a(1).

[284] *Official Journal of the European Union* (2009). Regulation (EC) No 1060/2009 (as amended to 22/05/14), Article 7(1).

[285] *Official Journal of the European Union* (2009). Regulation (EC) No 1060/2009 (as amended to 22/05/14), Article 7(4).

[286] *Official Journal of the European Union* (2009). Regulation (EC) No 1060/2009 (as amended to 22/05/14), Article 7(5).

[287] *Official Journal of the European Union* (2009). Regulation (EC) No 1060/2009 (as amended to 22/05/14), Article 8(1), and Annex I Section E, Part I, Point 5.

[288] *Official Journal of the European Union* (2009). Regulation (EC) No 1060/2009 (as amended to 22/05/14), Article 8(3).

[289] *Official Journal of the European Union* (2009). Regulation (EC) No 1060/2009 (as amended to 22/05/14), Article 8(5).

[290] *Official Journal of the European Union* (2009). Regulation (EC) No 1060/2009 (as amended to 22/05/14), Article 8(5).

[291] *Official Journal of the European Union* (2009). Regulation (EC) No 1060/2009 (as amended to 22/05/14), Article 8c(1).

[292] *Official Journal of the European Union* (2009). Regulation (EC) No 1060/2009 (as amended to 22/05/14), Article 8c(2).

[293] *Official Journal of the European Union* (2009). Regulation (EC) No 1060/2009 (as amended to 22/05/14), Article 10(1).

[294] *Official Journal of the European Union* (2009). Regulation (EC) No 1060/2009 (as amended to 22/05/14), Article 11(1).

[295] *Official Journal of the European Union* (2009). Regulation (EC) No 1060/2009 (as amended to 22/05/14), Annex I Section E, Part I.

[296] *Official Journal of the European Union* (2009). Regulation (EC) No 1060/2009 (as amended to 22/05/14), Article 11(3), and Annex I Section E, Part 2, Point 2.

[297] *Official Journal of the European Union* (2009). Regulation (EC) No 1060/2009 (as amended to 22/05/14), Article 11(2).

[298] *Official Journal of the European Union* (2009). Regulation (EC) No 1060/2009 (as amended to 22/05/14), Article 23e(1).

[299] *Official Journal of the European Union* (2009). Regulation (EC) No 1060/2009 (as amended to 22/05/14), Article 23e(2).

[300] *Official Journal of the European Union* (2009). Regulation (EC) No 1060/2009 (as amended to 22/05/14), Article 23e(3).

[301] *Official Journal of the European Union* (2009). Regulation (EC) No 1060/2009 (as amended to 22/05/14), Article 23e(4).

[302] *Official Journal of the European Union* (2009). Regulation (EC) No 1060/2009 (as amended to 22/05/14), Article 23e(5).

[303] *Official Journal of the European Union* (2009). Regulation (EC) No 1060/2009 (as amended to 22/05/14), Article 23e(6).

[304] *Official Journal of the European Union* (2009). Regulation (EC) No 1060/2009 (as amended to 22/05/14), Article 23e(8).

[305] European Securities and Markets Authority (2015). CRA Authorisation, Paris, 01/12/15. <https://www.esma.europa.eu/supervision/credit-rating-agencies/risk>

[306] European Commission (2008). Improved EU framework for investment funds – Frequently Asked Questions, MEMO/08/510, Brussels, 16/07/08, pp.1-2 and 4. http://europa.eu/rapid/press-release_MEMO-08-510_en.htm?locale=fr.

[307] European Commission (2014). Undertakings for collective investment in transferable securities – amended Directive (UCITS V): Frequently asked questions, MEMO/14/298, Brussels, 15/04/14, p.2. http://europa.eu/rapid/press-release_MEMO-14-298_en.htm?locale=en.

[308] *Official Journal of the European Union* (2009). Directive 2009/65/EC of the European Parliament and of the Council of 13 July 2009 on the coordination of laws, regulations and administrative provisions relating to undertakings for collective investment in transferable securities (UCITS) (recast), L302/32-L302/96, as amended to 28/08/14, Article 5(4).

[309] *Official Journal of the European Union* (2009). Directive 2009/65/EC (as amended to 28/08/14), Article 5(4).

[310] *Official Journal of the European Union* (2009). Directive 2009/65/EC (as amended to 28/08/14), Article 14a(1).

[311] *Official Journal of the European Union* (2009). Directive 2009/65/EC (as amended to 28/08/14), Article 14a(3).

[312] *Official Journal of the European Union* (2009). Directive 2009/65/EC (as amended to 28/08/14), Article 14b(1).

[313] *Official Journal of the European Union* (2009). Directive 2009/65/EC (as amended to 28/08/14), Article 14b(1)(b).

[314] *Official Journal of the European Union* (2009). Directive 2009/65/EC (as amended to 28/08/14), Article 14b(4).

[315] *Official Journal of the European Union* (2009). Directive 2009/65/EC (as amended to 28/08/14), Article 16(1).

[316] *Official Journal of the European Union* (2009). Directive 2009/65/EC (as amended to 28/08/14), Articles 17(2)(b) and 15.

[317] *Official Journal of the European Union* (2009). Directive 2009/65/EC (as amended to 28/08/14), Articles 18(1)(b) and 15.

[318] *Official Journal of the European Union* (2009). Directive 2009/65/EC (as amended to 28/08/14), Annex II.

[319] *Official Journal of the European Union* (2009). Directive 2009/65/EC (as amended to 28/08/14), Article 21(2).

[320] *Official Journal of the European Union* (2009). Directive 2009/65/EC (as amended to 28/08/14), Articles 21(5) and 21(2).

[321] *Official Journal of the European Union* (2009). Directive 2009/65/EC (as amended to 28/08/14), Article 27.

[322] *Official Journal of the European Union* (2009). Directive 2009/65/EC (as amended to 28/08/14), Article 22(1).

[323] *Official Journal of the European Union* (2009). Directive 2009/65/EC (as amended to 28/08/14), Article 22(2).

[324] *Official Journal of the European Union* (2009). Directive 2009/65/EC (as amended to 28/08/14), Article 22(3).

[325] *Official Journal of the European Union* (2009). Directive 2009/65/EC (as amended to 28/08/14), Article 22(4).

[326] *Official Journal of the European Union* (2009). Directive 2009/65/EC (as amended to 28/08/14), Article 22(5)(a).

[327] *Official Journal of the European Union* (2009). Directive 2009/65/EC (as amended to 28/08/14), Article 22(5)(b).

[328] *Official Journal of the European Union* (2009). Directive 2009/65/EC (as amended to 28/08/14), Article 22(6).

[329] *Official Journal of the European Union* (2009). Directive 2009/65/EC (as amended to 28/08/14), Article 23(1).

[330] *Official Journal of the European Union* (2009). Directive 2009/65/EC (as amended to 28/08/14), Article 23(2).

[331] *Official Journal of the European Union* (2009). Directive 2009/65/EC (as amended to 28/08/14), Article 25(1).

[332] *Official Journal of the European Union* (2009). Directive 2009/65/EC (as amended to 28/08/14), Article 25(2).

[333] *Official Journal of the European Union* (2009). Directive 2009/65/EC (as amended to 28/08/14), Recital 27, and Articles 37 and 38(1).

[334] *Official Journal of the European Union* (2009). Directive 2009/65/EC (as amended to 28/08/14), Article 51(1).

[335] *Official Journal of the European Union* (2009). Directive 2009/65/EC (as amended to 28/08/14), Article 88(1).

[336] *Official Journal of the European Union* (2009). Directive 2009/65/EC (as amended to 28/08/14), Article 56(2).

[337] *Official Journal of the European Union* (2009). Directive 2009/65/EC (as amended to 28/08/14), Article 68(1).

[338] *Official Journal of the European Union* (2009). Directive 2009/65/EC (as amended to 28/08/14), Article 69(1).

[339] *Official Journal of the European Union* (2009). Directive 2009/65/EC (as amended to 28/08/14), Article 72.

[340] *Official Journal of the European Union* (2009). Directive 2009/65/EC (as amended to 28/08/14), Article 74.

[341] *Official Journal of the European Union* (2009). Directive 2009/65/EC (as amended to 28/08/14), Articles 83(1), 83(2)(a) and 90.

[342] *Official Journal of the European Union* (2009). Directive 2009/65/EC (as amended to 28/08/14), Article 86.

[343] *Official Journal of the European Union* (2009). Directive 2009/65/EC (as amended to 28/08/14), Articles 84(2)(a), 85 and 90.

[344] *Official Journal of the European Union* (2009). Directive 2009/65/EC (as amended to 28/08/14), Article 98(1).

[345] *Official Journal of the European Union* (2009). Directive 2009/65/EC (as amended to 28/08/14), Article 98(2).

[346] *Official Journal of the European Union* (2009). Directive 2009/65/EC (as amended to 28/08/14), Article 99(1).

[347] *Official Journal of the European Union* (2009). Directive 2009/65/EC (as amended to 28/08/14), Article 99(6).

[348] *Official Journal of the European Union* (2009). Directive 2009/65/EC (as amended to 28/08/14), Article 99(7).

[349] *Official Journal of the European Union* (2009). Directive 2009/65/EC (as amended to 28/08/14), Article 99c(1).

[350] *Official Journal of the European Union* (2009). Directive 2009/65/EC (as amended to 28/08/14), Article 99e(1).

[351] *Official Journal of the European Union* (2009). Directive 2009/65/EC (as amended to 28/08/14), Article 102(1).

[352] *Official Journal of the European Union* (2009). Directive 2009/65/EC (as amended to 28/08/14), Article 102(2).

[353] *Official Journal of the European Union* (2009). Directive 2009/65/EC (as amended to 28/08/14), Article 102(5).

[354] *Official Journal of the European Union* (2009). Directive 2009/65/EC (as amended to 28/08/14), Article 107(2).

[355] *Official Journal of the European Union* (2009). Directive 2009/65/EC (as amended to 28/08/14), Article 107(3).

[356] *Official Journal of the European Communities* (1985). Council Directive 85/611/EEC of 20 December 1985 on the coordination of laws, regulations and administrative provisions relating to undertakings for collective investment in transferable securities (UCITS), L375/3-L375/17, as amended to 19/03/08, Article 57(1).

[357] *Official Journal of the European Union* (2011). Directive 2011/61/EU of the European Parliament and of the Council of 8 June 2011 on Alternative Investment Fund Managers and amending Directives 2003/41/EC and 2009/65/EC and Regulations (EC) No 1060/2009 and (EU) No 1095/2010, L174/1-L174/73, as amended to 12/06/14, Article 70.

[358] *Official Journal of the European Union* (2011). Directive 2011/61/EU (as amended to 12/06/14), Article 66(1)-(3).

[359] *Official Journal of the European Union* (2011). Directive 2011/61/EU (as amended to 12/06/14), Recital 4.

[360] *Official Journal of the European Union* (2011). Directive 2011/61/EU (as amended to 12/06/14), Recital 3.

[361] *Official Journal of the European Union* (2013). Regulation (EU) No 345/2013 of the European Parliament and of the Council of 17 April 2013 on European venture capital funds, L115/1-L115/17, Article 28.

[362] *Official Journal of the European Union* (2013). Regulation (EU) No 345/2013, Article 2(1)(a); *Official Journal of the European Union* (2011). Directive 2011/61/EU (as amended to 12/06/14), Article 3(2)(b).

[363] *Official Journal of the European Union* (2013). Regulation (EU) No 345/2013, Article 4.

[364] Baber, G. (2015). Venture capital in Europe: something ventured, something gained? *Company Lawyer*, 36(10), 310-313, at 313.

[365] *Official Journal of the European Union* (2013). Regulation (EU) No 346/2013 of the European Parliament and of the Council of 17 April 2013 on European social entrepreneurship funds, L115/18-L115/38, Article 29.

[366] *Official Journal of the European Union* (2013). Regulation (EU) No 346/2013, Article 4.

[367] *Official Journal of the European Union* (2013). Regulation (EU) No 346/2013, Article 2(1)(a); *Official Journal of the European Union* (2011). Directive 2011/61/EU (as amended to 12/06/14), Article 3(2)(b).

[368] *Official Journal of the European Union* (2013). Regulation (EU) No 346/2013, Article 3(1)(a)-(b).

[369] European Commission (2011). European Social Entrepreneurship Funds – Frequently Asked Questions, MEMO/11/881, Brussels, 07/12/11, p.3. <http://europa.eu/rapid/press-release_MEMO-11-881_en.pdf>

[370] *Official Journal of the European Union* (2015). Regulation (EU) 2015/760 of the European Parliament and of the Council of 29 April 2015 on European long-term investment funds, L123/98-L123/121, Article 38.

[371] *Official Journal of the European Union* (2015). Regulation (EU) 2015/760, Article 6(1).

[372] *Official Journal of the European Union* (2015). Regulation (EU) 2015/760, Article 13(1).

[373] *Official Journal of the European Union* (2015). Regulation (EU) 2015/760, Article 10.

[374] *Official Journal of the European Union* (2015). Regulation (EU) 2015/760, Article 9(1).

[375] *Official Journal of the European Union* (2009). Directive 2009/65/EC (as amended to 28/08/14), Article 50(1).

[376] European Commission (2013). European Long-term Investment Funds – frequently asked questions, MEMO/13/611, Brussels, 26/06/13, p.2. <http://europa.eu/rapid/press-release_MEMO-13-611_en.pdf>

[377] *Official Journal of the European Union* (2015). Regulation (EU) 2015/760, Article 13(1).

[378] *Official Journal of the European Union* (2014). Regulation (EU) No 1286/2014 of the European Parliament and of the Council of 26 November 2014 on key information documents for packaged retail and insurance-based investment products (PRIIPs), L352/1-L352/23, Article 5(1).

[379] *Official Journal of the European Union* (2014). Regulation (EU) No 1286/2014, Article 8(3).

[380] *Official Journal of the European Union* (2009). Directive 2009/65/EC (as amended to 28/08/14), Article 78(2).

[381] *Official Journal of the European Union* (2009). Directive 2009/65/EC (as amended to 28/08/14), Article 78(3).

[382] *Official Journal of the European Union* (2014). Regulation (EU) No 1286/2014, Article 32(1).

[383] *Official Journal of the European Union* (2014). Regulation (EU) No 1286/2014, Article 34.

[384] European Commission (2016). Proposal for a Directive of the European Parliament and of the Council amending Directive 2014/65/EU on markets in financial instruments as regards certain dates, COM(2016) final, Brussels, 10/02/16, Article 1(2)-(3). http://ec.europa.eu/finance/securities/docs/isd/mifid/160210-directive-amending-mifid_en.pdf.

[385] European Commission (2016). Proposal for a Regulation of the European Parliament and of the Council amending Regulation (EU) No 600/2014 on markets in financial

instruments, Regulation (EU) No 596/2014 on market abuse and Regulation (EU) No 909/2014 on improving securities settlement in the European Union and on central securities depositories as regards certain dates, COM(2016) final, Brussels, 10/02/16, Article 1(9)(a). http://ec.europa.eu/finance/securities/docs/isd/mifid/160210-regulation-amending-mifir_en.pdf.

[386] European Commission (2016). Press release: Commission extends by one year the application date for the MiFID II package, IP/16/265, Brussels, 10/02/04. http://europa.eu/rapid/press-release_IP-16-265_en.htm?locale=en.

[387] Baber, G. (2016). Banking in the European Union: hard Acts to follow? *Company Lawyer*, 37(3), 82-84, at 84.

[388] *Official Journal of the European Communities* (1998). Directive 98/26/EC of the European Parliament and of the Council of 19 May 1998 on settlement finality in payment and securities settlement systems, L166/45-L166/50, as amended to 28/08/14, Articles 1 and 2(a).

[389] *Official Journal of the European Communities* (1998). Directive 98/26/EC (as amended to 28/08/14), Article 7.

[390] *Official Journal of the European Communities* (1998). Directive 98/26/EC (as amended to 28/08/14), Article 9(1).

[391] *Official Journal of the European Communities* (1998). Directive 98/26/EC (as amended to 28/08/14), Article 10a.

[392] *European Commission (2010).* Proposal for a Directive of the European Parliament and of the Council amending Directive 97/9/EC of the European Parliament and of the Council on investor-compensation schemes, COM(2010) 371 final, Brussels, 12/07/10, Recital 3. http://ec.europa.eu/internal_market/securities/docs/isd/dir-97-9/proposal-modification_en.pdf.

[393] *European Commission (2010).* Proposal for a Directive of the European Parliament and of the Council amending Directive 97/9/EC of the European Parliament and of the Council on investor-compensation schemes, Recital 4.

[394] *European Commission (2010).* Proposal for a Directive of the European Parliament and of the Council amending Directive 97/9/EC of the European Parliament and of the Council on investor-compensation schemes, Article 1(4).

[395] *European Commission (2010).* Proposal for a Directive of the European Parliament and of the Council amending Directive 97/9/EC of the European Parliament and of the Council on investor-compensation schemes, Articles 1(7) and 1(2)(b)-(c).

[396] *Official Journal of the European Union* (2014). Directive 2014/49/EU of the European Parliament and of the Council of 16 April 2014 on deposit guarantee schemes (recast), L173/149-L173/178, as corrected to 30/12/14, Article 3(1)-(3).

[397] *Official Journal of the European Union* (2014). Directive 2014/49/EU (as corrected to 30/12/14), Article 3(4)-(5).

[398] *Official Journal of the European Union* (2014). Directive 2014/49/EU (as corrected to 30/12/14), Article 14(1).

[399] *Official Journal of the European Union* (2014). Directive 2014/49/EU (as corrected to 30/12/14), Article 14(2).

[400] *Official Journal of the European Union* (2014). Directive 2014/49/EU (as corrected to 30/12/14), Article 15(1).

[401] *Official Journal of the European Union* (2014). Directive 2014/49/EU (as corrected to 30/12/14), Article 15(2).

[402] *Official Journal of the European Union* (2014). Directive 2014/49/EU (as corrected to 30/12/14), Article 6(1).

[403] *Official Journal of the European Union* (2014). Directive 2014/49/EU (as corrected to 30/12/14), Article 5(1).

[404] *Official Journal of the European Union* (2009). Directive 2009/14/EC of the European Parliament and of the Council of 11 March 2009 amending Directive 94/19/EC on deposit-guarantee schemes as regards the coverage level and the payout delay, L68/3-L68/7, Article 1(3)(c).

[405] *Official Journal of the European Union* (2014). Directive 2014/49/EU (as corrected to 30/12/14), Article 16(1).

[406] *Official Journal of the European Union* (2014). Directive 2014/49/EU (as corrected to 30/12/14), Article 16(2)-(3).

[407] *Official Journal of the European Union* (2009). Directive 2009/14/EC, Article 1(6)(a).

[408] *Official Journal of the European Union* (2014). Directive 2014/49/EU (as corrected to 30/12/14), Article 8(1).

[409] *Official Journal of the European Union* (2014). Directive 2014/49/EU (as corrected to 30/12/14), Article 8(2).

[410] *Official Journal of the European Union* (2003). Directive 2002/87/EC of the European Parliament and of the Council of 16 December 2002 on the supplementary supervision of credit institutions, insurance undertakings and investment firms in a financial conglomerate and amending Council Directives 73/239/EEC, 79/267/EEC, 92/49/EEC, 92/96/EEC, 93/6/EEC and 93/22/EEC, and Directives 98/78/EC and 2000/12/EC of the European Parliament and of the Council, L35/1-L35/27, as amended to 27/06/13, Article 2(14).

[411] *Official Journal of the European Union* (2003). Directive 2002/87/EC (as amended to 27/06/13), Articles 5(2)(b) and 5(3).

[412] *Official Journal of the European Union* (2003). Directive 2002/87/EC (as amended to 27/06/13), Article 5(2)(c).

[413] *Official Journal of the European Union* (2003). Directive 2002/87/EC (as amended to 27/06/13), Article 10(1).

[414] *Official Journal of the European Union* (2003). Directive 2002/87/EC (as amended to 27/06/13), Article 11(1).

[415] *Official Journal of the European Union* (2003). Directive 2002/87/EC (as amended to 27/06/13), Article 6(2).

[416] *Official Journal of the European Union* (2003). Directive 2002/87/EC (as amended to 27/06/13), Annex I, Title II.

[417] *Official Journal of the European Union* (2003). Directive 2002/87/EC (as amended to 27/06/13), Articles 7(5) and 8(5).

[418] *Official Journal of the European Union* (2003). Directive 2002/87/EC (as amended to 27/06/13), Article 9(2)(d).

[419] *Official Journal of the European Union* (2003). Directive 2002/87/EC (as amended to 27/06/13), Article 9(4).

[420] *Official Journal of the European Union* (2003). Directive 2002/87/EC (as amended to 27/06/13), Article 9a.

[421] *Official Journal of the European Union* (2010). Regulation (EU) No 1093/2010 of the European Parliament and of the Council of 24 November 2010 establishing a European Supervisory Authority (European Banking Authority), amending Decision No 716/2009/EC and repealing Commission Decision 2009/78/EC, L331/12-L331/47, as amended to 30/07/14, Article 56; *Official Journal of the European Union* (2010). Regulation (EU) No 1094/2010 of the European Parliament and of the Council of 24 November 2010 establishing a European Supervisory Authority (European Insurance and Occupational Pensions Authority), amending Decision No 716/2009/EC and repealing Commission Decision 2009/79/EC, L331/48-L331/83, as amended to 22/05/14, Article 56; *Official Journal of the European Union* (2010). Regulation (EU) No 1095/2010 of the European Parliament and of the Council of 24 November 2010 establishing a European Supervisory Authority (European Securities and Markets Authority) amending Decision No 716/2009/EC and repealing Commission Decision 2009/77/EC, L331/84-L331/119, as amended to 22/05/14, Article 56.

[422] *Official Journal of the European Union* (2003). Directive 2002/87/EC (as amended to 27/06/13), Article 9b(1).

[423] *Official Journal of the European Union* (2003). Directive 2002/87/EC (as amended to 27/06/13), Article 9b(2).

[424] *Official Journal of the European Union* (2003). Directive 2002/87/EC (as amended to 27/06/13), Article 12(1)(a).

[425] *Official Journal of the European Union* (2003). Directive 2002/87/EC (as amended to 27/06/13), Article 12(1).

[426] *Official Journal of the European Union* (2003). Directive 2002/87/EC (as amended to 27/06/13), Article 12a(1).

[427] *Official Journal of the European Union* (2003). Directive 2002/87/EC (as amended to 27/06/13), Article 12b(1).

[428] *Official Journal of the European Union* (2003). Directive 2002/87/EC (as amended to 27/06/13), Article 14(1).

[429] *Official Journal of the European Union* (2003). Directive 2002/87/EC (as amended to 27/06/13), Article 16.

[430] *Official Journal of the European Communities* (2002). Directive 2002/47/EC of the European Parliament and of the Council of 6 June 2002 on financial collateral arrangements, L168/43-L168/50, as amended to 12/06/14, Article 3(1).

[431] *Official Journal of the European Communities* (2002). Directive 2002/47/EC (as amended to 12/06/14), Article 3(1).

[432] *Official Journal of the European Communities* (2002). Directive 2002/47/EC (as amended to 12/06/14), Article 1(4)(a).

[433] *Official Journal of the European Communities* (2002). Directive 2002/47/EC (as amended to 12/06/14), Article 1(2)(a)-(d).

[434] *Official Journal of the European Communities* (2002). Directive 2002/47/EC (as amended to 12/06/14), Article 4(1)(c).

[435] *Official Journal of the European Communities* (2002). Directive 2002/47/EC (as amended to 12/06/14), Article 4(2).

[436] *Official Journal of the European Communities* (2002). Directive 2002/47/EC (as amended to 12/06/14), Article 5(6).

[437] *Official Journal of the European Communities* (2002). Directive 2002/47/EC (as amended to 12/06/14), Article 9a.

[438] The Evaluation Partnership Limited (2006). Framework contract No RTD-JRC/00-06: Evaluation of the E-money Directive (2006/46/EC) – Final Report, Twickenham, 17/02/06, pp.2, 4 and 8. http://ec.europa.eu/internal_market/payments/docs/emoney /evaluation_en.pdf.

[439] *Official Journal of the European Union* (2009). Directive 2009/110/EC of the European Parliament and of the Council of 16 September 2009 on the taking up, pursuit and prudential supervision of the business of electronic money institutions amending Directives 2005/60/EC and 2006/48/EC and repealing Directive 2000/46/EC, L267/7-L267/17, Recital 2.

[440] *Official Journal of the European Union* (2009). Directive 2009/110/EC, Recital 4.

[441] *Official Journal of the European Union* (2009). Directive 2009/110/EC, Article 2(1).

[442] *Official Journal of the European Union* (2009). Directive 2009/110/EC, Article 2(2).

[443] *Official Journal of the European Union* (2009). Directive 2009/110/EC, Article 4.

[444] *Official Journal of the European Union* (2009). Directive 2009/110/EC, Article 5(1)-(5).

[445] *Official Journal of the European Union* (2007). Directive 2007/64/EC of the European Parliament and of the Council of 13 November 2007 on payment services in the internal market amending Directives 97/7/EC, 2002/65/EC, 2005/60/EC and 2006/48/EC and repealing Directive 97/5/EC, L319/1-L319/36, as amended to 17/11/09, Article 8(3).

[446] *Official Journal of the European Union* (2009). Directive 2009/110/EC, Article 7(1).

[447] *Official Journal of the European Union* (2007). Directive 2007/64/EC (as amended to 17/11/09), Article 9(1).

[448] *Official Journal of the European Union* (2007). Directive 2007/64/EC (as amended to 17/11/09), Article 9(2).

[449] Devnani, S., Godschalk, H., Klinger, H., Korus, K., Mantovani, I., Muller, P., Reifner, U., Riefa, C., Sinn, M. & Tiffe, A. (2013). Study on the impact of Directive 2007/64/EC on payment services in the internal market and on the application of Regulation (EC) No 924/2009 on cross-border payments in the Community, Contract MARKT/2011/120/H3/ST/OP: Final Report – Prepared by London Economics and institut für finanzdienstleistungen e.V. in association with PaySys Consultancy GmbH, February 2013, Paragraphs 5-6, p.ix. http://ec.europa.eu/finance/payments/ docs/framework/130724_study-impact-psd-annex_en.pdf.

[450] *Official Journal of the European Union* (2015). Directive (EU) 2015/2366 of the European Parliament and of the Council of 25 November 2015 on payment services in the internal market, amending Directives 2002/65/EC, 2009/110/EC and 2013/36/EU and Regulation (EU) No 1093/2010, and repealing Directive 2007/64/EC, L337/35-L337/127, Recital 4.

[451] *Official Journal of the European Union* (2015). Directive (EU) 2015/2366, Recital 6.

[452] *Official Journal of the European Union* (2015). Directive (EU) 2015/2366, Recital 33.

[453] *Official Journal of the European Union* (2015). Directive (EU) 2015/2366, Recital 34.

[454] *Official Journal of the European Union* (2015). Directive (EU) 2015/2366, Recital 2.

[455] *Official Journal of the European Union* (2015). Regulation (EU) No 2015/751 of the European Parliament and of the Council of 29 April 2015 on interchange fees for card-based transactions, L123/1-L123/15, Article 2(10).

[456] *Official Journal of the European Union* (2015). Regulation (EU) No 2015/751, Article 3(1).

[457] *Official Journal of the European Union* (2015). Regulation (EU) No 2015/751, Article 4.

[458] *Official Journal of the European Union* (2015). Regulation (EU) No 2015/751, Article 3(2)(a).

[459] *Official Journal of the European Union* (2015). Regulation (EU) No 2015/751, Article 4.

[460] European Commission (2013). Payment Services Directive and Interchange fees Regulation: frequently asked questions, MEMO/13/71, Brussels, 24/07/13, p.8. http://europa.eu/rapid/press-release_MEMO-13-719_en.pdf.

[461] European Commission (2013). Payment Services Directive and Interchange fees Regulation: frequently asked questions, p.6.

[462] *Official Journal of the European Union* (2015). Regulation (EU) No 2015/751, Article 7(1).

[463] *Official Journal of the European Union* (2015). Regulation (EU) No 2015/751, Article 12(1).

[464] *Official Journal of the European Union* (2015). Directive (EU) 2015/2366, Article 116.

[465] *Official Journal of the European Union* (2015). Directive (EU) 2015/2366, Article 115(1)-(2).

[466] *Official Journal of the European Union* (2015). Directive (EU) 2015/2366, Article 114.

[467] *Official Journal of the European Union* (2015). Directive (EU) 2015/2366, Article 1(1).

[468] *Official Journal of the European Union* (2015). Directive (EU) 2015/2366, Article 1(1)(a)-(b).

[469] *Official Journal of the European Union* (2015). Directive (EU) 2015/2366, Article 7.

[470] *Official Journal of the European Union* (2015). Directive (EU) 2015/2366, Articles 28(1)(e), 5(1)(b) and 5(1)(e).

[471] *Official Journal of the European Union* (2015). Directive (EU) 2015/2366, Article 30(2)-(3).

[472] *Official Journal of the European Union* (2015). Directive (EU) 2015/2366, Article 30(1).

[473] *Official Journal of the European Union* (2015). Directive (EU) 2015/2366, Article 46.

[474] *Official Journal of the European Union* (2015). Directive (EU) 2015/2366, Article 4(18).

[475] *Official Journal of the European Union* (2015). Directive (EU) 2015/2366, Annex I, Point 7.

[476] *Official Journal of the European Union* (2015). Directive (EU) 2015/2366, Annex II.

[477] *Official Journal of the European Union* (2015). Directive (EU) 2015/2366, Article 4(19).

[478] *Official Journal of the European Union* (2015). Directive (EU) 2015/2366, Annex I, Point 8.

[479] *Official Journal of the European Union* (2015). Directive (EU) 2015/2366, Article 33.

[480] *Official Journal of the European Union* (2015). Directive (EU) 2015/2366, Article 67.

[481] *Official Journal of the European Union* (2015). Directive (EU) 2015/2366, Article 67(2)(a).

[482] *Official Journal of the European Union* (2015). Directive (EU) 2015/2366, Article 67(2)(e).

[483] *Official Journal of the European Union* (2014). Directive 2014/59/EU of the European Parliament and of the Council of 15 May 2014 establishing a framework for the recovery and resolution of credit institutions and investment firms and amending Council Directive 82/891/EEC, and Directives 2001/24/EC, 2002/47/EC, 2004/25/EC, 2005/56/EC, 2007/36/EC, 2011/35/EU, 2012/30/EU and 2013/36/EU, and Regulations (EU) No 1093/2010 and (EU) No 648/2012, of the European Parliament and of the Council, L173/190-L173/348, Recital 119.

[484] *Official Journal of the European Union* (2014). Directive 2014/59/EU, Article 2(1)(23).

[485] *Official Journal of the European Union* (2014). Directive 2014/59/EU, Article 117(1).

[486] *Official Journal of the European Communities* (2001). Directive 2001/24/EC of the European Parliament and of the Council of 4 April 2001 on the reorganisation and winding up of credit institutions, L125/15-L125/23, as amended to 12/06/14, Article 1(3).

[487] *Official Journal of the European Union* (2014). Directive 2014/59/EU, Article 117(1).

[488] *Official Journal of the European Communities* (2001). Directive 2001/24/EC (as amended to 12/06/14), Article 1(4).

[489] *Official Journal of the European Union* (2014). Directive 2014/59/EU, Article 117(1).

[490] *Official Journal of the European Communities* (2001). Directive 2001/24/EC (as amended to 12/06/14), Article 1(5)-(6).

[491] *Official Journal of the European Communities* (2001). Directive 2001/24/EC (as amended to 12/06/14), Article 33.

[492] *Official Journal of the European Union* (2014). Directive 2014/59/EU, Article 84.

[493] *Official Journal of the European Union* (2014). Directive 2014/59/EU, Article 117(2).

[494] *Official Journal of the European Communities* (2001). Directive 2001/24/EC (as amended to 12/06/14), Article 2.

[495] *Official Journal of the European Union* (2014). Directive 2014/59/EU, Article 117(3)-(4).

[496] *Official Journal of the European Communities* (2001). Directive 2001/24/EC (as amended to 12/06/14), Articles 25-26.

[497] *Official Journal of the European Union* (2014). Directive 2014/59/EU, Articles 68(1) and 68(3).

[498] *Official Journal of the European Union* (2014). Directive 2014/59/EU, Articles 71(1) and 2(1)(23).

[499] *Official Journal of the European Communities* (2001). Directive 2001/24/EC of the European Parliament and of the Council of 4 April 2001 on the reorganisation and winding up of credit institutions, L125/15-L125/23, original version, Recital 1.

[500] *Official Journal of the European Communities* (2001). Directive 2001/24/EC (original version), Recital 2.

[501] *Official Journal of the European Union* (2014). Directive 2014/59/EU, Recital 1.

[502] *Official Journal of the European Union* (2014). Directive 2014/59/EU, Recital 2.

[503] *Official Journal of the European Union* (2014). Directive 2014/59/EU, Articles 1(1) and 2(1)(23).

[504] *Official Journal of the European Union* (2014). Directive 2014/59/EU, Article 5(1).

[505] *Official Journal of the European Union* (2014). Directive 2014/59/EU, Article 5(2).

[506] *Official Journal of the European Union* (2014). Directive 2014/59/EU, Article 5(5), and Annex, Section A, Points 1-3.

[507] *Official Journal of the European Union* (2014). Directive 2014/59/EU, Article 5(6).

[508] *Official Journal of the European Union* (2014). Directive 2014/59/EU, Article 7(1).

[509] *Official Journal of the European Union* (2014). Directive 2014/59/EU, Articles 7(2)-(3), 8(2) and 8(4).

[510] *Official Journal of the European Union* (2014). Directive 2014/59/EU, Articles 2(1)(1) and 37(9).

[511] *Official Journal of the European Union* (2014). Directive 2014/59/EU, Article 31(1).

[512] *Official Journal of the European Union* (2014). Directive 2014/59/EU, Article 31(2).

[513] *Official Journal of the European Union* (2014). Directive 2014/59/EU, Article 32(1).

[514] *Official Journal of the European Union* (2014). Directive 2014/59/EU, Article 34(1).

[515] *Official Journal of the European Union* (2014). Directive 2014/59/EU, Article 37(3).

[516] *Official Journal of the European Union* (2014). Directive 2014/59/EU, Article 38(1).

[517] *Official Journal of the European Union* (2014). Directive 2014/59/EU, Article 38(2).

[518] *Official Journal of the European Union* (2014). Directive 2014/59/EU, Article 40(1).

[519] *Official Journal of the European Union* (2014). Directive 2014/59/EU, Article 40(2).

[520] *Official Journal of the European Union* (2014). Directive 2014/59/EU, Article 40(3).

[521] *Official Journal of the European Union* (2014). Directive 2014/59/EU, Article 42(1).

[522] *Official Journal of the European Union* (2014). Directive 2014/59/EU, Article 42(2).

[523] *Official Journal of the European Union* (2014). Directive 2014/59/EU, Article 42(3).

[524] *Official Journal of the European Union* (2014). Directive 2014/59/EU, Article 43(1).

[525] *Official Journal of the European Union* (2014). Directive 2014/59/EU, Article 63(1).

[526] *Official Journal of the European Union* (2014). Directive 2014/59/EU, Article 44(2).

[527] Parris, M. (2016). Brexit would mean we don't give a damn, *The Times*, 20/02/16, 71838, 23.

Chapter Five

A FEW THOUGHTS

ABSTRACT

The United Kingdom's Prime Minister, the Right Honourable Margaret Thatcher MP, outlined a vision for the future of Europe from a British perspective, in her speech at Bruges in September 1988. This view captured some of the essential elements of what European values are. The Prime Minister's address was ignored by other leaders, who rushed towards an ideological but unworkable Economic and Monetary Union to which most Member States are tied. The GFC highlighted some of the problems with the arrangements for Economic and Monetary Union, to which the Commission responded in June 2015 by proposing a heavy programme of integration that transfers further powers to the EU's institutions. These plans are due to be completed by 2025.

The Commission's proposals are not wholly in the interests of Europe's citizens – for taken in their entirety they are inflexible, burdensome, and expensive to set up and to maintain. This puts foreign investment at risk, as investors can only expect to receive small returns over the next few years. It is only when Europe's leaders wake up to the fact that the rest of the world knows that they are pursuing Utopian goals, that changes in a sensible direction will be able to take place.

Keywords: European, Thatcher, Delors, Commission, Utopia, economic, monetary, fiscal

INTRODUCTION

In May 1979, The Right Honourable Margaret Thatcher MP was installed as the Prime Minister of the United Kingdom. Although too young to vote, I recall this event as being a pivotal moment that was greeted with much enthusiasm in the Conservative constituency in which I lived. Whilst Mrs. Thatcher's policies for the country were not perfect, she proved to be competent and effective in this role – putting her view of the national interest over personal ambition and, eventually, in November 1990, losing office as a result of actions of colleagues within the Conservative Party who held different views to hers.

One issue of relevance to Mrs. Thatcher's removal from office, was the diversity of opinions on Europe within the Conservative Party. The urgency of this matter was reinforced by developing ideas on the proposed Economic and Monetary Union for Member States of the European Community (as it then was). These plans were contained in the 'Report on economic and monetary union in the European Community,' which the Committee for the Study of Economic and Monetary Union published in April 1989 under the Chairmanship of the then President of the Commission, Mr. Jacques Delors[1007].

Mrs. Thatcher had already 'crossed swords' with Mr. Delors, culminating in her 'Speech to the College of Europe' in September 1988 – widely known as 'the Bruges Speech.' Although this address lacked depth, it was a brave attempt by the Prime Minister to define the United Kingdom's relationship with the European Community (as it then was), and to demonstrate that the vision of some of the EU's founding fathers as a federally-run United States of Europe was not shared by all Britons.

THE BRUGES SPEECH

After making complementary comments concerning the College of Europe and the city of Bruges, Mrs. Thatcher, in her customary way, reaches the point without prevarication.

> I want to start by disposing of some myths about my country, Britain, and its relationship with Europe and to do that, I must say something about the identity of Europe itself. Europe is not the creation of the Treaty of Rome. Nor is the European idea the property of any group or institution. We British are as much heirs to the legacy of European culture as any other nation. Our links to the rest of Europe, the continent of Europe have been the dominant factor in our history [1].

There follows some examples of the historic connection between the United Kingdom and the rest of Europe. Next, the speech makes some pertinent remarks concerning the European Community.

> The European Community belongs to *all* its members. It must reflect the traditions and aspirations of *all*[1008] its members. ... Britain does not dream of some cosy, isolated existence on the fringes of the European Community. Our destiny is in Europe, as part of the Community. That is not to say that our future lies only in Europe, but nor does that of France or Spain or, indeed, of any other member. The Community is not an end in itself. Nor is it an institutional device to be constantly modified according to the dictates of some abstract intellectual concept. Nor must it be ossified by endless regulation. The European Community is a practical means by which Europe can ensure the future prosperity and security of its people in a world in which there are many other powerful nations and groups of nations. We Europeans cannot afford to waste our energies on internal disputes or arcane institutional debates. They are no substitute for effective action. Europe has to be ready both to contribute in full measure to its own security and to compete commercially and industrially in a world in which success goes to the countries which encourage individual initiative and enterprise, rather than those which

---

[1007] The 'Report on economic and monetary union in the European Community' is available from the University of Pittsburgh's Archive of European Integration, at http://aei.pitt.edu/1007/1/monetary_delors.pdf. Membership of the Committee for the Study of Economic and Monetary Union included Baron Lamfalussy and Mr. de Larosière, both of whom achieved subsequent renown – see the sections entitled 'The Lamfalussy Process' in Chapter 1 and 'The de Larosière Report' in Chapter 3 (Committee for the Study of Economic and Monetary Union (1989), Report on economic and monetary union in the European Community, p.40).

[1008] Emphasis original.

attempt to diminish them. This evening I want to set out some guiding principles for the future which I believe will ensure that Europe does succeed, not just in economic and defence terms but also in the quality of life and the influence of its peoples [2].

Having taken responsibility for the United Kingdom's future within Europe, i.e., 'Our destiny is in Europe, as part of the Community' and 'We Europeans', Mrs. Thatcher links success to the encouragement of 'individual initiative and enterprise' and lays down 'guiding principles.' These are: (i) "[W]illing and active cooperation between independent sovereign states is the best way to build a successful European Community," (ii) "Community policies must tackle present problems in a *practical*[1009] way," (iii) "the need for Community policies which encourage enterprise," (iv) "Europe should not be protectionist," and (v) "Europe must continue to maintain a sure defence through NATO[1010]" [3]. This approach shows an awareness that the European Community should be outward-looking rather than introspective, whilst bearing some of the responsibility for economic progress on the territories of its Member States. Fortunately, the EU has done the latter (if not the former), with its application of structural funds to countries and regions in need[1011].

Finally, the speech considers the British approach as the Prime Minister perceived it to be.

> Mr. Chairman, I believe it is not enough just to talk in general terms about a European vision or ideal. If we believe in it, we must chart the way ahead and identify the next steps. And this is what I have tried to do this evening. This approach does not require new documents: they are all there, the North Atlantic Treaty, the Revised Brussels Treaty and the Treaty of Rome, texts written by far-sighted men, a remarkable Belgian – Paul Henri Spaak – among them. However far we may want to go, the truth is that we can only get there one step at a time. And what we need now is to take decisions on the next steps forward, rather than let ourselves be distracted by Utopian goals. Utopia never comes, because we know we should not like it if it did. Let Europe be a family of nations, understanding each other better, appreciating each other more, doing more together but relishing our national identity no less than our common European endeavour. Let us have a Europe that plays its part in the wider world, which looks outward not inward, and which preserves that Atlantic community – that Europe on both sides of the Atlantic – which is our noblest inheritance and our greatest strength. May I thank you for the privilege of delivering this lecture in this great hall to this great college [4].

Mrs. Thatcher's reference to 'Utopian goals' may have included that of Economic and Monetary Union, which did seem fairly Utopian at the time of the Bruges speech. If this was the case, then 'Utopia' did arrive – in January 1999. It has proved to be far from ideal.

Is it possible to learn from these comments? Rather than pursuing idyllic objectives, it is wise to set sensible goals, and attempt to fulfil these step-by-step.

[1009] Emphasis original.

[1010] 'NATO' is an abbreviation for the North Atlantic Treaty Organization'.

[1011] The EU is still funding regional projects. For example, the Commission has recently launched the "PEACE IV" Programme for peace and reconciliation in Northern Ireland and in the lands of Ireland close to its border with the United Kingdom – to which the EU is contributing almost 270 million Euros (European Commission (2016), Double announcements on Northern Ireland from Commissioner Crețu, <http://ec.europa.eu/regional_policy/en/newsroom/news/2016/01/18-01-2016-double-announcements-on-northern-ireland-from-commissioner-cretu>).

The Commission's document of June 2015, entitled 'Completing Europe's Economic and Monetary Union', sets out a 3 stage plan to be fulfilled "at the latest by 2025," for the completion of the Economic and Monetary Union that was initiated by the European Council in June 1988[1012] [5, 6]. 4 days after the publication of this document (on 22nd June 2015), the European Council conferred the title of "Honorary Citizen of Europe" on Mr. Delors, in recognition of "his remarkable contribution to the development of the European project" [7]. Given Mr. Delors' integral involvement with the planning and introduction of 'Utopia', the European Council's conferral upon him of an honour that only 2 others have received beforehand[1013] is a sign of its firm belief that this 'Utopia' can be made as blissful for the EU's citizens as its predecessor of June 1988 would have wished for. If the Commission has any reasonable chance of achieving this – even in part – then it will need to undertake the project step-by-step. It has started by publishing the plan, to which the next section will turn.

COMPLETING EUROPE'S ECONOMIC AND MONETARY UNION

The Commission's Report entitled 'Completing Europe's Economic and Monetary Union "reflects the personal deliberations and discussions of the five Presidents," i.e., Dr. Draghi and Messrs. Dijsselbloem, Juncker, Schulz and Tusk [8]. They consider that it will provide a beneficial framework for all inhabitants of the Eurozone.

> A complete EMU [Economic and Monetary Union] is not an end in itself. It is a means to create a better and fairer life for all citizens, to prepare the [European?]. Union for future global challenges and to enable each of its members to prosper [9].

The next paragraph is devoted to preening, perhaps to encourage confidence in the readers of the document.

> The euro is a successful and stable currency. It is shared by 19 EU Member States and more than 330 million citizens. It has provided its members with price stability and shielded them against external instability. Despite the recent [global financial]. crisis, it remains the second most important currency in the world, with a share of almost a quarter of global foreign exchange reserves, and with almost sixty countries and territories around the world either directly or indirectly pegging their currency to it [10].

3 paragraphs below this, the Report summarises the agenda.

> Europe's Economic and Monetary Union (EMU) today is like a house that was built over decades but only partially finished. When the storm hit, its walls and roof had to be stabilized quickly. It is now high time to reinforce its foundations and turn it into what EMU was meant to be: a place of prosperity based on balanced economic growth and price stability, a competitive social market economy, aiming at full employment and social progress. To achieve this, we will need to take further steps to complete EMU [11].

[1012] Thus, it is submitted that the Commission wishes to perfect 'Utopia' by 2025, for which it has support of the Presidents of the European Council, the Parliament, the European Central Bank and the Eurogroup.
[1013] Previous recipients of the 'Honorary Citizen of Europe' award are Messrs. Jean Monnet and Helmut Kohl.

The Economic and Monetary Union involves sacrifice, in return for promised benefits.

> The euro is more than just a currency. It is a *political* and economic project. All members of our Monetary Union *have given up* their previous national currencies *once and for all* and *permanently* share monetary sovereignty with the other euro area countries. In return, countries gain the benefits of using a credible and stable currency with a large, competitive and powerful single market. This *common destiny*[1014] requires solidarity in times of crisis and respect for commonly agreed rules from all members [12].

As the italicised words show, the Economic and Monetary Union involves an irreversible transfer of monetary sovereignty from its member countries to the institutions – i.e., to the European Council, the Council, the Parliament, the Commission and the European Central Bank. Is this really what countries want?

Once the control of monetary policy has been relinquished to the European Central Bank, then there is a risk that divergent fiscal policies of participating states could destabilize the Eurozone. Thus, there needs to be fiscal co-ordination amongst participant countries, and, ultimately, the transfer of fiscal powers to the institutions.

> [Member countries] must be able to absorb shocks internally through having suitably resilient economies and sufficient fiscal buffers over the economic cycle. This is because, with monetary policy set uniformly for the whole euro area, national fiscal policies are vital to stabilize the economy whenever a local shock occurs. And with all countries sharing a single exchange rate, they need flexible economics that can react quickly to downturns. Otherwise they risk that recessions leave deep and permanent scars. Yet price adjustment will never occur as quickly as exchange rate adjustment. And we have seen that market pressures can deprive countries of their fiscal stabilisers in a slump. For all economies to be permanently better off inside the euro area, they also need to be able to share the impact of shocks through risk-sharing within the EMU. In the short-term, this risk-sharing can be achieved through integrated financial and capital markets (private risk-sharing) combined with the necessary common backstops, i.e., a last-resort financial safety net, to the Banking Union. In the medium term, *as economic structures converge towards the best standards in Europe*[1015], public risk-sharing should be enhanced through a mechanism of fiscal stabilisation for the euro area as a whole [13].

Making promises that are built on contingencies is often unwise. Hence, the idea of 'as economic structures converge towards the best standards in Europe' should be treated cautiously. In any event, what are 'the best standards in Europe'? I would like to say 'those of the United Kingdom,' but others would disagree. Terms such as this need to be carefully defined, and reasons provided as to why they are used.

So, how does the Report propose to accomplish completion of the Economic and Monetary Union?

> Progress must happen on four fronts: first, towards a genuine Economic Union that ensures each economy has the structural features to prosper within the Monetary Union. Second towards a Financial Union that guarantees the integrity of our currency across the

---

[1014] Emphasis added.
[1015] Emphasis added.

Monetary Union and increases risk-sharing with the private sector. This means completing the Banking Union and accelerating the Capital Markets Union. Third, towards a Fiscal Union that delivers both fiscal sustainability and fiscal stabilisation. And finally towards a Political Union[1016] that provides the foundation for all of the above through genuine democratic accountability, legitimacy and institutional strengthening [14].

This passage is reminiscent of Professor Giandomenico Majone's[1017] proposition of 'Europe's Impossible Trinity', in which there can only simultaneously be 2 of the following 3 items: national democracy (the 'nation-state'), integrated national economies, and transnational democracy [15]. Professor Majone writes the following.

In the EU the problem is not a diminution of democracy at the national level. At issue, rather, is a 'democratic deficit' at the supranational level, that is, the absence or incomplete development of democratic institutions and processes that the citizens of the [European]. Union take for granted in their own country. ... [W]hile the majority of the citizens of the EU support deep economic integration because of its obvious advantages in terms of consumer choice and the free movement of people, goods and services, there is no evidence that even a sizeable majority are in favor of establishing a European superstate. Hence the strategy of integration by stealth adopted by the supranational institutions [16].

It seems pertinent, in the light of these comments, to look at the Fiscal Union and the Political Union that the Commission's Report is proposing.

In recent years, the so-called 'Six-Pack'[1018], the 'Two-Pack'[1019] and the Treaty on Stability, Coordination and Governance[1020] have brought significant improvements to the

---

[1016] Emphasis original.

[1017] Dr. Majone is Emeritus Professor of Public Policy at the European University Institute (in Florence), and is a Visiting Professor there and at the University of Pittsburgh.

[1018] The 'Six-Pack' came into force on 13th December 2011, and comprises 5 Regulations and one Directive, as follows: (i) Regulation (EU) No 1173/2011 of the European Parliament and of the Council of 16 November 2011 on the effective enforcement of budgetary surveillance in the euro area, (ii) Regulation (EU) No 1174/2011 of the European Parliament and of the Council of 16 November 2011 on enforcement measures to correct excessive macroeconomic imbalances in the euro area, (iii) Regulation (EU) No 1175/2011 of the European Parliament and of the Council of 16 November 2011 amending Council Regulation (EC) No 1466/97 on the strengthening of the surveillance of budgetary positions and the surveillance and coordination of economic policies, (iv) Regulation (EU) No 1176/2011 of the European Parliament and of the Council of 16 November 2011 on the prevention and correction of macroeconomic balances, (v) Council Regulation (EU) No 1177/2011 of 8 November 2011 amending Regulation (EU) No 1467/97 on speeding up and clarifying the implementation of the excessive deficit procedure, and (vi) Council Directive 2011/85/EU of 8 November 2011 on requirements for budgetary frameworks of the Member States (European Commission (2013), Six-pack? Two-pack? Fiscal compact? A short guide to the new EU fiscal governance, <http://ec.europa.eu/economy_finance/articles/governance/2012-03-14_six_pack_en.htm>; European Parliament (2015), Evaluating EU Economic Governance: Elements for the debate on the "Six-Pack" and "Two-Pack," January 2015, Table 2, p.8, <http://www.europarl.europa.eu/RegData/etudes/BRIE/2015/536374/EPRS_BRI% 282015%29536374_REV1_EN.pdf>).

[1019] The 'Two-Pack' entered into force on 30th May 2013, and consists of the following 2 Regulations: (i) Regulation (EU) No 472/2013 of the European Parliament and of the Council of 21 May 2013 on the strengthening of economic and budgetary surveillance of Member States in the euro area experiencing or threatened with serious difficulties with respect to their financial stability, and (ii) Regulation (EU) No 473/2013 of the European Parliament and of the Council of 21 May 2013 on common provisions for monitoring and assessing draft budgetary plans and ensuring the correction of excessive deficit of the Member

framework for fiscal policies in the EMU. Together they drive our efforts to prevent budgetary imbalances, to focus on debt developments and on better enforcement mechanisms, as well as on national ownership of EU rules. This new governance framework already provides for ample *ex ante*[1021] coordination of annual budgets of euro area Member States and enhances the surveillance of those experiencing financial difficulties. Every Member State must stick to the rules, or the credibility of this framework is at risk. The rules are admittedly complex, but the forthcoming review of the 'Six-Pack' and 'Two-Pack' should be an opportunity to improve clarity, transparency, compliance and legitimacy, while preserving their stability-oriented nature [17].

Whilst it is well-known that the introduction and the ratification of the Treaty on Stability, Coordination and Governance have not been free from controversy, it is also doubtful that the EU is able to proceed with any further integration over this area without changes to the Treaties. In January 2015, the Parliament made the following observations.

The "Two-Pack" and "Six-Pack" mark the latest stage of the legislative framework for Economic and Monetary Union (EMU). The process of fiscal integration has gone through a dramatic quickening of the pace in recent years, driven by the threat of the recent financial and sovereign debt crisis. Recent developments have highlighted again the challenges created by the asymmetry between a fully-fledged monetary policy and an economic governance which is in the hands of the Member States. The strengthening of economic governance is conceived, along with the Banking Union, as a project designed to preserve the stability of the euro. The "Two-Pack" and the "Six-Pack" have gone to the limits of EU competence in the field of economic policy. Any further deepening of the Economic or Monetary Union might, therefore, either require Treaty change or recourse

---

States in the euro area (European Commission (2013), 'Two-Pack' enters into force, completing budgetary surveillance cycle and further improving economic governance for the euro area, <http://europa.eu/rapid/press-release_MEMO-13-457_en.htm>; European Parliament (2015), Evaluating EU Economic Governance: Elements for the debate on the "Six-Pack" and "Two-Pack," January 2015, Table 2, p.8, <http://www.europarl.europa.eu/
RegData/etudes/BRIE/2015/536374/EPRS_BRI%282015%29536374_REV1_EN.pdf>).

[1020] The Treaty on Stability, Coordination and Governance in the Economic and Monetary Union is available from website of the Council and of the European Council, at http://www.consilium.europa.eu/en/workarea/downloadAsset.aspx?id=27066. This Treaty was agreed on 2nd March 2012, and entered into force on 1st January 2013 (Treaty on Stability, Coordination and Governance in the Economic and Monetary Union, Articles 14(2) and 16). The Contracting States to the Treaty agree "to strengthen the economic pillar of the economic and monetary union by adopting a set of rules intended to foster budgetary discipline through a fiscal compact, to strengthen the coordination of their economic policies and to improve the governance of the euro area, thereby supporting the achievement of the European Union's objectives for sustainable growth, employment, competitiveness and social cohesion" (Treaty on Stability, Coordination and Governance in the Economic and Monetary Union, Article 1(1)). The Contracting States are Austria, Belgium, Bulgaria, Cyprus, Denmark, Estonia, Finland, France, Germany, Greece, Hungary, Ireland, Italy, Latvia, Lithuania, Luxembourg, Malta, the Netherlands, Poland, Portugal, Romania, Slovenia, Slovakia, Spain and Sweden. Thus, it has been adopted by some Member States that are currently outside the Eurozone, in addition to the 19 countries that are within it. Furthermore, Croatia, the Czech Republic and the United Kingdom are able to adopt the Treaty, as it is "open to accession to Member States of the European Union other than the Contracting Parties" (Treaty on Stability, Coordination and Governance in the Economic and Monetary Union, Article 15). The Treaty may become mainstream EU law, as "[w]ithin five years, at most, of the date of entry into force of this Treaty [i.e., by 1st January 2018], on the basis of an assessment of the experience with its implementation, the necessary steps shall be taken, in accordance with the Treaty on the European Union and the Treaty on the Functioning of the European Union, with the aim of incorporating the substance of this Treaty into the legal framework of the European Union" (Treaty on Stability, Coordination and Governance in the Economic and Monetary Union, Article 16).

[1021] '*Ex ante*' means 'beforehand', i.e., the co-ordination of budgets of Member States before they are finalized.

to the intergovernmental method – both options which would raise the issue of parliamentary control. The sensitivity of the issue is also reflected in the involvement of national constitutional courts [18].

How does the Commission's Report address this issue?

In the short run (Stage 1), the current governance framework should be strengthened through the creation of an advisory European Fiscal Board. This new advisory entity would coordinate and complement the national fiscal councils that have been set up in the context of the EU Directive on budgetary frameworks[1022]. It would provide a public and independent assessment, at European level, of how budgets – and their execution – perform against the economic objectives and recommendations set out in the EU fiscal governance framework. The composition of the [European Fiscal]. Board should be pluralistic and draw from a wide range of expertise. The mandate of this new European Fiscal Board should rest on a number of guiding principles as set out in Annex 3. Such a European Fiscal Board should lead to better compliance with the common fiscal rules, a more informed public debate, and stronger coordination of national fiscal policies [19].

The proposed European Fiscal Board's guiding principles are as follows.

[1.]. It should coordinate the network of national fiscal councils and conform to the same standard of independence [2]. It should advise, not implement policy. Enforcing the rules should remain the task of the European Commission, which should be able to deviate from the views of the European Fiscal Board provided that it has justifiable reasons and explains them [3]. It should form an economic, rather than a legal, judgement on the appropriate fiscal stance, both at national and euro area levels, against the background of EU fiscal rules. This should be done on the basis of the rules set in the Stability and Growth Pact (SGP) [4]. It should be able to issue opinions when it considers it [to be]. necessary, including in particular in connection with the assessment of Stability Programmes and presentation of the annual Draft Budget Plans and the execution of national budgets [5]. It should provide an *ex post*[1023] evaluation of how the governance framework was implemented [20].

But, is there any real need for this advisory European Fiscal Board? If the development of the ESAs has set a precedent, then, an economic wobble[1024] affecting the Eurozone over the coming years may lead to the commissioning of a Report, to be chaired by an academic or another professional who is known to the Commission[1025], which recommends that the Board be given the power to issue RTSs and ITSs that the Commission is empowered to adopt[1026].

[1022] This is Council Directive 2011/85/EU of 8 November 2011 on requirements for budgetary frameworks of the Member States, which is part of the 'Six-Pack': see fn 1018.

[1023] *'Ex post'* means 'after the event' – which is the opposite of *'ex ante'*: see fn 1021.

[1024] The GFC was much more than a 'wobble'. Nonetheless, as the Commission considers the ESAs to be successful, it would take less than a crisis to precipitate a similar development over another area (European Commission (2014), European Commission (2014b), Report from the Commission to the European Parliament and the Council on the operation of the European Supervisory Authorities (ESAs) and the European System of Financial Supervision (ESFS), p.2, <http://ec.europa.eu/finance/general-policy/docs/committees/140808-esfs-review_en.pdf>). See Chapter 3, for information concerning the role of the ESAs.

[1025] See fn 1007.

[1026] On the Commission's behalf, the commissioning Commissioner commissions a Commission-friendly Report from the commissioned.

In spite of this, EU leaders show determination to proceed with fiscal reforms.

There are many ways for a currency union to progress towards a Fiscal Union. Yet, while the degree to which currency unions have common budgetary instruments differs, all mature Monetary Unions have put in place a common macroeconomic stabilisation function to better deal with shocks that cannot be managed at the national level alone. This would be a natural development for the euro area in the longer term (Stage 2) and under the conditions explained above, i.e., as the culmination of a process of convergence and further pooling of decision-making on national budgets. The objective of automatic stabilisation at the euro area level would not be to actively fine-tune the economic cycle at euro area level. Instead, it should improve the cushioning of large macroeconomic shocks and thereby make EMU overall more resilient. The exact design of such euro area stabilisers requires more in-depth work. This should be one of the tasks of the proposed expert group [21].

This is integration by stealth. How can one 'progress towards a Fiscal Union' without harmonising national fiscal policy? Rather than making the incremental changes outlined in the Commission's Report, would it be more honest for EU leaders to propose the foundation of a European Fiscal Authority? This step would need to come in a true Fiscal Union, so why conceal it from the public?

The answer to this question is that few people would support such a development. Therefore, the next steps towards the Fiscal Union need to be discreet[1027]. The Report states the following.

A prospective [macroeconomic] stabilisation function could, for example, build on the European Fund for Strategic Investments as a first step, by identifying a pool of financing sources and investment projects specific to the euro area, to be tapped into according to the business cycle. Various additional sources of financing should be considered. It will be important to ensure that the design of such stabilisation function rests on the following principles [1]. It should not lead to permanent transfers between countries or to transfers in one direction only, which is why converging towards Economic Union is a precondition for participation. It should also not be conceived as a way to equalize incomes between Member States [2]. It should neither undermine the incentives for sound fiscal policy-making at the national level, nor the incentives to address national structural weaknesses. Accordingly, and to prevent moral hazard, it should be tightly linked to compliance with the broad EU governance framework and to progress in converging towards the common standards described in Section 2 [of the Report, which is entitled 'Towards Economic Union – Convergence, Prosperity and Social Cohesion'] [3]. It should be developed within the framework of the European Union. This would guarantee that it is consistent with the existing EU fiscal framework and with procedures for the coordination of economic policies. It should be open and transparent *vis-à-vis* all EU Member States [4]. It should not be an instrument for crisis management. The European Stability Mechanism (ESM) already performs that function. Instead, its role should be to improve the overall economic resilience of EMU and individual euro area countries. It would thus help to prevent crises and actually make future inventions by the ESM less likely [22].

[1027] The Russians call this 'Шаг за шагом' – step-by-step – until the eventual goal of Fiscal Union is achieved.

Thus, the macroeconomic stabilisation function is to be a mini-IMF for Eurozone countries. Countries donate funds to it, and are able to draw on this money as and when the stabilisation function approves this – in accordance with its rules of operation. The claim in point [3] that the macroeconomic stabilisation function should be 'developed within the framework of the European Union', implies that its establishment would not require substantial changes to the TFEU and/or the TEU. Eurozone countries might choose to proceed in a similar way to the Treaty on Stability, Coordination and Governance – i.e., set up the function according to an agreement outside the EU legal framework in order to circumvent the need for additions and/or modifications to provisions of the Treaties, and then incorporate it into the mainstream EU structure – once countries have worked out how to operate it as effectively and efficiently as is reasonably possible.

The next section of the Report is entitled 'Democratic Accountability, Legitimacy and Institutional Strengthening' [23]. This is more tactful than the possible alternative title 'Towards Political Union – Making the Eurozone's Institutions More Authoritative, whilst Enhancing their Accountability to the Public'. The Commission's Report suggests a number of initiatives.

First practical steps have been initiated by the European Parliament to strengthen parliamentary oversight as part of the European Semester. 'Economic dialogues' between the European Parliament and the Council, the Commission and the Eurogroup have taken place in line with the provisions of the 'Six-Pack'[1028] and the 'Two-Pack'[1029] legislation. This has already been part of the latest European Semester rounds. These dialogues may be enhanced by agreeing on dedicated time-slots during the main steps of the Semester cycle. A new form of inter-parliamentary cooperation was established to bring together European and national actors. This takes place within the European Parliamentary Week organised by the European Parliament in co-operation with national Parliaments, which includes representatives from national Parliaments for in-depth discussions on policy priorities. The 'Two-Pack' also enshrined the right for a national Parliament to convene a Commissioner for a presentation of the Commission's opinion on a draft budgetary plan or of its recommendation to a Member State in Excessive Debt Procedure – a right that should be exercised more systemically than at present [24].

The Parliament's initiative to discuss issues of policy with representatives from the parliaments of Eurozone countries is a good one. At best, if each MP and MEP reasonably represents his/her constituents, and there is overlap between the constituencies of the MEP and the MP in question, then a majority of these constituents may benefit from the results of those discussions.

The presentation by a Commissioner to a national parliament in relation to the latter's draft budgetary plan may be insufficiently interrogative – i.e., the former may give instructions to the latter that may not be queried. The accountability of the executive to the legislature is a widely-accepted aspect of democracy, which should apply in the Member States – in so far as the issues under consideration are relevant to them (as national budgets are) – as well to the Parliament. In return, delegates to any national parliament should extend a (compulsory) code of courteous conduct to representatives of the Commission whom they have invited to speak there.

[1028] See fn 1018, for the 5 Regulations and one Directive of the 'Six-Pack'.
[1029] See fn 1019, for the 2 Regulations of the 'Two-Pack'.

We could further strengthen the timing and added value of these parliamentary moments in line with the renewed European Semester outlined in Annex 2. In particular, the European Commission could engage with the European Parliament at a plenary debate before the Annual Growth Survey is presented, and continue the debate following its adoption. Moreover, a second dedicated plenary debate could be held upon presentation by the Commission of the Country-Specific Recommendations, in accordance with the relevant provisions of the 'Six-Pack' on economic dialogue. At the same time, the Commission and Council representatives could participate in inter-parliamentary meetings in particular in the context of the European Parliamentary Week. This new practice could be progressively agreed upon in more detail between EU institutions (Commission, Ecofin Council, Eurogroup and the European Parliament) in full respect of their respective institutional rule, in the form of a non-binding interinstitutional agreement [25].

Annex 2 of the Report lays down a European Semester programme, which sets a Eurozone agenda followed by a national budgetary programme for each country within the scope of that agenda. This is analogous to legislative practice in the areas of shared competence between the EU and the Member States, in which the latter may "exercise their competence to the extent that the [European]. Union has not exercised its competence"[1030] [26]. The process is as follows.

The first stage (November of year 'n-1' to February of year 'n') would be devoted to assessing the situation in the euro area as a whole. The Commission's Annual Growth Survey (AGS) would be the basis for this discussion and would draw on a number of thematic reports, such as the Alert Mechanism Report, the annual report of the European Systemic Risk Board, the Joint Employment and Social Report, as well as the views of a new European Fiscal Board and the new euro area system of Competitiveness Authorities. Together, these reports would give a complete picture of euro area challenges. The AGS would be presented to and discussed by the European Parliament. At the same time as the AGS, the Commission would present a dedicated recommendation for action within the euro area, as well as a list of Member States it considers for 'in-depth reviews', according to the Macroeconomic Imbalance Procedure (MIP). These documents would be discussed within the European Parliament within the framework of the economic dialogue, as foreseen by the 'Six-Pack' legislation, and within the different formations of the Council and the Eurogroup. This means that by [the] end [of] February every year a genuine discussion will have taken place on the priorities set for the EU, and the euro area in particular, for the coming year. The following stage (March to July of year 'n') would be devoted to reviewing and assessing the performance and policies of the Member States in the light of these priorities. This is the phase where Member States should systematically involve national Parliaments, together with social partners and civil society, in the discussion of national priorities. This stage will start with the publication of the Commission's Country Reports, which summarise Member States' challenges and performance. This stage would end with the adoption of County-Specific Recommendations which should clearly take into account the euro area dimension agreed in the first stage. EU-level social partners could be

---

[1030] See fn 83 in the subsection entitled 'UCITS', in the section entitled 'Securities Legislation' in Chapter 1, for a discussion of the nature of 'maximum harmonisation' in the context of shared competence and exclusive competence.

involved in discussions earlier, for instance through a renewed Tripartite Social Summit and Macroeconomic Dialogue, to maximise their contributions to the new process [27].

Although this process is clear, it provides the Commission and its Euro-level advisors with *carte blanche* to decide central policy, with only nominal accountability to the European Parliament. National democracy for Eurozone countries is confined to the second part of the process – which constrains domestic parliamentary discretion. Any government in the United Kingdom would refuse to accept this model, and for good reason. It is centralizing, and relegates the role of national authorities to that of minor players. To take one example, it would be a shame to see the magnificent Parliament of Budapest – the design of which was enlightened by that of the equally impressive Houses of Parliament in London – confined to discussing niceties that are left in the spaces remaining from the Commission's Country Report for Hungary. A Euro-level promise of financial stability for Eurozone countries is not worth this.

In summary, the Commission's Report, which had been agreed with the Presidents of the other leading institutions of the EU and of the Eurozone, puts forward a substantial programme of integration – some of it by stealth – which transfers power to the institutions, in order to complete the Economic and Monetary Union and to develop other elements of unification across the Eurozone. There are a few constructive suggestions, most notably a dialogue between MEPs and MPs that may lead to the concerns of constituents of countries within the Eurozone being discussed, with the possibility of agreed action being taken by their democratic representatives.

It would not be right for this programme of centralization to be an outcome of the response to the GFC from within the EU. The preservation of the Euro is a matter of Euro-pride; if it leads to the implementation of ideological measures, such as some of those contained within, and others that may be pursuant to, the Report, then the time for the Euro-project to mature is not here. Instead, it is the time for alternative strategies to be tabled and discussed.

RECOMMENDED ALTERNATIVE STRATEGIES?

One of the most notable absences from the TFEU and the TEU is a set of Articles that would enable Member States which are participating in the Economic and Monetary Union, to be able to leave it. This omission remains current EU policy, as the Commission's Report states: "All members of our Monetary Union have given up their previous national currencies once and for all and permanently share monetary sovereignty with the other euro area countries" [28].

It is beyond the scope of this work to analyse the admission procedure which took place in each of the Member States that joined the EU since the turn of the millennium – the governments of these jurisdictions signed Accession Treaties that committed their countries to the Economic and Monetary Union from the date of their accession[1031]. It is submitted that

---

[1031] See fn 528 in the subsection entitled 'Comments on the concept of the CMU and on the timing of its introduction', in the section entitled 'The Capital Markets Union' in Chapter 4, for the way in which the TFEU and the Act of accession of the particular country provide for this; Croatia is given as an example.

the negotiators from those states were so keen to join the EU that they did not fully consider the implications of the compulsory Economic and Monetary Union that was to be imposed on them as part of the deal. As accession countries are required to implement the whole of the *acquis communautaire*[1032], this result was unavoidable by the time that those countries joined the EU[1033] – a 'take it or leave it' phenomenon[1034].

This unfortunate situation provides today's leaders of these states with a problem. Their predecessors have committed the relevant jurisdiction to joining the Economic and Monetary Union – either actually or potentially – and they now cannot withdraw from this without leaving the EU.

This situation is compounded by 2 other factors: 1) the incompetence of the Commission under the charge of Mr. Delors, and 2) the occurrence of the GFC. The Delors Commission committed countries to a Monetary Union, but without an accompanying Fiscal Union. The European Central Bank subsequently pursued financial stability with targets of low inflation, which reduced the ability of some of the Member States' governments to be able to induce conditions for growth there – resulting in recessionary conditions and high unemployment. The GFC precipitated debt crises in some Member States, which have proved to be difficult to address – given the central control of monetary policy and the currency union.

The most surprising result of these events is the current Commission's puzzling claim that this record is one of success, and that the Economic and Monetary Union needs to be 'completed.' It is not "like a house that was built over decades but only partially finished" [29]. It is like a rapidly-built naval vessel that is sent into a battle at sea, which proves to be tougher than expected. The ship returns to port damaged. It is then reinforced so heavily that, although it becomes almost indestructible, it can only move slowly through the water and is therefore outmanoevered.

So, how can countries be helped out of their dilemma of being unable to withdraw from an unworkable Economic and Monetary Union, whilst remaining within the EU? There need to be changes to the TEU and to the TFEU, which enable Eurozone countries to be able to withdraw from the Economic and Monetary Union. However, this is likely to be opposed by a few Eurozone countries, the Commission and the European Central Bank; therefore, reasonable changes to these Treaties would not occur in practice. Furthermore, leaders of Member States that would like to withdraw from the Economic and Monetary Union may be considered to be 'un-European' by some of their colleagues. Such an 'un-European' classification is nonsense. Mrs. Thatcher said: "The European Community is *one*[1035] manifestation of that European identity, but it is not the only one" [30]. This applies to the Economic and Monetary Union, too.

Assuming that the European Council will approve the proposals in the Commission's Report – which it is likely to do (if it has not done so already), it will only become clear with time whether or not these plans are right for the EU. It is submitted that the proposed Economic and Monetary Union is unlikely to attract substantial foreign investment over the next few years, because it is inflexible, burdensome, and expensive to set up and to maintain. Consequently, investors are likely to receive small returns on their money. It is only when the

---

[1032] The *acquis communautaire* is the entire collection of EU law that is in force.
[1033] The Economic and Monetary Union became operational on 1st January 1999.
[1034] The following countries are affected in this way: Bulgaria, Croatia, Cyprus, the Czech Republic, Estonia, Hungary, Latvia, Lithuania, Malta, Poland, Romania, Slovakia, and Slovenia.
[1035] Emphasis original.

Eurozone, and especially its leaders, wakes up to the fact that the rest of the world knows that it is pursuing an unrealizable ideology, that change in a more constructive direction will be able to take place.

CONCLUSION

The views of the development of the European Community (as it then was) of Mrs. Thatcher and Mr. Delors diverged. The approach of the latter has been pursued by later EU administrations, culminating in an unworkable Economic and Monetary Union to which most countries within the EU are tied. The heavy, bureaucratic nature of this arrangement has been augmented by the unexpected occurrence of the GFC and the Eurozone's difficulties in responding to it satisfactorily. No change in direction for the Eurozone is expected in the short-term future.

Mrs. Thatcher's view of an outward-looking, enterprise-rich Europe of which the European Community is just one manifestation, is in tune with the continent's history and with many of the people within it – including the author. In years of yore, British, Dutch, French, Portuguese and Spanish explorers and traders travelled the seas and lands of the world. In later times, the *Pax Britannica* was legendary. Thanks largely to the development of the European Project, there has, since 1945, been a *Pax Europa*. Current inward-looking policies by EU leaders threaten to erode this. A class of innovations similar to those of Messrs. Adenauer, Monnet, Schuman, Spaak, and other founding fathers of the European Project, are needed – but appropriate to the world around us today – in 2016.

You might: (i) look across the choppy sea to the coast of Northern Ireland from the Rhinns of Galloway – perhaps from Knockinaam Lodge in the footsteps of Sir Winston Churchill, (ii) admire the peaceful scene of Limoni Bay in the sunshine from the Kardamyli to Areopolis road, (iii) cruise across Lake Onega on a lazy June day to see the elaborate wooden churches of Kizhi Island, or (iv) view the sublime golden sunset at Urbino in November. If you do, you would know that you are in Europe.

REFERENCES

[1]   Thatcher, M. (1988). Speech to the College of Europe ("The Bruges Speech"), Bruges, 20/09/88. http://www.margaretthatcher.org/document/107332.

[2]   Thatcher, M. (1988). Speech to the College of Europe ("The Bruges Speech").

[3]   Thatcher, M. (1988). Speech to the College of Europe ("The Bruges Speech").

[4]   Thatcher, M. (1988). Speech to the College of Europe ("The Bruges Speech").

[5]   *European Commission (2015).* Completing Europe's Economic and Monetary Union: Report by Jean-Claude Juncker in close cooperation with Donald Tusk, Jeroen Dijsselbloem, Mario Draghi and Martin Schulz, Brussels, 22/06/15, Annex 1, pp.20-21. <http://ec.europa.eu/priorities/economic-monetary-union/docs/5-presidents-report_en.pdf>

[6]   Committee for the Study of Economic and Monetary Union (1989). Report on economic and monetary union in the European Community: Presented April, 17, 1989, p.3. <http://aei.pitt.edu/1007/1/monetary_delors.pdf>

[7]   European Council (2015). Cover Note from the General Secretariat of the Council to Delegations, EUCO 22/15, Brussels, 26/06/15, p.8. www.consilium.europa.eu/en/meetings/european-council/2015/06/EUCO-conclusions-pdf/.

[8]   *European Commission (2015).* Completing Europe's Economic and Monetary Union, p.2.

[9]   *European Commission (2015).* Completing Europe's Economic and Monetary Union, p.2.

[10] *European Commission (2015).* Completing Europe's Economic and Monetary Union, p.4.

[11] *European Commission (2015).* Completing Europe's Economic and Monetary Union, p.4.

[12] *European Commission (2015).* Completing Europe's Economic and Monetary Union, p.4.

[13] *European Commission (2015).* Completing Europe's Economic and Monetary Union, p.4.

[14] *European Commission (2015).* Completing Europe's Economic and Monetary Union, pp.4-5.

[15] Majone, G. (2005). Dilemmas of European Integration: The Ambiguities & Pitfalls of Integration by Stealth. Oxford: Oxford University Press, p.187, and Figure 9.2, p.188.

[16] Majone, G. (2005). Dilemmas of European Integration: The Ambiguities & Pitfalls of Integration by Stealth. Oxford: Oxford University Press, p.187.

[17] *European Commission (2015).* Completing Europe's Economic and Monetary Union, p.14.

[18] European Parliament (2015). Evaluating EU Economic Governance: Elements for the debate on the "Six-Pack" and "Two-Pack," January 2015, p.1. http://www.europarl.europa.eu/RegData/etudes/BRIE/2015/536374/EPRS_BRI%282015%29536374_REV1_EN.pdf.

[19] European Commission (2015), Completing Europe's Economic and Monetary Union, p.14.

[20] *European Commission (2015).* Completing Europe's Economic and Monetary Union, Annex 3, p.23.

[21] *European Commission (2015).* Completing Europe's Economic and Monetary Union, p.14.

[22] *European Commission (2015).* Completing Europe's Economic and Monetary Union, pp.6 and 15.

[23] *European Commission (2015).* Completing Europe's Economic and Monetary Union, p.16.

[24] *European Commission (2015).* Completing Europe's Economic and Monetary Union, p.17.

[25] *European Commission (2015).* Completing Europe's Economic and Monetary Union, p.17.

[26] *Official Journal of the European Union* (2012). Consolidated version of the Treaty on the Functioning of the European Union, C326/47-C326/199, Article 2(2).

[27] *European Commission (2015).* Completing Europe's Economic and Monetary Union, Annex 2, p.22.

[28] *European Commission (2015).* Completing Europe's Economic and Monetary Union, p.4.

[29] *European Commission (2015).* Completing Europe's Economic and Monetary Union, p.4.

[30] Thatcher, M. (1988). Speech to the College of Europe ("The Bruges Speech").

BIBLIOGRAPHY

Baber, G. (2010). The Impact of Legislation and Regulation on the Freedom of Movement of Capital in Estonia, Poland and Latvia. Newcastle-upon-Tyne: Cambridge Scholars Publishing.

Baber, G. (2012a). From MiFID to MiFID II: A steady transition. *Company Lawyer*, 33(10), 316-317.

Baber, G. (2012b). International financial regulation: order or chaos? *Company Lawyer*, 33(1), 17-18.

Baber, G. (2012c). Preferred stock: wisely named? *Company Lawyer*, 33(5), 129-130.

Baber, G. (2013a). The EMIR of Strasbourg: A three-year journey from Pittsburgh. *Company Lawyer*, 34(4), 117-119.

Baber, G. (2013b). The EMIR of Strasbourg: changing the financial landscape of the EEA. *Company Lawyer*, 34(9), 285-286.

Baber, G. (2013c). UK Banking and the Financial Crisis: What lessons have we learned? BPP Law School Opinion Piece, April 2013, 1-10.

Baber, G. (2014a). Legislative and regulatory responses to the global financial crisis from within the United Kingdom. *Journal of Financial Crime*, 21(2), 124-148.

Baber, G. (2014b). The Free Movement of Capital and Financial Services: An Exposition? Newcastle-upon-Tyne: Cambridge Scholars Publishing.

Baber, G. (2014c). The Prudential Regulation Authority: special measures for special times. *Company Lawyer*, 35(12), 353-360.

Baber, G. (2015a). Banking law in the EU: has the law come of age? *Company Lawyer*, 36(12), 369-370.

Baber, G. (2015b). Deposit guarantee and bank recovery: leads from the financial crisis? Company Lawyer, 36(3), 83-85.

Baber, G. (2015c). "The European Union's legislative response to the global financial crisis: A perspective taken from 2015." In *The Global Financial Crisis: Causes, Consequences and Impact on Economic Growth*, edited by J. Barnett, 89-158. New York: Nova Science Publishers, Inc.

Baber, G. (2015d). Venture capital in Europe: something ventured, something gained? *Company Lawyer,* 36(10), 310-313.

Baber, G. (2016). Banking in the European Union: hard Acts to follow? *Company Lawyer*, 37(3), 82-84.

Basel Committee on Banking Supervision (2010). Report and Recommendations of the Cross-border Bank Resolution Group: March 2010. Basel: Bank for International Settlements. http://www.bis.org/publ/bcbs169.pdf.

Basel Committee on Banking Supervision (2015). Ninth progress report on adoption of the Basel regulatory framework: October 2015. Basel: Bank for International Settlements. http://www.bis.org/bcbs/publ/d338.pdf.

Committee for the Study of Economic and Monetary Union (1989). Report on economic and monetary union in the European Community: Presented April, 17, 1989. http://aei.pitt.edu/1007/1/monetary_delors.pdf.

Devnani, S., Godschalk, H., Klinger, H., Korus, K., Mantovani, I., Muller, P., Reifner, U., Riefa, C., Sinn, M. & Tiffe, A. (2013). Study on the impact of Directive 2007/64/EC on payment services in the internal market and on the application of Regulation (EC) No 924/2009 on cross-border payments in the Community, Contract MARKT/ 2011/120/H3/ST/OP: Final Report – Prepared by London Economics and institut für finanzdienstleistungen e.V. in association with PaySys Consultancy GmbH, February 2013. http://ec.europa.eu/finance/payments/docs/framework/130724_study-impact-psd-annex_en.pdf.

Dixon, H. (2014). Unlocking Europe's capital markets union. Centre for European Reform, October 2014, 1-8.

European Banking Authority (2015a). Consultation Paper: Draft Regulatory Technical Standards on separation of payment card schemes and processing entities under Article 7(6) of Regulation (EU) 2015/761, EBA/CP/2015/24, London, 08/12/15. https://www.eba.europa.eu/documents/10180/1303831/EBA-CP-2015-24+%28CP+on+RTS+on+separation+under+IFR+%29.pdf.

European Banking Authority (2015b). Top Management, London, 10/12/15. http://www.eba.europa.eu/about-us/organisation/top-management.

European Banking Authority (2016). Joint Committee, London. 14/03/16. http://www.eba.europa.eu/about-us/organisation/joint-committee.

European Central Bank (2015). Financial Integration in Europe: April 2015, Frankfurt am Main, https://www.ecb.europa.eu/pub/pdf/other/financialintegrationineurope201504.en.pdf# page=6&zoom=auto,-14,792.

European Central Bank (2016). ECB Banking Supervision: SSM priorities 2016, Frankfurt am Main, 06/01/16. https://www.bankingsupervision.europa.eu/ecb/pub/pdf/publication_supervisory_priorities_2016.en.pdf.

European Commission (1985). Completing the internal market, COM(85) 310 final, 14/06/85. http://europa.eu/documents/comm/white_papers/pdf/com1985_0310_f_en.pdf.

European Commission (1999). Financial Services: Implementing the framework for financial markets: Action Plan, COM(1999)232, 11/05/99. http://ec.europa.eu/internal_market/finances/docs/actionplan/index/action_en.pdf.

European Commission (2001a). *Final Report of the Committee of Wise Men on the Regulation of European Securities Markets*, Brussels, 15/02/01. http://ec.europa.eu/finance/securities/docs/lamfalussy/wisemen/final-report-wise-men_en.pdf.

European Commission (2001b). Press release: Financial services: Commission proposes Directive on insider dealing and market manipulation, IP/01/758, Brussels, 30/05/01. http://europa.eu/rapid/press-release_IP-01-758_en.htm?locale=en.

European Commission (2001c). Proposed Directive on Prospectuses – Frequently Asked Questions, MEMO/01/204, Brussels, 30/05/01. http://europa.eu/rapid/press-release_MEMO-01-204_en.htm?locale=en.

European Commission (2001d). The Market Abuse Directive – Frequently Asked Questions, MEMO/01/203, Brussels, 30/05/01. http://europa.eu/rapid/press-release_MEMO-01-203_en.htm?locale=en.

European Commission (2001e). The Proposed Prospectus Directive: Frequently asked questions, MARKT F2/HGD/NDB D(2001), Brussels, 28/09/01. http://ec.europa.eu/internal_market/securities/docs/prospectus/2001-09-faq_en.pdf.

European Commission (2002a). Press release: Investment services: proposed new Directive would protect investors and help investment firms operate EU-wide, IP/02/1706, Brussels, 19/11/02. http://europa.eu/rapid/press-release_IP-02-1706_en.htm?locale=en.

European Commission (2002b). Proposal for Directive on investment services and regulated markets – frequently asked questions, MEMO/02/257, Brussels, 19/11/02. http://europa.eu/rapid/press-release_MEMO-02-257_en.htm?locale=en.

European Commission (2003). Press release: Securities markets: Commission proposes Directive to increase investor protection and transparency, IP/03/436, Brussels, 26/03/03. http://europa.eu/rapid/press-release_IP-03-436_en.htm?locale=en.

European Commission (2004a). Press release: Financial services: final adoption of Transparency Directive will help investors and boost trust in markets, IP/04/1508, Brussels, 17/12/04. http://europa.eu/rapid/press-release_IP-04-1508_en.htm?locale=en.

European Commission (2004b). Press release: Investment Services: final adoption of Directive is boost for investment firms and their clients, IP/04/546, Brussels, 27/04/04. http://europa.eu/rapid/press-release_IP-04-546_en.htm?locale=en.

European Commission (2007). Review of the Lamfalussy process – Strengthening supervisory convergence, COM(2007) 727 final, 20/11/07. http://eur-lex.europa.eu/legal-content/EN/TXT/HTML/?uri=URISERV:l32056&from=CS.

European Commission (2008a). Improved EU framework for investment funds – Frequently Asked Questions, MEMO/08/510, Brussels, 16/07/08. http://europa.eu/rapid/press-release_MEMO-08-510_en.htm?locale=fr.

European Commission (2008b). Lamfalussy League Table – Transposition of Lamfalussy Directives: State of play as at 19/12/2008. http://ec.europa.eu/finance/securities/docs/transposition/table_en.pdf.

European Commission (2009). The High-Level Group on Financial Supervision in the EU, Chaired by Jacques de Larosière: Report, Brussels, 25/02/09. http://ec.europa.eu/internal_market/finances/docs/de_larosiere_report_en.pdf.

European Commission (2010). Proposal for a Directive of the European Parliament and of the Council amending Directive 97/9/EC of the European Parliament and of the Council on investor-compensation schemes, COM(2010) 371 final, Brussels, 12/07/10. http://ec.europa.eu/internal_market/securities/docs/isd/dir-97-9/proposal-modification_en.pdf.

European Commission (2011a). European Social Entrepreneurship Funds – Frequently Asked Questions, MEMO/11/881, Brussels, 07/12/11. http://europa.eu/rapid/press-release_MEMO-11-881_en.pdf.

European Commission (2011b). Regulation on Short Selling and Credit Default Swaps – Frequently Asked Questions, MEMO/11/713, Brussels, 19/10/11. http://europa.eu/rapid/press-release_MEMO-11-713_en.htm?locale=en.

European Commission (2013a). European Long-term Investment Funds – frequently asked questions, MEMO/13/611, Brussels, 26/06/13. http://europa.eu/rapid/press-release_MEMO-13-611_en.pdf.

European Commission (2013b). Payment Services Directive and Interchange fees Regulation: frequently asked questions, MEMO/13/71, Brussels, 24/07/13. http://europa.eu/rapid/press-release_MEMO-13-719_en.pdf.

European Commission (2013c). Six-pack? Two-pack? Fiscal compact? A short guide to the new EU fiscal governance. http://ec.europa.eu/economy_finance/articles/governance/2012-03-14_six_pack_en.htm.

European Commission (2013d). 'Two-Pack' enters into force, completing budgetary surveillance cycle and further improving economic governance for the euro area, MEMO/13/457, Brussels, 27/05/13. http://europa.eu/rapid/press-release_MEMO-13-457_en.htm.

European Commission (2014a). Commission Recommendation of 12.3.2014 on a new approach to business failure and insolvency, C(2014) 1500 final, Brussels, 12/03/14. http://ec.europa.eu/justice/civil/files/c_2014_1500_en.pdf.

European Commission (2014b). Regulation on securities settlement and on Central Securities Depositories in the EU ('CSD Regulation') – Frequently Asked Questions, MEMO/14/312, Brussels, 16/04/14. http://europa.eu/rapid/press-release_MEMO-14-312_en.htm?locale=en.

European Commission (2014c). Report from the Commission to the European Parliament and the Council on the operation of the European Supervisory Authorities (ESAs) and the European System of Financial Supervision (ESFS), COM(2014) 509 final, Brussels, 08/08/14. http://ec.europa.eu/finance/general-policy/docs/committees/140808-esfs-review_en.pdf.

European Commission (2014d). Undertakings for collective investment in transferable securities – amended Directive (UCITS V): Frequently asked questions, MEMO/14/298, Brussels, 15/04/14. http://europa.eu/rapid/press-release_MEMO-14-298_en.htm?locale=en.

European Commission (2015a). Commission Delegated Regulation (EU) …/… of 30.11.2015 supplementing Directive 2003/71/EC of the European Parliament and of the Council with regard to regulatory technical standards for approval and publication of the prospectus and dissemination of advertisements and amending Commission Regulation (EC) No 809/2004, C(2015) 8379 final, Brussels, 30/11/15. http://ec.europa.eu/finance/securities/docs/prospectus/151130-delegated-regulation_en.pdf.

European Commission (2015b). Commission Staff Working Document: Economic Analysis, Accompanying the document 'Communication from the Commission to the European Parliament, the Council, the European Economic and Social Committee and the Committee of the Regions – Action Plan on Building a Capital Markets Union,' SWD(2015) 183 final, Brussels, 30/09/15. http://ec.europa.eu/finance/capital-markets-union/docs/building-cmu-economic-analysis_en.pdf.

European Commission (2015c). Commission Staff Working Document: Feedback Statement on the Green Paper "Building a Capital Markets Union," Accompanying the document 'Communication for the Commission to the European Parliament, the Council, the European Economic and Social Committee and the Committee of the Regions – Action Plan on Building a Capital Markets Union,' SWD(2015) 184 final, Brussels, 30/09/15.

http://ec.europa.eu/finance/consultations/2015/capital-markets-union/docs/summary-of-responses_en.pdf.

European Commission (2015d). Commission Staff Working Document: Initial reflections on the obstacles to the development of deep and integrated EU capital markets, Accompanying the document 'Green Paper: Building a Capital Markets Union,' SWD(2015) 13, Brussels, 18/02/15. http://ec.europa.eu/finance/consultations/2015/capital-markets-union/docs/staff-working-document_en.pdf.

European Commission (2015e). Communication from the Commission to the European Parliament and the Council: A Fair and Efficient Corporate Tax System in the European Union: 5 Key Areas for Action, COM(2015) 302 final, Brussels, 17/06/15. http://ec.europa.eu/taxation_customs/resources/documents/taxation/company_tax/fairer_corporate_taxation/com_2015_302_en.pdf.

European Commission (2015f). Communication from the Commission to the European Parliament, the Council, the European Economic and Social Committee and the Committee of the Regions – Action Plan on Building a Capital Markets Union, COM(2015) 468 final, Brussels, 30/09/15. http://ec.europa.eu/finance/capital-markets-union/docs/building-cmu-action-plan_en.pdf.

European Commission (2015g). Completing Europe's Economic and Monetary Union: Report by Jean-Claude Juncker in close cooperation with Donald Tusk, Jeroen Dijsselbloem, Mario Draghi and Martin Schulz, Brussels, 22/06/15, http://ec.europa.eu/priorities/economic-monetary-union/docs/5-presidents-report_en.pdf.

European Commission (2015h). Consultation Document: Review of the Prospectus Directive, Brussels, 18/02/15. http://ec.europa.eu/finance/consultations/2015/prospectus-directive/docs/consultation-document_en.pdf.

European Commission (2015i). Green Paper: Building a Capital Markets Union, COM(2015) 63 final, Brussels, 18/02/15. http://ec.europa.eu/finance/consultations/2015/capital-markets-union/docs/green-paper_en.pdf.

European Commission (2015j). Implementing Technical Standards supplementing Regulation (EU) 575/2013 (CRR) and Directive 2013/36/EU (CRD): State of play, Brussels, 18/12/15. http://ec.europa.eu/finance/bank/docs/regcapital/acts/overview-crr-crdiv-its_en.pdf.

European Commission (2015k). Proposal for a Regulation of the European Parliament and of the Council on the prospectus to be published when securities are offered to the public or admitted to trading, COM(2015) 583 final, Brussels, 30/11/15. http://eur-lex.europa.eu/resource.html?uri=cellar:036c16c7-9763-11e5-983e-01aa75ed71a1.0006.02/DOC_1&format=PDF.

European Commission (2015l). Regulatory Technical Standards supplementing Regulation (EU) 575/2013 (CRR) and Directive 2013/36/EU (CRD): State of play, Brussels, 19/11/15. http://ec.europa.eu/finance/bank/docs/regcapital/acts/overview-crr-crdiv-rts_en.pdf.

European Commission (2015m). Re-launch of the Common Consolidated Corporate Tax Base (CCCTB). http://ec.europa.eu/taxation_customs/common/consultations/tax/relaunch_ccctb_en.htm.

European Commission (2016a). Double announcements on Northern Ireland from Commissioner Crętu. http://ec.europa.eu/regional_policy/en/newsroom/news/2016/01/18-01-2016-double-announcements-on-northern-ireland-from-commissioner-cretu.

European Commission (2016b). Press release: Commission extends by one year the application date for the MiFID II package, IP/16/265, Brussels, 10/02/04. http://europa.eu/rapid/press-release_IP-16-265_en.htm?locale=en.

European Commission (2016c). Proposal for a Directive of the European Parliament and of the Council amending Directive 2014/65/EU on markets in financial instruments as regards certain dates, COM(2016) final, Brussels, 10/02/16. http://ec.europa.eu/finance/securities/docs/isd/mifid/160210-directive-amending-mifid_en.pdf.

European Commission (2016d). Proposal for a Regulation of the European Parliament and of the Council amending Regulation (EU) No 600/2014 on markets in financial instruments, Regulation (EU) No 596/2014 on market abuse and Regulation (EU) No 909/2014 on improving securities settlement in the European Union and on central securities depositories as regards certain dates, COM(2016) final, Brussels, 10/02/16. http://ec.europa.eu/finance/securities/docs/isd/mifid/160210-regulation-amending-mifir_en.pdf.

European Communities (1986). The Single European Act, Luxembourg, 17/02/86.

European Council (2012). Treaty on Stability, Coordination and Governance in the Economic and Monetary Union between the Kingdom of Belgium, the Republic of Bulgaria, the Kingdom of Denmark, the Federal Republic of Germany, the Republic of Estonia, Ireland, the Hellenic Republic, the Kingdom of Spain, the French Republic, the Italian Republic, the Republic of Cyprus, the Republic of Latvia, the Republic of Lithuania, the Grand Duchy of Luxembourg, Hungary, Malta, the Kingdom of the Netherlands, the Republic of Austria, the Republic of Poland, the Portuguese Republic, Romania, the Republic of Slovenia, the Slovak Republic, the Republic of Finland and the Kingdom of Sweden, Brussels, 02/03/12. http://www.consilium.europa.eu/en/workarea/downloadAsset.aspx?id=27066.

European Council (2015). Cover Note from the General Secretariat of the Council to Delegations, EUCO 22/15, Brussels, 26/06/15. www.consilium.europa.eu/en/meetings/european-council/2015/06/EUCO-conclusions-pdf/.

European Court of Justice (1979). 120/78 Rewe-Zentral v Bundesmonopolverwaltung für Branntwein [1979]. ECR 649.

European Court of Justice (2002). C367/98 Commission v Portugal [2002]. I-4731.

European Court of Justice (2003). C463/00 Commission v Spain [2003]. I-4581.

European Insurance and Occupational Pensions Authority (2015). EIOPA Organigram 2015, Frankfurt am Main, 10/12/15. https://eiopa.europa.eu/Publications/Administrative/EIOPA%20Organigram%202015%2011.pdf.

European Insurance and Occupational Pensions Authority (2016). Joint Committee, Frankfurt am Main, 14/03/16. https://eiopa.europa.eu/about-eiopa/organisation/joint-committee.

European Parliament (2015). Evaluating EU Economic Governance: Elements for the debate on the "Six-Pack" and "Two-Pack." January 2015. http://www.europarl.europa.eu/RegData/etudes/BRIE/2015/536374/EPRS_BRI%282015%29536374_REV1_EN.pdf.

European Securities and Markets Authority (2015a). Commission des opérations de bourse – Press Release: The Creation of the Forum of European Securities Commissions (FESCO), FD1047, 09/12/97. http://www.esma.europa.eu/system/files/FD1047.pdf.

European Securities and Markets Authority (2015b). Competent Authorities for Central Securities Depositories (CSDs) designated in accordance with Article 11(1) of Regulation

(EU) No 909/2014 (CSDR), Paris, 22/07/15. https://www.esma.europa.eu/sites/default/files/library/competentauthoritiesundercsdr.pdf.

European Securities and Markets Authority (2015c). CRA Authorisation, Paris, 01/12/15. https://www.esma.europa.eu/supervision/credit-rating-agencies/risk.

European Securities and Markets Authority (2015d). Draft technical standards under CSDR: Annex II to the Final Report on the draft technical standards under the Regulation No 909/2014 of the European Parliament and of the Council of 23 July 2014 on improving securities settlement in the European Union and on central securities depositories and amending Directives 98/26/EC and 2014/65/EU and Regulation (EU) No 236/2012 (CSDR), ESMA/2015/1457/Annex II, Paris, 28/09/15. https://www.esma.europa.eu/sites/default/files/library/2015/11/2015-esma-1457_-_annex_ii_-_csdr_ts_on_csd_requirements_and_internalised_settlement.pdf.

European Securities and Markets Authority (2015e). Final Report: Draft technical standards on the Market Abuse Regulation, ESMA/2015/1455, Paris, 28/09/15. https://www.esma.europa.eu/sites/default/files/library/2015/11/2015-esma-1455_-_final_report_mar_ts.pdf.

European Securities and Markets Authority (2015f). List of Central Counterparties authorised to offer services and activities in the Union, Paris, 30/10/15. https://www.esma.europa.eu/sites/default/files/library/ccps_authorised_under_emir.pdf.

European Securities and Markets Authority (2015g). Who is who, Paris, 10/12/15. https://www.esma.europa.eu/page/Whos-who.

European Securities and Markets Authority (2016a). Joint Committee, Paris, 14/03/16. https://www.esma.europa.eu/sections/joint-committee.

European Securities and Markets Authority (2016b). List of third-country Central Counterparties recognised to offer services and activities in the Union, Paris, 27/01/16. https://www.esma.europa.eu/sites/default/files/library/third-country_ccps_recognised_under_emir.pdf.

European Securities and Markets Authority (2016c). Market Abuse and Accepted Practices, Paris, 25/01/16. https://www.esma.europa.eu/regulation/trading/market-abuse.

European Securities and Markets Authority (2016d). OTC derivatives and clearing obligation, Paris, 15/02/16. https://www.esma.europa.eu/regulation/post-trading/otc-derivatives-and-clearing-obligation.

European Securities and Markets Authority (2016e). Questions and Answers: Implementation of the Regulation (EU) No 648/2012 on OTC derivatives, central counterparties and trade repositories (EMIR), ESMA/2016/293, Paris, 16/02/16. https://www.esma.europa.eu/sites/default/files/library/2016-293_qa_xvi_on_emir_implementation.pdf.

European Systemic Risk Board (2015). Permanent members of the ESRB General Board, Frankfurt am Main, 07/12/15. https://www.esrb.europa.eu/pub/pdf/other/Perm_memb_GB.pdf?4571846b1be15137940de88b5ddadae4.

European Union (2015). Traité instituant la Communauté Économique Européenne et documents annexes, 25/03/57. http://eur-lex.europa.eu/legal-content/FR/TXT/PDF/?uri=CELEX:11957E/TXT&qid=1435339846434&from=EN.

Financial Stability Board (2011a). Consumer Finance Protection with particular focus on credit, Basel, 26/10/11. http://www.financialstabilityboard.org/wp-content/uploads/r_111026a.pdf.

Financial Stability Board (2011b). Key Attributes of Effective Resolution Regimes for Financial Institutions, Basel, October 2011. http://www.financialstabilityboard.org/wp-content/uploads/r_111104cc.pdf?page_moved=1.

Financial Stability Board (2012). Enhancing the Risk Disclosures of Banks: Report of the Enhanced Disclosure Task Force, Basel, 29/10/12. http://www.financialstabilityboard.org/wp-content/uploads/r_121029.pdf?page_moved=1.

Financial Stability Board (2014). Key Attributes of Effective Resolution Regimes for Financial Institutions, Basel, 15/10/14. http://www.financialstabilityboard.org/wp-content/uploads/r_141015.pdf.

Financial Stability Board (2015a). FSB Members. http://www.financialstabilityboard.org/about/fsb-members/.

Financial Stability Board (2015b). Implementation and effects of the G20 financial regulatory reforms: Report of the Financial Stability Board to G20 Leaders, 09/11/15. http://www.financialstabilityboard.org/wp-content/uploads/Report-on-implementation-and-effects-of-reforms-final.pdf.

Financial Stability Board (2015c). Letter from the Chairman of the Financial Stability Board to G20 Finance Ministers and Central Bank Governors: Financial Reforms – Finishing the Post-Crisis Agenda and Moving Forward, 04/02/15. http://www.financialstabilityboard.org/wp-content/uploads/FSB-Chair-letter-to-G20-February-2015.pdf.

Financial Stability Board (2015d). Letter from the Chairman of the Financial Stability Board to G20 Finance Ministers and Central Bank Governors: Financial Reforms – Progress on the Work Plan for the Antalya Summit, 05/10/15. http://www.financialstabilityboard.org/wp-content/uploads/FSB-Chairs-letter-to-G20-Mins-and-Govs-5-October-2015.pdf.

Financial Stability Board (2015e). Letter from the Chairman of the Financial Stability Board to G20 Leaders: Financial Reforms – Achieving and Sustaining Resilience for All, 09/11/15. http://www.financialstabilityboard.org/wp-content/uploads/FSB-Chairs-letter-to-G20-Leaders-9-Nov.pdf.

Financial Stability Board (2015f). Principles for Cross-border Effectiveness of Resolution Actions. 03/11/15. http://www.financialstabilityboard.org/wp-content/uploads/Principles-for-Cross-border-Effectiveness-of-Resolution-Actions.pdf.

G20 (2007). The Group of Twenty: a History. http://www.g20.utoronto.ca/docs/g20history.pdf.

G20 (2008). Declaration Summit on Financial Markets and the World Economy, Washington D.C., 15/11/08. https://g20.org/wp-content/uploads/2014/12/Washington_Declaration_0.pdf.

G20 (2009a). Declaration on Strengthening the Financial System – London Summit, London, 02/04/09. www.g20.utoronto.ca/2009/2009ifi.pdf.

G20 (2009b). London Summit – Leaders' Statement, London, 02/04/09. https://www.imf.org/external/np/sec/pr/2009/pdf/g20_040209.pdf.

G20 (2009c). Leaders' Statement: The Pittsburgh Summit, Pittsburgh, 25/09/09. https://g20.org/wp-content/uploads/2014/12/Pittsburgh_Declaration_0.pdf.

G20 (2010a). Innovative Financial Inclusion: Principles and Report on Innovative Financial Inclusion from the Access through Innovation Sub-Group of the G20 Financial Inclusion

Experts Group, 25/05/10. http://www.gpfi.org/sites/default/files/documents/Principles%20and%20Report%20on%20Innovative%20Financial%20Inclusion_0.pdf.

G20 (2010b). Toronto Summit: Declaration, Toronto, 27/06/10. http://www.g20.utoronto.ca/2010/g20_declaration_en.pdf.

G20 (2010c). The G20 Seoul Summit Leaders' Declaration, Seoul, 12/11/10. https://g20.org/wp-content/uploads/2014/12/Seoul_Summit_Leaders_Declaration.pdf.

G20 (2010d). The Seoul Summit Document, Seoul, 12/11/10. https://g20.org/wp-content/uploads/2014/12/Seoul_Summit_Document.pdf.

G20 (2011). Cannes Summit final declaration – Building our Common Future: Renewed Collective Action For the Benefit of All, Cannes, 04/11/11. https://g20.org/wp-content/uploads/2014/12/Declaration_eng_Cannes.pdf.

G20 (2012). G2012 Los Cabos México: G20 Leaders Declaration, Los Cabos, 19/06/12. http://www.g20.utoronto.ca/2012/2012-0619-loscabos.pdf.

G20 (2013). Russia G20: G20 Leaders' Declaration, St. Petersburg, 06/09/13. https://g20.org/wp-content/uploads/2014/12/Saint_Petersburg_Declaration_ENG_0.pdf.

G20 (2014). G20 Australia 2014: G20 Leaders' Communiqué – Brisbane Summit, Brisbane, 16/11/14. https://g20.org/wp-content/uploads/2014/12/brisbane_g20_leaders_summit_communique1.pdf.

G20 (2015a). G20 Members. < https://g20.org/about-g20/g20-members/>.

G20 (2015b). G20 Turkey 2015: G20 Leaders Communiqué – Antalya Summit, Antalya, 16/11/15. <http://www.g20.utoronto.ca/2015/151116-communique.html>

Global Partnership for Financial Inclusion (2011). GPFI Report to the Leaders: G20 Leaders Summit, Cannes, 05/11/11. http://www.gpfi.org/sites/default/files/documents/GPFI%20report%20to%20G-20.pdf.

Global Partnership for Financial Inclusion (2012), The G20 Basic Set of Financial Inclusion Indicators. http://www.gpfi.org/sites/default/files/G20%20Basic%20Set%20of%20Financial%20Inclusion%20Indicators.pdf.

International Monetary Fund (2015). International Monetary Fund Factsheet: IMF Quotas: 24/09/15. http://www.imf.org/external/np/exr/facts/pdf/quotas.pdf.

Joint Committee of the European Supervisory Authorities (2014). Joint Guidelines on the convergence of supervisory practices relating to the consistency of supervisory coordination arrangements for financial conglomerates, JC/GL/2014/01, 22/12/14. https://www.eba.europa.eu/documents/10180/936042/JC+GL+2014+01+%28Joint+Guidelines+on+coordination+arrangements+for+financi....pdf.

Joint Committee of the European Supervisory Authorities (2015a). Joint Committee: List of Identified Financial Conglomerates as per 31 December 2014 figures. JC 2015 079, 19/10/15. http://www.eba.europa.eu/documents/10180/1294818/JC+2015+079+%282015+list+of+identified+Financial+Conglomerates%29_Final.pdf.

Joint Committee of the European Supervisory Authorities (2015b). Second Consultation Paper: Draft Regulatory Technical Standards on risk-management techniques for OTC-derivative contracts not cleared by a CCP under Article 11(15) of Regulation (EU) No 648/2012, JC/CP/2015/002, 10/06/15. https://www.eba.europa.eu/documents/10180/1106136/JC-CP-2015-002+JC+CP+on+Risk+Management+Techniques+for+OTC+derivatives+.pdf.

Juncker, J.-C. (2014). A New Start for Europe: My Agenda for Jobs, Growth, Fairness and Democratic Change – Political Guidelines for the next European Commission, Strasbourg, 15/07/14. http://ec.europa.eu/priorities/docs/pg_en.pdf.

Kaya, O. (2015). Capital Markets Union: An ambitious goal, but few quick wins. Deutsche Bank Research: EU Monitor – Global financial markets, 02/11/15, 1-20.

Lannoo, K. (2015a). Detailed CMU Action Plan, but more (ambition) is required. ECMI Commentary, No.39/2 October 2015, 1-3.

Lannoo, K. (2015b). Which Union for Europe's Capital Markets? ECMI Policy Brief, No.22/February 2015, 1-9.

Lannoo, K., Pollack, A., & Staehr, O. (2015). Keep capital markets union simple. ECMI Commentary, No.38/July 2015, 1-2.

Majone, G. (2005). Dilemmas of European Integration: The Ambiguities & Pitfalls of Integration by Stealth. Oxford: Oxford University Press.

Morland, M. (2015). Times cartoons: Dave and the Beanstalk, The Times, 29/12/15, 71792, 27.

Official Journal of the European Communities (1977). First Council Directive 77/780/EEC of 12 December 1977 on the coordination of laws, regulations and administrative provisions relating to the taking up and pursuit of the business of credit institutions, L322/30-L322/37; amended by: *Official Journal of the European Communities* (1989), Second Council Directive 89/646/EEC of 15 December 1989 on the coordination of laws, regulations and administrative provisions relating to the taking up and pursuit of the business of credit institutions and amending Directive 77/780/EEC; corrected by: *Official Journal of the European Communities* (1990), Corrigendum to the second Council Directive 89/646/EEC of 15 December 1989 on the coordination of laws, regulations and administrative provisions relating to the taking up and pursuit of the business of credit institutions and amending Directive 77/780/EEC, L158/87; *Official Journal of the European Communities* (1990), Corrigendum to the second Council Directive 89/646/EEC of 15 December 1989 on the coordination of laws, regulations and administrative provisions relating to the taking up and pursuit of the business of credit institutions and amending Directive 77/780/EEC, L258/35; repealed by: *Official Journal of the European Communities* (2000), Directive 2000/12/EC of the European Parliament and of the Council of 20 March 2000 relating to the taking up and pursuit of the business of credit institutions, L126/1-L126/59.

Official Journal of the European Communities (1978). Fourth Council Directive 78/660/EEC of 25 July 1978 based on Article 54(3)(g) of the Treaty on the annual accounts of certain types of companies, L222/11-L222/31; amended by: *Official Journal of the European Communities* (1979), Act concerning the conditions of accession of the Hellenic Republic and the adjustments to the Treaties, L291/17-L291/177; *Official Journal of the European Communities* (1983), Seventh Council Directive 83/349/EEC of 13 June 1983 based on the Article 54(3)(g) of the Treaty on consolidated accounts, L193/1-L193/17; *Official Journal of the European Communities* (1984), Council Directive 84/569/EEC of 27 November 1984 revising the amounts expressed in ECU in Directive 78/660/EEC, L314/28; *Official Journal of the European Communities* (1985), Act concerning the conditions of accession of the Kingdom of Spain and the Portuguese Republic and the adjustments to the Treaties, L302/23-L302/465; *Official Journal of the European Communities* (1989), Eleventh Council Directive 89/666/EEC of 21 December 1989 concerning disclosure requirements in respect of branches opened in a Member State by certain types of company governed by the law of another State, L395/36-L395/39; *Official Journal of the European Communities* (1990), Council Directive 90/604/EEC of 8 November 1990 amending Directive 78/660/EEC on annual accounts and Directive 83/349/EEC on consolidated accounts as concerns the exemptions for small and medium-sized companies and the publication of accounts in ecus, L317/57-L317/59; *Official Journal of the European Communities* (1990), Council Directive 90/605/EEC of 8 November 1990 amending Directive 78/66//EEC on annual accounts and Directive 83/349/EEC on consolidated accounts as regards the scope of those Directives, L317/60-L317/62; *Official Journal of the European Communities* (1994), Council Directive 94/8/EC of 21 March 1994 amending Directive 78/660/EEC as regards the revision of amounts expressed in ecus, L82/33-L82/34; *Official Journal of the European Communities* (1994), Act concerning the conditions of accession of the Kingdom of Norway, the Republic of Austria, the Republic of Finland and the Kingdom of Sweden and the adjustments to the Treaties on which the European Union is founded, C241/21-C241/370, adapted by: *Official Journal of the European Communities* (1995), Decision 95/1/EC, Euratom, ECSC, of 1 January 1995 adjusting the instruments concerning the accession of new Member States to the European Union, L1/1-L1/219; *Official Journal of the European Communities* (1999), Council Directive 1999/60/EC of 17 June 1999 amending Directive 78/660/EEC as regards amounts expressed in ecus, L162/65-L162/66; *Official Journal of the European Communities* (2001), Directive 2001/65/EC of the European Parliament and of the Council of 27 September 2001 amending Directives 78/660/EEC, 83/349/EEC and 86/635/EEC as regards the valuation rules for the annual and consolidated accounts of certain types of companies as well as of banks and other financial institutions, L283/28-L283/32; *Official Journal of the European Communities* (2003), Council Directive 2003/38/EC of 13 May 2003 amending Directive 78/660/EEC on the annual accounts of certain types of companies as regards amounts expressed in euro, L120/22-L120/23; *Official Journal of the European Union* (2003), Directive 2003/51/EC of the European Parliament and of the Council of 18 June 2003 amending Directives 78/660/EEC, 83/349/EEC, 86/635/EEC and 91/674/EEC on the annual and consolidated accounts of certain types of companies, banks and other financial institutions and insurance undertakings, L178/16-L178/22; *Official Journal of the European Union* (2003), Act concerning the conditions of accession of the Czech Republic, the Republic of Estonia, the Republic of Cyprus, the Republic of Latvia, the Republic of Lithuania, the Republic of Hungary, the Republic of Malta, the Republic of Poland, the Republic of Slovenia and the Slovak Republic and the adjustments to the Treaties on which the European Union is founded, L236/33-L236/955; *Official Journal of the European Union* (2006), Directive 2006/43/EC of the European Parliament and of the Council of 17 May 2006 on statutory audits of annual accounts and consolidated accounts, amending Council Directives 78/660/EEC and 83/349/EEC and repealing Council Directive 84/253/EEC, L157/87-L157/107; *Official Journal of the European Union* (2006), Directive 2006/46/EC of the European Parliament and of the Council of 14 June 2006 amending Council Directives 78/660/EEC on the annual accounts of certain types of companies, 83/349/EEC on consolidated accounts, 86/635/EEC on the annual accounts and consolidated accounts of banks and other financial institutions and 91/674/EEC on the annual accounts and consolidated accounts of insurance undertakings,

L224/1-L224/7; *Official Journal of the European Union* (2006), Council Directive 2006/99/EC of 20 November 2006 adapting certain Directives in the field of company law, by reason of the accession of Bulgaria and Romania, L363/137-L363/140; *Official Journal of the European Union* (2009), Directive 2009/49/EC of the European Parliament and of the Council of 18 June 2009 amending Council Directives 78/660/EEC and 83/349/EEC as regards certain disclosure requirements for medium-sized companies and the obligation to draw up consolidated accounts, L164/42-L164/44; *Official Journal of the European Union* (2012), Directive 2012/6/EU of the European Parliament and of the Council of 14 March 2012 amending Council Directive 78/660/EEC on the annual accounts of certain types of companies as regards micro-entities, L81/3-L81/6; *Official Journal of the European Union* (2013), Council Directive 2013/24/EU of 13 May 2013 adapting certain directives in the field of company law, by reason of the accession of the Republic of Croatia, L158/365-L158/367; repealed by: *Official Journal of the European Union* (2013), Directive 2013/34/EU of the European Parliament and of the Council of 26 June 2013 on the annual financial statements, consolidated financial statements and related reports of certain types of undertakings, amending Directive 2006/43/EC of the European Parliament and of the Council and repealing Council Directives 78/660/EEC and 83/349/EEC, L182/19-L182/76.

Official Journal of the European Communities (1983). Seventh Council Directive 83/349/EEC of 13 June 1983 based on the Article 54(3)(g) of the Treaty on consolidated accounts, L193/1-L193/17, amended by: *Official Journal of the European Communities* (1985), Act concerning the conditions of accession of the Kingdom of Spain and the Portuguese Republic and the adjustments to the Treaties, L302/23-L302/465; *Official Journal of the European Communities* (1989), Eleventh Council Directive 89/666/EEC of 21 December 1989 concerning disclosure requirements in respect of branches opened in a Member State by certain types of company governed by the law of another State, L395/36-L395/39; *Official Journal of the European Communities* (1990), Council Directive 90/604/EEC of 8 November 1990 amending Directive 78/660/EEC on annual accounts and Directive 83/349/EEC on consolidated accounts as concerns the exemptions for small and medium-sized companies and the publication of accounts in ecus, L317/57-L317/59; *Official Journal of the European Communities* (1990), Council Directive 90/605/EEC of 8 November 1990 amending Directive 78/66//EEC on annual accounts and Directive 83/349/EEC on consolidated accounts as regards the scope of those Directives, L317/60-L317/62; *Official Journal of the European Communities* (1994), Act concerning the conditions of accession of the Kingdom of Norway, the Republic of Austria, the Republic of Finland and the Kingdom of Sweden and the adjustments to the Treaties on which the European Union is founded, C241/21-C241/370, adapted by: *Official Journal of the European Communities* (1995), Decision 95/1/EC, Euratom, ECSC, of 1 January 1995 adjusting the instruments concerning the accession of new Member States to the European Union, L1/1-L1/219; *Official Journal of the European Communities* (2001), Directive 2001/65/EC of the European Parliament and of the Council of 27 September 2001 amending Directives 78/660/EEC, 83/349/EEC and 86/635/EEC as regards the valuation rules for the annual and consolidated accounts of certain types of companies as well as of banks and other financial institutions, L283/28-L283/32; *Official Journal of the European Union* (2003), Directive 2003/51/EC of the European Parliament and of the Council of 18 June 2003 amending Directives

78/660/EEC, 83/349/EEC, 86/635/EEC and 91/674/EEC on the annual and consolidated accounts of certain types of companies, banks and other financial institutions and insurance undertakings, L178/16-L178/22; *Official Journal of the European Union* (2003), Act concerning the conditions of accession of the Czech Republic, the Republic of Estonia, the Republic of Cyprus, the Republic of Latvia, the Republic of Lithuania, the Republic of Hungary, the Republic of Malta, the Republic of Poland, the Republic of Slovenia and the Slovak Republic and the adjustments to the Treaties on which the European Union is founded, L236/33-L236/955; *Official Journal of the European Union* (2006), Directive 2006/43/EC of the European Parliament and of the Council of 17 May 2006 on statutory audits of annual accounts and consolidated accounts, amending Council Directives 78/660/EEC and 83/349/EEC and repealing Council Directive 84/253/EEC, L157/87-L157/107; *Official Journal of the European Union* (2006), Directive 2006/46/EC of the European Parliament and of the Council of 14 June 2006 amending Council Directives 78/660/EEC on the annual accounts of certain types of companies, 83/349/EEC on consolidated accounts, 86/635/EEC on the annual accounts and consolidated accounts of banks and other financial institutions and 91/674/EEC on the annual accounts and consolidated accounts of insurance undertakings, L224/1-L224/7; *Official Journal of the European Union* (2006), Council Directive 2006/99/EC of 20 November 2006 adapting certain Directives in the field of company law, by reason of the accession of Bulgaria and Romania, L363/137-L363/140; *Official Journal of the European Union* (2009), Directive 2009/49/EC of the European Parliament and of the Council of 18 June 2009 amending Council Directives 78/660/EEC and 83/349/EEC as regards certain disclosure requirements for medium-sized companies and the obligation to draw up consolidated accounts, L164/42-L164/44; *Official Journal of the European Union* (2013), Council Directive 2013/24/EU of 13 May 2013 adapting certain directives in the field of company law, by reason of the accession of the Republic of Croatia, L158/365-L158/367; corrected by: *Official Journal of the European Communities* (1983), Corrigendum to Seventh Council Directive 83/349/EEC of 13 June 1983 based on the Article 54(3)(g) of the Treaty on consolidated accounts, L211/31; repealed by: *Official Journal of the European Union* (2013), Directive 2013/34/EU of the European Parliament and of the Council of 26 June 2013 on the annual financial statements, consolidated financial statements and related reports of certain types of undertakings, amending Directive 2006/43/EC of the European Parliament and of the Council and repealing Council Directives 78/660/EEC and 83/349/EEC, L182/19-L182/76.

Official Journal of the European Communities (1985). Council Directive 85/611/EEC of 20 December 1985 on the coordination of laws, regulations and administrative provisions relating to undertakings for collective investment in transferable securities (UCITS), L375/3-L375/17; amended by: *Official Journal of the European Communities* (1988), Council Directive 88/220/EEC of 22 March 1988 amending, as regards the investment policies of certain UCITS, Directive 85/611/EEC on the coordination of laws, regulations and adminsitrative provisions relating to undertakings for collective investments in transferable securities (UCITS), L100/31-L100/32; *Official Journal of the European Communities* (1995), European Parliament and Council Directive 95/26/EC of 29 June 1995 amending Directives 77/780/EEC and 89/646/EEC in the field of credit institutions, Directives 73/239/EEC and 92/49/EEC in the field of non-life insurance, Directives 79/267/EEC and 92/96/EEC in the field of life assurance, Directive 93/22/EEC in the field of investment firms and Directive 85/611/EEC in the field of undertakings for collective investment in transferable securities (Ucits), with a view to reinforcing prudential supervision, L168/7-L168/13; *Official Journal of the European Communities* (2000), Directive 2000/64/EC of the European Parliament and of the Council of 7 November 2000 amending Council Directives 85/611/EEC, 92/49/EEC, 92/96/EEC and 93/22/EEC as regards exchange of information with third countries, L290/27-L290/28; *Official Journal of the European Communities* (2002), Directive 2001/107/EC of the European Parliament and of the Council of 21 January 2002 amending Council Directive 85/611/EEC on the coordination of laws, regulations and administrative provisions relating to undertakings for collective investment in transferable securities (UCITS) with a view to regulating management companies and simplified prospectuses, L41/20-L41/34; *Official Journal of the European Communities* (2002), Directive 2001/108/EC of the European Parliament and of the Council of 21 January 2002 amending Council Directive 85/611/EEC on the coordination of laws, regulations and administrative provisions relating to undertakings for collective investment in transferable securities (UCITS), with regards to investments of UCITS, L41/35-L41/42; *Official Journal of the European Union* (2004), Directive 2004/39/EC of the European Parliament and of the Council of 21 April 2004 on markets in financial instruments amending Council Directives 85/611/EEC and 93/6/EEC and Directive 2000/12/EC of the European Parliament and of the Council and repealing Council Directive 93/22/EEC, L145/1-L145/44; *Official Journal of the European Union* (2005), Directive 2005/1/EC of the European Parliament and of the Council of 9 March 2005 amending Council Directives 73/239/EEC, 85/611/EEC, 91/675/EEC, 92/49/EEC and 93/6/EEC and Directives 94/19/EC, 98/78/EC, 2000/12/EC, 2001/34/EC, 2002/83/EC and 2002/87/EC in order to establish a new organisational structure for financial services committees, L79/9-L79/17; *Official Journal of the European Union* (2008), Directive 2008/18/EC of the European Parliament and of the Council of 11 March 2008 amending Council Directive 85/611/EEC on the coordination of laws, regulations and administrative provisions relating to undertakings for collective investment and transferable securities (UCITS), as regards the implementing powers conferred on the Commission, L76/42-L76/43; corrected by: *Official Journal of the European Union* (2005), Corrigendum to Directive 2004/39/EC of the European Parliament and of the Council of 21 April 2004 on markets in financial instruments amending Council Directives 85/611/EEC and 93/6/EEC and Directive 2000/12/EC of the European Parliament and of the Council and repealing Council Directive 93/22/EEC, L45/18; repealed by: *Official Journal of the European Union* (2009), Directive 2009/65/EC of the European Parliament and of the Council of 13 July 2009 on the coordination of laws, regulations and administrative provisions relating to undertakings for collective investment in transferable securities (UCITS) (recast), L302/32-L302/96.

Official Journal of the European Communities (1986). Council Directive 86/635/EEC of 8 December 1986 on the annual accounts and consolidated accounts of banks and other financial institutions, L372/1-L372/17, amended by: *Official Journal of the European Communities* (2001), Directive 2001/65/EC of the European Parliament and of the Council of 27 September 2001 amending Directives 78/660/EEC, 83/349/EEC and 86/635/EEC as regards the valuation rules for the annual and consolidated accounts of certain types of companies as well as of banks and other financial institutions, L283/28-

L283/32; *Official Journal of the European Union* (2003), Directive 2003/51/EC of the European Parliament and of the Council of 18 June 2003 amending Directives 78/660/EEC, 83/349/EEC, 86/635/EEC and 91/674/EEC on the annual and consolidated accounts of certain types of companies, banks and other financial institutions and insurance undertakings, L178/16-L178/22; *Official Journal of the European Union* (2006), Directive 2006/46/EC of the European Parliament and of the Council of 14 June 2006 amending Council Directives 78/660/EEC on the annual accounts of certain types of companies, 83/349/EEC on consolidated accounts, 86/635/EEC on the annual accounts and consolidated accounts of banks and other financial institutions and 91/674/EEC on the annual accounts and consolidated accounts of insurance undertakings, L224/1-L224/7.

Official Journal of the European Communities (1987). Council Decision 87/373/EEC of 13 July 1987 laying down the procedures for the exercise of implementing powers conferred on the Commission, L197/33-L197/35; repealed by: *Official Journal of the European Communities* (1999), Council Decision 1999/468/EC of 28 June 1999 laying down the procedures for the exercise of implementing powers conferred on the Commission, L184/23-L184/26.

Official Journal of the European Communities (1989). Second Council Directive 89/646/EEC of 15 December 1989 on the coordination of laws, regulations and administrative provisions relating to the taking up and pursuit of the business of credit institutions and amending Directive 77/780/EEC, corrected by: *Official Journal of the European Communities* (1990), Corrigendum to the Second Council Directive 89/646/EEC of 15 December 1989 on the coordination of laws, regulations and administrative provisions relating to the taking up and pursuit of the business of credit institutions and amending Directive 77/780/EEC, L83/128; *Official Journal of the European Communities* (1990), Corrigendum to the Second Council Directive 89/646/EEC of 15 December 1989 on the coordination of laws, regulations and administrative provisions relating to the taking up and pursuit of the business of credit institutions and amending Directive 77/780/EEC, L258/35; *Official Journal of the European Communities* (1997), Corrigendum to the Second Council Directive 89/646/EEC of 15 December 1989 on the coordination of laws, regulations and administrative provisions relating to the taking up and pursuit of the business of credit institutions and amending Directive 77/780/EEC, L311/34; repealed by: *Official Journal of the European Communities* (2000), Directive 2000/12/EC of the European Parliament and of the Council of 20 March 2000 relating to the taking up and pursuit of the business of credit institutions, L126/1-L126/59.

Official Journal of the European Communities (1992). Council Directive 92/30/EEC of 6 April 1992 on the supervision of credit institutions on a consolidated basis, L110/52-L110/58, corrected by: *Official Journal of the European Communities* (1992), Corrigendum of Council Directive 92/30/EEC of 6 April 1992 on the supervision of credit institutions on a consolidated basis, L280/54; repealed by: *Official Journal of the European Communities* (2000), Directive 2000/12/EC of the European Parliament and of the Council of 20 March 2000 relating to the taking up and pursuit of the business of credit institutions, L126/1-L126/59.

Official Journal of the European Communities (1993a). Council Directive 93/6/EEC of 15 March 1993 on the capital adequacy of investments firms and credit institutions, L141/1-L141/26, amended by: *Official Journal of the European Communities* (1998), Directive

98/31/EC of the European Parliament and of the Council of 22 June 1998 amending Council Directive 93/6/EEC on the capital adequacy of investment firms and credit institutions, L204/13-L204/25; *Official Journal of the European Communities* (1998), Directive 98/33/EC of the European Parliament and of the Council of 22 June 1998 amending Article 12 of Council Directive 77/780/EEC on the taking up and pursuit of the business of credit institutions, Articles 2, 5, 6, 7, 8 of and Annexes II and III to Council Directive 89/647/EEC on a solvency ratio for credit institutions and Article 2 of and Annex II to Council Directive 93/6/EEC on the capital adequacy of investment firms and credit institutions, L204/29-L204/36; *Official Journal of the European Union* (2003), Directive 2002/87/EC of the European Parliament and of the Council of 16 December 2002 on the supplementary supervision of credit institutions, insurance undertakings and investment firms in a financial conglomerate and amending Council Directives 73/239/EEC, 79/267/EEC, 92/49/EEC, 92/96/EEC, 93/6/EEC and 93/22/EEC, and Directives 98/78/EC and 2000/12/EC of the European Parliament and of the Council, L35/1-L35/27; *Official Journal of the European Union* (2004), Directive 2004/39/EC of the European Parliament and of the Council of 21 April 2004 on markets in financial instruments amending Council Directives 85/611/EEC and 93/6/EEC and Directive 2000/12/EC of the European Parliament and of the Council and repealing Council Directive 93/22/EEC, L145/1-L145/44; *Official Journal of the European Union* (2005), Directive 2005/1/EC of the European Parliament and of the Council of 9 March 2005 amending Council Directives 73/239/EEC, 85/611/EEC, 91/675/EEC, 92/49/EEC and 93/6/EEC and Directives 94/19/EC, 98/78/EC, 2000/12/EC, 2001/34/EC, 2002/83/EC and 2002/87/EC in order to establish a new organisational structure for financial services committees, L79/9-L79/17; corrected by: *Official Journal of the European Communities* (1998), Corrigendum to Directive 98/31/EC of the European Parliament and of the Council of 22 June 1998 amending Council Directive 93/6/EEC on the capital adequacy of investment firms and credit institutions, L248/20; *Official Journal of the European Union* (2005), Corrigendum to Directive 2004/39/EC of the European Parliament and of the Council of 21 April 2004 on markets in financial instruments amending Council Directives 85/611/EEC and 93/6/EC and Directive 2000/12/EC of the European Parliament and of the Council and repealing Council Directive 93/22/EEC, L45/18; repealed by: *Official Journal of the European Union* (2006), Directive 2006/49/EC of the European Parliament and of the Council of 14 June 2006 on the capital adequacy of investment firms and credit institutions (recast), L177/201-L177/255.

Official Journal of the European Communities (1993b). Council Directive 93/22/EEC of 10 May 1993 on investment services in the securities field, L141/27-L141/46, amended by: *Official Journal of the European Communities* (1997), Directive 97/9/EC of the European Parliament and of the Council of 3 March 1997 on investor-compensation schemes, L84/22-L84/31; *Official Journal of the European Communities* (2000), Directive 2000/64/EC of the European Parliament and of the Council of 7 November 2000 amending Council Directives 85/611/EEC, 92/49/EEC, 92/96/EEC and 93/22/EEC as regards exchange of information with third countries, L290/27-L290/28; *Official Journal of the European Union* (2003), Directive 2002/87/EC of the European Parliament and of the Council of 16 December 2002 on the supplementary supervision of credit institutions, insurance undertakings and investment firms in a financial conglomerate and amending Council Directives 73/239/EEC, 79/267/EEC, 92/49/EEC, 92/96/EEC, 93/6/EEC and

93/22/EEC, and Directives 98/78/EC and 2000/12/EC of the European Parliament and of the Council, L35/1-L35/27; corrected by: *Official Journal of the European Communities* (1993), Corrigendum to Council Directive 93/22/EEC of 10 May 1993 on investment services in the securities field, L141/32; *Official Journal of the European Communities* (1993), Corrigendum to Council Directive 93/22/EEC of 10 May 1993 on investment services in the securities field, L194/27; repealed by: *Official Journal of the European Union* (2004), Directive 2004/39/EC of the European Parliament and of the Council of 21 April 2004 on markets in financial instruments amending Council Directives 85/611/EEC and 93/6/EEC and Directive 2000/12/EC of the European Parliament and of the Council and repealing Council Directive 93/22/EEC, L145/1-L145/44.

Official Journal of the European Communities (1994). Directive 94/19/EC of the European Parliament and of the Council of 30 May 1994 on deposit-guarantee schemes, L135/5-L135/14, amended by: *Official Journal of the European Union* (2005), Directive 2005/1/EC of the European Parliament and of the Council of 9 March 2005 amending Council Directives 73/239/EEC, 85/611/EEC, 91/675/EEC, 92/49/EEC and 93/6/EEC and Directives 94/19/EC, 98/78/EC, 2000/12/EC, 2001/34/EC, 2002/83/EC and 2002/87/EC in order to establish a new organisational structure for financial services committees, L79/9-L79/17; *Official Journal of the European Union* (2009), Directive 2009/14/EC of the European Parliament and of the Council of 11 March 2009 amending Directive 94/19/EC on deposit-guarantee schemes as regards the coverage level and the payout delay, L68/3-L68/7; repealed by: *Official Journal of the European Union* (2014), Directive 2014/49/EU of the European Parliament and of the Council of 16 April 2014 on deposit guarantee schemes (recast), L173/149-L173/178.

Official Journal of the European Communities (1995). European Parliament and Council Directive 95/26/EC of 29 June 1995 amending Directives 77/780/EEC and 89/646/EEC in the field of credit institutions, Directives 73/239/EEC and 92/49/EEC in the field of non-life insurance, Directives 79/267/EEC and 92/96/EEC in the field of life assurance, Directive 93/22/EEC in the field of investment firms and Directive 85/611/EEC in the field of undertakings for collective investments in transferable securities (Ucits), with a view to reinforcing prudential supervision, L168/7-L168/13, amended by: *Official Journal of the European Communities* (2000), Directive 2000/12/EC of the European Parliament and of the Council of 20 March 2000 relating to the taking up and pursuit of the business of credit institutions, L126/1-L126/59; *Official Journal of the European Communities* (2002), Directive 2002/83/EC of the European Parliament and of the Council of 5 November 2002 concerning life assurance, L345/1-L345/51.

Official Journal of the European Communities (1997). Directive 97/9/EC of the European Parliament and of the Council of 3 March 1997 on investor-compensation schemes, L84/22-L84/31.

Official Journal of the European Communities (1998a). Directive 98/26/EC of the European Parliament and of the Council of 19 May 1998 on settlement finality in payment and securities settlement systems, L166/45-L166/50, amended by: *Official Journal of the European Union* (2009), Directive 2009/44/EC of the European Parliament and of the Council of 6 May 2009 amending Directive 98/26/EC on settlement finality in payment and securities settlement systems and Directive 2002/47/EC on financial collateral arrangements as regards linked systems and credit claims, L146/37-L146/43; *Official Journal of the European Union* (2010), Directive 2010/78/EU of the European

Parliament and of the Council of 24 November 2010 amending Directives 98/26/EC, 2002/87/EC, 2003/6/EC, 2003/41/EC, 2003/71/EC, 2004/39/EC, 2004/109/EC., 2005/60/EC, 2006/48/EC, 2006/49/EC and 2009/65/EC in respect of the powers of the European Supervisory Authority (European Banking Authority), the European Supervisory Authority (European Insurance and Occupational Pensions Authority) and the European Supervisory Authority (European Securities and Markets Authority), L331/120-L331/161; *Official Journal of the European Union* (2012), Regulation (EU) No 648/2012 of the European Parliament and of the Council of 4 July 2012 on OTC derivatives, central counterparties and trade repositories, L201/1-L201/59; *Official Journal of the European Union* (2014), Regulation (EU) No 909/2014 of the European Parliament and of the Council of 23 July 2014 on improving securities settlement in the European Union and on central securities depositories and amending Directives 98/26/EC and 2014/65/EU and Regulation (EU) No 236/2012, L257/1-L257/72.

Official Journal of the European Communities (1998b). Directive 98/78/EC of the European Parliament and of the Council of 27 October 1998 on the supplementary supervision of insurance undertakings in an insurance group, L330/1-L330/12, amended by: *Official Journal of the European Union* (2003), Directive 2002/87/EC of the European Parliament and of the Council of 16 December 2002 on the supplementary supervision of credit institutions, insurance undertakings and investment firms in a financial conglomerate and amending Council Directives 73/239/EEC, 79/267/EEC, 92/49/EEC, 92/96/EEC, 93/6/EEC and 93/22/EEC, and Directives 98/78/EC and 2000/12/EC of the European Parliament and of the Council, L35/1-L35/27; *Official Journal of the European Union* (2005), Directive 2005/1/EC of the European Parliament and of the Council of 9 March 2005 amending Council Directives 73/239/EEC, 85/611/EEC, 91/675/EEC, 92/49/EEC and 93/6/EEC and Directives 94/19/EC, 98/78/EC, 2000/12/EC, 2001/34/EC, 2002/83/EC and 2002/87/EC in order to establish a new organisational structure for financial services committees, L79/9-L79/17; *Official Journal of the European Union* (2005), Directive 2005/68/EC of the European Parliament and of the Council of 16 November 2005 on reinsurance and amending Council Directives 73/239/EEC, 92/49/EEC as well as Directives 98/78/EC and 2002/83/EC, L323/1-L323/50; *Official Journal of the European Union* (2011), Directive 2011/89/EU of the European Parliament and of the Council of 16 November 2011 amending Directives 98/78/EC, 2002/87/EC, 2006/48/EC and 2009/138/EC as regards the supplementary supervision of financial entities in a financial conglomerate, L326/113-L326/141.

Official Journal of the European Communities (1999). Council Decision 1999/468/EC of 28 June 1999 laying down the procedures for the exercise of implementing powers conferred on the Commission, L184/23-L184/26, amended by: *Official Journal of the European Union* (2006), Council Decision 2006/512/EC of 17 July 2006 amending Decision 1999/468/EC laying down the procedures for the exercise of implementing powers conferred on the Commission, L200/11-L200/13; repealed by: *Official Journal of the European Union* (2011), Regulation (EU) No 182/2011 of the European Parliament and of the Council of 16 February 2011 laying down the rules and general principles concerning mechanisms for control by Member States of the Commission's exercise of implementing powers, L55/13-L55/18.

Official Journal of the European Communities (2000a). Council Regulation (EC) No 1346/2000 of 29 May 2000 on insolvency proceedings, L160/1-L160/18, amended by:

Official Journal of the European Union (2003), Act concerning the conditions of accession of the Czech Republic, the Republic of Estonia, the Republic of Cyprus, the Republic of Latvia, the Republic of Lithuania, the Republic of Hungary, the Republic of Malta, the Republic of Poland, the Republic of Slovenia and the Slovak Republic and the adjustments to the Treaties on which the European Union is founded, L236/33-L236/955; *Official Journal of the European Union* (2005), Council Regulation (EC) No 603/2005 of 12 April 2005 amending the lists of insolvency proceedings, winding-up proceedings and liquidators in Annexes A, B and C to Regulation (EC) No 1346/2000 on insolvency proceedings, L100/1-L100/8; *Official Journal of the European Union* (2006), Council Regulation (EC) No 694/2006 of 27 April 2006 amending the lists of insolvency proceedings, winding-up proceedings and liquidators in Annexes A, B and C to Regulation (EC) No 1346/2000 on insolvency proceedings, L121/1-L121/13; *Official Journal of the European Union* (2006), Council Regulation (EC) No 1791/2006 of 20 November 2006 adapting certain Regulations and Decision in the fields of free movement of goods, freedom of movement of persons, company law, competition policy, agriculture (including veterinary and phyto sanitary legislation), transport policy, taxation, statistics, energy, environmnet, cooperation in the fields of justice and home affairs, customs union, external relations, common foreign and security policy and institutions, by reason of the accession of Bulgaria and Romania, L363/1-363/80; *Official Journal of the European Union* (2007), Council Regulation (EC) No 681/2007 of 13 June 2007 amending the lists of insolvency proceedings, winding-up proceedings and liquidators in Annexes A, B and C to Regulation (EC) No 1346/2000 on insolvency proceedings, L159/1-L159/13; *Official Journal of the European Union* (2008), Council Regulation (EC) No 788/2008 of 24 July 2008 amending the lists of insolvency proceedings and winding-up proceedings in Annexes A and B to Regulation (EC) No 1346/2000 on insolvency proceedings and codifying Annexes A, B and C to that Regulation, L213/1-L213/13; *Official Journal of the European Union* (2010), Implementing Regulation of the Council (EU) No 210/2010 of 25 February 2010 amending the lists of insolvency proceedings, winding-up proceedings and liquidators in Annexes A, B and C to Regulation (EC) No 1346/2000 on insolvency proceedings and codifying Annexes A, B and C to that Regulation, L65/1-L65/13; *Official Journal of the European Union* (2011), Council Implementing Regulation (EU) No 583/2011 of 9 June 2011 amending the lists of insolvency proceedings, winding-up proceedings and liquidators in Annexes A, B and C to Regulation (EC) No 1346/2000 on insolvency proceedings and codifying Annexes A, B and C to that Regulation, L160/52-L160/64; *Official Journal of the European Union* (2013), Council Regulation (EU) No 517/2013 of 13 May 2013 adapting certain regulations and decisions in the fields of free movement of goods, freedom of movement for persons, company law, competition policy, agriculture, food safety, veterinary and phytosanitary policy, transport policy, energy, taxation, statistics, trans-European networks, judiciary and fundamental rights, justice, freedom and security, environment, customs union, external relations, foreign, security and defence policy and institutions, by reason of the accession of the Republic of Croatia, L158/1-L158/71; *Official Journal of the European Union* (2014), Council Implementing Regulation (EU) No 663/2014 of 5 June 2014 replacing Annexes A, B and C to Regulation (EC) No 1346/2000 on insolvency proceedings, L179/4-L179/16; corrected by: *Official Journal of the European Union* (2007), Corrigendum to Council Regulation (EC) No 603/2005 of 12 April 2005 amending the lists of insolvency proceedings, winding-up proceedings and liquidators in Annexes A, B and C to Regulation (EC) No 1346/2000 on insolvency proceedings, L49/36.

Official Journal of the European Communities (2000b). Directive 2000/12/EC of the European Parliament and of the Council of 20 March 2000 relating to the taking up and pursuit of the business of credit institutions, L126/1-L126/59, amended by: *Official Journal of the European Communities* (2000), Directive 2000/28/EC of the European Parliament and of the Council of 18 September 2000 amending Directive 2000/12/EC relating to the taking up and pursuit of the business of credit institutions, L275/37-L275/38; *Official Journal of the European Union* (2003), Directive 2002/87/EC of the European Parliament and of the Council of 16 December 2002 on the supplementary supervision of credit institutions, insurance undertakings and investment firms in a financial conglomerate and amending Council Directives 73/239/EEC, 79/267/EEC, 92/49/EEC, 92/96/EEC, 93/6/EEC and 93/22/EEC, and Directives 98/78/EC and 2000/12/EC of the European Parliament and of the Council, L35/1-L35/27; *Official Journal of the European Union* (2003), Act concerning the conditions of accession of the Czech Republic, the Republic of Estonia, the Republic of Cyprus, the Republic of Latvia, the Republic of Lithuania, the Republic of Hungary, the Republic of Malta, the Republic of Poland, the Republic of Slovenia and the Slovak Republic and the adjustments to the Treaties on which the European Union is founded, L236/33-L236/955; *Official Journal of the European Union* (2004), Commission Directive 2004/69/EC of 27 April 2004 amending Directive 2000/12/EC of the European Parliament and of the Council as regards the definition of 'multilateral development banks', L125/44; *Official Journal of the European Union* (2004), Directive 2004/39/EC of the European Parliament and of the Council of 21 April 2004 on markets in financial instruments amending Council Directives 85/611/EEC and 93/6/EEC and Directive 2000/12/EC of the European Parliament and of the Council and repealing Council Directive 93/22/EEC, L145/1-L145/44; *Official Journal of the European Union* (2005), Directive 2005/1/EC of the European Parliament and of the Council of 9 March 2005 amending Council Directives 73/239/EEC, 85/611/EEC, 91/675/EEC, 92/49/EEC and 93/6/EEC and Directives 94/19/EC, 98/78/EC, 2000/12/EC, 2001/34/EC, 2002/83/EC and 2002/87/EC in order to establish a new organisational structure for financial services committees, L79/9-L79/17; *Official Journal of the European Union* (2006), Commission Directive 2006/29/EC of 8 March 2006 amending Directive 2000/12/EC of the European Parliament and of the Council as regards exclusion or inclusion of certain institutions from the scope of application, L70/50-L70/51; corrected by: *Official Journal of the European Union* (2005), Corrigendum to Directive 2000/12/EC of the European Parliament and of the Council of 20 March 2000 relating to the taking up and pursuit of the business of credit institutions, L290/30; *Official Journal of the European Union* (2005), Corrigendum to Directive 2004/39/EC of the European Parliament and of the Council of 21 April 2004 on markets in financial instruments amending Council Directives 85/611/EEC and 93/6/EEC and Directive 2000/12/EC of the European Parliament and of the Council and repealing Council Directive 93/22/EEC, L45/18; repealed by: *Official Journal of the European Union* (2006), Directive 2006/48/EC of the European Parliament and of the Council of 14 June 2006 relating to the taking up and pursuit of the business of credit institutions (recast), L177/1-L177/200.

Official Journal of the European Communities (2000c). Directive 2000/46/EC of the European Parliament and of the Council of 18 September 2000 on the taking up, pursuit and prudential supervision of the business of electronic money institutions, L275/39-L275/43, repealed by: *Official Journal of the European Union* (2009), Directive 2009/110/EC of the European Parliament and of the Council of 16 September 2009 on the taking up, pursuit and prudential supervision of the business of electronic money institutions amending Directives 2005/60/EC and 2006/48/EC and repealing Directive 2000/46/EC, L267/7-L267/17.

Official Journal of the European Communities (2001a). Commission Decision 2001/527/EC of 6 June 2001 establishing the Committee of European Securities Regulators, L191/43-L191/44, amended by: *Official Journal of the European Union* (2004), Commission Decision of 5 November 2003 amending Decision 2001/527/EC establishing the Committee of European Securities Regulators, L3/32; repealed by: *Official Journal of the European Union* (2009), Commission Decision of 23 January 2009 establishing the Committee of European Securities Regulators, L25/18-L25/22.

Official Journal of the European Communities (2001b). Commission Decision 2001/528/EC of 6 June 2001 establishing the European Securities Committee, L191/45-L191/46, amended by: *Official Journal of the European Union* (2004), Commission Decision of 5 November 2003 amending Decision 2001/528/EC establishing the European Securities Committee, L/33.

Official Journal of the European Communities (2001c). Directive 2001/24/EC of the European Parliament and of the Council of 4 April 2001 on the reorganisation and winding up of credit institutions, L125/15-L125/23, amended by: *Official Journal of the European Union* (2014), Directive 2014/59/EU of the European Parliament and of the Council of 15 May 2014 establishing a framework for the recovery and resolution of credit institutions and investment firms and amending Council Directive 82/891/EEC, and Directives 2001/24/EC, 2002/47/EC, 2004/25/EC, 2005/56/EC, 2007/36/EC, 2011/35/EU, 2012/30/EU and 2013/36/EU, and Regulations (EU) No 1093/2010 and (EU) No 648/2012, of the European Parliament and of the Council, L173/190-L173/348.

Official Journal of the European Communities (2001d). Directive 2001/34/EC of the European Parliament and of the Council of 28 May 2001 on the admission of securities to official stock exchange listing and on information to be published on those securities, L184/1-L184/66, amended by: *Official Journal of the European Union* (2003), Directive 2003/6/EC of the European Parliament and of the Council of 28 January 2003 on insider dealing and market manipulation (market abuse), L96/16-L96/25; *Official Journal of the European Union* (2003), Directive 2003/71/EC of the European Parliament and of the Council of 4 November 2003 on the prospectus to be published when securities are offered to the public or admitted to trading and amending Directive 2001/34/EC, L345/64-L345/89; *Official Journal of the European Union* (2004), Directive 2004/109/EC of the European Parliament and of the Council of 15 December 2004 on the harmonisation of transparency requirements in relation to information about issuers whose securities are admitted to trading on a regulated market and amending Directive 2001/34/EC, L390/38-L390/57; *Official Journal of the European Union* (2005), Directive 2005/1/EC of the European Parliament and of the Council of 9 March 2005 amending Council Directives 73/239/EEC, 85/611/EEC, 91/675/EEC, 92/49/EEC and 93/6/EEC and Directives 94/19/EC, 98/78/EC, 2000/12/EC, 2001/34/EC, 2002/83/EC and

2002/87/EC in order to establish a new organisational structure for financial services committees, L79/9-L79/17.

Official Journal of the European Communities (2002a). Consolidated version of the Treaty Establishing the European Community, C325/33-C326/184, amended by: *Official Journal of the European Union* (2007), Treaty of Lisbon amending the Treaty on European Union and the Treaty Establishing the European Community, C306/1-C306/271; renamed: Treaty on the Functioning of the European Union.

Official Journal of the European Communities (2002b). Directive 2002/47/EC of the European Parliament and of the Council of 6 June 2002 on financial collateral arrangements, L168/43-L168/50, amended by: *Official Journal of the European Union* (2009), Directive 2009/44/EC of the European Parliament and of the Council of 4 May 2009 amending Directive 98/26/EC on settlement finality in payment and securities settlement systems and Directive 2002/47/EC on financial collateral arrangements as regards linked systems and credit claims, L146/37-L146/43; *Official Journal of the European Union* (2014), Directive 2014/59/EU of the European Parliament and of the Council of 15 May 2014 establishing a framework for the recovery and resolution of credit institutions and investment firms and amending Council Directive 82/891/EEC, and Directives 2001/24/EC, 2002/47/EC, 2004/25/EC, 2005/56/EC, 2007/36/EC, 2011/35/EU, 2012/30/EU and 2013/36/EU, and Regulations (EU) No 1093/2010 and (EU) No 648/2012, of the European Parliament and of the Council, L173/190-L173/348.

Official Journal of the European Communities (2002c). Directive 2002/65/EC of the European Parliament and of the Council of 23 September 2002 concerning the distance marketing of consumer financial services and amending Council Directive 90/619/EEC and Directives 97/7/EC and 98/27/EC, L271/16-L271/24, amended by: *Official Journal of the European Union* (2005), Directive 2005/29/EC of the European Parliament and of the Council of 11 May 2005 concerning unfair business-to-consumer commercial practices in the internal market and amending Council Directive 84/450/EEC, Directives 97/7/EEC, 98/22/EC and 2002/65/EC of the European Parliament and of the Council and Regulation (EC) No 2006/2004 of the European Parliament and of the Council ('Unfair Commercial Practices Directive'), L149/22-L149/39; *Official Journal of the European Union* (2007), Directive 2007/64/EC of the European Parliament and of the Council of 13 November 2007 on payment services in the internal market amending Directives 97/7/EC, 2002/65/EC, 2005/60/EC and 2006/48/EC and repealing Directive 97/5/EC, L319/1-L319/36.

Official Journal of the European Communities (2002d). Regulation (EC) No 1606/2002 of the European Parliament and of the Council of 19 July 2002 on the application of international accounting standards, L243/1-L243/4, amended by: *Official Journal of the European Union* (2008), Regulation (EC) No 297/2008 of the European Parliament and of the Council of 11 March 2008 amending Regulation (EC) No 1606/2002 on the application of international accounting standards, as regards the implementing powers conferred on the Commission, L97/62-L97/63.

Official Journal of the European Union (2003a). Directive 2002/87/EC of the European Parliament and of the Council of 16 December 2002 on the supplementary supervision of credit institutions, insurance undertakings and investment firms in a financial conglomerate and amending Council Directives 73/239/EEC, 79/267/EEC, 92/49/EEC, 92/96/EEC, 93/6/EEC and 93/22/EEC, and Directives 98/78/EC and 2000/12/EC of the

European Parliament and of the Council, L35/1-L35/27, amended by: *Official Journal of the European Union* (2005), Directive 2005/1/EC of the European Parliament and of the Council of 9 March 2005 amending Council Directives 73/239/EEC, 85/611/EEC, 91/675/EEC, 92/49/EEC and 93/6/EEC and Directives 94/19/EC, 98/78/EC, 2000/12/EC, 2001/34/EC, 2002/83/EC and 2002/87/EC in order to establish a new organisational structure for financial services committees, L79/9-L79/17; *Official Journal of the European Union* (2008), Directive 2008/25/EC of the European Parliament and of the Council of 11 March 2008 amending Directive 2002/87/EC on the supplementary supervision of credit institutions, insurance undertakings and investment firms in a financial conglomerate, as regards the implementing powers conferred on the Commission, L81/40-L81/41; *Official Journal of the European Union* (2010), Directive 2010/78/EU of the European Parliament and of the Council of 24 November 2010 amending Directives 98/26/EC, 2002/87/EC, 2003/6/EC, 2003/41/EC, 2003/71/EC, 2004/39/EC, 2004/109/EC., 2005/60/EC, 2006/48/EC, 2006/49/EC and 2009/65/EC in respect of the powers of the European Supervisory Authority (European Banking Authority), the European Supervisory Authority (European Insurance and Occupational Pensions Authority) and the European Supervisory Authority (European Securities and Markets Authority), L331/120-L331/161; *Official Journal of the European Union* (2011), Directive 2011/89/EU of the European Parliament and of the Council of 16 November 2011 amending Directives 98/78/EC, 2002/87/EC, 2006/48/EC and 2009/138/EC as regards the supplementary supervision of financial entities in a financial conglomerate, L326/113-L326/141; *Official Journal of the European Union* (2013), Directive 2013/36/EU of the European Parliament and of the Council of 26 June 2013 on access to the activity of credit institutions and the prudential supervision of credit institutions and investment firms, amending Directive 2002/87/EC and repealing Directives 2006/48/EC and 2006/49/EC, L176/338-L176/436.

Official Journal of the European Union (2003b). Directive 2003/6/EC of the European Parliament and of the Council of 28 January 2003 on insider dealing and market manipulation (market abuse), L96/16-L96/25, amended by: *Official Journal of the European Union* (2008), Directive 2008/26/EC of the European Parliament and of the Council of 11 March 2008 amending Directive 2003/6/EC on insider dealing and market manipulation (market abuse), as regards the implementing powers conferred on the Commission, L81/42-L81/44; *Official Journal of the European Union* (2010), Directive 2010/78/EU of the European Parliament and of the Council of 24 November 2010 amending Directives 98/26/EC, 2002/87/EC, 2003/6/EC, 2003/41/EC, 2003/71/EC, 2004/39/EC, 2004/109/EC., 2005/60/EC, 2006/48/EC, 2006/49/EC and 2009/65/EC in respect of the powers of the European Supervisory Authority (European Banking Authority), the European Supervisory Authority (European Insurance and Occupational Pensions Authority) and the European Supervisory Authority (European Securities and Markets Authority), L331/120-L331/161; repealed by: *Official Journal of the European Union* (2014), Regulation (EU) No 596/2014 of the European Parliament and of the Council of 16 April 2014 on market abuse (market abuse regulation) and repealing Directive 2003/6/EC of the European Parliament and of the Council and Commission Directives 2003/124/EC, 2003/125/EC and 2004/72/EC, L173/1-L173/61.

Official Journal of the European Union (2003c). Directive 2003/71/EC of the European Parliament and of the Council of 4 November 2003 on the prospectus to be published when securities are offered to the public or admitted to trading and amending Directive 2001/34/EC, L345/64-L345/89, amended by: *Official Journal of the European Union* (2008), Directive 2008/11/EC of the European Parliament and of the Council of 11 March 2008 amending Directive 2003/71/EC on the prospectus to be published when securities are offered to the public or admitted to trading, as regards the implementing powers conferred on the Commission, L76/37-L76/38; *Official Journal of the European Union* (2010), Directive 2010/73/EU of the European Parliament and of the Council of 24 November 2010 amending Directives 2003/71/EC on the prospectus to be published when securities are offered to the public or admitted to trading and 2004/109/EC on the harmonisation of transparency requirements in relation to information about issuers whose securities are admitted to trading on a regulated market, L327/1-L327/12; *Official Journal of the European Union* (2010), Directive 2010/78/EU of the European Parliament and of the Council of 24 November 2010 amending Directives 98/26/EC, 2002/87/EC, 2003/6/EC, 2003/41/EC, 2003/71/EC, 2004/39/EC, 2004/109/EC., 2005/60/EC, 2006/48/EC, 2006/49/EC and 2009/65/EC in respect of the powers of the European Supervisory Authority (European Banking Authority), the European Supervisory Authority (European Insurance and Occupational Pensions Authority) and the European Supervisory Authority (European Securities and Markets Authority), L331/120-L331/161; *Official Journal of the European Union* (2013), Directive 2013/50/EU of the European Parliament and of the Council of 22 October 2013 amending Directive 2004/109/EC of the European Parliament and of the Council on the harmonisation of transparency requirements in relation to information about issuers whose securities are admitted to trading on a regulated market, Directive 2003/71/EC of the European Parliament and of the Council on the prospectus to be published when securities are offered to the public or admitted to trading and Commission Directive 2007/14/EC laying down detailed rules for the implementation of certain provisions of Directive 2004/109/EC, L294/13-L294/27; *Official Journal of the European Union* (2014), Directive 2014/51/EU of the European Parliament and of the Council of 16 April 2014 amending Directives 2003/71/EC and 2009/138/EC and Regulations (EC) No 1060/2009, (EU) No 1094/2010 and (EU) No 1095/2010 in respect of the powers of the European Supervisory Authority (European Insurance and Occupational Pensions Authority) and the European Supervisory Authority (European Securities and Markets Authority), L153/1-L153/61.

Official Journal of the European Union (2003d). Commission Regulation (EC) No 2273/2003 of 22 December 2003 implementing Directive 2003/6/EC of the European Parliament and of the Council as regards exemptions for buy-back programmes and stabilisation of financial instruments, L336/33-L336/38; repealed by: *Official Journal of the European Union* (2014), Regulation (EU) No 596/2014 of the European Parliament and of the Council of 16 April 2014 on market abuse (market abuse regulation) and repealing Directive 2003/6/EC of the European Parliament and of the Council and Commission Directives 2003/124/EC, 2003/125/EC and 2004/72/EC, L173/1-L173/61.

Official Journal of the European Union (2004a). Commission Decision 2004/5/EC of 5 November 2003 establishing the Committee of European Banking Supervisors, L3/28-L3/29; repealed by: *Official Journal of the European Union* (2009), Commission Decision 2009/78/EC of 23 January 2009 establishing the Committee of European Banking Supervisors, L25/23-L25/27; repealed by: *Official Journal of the European*

Union (2009), Commission Decision 2009/78/EC of 23 January 2009 establishing the Committee of European Banking Supervisors, L25/23-L25/27.

Official Journal of the European Union (2004b). Commission Decision 2004/6/EC of 5 November 2003 establishing the Committee on European Insurance and Occupational Pensions Supervisors, L3/30-L3/31; repealed by: *Official Journal of the European Union* (2009), Commission Decision of 23 January 2009 establishing the Committee of European Insurance and Occupational Pensions Supervisors, L25/28-L25/32; repealed by: *Official Journal of the European Union* (2009), Commission Decision 2009/79/EC of 23 January 2009 establishing the Committee of European Insurance and Occupational Pensions Supervisors, L25/28-L25/32.

Official Journal of the European Union (2004c). Commission Regulation (EC) No 809/2004 of 29 April 2004 implementing Directive 2003/71/EC of the European Parliament and of the Council as regards information contained in prospectuses as well as the format, incorporation by reference and publication of such prospectuses and dissemination of advertisements, L149/1-L149/126, amended by: *Official Journal of the European Union* (2006), Commission Regulation (EC) No 1787/2006 of 4 December 2006 amending Commission Regulation (EC) 809/2004 implementing Directive 2003/71/EC of the European Parliament and of the Council as regards information contained in prospectuses as well as the format, incorporation by reference and publication of such prospectuses and dissemination of advertisements, L337/17-L337/20; *Official Journal of the European Union* (2007), Commission Regulation (EC) No 211/2007 of 27 February 2007 amending Regulation (EC) No 809/2004 implementing Directive 2003/71/EC of the European Parliament and of the Council as regards financial information in prospectuses where the issuer has a complex financial history or has made a significant financial commitment, L61/24-L61/27; *Official Journal of the European Union* (2008), Commission Regulation (EC) No 1289/2008 of 12 December 2008 amending Commission Regulation (EC) No 809/2004 implementing Directive 2003/71/EC of the European Parliament and of the Council as regards elements related to prospectus and advertisements, L340/17-L340/19; *Official Journal of the European Union* (2012), Commission Delegated Regulation (EU) No 311/2012 of 21 December 2011 amending Regulation (EC) No 809/2004 implementing Directive 2003/71/EC of the European Parliament and of the Council as regards elements related to prospectuses and advertisements, L103/13-L103/14; *Official Journal of the European Union* (2012), Commission Delegated Regulation (EU) No 486/2012 of 30 March 2012 amending Regulation (EC) No 809/2004 as regards the format and the content of the prospectus, the base prospectus, the summary and the final terms and as regards the disclosure requirements, L150/1-L150/65; *Official Journal of the European Union* (2012), Commission Delegated Regulation (EU) No 862/2012 of 4 June 2012 amending Regulation (EC) No 809/2004 as regards information on the consent to use the prospectus, information on underlying indexes and the requirement for a report prepared by independent accountants or auditors, L256/4-L256/13; *Official Journal of the European Union* (2013), Commission Delegated Regulation (EU) No 621/2013 of 21 March 2013 correcting the Polish version of Regulation (EC) No 809/2004 implementing Directive 2003/71/EC of the European Parliament and of the Council as regards information contained in prospectuses as well as the format, incorporation by reference and publication of such prospectuses and dissemination of advertisements, L177/14; *Official Journal of the European Union* (2013), Commission Delegated Regulation (EU)

No 759/2013 of 30 April 2013 amending Regulation (EC) No 809/2004 as regards the disclosure requirements for convertible and exchangeable debt securities, L213/1-L213/9; *Official Journal of the European Union* (2015), Commission Delegated Regulation (EU) No 2015/1604 of 12 June 2015 amending Regulation (EC) No 809/2004 implementing Directive 2003/71/EC of the European Parliament and of the Council as regards elements related to prospectuses and advertisements, L249/1-L249/2; corrected by: *Official Journal of the European Union* (2004), Corrigendum to Commission Regulation (EC) No 809/2004 of 29 April 2004 implementing Directive 2003/71/EC of the European Parliament and of the Council as regards information contained in prospectuses as well as the format, incorporation by reference and publication of such prospectuses and dissemination of advertisements, L215/3-L215/103.

Official Journal of the European Union (2004d). Directive 2004/39/EC of the European Parliament and of the Council of 21 April 2004 on markets in financial instruments amending Council Directives 85/611/EEC and 93/6/EEC and Directive 2000/12/EC of the European Parliament and of the Council and repealing Council Directive 93/22/EEC, L145/1-L145/44, amended by: *Official Journal of the European Union* (2006), Directive 2006/31/EC of the European Parliament and of the Council of 5 April 2006 amending Directive 2004/39/EC on markets in financial instruments, as regards certain deadlines, L114/60-L114/63; *Official Journal of the European Union* (2007), Directive 2007/44/EC of the European Parliament and of the Council of 5 September 2007 amending Council Directive 92/49/EEC and Directives 2002/83/EC, 2004/39/EC, 2005/68/EC and 2006/48/EC as regards procedural rules and evaluation criteria for the prudential assessment of acquisitions and increase of holdings in the financial sector, L247/1-L247/16; *Official Journal of the European Union* (2008), Directive 2008/10/EC of the European Parliament and of the Council of 11 March 2008 amending Directive 2004/39/EC on markets in financial instruments as regards the implementing powers conferred on the Commission, L76/33-L76/36; *Official Journal of the European Union* (2010), Directive 2010/78/EU of the European Parliament and of the Council of 24 November 2010 amending Directives 98/26/EC, 2002/87/EC, 2003/6/EC, 2003/41/EC, 2003/71/EC, 2004/39/EC, 2004/109/EC, 2005/60/EC, 2006/48/EC, 2006/49/EC and 2009/65/EC in respect of the powers of the European Supervisory Authority (European Banking Authority), the European Supervisory Authority (European Insurance and Occupational Pensions Authority) and the European Supervisory Authority (European Securities and Markets Authority), L331/120-L331/161; corrected by: *Official Journal of the European Union* (2005), Corrigendum to Directive 2004/39/EC of the European Parliament and of the Council of 21 April 2004 on markets in financial instruments amending Council Directives 85/611/EEC and 93/6/EEC and Directive 2000/12/EC of the European Parliament and of the Council and repealing Council Directive 93/22/EEC, L45/18; *Official Journal of the European Union* (2014), Corrigendum to Directive 2010/78/EU of the European Parliament and of the Council of 24 November 2010 amending Directives 98/26/EC, 2002/87/EC, 2003/6/EC, 2003/41/EC, 2003/71/EC, 2004/39/EC, 2004/109/EC, 2005/60/EC, 2006/48/EC, 2006/49/EC and 2009/65/EC in respect of the powers of the European Supervisory Authority (European Banking Authority), the European Supervisory Authority (European Insurance and Occupational Pensions Authority) and the European Supervisory Authority (European Securities and Markets Authority), L54/23; repealed by: *Official Journal of the European Union* (2014),

Directive 2014/65/EU of the European Parliament and of the Council of 15 May 2014 on markets in financial instruments and amending Directive 2002/92/EC and Directive 2011/61/EU (recast), L173/349-L173/496.

Official Journal of the European Union (2004e). Directive 2004/109/EC of the European Parliament and of the Council of 15 December 2004 on the harmonisation of transparency requirements in relation to information about issuers whose securities are admitted to trading on a regulated market and amending Directive 2001/34/EC, L390/38-L390/57, amended by: *Official Journal of the European Union* (2008), Directive 2008/22/EC of the European Parliament and of the Council of 11 March 2008 amending Directive 2004/109/EC on the harmonisation of transparency requirements in relation to information about issuers whose securities are admitted to trading on a regulated market, as regards the implementing powers conferred on the Commission, L76/50-L76/53; *Official Journal of the European Union* (2010), Directive 2010/73/EU of the European Parliament and of the Council of 24 November 2010 amending Directives 2003/71/EC on the prospectus to be published when securities are offered to the public or admitted to trading and 2004/109/EC on the harmonisation of transparency requirements in relation to information about issuers whose securities are admitted to trading on a regulated market, L327/1-L327/12; *Official Journal of the European Union* (2010), Directive 2010/78/EU of the European Parliament and of the Council of 24 November 2010 amending Directives 98/26/EC, 2002/87/EC, 2003/6/EC, 2003/41/EC, 2003/71/EC, 2004/39/EC, 2004/109/EC., 2005/60/EC, 2006/48/EC, 2006/49/EC and 2009/65/EC in respect of the powers of the European Supervisory Authority (European Banking Authority), the European Supervisory Authority (European Insurance and Occupational Pensions Authority) and the European Supervisory Authority (European Securities and Markets Authority), L331/120-L331/161; *Official Journal of the European Union* (2013), Directive 2013/50/EU of the European Parliament and of the Council of 22 October 2013 amending Directive 2004/109/EC of the European Parliament and of the Council on the harmonisation of transparency requirements in relation to information about issuers whose securities are admitted to trading on a regulated market, Directive 2003/71/EC of the European Parliament and of the Council on the prospectus to be published when securities are offered to the public or admitted to trading and Commission Directive 2007/14/EC laying down detailed rules for the implementation of certain provisions of Directive 2004/109/EC, L294/13-L294/27.

Official Journal of the European Union (2005a). Directive 2005/1/EC of the European Parliament and of the Council of 9 March 2005 amending Council Directives 73/239/EEC, 85/611/EEC, 91/675/EEC, 92/49/EEC and 93/6/EEC and Directives 94/19/EC, 98/78/EC, 2000/12/EC, 2001/34/EC, 2002/83/EC and 2002/87/EC in order to establish a new organisational structure for financial services committees, L79/9-L79/17.

Official Journal of the European Union (2005b). Directive 2005/60/EC of the European Parliament and of the Council of 26 October 2005 on the prevention of the use of the financial system for the purpose of money laundering and terrorist financing, L309/15-L309/36, amended by: *Official Journal of the European Union* (2007), Directive 2007/64/EC of the European Parliament and of the Council of 13 November 2007 on payment services in the internal market amending Directives 97/7/EC, 2002/65/EC, 2005/60/EC and 2006/48/EC and repealing Directive 97/5/EC, L319/1-L319/36; *Official Journal of the European Union* (2008), Directive 2008/20/EC of the European Parliament and of the Council of 11 March 2008 amending Directive 2005/60/EC on the prevention of the use of the financial system for the purpose of money laundering and terrorist financing, as regards the implementing powers conferred on the Commission, L76/46-L76/47; *Official Journal of the European Union* (2009), Directive 2009/110/EC of the European Parliament and of the Council of 16 September 2009 on the taking up, pursuit and prudential supervision of the business of electronic money institutions amending Directive 2005/60/EC and 2006/48/EC and repealing Directive 2000/46/EC, L267/7-L267/17; *Official Journal of the European Union* (2010), Directive 2010/78/EU of the European Parliament and of the Council of 24 November 2010 amending Directives 98/26/EC, 2002/87/EC, 2003/6/EC, 2003/41/EC, 2003/71/EC, 2004/39/EC, 2004/109/EC, 2005/60/EC, 2006/48/EC, 2006/49/EC and 2009/65/EC in respect of the powers of the European Supervisory Authority (European Banking Authority), the European Supervisory Authority (European Insurance and Occupational Pensions Authority) and the European Supervisory Authority (European Securities and Markets Authority), L331/120-L331/161; repealed by: *Official Journal of the European Union* (2015), Directive (EU) 2015/849 of the European Parliament and of the Council of 20 May 2015 on the prevention of the use of the financial system for the purposes of money laundering or terrorist financing, amending Regulation (EU) No 648/2012 of the European Parliament and of the Council, and repealing Directive 2005/60/EC of the European Parliament and of the Council and Commission Directive 2006/70/EC, L141/73-L141/117.

Official Journal of the European Union (2006a). Commission Directive 2006/73/EC of 10 August 2006 implementing Directive 2004/39/EC of the European Parliament and of the Council as regards organisational requirements and operating conditions for investment firms and defined terms for the purposes of that Directive, L241/26-L241/58.

Official Journal of the European Union (2006b). Commission Regulation (EC) No 1287/2006 of 10 August 2006 implementing Directive 2004/39/EC of the European Parliament and of the Council as regards record-keeping obligations for investment firms, transaction reporting, market transparency, admission of financial instruments to trading, and defined terms for the purposes of that Directive, L241/1-L241/25.

Official Journal of the European Union (2006c). Directive 2006/48/EC of the European Parliament and of the Council of 14 June 2006 relating to the taking up and pursuit of the business of credit institutions (recast), L177/1-L177/200, amended by: *Official Journal of the European Union* (2007), Commission Directive 2007/18/EC of 27 March 2007 amending Directive 2006/48/EC of the European Parliament and of the Council as regards the exclusion or inclusion of certain instructions from its scope of application and the treatment of exposures to multilateral development banks, L87/9-L87/10; *Official Journal of the European Union* (2007), Directive 2007/44/EC of the European Parliament and of the Council of 5 September 2007 amending Council Directive 92/49/EEC and Directives 2002/83/EC, 2004/39/EC, 2005/68/EC and 2006/48/EC as regards procedural rules and evaluation criteria for the prudential assessment of acquisitions and increase in holdings in the financial sector, L247/1-L247/16; *Official Journal of the European Union* (2007), Directive 2007/64/EC of the European Parliament and of the Council of 13 November 2007 on payment services in the internal market amending Directives 97/7/EC, 2002/65/EC, 2005/60/EC and 2006/48/EC and repealing Directive 97/5/EC, L319/1-L319/36; *Official Journal of the European Union* (2008), Directive 2008/24/EC of the European Parliament and of the Council of 11 March 2008 amending Directive 2006/48/EC relating to the taking up and pursuit of the business of credit institutions, as regards the implementing powers conferred on the Commission, L81/38-L81/39; *Official Journal of the European Union* (2009), Commission Directive 2009/83/EC of 27 July 2009 amending certain Annexes to Directive 2006/48/EC of the European Parliament and of the Council as regards technical provisions concerning risk management, L196/14-L196/21; *Official Journal of the European Union* (2009), Directive 2009/110/EC of the European Parliament and of the Council of 16 September 2009 on the taking up, pursuit and prudential supervision of the business of electronic money institutions amending Directive 2005/60/EC and 2006/48/EC and repealing Directive 2000/46/EC, L267/7-L267/17; *Official Journal of the European Union* (2009), Directive 2009/111/EC of the European Parliament and of the Council of 16 September 2009 amending Directives 2006/48/EC, 2006/49/EC and 2007/64/EC as regards banks affiliated to central institutions, certain own funds items, large exposures, supervisory arrangements, and crisis management, L302/97-L302/119; *Official Journal of the European Union* (2010), Commission Directive 2010/16/EU of 9 March 2010 amending Directive 2006/48/EC of the European Parliament and of the Council as regards the exclusion of a certain institution from the scope of application, L60/15-L60/16; *Official Journal of the European Union* (2010), Directive 2010/76/EU of the European Parliament and of the Council of 24 November 2010 amending Directives 2006/48/EC and 2006/49/EC as regards capital requirements for the trading book and for re-securitisations, and the supervisory review of remuneration policies, L329/3-L329/35; *Official Journal of the European Union* (2010), Directive 2010/78/EU of the European Parliament and of the Council of 24 November 2010 amending Directives 98/26/EC, 2002/87/EC, 2003/6/EC, 2003/41/EC, 2003/71/EC, 2004/39/EC, 2004/109/EC, 2005/60/EC, 2006/48/EC, 2006/49/EC and 2009/65/EC in respect of the powers of the European Supervisory Authority (European Banking Authority), the European Supervisory Authority (European Insurance and Occupational Pensions Authority) and the European Supervisory Authority (European Securities and Markets Authority), L331/120-L331/161; *Official Journal of the European Union* (2011), Directive 2011/89/EU of the European Parliament and of the Council of 16 November 2011 amending Directives 98/78/EC, 2002/87/EC, 2006/48/EC and 2009/138/EC as regards the supplementary supervision of financial entities in a financial conglomerate, L326/113-L326/141; *Official Journal of the European Union* (2012), Treaty between the Kingdom of Belgium, the Republic of Bulgaria, the Czech Republic, the Kingdom of Denmark, the Federal Republic of Germany, the Republic of Estonia, Ireland, the Hellenic Republic, the Kingdom of Spain, the French Republic, the Italian Republic, the Republic of Cyprus, the Republic of Latvia, the Republic of Lithuania, the Grand Duchy of Luxembourg, the Republic of Hungary, the Republic of Malta, the Kingdom of the Netherlands, the Republic of Austria, the Republic of Poland, the Portuguese Republic, Romania, the Republic of Slovenia, the Slovak Republic, the Republic of Finland, the Kingdom of Sweden, the United Kingdom of Great Britain and Northern Ireland (Member States of the European Union) and the Republic of Croatia concerning the accession of the Republic of Croatia to the European Union, L112/10-L112/110; corrected by: *Official Journal of the European Union* (2011), Corrigendum to Directive 2010/78/EU of the European Parliament and of the Council of 24 November 2010 amending Directives 98/26/EC, 2002/87/EC, 2003/6/EC, 2003/41/EC, 2003/71/EC,

2004/39/EC, 2004/109/EC, 2005/60/EC, 2006/48/EC, 2006/49/EC and 2009/65/EC in respect of the powers of the European Supervisory Authority (European Banking Authority), the European Supervisory Authority (European Insurance and Occupational Pensions Authority) and the European Supervisory Authority (European Securities and Markets Authority), L170/43; repealed by: *Official Journal of the European Union* (2013), Directive 2013/36/EU of the European Parliament and of the Council of 26 June 2013 on access to the activity of credit institutions and the prudential supervision of credit institutions and investment firms, amending Directive 2002/87/EC and repealing Directives 2006/48/EC and 2006/49/EC, L176/338-L176/436.

Official Journal of the European Union (2006d). Directive 2006/49/EC of the European Parliament and of the Council of 14 June 2006 on the capital adequacy of investment firms and credit institutions (recast), L177/201-L177/255, amended by: *Official Journal of the European Union* (2008), Directive 2008/23/EC of the European Parliament and of the Council of 11 March 2008 amending Directive 2006/49/EC on the capital adequacy of investment firms and credit institutions, as regards the implementing powers conferred on the Commission, L76/54-L76/55; *Official Journal of the European Union* (2009), Commission Directive 2009/27/EC of 7 April 2009 amending certain Annexes to Directive 2006/49/EC of the European Parliament and of the Council as regards technical provisions concerning risk management, L94/97-L94/99; *Official Journal of the European Union* (2009), Directive 2009/111/EC of the European Parliament and of the Council of 16 September 2009 amending Directives 2006/48/EC, 2006/49/EC and 2007/64/EC as regards banks affiliated to central institutions, certain own funds items, large exposures, supervisory arrangements, and crisis management, L302/97-L302/119; *Official Journal of the European Union* (2010), Directive 2010/76/EU of the European Parliament and of the Council of 24 November 2010 amending Directives 2006/48/EC and 2006/49/EC as regards capital requirements for the trading book and for re-securitisations, and the supervisory review of remuneration policies, L329/3-L329/35; *Official Journal of the European Union* (2010), Directive 2010/78/EU of the European Parliament and of the Council of 24 November 2010 amending Directives 98/26/EC, 2002/87/EC, 2003/6/EC, 2003/41/EC, 2003/71/EC, 2004/39/EC, 2004/109/EC, 2005/60/EC, 2006/48/EC, 2006/49/EC and 2009/65/EC in respect of the powers of the European Supervisory Authority (European Banking Authority), the European Supervisory Authority (European Insurance and Occupational Pensions Authority) and the European Supervisory Authority (European Securities and Markets Authority), L331/120-L331/161; repealed by: *Official Journal of the European Union* (2013), Directive 2013/36/EU of the European Parliament and of the Council of 26 June 2013 on access to the activity of credit institutions and the prudential supervision of credit institutions and investment firms, amending Directive 2002/87/EC and repealing Directives 2006/48/EC and 2006/49/EC, L176/338-L176/436.

Official Journal of the European Union (2006e). Regulation (EC) No 1786/2006 of the European Parliament and of the Council of 15 November 2006 on information on the payer accompanying transfers of funds, L345/1-L345/9, corrected by: *Official Journal of the European Union* (2007), Corrigendum to Regulation (EC) No 1786/2006 of the European Parliament and of the Council of 15 November 2006 on information on the payer accompanying transfers of funds, L323/59.

Official Journal of the European Union (2007a). Commission Directive 2007/14/EC of 8 March 2007 laying down detailed rules for the implementation of certain provisions of Directive 2004/109/EC on the harmonisation of transparency requirements in relation to information about issuers whose securities are admitted to trading on a regulated market, L69/27-L69/36, amended by: *Official Journal of the European Union* (2013), Directive 2013/50/EU of the European Parliament and of the Council of 22 October 2013 amending Directive 2004/109/EC of the European Parliament and of the Council on the harmonisation of transparency requirements in relation to information about issuers whose securities are admitted to trading on a regulated market, Directive 2003/71/EC of the European Parliament and of the Council on the prospectus to be published when securities are offered to the public or admitted to trading and Commission Directive 2007/14/EC laying down detailed rules for the implementation of certain provisions of Directive 2004/109/EC, L294/13-L294/27.

Official Journal of the European Union (2007b). Directive 2007/36/EU of the European Parliament and of the Council of 11 July 2007 on the exercise of certain rights of shareholders in listed companies, L184/17-L184/24, amended by: *Official Journal of the European Union* (2014), Directive 2014/59/EU of the European Parliament and of the Council of 15 May 2014 establishing a framework for the recovery and resolution of credit institutions and investment firms and amending Council Directive 82/891/EEC, and Directives 2001/24/EC, 2002/47/EC, 2004/25/EC, 2005/56/EC, 2007/36/EC, 2011/35/EU, 2012/30/EU and 2013/36/EU, and Regulations (EU) No 1093/2010 and (EU) No 648/2012, of the European Parliament and of the Council, L173/190-L173/348.

Official Journal of the European Union (2007c). Directive 2007/64/EC of the European Parliament and of the Council of 13 November 2007 on payment services in the internal market amending Directives 97/7/EC, 2002/65/EC, 2005/60/EC and 2006/48/EC and repealing Directive 97/5/EC, L319/1-L319/36, amended by: *Official Journal of the European Union* (2009), Directive 2009/111/EC of the European Parliament and of the Council of 16 September 2009 amending Directives 2006/48/EC, 2006/49/EC and 2007/64/EC as regards banks affiliated to central institutions, certain own funds items, large exposures, supervisory arrangements, and crisis management, L302/97-L302/119; corrected by: *Official Journal of the European Union* (2009), Corrigendum to Directive 2007/64/EC of the European Parliament and of the Council of 13 November 2007 on payment services in the internal market amending Directives 97/7/EC, 2002/65/EC, 2005/60/EC and 2006/48/EC and repealing Directive 97/5/EC, L187/5; repealed by: *Official Journal of the European Union* (2015), Directive (EU) 2015/2366 of the European Parliament and of the Council of 25 November 2015 on payment services in the internal market, amending Directives 2002/65/EC, 2009/110/EC and 2013/36/EU and Regulation (EU) No 1093/2010, and repealing Directive 2007/64/EC, L337/35-L337/127.

Official Journal of the European Union (2009a). Commission Decision 2009/77/EC of 23 January 2009 establishing the Committee of European Securities Regulators, L25/18-L25/22; repealed by: *Official Journal of the European Union* (2010), Regulation (EU) No 1095/2010 of the European Parliament and of the Council of 24 November 2010 establishing a European Supervisory Authority (European Securities and Markets Authority) amending Decision No 716/2009/EC and repealing Commission Decision 2009/77/EC, L331/84-L331/119.

Official Journal of the European Union (2009b). Commission Decision 2009/78/EC of 23 January 2009 establishing the Committee of European Banking Supervisors, L25/23-L25/27; repealed by: *Official Journal of the European Union* (2010), Regulation (EU) No 1093/2010 of the European Parliament and of the Council of 24 November 2010 establishing a European Supervisory Authority (European Banking Authority), amending Decision No 716/2009/EC and repealing Commission Decision 2009/78/EC, L331/12-L331/47.

Official Journal of the European Union (2009c). Commission Decision 2009/79/EC of 23 January 2009 establishing the Committee of European Insurance and Occupational Pensions Supervisors, L25/28-L25/32; repealed by: *Official Journal of the European Union* (2010), Regulation (EU) No 1094/2010 of the European Parliament and of the Council of 24 November 2010 establishing a European Supervisory Authority (European Insurance and Occupational Pensions Authority), amending Decision No 716/2009/EC and repealing Commission Decision 2009/79/EC, L331/48-L331/83.

Official Journal of the European Union (2009d). Directive 2009/14/EC of the European Parliament and of the Council of 11 March 2009 amending Directive 94/19/EC on deposit-guarantee schemes as regards the coverage level and the payout delay, L68/3-L68/7; repealed by: *Official Journal of the European Union* (2014), Directive 2014/49/EU of the European Parliament and of the Council of 16 April 2014 on deposit guarantee schemes (recast), L173/149-L173/178.

Official Journal of the European Union (2009e). Directive 2009/65/EC of the European Parliament and of the Council of 13 July 2009 on the coordination of laws, regulations and administrative provisions relating to undertakings for collective investment in transferable securities (UCITS) (recast), L302/32-L302/96, amended by: *Official Journal of the European Union* (2010), Directive 2010/78/EU of the European Parliament and of the Council of 24 November 2010 amending Directives 98/26/EC, 2002/87/EC, 2003/6/EC, 2003/41/EC, 2003/71/EC, 2004/39/EC, 2004/109/EC., 2005/60/EC, 2006/48/EC, 2006/49/EC and 2009/65/EC in respect of the powers of the European Supervisory Authority (European Banking Authority), the European Supervisory Authority (European Insurance and Occupational Pensions Authority) and the European Supervisory Authority (European Securities and Markets Authority), L331/120-L331/161; *Official Journal of the European Union* (2011), Directive 2011/61/EU of the European Parliament and of the Council of 8 June 2011 on Alternative Investment Fund Managers and amending Directives 2003/41/EC and 2009/65/EC and Regulations (EC) No 1060/2009 and (EU) No 1095/2010, L174/1-L174/73; *Official Journal of the European Union* (2013), Directive 2013/14/EU of the European Parliament and of the Council of 21 May 2013 amending Directive 2003/41/EC on the activities and supervision of institutions for occupational retirement provision, Directive 2009/65/EC on the coordination of laws, regulations and administrative provisions relating to undertakings for collective investment in transferable securities (UCITS) and Directive 2011/61/EU on Alternative Investment Funds Managers in respect of over-reliance on credit ratings, L145/1-L145/3; *Official Journal of the European Union* (2014), Directive 2014/91/EU of the European Parliament and of the Council of 23 July 2014 amending Directive 2009/65/EC on the coordination of laws, regulations and administrative provisions relating to undertakings for collective investment in transferable securities

(UCITS) as regards depositary functions, remuneration policies and sanctions, L257/186-L257/213.

Official Journal of the European Union (2009f). Directive 2009/110/EC of the European Parliament and of the Council of 16 September 2009 on the taking up, pursuit and prudential supervision of the business of electronic money institutions amending Directives 2005/60/EC and 2006/48/EC and repealing Directive 2000/46/EC, L267/7-L267/17.

Official Journal of the European Union (2009g). Directive 2009/138/EC of the European Parliament and of the Council of 25 November 2009 on the taking-up and pursuit of the business of Insurance and Reinsurance (Solvency II) (recast), L335/1-L335/155, amended by: *Official Journal of the European Union* (2011), Directive 2011/89/EU of the European Parliament and of the Council of 16 November 2011 amending Directives 98/78/EC, 2002/87/EC, 2006/48/EC and 2009/138/EC as regards the supplementary supervision of financial entities in a financial conglomerate, L326/113-L326/141; *Official Journal of the European Union* (2012), Directive 2012/23/EU of the European Parliament and of the Council of 12 September 2012 amending Directive 2009/138/EC (Solvency II) as regards the date for its transposition and the date of its application, and the date of repeal of certain Directives, L249/1-L249/2; *Official Journal of the European Union* (2013), Council Directive 2013/23/EU of 13 May 2013 adapting certain directives in the field of financial services, by reason of the accession of the Republic of Croatia, L158/362-L158/364; *Official Journal of the European Union* (2013), Directive 2013/58/EU of the European Parliament and of the Council of 11 December 2013 amending Directive 2009/138/EC (Solvency II) as regards the date for its transposition and the date of its application, and the date of repeal of certain Directives (Solvency I), L341/1-L341/3; *Official Journal of the European Union* (2014), Directive 2014/51/EU of the European Parliament and of the Council of 16 April 2014 amending Directives 2003/71/EC and 2009/138/EC and Regulations (EC) No 1060/2009, (EU) No 1094/2010 and (EU) No 1095/2010 in respect of the powers of the European Supervisory Authority (European Insurance and Occupational Pensions Authority) and the European Supervisory Authority (European Securities and Markets Authority), L153/1-L153/61; corrected by: *Official Journal of the European Union* (2014), Corrigendum to Directive 2009/138/EC of the European Parliament and of the Council of 25 November 2009 on the taking-up and pursuit of the business of Insurance and Reinsurance (Solvency II), L219/66.

Official Journal of the European Union (2009h). Regulation (EC) No 1060/2009 of the European Parliament and of the Council of 16 September 2009 on credit rating agencies, L302/1-L302/31, amended by: *Official Journal of the European Union* (2011), Regulation (EU) No 513/2011 of the European Parliament and of the Council of 11 May 2011 amending Regulation (EC) No 1060/2009 on credit rating agencies, L145/30-L145/56; *Official Journal of the European Union* (2011), Directive 2011/61/EU of the European Parliament and of the Council of 8 June 2011 on Alternative Investment Fund Managers and amending Directives 2003/41/EC and 2009/65/EC and Regulations (EC) No 1060/2009 and (EU) No 1095/2010, L174/1-L174/73; *Official Journal of the European Union* (2013), Regulation (EU) No 462/2013 of the European Parliament and of the Council of 21 May 2013 amending Regulation (EC) No 1060/2009 on credit rating agencies, L146/1-L146/33; *Official Journal of the European Union* (2014), Directive

2014/51/EU of the European Parliament and of the Council of 16 April 2014 amending Directives 2003/71/EC and 2009/138/EC and Regulations (EC) No 1060/2009, (EU) No 1094/2010 and (EU) No 1095/2010 in respect of the powers of the European Supervisory Authority (European Insurance and Occupational Pensions Authority) and the European Supervisory Authority (European Securities and Markets Authority), L153/1-L153/61.

Official Journal of the European Union (2010a). Regulation (EU) No 1092/2010 of the European Parliament and of the Council of 24 November 2010 on European Union macro-prudential oversight of the financial system and establishing a European Systemic Risk Board, L331/1-L331/11.

Official Journal of the European Union (2010b). Regulation (EU) No 1093/2010 of the European Parliament and of the Council of 24 November 2010 establishing a European Supervisory Authority (European Banking Authority), amending Decision No 716/2009/EC and repealing Commission Decision 2009/78/EC, L331/12-L331/47, amended by: *Official Journal of the European Union* (2013), Regulation (EU) No 1022/2013 of the European Parliament and of the Council of 22 October 2013 amending Regulation (EU) No 1093/2010 establishing a European Supervisory Authority (European Banking Authority) as regards the conferral of specific tasks on the European Central Bank pursuant to Council Regulation (EU) No 1024/2013, L287/5-L287/14; *Official Journal of the European Union* (2014), Directive 2014/17/EU of the European Parliament and of the Council of 4 February 2014 on credit agreements for consumers relating to residential immovable property and amending Directives 2008/48/EC and 2013/36/EU and Regulation (EU) No 1093/2010, L60/34-L60/85; *Official Journal of the European Union* (2014), Directive 2014/59/EU of the European Parliament and of the Council of 15 May 2014 establishing a framework for the recovery and resolution of credit institutions and investment firms and amending Council Directive 82/891/EEC, and Directives 2001/24/EC, 2002/47/EC, 2004/25/EC, 2005/56/EC, 2007/36/EC, 2011/35/EU, 2012/30/EU and 2013/36/EU, and Regulations (EU) No 1093/2010 and (EU) No 648/2012, of the European Parliament and of the Council, L173/190-L173/348; *Official Journal of the European Union* (2014), Regulation (EU) No 806/2014 of the European Parliament and of the Council of 15 July 2014 establishing uniform rules and a uniform procedure for the resolution of credit institutions and certain investment firms in the framework of a Single Resolution Mechanism and a Single Resolution Fund and amending Regulation (EU) No 1093/2010, L225/1-L225/90.

Official Journal of the European Union (2010c). Regulation (EU) No 1094/2010 of the European Parliament and of the Council of 24 November 2010 establishing a European Supervisory Authority (European Insurance and Occupational Pensions Authority), amending Decision No 716/2009/EC and repealing Commission Decision 2009/79/EC, L331/48-L331/83; amended by: *Official Journal of the European Union* (2014), Directive 2014/51/EU of the European Parliament and of the Council of 16 April 2014 amending Directives 2003/71/EC and 2009/138/EC and Regulations (EC) No 1060/2009, (EU) No 1094/2010 and (EU) No 1095/2010 in respect of the powers of the European Supervisory Authority (European Insurance and Occupational Pensions Authority) and the European Supervisory Authority (European Securities and Markets Authority), L153/1-L153/61.

Official Journal of the European Union (2010d). Regulation (EU) No 1095/2010 of the European Parliament and of the Council of 24 November 2010 establishing a European

Supervisory Authority (European Securities and Markets Authority) amending Decision No 716/2009/EC and repealing Commission Decision 2009/77/EC, L331/84-L331/119, amended by: *Official Journal of the European Union* (2011), Directive 2011/61/EU of the European Parliament and of the Council of 8 June 2011 on Alternative Investment Fund Managers and amending Directives 2003/41/EC and 2009/65/EC and Regulations (EC) No 1060/2009 and (EU) No 1095/2010, L174/1-L174/73; *Official Journal of the European Union* (2014), Directive 2014/51/EU of the European Parliament and of the Council of 16 April 2014 amending Directives 2003/71/EC and 2009/138/EC and Regulations (EC) No 1060/2009, (EU) No 1094/2010 and (EU) No 1095/2010 in respect of the powers of the European Supervisory Authority (European Insurance and Occupational Pensions Authority) and the European Supervisory Authority (European Securities and Markets Authority), L153/1-L153/61.

Official Journal of the European Union (2010e). Council Regulation (EU) No 1096/2010 of 17 November 2010 conferring specific tasks upon the European Central Bank concerning the functioning of the European Systemic Risk Board, L331/162-L331/164.

Official Journal of the European Union (2011a). Directive 2011/61/EU of the European Parliament and of the Council of 8 June 2011 on Alternative Investment Fund Managers and amending Directives 2003/41/EC and 2009/65/EC and Regulations (EC) No 1060/2009 and (EU) No 1095/2010, L174/1-L174/73; amended by: *Official Journal of the European Union* (2013), Directive 2013/14/EU of the European Parliament and of the Council of 21 May 2013 amending Directive 2003/41/EC on the activities and supervision of institutions for occupational retirement provision, Directive 2009/65/EC on the coordination of laws, regulations and administrative provisions relating to undertakings for collective investment in transferable securities (UCITS) and Directive 2011/61/EU on Alternative Investment Funds Managers in respect of over-reliance on credit ratings, L145/1-L145/3; *Official Journal of the European Union* (2014), Directive 2014/65/EU of the European Parliament and of the Council of 15 May 2014 on markets in financial instruments and amending Directive 2002/92/EC and Directive 2011/61/EU (recast), L173/349-L173/496.

Official Journal of the European Union (2011b). Regulation (EU) No 182/2011 of the European Parliament and of the Council of 16 February 2011 laying down the rules and general principles concerning mechanisms for control by Member States of the Commission's exercise of implementing powers, L55/13-L55/18.

Official Journal of the European Union (2012a). Act concerning the conditions of accession of the Republic of Croatia and the adjustments to the Treaty on European Union, the Treaty on the Functioning of the European Union and the Treaty Establishing the European Atomic Energy Community, L112/21-L112/91.

Official Journal of the European Union (2012b). Charter of Fundamental Rights of the European Union, C326/391-C326/407.

Official Journal of the European Union (2012c). Commission Delegated Regulation (EU) No 486/2012 of 20 March 2012 amending Regulation (EC) No 809/2004 as regards the format and the content of the prospectus, the base prospectus, the summary and the final terms and as regards the disclosure requirements, L150/1-L150/65.

Official Journal of the European Union (2012d). Commission Delegated Regulation (EU) No 918/2012 of 5 July 2012 supplementing Regulation (EU) No 236/2012 of the European Parliament and the Council on short selling and certain aspects of credit default swaps with regard to definitions, the calculation of net short positions, covered sovereign credit default swaps, notification thresholds, liquidity thresholds for suspending restrictions, significant falls in the value of financial instruments and adverse events, L274/1-L274/15, amended by: *Official Journal of the European Union* (2015), Commission Delegated Regulation (EU) 2015/97 of 17 October 2014 correcting Delegated Regulation (EU) No 918/2012 as regards the notification of significant net short positions in sovereign debt, L16/22.

Official Journal of the European Union (2012e). Commission Implementing Regulation (EU) No 827/2012 of 29 June 2012 laying down implementing technical standards with regard to the means for public disclosure of net position in shares, the format of the information to be provided to the European Securities and Markets Authority in relation to net short positions, the types of agreements, arrangements and measures to adequately ensure that shares or sovereign debt instruments are available for settlement and the dates and period for the determination of the principal venue for a share according to Regulation (EU) No 236/2012 of the European Parliament and of the Council on short selling and certain aspects of credit default swaps, L251/11-L251/18.

Official Journal of the European Union (2012f). Consolidated version of the Treaty on European Union, C326/13-C326/45.

Official Journal of the European Union (2012g). Consolidated version of the Treaty on the Functioning of the European Union, C326/47-C326/199.

Official Journal of the European Union (2012h). Regulation (EU) No 236/2012 of the European Parliament and of the Council of 14 March 2012 on short selling and certain aspects of credit default swaps, L86/1-L86/24, amended by: *Official Journal of the European Union* (2014), Regulation (EU) No 909/2014 of the European Parliament and of the Council of 23 July 2014 on improving securities settlement in the European Union and on central securities depositories and amending Directives 98/26/EC and 2014/65/EU and Regulation (EU) No 236/2012, L257/1-L257/72.

Official Journal of the European Union (2012i). Regulation (EU) No 648/2012 of the European Parliament and of the Council of 4 July 2012 on OTC derivatives, central counterparties and trade repositories, L201/1-L201/59, amended by: *Official Journal of the European Union* (2013), Regulation (EU) No 575/2013 of the European Parliament and of the Council of 26 June 2013 on prudential requirements for credit institutions and investment firms and amending Regulation (EU) No 648/2012, L176/1-L176/337; *Official Journal of the European Union* (2013), Commission Delegated Regulation (EU) No 1002/2013 of 12 July 2013 amending Regulation (EU) No 648/2012 of the European Parliament and of the Council on OTC derivatives, central counterparties and trade repositories with regard to the list of exempted entitites, L279/2-L279/3; *Official Journal of the European Union* (2014), Directive 2014/59/EU of the European Parliament and of the Council of 15 May 2014 establishing a framework for the recovery and resolution of credit institutions and investment firms and amending Council Directive 82/891/EEC, and Directives 2001/24/EC, 2002/47/EC, 2004/25/EC, 2005/56/EC, 2007/36/EC, 2011/35/EU, 2012/30/EU and 2013/36/EU, and Regulations (EU) No 1093/2010 and (EU) No 648/2012, of the European Parliament and of the Council, L173/190-L173/348; *Official Journal of the European Union* (2015), Directive (EU) 2015/849 of the European Parliament and of the Council of 20 May 2015 on the prevention of the use of financial resources for the purpose of money laundering or terrorist financing, amending

Regulation (EU) No 648/2012 of the European Parliament and of the Council, and repealing Directive 2005/60/EC of the European Parliament and of the Council and Commission Directive 2006/70/EC, L141/73-L141/117; *Official Journal of the European Union* (2015), Commission Delegated Regulation (EU) 2015/1515 of 5 June 2015 amending Regulation (EU) No 648/2012 of the European Parliament and of the Council as regards the extension of the transitional periods related to pension scheme arrangements, L239/63-L239/64; *Official Journal of the European Union* (2015), Regulation (EU) 2015/2365 of the European Parliament and of the Council of 25 November 2015 on transparency of securities financing transactions and of reuse and amending Regulation (EU) No 648/2012, L337/1-L337/34.

Official Journal of the European Union (2013a). Commission Delegated Regulation (EU) No 149/2013 of 19 December 2012 supplementing Regulation (EU) No 648/2012 of the European Parliament and of the Council with regard to regulatory technical standards on indirect clearing arrangements, the clearing obligation, the public register, access to a trading venue, non-financial counterparties, and risk mitigation techniques for OTC derivatives contracts not cleared by a CCP, L52/11-L52/24.

Official Journal of the European Union (2013b). Commission Delegated Regulation (EU) No 153/2013 of 19 December 2012 supplementing Regulation (EU) No 648/2012 of the European Parliament and of the Council with regard to regulatory technical standards on requirements for central counterparties, L52/41-L52/74.

Official Journal of the European Union (2013c). Council Regulation (EU) No 1024/2013 of 15 October 2013 conferring specific tasks on the European Central Bank concerning policies relating to the prudential supervision of credit institutions, L287/63-L287/69.

Official Journal of the European Union (2013d). Directive 2013/14/EU of the European Parliament and of the Council of 21 May 2013 amending Directive 2003/41/EC on the activities and supervision of institutions for occupational retirement provision, Directive 2009/65/EC on the coordination of laws, regulations and administrative provisions relating to undertakings for collective investment in transferable securities (UCITS) and Directive 2011/61/EU on Alternative Investment Funds Managers in respect of over-reliance on credit ratings, L145/1-L145/3.

Official Journal of the European Union (2013e). Directive 2013/34/EU of the European Parliament and of the Council of 26 June 2013 on the annual financial statements, consolidated financial statements and related reports of certain types of undertakings, amending Directive 2006/43/EC of the European Parliament and of the Council and repealing Council Directives 78/660/EEC and 83/349/EEC, L182/19-L182/76, amended by: *Official Journal of the European Union* (2014), Directive 2014/95/EU of the European Parliament and of the Council of 22 October 2014 amending Directive 2013/34/EU as regards disclosure of non-financial and diversity information by certain large undertakings and groups, L330/1-L330/9; *Official Journal of the European Union* (2014), Council Directive 2014/102/EU of 7 November 2014 adapting Directive 2013/34/EU of the European Parliament and of the Council on the annual financial statements, consolidated financial statements and related reports of certain types of undertakings, by reason of the accession of the Republic of Croatia, L334/86-L334/87.

Official Journal of the European Union (2013f). Directive 2013/36/EU of the European Parliament and of the Council of 26 June 2013 on access to the activity of credit institutions and the prudential supervision of credit institutions and investment firms, amending Directive 2002/87/EC and repealing Directives 2006/48/EC and 2006/49/EC, L176/338-L176/436, amended by: *Official Journal of the European Union* (2014), Directive 2014/17/EU of the European Parliament and of the Council of 4 February 2014 on credit agreements for consumers relating to residential immovable property and amending Directives 2008/48/EC and 2013/36/EU and Regulation (EU) No 1093/2010, L60/34-L60/85; *Official Journal of the European Union* (2014), Directive 2014/59/EU of the European Parliament and of the Council of 15 May 2014 establishing a framework for the recovery and resolution of credit institutions and investment firms and amending Council Directive 82/891/EEC, and Directives 2001/24/EC, 2002/47/EC, 2004/25/EC, 2005/56/EC, 2007/36/EC, 2011/35/EU, 2012/30/EU and 2013/36/EU, and Regulations (EU) No 1093/2010 and (EU) No 648/2012, of the European Parliament and of the Council, L173/190-L173/348; corrected by: *Official Journal of the European Union* (2013), Corrigendum to Directive 2013/36/EU of the European Parliament and of the Council of 26 June 2013 on access to the activity of credit institutions and the prudential supervision of credit institutions and investment firms, amending Directive 2002/87/EC and repealing Directives 2006/48/EC and 2006/49/EC, L208/73.

Official Journal of the European Union (2013g). Directive 2013/50/EU of the European Parliament and of the Council of 22 October 2013 amending Directive 2004/109/EC of the European Parliament and of the Council on the harmonisation of transparency requirements in relation to information about issuers whose securities are admitted to trading on a regulated market, Directive 2003/71/EC of the European Parliament and of the Council on the prospectus to be published when securities are offered to the public or admitted to trading and Commission Directive 2007/14/EC laying down detailed rules for the implementation of certain provisions of Directive 2004/109/EC, L294/13-L294/27.

Official Journal of the European Union (2013h). Regulation (EU) No 345/2013 of the European Parliament and of the Council of 17 April 2013 on European venture capital funds, L115/1-L115/17.

Official Journal of the European Union (2013i). Regulation (EU) No 346/2013 of the European Parliament and of the Council of 17 April 2013 on European social entrepreneurship funds, L115/18-L115/38.

Official Journal of the European Union (2013j). Regulation (EU) No 575/2013 of the European Parliament and of the Council of 26 June 2013 on prudential requirements for credit institutions and investment firms and amending Regulation (EU) No 648/2012, L176/1-L176/337, amended by: *Official Journal of the European Union* (2015), Commission Delegated Regulation (EU) 2015/62 of 10 October 2014 amending Regulation (EU) No 575/2013 of the European Parliament and of the Council with regard to the leverage ratio, L11/37-L11/43; corrected by: *Official Journal of the European Union* (2013), Corrigendum to Regulation (EU) No 575/2013 of the European Parliament and of the Council of 26 June 2013 on prudential requirements for credit institutions and investment firms and amending Regulation (EU) No 648/2012, L208/68-L208/72; *Official Journal of the European Union* (2013), Corrigendum to Regulation (EU) No 575/2013 of the European Parliament and of the Council of 26 June 2013 on prudential requirements for credit institutions and investment firms and amending Regulation (EU) No 648/2012, L321/6-L321/342.

Official Journal of the European Union (2013k). Council Regulation (EU) No 1024/2013 of 15 October 2013 conferring specific tasks on the European Central Bank concerning policies relating to the prudential supervision of credit institutions, L287/63-L287/89.

Official Journal of the European Union (2014a). Commission Delegated Regulation (EU) No 382/2014 of 7 March 2014 supplementing Directive 2003/71/EC of the European Parliament and of the Council with regard to regulatory technical standards for publication of supplements to the prospectus, L111/36-L111/39.

Official Journal of the European Union (2014b). Commission Delegated Regulation (EU) No 524/2014 of 12 March 2014 supplementing Directive 2013/36/EU of the European Parliament and of the Council with regard to regulatory technical standards specifying the information that competent authorities of home and host Member States supply to one another, L148/6-L148/14.

Official Journal of the European Union (2014c). Commission Delegated Regulation (EU) No 530/2014 of 12 March 2014 supplementing Directive 2013/36/EU of the European Parliament and of the Council with regard to regulatory technical standards further defining material exposures and thresholds for internal approaches to specific risk in the trading book, L148/50-L148/51.

Official Journal of the European Union (2014d). Commission Implementing Regulation (EU) No 620/2014 of 4 June 2014 laying down implementing technical standards with regard to information exchange between competent authorities of home and host Member States, according to Directive 2013/36/EU of the European Parliament and of the Council, L172/1-L172/25.

Official Journal of the European Union (2014e). Directive 2014/49/EU of the European Parliament and of the Council of 16 April 2014 on deposit guarantee schemes (recast), L173/149-L173/178, corrected by: *Official Journal of the European Union* (2014), Corrigendum to Directive 2014/49/EU of the European Parliament and of the Council of 16 April 2014 on deposit guarantee schemes, L212/47; *Official Journal of the European Union* (2014), Corrigendum to Directive 2014/49/EU of the European Parliament and of the Council of 16 April 2014 on deposit guarantee schemes, L309/37.

Official Journal of the European Union (2014f). Directive 2014/57/EU of the European Parliament and of the Council of 16 April 2014 on criminal sanctions for market abuse (market abuse directive), L173/179-L173/189.

Official Journal of the European Union (2014g). Directive 2014/59/EU of the European Parliament and of the Council of 15 May 2014 establishing a framework for the recovery and resolution of credit institutions and investment firms and amending Council Directive 82/891/EEC, and Directives 2001/24/EC, 2002/47/EC, 2004/25/EC, 2005/56/EC, 2007/36/EC, 2011/35/EU, 2012/30/EU and 2013/36/EU, and Regulations (EU) No 1093/2010 and (EU) No 648/2012, of the European Parliament and of the Council, L173/190-L173/348.

Official Journal of the European Union (2014h). Directive 2014/65/EU of the European Parliament and of the Council of 15 May 2014 on markets in financial instruments and amending Directive 2002/92/EC and Directive 2011/61/EU (recast), L173/349-L173/496, amended by: *Official Journal of the European Union* (2014), Regulation (EU) No 909/2014 of the European Parliament and of the Council of 23 July 2014 on improving securities settlement in the European Union and on central securities depositories and amending Directives 98/26/EC and 2014/65/EU and Regulation (EU) No 236/2012, L257/1-L257/72.

Official Journal of the European Union (2014i). Directive 2014/91/EU of the European Parliament and of the Council of 23 July 2014 amending Directive 2009/65/EC on the coordination of laws, regulations and administrative provisions relating to undertakings for collective investment in transferable securities (UCITS) as regards depositary functions, remuneration policies and sanctions, L257/186-L257/213.

Official Journal of the European Union (2014j). Regulation (EU) No 596/2014 of the European Parliament and of the Council of 16 April 2014 on market abuse (market abuse regulation) and repealing Directive 2003/6/EC of the European Parliament and of the Council and Commission Directives 2003/124/EC, 2003/125/EC and 2004/72/EC, L173/1-L173/61.

Official Journal of the European Union (2014k). Regulation (EU) No 600/2014 of the European Parliament and of the Council of 15 May 2014 on markets in financial instruments and amending Regulation (EU) No 648/2012, L173/84-L173/148, corrected by: *Official Journal of the European Union* (2015), Corrigendum to Regulation (EU) No 600/2014 of the European Parliament and of the Council of 15 May 2014 on markets in financial instruments and amending Regulation (EU) No 648/2012, L270/4.

Official Journal of the European Union (2014l). Regulation (EU) No 909/2014 of the European Parliament and of the Council of 23 July 2014 on improving securities settlement in the European Union and on central securities depositories and amending Directives 98/26/EC and 2014/65/EU and Regulation (EU) No 236/2012, L257/1-L257/72.

Official Journal of the European Union (2014m). Regulation (EU) No 1286/2014 of the European Parliament and of the Council of 26 November 2014 on key information documents for packaged retail and insurance-based investment products (PRIIPs), L352/1-L352/23, corrected by: Corrigendum to Regulation (EU) No 1286/2014 of the European Parliament and of the Council of 26 November 2014 on key information documents for packaged retail and insurance-based investment products (PRIIPs), L358/50.

Official Journal of the European Union (2015a). Commission Delegated Regulation (EU) 2015/61 of 17 December 2014 supplementing Directive 2004/109/EC of the European Parliament and of the Council with regard to certain regulatory technical standards on major holdings, L120/2-L120/5.

Official Journal of the European Union (2015b). Commission Delegated Regulation (EU) 2015/2205 of 6 August 2015 supplementing Regulation (EU) No 648/2012 of the European Parliament and of the Council with regard to regulatory technical standards on the clearing obligation, L314/13-L314/21.

Official Journal of the European Union (2015c). Directive (EU) 2015/849 of the European Parliament and of the Council of 20 May 2015 on the prevention of the use of the financial system for the purposes of money laundering or terrorist financing, amending Regulation (EU) No 648/2012 of the European Parliament and of the Council, and repealing Directive 2005/60/EC of the European Parliament and of the Council and Commission Directive 2006/70/EC, L141/73-L141/117.

Official Journal of the European Union (2015d). Directive (EU) 2015/2366 of the European Parliament and of the Council of 25 November 2015 on payment services in the internal market, amending Directives 2002/65/EC, 2009/110/EC and 2013/36/EU and Regulation (EU) No 1093/2010, and repealing Directive 2007/64/EC, L337/35-L337/127.

Official Journal of the European Union (2015e). Regulation (EU) 2015/751 of the European Parliament and of the Council of 29 April 2015 on interchange fees for card-based transactions, L123/1-L123/15.

Official Journal of the European Union (2015f). Regulation (EU) 2015/760 of the European Parliament and of the Council of 29 April 2015 on European long-term investment funds, L123/98-L123/121.

Official Journal of the European Union (2015g). Regulation (EU) 2015/2365 of the European Parliament and of the Council of 25 November 2015 on transparency of securities financing transactions and of reuse and amending Regulation (EU) No 648/2012, L337/1-L337/34.

Organisation for Economic Co-operation and Development (2015a). Convention on Mutual Administrative Assistance in Tax Matters. <http://www.oecd.org/ctp/exchange-of-tax-information/conventiononmutualadministrativeassistanceintaxmatters.htm>

Organisation for Economic Co-operation and Development (2015b). Global Forum on Transparency and Exchange of Information for Tax Purposes: Peer Reviews. http://www.oecd-ilibrary.org/taxation/global-forum-on-transparency-and-exchange-of-information-for-tax-purposes-peer-reviews_2219469x.

Parris, M. (2016). Brexit would mean we don't give a damn, The Times, 20/02/16, 71838, 23.

Standard and Poor's Rating Services (2016). Standard & Poor's Ratings Definitions. https://www.standardandpoors.com/en_US/web/guest/article/-/view/sourceId/504352.

Stern, H. G., & Feldman, R. J. (2009). Too Big to Fail: The Hazards of Bank Bailouts (paperback edition). Washington D.C.: Brookings Institution Press.

Thatcher, M. (1988). Speech to the College of Europe ("The Bruges Speech"), Bruges, 20/09/88. http://www.margaretthatcher.org/document/107332.

The Evaluation Partnership Limited (2006). Framework contract No RTD-JRC/00-06: Evaluation of the E-money Directive (2006/46/EC) – Final Report, Twickenham, 17/02/06. http://ec.europa.eu/internal_market/payments/docs/emoney/evaluation_en.pdf.

The Giovannini Group (2001). Cross-Border Clearing and Settlement Arrangements in the European Union, Brussels, April 2001. http://www.ebf-fbe.eu/uploads/First%20 Giovannini%20Report%20on%20Clearing%20&%20Settlement%20in%20the%20EU% 20%282001%29.pdf.

The Giovannini Group (2003). The Giovannini Group: Second Report on EU Clearing and Settlement Arrangements, Brussels, April 2003. http://ec.europa.eu/internal_market/ financial-markets/docs/clearing/second_giovannini_report_en.pdf.

Tietmeyer, H. (1999). International Cooperation and Coordination in the Area of Financial Market Supervision and Surveillance, Report by Hans Tietmeyer, President of the Deutsche Bundesbank, 11/02/99. http://www.financialstabilityboard.org/wp-content/uploads/r_9902.pdf.

Valiante, D. (2015). Light and shadows in Europe's new Action Plan for Capital Markets Union. ECMI Commentary, No.40/5 October 2015, 1-4.

World Bank (2009). Development Committee: Enhancing Voice and Participation of Developing and Transition Countries in the World Bank Group: Update and Proposals for Discussion, DC2009-0011, 29/09/09. http://siteresources.worldbankorg/DEV COMMINT/Documentation/22335196/DC2009-0011(E)Voice.pdf.

ABOUT THE AUTHOR

Dr. Graeme Scott Baber

B.A., M.A. (Oxon.); LL.B., B.Sc.(Economics), LL.M., M.Sc.(Development Finance),
Ph.D. (Lond.); Pg.C., M.B.A., M.Sc.(Strategic Focus) (Heriot-Watt); M.Sc.(Computer
Science) (Herts.); P.G.C.P.E. (BPP)

Graeme Baber is an independent legal researcher, specializing in international, European Union and United Kingdom financial law. He has published 2 monographs with Cambridge Scholars Publishing, entitled *The Impact of Legislation and Regulation on the Freedom of Movement of Capital in Estonia, Poland and Latvia* and *The Free Movement of Capital and Financial Services: An Exposition?*, and is currently writing a series of legal essays with that publisher. Graeme has also published chapters for edited collections and many learned articles. He is an experienced teacher of university students. Graeme's other interests comprise musical performance on organ and pianoforte – especially the works of Johann Sebastian Bach and Joseph Haydn. He is also a composer of both sacred and secular pieces, and a keen scenic and garden photographer.

INDEX

D

E

G

H

I

S

T

U

V

W